Cultural Anthropology

Understanding a World in Transition

2nd Edition

Publisher and Marketing Manager: Richard Schofield

Project Development: Della Brackett

Managing Editor: Joyce Bianchini

Permissions Coordinator: Esther Scannell

Design and Illustrations: Rachel Weathersbee

Typesetter: Suzanne Schmidt

Softcover ISBN:	978-1-61882-176-8
Looseleaf ISBN:	978-1-59602-692-6
TEXTBOOK-Plus Bundle ISBN:	978-1-59602-692-6
eBOOK-Plus ISBN:	978-1-61882-046-4

Cultural Anthropology

Understanding a World in Transition

2nd Edition

Sheldon Smith and Philip D. Young

Brief Table of Contents

Table of Contents

Chapter 2
Human Biological and Cultural Evolution

76

Chapter 3
Development of
Anthropological Theory

112

Chapter 4
Bands and Tribes:
Remote Peripheries

152

Chapter 5
Chiefdoms and Pre-Modern States: Core-Periphery Relations   182

Chapter 6
The Modern World: Capitalism, World Systems, and Globalization

Chapter 7
Ethnicity, Ethnic Conflict, and Social Movements — 244

Chapter 8
Africa: Overcoming a Colonial Legacy

278

Chapter 9
The Middle East:
Ethnicity, Oil, and Conflict 316

Chapter 10
Asia:
The Emerging Tigers   352

Chapter 11

Latin America: Political Bosses,
Dependency, and Democratic Reform   390

Chapter 12
Global Problems, International Development, and Anthropology in the Third Millennium   428

Preface

In the years from the end of World War II until the collapse of the Soviet Union, interests around the world were focused on the potential threat of atomic war and the destruction of the planet. Since the events of September 11, 2001, that threat has been replaced by the realities of terrorism and the ongoing wars in Iraq and Afghanistan. A few short years ago, Americans generally were unaware of al Qaeda and had limited understanding of Islam and the cultures of the people who practice it. Today Americans are aware. Nevertheless, the more mundane—but equally critical—issues of political, economic, demographic, and ecological transitions throughout the world still maintain relevance. These transitions bring promises, and they bring threats. With the recent economic crises both here and abroad, our portfolio of interests has shifted from global war to much more local issues and problems of human adaptation; these local issues, however, are driven by global change.

Anthropology has a unique contribution to make to the study of global change, for it is the preeminent discipline in the study of culture change through time and space. In the period directly after World War II, anthropologists such as Robert Redfield, George Foster, John Gillin, Oscar Lewis, and Margaret Mead were at the forefront in explaining a changing world, one that described the influence of "modernization" on traditional societies. With the age of postmodernism, however, the concept of modernization became less relevant as anthropologists began to doubt that modern ideas made life in traditional societies better. Anthropologists, borrowing heavily from the field of literary criticism, turned to critiques of modernity and the objectivity of ethnographic science. Questions of what the true "other" really was came to dominate the discipline for a time. These critiques of ethnography and philosophical musing about "otherness" served one useful purpose: They forced anthropologists to examine carefully both their methods of data collection and their theoretical assumptions.

As so often happens in world history, our world is again going through dramatic and rapid changes, and anthropology has renewed its interest in the study of sociocultural change. These changes are no longer driven by Western technology and culture but by the global marketplace, which is having a dramatic impact on political and ecological systems around the world. Out of the self-examination precipitated by the postmodern critique has come a renewed theoretical and methodological vigor within the field, precisely what is needed to move into the realm of analysis of global systems.

We both have been interested in how anthropology can be used to interpret contemporary global issues since our years in graduate school and before. We both lived outside of the United States before we took the plunge of becoming professional students of culture. While we both share interests in the more traditional fields of anthropology—such as prehistory, kinship studies, linguistics, and many other fascinating areas of the discipline—it has been the day-to-day issues of human survival and adaptation that have most intrigued us.

Anthropologists, other social scientists, and historians have increasingly been involved in the analysis of global change, and we have been able to rely on the developing body of theory and case studies to write our textbook. We examine social change by focusing on three major transitions: a globally driven economic transition to capitalism, a political transition that involves democratic reform movements, and an ecological transition to smaller families. These transitions, which can be viewed as empirical changes in systems or ideological shifts in what people believe, often bring a mixed bag of positive and negative outcomes.

Our global approach, with its emphasis on these transitions, allows us to discuss current issues across this changing world. It is common to hear and read international news commentators using the term *transition* to describe international issues such as changes in the political structures of Russia, Eastern Europe, and China; however, it is also common to have the same concept used by local newspeople to describe changing communities here in the United States. It is just as common to find local journalists in places like Puebla, Mexico, writing articles in the local *Sol de Puebla* that are remarkably "anthropological" and examining the impact of international trade on local communities and ecosystems. These concepts, so central to modern cultural anthropology, are now the analytic tools used by international experts, other social scientists, journalists, newscasters, and students of change around the world.

In this book, we take advantage of anthropology's holistic and interdisciplinary approaches in our presentation of a world in transition. The book connects with theoretical points of view found in contemporary economics, political science, geography, psychology, history, global studies, and peace studies. In part, we can connect to other disciplines because anthropology has been embraced by these disciplines; in turn, anthropology has become increasingly multidisciplinary, absorbing ideas from other disciplines and integrating them into new theoretical perspectives.

One of these perspectives, called political ecology, provides a framework for analyzing the relationship between productive activity, trade, power, and ecological adaptation in both the preindustrial world and in the contemporary world, and in traditional societies and in modern societies. We utilize this perspective throughout the book, providing the reader with a unified view of how the world works, rather than a collection of topics to learn.

Political ecology combines human (or cultural ecology) and political economy. Human ecology asks questions about adaptation. Its principal concern has been with the interactions between humans and their biophysical environment. A key element in our political ecology approach is the notion that adaptation is a mental process, or what John Bennett has referred to as "minding." Political economy examines questions regarding the institutions of human societies. Its focus has been on the links between productive activity, trade, and the distribution of power in societies. A critical factor in the political economy perspective is the importance of trade, which is an obvious variable for human society in a globalizing age, and a sometimes overlooked factor in connecting societies throughout history and prehistory. In this book, we also take a regional approach and examine how globalization is transforming societies in six regions of the world. Grounding our discussion in the political ecology framework, we look at the development of American and European societies, Africa, the Middle East, Asia, and Latin America, describing both the age-old adaptations and the contemporary problems facing these regions—problems we read or hear about in our daily news. Our political ecology approach highlights the connections between human ecological processes and the political and economic transformations that are occurring in modern states.

Our book also effectively integrates archaeology and history to provide the reader with a sense of continuity from ancient to modern times. This historical context is essential to understanding the dynamics of culture change, ethnic conflict, and indigenous rights issues.

In addition to global, interdisciplinary, holistic, and regional approaches, the text also gives an emphasis to ethnic diversity and ethnic conflict. Chapter 7, "Ethnicity, Ethnic Conflict, and Social Movements," examines the concept of ethnicity and analyzes ethnic conflict and indigenous and ethnic rights movements within the framework of social movements theory. The framework allows us to contextualize social movements, ranging from civil rights movements to indigenous rights movements to ethnonationalism, and to give them meaning in light of global changes. These topics are explored in every regional chapter. While our interest is in current issues, we do not slight traditional topics in anthropology. The first half of the book examines the history of anthropological thought and explores basic questions: What is culture? What is community? How do we study culture? How does language influence cultural perception? How do cultural misunderstandings come about? How are distinct types of societies organized? How did the state come into existence? We also examine other traditional topics such as kinship, religion, marriage, systems of production, and exchange within the context of case studies presented in the regional chapters.

The theoretical approach of the text is easily learned, applied, and used. We suggest using international newspapers, such as the *New York Times*, the *Washington Post* the *Los Angeles Times*, or the *Christian Science Monitor* as adjunct reading. The ideas in the book soon mesh with the current events reports, rendering complex global issues comprehensible. In part, this is because we integrate current events into the text from the very beginning in the form of case studies and ecological maladaptation boxes. These present the complex political, economic, and demographic shifts involved in the development of ecological issues and problems around the world.

Our text is deliberately brief enough to be suitable for use in a quarter system, yet its content is provocative enough to provide plenty of material for discussion in semester-long courses. Anthropology has never been an ivory tower discipline, and this is not an ivory tower book. It demands much of students and instructors, but it steps directly into a world with which we must become familiar in the next decades of the new millennium.

We have had a great deal of help in our quest. It has been gratifying to find that so many of our colleagues share our interest in an anthropology that deals with transitions we are experiencing. We wish to thank several individuals who helped along the way, while at the same time absolving them of any responsibility for the final product.

At the University of Oregon, Harry Wolcott provided insightful comments on the first three chapters, and Vernon Dorjahn made his expertise available on the Africa chapter. Jess Hollenback and Mark Chavalas provided valuable advice on sections dealing with the religions of the Middle East and Asia.

Several colleagues on various campuses served as reviewers of an earlier version of the manuscript and provided many useful comments and suggestions, many of which are reflected in the current text. For their efforts, we sincerely thank: James Armstrong of SUNY at Plattsburgh; Raymond Bucko of Le Moyne College, Syracuse New York; Charles Ellenbaum, College of Du Page, Glen Ellyn, Illinois; Northampton, Massachusetts; Paul Magnarella, University of Florida at Gainesville; Richard Moore, Ohio Sate University, Columbus; Edward Reeves of Morehead State University, Morehead, Kentucky; and Richard Wilk of Indian University at Bloomington.

Finally, both of us would like to acknowledge our intellectual debts to several individuals who have, knowingly or not, influenced our thinking and the development of our ideas over the years. Patrick Gallagher's charismatic enthusiasm for anthropology strongly influenced Sheldon's choice of an anthropology major at the George Washington University in the early 1960s. John W. Bennet, Distinguished Professor Emeritus at Washington University in St. Louis, has helped keep that interest burning and directed it through almost two decades of professional research, writing, and teaching. The intellectual stimulus for much of this book can be traced to Professor Bennett's influence as one of the outstanding scholars of contemporary anthropology.

Phil Young spent both his undergraduate and graduate days at the University of Illinois at Urbana, where he was influenced in various ways by an intellectually powerful cast of characters: Joseph B. Casagrande, Julian Steward, Donald Lathrap, Ken Hale, F. K. Lehman, and Oscar Lewis. They are undoubtedly responsible for Phil's lifelong eclecticism. At the University of Oregon, where he has spent most of his career, Phil would like to acknowledge the intellectual stimulation provided over the years by numerous colleagues, but in particular Homer Barnett and Harry Wolcott in the Anthropology Department, Rob Proudfoot in the International Studies Program, and Colette Grinvald, Talmy Givón, and Scott DeLancey in the Linguistics Department.

Instructor Supplements ● ● ● ●

A complete teaching package is available to instructors who adopt this book. This package includes an **instructor's manual, test bank, course management software,** and **PowerPoint slides.**

- **Instructor's Manual** A comprehensive manual provides a wealth of teaching suggestions, objectives and resources, class activities, and discussion questions.

- **Test Bank** An extensive test bank of over one thousand questions is available to instructors in both hard copy and electronic form. Each chapter consists of fifty multiple choice, twenty true/false, and five essay questions. Each question is referenced to the appropriate text section/topic to make test creation quick and easy.

- **Course Management Software** BVT's Course Management Software (Respondus) allows for the creation of randomly generated tests and quizzes that can be downloaded directly into a wide variety of course management environments such as Blackboard, Web CT, Desire 2 Learn, Angel, E Learning, and others.

- **PowerPoint™ slides** A set of PowerPoint slides includes charts, tables, and graphs from the text, as well as overview slides and bullet-pointed lists designed to guide lectures and discussions.

Student Resources ● ● ● ●

Student resources are available for this textbook at www.BVTLab.com. These resources are geared towards students needing additional assistance as well as those seeking complete mastery of the content. The following resources are available:

- **Practice Questions** Students can work through hundreds of practice questions online. Questions are multiple choice or true/false format and are graded instantly for immediate feedback.

- **Flashcards** BVT*Lab* includes sets of flashcards for each chapter that reinforce the key terms and concepts from the textbook.

- **Chapter Summaries** A convenient and concise chapter summary is available as a study aid for each chapter.

- **Study Guide** A thorough and practical student study guide includes learning objectives, chapter outlines, questions, and ideas that help the student review the material presented in this text. The study guide is available in both physical and online formats.

BVT*Lab*

BVT*Lab* is a simple, robust, online lab for college instructors and their students. It is an affordable option for students, with student lab fees costing only $19.99 for a full-semester course. Even if you do not use the lab as your online classroom, your students can still take advantage of the many student resources available In the lab.

BVT*Lab* for Instructors

Course Setup

BVT*Lab* has an easy-to-use, intuitive interface that allows instructors to quickly set up their courses and grade books, and replicate them from section to section and semester to semester. Multiple choice and true/false questions can be delivered online as practice questions, homework assignments, quizzes, and tests—each of which draws from a separate bank of questions. Homework, quizzes, and tests have assigned start and end times; tests can be proctored in the computer lab or self-proctored for distance learners. Instructors can preview and manually select questions assigned to students, or they can use the "quick-pick" feature in BVT*Lab* to generate sets of questions.

Grade Book

Using an assigned passcode, students register into the grade book. All homework, quizzes, and tests are automatically graded and recorded in the grade book. In addition, instructors can manually enter or modify scores, with provisions for extra credit, attendance, and participation grades. Grade books can be printed, or downloaded for transfer to various school course management systems.

Communication Tools

Instructors can post discussion threads to a class forum and then monitor and moderate student replies. Important notifications can also be sent directly to each student via email.

BVT*Lab* for Students

BVT*Lab* is a comprehensive online learning environment designed to help students succeed. It provides a complete online classroom, as well as the practice questions, learning aids, and communication tools that students need for success. For classes taught within the lab, students can view their grades for all completed work and also review prior homework and quizzes to identify areas that require additional study.

An online discussion forum allows students to interact with each other and the instructor to explore challenging concepts and share other resources, while providing an online community for distance learning.

Even if a class is not taught in the lab, students are always welcome to login as a guest and explore the many student resources described above.

BVT Online Student Bookstore ● ● ● ●

For convenience and savings, students have the added option of purchasing this textbook and associated resources in the following formats at www.BVT*Lab*.com:

- Two-color, hardcover textbook
- Two-color, softcover textbook
- Loose-leaf black & white textbook
- eBook subscription (six months)
- BVT*Lab*
- Online student resource package
- Study guide—hard copy or eBook subscription

Customization ● ● ● ●

BVT's Custom Publishing Division can help you modify this book's content to satisfy your specific instructional needs. The following are examples of customization:

- Rearrangement of chapters to follow the order of your syllabus
- Deletion of chapters not covered in your course
- Addition of paragraphs, sections or chapters you or your colleagues have written for this course
- Editing of the existing content, down to the word level
- Addition of handouts, lecture notes, syllabus, etc.
- Incorporation of student worksheets into the textbook
- Study guide—hard copy or eBook subscription

All of these customizations will be professionally typeset to produce a seamless textbook of the highest quality, with an updated table of contents to reflect the customized content.

About the Author ● ● ● ●

Sheldon Smith was born in Port of Spain, Trinidad, in 1940 and grew up in Latin America. He moved to the United States at age fourteen. His father was a U.S. diplomat, and Smith planned to follow in his father's footsteps. However, his study of Anthropology became his major focus. Smith holds a B.A. in Sociology/Anthropology from George Washington University (1959–1963). He completed his masters and doctorate in Anthropology from the University of Oregon (1964–1969). He has spent most of his career at the University of Wisconsin, La Crosse, and has carried out extensive field research in Columbia.

An Open Invitation to Our Readers ● ● ● ●

We feel it is imperative to make sure that our textbook is as current, relevant, and engaging as possible, as well as providing the greatest utility benefit to instructors and students alike. If you have any comments and/or suggestions from which future editions of this book may benefit, please let us know. We welcome your emails and will give due consideration to each and every one. Please send your communications to: **contactus@bvtpublishing.com**.

Introduction
Studying Anthropology

Anthropology in the Twenty-First Century

All disciplines have their stereotypes. Psychologists are pictured working with beleaguered patients to find what went wrong with the mother/father/child relationship. Sociologists are viewed working with urban elites and masses to solve issues based on class biases. Paleontologists dig up the bones of dinosaurs to uncover the secrets of biological evolution, and cultural anthropologists are viewed trying to understand how "primitive peoples" live around the world. We begin here by arguing that all of these disciplines are much broader than as portrayed above. This is a book about cultural anthropology, a discipline that was once called "ethnography" when its subject was pre-modern or primitive people around the world. The study of "primitive man" was what made the discipline of interest to both students and the public in the early twentieth century. After World War II, however, the term ethnography was slowly replaced by the term cultural anthropology, and the discipline has expanded to include all of the people of world. The study of primitive man is now looked at as a historical, and somewhat ethnocentric, phase (a term to be explained shortly) of cultural anthropology.

Cultural anthropology today is a very broad topic, and the discipline has expanded exponentially from the late nineteenth and early twentieth centuries, when the topic of primitive man was its focus. Today, the study of primitive man has been reduced to only one or two chapters in cultural anthropology books; but as was true sixty years ago, the key subject is still culture. Culture is central to cultural anthropology, but it is difficult to define like many key concepts in the social sciences. (Other social science concepts that are difficult to define are economy, power, and personality). Culture is a concept that has been so successful in cultural anthropology that it has been adopted by many other disciplines.

What makes cultural anthropology such an effective discipline is its field research or ethnography. Such anthropological luminaries as Franz Boas, Bronislaw Malinowski, Ruth Benedict, and Margaret Mead developed ethnographic field research techniques. For these writers and their followers, research consisted of getting into the mind of the informant. While most social sciences depend on quantitative research techniques, ethnography requires a humanistic or non-quantitative knowledge of human culture. (This is a subject we will return to; for a history of the subject see Harris 1968.)

Contemporary cultural anthropology has expanded way beyond the study of primitive societies. A survey of the Internet soon reveals that the range of ethnographic or cultural anthropological research and writing in the twenty-first century is extraordinary. A few surprising topics include work by anthropologists in the inner city on crack dealers, the study of the acquisition and marketing of human body parts, the culture of international markets, aid in developing countries, and research on violence around the world. These and other cultural anthropology topics are found in Jeremy MacClancy's recent edited volume *Exotic No More: Anthropology on the Front Lines.* To those who think of anthropology as the study of stones, bones, and "primitive" peoples, the topics of modern cultural anthropology may come as a bit of a surprise.

While a brief survey reveals all types of anthropology that are not traditional, deeper knowledge of the history of the disciplines shows that research on controversial and difficult issues is nothing new, but has characterized the discipline from its beginnings. After all, the central question asked by cultural anthropologists is "what does it mean to be human?" To answer that question, anthropologists have researched evidence for all kinds of interesting problems that have faced humankind since Australopithecus, the first ancestors of *Homo sapiens*, appeared on earth. While humans have had many successes, today we worry about our own survival; and we find that the writings of anthropologists about the disappearances of ancient civilizations, such as the Indus people of Harappa-Mohenjo Daro, the Ancient Egyptians, the Aztec, the Maya, the Inca and the cliff dwellers of the American Southwest may shed light on threats to our own survival. As is true for modern cultures, all of these ancient civilizations suffered from over-exploitation of resources. However, anthropologists do not just study how societies ceased to be—they also study how they came into being through cultural evolution. Anthropologists have formed a simple evolutionary typology—from bands of hunters, tribes in simple agrarian societies limited to slash and burn agriculture, chiefdoms and civilizations with complex irrigation agriculture. Bands, tribes, chiefdoms, and civilizations form a typology of social complexity around which this book is organized. We also will look at other typologies that cross cut bands, tribes, chiefdoms and states, such as those having to do with kinship, community organization, child training practices and personalities, types of art, technology, and much else.

Recently, many anthropologists have focused on the threats to human societies that have to do with global economic changes, known as globalization, such as we read about for the cultures of Guatemala, Haiti and Indonesia. What anthropologists often discover is that globalization causes people to make changes to their own way of life that damage their environments and to which people cannot, subsequently, adapt. Quoting Marshall Sahlins, one of the leaders of modern anthropology, "Lots of things people do are truly stupid, if understandable, and many cultures have gone to the wall" (1977, 221).

■Cultures can be assimilated by more powerful or attractive cultures or a culture may fight to maintain its own cultural integrity. Americans are still surprised at how Moslems around the world have responded to fears of their assimilation by non-Moslems.

Yet not all cultures self-destruct. Some cultures are attacked by other cultures and destroyed. Americans with some sense of history are familiar with their own ancestors' actions in destroying many American Indian cultures. Cultures can, also, be assimilated by more powerful or attractive cultures, such as is happening around the world; or a culture may fight to maintain its own cultural integrity. Americans are still surprised at how Moslems around the world have responded to fears of their assimilation by non-Moslems. Today, 9/11 has become shorthand for fears, most of them imaginary, of attacks on American societies by radical religious movements around the world.

We know that crises seem to be everywhere. Scientists are central to our understanding of their complexity; and because anthropology is an extremely broad discipline, there appear to be few "global topics" in which anthropologists are not involved. Researchers in anthropology and other sciences show that humans around the world have been constantly challenged by the problem of survival. Among the problems studied are overpopulation and the unsustainable use of resources needed for our survival: rapid depletion of nearly all of the usable resources of the land, the rivers, and the seas; massive deforestation; soil erosion; species extinction; and toxic chemical pollution of the air we breathe, the water we drink, and the foods, be they plant or animal, which we consume. Thanks to the research of anthropologists and many other scientists we know that pollution and deforestation seem to be contributing to global warming. Hunger and poverty are becoming more common in some regions as human populations continue to increase, while in other regions just the opposite is happening as populations shrink and people suffer from epidemics of overeating. Over one-third of all Americans are obese, and the lives of Americans of the future may be shorter than those of today. While democracy has recently replaced dictatorships in many societies around the world, in others ethnic conflict and corruption appear endemic. These problems are no longer local, isolated instances; they are worldwide, brought on by the excesses of the expansion of a global economy (globalization) in which we are all involved, directly or indirectly, and whether we like it or not.

Will the cultures of the twenty-first century go to the wall? Are rich societies threatening the ways of life of others by dragging them into a global economy? Or will globalization bring answers that are needed by threatened societies? Can anthropologists supply a few of the answers in helping threatened cultures survive?

The study of anthropology can go a long way toward providing a few answers to these questions, but there are many other questions that anthropologists have studied over the last century and a half that are much less dramatic. Among a few of these are questions asked in the age of "classic anthropology," which lasted roughly from the beginning of the twentieth century until the early 1970s: How did mankind originate? How did languages evolve? How do children become adults? What is the role of sexuality in the

■Are rich societies threatening the ways of life of others by dragging them into a global economy?

development of social systems? How did legal systems evolve? What is the function of religion? How did art come about? Research on such topics continue on today, and continue to play a large role, but many contemporary anthropologists also conduct research on such topics as business enterprises and marketing, education, law, and many other important topics that will be discussed in this book. The age of "global anthropology," which is now upon us, should not obscure the thousands of topics studied by anthropologists around the world.

The breadth of anthropology is absorbing, for the definition of anthropology is nothing less than "the study of humankind." While this definition differs from earlier definitions only in its political correctness (anthropology used to be defined as the study of *man*kind), the major concerns of the discipline have shifted significantly as the world has changed. For example, the traditional preoccupation of ethnographers with describing and interpreting kinship terminological systems, descent systems, and rules of marriage and postmarital residence—an understandable focus of interest when studying small-scale societies that were apparently isolated socially from the world beyond their boundaries—has seemingly all but disappeared, even though it was very important to the age of classic anthropology and the study of "primitive man." Modern cultural anthropologists still consider kinship important to an understanding of the workings of many, if not most, cultures; but kinship studies have been reformulated as studies of gender roles and relations, power, inequality, and difference (Peletz 1995). In general, anthropologists have not so much turned their attention away from studies of societies of intimates (Givón 1979); rather, they have increasingly focused on the larger scale interconnections of communities, regions, and states and the consequences of these for societies of all sizes and cultural persuasions. This is what we mean by "global anthropology."

Many anthropologists are disturbed by the changes they see in our modernizing world. Several years ago, I (SS) received a letter from a senior anthropologist, now deceased, who felt deeply distressed by changes he had helped bring about in East Africa. (When recounting personal experiences in the text, (SS) after the "I" stands for Sheldon Smith and (PY) stands for Philip Young.) He viewed modernization as a destroyer of traditional communities. However, he had worked for international organizations to "improve life" among pastoral nomads, and in improving their lives, had undermined their traditions. There is no doubt that modernization has introduced new ideas which allow (or force) native peoples to become subordinate to the will of outsiders, threaten their customs and their habitats, and have the potential to alter completely their way of life. In this text, we will consider many changes in traditional life ways from our anthropological perspective; but we must also keep in mind that for some people, the disappearance of traditions may not be lamented, as illustrated in the personal account in the following case study.

■Modernization has the potential to completely alter a culture's way of life.

Case
Study

Jardín, Colombia, a Personal Account

Almost three decades ago, in 1984, I (SS) took a bus from the city of Medellín, Colombia, to the small town of Jardín for a three-week research project. My brother had written his dissertation on the coffee farmers of the region, and I had visited the region when I was just a teenager and a member of the Boy Scouts of Colombia (my father was the U.S. Consul assigned to Medellín, and my family lived there from 1953–1957). The name *Jardín* means garden in Spanish. Our boy scout troop camped outside of Jardín in December 1956. At the time, my images of Jardín were of a remote, quiet, Andean town of whitewashed walls and red tile roofs set in a valley as green as emeralds. Later that year, my high school friends and I had gone into the town one weekend and watched and participated in dancing the *bambuco* (a traditional dance) with local girls. Many years later, my brother, Richard, lived in a nearby town while working for the Peace Corps, and subsequently spent several years in Jardín where he had made many friends, which is a prerequisite for anthropological research. His research was the basis for his dissertation, *Los Cafeteros* or the *Coffee Growers* (1974).

In 1984, I collected information on the changes that had occurred in the region since my brother's research in the late 1960s and my own visit almost twenty years prior. I was astonished. In 1956, only a few of the wealthiest locals had access to battery powered short wave radios. By 1984, most of the middle class families in the town, and most of the coffee farmers in the countryside, had television sets, VCRs, and boom boxes. A local radio station played Colombian versions of the Grateful Dead. Television brought soap operas depicting upper class Colombian culture to the wives of coffee farmers, and on Saturday nights, those wives dressed up like their favorite actresses and came into downtown Jardín for coffee or a rum drink. No one danced the bambuco in the town's *cantinas* (taverns) anymore; and when asked about the traditional music I had enjoyed so much as a teenager, young people told me *"ah, esta es la musica de nuestros padres"* (that is the music of our parents). What did they listen to? American rock and roll sung in Colombian Spanish by local rock bands.

Not long after my short stay, I learned that the people of Jardín were threatened by the power of the Medellín and Cali drug cartels, and the dangers of being kidnapped prevented my return. The cartels were finally destroyed in the 1990s. Americans I knew blamed Colombians for the importation of drugs into the United States, but the people of Jardín I met had a different perspective than did Americans. Many of the people I talked to felt that Colombian culture was being corrupted by American demands for drugs and that Americans had to gain control over their own problem. The best the people of Jardín could do was to protect their own children from drugs by jailing drug dealers, who were not welcome in the town.

I was disturbed by many of the changes since 1956. I missed the traditional music and dances, and I felt the community was threatened by the power of the "kings of cocaine," as two American writers described them (Gugliotta and Leen 1989). The young people I met did not feel the same about the change in musical tastes although they were angry with the drug dealers and American images of Colombians as seen on American television programs such as *Miami Vice*, a popular program that depicted Colombians as importers of drugs from South America.

My own contact with Colombians in the 1950s had been of a very different culture, one in which drugs played almost no role while family and community were central and traditions were venerated. However, by 1984, the traditions with which I was familiar had faded. While the past was important, the haunting folk songs of the past were no longer played in public. In 1984, the people of the town used modern technology to protect and preserve their traditions. VCRs and camcorders recorded the old dances for posterity. Today, the people of Jardín watch television to see who is going to win a competition in Bogota as the best *bambuco* dancers in the country, but they do not know the steps anymore (not unlike Americans watching Appalachian folk dances and listening to their music on television). Coffee brokers use computers to study market conditions and try to gauge the best times to buy or sell coffee. American buyers for Starbucks are in constant communication with coffee brokers to find out where the best coffee beans are grown and when to buy. Juan Valdez, who is from this region of Colombia, appears on your television sets advertising fine Colombian coffees. Most astonishing to this writer, Jardín has a site on the Internet, where one can visit the same

town via Google and even contact residents through e-mail. Also of interest is how young Columbian scholars, writing about the cultural history of their country, now draw on the writings of an earlier generation of anthropologists about the Columbian ethnic populations.

While rural Colombia is threatened with the homogenization of its popular culture by "media" culture (what shows up on television), globalization does not make Colombian culture disappear. Instead, what is happening is the emergence of a new culture that is neither traditional nor modern but combines both. As one moves the radio dial, stations play traditional folk music or modern Colombian rock and roll. One cantina in downtown Jardín plays *"El Dueto de Antaño"* (the *Duet of the Past* or of *yesteryear)*, while another plays Mexican golden oldies, and a third plays hard rock or hip hop. Since all three cantinas face the same park, where their loudspeakers are hung from oak trees, a listener can hear expressions of three subcultures at once.

My image of Jardín as a remote Colombian town was shaken up even further recently when I was looking through a magazine published by *Nature Conservancy.* In it I found an article describing how a resident of the municipality had donated 124 acres of land to the Nature Conservancy to protect a population of yellow-eared parrots, a species whose existence is threatened, and that Jardín is on a network of regions in Colombia that are trying to preserve nature.

Anthropologists have visited the village of Jardín, the city of Medellín, and many other regions in the state of Antioquia and throughout Colombia over the last century. Since the 1950s, the topic of anthropology has been taught at several Colombian universities; and bibliographies of the work of anthropologists in Colombia would fill many book shelves. For the graduate student looking for a fresh subject, it appears that anthropologists have studied every region of the world. Of course, some regions have been studied in much greater depth than others. Some countries, such as Mexico, now produce their own cultural anthropology students who study the topic in their own universities and become researchers and instructors in anthropology at local universities. While anthropology was once considered an esoteric subject, its subject matter has become of worldwide importance.

Just what is anthropology and why has it stirred up so much interest?

What is Anthropology?

anthropology

The study of humankind

Anthropology is the study of humankind and all its manifestations in all times and places. Anthropologists study the biological, cultural, linguistic, and prehistoric aspects of humans, but they do not do it alone. They incorporate and utilize accumulated knowledge from many sources in their search for answers to why humans think and believe and behave in so many diverse ways. Not all anthropologists do field research. Many find it more productive to work on published sources found in libraries. However, because of the vast number of publications on thousands of subjects, there is a sense in which the anthropologist working in the library or the national archives is as much "in the field" as one who is living in a small thatched-roof hut in a tiny tropical forest village several hours (or days) walk from anywhere else.

Anthropology has been called multidisciplinary, or interdisciplinary, because it is a discipline that makes use of the collected knowledge of other academic disciplines in a search for a better understanding of the human condition. An anthropologist specializing in medical research on AIDS makes use of written documents, such as medical reports found in medical libraries and computerized databases. He or she studies the accumulated knowledge of the medical community and pours over what epidemiologists have to say, examines the reports of sociologists, social workers, demographers and possibly even political scientists and economists. The researcher uses the specialists of these other disciplines as (proxy) informants, in much the same way that the anthropologist in the field might interview a native specialist to learn about local beliefs concerning illness and health.

ANTHROPOLOGY AS A SCIENCE OF PROCESS AND CONNECTIVITY

Anthropology is a fascinating and eclectic discipline that studies all forms of human adaptation. Most anthropology is based on human evolution, which has many distinct perspectives. People with just a passing acquaintance with anthropology are aware of the evolutionary aspect of anthropology which focuses on the study of biological adaptations and human origins. Most people are aware that anthropologists have studied how humans evolved from an early chimpanzee-like ancestor to modern Homo sapiens; but the study of culture is central to the understanding of evolution, which is not just a physiological process. Human evolution is an intellectual process as well. Anthropologists are interested in culture as an adaptive response to physical habitats and external pressures (such as trade, colonialism, warfare, hegemony) through time. This interest in the adaptive responses of people in very distinct societies over hundreds of thousands of years has led anthropology to be a very broad social science with an unusually holistic worldview.

Eric Wolf, one of the most prominent anthropologists of the twentieth century, argued that anthropology is a very special science because it never became highly specialized. It is a type of political economy and contrasts with the narrower perspectives of the other social sciences. Wolf states that political economy was

> … a field of inquiry concerned with "the wealth of nations," the production and distribution of wealth within and between political entities and the classes composing them. (Wolf 1982, 8)

As a modern heir of political economy, it most closely resembles the point of view once espoused by Saint Simon and August Comte before the distinct social sciences came into being during the nineteenth and twentieth centuries. Sociology came to focus on the study of how close social relationships (solidarity) hold societies together. Economics specialized in the study of how markets work, as though they were disconnected from society. Political science moved in the direction of creating a market model of the political process, treating economy and ideology as external "environments," but mostly ignoring anything which is not driven by political decision making. These specializations in the study of complex processes led to 1) viewing human social relations (solidarity, markets, and political decisions) as "causal in their own right"; and 2) viewing categories, such as communities and nation states, as "real." Social relations became causes that were severed from economic, political, and ideological processes and connections. Society and culture were conceptualized as autonomous, self-regulating, and bounded. According to Wolf, anthropology retained a pre-specialized interest in the holistic nature of humankind.

In 1982, Wolf published his *Europe and the People without History*, where he most carefully showed that, while anthropology has changed through many schools of thought, it is the primary heir of political economy through its emphasis on "process" and "connectivity." He showed that anthropology has retained a holistic approach. By **process** he meant the focus by anthropologists on the problems of human adaptation to physical habitats (technological changes, impact on the environment), while **connectivity** refers to the "adaptations" of cultures to each other (communication, peace, trade, war). While some anthropologists would like to narrow anthropology to the highly specific ethnographic study of single societies, Wolf argued quoting Alexander Lesser, that anthropology views human societies not as closed systems but as open systems which are connected to each

process

The focus by anthropologists on the problems of human adaptation to physical habitats

connectivity

The "adaptations" of cultures to each other

other (Wolf 1982,19). Cultures, societies, or nation states should not be viewed as bounded or as self perpetuated "designs for living." Wolf emphasized the importance of understanding the dynamics of process and connectivity rather than simply creating categories such as *societies, cultures, nations, bands, tribes, chiefdoms, states, etc.* Often such categories are misused to explain complex events. Echoing Karl Marx, Wolf prefers an anthropology that bares the laws or regularities surrounding the production of wealth.

While Wolf showed why anthropology remained similar to political economy, his book also marked the transition from the age of "classic anthropology" to the age of "global anthropology." His life was cut short in 1999, the same year he published his influential *Envisioning Power,* a book that featured his life-long interest in the nature of politics and power. Wolf contributed to the age of classic anthropology, which focused on the nature of culture, by stressing his own unique ecological view of power relationships; but by 1982, his vision had matured beyond ecology to see all cultures as connected not only to their habitats but to each other through trade and communication. Wolf's book insisted that the societies of the world had always been connected to each other, a view echoed in the historians Robert McNeil and William McNeil's (son and father) 2003 brief world history called *The Human Web.* Most historians and anthropologists tended to the Eurocentric view that world trade began with the discovery of the New World in 1492; but Wolf and the two McNeils wrote that international trade was nothing new, but had been going on for thousands of years, and could be traced to the very beginnings of civilization in the Middle East.

In his work, Wolf bridged classic and global anthropology. While his early work was rooted in classic anthropology, he already understood the importance of global connections. Examples are *Sons of the Shaking Earth* (1959) and *Peasants* (1966) where he rooted societies in their ecosystems but moved on to show the critical nature of trade in connecting societies to each other. In these early works, he introduced the reader to a global perspective of humanity that was very different from his predecessors, and even from his own earlier work.

This book divides the history of anthropology into three phases borrowing key words from archaeology. The first phase, which will only be presented in a brief summary, can be called its **formative phase**. This is the period when anthropologists were primarily trained to collect, classify, and describe cultural and biological materials for museums. The interest of formative anthropologists was to explain to the public what their displays represented, a tremendous task that occurred primarily in the nineteenth century. While curiosity in human origins and foreign cultures pre-dates the nineteenth century, financial resources only came available for such luxuries as museums and universities as societies became industrialized. The next phase, the **classic,** came about as anthropologists turned from their work in museums to the task of education as colleges and universities employed them, beginning just before World War I to just a few decades after World War II. The generation of classic anthropology attempted to answer the question of how the cultures being described worked. A variety of theories were developed, such as functionalism, cultural ecology, Freudian psychology, idealism, and materialism, to name only a few. The phase we are now in can be called **global anthropology**. It has its roots in classic anthropology but seeks to answer questions on the nature of culture by reaching out to global processes. While we have selected Eric Wolf as representing the transition from classic to global anthropology, many classic theoreticians—such as Richard N. Adams, John W. Bennett, and Fredrik Barth—were critical of classic anthropology for its **reductionism,** the tendency to explain human

formative phase

In the history of anthropology, the period in which anthropologists were primarily trained to collect, classify, and describe cultural and biological materials for museums; primarily occurred in the nineteenth century

classic phase

In the history of anthropology, the period in which anthropologists became employed in colleges and universities; began just before World War I and lasted until a few decades after World War II

global anthropology

The current phase of anthropological history, which seeks to answer questions about the nature of culture by reaching out to global processes

reductionism

The tendency to explain human communities through theories that viewed them as though they existed in isolation

■Anthropolgist Reo Fortune spent five months working with the Dobu people of the Pacific and researched kinship, marriage, sex, and sorcery.

communities through theories that viewed them as though they existed in isolation. The key to understanding the difference between classic and global anthropology is not to think of the latter as superior to the former, but to think of classic anthropology as a stepping-stone to global anthropology, just as formative anthropology was a stepping-stone to classic anthropology.

In the formative period, which dates back to little over a century or more ago, we find the anthropologist stepping from the museum and into the classroom with an enormous body of information on the cultures of the world that was continuously growing. The movement into the classic can be identified by anthropologists trying to overcome ethnocentrism. This meant trying to avoid imposing American or European models of society and culture on studies made throughout the world by a growing number of trained ethnographers. Reo Fortune is a good example of a classic anthropologist. Working with the Dobu of the Pacific, he limited himself to a single village of about 25 people, and generalized from that sample to an entire society of about 2,500 people (Fortune 1932). While he took samples of the larger society by traveling throughout Dobu territory, he only lived among these people for five months and restricted his research to kinship, marriage, sex, and sorcery, which he theorized were linked. Unlike today's global anthropologists, he purposefully avoided any records kept by missionaries or European colonial administrators, thinking their writings might be tainted, while he and his colleagues considered his comments to be "scientific." Yet he would use such ethnocentric terms as "puritanical" and "savage" in reference to sex and sorcery, thus viewing "primitives" of the Pacific from the reference point of early twentieth century England. While anthropology has become increasingly more global since the 1970s, the writers of formative and classic anthropology, ethnocentric though some of them were, cannot be abandoned because their writings form a base for contemporary anthropology.

THE SUBDISCIPLINES OF ANTHROPOLOGY

The discipline of anthropology encompasses four major subdisciplines, with specialties within each, and quite a diversity of theoretical perspectives. These disciplines also subdivide and sometimes overlap. The following explains the major divisions of anthropology.

Biological Anthropology: The Study of Physical Change   Biological anthropology and archaeology are methodologically closer to the natural sciences than linguistic and cultural anthropology. The former are geared to the "long view" of human history, whereas cultural anthropology operates in the "current history" of recent centuries. Biological anthropology, in many respects, closely resembles the field of biology, except that anthropologists focus on human beings, their ancestors, and their primate relatives, and not on nonhuman life forms. The evolution of *Homo sapiens sapiens* (modern humans) is a major interest of biological anthropologists, as is the range of human biological variation, which itself is a product of evolution. Human evolution is the heart of biological anthropology. Within the sub-discipline of biological anthropology are three broad but closely related specialties.

Physiological Anthropology, Paleoanthropology, and Primatology

Physiological anthropology is concerned with the physical make up of human beings (and their primate cousins: monkeys, chimpanzees, gorillas, and gibbons). Anthropologists in this field tend to share many of the interests of biologists interested in humans. Their general focus is on how the human body functions and adapts. Medical anthropologists, for example, may work in the tropical areas of Central America, Southeast Asia, and elsewhere trying to find out why certain kinds of diseases occur in the tropics. They may work in highland Peru to find out why certain populations are characterized by aggression and *hypoglycemia* (an abnormally low level of glucose in the blood), and if there is a relationship between the two. They may study the diet and nutritional status of human populations under various environmental conditions. Or, they may use X-ray technology to find out what was in the digestive tract of a mummified Egyptian pharaoh or the recently discovered Mesolithic Man of the Alps. Some may work like Temperance Brennan, in the television show *Bones*, as pathologists specializing in **forensic anthropology** identifying human skeletal remains that may be evidence of a crime. The vast amount of data that anthropologists have accumulated on human biological variation, past and present, is what makes it possible for the forensic anthropologist to decide to what population (race) an individual belonged and whether the remains are ancient or modern, as well as identifying sex and approximate age. After World War II, the identification of many of the remains of American soldiers was done at the Department of Physical Anthropology of the Smithsonian Institute in Washington, D.C. Recently biological anthropologists worked with the governments of Argentina and Guatemala to determine how government critics were killed during the "dirty war" of a decade ago, and in Bosnia and Kosovo to identify victims of **genocide.**

Paleoanthropology is the aspect of biological anthropology with which most people are familiar. A common response when an anthropologist introduces him or herself to someone who lacks familiarity with anthropology is, "oh, you are one of those people who studies bones, like Richard Leakey." I (SS) clearly remember one time as a young anthropology instructor when some La Crosse city officials asked me to identify what they thought were the bones of an ancient mastodon, but turned out to be those of a recently deceased cow. On another occasion I was asked to identify what local police thought was a human foot. I examined it and not only identified it as human but, more precisely, as that of an adolescent boy or girl. Later, forensic experts in Madison identified the same remain as the foot of a young bear. Since that latter experience, I have avoided trying to do the things that biological anthropologists are trained to do; I stick to my sociocultural interests.

forensic anthropology

The identification of human skeletal remains that may be evidence of a crime

genocide

The systematic extermination of a people group

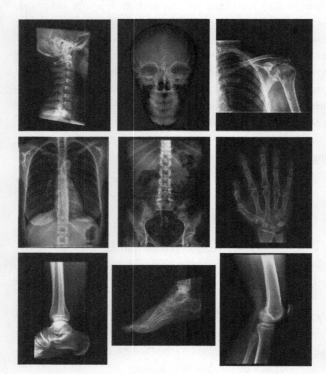

■ The evolution of *Homo sapiens sapiens* (modern humans) is a major interest of biological anthropologists, as is the range of human biological variation, which itself is a product of evolution.

paleoecology

The relations and interactions between ancient life forms and their environment

hominids

Primates, including humans and their ancestors, belonging to the family *hominidae*

artifacts

Items created by humans that have definite forms and functions created by culture

historical archaeology

A subfield of archaeology that examines the sites occupied by human populations during the historic period, and the artifacts the sites contain, in order to supplement the written records of history

Paleoanthropology is very close in both methods and interests to paleontology, the branch of geology that studies the evolution of early life forms. The focus is on what human fossil remains and those of our primate ancestors can tell us about the evolutionary history of humans. It is not at all unusual to find paleoanthropologists working with paleontologists to recreate the **paleoecology** of a region's ancient ecosystems. Today, museums can re-create the interaction of plants and animals from very ancient times.

Other important questions asked by paleoanthropologists usually have to do with human or primate origins and evolution. The term "primate" is applied to the *order* in biological taxonomy that includes all of humanity's ancestors and present day relatives such as lemurs, gibbons, monkeys, and apes. Most of the paleoanthropologist's work is done by using methods of excavation closely related to those of archaeology. Paleoanthropologists tend to concentrate on fossil remains, such as the mineralized skeletons of ancient **hominids** (humans and our relatives) and other primates. While the implications of the discoveries of paleoanthropologists are often controversial and hard to understand, the fact of evolutionary change itself is not a matter of controversy among scientists. Like paleontology, paleoanthropology is a fascinating discipline whose subject matter helps fill out the knowledge anthropologists have accumulated on how humans evolved.

Primatology is closely related to paleoanthropology. Primatologists may study the comparative anatomy of both living and fossil primates in order to ascertain similarities and differences between our primate relatives and us. Some primatologists study the behavior of living primates in much the same way as ethnographers study human cultures. The major difference is that they cannot ask questions of their subjects. Primate behavior specialists are interested in such questions as the extent to which some forms of behavior common to humans and other primate species may be a result of the common biological heritage of primates rather than cultural learning.

Archaeology: The Long View of Culture Change

Archaeology, in many respects, is the oldest sub-discipline of anthropology. Although archaeology also involves the study of human origins and evolution, it differs from paleoanthropology in that the subject matter is not the fossil record but rather the **artifacts** that human beings have left behind. Artifacts are those things created by human beings that have definite forms and functions created by culture. Archaeology takes the long view of culture change, roughly from three or four million years ago when the first artifacts appear to when the historical record takes over and allows us to read about events. **Historical archaeology** is a special subfield of archaeology which examines the sites occupied by human populations during the historic period, and the artifacts these sites contain, in order to supplement the written records of history.

While archaeology is identified most clearly within anthropology with the study of prehistoric cultures, its methods of scientific excavation are often borrowed by other disciplines for research purposes; and its boundaries extend to classical, biblical, and historical archaeology. For example, archaeology has been used recently to excavate early biblical monuments in the Near East and colonial structures in the United States, such as plantations in Georgia

■Artifacts are those things created by human beings which have definite forms and functions, such as the pottery found at this excavation site.

and Florida, which are clearly historical. The Mississippi Valley Archaeology Center of the University of Wisconsin, La Crosse recently excavated a nineteenth century boat and a fort found just south of La Crosse near Prairie de Chien. It is an open question here whether these researchers are dabbling in archaeology, anthropology, history, or biblical studies. What is important is that scholars cross into each other's disciplines. Their activities should remind us just how permeable those boundaries are and how important it is not to make the boundaries between disciplines more real than they are.

Linguistic Anthropology: A Look into Logic and the Mind

Another important subdiscipline of anthropology is linguistics, which is closely related to cultural anthropology. Linguistics is the scientific study of language. **Linguistic anthropology** focuses on the multifaceted relationship between language and culture. It is the anthropologist's way of discerning the logic of other people's reality. It is a way of trying to see things from the emic or native point of view, so to speak, whether the natives are hunters and gatherers of the Kalahari Desert, Quechua-speaking villagers in the Peruvian Andes, or our next-door neighbors. To paraphrase Pogo, we have met the natives and they are us. The study of languages and the nature of the relationship between that language a people speak, their culture, and their thought patterns has long been a part of anthropology. In many respects it really is hard to make a sharp division between linguistics and cultural anthropology. However, the study of language is certainly not now, and never has been, confined to the field of anthropology. The pre-twentieth century roots of linguistics are to be found in philosophy and philology, both of which attempt to decipher the meaning of words and how they change through time. Today linguistics has become a discipline with departmental status at many universities; or it may be associated with departments of English or psychology, depending on the history of the institution and the research foci of the linguists. Both linguistics and cultural anthropology have close relationships to the emerging interdisciplinary field of **cognitive science**.

■Another important reason why the study of linguistics is important to anthropology is that the culture and social organization of a society can be understood only through an understanding of the language of that culture.

Within the broad field of linguistic anthropology are several divisions of labor. **Comparative linguistics** (also called historical linguistics) focuses on the origins of different languages and the genetic relationships among languages. Linguistic anthropologists such as Floyd Lounsbury, Joseph Greenberg, and Terence Kaufman, each in their own way, have been leaders in this field. **Ethnolinguistics** (also called ethnosemantics) is the study of the ways in which people of different cultures organize, categorize, and classify everything that makes up their world. Brent Berlin, Cecil Brown, and Eugene Hunn are among the outstanding scholars in this field. **Sociolinguists** study the particular ways in which language is used in social interaction to mark, for example, *status* and *role* relationships. The works of William Labov are classics in this field.

There are several reasons why anthropologists, particularly cultural anthropologists, have an interest in linguistics. In a great many societies in which anthropologists do research, the languages are unwritten. That is, there is no tradition of literacy. Under such circumstances, the anthropologist may be the first one to record the language using

linguistic anthropology

The study of the relationship between language and culture

cognitive science

The scientific study of cognition

comparative linguistics

The study of the origins of different languages and the genetic relationships among languages

ethnolinguistics

The study of the ways in which people from different cultures organize, categorize, and classify the things that make up their worlds

sociolinguistics

The study language in relation to its social context

phonetic alphabet

An alphabet based on the sounds of a spoken language

phoneme

A unit of sound that has no meaning

morpheme

A unit of sound that has meaning

lexicon

The vocabulary of a particular language

grammar

The way the sentences of a language are constructed

a **phonetic alphabet** to record the sounds. Ideally, this is followed by *phonemic* and *morphological* (a **phoneme** is a unit of sound that does not carry meaning, while a **morpheme** is a unit of sound that contains or carries meaning) analysis and the compilation of a **lexicon** or dictionary and a **grammar** of the language.

The anthropologist often becomes the only specialist in the study of a rare language; and even if the language is not rare, he or she may still be among the few to have studied it. Another important reason why the study of linguistics is important to anthropology is that the culture and social organization of a society can be understood only through an understanding of the language, for neither culture nor social organization are directly observable (both are abstractions from behavior the researcher thinks important). For example, the way in which people classify their relatives differs significantly from society to society. An anthropologist who does not understand the language will not be able to understand basic kinship patterns that are fundamental to social organization. As an example, among the Ngóbe of Panama, father's brother and mother's brother are perceived as distinct from each other; but a father, his brother, and mother's sister's husband are perceived as the same kind of social person and accordingly referred to by the same kinship term. This is quite unlike the American kinship system where the father's brother, mother's brother, mother's sister's husband and father's sister's husband are all perceived to be the same kind of relative—and all are referred to as 'uncle', from which father is distinguished. The way kin are classified can provide important clues to the structure and content of certain role relationships within societies. In American culture, aunt and uncle are special kinsmen on whom one can rely for help. They are particularly important during special occasions such as birthdays, Christmas, marriage, birth, and death. In other cultures, aunts and uncles on the mother's side or father's may be given much greater or lesser importance. For example, among the Cherokee who are matrilineal, the mother and mother's sister are both called mother but are distinguished from the father's sister. Among the Crow that are patrilineal, father and father's brother are called father and are distinguished from mother's brother. Anthropologists have long understood that in some societies where kinship and social organization amount to the same thing, kinship terms are extremely important. For example, the killing of a father's brother may require his son to avenge his father's death. This may be true even if the father was originally killed because he had committed murder. Or, the son may demand blood wealth (called *wergild* in the kinship literature).

Finally, linguistics is important to the anthropologist because it is a way to gain some understanding of the workings of the human mind. In the next chapter we will find that a language is a highly specific code, one that is governed by what may be broad and genetically based rules. These rules may have a lot to do with the basic operation of the brain, that is, with cognitive processes; and by studying a language, we gain some understanding of the way in which these complex codes work. Furthermore, it appears that many aspects of culture are also governed by rules, which parallel rules of language; and by studying the structure of language, we gain insights into the operation of how the mind helps organize culture. However, language and culture are both abstractions from raw data, and the attempt to link causal relationships between the two (does language cause culture or vice versa?) leads to frustration.

Cultural Anthropology: The Anthropology of Current History

The broadest of the sub-disciplines of anthropology, in terms of areas of specialization and theoretical perspectives, as well as number of practitioners, is cultural anthropology, also called sociocultural anthropology. It is also the subdiscipline that is least well understood by the well-educated layperson. For thirty years, when asked what I (PY) did for a living, if I responded, "I am a cultural anthropologist" most people on planes, trains, buses, and in the local bars either responded with "well, that's very interesting," meaning they didn't have the foggiest idea of what I did, or they asked "have you dug up any interesting bones lately?" When someone seemed genuinely interested, I took the trouble to explain. For most people, the study of living people is something they associate with psychology or sociology; some feel quite uncomfortable with the very idea that anyone would make a living by studying how other people live.

The term "sociocultural" is a combination of the words *society* and *culture* and is often used as shorthand for the two. To the cultural anthropologist, culture and society are analytically distinct phenomena that, like language and culture, are derived from the same observations of people. They are so tightly entwined in real life as to be inseparable; thus questions about the relationship between culture and society usually lead to dead ends. As discussed earlier, when a cultural anthropologist conducts field research among a particular group of people, the endeavor is called **ethnography** and the researcher an **ethnographer.** He or she may wish to call their observations society, culture, or sociocultural; but these terms are meaningless to the people studied, as are the terms ethnography or ethnographer. One of the most difficult problems experienced by ethnographers is trying to explain to the people being studied just what the objectives of the researcher might be. In volatile regions of the world, the ethnographer may find his or her work difficult to explain and dangerous to carry out.

When an anthropologist makes a comparison of the features of any two or more societies or cultures, the activity is called **ethnology**, or comparative ethnography. Such comparisons may be qualitative (looking only for the presence or absence of particular features) or quantitative (for example, counting instances of co-occurrences of two or more features and using statistical methods to determine the degree of significance of resulting correlations).

Cultural anthropology, during its classic period, was subdivided into subdisciplines, many of which continue to be used today in the age of global anthropology. Among these subdisciplines is **social anthropology,** usually the study of kinship, but also overlapping into the following specializations: **political anthropology** (the study of the emergence and development of public policy and political culture); **economic anthropology** (the comparative study of economic systems); **human** or **cultural ecology** (the relationship of cultural systems to physical habitats); the **anthropology of religion** (the comparative study of how humans view the supernatural); and the **anthropology of art** (primarily the study of folk art) and other specializations found in the section on classic anthropology following Chapter 2. Global or contemporary anthropology, another subdivision of cultural anthropology, is made up of disciplines that emerged in importance during and after the 1970s, many of which also began to emerge in the age of classic anthropology, such as **applied anthropology,** which emerged directly after World War II but did not become popular until the latter part of the twentieth century; **medical anthropology** (applied biological anthropology); **legal anthropology** (comparative law); **ethnoscience** or **cognitive anthropology** (the study of folk taxonomies of human and natural phenomena)— to name a few of the topics taken up in the section on global anthropology. Every generation of anthropologists has brought with it new terms that became popular and then faded in importance. When looking through the literature, it is important to keep in mind that the essence of most all of cultural anthropology, regardless of specialization, is the study of social and cultural manifestations of living populations. Of recent importance

---

ethnography

Field research conducted by a cultural anthropologist among a particular group of people

ethnographer

The researcher who conducts field research among a particular group of people

ethnology

The comparison of the features of two or more societies or cultures

social anthropology

The study of kinship

political anthropology

The study of the emergence and development of public policy and political culture

economic anthropology

The comparative study of economic systems

human or cultural ecology

The study of the relationship between cultural systems and physical habitats

is the emergence of **ethnohistory** as a special field of cultural anthropology that attempts to understand the lives of past populations through judicious, if tedious, analysis and interpretation of a combination of historical records and archaeological data and that belongs to both classic and global anthropology.

Cultural anthropology is similar to other social sciences, such as sociology, political science, psychology, and economics. However, it is much broader and tends to incorporate aspects of these disciplines. Eric Wolf has argued that modern cultural anthropology is a type of history, one that differs from history itself through the application of the scientific method. This observation should not imply that historians do not use the scientific method, for many do. To explain cultural anthropology more clearly, we call it a social science of current history. By current, we mean anything within the last two to three hundred years. By science, we are stressing ethnographic field research. It is here that historians and cultural anthropologists can be most clearly distinguished. Historians do not do field research, while cultural anthropologists are expected to do field research. Field research sets the discipline apart from other social sciences. Field research also creates sets of ethical problems that have been difficult to resolve. Field research in cultural anthropology requires becoming accepted by some group of people and gaining their trust sufficiently to understand their way of life from the inside; this form of research is called participant observation. Ideally, the researcher should be able to achieve an "etic" point of view ("emic" and "etic" and the problems entailed with participant observation are explained further on). Participant observation is a powerful tool. While developed by ethnographers, participant observation has been adopted by researchers in other disciplines such as political science, sociology, economics, and psychology, as well as studies of areas such as Latin America, Europe, the Middle East, Africa, and Asia.

Anthropology is made up of many subdisciplines in addition to cultural anthropology. Among the most important is biological or physical anthropology, which studies the biological changes in humans over millions of years. Archaeology is well known to the public. It depends on the study of artifacts or elements of culture created by humans. It takes the "long view" of culture change over the last three to four million years. We have already touched on linguistics, which uses science to study languages.

Cultural anthropology is less involved with the study of the past and is restricted to the recent neighborhood of time, the last two to three hundred years. Ethnohistory,

■Sociocultural anthropology applied specializations lends itself to college campuses with international studies programs. Posing here is William Balee, Anthropology professor at Tulane University with an indigenous land consultant in Brazil.

ethnohistory

The study of the lifeways of past populations

mentioned above, attempts to study ethnographic writings belonging to the past. For example, explorers in the New World created an extensive literature describing their discoveries to European readers. More recently, American and European writers have tried to describe the impact of European capitalism on native populations around the world. This is roughly the period within which capitalism has evolved, called the age of modernization or globalization.

Many anthropology texts tend to view capitalism, modernization, and globalization as negative forces that disrupt traditional societies. While this is true in certain respects, all societies everywhere are making changes to accommodate economic development, some for the better and some for the worse. Yet everywhere, these are changes that are beyond anyone's control. Even if we wanted to protect traditional societies, we lack the tools to do so. All people, including us, lack the means to protect themselves from modernization or globalization. While we believe that it is better for people to judge how far they will accommodate to global pressures for change, no one really knows how to block cultural change.

Classic and Global Anthropology

In this book, we will include material from biological, linguistic, and archaeological anthropology; but we will do so from the point of view of cultural anthropology. A century and a half ago, anthropology meant the study of human origins in order to prove the superiority of Western civilization. Most studies were from biological, linguistic, and archaeological anthropology; cultural anthropology did not yet exist. Anthropology assumed the superiority of Western Civilization, primarily as expressed in post-Civil War America and Victorian Great Britain. Today, anthropology means almost the opposite of what it once did. Today, anthropology tends to be associated with ideas on human equality and on the damage created by ethnocentrism, when one culture (European and/or American) considers itself superior to others cultures. In most of this book, unless otherwise stressed, the term "anthropology" will be used to mean contemporary cultural anthropology with only brief introductions to archaeology, biological anthropology, and linguistics.

We are going to distinguish "classic" from "global anthropology" in the chapters that follow. Classic anthropology coincides with the age of "modernization" and was the study of largely non-modern societies around the world from the turn of the twentieth century to the 1970s. Global anthropology does not contradict classic anthropology, and many continue to study the problems asked during the age of classic anthropology. However, global anthropology differs from classic anthropology in how culture is viewed and the goal in studying peoples around the world. There are many exceptions to the following, but the age of classic anthropology was a search for "pure" culture among so called "primitive" peoples who had not been influenced by the modern world and who were thought to be isolated. Classic anthropologists thought they could find out how pre-modern societies operated by studying native populations in remote parts of the world. The age of global anthropology, which we are now in, rejects the idea that there is

■ The age of classic anthropology was a search for "pure" culture among so called "primitive" peoples who had not been influenced by the modern world and who were thought to be isolated.

such a thing as pure culture and the distinctions between "modern" and "primitive" are no longer made. Contemporary anthropologists are just as apt to do their research in American and European or other "complex" cultures, as they are "non-Western cultures." The idea of "pure culture" is no longer central to research because anthropologists recognize that all cultures have been in communication with each other for thousands of years, and that there never was such a thing as a "pure culture." In addition, all cultures around the world are components in a global world; there is no such thing as an isolated, "primitive" or "simple" society. Such a society may never have existed, except in the imagination of classic anthropologists. For some anthropologists, the changes introduced by globalization are for the better; but for many others the changes may not be so. The very meaning of what is better and what is worse is central to many debates in global anthropology and other related disciplines.

In addition to trying to find pure cultures, both anthropologists and sociologists thought that the study of primitive societies would give them insights into how societies function. In the 1930s, functionalism, a theoretical perspective that pervaded the social sciences, assumed that societies could be broken down into their components and that the study of the interaction of these components would clarify how societies "function." Another important term that appeared during this time was "holistic," a term that meant roughly the same as "functionally integrated." Functionalism and holism meant much the same thing, and it was assumed that these characteristics were best studied in small or primitive societies. The component that dominated all such societies was the economy. The evolution of society could be understood as going from simple economic exchanges to complicated ones. For example, political activities in hunting societies were dominated by reciprocity or gift giving, while political activities in agricultural societies were dominated by redistribution (in the hands of a "big man") and states were characterized by states based on irrigation agriculture where peasants did all the work and were ruled by managerial elites. The holistic nature of such societies became central to how anthropologists viewed all societies, including American and European societies. However, with the maturation of classic anthropology, and the appearance of Eric Wolf's work (see below), the isolated nature of "primitive" societies around the world came to be questioned. The idea that societies were governed by their economies also lost its appeal as the complexity of all societies became increasingly apparent. Primitive societies, it turns out, were never simple and probably not primitive. The specializations (topics) of the classic remain with us, but they have matured from the study of pre-modern, "simple" or primitive societies to contemporary societies in a global world. The term "holistic" has also changed in meaning, from the idea that cultures were bounded and that their distinct "systems" reinforced one another to the idea that people experience cultures as though they were integrated, but that the experience of integration is an illusion.

Like classic anthropology, global anthropology has its subdivisions, many of which grew out of the subdisciplines of the classic and will be presented in the chapters where they appear to best belong. Examples of global anthropological specialization are applied anthropology, development anthropology, environmental anthropology, feminist studies, gender studies, medical anthropology, and many other topics we will touch on.

Global anthropology is grounded in the same ethnographic training that characterized classic anthropology and depends on the trust of informants. We do not want to suggest that "classic anthropology" was "then," and "global anthropology" is "now," or that the two are exclusive to each other. The following chapters begin with classic anthropology and move into global anthropology. While classic anthropologists lived and wrote in a pre-global time period, the intellectual problems they faced were not unlike those of today. The ethical tangles of whether to put on paper information that might be used to exploit informants and break the trust established in field research today is no different than fifty or a hundred years ago. The problems of how an outsider becomes an insider are the same. The many ways of how to understand culture were first formulated by classic anthropologists; the definitions of economic, political, psychological, and other anthropologies were first made by classic anthropologists and are useful today. As was true during the classic, in the global age defining where we stand and what we do is by no means a straightforward operation for there are many theoretical debates and strong disagreements. We are going to explain different points of view, but we will not take sides.

One of the most important subfields of global anthropology is applied anthropology. Applied anthropology is the use of anthropological knowledge to solve the problems of human societies around the world. Applied studies have become very popular among students who are interested in the discipline but do not want to teach. It is also a viable option in these times when jobs in academic anthropology are hard to find. The difference between the cultural anthropologist doing basic research and the applied anthropologist lies in the questions asked. The cultural anthropologist (classic or global) will have an interest in testing some aspect of a scientific theory. This requires being able to spell out the theory clearly and the hypotheses that are derived from it. The applied anthropologist, although trained in theory, has greater interest in the resolution of human problems such as hunger, poverty, or the destruction of ecosystems. Back issues of the journals *Human Organization*, and *Human Ecology* provide a sampling of the kinds of problems addressed by applied anthropologists: groundwater management in Baluchistan, weight concerns between African-American and White female adolescents, the use of family planning among the poor in the United States, the impact of commercial fishing on oceanic ecosystems, common property rights in the state of Kerela in India, deforestation in the Philippines and the Ecuadorian Amazon, pest-management in Egypt, mortality in rural Australia, discrimination against Ethiopian Jews in Israel, peacemaking in Mindanao, mental illness in Mexico, the impact of cattle ranching on the little Colorado River Basin, and so on.

Culture with a Big "C"

culture

The shared knowledge, beliefs and patterns for behavior, the resulting behavior, and the resulting material products

Whether dealing with classic or global anthropology, it is fair to say that cultural anthropologists are not in complete agreement about how to define or understand the primary objective of their analysis: **culture.** The concept of culture is basic to anthropology; but like the concepts of *personality* in psychology and *power* in political science, definitions tend to differ from writer to writer. Exactly what is culture? There is some agreement that culture has been humankinds' primary means of adaptation for the past several thousand years, yet it is a concept notoriously difficult to define. We have ceased to change biologically in any significant way; and while there have been a few minor biologically adaptive trends in the last ten thousand years, we adapt to nature through culture, which constantly changes. Culture is often expressed and usually transmitted through language, but it is much more than language. Large-scale complex cultures are usually composed of several different *sub-cultural* realities. These sub-cultures may be based on ethnicity (e.g., Mexican-Americans), religion (e.g., Catholics or Jews), or even occupation (e.g., longshoremen—see Pilcher, 1972).

The classic, and, so far as we know, first anthropological definition of culture was that of Edward B. Tylor who wrote the following in 1871:

"Culture or Civilization, taken in its wide ethnographic sense, is that complex whole which includes knowledge, belief, art, morals, law, custom, and any other capabilities and habits acquired by man as a member of society" (Tylor 1958, 1 [1871])

From this rather all-encompassing beginning, which appears to take in everything, *including* the kitchen sink, the quest for an agreed-upon definition of anthropology's central concept has continued. In 1952, two classic anthropologists, Alfred Kroeber and Clyde Kluckhohn compiled over 150 definitions of culture, provided some historical background on the origin and use of the term, classified the definitions in broad categories, and provided a definition of their own. Their classification contained the following categories: descriptive (emphasis on broad definitions with lists of content); historical (emphasis on tradition); normative (emphasis on rules or ideals); psychological (emphasis on habits and learning); structural (emphasis on patterning); genetic (based on D.N.A.); mental (emphasis on ideas, symbols); material (culture as product); and finally, incomplete definitions (unsystematic or metaphorical). As Borofsky (1994, 3) points out, the Kroeber and Kluckhohn definition of culture seems to have proven too broad and cumbersome and is seldom cited.

Modern definitions of culture are of two general types. The first type is ideational: culture is defined as being purely in the mind, while behavior and artifacts are left out. These are considered to be manifestations of culture, but should not be confused with culture. The second type includes the behavioral and material as well as the mental. Definitions of the first type, what we refer to as culture with a "small c," deliberately distinguish internalized mental configurations from the behavior, institutions, and material products that result from them. Definitions of the second type, those that include our internalized mental rules for behavior, the behavior itself, and usually the material products of our endeavors here are considered to be culture with a big "C." Here the links among mental rules, behavior, and material culture are stressed and at least part of what we mean by "culture is directly observable." We will use a definition of the second type in this book.

Culture is shared knowledge, beliefs and patterns for behavior, the resulting behavior, and the resulting material products.

Thus, culture in our definition is partly a symbolic phenomenon that exists in the mind and a code of sorts that governs the way we act in particular contexts. Culture is also partly the patterned behavior that people in a society engage in as a result of shared ideas about what is appropriate. In addition, the shared knowledge of a society's members results in the production of the material goods of a culture, some of which may be purely utilitarian, while others may be have purely symbolic meaning, and a whole lot are both useful and symbolic.

Culture, then, is both idea and thing. As an example, think of what went into building a 1956 Chevrolet more than a half-century ago. Designers and engineers first made blueprints determining the car's style and mechanical details. The car was first an idea, and then it was manufactured into an object, which caught on and became very popular. That car is no longer accepted as a design for automobiles. It was too large and consumed too much fuel to meet today's needs, but both the idea and its manifestation as an automobile are a part of American culture. Today, the same car may stand in a museum as an example of mid-twentieth century automobiles. The car has very different symbolic meanings for visitors to the museum. It is not the same car to an adolescent today as it would be to an adult who was an adolescent when the car was first manufactured. Culture is a constantly changing phenomenon.

Earlier we wrote that *society* has often been confused with culture and vice versa. In many anthropology and sociology texts, the definitions overlap to the point where it is hard to distinguish the two. While the two concepts can often be interchanged when writing, they do not mean the same and they should be distinguished. Society is a phenomenon that can be sensed: that is, it can be touched and measured, but culture is a mental phenomenon and can only be visualized. Keesing (1976, 568) defines society as, simply, "a population marked by relative separation from surrounding populations and a distinctive culture." This is what we will mean when we refer to society. The members of a society are the carriers of its culture, but they are not the culture.

These two abstractions are confusing because what they mean is very close, but society would be people dancing or interacting in some way while culture would be the idea of dancing or behavioral interaction in the mind. We can see two people dancing (social interaction), and we can see the Chevrolet (material culture). However, we cannot see the ideas that brought the car into existence or that brought dance steps into being, nor can we directly observe all that there is to know about the cultural significance of dancing or cars in any particular culture. Social institutions such as marriage are also manifestations of culture. While we can observe people getting married, we cannot directly observe the rules of marriage in a society. We must remember, also, that behavior itself does not always reflect cultural ideals, that is, the way in which people believe they *ought* to behave. It does reflect, in a sense, the playing out of individual understandings of cultural ideals, although we must also remember that any instance of behavior may be a deliberate violation of the cultural rules. The reader should be able to appreciate how difficult it is for the anthropologist to extract culture from perceived behavior while at the same time understanding the power of the two concepts.

It is important to remember that society and culture are analytically distinct concepts invented by sociologists and anthropologists in order to communicate about what they

■Society and culture are often confused. Society would be people dancing or interacting in some way while culture would be the idea of dancing or behavioral interaction in the mind.

are studying. And, while they have been introduced to the mass media by sociologists and anthropologists, they are also recent introductions to our language. In a good many societies, the words "culture," "society," and "sociocultural" either do not exist, or they mean very different things. The word for society in Colombia, *sociedad*, does not refer to a group of those who share a common culture, but rather to something like "the moral order," an abstraction of ideal cultural rules, something to live up to. When in Colombia, one must be aware that *sociedad* does not mean "society" in the anthropologist's sense. The same is true for "culture." The word for culture in Colombian Spanish is *cultura* and refers to high culture: poetry, classical music, ballet, and so on. This use is also the traditional use of the word in the United States, but the word "culture" is slowly being used more and more as sociologists and anthropologists use it.

CHARACTERISTICS OF CULTURE

Now that we have defined culture, as we will use the term, we need also to examine briefly the main characteristics of culture as defined by both classic and global anthropology. Culture is shared, transmitted across generations through learning (not biologically), and patterned. Individual behavior that departs from the accepted cultural norms is idiosyncratic. None of these three major characteristics of culture—shared, learned, and patterned—should be taken to mean that culture is tightly bounded and static or unchanging, and no modern anthropologist would take them to mean this. The fact that cultures change, sometimes slowly and sometimes rapidly, has been known, although not always emphasized, since the early days of anthropology. Perhaps it would be wise to add as a fourth characteristic of culture—that it is flexible. Before summarizing the general characteristics of culture, we should present a weakness to the concept, which is addressed by John W. Bennett in his 1998 book of essays *Classic Anthropology* (Bennett 1998,14). Bennett points out that culture, no matter how defined, is an "analytic construct" and not something "real." Most cultural anthropologists, after giving their definition of culture, then turn to a descriptive or theoretical analysis of a problem and use other terms more appropriate to their study such as class, role, belief, and other terms found throughout this book and summarized in the glossary. The danger of using the concept of culture as something real is that of **reification,** which means making an abstraction into something concrete with cause and effect aspects (an example is the statement that "culture causes warfare." Another danger in thinking of culture as something concrete is the danger of "determinism," which means explaining an abstraction through another abstraction, as in "culture is determined by economy" or "culture is determined by environment." Economic or environmental determinism are but two examples of those found in the anthropological literature; culture is much too complex a phenomenon to reduce down to a single set of causes, a problem we will avoid.

reification

Turning an abstract idea into a concrete idea with cause-and-effect aspects

Shared   One of the dangers of the concept of culture is to think of everyone in a culture sharing the same ideas in common. This definition is common to anthropology texts, but it is easy to show that members of a society do not usually share completely all beliefs and knowledge that constitute a part of culture. Culture is more likely to be shared in small-scale societies with relatively few members than in large-scale complex societies with hundreds of thousands, or even millions, of members and probably numerous subcultures, but even small-scale societies allow a great deal of variation in beliefs. To say that culture is shared is to say that it is an attribute of groups rather than individuals. What is shared as a part of culture can be described as a set of central ideas or images or prototypes with their attached symbolic meanings and a permissible range of alternatives. This is what allows people to have a reasonable set of expectations about the behavior of others in a given social interaction, to recognize permissible deviations from the ideal behavior as well as culturally inappropriate behaviors. It is also what creates problems in social interaction between members of different cultures where expected behaviors and the symbolic meaning of them are not the same. Roger Keesing describes these cultural patterns as "patterns of assumption, perception, and custom." He provides a telling example of the misunderstanding that can result in a situation of cross-cultural interaction:

> "A Bulgarian woman was serving dinner to a group of her American husband's friends, including an Asian student. After her guests had cleaned their plates, she asked if any would like a second helping: A Bulgarian hostess who let a guest go hungry would be disgraced. The Asian student accepted a second helping, and then a third—as the hostess anxiously prepared another batch in the kitchen. Finally, in the midst of his fourth helping, the Asian student slumped to the floor; but better that, in his country, than to insult his hostess by refusing food that had been offered." (1976, 1)

Despite the obvious cultural misunderstandings shown in this example, we should not conclude that different cultures do not share any rules, patterns, expectations, symbolic meanings, or behaviors in common. The modern view is that cultural boundaries are overlapping and permeable. This is an aspect of flexibility (see below). Diverse cultures may share common beliefs in the area of religion, for example. Islam in this respect unites a vast multitude of otherwise distinct cultures across northern Africa, through the Middle East and into Central Asia, China, Malaysia, Indonesia, and the Philippines. As Lapidus points out: "Though Islam is not often the totality of their lives, it permeates their self-conception, regulates their daily existence, provides the bonds of society...." (1988, xix)

■The largely unconscious process of natural language acquisition is a good example of how culture is passed across the generations through the cognitive process of learning.

Learned   Culture is not transmitted from one generation to the next genetically (or biologically). It is passed along across the generations through the complicated cognitive process of learning. Learning takes place through language and observation. Humans are capable of symbolic learning. Humans, unlike most animals, can learn that one thing stands for (symbolizes) something else. Another part of the learning process is the ability to generalize, to discern patterns and formulate rules from specific instances. This is a largely unconscious process; natural language acquisition by children is a good example. While much of the learning that makes up the transmission of culture is from members of older generations to members of younger ones, not all of it is. Parents do learn from their children and grandparents from their grandchildren, although they may be reluctant to admit it. Everyone also learns from their peer groups, members of their own generation. Children, for example, with slightly different (sub) cultural backgrounds, may compare notes and in the process arrive at a new synthesis. This is one of the sources of culture change. Cultural learning in a broad sense is knowledge transmitted among humans—and they need not share the same culture for this to occur. Culture contact is an important source of culture change (see Flexible, below). One of the most intriguing aspects of the learning process is that it is almost always imperfect. Consequently, subtle changes occur in what is understood and how things are done and are passed on. This is another source of culture change. The major sources of culture change are, of course, deliberate alterations in the way things are done that come to be agreed upon as useful responses to altered conditions—even though, in the long term, some such changes may turn out to be maladaptive. We will have more to say about culture change in Chapter 2, and most other chapters will contain examples of culture change.

Patterned   To say that there are patterns in culture means that there are agreed-upon rules and conventions that people follow or honor in the breach. It means that an outsider can observe repetitive behaviors associated with particular social contexts. It also means that one can consistently recognize the differences between pictorial art forms of contemporary China, for example, and those of the indigenous cultures of the Northwest Coast of North America. Some rules are carried around only in people's heads. This is the only way that culture patterns are maintained in non-literate societies. It is one of the ways the patterns are maintained in literate societies; the other way is by codification, that is, writing down the rules. Written laws, for example, are part of United States culture. Even when cultural rules and conventions are written down, they are still subject to change, and the rules for making changes may themselves be codified.

Flexible   All cultures change; most changes are adaptations. Cultures adapt to each other in response to altered contexts and circumstances. Change, not equilibrium, is the normal state of cultural systems. One of the significant alterations of context is when two (or more) cultures come in contact with one another, such as Spanish culture and Latin American culture after 1500 and the discovery of the New World. This always results in an interchange of ideas, knowledge, and goods. Not all the new ideas and knowledge or even all the new goods may be acceptable; but the potential is there, and culture change of some sort is sure to occur (Latin American populations by and large rejected Spanish culture and were forced to adopt it). Culture contact may, and often does, result in a relationship of domination and subordination—and much of this book will examine such relationships. Cultures also change in response to changes in their natural environment. Studies of this kind of change are the classic focus of human or cultural ecology. Such change is not always successful, and some cultures may die out as a result. Of course, one might well ask, how anyone can know if a culture has become extinct or simply transformed into something else that we do not recognize as a direct descendant of an earlier culture? There is no simple answer to this question.

THE PERSPECTIVE OF ANTHROPOLOGY

In addition to the concept of culture itself, the anthropological perspective, classic and global, is informed by three major organizing themes: *holism*, *comparison*, and the dilemma of *cultural relativism* versus *ethnocentrism*. In addition, there are many analytic concepts that anthropologists stress in presenting their descriptions and interpretations of cultures and societies. These may not be specified. They may be implicit in what is said, or they may be explicit. Those that we will examine are present in one form or another in most writings of cultural anthropologists. These are the contrast between the concepts of *ideal* and *real*, and the contrast between *emic* and *etic* views. We will discuss each, in turn, here; and they will be explicit or implicit in various other places throughout the book. It should be noted that anthropologists are not in complete agreement about the value of these themes to a modern anthropological perspective.

Holism   Holism in anthropology is the view that we must attempt to understand cultural features within their context. It brings together the four fields of anthropology. According to this view, which was developed by Franz Boas, the study of people must include biological, archaeological, linguistic, and cultural anthropology. The operating assumptions here are that different aspects of humans—their biological systems, languages, pre-histories and histories, cultures, and environments—have influenced one another. What may be enigmatic or puzzling in isolation will be understandable in the larger context. While simple cause-effect relationships do exist in nature, the holistic view assumes that they are relatively uncommon in cultural systems (scientists believe that simple single cause-one effect relationships are rare in nature).

Modern holism does not require the belief, attributed to early functionalists, that everything in culture and society is functionally related to everything else (this is the sense in which the term holism was used in the study of small tribes living on Pacific Islands). Holism originally applied to thinking of cultures as closed systems, but anthropologists today look at culture as composed of open systems that influence each other. The difference is open systems can be affected by outside forces while closed systems cannot. Classic anthropology looked at cultures as closed and ignored outside forces, such as trade and conflict. This is not to say there is no such thing as closed systems, for cultures often close themselves against outside forces when these are disruptive. An example is American Indian societies in the sixteenth century once their leaders became aware of the disruptive nature of European cultures. However, closed and open systems must be thought of as relative, for all societies can be relatively closed or relatively open. In general, the most open societies are American and European, while some societies in Africa, the Middle East, and Asia may be relatively closed. The problem of openness and closure helps to explain some of the features of terrorism and conflict covered in future chapters. Terrorism is a tool used to close societies and to insure their continued closure.

The emergence of global anthropology, with its greater emphasis on connectivity and process, has given holism new importance. Global anthropologists search for the interactions between political, economic, ideological, and ecological factors, thus making anthropology even more a holistic science than in the age of classic anthropology when these outside forces were ignored. Also of great importance is the way that the search for connectivity requires that anthropology attend to the findings of other disciplines, such as economics, political science, sociology, psychology, and history. Holism is a major research strategy of global anthropology, but its earlier meaning is still important for cultures have holistic characteristics. When anthropologists go into the field they try to understand how political, economic, social, and psychological subsystems fit together as they gather their ethnographic data. One of anthropology's major contributions to social science and history is that of synthesis: bringing together what political scientists, economists, sociologists, and psychologists specialize in studying. Holism, then, is the search for connections between cultures and within cultures.

Why is a holistic approach useful? Because most of the contemporary problems of the planet are the consequences of rapid culture change, and the problems we face on the planet are complex phenomena made up of interrelated systems, some of which may be connected (Smith 1993, 1994). However, holism today is a research strategy not an assumption about the nature of culture (a characteristic of classic anthropology). For example, the destruction of the planet's tropical forests is not solely an ecological issue but also holistically connected to other phenomena in addition to forest ecosystems. Threats to forest ecosystems are made up of political, economic, demographic, and other factors. For example, a decade ago in Brazil urban poverty forced

■ The destruction of the planet's tropical forests is not solely an ecological issue. It is holistically connected to other phenomena in addition to forest ecosystems. Threats to forest ecosystems rise from politics, economics, and demographic sources.

people to migrate to the rainforests. The Brazilian government, which was controlled by a wealthy elite, did not wish to democratize and found it cheaper to build roads into the Amazon than to deal directly with poverty and overcrowding in urban and some rural areas. Over the last decade, Brazil has gone through a democratizing revolution that has brought prosperity to the poor and has made all Brazilians much more aware of the environment. It is fascinating to learn how democracy and prosperity have made Brazilians much more aware of environmental degradation. The United Nations and other international organizations can pass all kinds of resolutions to protect nature; until poverty is reduced, however, the poor may be unable to comply.

Comparison   While holism promotes a global view with the examination of processes and connections, it also leads to the use of the comparative method. The comparative method means dissecting cultures and societies into components and features, and examining their similarities and differences. These contrasts are used to construct theories and testable hypotheses about the nature of culture. Holism and the comparative method form the essence of anthropological analysis, though they are not unique to the discipline. They appear to be universal features of the human thought process.

An example of the use of holism and the comparative method is found in the study of descent systems and kinship. For example, there is a relationship between certain types of descent and certain types of post-marital residence such that patrilineality (descent through the male line) and **patrilocality** (when a woman comes to live with her husband) are often found together. Sometimes, however, they are not. An important theoretical question is why they are found together; however, equally important, but perhaps more difficult, is the question of why they are not *always* found together. Holism and the comparative method attempt to determine how cultural variables are related to one another. Although the two methods have yielded some interesting correlations, and continue to be useful in generating hypotheses, there are three problems that one should be aware of in using the two methods. First, there is the problem of determining whether two features that occur together in different cultures are related functionally or historically. That is, are they similar because they are responding to the same "causes" or are they similar because they diffused from another part of the world together? In the past, if one chose a sample of cultures that were geographically distant from one another, the problem of historical borrowing was ignored. In today's world, this is not so easy to do because the flow of cultural ideas has increased tremendously.

There is also much more information available to the researcher. There once was a time when colonial authorities restricted access to archives; but as colonialism disappeared, once closed resources were open. A great deal of information regarding Latin America's indigenous peoples was collected by authorities in the sixteenth century for a wide variety of reasons and sealed in Catholic Church archives. Many of these have been opened and researchers are finding that many of their pet theories about the conquest of the New World do not fit new information available. For example,

patrilocality

The relocation of a woman to her husband's house upon marriage

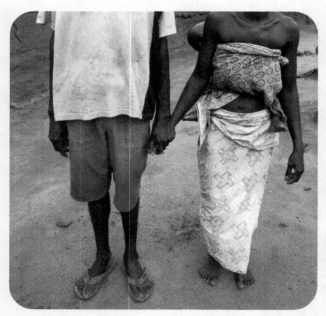

■Patrilocality is when a woman comes to live with her husband.

many tribes once thought to have been conquered by Spain actually joined with the Spaniards in the conquest and became their allies.

A second problem is that of insuring that cultural features are comparable. Cross-cultural comparison assumes that the units being compared are distinct cultures. However, as we have already seen, cultures are open systems with permeable and sometimes overlapping boundaries; their normal state is one of dynamic change rather than static equilibrium. How, then, do we determine that this is Culture A and that is Culture B, and that the two never influenced each other? Another example, can we compare tribes with no central authority and nation-states that have been centralized for the last century or two?

A third problem is the comparability of data. For example, do all reports of patrilocality refer to exactly the same phenomenon? It should be noted that some anthropologists use the term patrilocality to refer to all instances of post-marital residence where the husband resides with his own kin group and the wife goes to live either in the house of her husband's father or on the lands of the husband's kin; others distinguish living in the husband's father's house from simply living on the lands of the husband's kin and refer to the latter as **virilocality**. Do the terms mean the same thing or are they different? Further, is what different ethnographers report an ideal rule in one instance and a generalization based on widespread practice in another? In addition, written ethnographies are not identical the way cultural features are reported. Characteristics of distinct societies were researched for vastly different purposes, and many may not be comparable. For example, American anthropologists studying American Indian populations in the late nineteenth and early twentieth centuries were interested in salvaging the remains of peoples' cultures whose very existence was threatened, while British researchers in the islands of Melanesia did not have to worry about the survival of people they studied and could ask questions of living people about the relationship between sex and religion. Did the distinct interests of these researchers sway the way they described similar and different cultural practices?

Despite these problems, cross-cultural comparison, if used carefully, can yield some significant insights into the workings of cultural systems, particularly if one knows what the objectives of the original researchers were.

Cultural Relativism versus Ethnocentrism

Another feature of anthropology is cultural relativism. This perspective is the view that there is an internal rationale to the beliefs, behaviors, and practices of all cultures and that we should not impose value judgments on the customs of others. According to this argument, we should not judge others by our own standards. Ethnocentrism is the opposite perspective, according to which people tend to think their own cultures are superior to those of any other.

Cultural relativism is a slippery concept. The concept was developed in the study of small scale, tribal societies and does not work well in modern and highly industrial societies. That is why we prefer to distinguish extreme relativism from weak relativism. Extreme relativism was common in the early twentieth century when anthropologists worked primarily in small scale, tribal societies. Today, anthropologists may very well work in modern, industrial societies where extreme relativism would be considered a rather naive view given the features of modern societies. The concept was meant to describe warfare as well as cannibalism, infanticide, and female genital mutilation in tribal or peasant societies. It is doubtful that very many anthropologists ever subscribed to the strong version of cultural relativism for technologically advanced societies where warfare and human exploitation has horrific characteristics. Scale is a very important distinction between tribal and modern societies. Warfare, as practiced among the American Indian, the Aztec, and Maya were small-scale affairs where only a few hundred warriors and no innocent by-standers were killed. Compared to primitive warfare, modern warfare is on a scale where thousands or hundreds of thousands of soldiers and innocent civilians might die as was true for World War I, World War II, or the Vietnam conflict.

The weak version of cultural relativism—the version that we, and we believe most modern anthropologists, accept—argues that our best chance of achieving an understanding of the small scale societies we study should be by viewing people on their own terms, not ours. However, such acceptance will not work in modern and industrial societies, particularly in colonial settings. In modern societies, the scale of exploitation between elites and masses, and the scale of conflict as well as exploitation of natural resources does not compare to practices of tribal societies around the world.

The contrast between tribal and modern is easy to make. For example, in modern Guatemala, a powerful elite has held landless Maya Indians subject to extreme exploitation and degradation since the colonial period. Hundreds of thousands of people have died due to civil wars between elites and masses. During the prehistoric period, however, while warfare and exploitation were widespread, archaeological reports show that only comparatively few people died either of warfare or class exploitation. Another good example of relatively modern exploitation was the abuse of African Americans on cotton plantations in the Deep South between 1600 and 1960.

Slavery, conflict, and the exploitation of nature occurred in tribal societies, but they occurred on a far smaller scale than in modern societies. Among the American Indians, warfare might lead to the capture of enemies who were made into slaves, but these were not treated as slaves were in the American South. They were often adopted into the winner's family. Slaves could buy their freedom and even become warriors. In these societies, a weak version of cultural relativism is easy to apply; however, in modern and large scale societies, it does not work. Anthropologists find it easy to condemn warfare, sexual exploitation, and class stratification in modern societies. For example, for several decades anthropologists have condemned the destruction of tropical environments around the world and of the indigenous people who live in them, particularly the rainforests of South America, Africa, and Asia. Another clear example of behavior anthropologists (or most people) would condemn is Hitler and the Nazi attempt to eradicate six million Jews, as well as many East European peoples before and during World War II. Finally, a more recent example anthropologists condemn is the genocide of Southeast Asian people by the Pol Pot regime of Cambodia.

■Scale is a very important distinction between tribal and modern societies. The contrast between the nomadic and the contemporary is usually easy to make.

Why do anthropologists study warfare and such activities as pre- and extra-marital sex in tribal societies? Their study gives us an emic view (the view from within the culture) of these behaviors, which can be contextualized into tribal or small-scale religions and worldviews. The study of warfare and sex in large-scale societies is very difficult. For one thing, most men are not warriors. For another, the function of warfare as a means of elevating male prestige may be displaced into sports. Marvin Harris has suggested that sports in modern societies allow men to elevate their prestige above women, allowing them to exploit the fairer sex. Keep in mind, however, that Harris was writing about American culture in the twentieth century. In the twenty-first century, women's sports activities make this generalization more difficult to make. There have been some important changes in gender relations since Harris wrote his observations half a century ago. What do we make of the dominance of women in many corporations and educational institutions, as well as playing as well as men in certain sports such as tennis and golf? Recently, women have begun to display aggression in basketball and other sports in ways once reserved for men. Is all of this good or bad? Cultural relativism tells us it is neither: cultural behaviors change as societies modernize, and what was once normal is no longer that way.

The opposite of cultural relativism is ethnocentrism. Ethnocentrism is the view that one's own culture is superior to all others and that others' ways of believing and doing are wrong or inferior or at the least just plain weird, if harmless. It engenders distrust, sometimes hatred and sometimes violence. It is a view against which anthropologists have always argued, even if they were uncomfortable with the concept of cultural relativism itself. Ethnocentrism is a condition to be transcended if we are to achieve a more humane world. Paradoxically, it also seems to be a natural human response to cultural differences. All cultures of which we have records display ethnocentrism to some degree. This does not justify the attitude, but it does point out the difficulties in achieving tolerance between certain groups (for example, Palestinians and Israelis reject outsiders who admonish the use of stereotypes each of these have for one another). It seems to be part of the baggage of cultural boundary maintenance and tends to come to the fore under conditions of cultural stress. It is clearly manifest in situations of ethnic conflict. As you proceed through this book, you might think about whether ethnocentrism has increased in the modern world as cultures come into more frequent and intimate contact, or if it has decreased. If it has decreased, is the disappearance of ethnocentrism a sign of modernization?

Ideal and Real Culture Research by anthropologists shows that all of this is even more complex than suggested above because people do not always behave in the way they say they do. Anthropologists have developed terms to deal with this problem. **Ideal culture** embodies what people think they ought to do; **real culture** is what they actually do. In other words, there are ideal rules for behavior, agreed-upon by many. People can often tell you what they are, even if they don't personally agree with them. Everyone is aware that no one behaves in conformity with the ideals all the time, sometimes for good reasons and sometimes not. Ethnographers should record both cultural ideals and real behavior, but the matter is not quite this simple; and we will take it up again and examine the complexities in the next chapter in our discussion of field research. For now, we will just observe that cultural ideals constitute an emic or insider view because only the people themselves can provide you an account of these—and, again, because cultures are dynamic systems, there may not be complete agreement. If by real we mean what the researcher observes, then we can, for the moment, call this an etic view.

ideal culture

What people think they ought to do

real culture

What people actually do

Emic and Etic   As we have indicated above, the emic view of things is that of insiders, the members of a culture; and the etic view is that of outsiders, usually but not always scientific observers like anthropologists. Both views have utility. However, the contrast between emic and etic is not as straightforward as simply insider/outsider and has generated controversy among anthropologists about both the utility of the concepts and what they mean. (See T. Headland, K. Pike, and M. Harris, eds., 1990, *Emics and Etics*, for presentations of various points of view that will add to the discussion below.) Hereafter we add to our discussion above by pointing out some other ways in which the concepts of emic and etic have been used to refer to types of analysis.

Kenneth Pike, a linguist, pointed out that there is a duality to anthropology in that it attempts to state what the native thinks about culture as an insider and at the same time creates a more mechanistic view from the outside which compares the culture studied to other cultures (1954). The first point of view is called **emic analysis,** and the second is **etic analysis.** The etic model uses cross-cultural categories to characterize entire societies, often put into an evolutionary or economic perspective. The native would often not recognize the way that his/her culture is described in the second model, but the first description should be familiar.

As an example, in my (SS) study of plantation economies of Central America (1982), I created an economic model of the south coast of Guatemala, which showed that large sugar mills, called *ingenios*, and smaller supplier plantations, called *fincas*, controlled the lives of hundreds of thousands of landless laborers. This was an etic model and was a comparative study using material from plantation studies from the American south, the Caribbean, Africa, and Southeast Asia. My etic model connected the local workers to the fincas, the fincas to the ingenios, and these to the world economy. I doubt if any of my informants would have recognized themselves in my published observations. Several owners of the fincas who read my study angrily denied their participation in such an exploitative system and were often proud of how they dealt with their own laborers. However, a *colono*, or resident laborer living on a cotton plantation, would have agreed about his exploitation by the plantation owners.

In contrast to my surveys of the Guatemalan coast, which involved close to one hundred interviews, was the emic biography of a single day laborer on a plantation found in Sidney Mintz' *Worker in the Cane* (1974 [1960]). His narrative is the poignant story of the life of a sugar worker in Puerto Rico. Mintz' approach would be considered humanistic rather than scientific; but while some anthropologists would argue that one approach is better than the other, the two approaches are best seen as complementary. Each approach gives the other greater depth. Because of the use of emic research such as that produced by Mintz and Clifford Geertz (whose work is discussed in Chapter 2), many anthropologists argued anthropology was closer to the humanities, while others who used survey approaches argued that theirs was a science. However, the history of anthropology has been made up of both emic and etic studies because the topic of the research—culture—can be understood both "up close" and "from a distance."

One of the difficulties of anthropology is that writers sometimes may ascribe subjective judgments derived from their own culture to the people involved in his/her study. For example, the researcher may feel that the owner of a finca exploits a sugar cane worker; but in interviews, the informant may not

emic analysis

The analysis of what a native thinks about his culture as an insider

etic analysis

The comparative analysis of a culture with other cultures by an outsider to the cultures

view his relationship to the owner of the estate as one of exploitation, and may be proud of his occupation. The question is, should the anthropologist pass on his/her judgment about the morality of the situation he/she is studying or leave it up to the reader to decide. Should either one be passing moral judgments as "students of society"? Here we touch on the complexity of what is and what is not ethnocentrism, and when cultural relativism is "hard" or "soft." The question may not have an answer, but the anthropologist may be the only person to ever study a difficult human situation. The question what to do with his or her knowledge of a situation involving ambiguous issues of exploitation is very common to the discipline.

Perhaps the anthropologist may wish to avoid discussing his or her informants and instead present the question abstractly by writing or lecturing about "plantation systems" as exploitative. But are they? This may not appear to be a problem to the reader. However, from a hard science point of view, the question is do economic "systems" have goals or values? Scientists argue that ascribing values to "systems"—whether human or physical—makes the writer guilty of **teleology**. Teleological reasoning means ascribing "telos" or historical goals to "things," such as economic systems, evolving species, or cosmic events. According to a "hard science" point of view, it would appear fair enough to ascribe goals and values to people who are actors, but not to the systems within which they act. Many would argue that ignoring the exploitation of his or her fellows produces a "science" that has little relevance to most people. Most anthropologists would agree, but it doesn't take a great deal to see that anthropology is a discipline torn between appearing scientific or humanistic. That is why we would like to think of anthropology as a humanistic science, despite the ambiguous nature of the definition.

> **teleology**
>
> The ascription of values to "systems," whether human or physical

Anthropology, Modernization, and Globalization

Anthropology has long had a tradition of studying culture change. In the period directly after World War II, the study of culture change had as its focus the impact of "modern" societies on "traditional" societies (that is, the impact of technologically advanced societies on those not so advanced). Up until the late 1970s, anthropologists and others stressed how changing sources of production influenced other aspects of culture (distinctions were made between core or infrastructure, structure and superstructure). The importance of the sources of production perspective permeated all the social sciences, as well as history. Central to modernization theory was the acceptance of the importance of science and secularization. These were supposed to reduce the importance of religion and ethnic identity.

We have argued that the study of culture is complex and ambiguous. If we add the changing nature of culture, we underscore how complicated research really is, especially when the very idea of culture change is itself changing because we are living through the process of globalization, a term which means (among other things) the connecting of every household in the world with every other household through the electronic media and trade. Not long ago, culture change was explained as a form of cultural evolution, with single societies evolving through time. Today, however, globalization locks different societies, nation states, or peoples to each other. Computers, long distance telecommunication, the use of satellites, the vanishing cost of transmitting information, and industrial robotics—all these processes are changing every society in the world. Culture change no longer means the impact of industrial societies on developing societies but rather the impact of globalization on all the peoples of the world, for better or for worse.

The world is being re-made today not so much by forces that have only recently become important but by forces that were long ignored, and which we take up in this book. Modernization theories that only focused on "sources of production" ignored trade and property rights. In addition to ignoring trade and property rights, we discover that ethnic identity and religion are other factors that have been ignored. The sudden outbreak of ethnic violence in the forms of "ethnic cleansing" and "ethnonationalism" in places like Yugoslavia have forced anthropologists, social scientists, and historians to examine many of their assumptions. Ethnicity and religion, according to the age of classic anthropology, were supposed to disappear as societies modernized and became more secular; however, far from disappearing, they have become much more important.

The reason why globalization is associated with the resurgence of ethnic identity and religion is not fully understood. In many places, such as rural Mexico, Colombia, and much of Latin America, religion and ethnicity never disappeared but tended to be ignored by researchers who assumed that as societies evolved, they became more secular. In addition, it was assumed that indigenous peoples, such as the Maya, Quechua, Aymara, and other "Indian" populations would abandon their traditional identities as they modernized. Much to researchers' surprise, in the 1990s, not only were indigenous peoples not abandoning their identities but also they became interested in maintaining their traditions. They often sought out the ethnographic work of anthropologists of earlier generations to learn about their own traditions. In other regions, such as the Middle East, and parts of Africa and Asia, secularization came to be viewed as a threat. Islam and other religions such as Buddhism and non-western forms of Christianity became more aggressive in defining themselves. Ethnic identities began to become central to politics.

Globalization is changing anthropology, but many anthropologists resist and present fiercely anti-globalization perspectives due to threats to traditional societies, which they wish to preserve. Many of these have embraced post-modernism (explained in Chapter 2) and its anti-global perspective, while others, such as ourselves, view globalization as one of many systems of change that have transformed the nature of culture over the long millennia since the origins of the first hunters and food gatherers.

Anthropologists are learning how to use computers, the Internet, and the other technologies of the age to deal with the global issues brought on by globalization. More important than technology in facing the complex problems brought on by globalization, however, is the multidisciplinary perspective of modern anthropology. While the anthropology of forty years ago focused mainly on such topics as kinship relations, descent systems and residence rules, and other descriptions of the internal dynamics of small scale cultures, the anthropology of today—and tomorrow—is challenged to find ways to help societies sort through a variety of transitions to different but satisfying lives. This will by no means be a simple task. There are issues of the environment, of political and economic change, of gender, issues dealing with ethnic relations, and much, much more. The big question is, can anthropology rise to this challenge? We believe that anthropology's multidisciplinary approach is exactly what is needed as long as researchers remain objective. This book will be an extended elaboration of our view.

This book is about globalization and other transitions. Humans have passed through three great transitions (Bennett 1998, 78). The first was from an existence based entirely on hunting and food gathering to one in which horticulture, agriculture, and pastoralism

food extraction

The hunting and gathering of food

food production

The creation of food through horticulture, agriculture, and pastoralism

dominated and early civilizations developed. This shift may be referred to as the transition from **food extraction** to **food production,** and it had profound environmental consequences (to be discussed later). The second transition began with the age of discovery, *circa* AD 1492, which saw the beginnings of worldwide trade, mercantilism and monopoly capitalism. Out of this transition emerged the modern world system of the late industrial era. The *modern world system* was composed of a wealthy European-American core and a poor periphery whose resources were monopolized and exploited by the core. The third transition we see began in the mid 1980s when the Soviet Union began to fall apart, which is called "globalization." Globalization is hard to describe because we are in its very beginning stages. It is a transition in which the monopoly over the resources of the planet by the rich core is ending and new cores and peripheries are emerging around the world. Many new economic opportunities are opening in both cores and peripheries, but with them come unprecedented threats to ecosystems and human rights. At the same time, electronic technology is fostering the rapid development of a vast network of worldwide communication links that permit information transfer at speeds undreamed of, except by writers of science fiction, even fifteen years ago.

A Problem Driven Discipline

It has been over forty years since my (SS) first introduction to field work in anthropology. In the summer of 1966, I drove with a team of graduate students to coastal Guatemala where I spent four months doing a detailed study of the plantations around the coastal town of Santa Catalina Siquinala. I began my ethnographic fieldwork by interviewing administrators and workers. I collected census data, economic information, and surveys on the political structure of the south coast.

As I became involved in my research, I became very concerned with what I learned. I learned that half of the workers on the plantation estates were Maya Indians brought down from their cool mountain homes by *contratistas* (contractors) to work off debts incurred during the religious ceremonies of the *cargo system.* The cargo system is a set of hierarchically arranged positions that entail religious (and in some communities, civil) obligations. These obligations last for one year, and every adult male is expected to hold one or more cargos during his lifetime. The obligations include sponsorship of ritual events that are based on both ancient Mayan and Catholic beliefs. Each Maya cargo holder carries a symbolic "cargo" of ritual duties acted out over a year and gives him and his family status in Maya communities. A man and his wife may, for example, take care of a local Catholic church for the year. Early studies of the cargo system, which I read about in graduate school, made it appear indigenous to the Mayan communities. To my surprise, the modern cargo system had become integrated into the plantation economy of the coast by 1966, and Indians had to pay off debts incurred during the ceremonies by working on the hot coastal plantations. The plantations grew sugar cane, most of which was sold to United States corporations in raw form and then refined to become the sugar you put on your breakfast cereal.

My research project became my master's thesis, and I hoped to return to the coast to expand the work into a PhD; but a revolution between the Maya Indians, non-Indian peasants, and the Guatemalan government exploded right in the region where I had done my research. One of the reasons for the violence was exploitation of the workers by plantation owners. In 1982, twenty-six people in the town of Siquinala were killed during a fight between the FAR (Armed Revolutionary Forces) and the government. Some of those killed were Mayan guerrilla fighters; and a few were landowners, many of whom I had interviewed. After years of U.S. support for the Guatemalan government, despite human rights abuses, American diplomats turned to trying to negotiate political changes to end the violence instead of supporting the government. The conflict came to an end in the 1980s and 1990s, but the plantation system that had been central to the conflict has changed little. Forty years later, the civil war has all but disappeared; but in its place there has emerged a very high homicide rate within the working classes, and a society that is still primarily composed of rich and poor.

The difficulties in achieving equitable changes in Guatemala and other developing countries have become central to the topics that characterize global anthropology. Anthropologists (and other social scientists) refer collectively to the processes and results of changes of roughly the last three decades as first *modernization* and then *globalization*. Whereas, in the classic years of anthropology, roughly from the beginning of last century to the late 1950s, it was possible to find remote Maya communities and to study them—as though they had evolved in isolation (an illusion even then); such is no longer possible. To understand the modern Maya, it is necessary to understand their relations with the national government and the national government's connections, in turn, to other governments; their relationships to transnational corporations in the sugar, cotton, and banana industries, as well as the Mayan traditional customs, beliefs, and habits and adaptations they have made to the global economy. This is an example of globalization, of the interconnectivity of societies in the modern world to each other. The term globalization must now include the transforming power of computers and mass communication. We are not just connected—the wiring of the connections is beginning to change the world.

Wolf wrote *Europeans and the People without History* in 1982, just a few years before globalization began to transform the planet. His book examines the world as it looked during the time period when it was dominated by a Euro-American "core" with a set of peripheries and semi-peripheries, which were often called "the third world": Latin America, Asia, and the Middle East. Since 1982, there have been some astonishing changes: the slow disintegration of the core, the collapse of the Soviet Union, and the economic transformation of a few third world societies into first world status, such as China and India. The elemental reason for the changes is the coupling of computers and global financial markets. Nation states, such as the United States, Great Britain, and France, no longer have control over the movement of investments and find it increasingly difficult to secure predictable jobs for their citizens, who blame globalization for a lack of jobs. At the same time, investors are demanding that unstable dictatorships, which once functioned with little interest or attention to efficiency, become democratic if they are to attract outside investment. Democratization is occurring in once very undemocratic places ranging from Russia to Chile. While parts of the world democratize, 9/11 has changed the nature of international relations and prompted the American invasions of Afghanistan and Iraq. In neither of these two places are things going according to plan. The Pentagon under the leadership of General Petreaus has turned increasingly to anthropologists with expertise in Iraq and Afghanistan.

These new changes are having results which are totally unpredictable: the core countries are becoming politically more unstable, including the United States and also France, Italy, and Great Britain. New pressures in these countries are producing clashes between ethnic groups that had been at peace for over a generation. In the former periphery, growing economies are putting tremendous pressures on environments. For example, as a part of its economic development, China has created a giant dam system to contain the waters

■9/11 has changed the nature of international relations and prompted the American invasions of Afghanistan and Iraq.

of the Yangtze River in order to create electrical power and prevent flooding, but this threatens to destroy thousands of villages and inflict severe damage on riverine ecosystems. It is becoming obvious that the spread of capitalism requires democracy to protect both human rights and the environment, but some regions are resisting.

There are, then, many problems for anthropologists to study. These problems are global and run the gamut from economic development to ethnic conflict, ethnonationalism, international terrorism, and human and environmental rights. Classic cultural anthropologists focused heavily on small-scale traditional societies, at least until the post World War II era. In that process, anthropology accumulated a great wealth of knowledge about the lifeways, social organization, and relationships to nature of these small-scale societies. As these societies become fewer, and less isolated, and global cultural anthropology turns more and more to studies of the more complex cultures and subcultures of the industrializing, industrial, and post-industrial world, we should neither abandon nor forget the knowledge gained from these earlier studies. For traditional societies contain some of the only examples available of truly sustainable relationships with nature. The answers to many current dilemmas may very well lie in the accumulated wisdom of these societies of intimates—in their indigenous knowledge, to use the current phrase.

Anthropology is a problem driven science, but it's history is also one of being drawn to classification and the formulation (not without some justification, of course) of categories such as band, tribe, chiefdom, state, nation, society, clan, lineage, politics, economics, kinship, and ethnicity, which have sometimes undergone a mysterious transformation from categories to explanations. This is an anthropology text that will focus on problems and give short shrift to categories as ends in themselves.

In this chapter we have examined the sub-disciplines and central concepts of anthropology. In the following two chapters, we will explore the methods and theories of modern cultural anthropology; and in the following chapters, we will begin with the research and theories of classic anthropology and then move into the age of global anthropology. Central to an explanation of globalization is the growth of trade and democracy. At the heart of this text the proposition that while trade and democracy are important, there are other transitions which are equally important and which can get lost, the most basic of which are transitions to values supporting human rights and the rights of nature.

■　■　❚❚

Chapter Summary

Studying Anthropology

Anthropology is a very broad field overlapping such distinct disciplines as biology, geology, paleontology, history, economics, sociology, philosophy, psychology, the arts and many others. Its focus is humankind that is both defined and studied holistically. A general division of labor is reflected in the four major sub-disciplines, which we have discussed. Yet most anthropologists are used to wearing several "hats" and maintaining an up-to-date working knowledge of other disciplines and sub-disciplines. For example, archaeologists must know considerable biological anthropology and geology, while applied anthropologists must know quite a lot about cultural anthropology, economics, and ecology; and cultural anthropologists should keep up on the work of applied anthropologists, and so on.

While this may seem a little confusing and contradictory, that is only true if one assumes that disciplines should be "pure." However, as we will come to appreciate, human beings are constantly reorganizing and re-categorizing their activities; it would be a mistake for students of the human condition not to do the same. In this text, rather than focus on things, we examine the global issues: process, connectivity, and adaptation. We will deliberately bring in much that is not traditional anthropology—philosophy, history, economics, international issues, and so on—because these are central to a global anthropology. Further, we agree with Eric Wolf's critique of the tendency of scholars to territorialize their disciplines and then to define themselves into corners. This brings us back to the observation that there is no such thing as pure anthropology, or pure any discipline (Wolf 1982). We do not believe it is possible to gain an adequate understanding of the human condition by defining and categorizing alone (although we all do both); however, it is necessary to add analyses of problems, processes, and connections.

In addition, in the following chapters we will gain better insights into human culture in its three guises: symbol, behavior, and adaptation. We will see that while human behavior has a biological basis, it is culture that determines much of what we do and how we do it. Anthropologists have long argued that human adaptation is primarily due to successful changes in culture, not biology. While anthropologists have studied cultural change through the Paleolithic, Mesolithic, Neolithic, and Present (the last ten thousand years), their approach has been Eurocentric (as though all of the cultures of the world spun off of European models, which is not true). What we do is to take up the new challenge of viewing anthropology as a global discipline with critical relationships to other social sciences and humanities. Anthropologists must develop a multifaceted and global approach to adaptation that incorporates all world cultures and, in doing so, borrows liberally from other disciplines with a global context.

The study of cultural change is what sets American cultural anthropology apart from the discipline as practiced in other countries. In the history of American anthropology, culture change has been written about through an evolutionary perspective looking for predictive laws. Sometimes it is written about as the study of patterns of change, avoiding evolutionary or Marxist interpretations (as were popular fifty years ago). Sometimes writers use the biographies of individuals to describe change over a lifetime. We have incorporated most approaches, but in this book we will interpret change through concepts derived from globalization. Globalization is the central theme in this text. From globalization we will examine property rights, modes of production, trade, human-habitat relations, ideology, and the links among them. Globalization can be looked at as the final phase of cultural evolution, one in which international trade and democracy are the dominant forces of adaptation.

Chapter
Terms

anthropology	7	global anthropology	9
anthropology of art	16	grammar	14
anthropology of religion	16	historical archaeology	12
applied anthropology	16	hominids	12
artifacts	12	human or cultural ecology	15
classic phase	9	ideal culture	30
cognitive anthropology	16	lexicon	14
cognitive science	13	linguistic anthropology	13
comparative linguistics	13	medical anthropology	16
connectivity	8	morpheme	14
culture	19	paleoecology	12
economic anthropology	15	patrilocality	27
emic analysis	31	phoneme	14
ethnographer	15	phonetic alphabet	14
ethnography	15	political anthropology	15
ethnohistory	17	process	8
ethnolinguistics	14	real culture	30
ethnology	15	reductionism	9
etic analysis	31	reification	22
food extraction	34	social anthropology	15
food production	34	sociolinguistics	14
forensic anthropology	11	teleology	32
formative phase	9	virilocality	28
genocide	11		

Chapter 1
Studying Cultures

Conducting research on any culture and then describing, analyzing, and interpreting your findings is a difficult but fascinating undertaking. In this chapter, we will examine three major aspects of the endeavor: perspectives on culture, language and culture relations, and fieldwork. In the last chapter we provided an operational definition of culture and discussed some of culture's major characteristics. In this chapter we will examine some perspectives and issues regarding ways to look at cultures or the features of them. It is impossible to get an understanding of any culture without also understanding the language; therefore, language and its study are included in this chapter. Language is the major (but not the only) form of communication in all human cultures. It is an important means by which culture is transmitted, and it is therefore important to understand something about how language functions and how it is related to culture. Fieldwork involves a number of data collection and analysis techniques. We'll begin with perspectives on culture, then have a look at language, and finally discuss fieldwork.

Perspectives on Cultures

In the last chapter, we were introduced to how anthropologists conceptualize culture as an adaptive response to ecosystems and technology. The context can be historical or evolutionary. In the following, we suggest that cultures can be looked at as adaptive strategies, communities, and regulators of time and space. These perspectives are useful when looking at cultures as components of global networks, as opposed to the view of classic anthropology that saw cultures as closed and functionally integrated. The next chapter will present the history of formative, classic, and global anthropology.

CULTURES AS ADAPTIVE STRATEGIES

Practitioners of classic anthropology from early in the twentieth century until after World War II tended to view cultures as closed and static. Since the 1970s, as anthropologists have adopted a more global perspective, they have exchanged a static for a dynamic view of culture. John W. Bennett, a major figure of the classic anthropology who created a conceptual framework for global anthropology, suggests that culture should be viewed as coping or adaptive strategies (1976, 1993). This approach, conforming to what we said about the flexibility of culture in the Introduction chapter, assumes that culture is a dynamic system with permeable boundaries. Culture is a theory about reality that we carry in our minds; and it is not one, but many alternative strategies to achieve goals that help us adapt to changes in our local environment and the larger world. Most of what we see happening in the world today confirms this view of cultures as ever-changing systems composed of alternative adaptations. Yet this view presents a dilemma to anthropologists who view themselves as sympathizing with societies whose members are fighting to preserve their cultural distinctiveness. During the classic period, cultures were seen as, if not unchanging, only very slowly changing. Globalization has produced rapid change in those cultures that anthropologists fondly called "traditional" and viewed as stable and desirable (with a few exceptions) ways of life. Some scholars reject globalization as a largely negative process and deny that it has benefits for members of traditional ways of life. At the same time, however, and with increasing speed, traditional ways of life are disappearing; in their place are appearing new cultures which blend the old and the new, that is, traditional and global. People who are members of traditional cultures are borrowing and inventing new ways to adapt to an ever-changing world.

Another important classic anthropologist who contributed considerably to a global perspective is Marshall Sahlins who advocates a new historical ethnography, taking into account how cultures incorporate modernization and globalization to their own advantage. He notes that Karl Marx argued that modernization destroys all traditional cultures by enculturating native populations to western norms. The error in this argument, says Sahlins, is in conceptualizing culture as *sui generis* (an isolated entity controlled by its own laws). He points out that all cultures are subject to external pressures, natural and social, and that adjustment to such pressures is a normal process. In this regard, he says, no culture is an entity unto itself (1994, 387). Sahlins spent most of his career studying natives of the Pacific. He argues that while the West may have dominated cultures of the Pacific Islands in the nineteenth century (Sahlins questions whether this was ever fully so), they now manipulate modernizing influences and their own past to their advantage when possible. Sahlins differs from many anthropologists studying the Pacific in that he pays attention to modern features, such as the Hula dance. In the following, Sahlins shows how Hawaiian communities both retain the past and adjust to the present:

> Hula schools (*halau hula*) have been flourishing in Hawaii since the early 1970s. Many function under the patronage of Laka, the ancient goddess of hula, are led by inspired teachers (*kemu*), and observe various rituals of training and performance. Hula schools are a significant element of what some participants are pleased to call "the Hawaiian renaissance."

> The local people articulate with the dominant cultural order even as they take their distance from it, jiving to the world beat while making their own music (Sahlins 1994, 389).

■Hula dancing is an important and integral part of the Hawaiian culture and hula schools or *halau hula*, have been flourishing since the 1970s.

These upbeat commentaries on culture change among indigenous Hawaiians are in stark contrast to commentaries of a decade ago that lamented the extinction of traditional cultures by Western civilization.

Rather than viewing "globalization" as a wholly negative process where traditional cultures are consumed by the West, the new assessment is that these cultures are adapting to globalization in ways that were not foreseen by classic anthropologists. Change, it seems, is an ever-present feature of culture despite the static, timeless picture presented by many classic ethnographies. It was common for classic anthropologists to write about the **ethnographic present** as though ethnography were like an unchanging photograph. This analytic fiction was common in the first part of the twentieth century. However, after World War II, the study of cultural change, with its focus on modernization and modernization theory became popular. Since the 1980s, globalization has sped up the processes of cultural change. Instead of an ethnographic present, anthropologists have come to realize that cultures have always been changing.

Anthropologists may mourn the passing of traditional ways of life; but we must realize that even as they scrupulously record the details of the cultures they study, these are in the process of becoming something new and different, and hopefully adaptive successes. We should also be aware that most ethnographers can only study small samples of a culture. Ethnographies of fifty years ago seem remarkably naïve when compared to modern ethnographies written by native researchers (many cultures today produce their own ethnographic researchers who may be anthropologists, journalists, or novelists). In this view, then, adaptive strategies are always altering specific cultural configurations. Cultures are abstractions with very fuzzy boundaries, not things. This highlights the need for anthropologists, when studying cultures, to focus on process and connectivity and not on idealized ways of living that may have been only temporary.

ethnographic present

The presentation of an ethnography as static and unchanging

CULTURES AS COMMUNITIES

Human beings interact together in social groups that can be observed and studied. It is common to refer to such groups as communities. When we think of a community, the first thing that may come to mind is a bounded geographic space occupied by a group of people whose behavior is similar. There is another interesting conceptualization, however, developed by two classic anthropologists, Conrad Arensberg and Solon Kimball. They argued that culture could be understood as community. Community studies were very popular from the 1930s through to the 1960s when "community" meant a closely delimited and bounded group of people living in village-like conditions. However, as more anthropologists began to study cultures as samples of much larger populations, such as nation states, the study of communities faded. Arensberg and Kimball argued that community is not just a settlement pattern but that it is a "master institution." Here we briefly survey their work.

Most anthropologists thought of communities as "settlement patterns" or an "aggregate of people who interact due to kinship or propinquity" (neighborliness), two popular definitions. However, Arensberg and Kimball argued that people in all cultures live in communities which are master variables, somewhat like genetic codes, that are passed down from generation to generation, or learned by foreigners. They argued that communities can be studied through observation and quantification, and that they are approachable through social science techniques. Arensberg and Kimball placed particular emphasis on the importance of the human community in anthropological research (Arensberg and Kimball 1972). For them, community is not a demographic unit, nor is it a geographical entity. More recently, Kimball and Partridge define community as the "systems of interaction regularities and cultural behaviors which exist within an environmental context" (1979, 1). A community is the symbolically determined way that human beings organize themselves in time and space. Arensberg and Kimball see the community as the most important model of culture:

■"Community" is defined by the "systems of interaction regularities and cultural behaviors which exist within an environmental context, such as these teenagers celebrating Canada Day.

> We believe the community to be … a master institution or master social system; a key to society; and a model, indeed, perhaps the most important model of culture … When we call the community a "master system" or "key" we mean that it provides the structure of roles, relationships, and activities embodying this pattern. We are impelled to call it a master pattern, master mold, or master system because it provides a cell like duplication; a repeated, stable form for the culture in each place where that culture occurs and in each generation of its people (1972, x).

With few exceptions, humans share a life in common with other members of an organized community. When, as children, we begin to move beyond the confines of the family into the larger society, one of the first things we do is to develop a cognitive map of our community. Once you understand how a culture organizes its communities, it is relatively easy to find your way around other similar communities you are just visiting. It is that mental or cognitive map which is the "master system" that Arensberg and Kimball view as a master system of culture. For them community residents adopt a master plan of all the roles and statuses of the community and how each resident relates to roles and statuses as they mature. One amazing aspect of community is how a person goes through a lifetime adjusting to different roles and statuses

■An example of a cognitive map is how we are conditioned by our culture to be able to navigate our way around in new environments with familiar attributes. If one grows up in a small town, and then travels to a larger city, one still understands a freeway system and how cities are generally laid out.

without being told what they are. Knowledge of community takes the form of a master map found in a person's mind. Like language, it is mostly learned without it being taught.

There is a long tradition of community studies in the social sciences, especially in anthropology. Most examples of this tradition are, in fact, studies of geographically situated communities in the common sense of the term and many, if not most of these studies, assume that the community studied represents a microcosm of the larger culture. From the 1930s until the late 1960s, anthropologists studied mostly rural communities around the world. Such studies included many fine contributions on the organization of American society. For example, Lloyd Warner, an anthropologist who taught at the University of Chicago during this time period, did a series called the Yankee City studies. These studies were of a small New England city and attracted a good deal of attention to the study of modern communities.

Is a community really a microcosm of the larger culture in which it is embedded? The answer is, it depends. Long ago, Arensberg (1961) pointed out that, whether one is studying a community as an object (as an entity in and of itself) or as a sample from which to generalize about some larger entity, there are four basic issues that must be addressed. First, there is the issue of *representativeness*. By what criteria does one choose a particular community as representative of many, if not most, communities within the larger society? Second is the issue of *completeness*. Given that communities often overlap one another, whether in physical space or in terms of interaction spheres, how does one decide where to construct the boundaries and say "this is a part of the community and this is not?" Third is the issue of *inclusiveness*. To what extent must the institutions of a given community mirror those of the larger society for it to be considered a fair sample? Fourth, there is the issue of *cohesiveness* or *solidarity*. How much cooperation and harmony must there be in order for the selected social group to be considered a community at all? In addition, how much factionalism must there be to mirror conditions in the larger society? None of these issues are easily responded to, and each becomes more complex and more problematic the more complex and subculturally divided the larger society is. Choosing a community of Kayapó horticulturists in the Amazonian tropical forest as representative, complete, inclusive, and cohesive in regard to Kayapó culture is undoubtedly less problematic than is choosing a community in the United States in order to sample American culture.

Despite these problems and other criticisms of the community study method, the tradition of community study has remained strong in cultural anthropology. Of the many reasons for this, two come readily to mind: the community is a manageable unit for the individual researcher (and most anthropological field research is still done by lone individuals); and communities are in many ways the laboratories of the anthropologist. They provide the data for the formulation of hypotheses (which can often be tested using survey methods) and for the testing of hypotheses.

The concept of community is an abstraction meant to call attention to different means by which people organize their day-to-day lives. There are many terms that are used in the anthropological literature to address different kinds of communities. As we will learn in Chapter 2 and the chapters that follow, a community may be a band of hunter-gatherers living in the Arctic or in Africa who lack any larger unit of organization (they do not have any form of tribe or state). Or the community may be a group of families living in a village within a larger tribe of agriculturalists or pastoralists, who also lack any centralized form of organization but are integrated through trade, exchange, and share a common religion. What political organization there is may be in the hands of a big man, who may be a trader or mature warrior and who delegates responsibilities to those with less authority. Or, the community may be organized into a set of unilineal (matrilineal or patrilineal) groupings whose kinship relations are traced by male or female links to previous generations of liked sex relations. Those in position of power are those who are oldest or have been granted ceremonial or other rights on the basis of their kinship connections to a founding ancestor. There are many possibilities on how authority is passed down to the next generation. In general, the more structured is kinship, the more structured is authority. Or in more structured societies, the central community may be a village within a system of state centralization with a king and court. These are but a few of the community types found in pre-industrial societies. Many other forms of community organization are possible in industrial societies when the claims of kinship at a local level are weak, but the claim of the state is strong, such as modern American or European societies, and so on. The typology can be expanded and extended depending on the level of analysis towards which the writer is striving. Phil (PY) has lived among the Ngóbe of Panama who live in tribes of kinsmen, while I (SS) have done research among plantation workers in Guatemala and coffee growing communities in Colombia, both of which are also members of nation states. Our research shows the wide variation in community types found in Latin America. These three examples show the importance of focusing on the nature of community. The tribal Ngóbe of Panama and the landless Mayan workers of Guatemala are very different from each other, and both are distinct from Colombian coffee growers; however, all three are Latin American. The adaptations of all three communities reflect their histories and the impact of globalization. A careless generalization might throw all three into the same category of modernizing people of third world countries, but a careful study of community organization shows the three do respond in different ways to globalization. Tribes are the least organized, chiefdoms are much more highly organized, and states are the most organized types of social systems. States in turn are more or less organized on the basis of technological complexity, with societies like ours being among the most complex in technology and social organization.

KINESICS: CULTURES AS REGULATORS OF TIME AND SPACE

In addition to examining how cultures (as communities) adapt to their habitats, another useful and empirical way to look at cultures is as regulators of time and space. This is the hallmark of Edward T. and Mildred Hall's research and writing (these two are known as "kinesiologists" and their work is called kinesics). The Halls' research rests on the observation that all mammals are territorial and have instinctive (biological) spacing mechanisms, which in humans are learned and depend on culture. Territoriality is the protection of space. It is a means of insuring species propagation and density regulation in a given

■ All mammals, including humans, are instinctively territorial to some degree. Territory provides a framework of spaces for the young to learn, to hide, and play, and for adults to acquire food and shelter, and to reproduce.

habitat. The territory provides a framework where there are spaces for the young to learn, hide, and play, and for adults to acquire food and shelter and to reproduce. Distance regulation also provides a framework for intra-species communication and protection against over-exploitation of the habitat. Territoriality is often tied to dominance hierarchies that are worked out through threat and violence among the members of a species who occupy a territory (among baboons the defense of territory is tied directly to male dominance and access to females).

In *Understanding Cultural Differences* (1990), Edward and Mildred Hall argue that we are in many ways like our mammalian relatives, but that we organize both space and time according to linguistic and cultural categories, not smell or aggression. Most of the rules governing time and space regulation are not explicit but are learned and passed down from one generation to another. The Halls divide up time and space more explicitly in their comparison of predominantly American and European cultures. They look at space regulation in terms of three categories: territoriality, personal space, and multisensory spatial experience.

They point out that Americans tend to be territorial about places that they label "mine" such as the layout of a cook's kitchen or a child's bedroom. In Germany, the Halls argue, territoriality is extended to possessions, such as the automobile. Touching a German's car may elicit a response as though the owner's body had been touched. Cultural differences are also evident in spatial arrangements as metaphors for power. For example, German and American businesses reserve the top floors of a building for high-ranking executives, while the French officials occupy a position in a middle office surrounded by subordinates on the same floor. The French sense of power has the individual in the center with lines of power radiating out, rather than at the apex of a hierarchy. Washington, D.C., which was designed by a French architect, is a good example of French symbolic subordination since the White House was built in the center and other political institutions were constructed around it (Hall and Hall 1990, 10).

Personal space is the personal use of space; it, too, is controlled by culture. The Halls argue that each person is surrounded by invisible "bubbles of space" which expand and contract, depending on relations to people nearby and the individual's emotional state, cultural background, and activity being performed. Changes in the bubble that run counter to cultural norms of comfort may evoke aggressive behavior. The Halls point out that in Germany, which is in northern Europe, the bubbles are very large and people keep their distance. In Italy, which is in southern Europe, the bubbles get smaller as one travels from north to south until they almost cease to exist. German travelers in southern Europe may feel a sense of entrapment when riding an elevator, bus, or other enclosed vehicles when traveling in Italy, or Spain, another country that has small bubbles of space use. Notice in the example below (see Language and Culture) of the coffee break in Tokyo, how the American moved away from the Arab, thinking he was standing too close. Mexicans' sense of space is much like Spaniards', and Americans traveling through Mexico may find that those they socialize with stand close. Male Americans often confuse a woman's overtures of friendship for signs of sexuality.

Finally, the Halls note that people perceive space through all of the senses: Auditory space is perceived by the ears; thermal space by the skin; kinesthetic space by the muscles; and olfactory space by the nose. This is what they mean by multisensory spatial experience. There are significant cultural differences in the way in which the senses are utilized to program spatial experience. Germans rely heavily on auditory screening, especially when they want to concentrate. French and Italians reject auditory screening and thrive on noisy interruptions; they tune in only to those social cues that interest them, ignoring all others. Americans and Germans find French and Italian cities very noisy, while French and Italians find German and American cities to be cold and aloof. It is easy to understand that such differences are likely to result in cross-cultural misunderstandings.

Time, like space, is culturally organized. There are many kinds of time systems. The Halls highlight two as producing modern cross-cultural misunderstandings: monochronic and polychronic time. Monochronic means paying attention to and doing only one thing at a time. Polychronic means experiencing many human sensations at the same time. In monochronic cultures, time is experienced in a linear way and is scheduled and compartmentalized making it possible for a person to concentrate on just one person at a time. Americans use monochronic time and classify activities by setting priorities. Here people are governed by time and do not like being interrupted. Monochronic time is an artifact of the industrial revolution. Hall and Hall argue that German and Swiss cultures are dominated by "the iron hand of monochronic time" (Hall and Hall 1990, 14).

Polychronic time is the antithesis of monochronic. Mexico is a good example of a culture with a polychronic view of time. Two Mexican businessmen standing on a corner talking would prefer to be late for their next appointment than abruptly end their conversation before its natural conclusion. Time and schedules are simply not as important as socialization with people. The Halls see links between the ways in which cultures conceptualize and regulate time, space, and information flow. Monochronic Americans traveling in Mexico may find the use of time and space upsetting. Appointments may mean very little and will be shifted around to accommodate to an individual's hierarchy of friends, family, and associates, and not to the dictates of a clock. The Halls believe that millions of dollars have been lost in international business because people belonging to monochronic and polychronic cultures do not understand one another. They provide the following example:

> A French salesman working for a French company that had recently been bought by Americans found himself with a new American manager who expected instant results and higher profits immediately. Because of the emphasis on personal relationships, it frequently takes years to develop customers in polychronic France, and, in family-owned firms, relations with customers may span generations. The American manager, not understanding this, ordered the salesman to develop new customers within three months. The salesman knew this was impossible and had to resign, asserting his legal right to take with him all the loyal customers he had developed over the years. Neither side understood what had happened (Hall and Hall 1990, 16–17).

The Halls make a good case for the cultural significance of time and space regulation, but of course there is more than that to cultural differences. Try a small experiment. The next time you are talking with a friend, especially one from another culture, think about personal space. See if you can determine your own and theirs by moving closer and then further away during the conservation. What does the other person do when you move closer and closer? How do you feel? What happens as you increase the distance between you and the other person?

■Children begin learning language from the time they are born, but that ability decreases after twelve to thirteen years of age.

Culture, Cognition, and Language

If we are to understand how cultures are acquired and how cultures change, we need to know something about how the human brain stores and processes information. Language is our best-known means of information storage, processing, and retrieval. As we will explain, children begin learning language from the time they are born, but that ability decreases after twelve to thirteen years of age. Is childhood language acquisition the only way we learn our culture? In fact, children learn more than language. They also learn appropriate behavior through observation. Anthropologists and other social scientists have long referred to the general process whereby children learn what their parents and others around them know as **enculturation** or **socialization** (the former term tends to be used by anthropologists while the second term tends to be used by sociologists). A great deal of language acquisition and enculturation occur without the learners or teachers being fully aware of the transmission of knowledge.

enculturation

The term used by anthropologists to describe the general process whereby children learn what their parents and others around them know

socialization

The term used by sociologists to describe the general process whereby children learn what their parents and others around them know

HELEN KELLER, FERAL CHILDREN, AND THE ACQUISITION OF CULTURE

What happens when normal acquisition is disrupted due to the lack of normal means of language and cultural acquisition? Anthropologists, psychologists, and neuroscientists have long searched for case studies on children who failed to learn language while young, or by means other than speech, such as sign language. The problem is there are actually very few documented cases, the most famous of which is the story of Helen Keller. Keller's story is useful because both Helen and her teacher, Anne Sullivan, recorded their experiences and later wrote books on them. When Helen Keller was nineteen months old, and was on the way to learning language, she became ill either with scarlet fever or meningitis. The illness left her both blind and deaf and unable to learn language through the normal processes of language acquisition. Anne Sullivan, who had already acquired a reputation for teaching children with learning disabilities, was hired to try to help Helen re-acquire language.

Descriptions of Helen at age seven, when Miss Sullivan first entered her life, disclose no human or cultural attributes. Anne Sullivan described her as "an unruly little animal." Anne Sullivan began teaching Helen by spelling words into her hands using American Sign Language (the same language that was used in the 1970s to teach chimpanzees and gorillas how to "talk"). While she learned to use a few words quickly, she did not grasp the more general idea that words stood for things. The first words she learned were "signs" not "symbols." This means she was conditioned to the use of words, much as a dog might learn to respond to a bell that stands for water. The difference between sign and symbol is important here. A sign can either be some form that resembles the item being signed, such as thunder being a sign of a rainstorm, or it can be a sound, visible form, or touch that becomes associated with the thing being signed, much as dogs can be conditioned to respond to a bell that stands for food. In a symbol, there is no relationship between the symbol and what it stands for and/or the relationship is not based on conditioning.

Anne Sullivan used a language developed for deaf mutes. She used the sign for water, which she "signed" on Helen's hand. Helen became conditioned to the sign, and would make it on Anne's hand when wanting water. There was, however, some point when the sign for water changed to a symbol. The point may have occurred when Helen suddenly understood that there was something "behind" the "sign." Anne Sullivan has described the miracle moment, which was put into a television play and a movie called *The Miracle Worker:*

I made Helen hold her mug under the spout while I pumped. As the cold water gushed forth, filling the mug, I spelled "w-a-t-e-r" into Helen's free hand. The word coming so close on the sensation of cold water rushing over her hand seemed to startle her. She dropped the mug and stood as one transfixed. A new light came into her face. She spelled "water" several times. Then she dropped on the handle and asked for its name and pointed to the pump and trellis, and suddenly turned around she asked for my name … in a few hours she had added thirty new words to her vocabulary (quoted in White 1949, 38–39).

There has been considerable debate among psychologists, linguists, and anthropologists as to what may have happened. As explained above, one popular interpretation is that the words that Helen Keller used changed from signs to symbols, and that she not only began to use language but also became a "culture bearer," or human being. Anne Sullivan's description can be put next to Helen Keller's memory of the event:

We walked down the path to the well-house, attracted by the fragrance of the honeysuckle with which it was covered. Someone was drawing water and my teacher placed my hand under the spout. As the cool stream gushed over one hand she spelled onto the other the word *water*, first slowly then rapidly. I stood still, my whole attention fixed on the motion of her fingers. Suddenly I felt a misty consciousness as of something forgotten—a thrill of returning thought; and somehow the mystery of language was revealed to me. I knew that "w-a-t-e-r" meant the wonderful cool something that was flowing over my hand. That living word awakened my soul, gave it light, hope, joy, set it free (quoted in White 1949, 38).

There have been other instances of children, without language and culture, found in the wild and known as feral children, such as Amala and Kamala, the wolf children discovered in India in the 1920s, and Victor, the wild boy of Aveylon discovered in southern France in 1800. All of these children are described as acting like wild animals unable to learn language. While many scholars believe the original studies on these children were spurious, they fit into a larger picture of what happens to children when they are not exposed to language or culture until too late in life (as mentioned above, thought to be about age thirteen). Beyond that age the brain loses its capacity to respond to the complex codes of language and culture. Both

■Helen Keller with her teacher Anne Sullivan, 1888.

clinical evidence and theory show that humans have a genetic propensity to learn language and culture, and that the brain of a newborn child responds to the code of language and culture in pre-determined ways. Charles Laughlin and Eugene D'Aquili have proposed that the brain controls language acquisition through theories of language. These theories govern different aspects of language.

THE BRAIN AS THEORY BUILDER

In their book, *Biogenetic Structuralism*, first published in 1974, Charles Laughlin and Eugene D'Aquili proposed a controversial theory about the nature of the brain and its relationship to language and culture. The theory has become the basis for the discipline of neuroscience. According to Laughlin and D'Aquili, the human brain is the ultimate taxonomizer and theory builder that responds to sounds and images by organizing them and storing them into the cells of the brain, a process that begins when the child is born. The child's brain, at birth, is programmed to learn the culture and language that form its environment. Laughlin and D'Aquili begin by arguing that the mind is a logic producing biological machine. It is responsible in all cultures for creating questions in philosophy, religion, myth, and ritual that deal with the large questions in life.

Laughlin and D'Aquili adopted the point of view of evolutionary biologists who argued that our basic emotions are part of the primitive brain underlying the neocortex, which first evolved during the age of the dinosaurs. Many emotional givens that psychologists think are part of the human mind are biologically based and are the products of evolu-

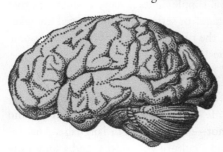

tion. Not only did Laughlin and D'Aquili argue that the brain is evolutionarily based, but they also argued that there is no such thing as "mind." Rather, the brain responds directly to stimuli. If the stimuli are not present, those parts of the brain that are tied to specific sense systems will not develop (this is true for kittens, monkeys, and humans, Wexler 2006).

The child does not learn by being taught, but learns through three major processes of enculturation: observation, practice (participation and repetitious imitation), and language acquisition. All are forms of learning. While a great deal of cultural learning undoubtedly takes place through the medium of spoken (and in literate cultures, written) language, it is likely that language as a mechanism for the transmission of cultural knowledge has been overrated, or at the very least, observation and participation have been slighted. We live and function in a literate culture. Much of what we learn is through written language. So it is natural for us to think that language is central and observation and participation considerably less important in learning what one needs to know to function effectively in one's culture—or, for that matter, to begin to understand another culture. Yet it is well known, for example, that students who learn another language in the classroom do not learn it as rapidly, or as thoroughly, nor can they use it as effectively as those who learn it within the cultural context in which it is spoken. Why should this be so? Maurice Block (1994) suggests that conceptual thought is not dependent on language alone (although there is constant interchange between language and conceptual thought once language is developed), but that much of our knowledge is non-linguistic and that concepts involve implicit networks of meanings that are based on experience, observation, and participation (Block 1994, 277–278, also Wexler 2006). For example, learning to play golf, to drive, or even to make bread has a lot to do with observation and practice and may have only minimal language involvement. As anyone who has tried it knows, you don't learn to play golf or to drive by reading the manuals; and you don't learn to make bread—at least not good bread—simply by reading the recipe.

As we shall see in the section below on fieldwork, cultural anthropologists rely heavily on participation and observation as means of learning about other cultures, and perhaps what is internalized and conceptualized in this way is at least as important in the production of ethnographic description as what is learned by talking about things in the local language after one learns it. Frederik Barth in his preface to Robert Pehrson's book, *The Social Organization of the Marri Baluch*, has pointedly illustrated this. Pehrson died while doing field work. Barth set about the task of compiling and analyzing Pehrson's field notes in order to produce the book that Pehrson would have produced had he lived. Barth undertook this task because Pehrson was his friend, they shared professional interests and views, and it was presumed that there were considerable similarities between the Baluch and the Pathan cultures that Barth had studied. Yet even after memorizing over two hundred typed pages of Pehrson's field notes in hopes of achieving some kind of understanding, Barth's attempts to write up the material in a coherent fashion were frustrated by the diversity of the data and the seeming lack of coherence. Yet Barth reports that Pehrson's field notes were quite detailed and impeccably professional. In desperation, Barth went to Pakistan and spent five weeks living with the Marri. After that brief time in the field, Barth was able to make sense of the notes and write the monograph. What had been missing? Barth reports the following:

> … it is singularly difficult to identify the critical supplementary data. I believe … that they are mainly connected with the concrete "stage" or setting in which social life takes place: the sizes of habitations, the uses of space, the physical as well as the conventional opportunities for conversation (Barth in Pehrson 1966, xi).

In other words, despite the attention given to detail in the notes of most anthropologists, much of the context within which social life takes place, is participated in, and observed, does not—and perhaps much of it cannot—get recorded in language. Anthropologists have long argued that to really understand a culture you must spend a long time living in it. There is apparently considerable truth in this maxim. However, we should emphasize that it is the interplay between language and other modes of learning that give us the whole picture.

CHARACTERISTICS OF LANGUAGE

All humans (with the exception of some born with certain types of genetic abnormalities) have the capacity to use language. This capacity is a part of our evolutionary and biological heritage. No other animal has the ability to use, or for that matter, to learn, human language in the way humans learn and use it. This is confirmed rather than disproved by all of the experimental attempts to teach human language (either spoken or sign language) to non-human primates. Thus, the ability to use language has a biological base; the ability to communicate in a *particular* language is learned. However, to say that languages are learned is not to say that they must be formally taught. In our literate society we tend to think that at least the grammar of a language, and perhaps much of the vocabulary, must be taught in school. But think about the fact that in hundreds

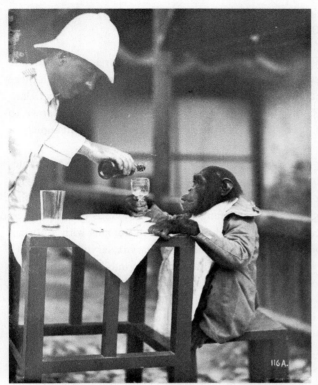

■In the Yerkes and Kohler experiment, the scientists attempted to directly teach English to gorillas and chimpanzees. However, all of the experimental attempts to teach human language have been unsuccessful.

of societies past and present, languages are simply learned by children as they grow up. Formal language training does not occur, and yet children rapidly become fluent and produce grammatically correct utterances. This attests to the innateness of our language ability; that is, the acquisition of language is based on biology, or to put it another way, on the way the human brain is put together.

Among linguists, cognitive scientists, and anthropologists, there is a difference of opinion as to whether language capacity is localized in a separate part of the brain and involves distinct cognitive processes or whether the capacity is more generalized and involves the same cognitive processes as those utilized in non-linguistic cognition (for example, seeing, hearing, smelling, tasting). The argument is complicated, the evidence is not clear-cut, and we need not resolve the issue here. No one disputes the fact that children do learn languages without formal instruction.

Human languages are incredibly diverse and complex in terms of their surface characteristics, such as the meanings attached to particular sequences of sounds, the inventory of significant sounds themselves, the ways in which sentences are structured, and the types and levels of meaning that may be attached to utterances. Yet, beneath this surface of diversity, all human languages share certain basic characteristics. Charles Hockett calls these universal characteristics of human language design features, and he originally listed thirteen (1960). Some other animal communication systems contain some of these features, but no other animal communication system that we know of contains all of them. The following lists these features, as modified to a standard list of nine in *Language Files:*

1) Mode of communication (vocal-auditory in the case of human and many animal systems);

2) Semanticity (the signals have meaning);

3) Pragmatic function (the communication serves a useful purpose);

4) Interchangeability (ability of individuals to both send and receive messages);

5) Cultural transmission (specific signals are learned rather than genetically transmitted);

6) Arbitrariness (form is not logically related to meaning);

7) Discreteness (complex messages built up out of smaller parts);

8) Displacement (ability to communicate about things not present in space or time); and

9) Productivity (ability to produce an infinite number of novel meaningful messages using a finite number of elements whose individual meanings are arbitrary). This

descriptive linguistics

The analysis of the structures of language into agreed-upon components in order to provide descriptions that are comparable

phone

A discreet sound that is part of a language

phonemes

The significant sounds in a language that convey meaning when speaking

phonology

The study of the phonemes of a language

allophone

A sound contained in a phoneme that has variations due to the context of other sounds in which it occurs

morphemes

Sounds that carry meaning, which are composed of phonemes

free morpheme

A word that stands alone and has meaning

bound morphemes

Units of meaning that must occur attached to another morpheme

infix

A bound morpheme that occurs within a word

is the feature Hockett termed *duality of patterning* (Jannedy, Poletto, and Weldon 1994, 20–21).

All communication systems contain the first three features; some non-human systems contain features four through seven (although there is disagreement about some of these). Importantly, only human languages contain eight and nine, and only human languages are known to contain all nine. It is the last two features that make human language a truly unique communication system.

People talk and listen, read and write. Linguists analyze the structures of languages into agreed-upon components in order to provide descriptions that are comparable. This endeavor is called **descriptive linguistics.** All languages contain a range of discreet sounds called **phones.** The study of these sounds is called phonetics. All humans with a normal vocal tract (lips, tongue, oral and nasal cavities, pharynx, larynx, vocal cords, trachea, and lungs) can produce, with practice, the sounds of all human languages. Granted, some sounds such as the clicks in some African Bantu languages are notoriously difficult for an English speaker to master. The significant sounds in a language—that is, those that make a difference in meaning when speaking—are called **phonemes.** The study of the phonemes of a language is called **phonology.** Some phonemes may be composed of **allophones**, sound variations due to the context of other sounds in which they occur. For example, in English the /t/ sound in [top] is really a [th] sound (aspirated /t/, that is, it has a puff of air following it) while the /t/ in [stop] is unaspirated. (In linguistic analysis, it is customary to use slashes to surround a sound or word rendered phonemically and brackets to surround a sound or word rendered phonetically.) [t] and [th] are allophones of /t/ in English. The phonemes of a language should not be confused with the signs (letters of the alphabet) used to represent them. While the written form of some languages is much closer to a phonemic representation than is English (which is what makes spelling so difficult in English), probably no written language has a writing system that precisely renders its phonemic representation. Phonemes call up a contrast in meaning between words, but do not carry meaning.

Sounds that carry meaning are called **morphemes**, which are composed of phonemes. The study of morphemes is called morphology. **Free morphemes** are what we commonly call words. They can stand alone and have meaning. **Bound morphemes** are those units of meaning that must occur attached to some other morpheme. An example from English is the morpheme -*ed*, as in finish*ed*, which carries the meaning *past tense*. In English, bound morphemes occur frequently as prefixes, that is, at the beginning of a word, and as suffixes, at the end of a word. A third type of bound morpheme occurs within a word and is called an **infix**. An infix is a bound morpheme that occurs within a word. Infixes are common in some North American Indian languages such as Navajo. Words are categorized as parts of speech such as nouns, verbs, prepositions, and adjectives.

All languages arrange their words in characteristic ways to form larger units of meaning called sentences, if they can stand independently, and phrases, if they must be part of a sentence. The study of the organization of words into phrases and sentences is called **syntactics**. This is what was called grammar when you were being taught "proper" English in school. Larger units of meaning contain systematically arranged parts of speech, which are given functional labels—such as subject, verb, and object. Different languages arrange these (and other) parts of a sentence in different ways. English declarative sentences, for example, characteristically have the arrangement Subject-Verb-Object while Ngóbere, the language of the Ngóbe people of Panama, has a Subject-Object-Verb arrangement.

The study of the meaning of words, phrases, sentences, and even larger units of discourse is called **semantics**. The meanings of a word may depend on the context in which it is used, as well as whether it is intended to be taken literally or metaphorically; the same is true of phrases and sentences. The ways in which metaphor is used in different cultures and in different social contexts is itself a topic of much anthropological and linguistic research.

There are many more fascinating details about language that could be addressed, but this is not an introduction to linguistics so we will leave it at this. The student should by now have some sense of the complexity and diversity of human languages as systems of communication. Perhaps it should also be noted that all languages change through time, often in quite systematic ways, and that many of today's languages have common ancestors in the past. The study of language change and the relationships of languages to one another is called historical or comparative linguistics.

We now turn to an as yet unresolved question among anthropologists and linguists, the relation between language and culture.

LINGUISTIC RELATIVITY: THE SAPIR-WHORF HYPOTHESIS

The Sapir-Whorf hypothesis states that there is a close relationship between the way in which members of a culture perceive their world and the way in which they use their language to communicate their perceptions (their world view). While there seems little doubt that a relationship exists between the categories of a language and those of a culture, Benjamin Lee Whorf went further than most other scholars of his day. He argued that speakers of different languages experience and perceive different realities because of the categories of their language. This idea was not entirely original with Whorf, having been suggested in the nineteenth century by Alexander Von Humboldt. As proof of his hypothesis, Whorf offered a contrast between several features of English and Hopi. For example, he noted that the Hopi language structures time as cyclical while English structures time as linear. Hopi categorizes action in terms of kind of validity (reporting, expecting, and speaking from previous knowledge), and so Whorf called it a "timeless" language; English categorizes action in terms of past, present, and future, thus focusing on time and segmenting it. Whorf also noted other differences between the ways in which Hopi and English categorized reality. He concluded that language influences patterns of thought and therefore of cultural behavior. In addition, more recent work on the Hopi language has shown that it not only has distinct tenses from English but that it also has unique metaphors for time: units of time including days, number of days, parts of the day, yesterday and tomorrow, days of the week, weeks, months, lunar phases, seasons, and the year (Malotki 1983). Whorf did not have all the information he needed about Hopi to prove his hypothesis, and many tests have been made to test this interesting proposition; but no one has managed to

---

syntactics

The study of the organization of words into phrases and sentences

semantics

The study of the meaning of words, phrases, sentences, and even larger units of discourse

prove or disprove Whorf. Still, modern anthropologists are interested in the influence of language on behavior.

Most anthropologists today would agree with what we can term a weak version of the Whorfian hypothesis, namely, that languages do express cultural emphases and nuances, but that the relationship goes both ways rather than being of the causal form "language structures cultural reality." The interdependence of language and culture can be seen in the possible misunderstandings that occur when individuals from different cultures attempt to communicate in the language of one or the other.

LANGUAGE AND CROSS-CULTURAL MISUNDERSTANDING

Cross-cultural misunderstandings often have their bases in idealized standards of proper behavior. When representatives of different cultures are unaware of each other's cultural expectations, many misunderstandings are possible. Cross-cultural conversations are a good way to illustrate this. The first example below is taken from an account by Elashmawi and Harris (1993). During a business conference at a Tokyo convention center, American John Smith is trying to build a network of personal relations by introducing himself to as many people as possible and engaging them in conversation during coffee breaks. Smith spots two men, one Japanese and the other Arab, and approaches them. The following conversation ensues.

Smith:	Good morning, gentlemen. I'm John Smith. (He extends his hand to the Arab man first and then to the Japanese.) Do you mind if I join you?
Mohammed:	(As he shakes Smith's hand with both of his) Welcome, please join us.
Suzuki:	(He steps backward and bows slightly. He shakes Mr. Smith's hand without saying anything, ready to exchange business cards.)
Mohammed:	Are you enjoying yourself in this wonderful country, Mr. Smith?
Smith:	Oh, sure; it's very nice here. What do you do Mr. ... ?
Mohammed:	Mohammed Rageh. I'm from Egypt and the president of my import company. We are here to look at some of the available products and meet our Japanese friends.
Smith:	(Turning to Suzuki.) And your name, sir?
Suzuki:	(He silently hands Smith his business card.)

(cont'd) ▶

Smith:	(After looking at it quickly) Oh, you're Mr. Suzuki.
Suzuki:	Yes, Sany Corporation.
Smith:	I see. (Puts Suzuki's card into his pocket and hands each man his business card.) Do you have a card, Mr. Mohammed?
Mohammed:	(Smiling) No, I don't carry them with me. Everyone knows me. (Moving closer to John to show his hospitality.) I'm the president.
Smith:	(Stepping back from Mohammed.) Oh, I understand.
Suzuki:	Mr. Smith, you are from the Blackford Company?
Smith:	Yes, I'm the marketing director in charge of the Southwestern Division.
Mohammed:	Well, should we all go have some coffee and enjoy our break time together?
Smith:	I'm sorry, but I have to talk to some other people. Maybe we'll get together later on. It was very nice to meet you. Goodbye.

John Smith walks away to meet more people, not realizing how little he understood the conversation in which he had just been engaged. Hidden beneath the words were different cultural expectations about both the style of the conversation and the appropriateness of the behavior accompanying it. Smith unknowingly offended both the Arab and the Japanese because of his insensitivity to their cultural expectations. His first blunder occurred when Mohammed asked John about his stay in Japan. John answered abruptly and then asked Mohammed what he did. Arabs like to establish personal relations with someone first before talking about business. Consequently, Mohammed thought John was brusque. The next clash occurred when Smith put away Mr. Suzuki's business card after merely glancing at it. In Japan it is customary to study a business card carefully to determine company name and rank, which are usually not discussed. By putting the card away, John offended Mr. Suzuki. On the other hand, Smith probably interpreted Mr. Suzuki's initial silence as rather standoffish behavior. Next, by moving away from Mohammed when Mohammed moved closer, Smith was unknowingly rejecting Mohammed's attempt to be hospitable; and he did so again when he declined to join Mohammed and Suzuki for coffee. Smith was undoubtedly made uncomfortable by Mohammed's closeness. This illustrates what was mentioned above about cultural differences in communication distance. Mr. Smith also offended by stating his own position in his company. That probably sounded, at least to Mr. Suzuki, as though Smith was bragging.

In our second example, taken from Harris and Moran (1987, 256), an American working for a transnational company in Greece is trying to follow his democratic cultural ideals, not realizing that his Greek employee has an ideal male standard of conduct called *filotimo*. Filotimo requires Greek men to act manly, to give orders and also to take them without complaining; but it also means that "a boss" must give orders that are exact and clear.

■ Verbal Conversation	■ Attribution
American: How long will it take you to finish this report?	American: I asked him to participate. Greek: His behavior makes no sense. He is the boss. Why doesn't he tell me exactly what he wants?
Greek: I do not know. How long should I take?	American: He doesn't want to be responsible. Greek: I asked him for an order.
American: You are in the best position to analyze time requirements.	American: I press him to take responsibility for his own actions. Greek: What nonsense! I better give him an answer.
Greek: Ten days.	American: He lacks the ability to estimate time. His estimate is totally inadequate.
American: Take fifteen. Is it agreed to? Greek: Okay, fifteen days.	American: I offer a contract. Greek: That is an order. I better take it.

(In fact, the report required thirty days, so the Greek, following filotimo and without complaining worked night and day; but he still needed one more day than the fifteen allotted.)

American. Where is the report?	American: I am making sure he fulfills his contract. Greek: He is demanding that the report be turned in.
Greek: It will be ready tomorrow.	
American: But we agreed it would be ready today.	American: That's what Greeks always say. I will get him to fulfill his contract.
Greek hands in his resignation.	Greek: The stupid incompetent boss! Not only did he give me bad orders, but he doesn't even appreciate that I did a 30-day job in sixteen days. I can't work for such a bully.

American: Why are Greeks always
irresponsible?

Greek: Americans pretend they are fair,
but they are really brutish.   (From Harris & Moran 1987, 256).

■   ■   ■

What these two examples illustrate is that language does not convey the same message
for everyone even though the words are the same. Cultural background provides the context for interpretation. Also, language does not convey all of the information that is necessary for understanding the message. In both of these examples, misunderstandings might
have been avoided if the participants had understood something about each other's cultural
expectations. It is not realistic to expect anyone to learn all the nuances of all the cultures
with which she or he might come in contact. However, it is reasonable to expect awareness
that there *are* cultural differences that are likely to make a difference.

Two things are essential in any attempt to achieve cross-cultural understanding. First,
you must realize that your own culturally based assumptions about human nature and
behavior are inherently ethnocentric. Consciously examine your own beliefs and expectations and accept the fact that those of others may be different, but not wrong. Second, try to
understand the behavior of someone from another culture within his or her cultural context
(cultural relativism). When approaching a cross-cultural situation, study body language and
the response of others to your statements, and be aware of your own reactions. It is possible
to mitigate misunderstanding by simply pointing out to members of other cultures that you
may have made a mistake, and that perhaps you and others in the group have different values and expectations. A discussion of how two cultures have distinct understandings of
human nature is a great learning tool and helps defuse explosive situations.

Doing Ethnography: Fieldwork

ethnographer

An anthropologist
conducting cultural
anthropology
research in the field

ethnography

A study produced by
an ethnographer

Anthropologists play different roles through time when doing research in cultural anthropology. When conducting research in the field, they call themselves **ethnographers** and
the studies they produce are called **ethnographies**. The terms are derived from the Greek
combining form *éthnos*, meaning people, and *graphos*, also a Greek term which means a
thing written or drawn. In essence, ethnography means, "to write about ethnic groups or
people." Ethnographers do detailed studies of different aspects of a peoples' culture, such as
kinship systems, economies, political systems, religions, and ideologies. The focus depends
upon individual theoretical or problem-oriented interests, or the cultural themes of the
society under study. That is to say, ethnography is always context-dependent and all ethnographies should be read with this in mind. An ethnography usually contains a description of
the findings, often from both an emic and an etic viewpoint; an analysis, which is a "systematic way to identify key factors and relationships among them" (Wolcott 1994, 10); and an
interpretation of what the data mean within some chosen framework of hypotheses or theories. These components of an ethnography—description, analysis, and interpretation—are
not mutually exclusive and often are not sharply separated (or even identified as such) in the
writings of ethnographers.

How does one achieve a relatively deep understanding of another culture? Is long-term residence in another society enough? Obviously not. Many Americans spend years overseas and never really achieve an understanding of the culture that surrounds them. Understanding requires active, systematic effort. It requires long-term field research during which, to the best of one's ability, one suspends one's own beliefs and tries to understand those of others. Learning the ways of another culture is a process that is never complete, often beset

Case Study

Eating in the Rain

In early 1964, I (PY) arrived in the small Panamanian town of San Felix on the edge of Ngóbe territory. Seven years before, while in the U.S. Army, I had taken a few days leave and visited Ngóbe country. At the end of that brief stay, the people I had met said, "Come back and see us." One of them was a man named Jacinto. I wrote a note to Jacinto saying I had returned and was in San Felix. A boy who was going up the mountain to a hamlet near to Jacinto's house agreed to carry the message. Two days later another boy brought Jacinto's reply: "I'm busy working in my fields. What do you want?" Not exactly the enthusiastic greeting I had been anticipating. Although disappointed that Jacinto had not come to town to meet me, I was eager to make arrangements to begin my research. One of the small storeowners in San Felix introduced me to Eduardo, a young Ngóbe man from the hamlet of Hato Pilon. I explained to Eduardo that I wished to go far up into the mountains to the hamlet of Cerro Mamita where Jacinto lived. The storeowner agreed to rent me a horse and I contracted Eduardo to be my guide.

We arrived at Cerro Mamita during a tropical rainstorm. Both of us were soaked to the skin and then some. A couple of boys came running out of a house and unsaddled the horses. Eduardo indicated to me that the house was Jacinto's. Jacinto came to the doorway, greeted me, and invited me in. After standing near the cooking fire on the floor in the center of the house to dry myself and my clothes, I took the seat I was offered on the bench to the right of the door as one faces out. Men always sit here. Eduardo had remained outside and seated himself on a rock near the house. It was still pouring rain. After some polite conversation, I was served a steaming hot meal by Jacinto's mother. A young girl took a large bowl of food out to Eduardo who was still sitting on the rock. He ate alone in the rain, occasionally conversing with Jacinto who remained inside the house. I asked Jacinto why Eduardo was sitting outside and eating in the rain. The response was less than enlightening: "Because he wants to." Having spent a full day in travel and conversation with Eduardo, I knew he was a

rational young man, so this odd behavior puzzled me. I knew there was something more here than met the eye. I didn't know what and at that point had no idea what the right questions might be to ask. But I did not forget the incident.

I successfully made arrangements to live in the hamlet of Cerro Mamita and begin my research. (I am leaving out a great many details that are not directly relevant here.) Over the weeks that followed, I began to collect as much genealogical data as possible. I also collected data on the terms Ngóbe use to refer to kinspersons and on which kinspersons are referred to by which terms. In small-scale societies like that of the Ngóbe, most social relations are based on kinship so both types of information are essential to understand what is going on. In the course of data collection I found that Jacinto and Eduardo were related by marriage. Eduardo was married to the daughter of Jacinto's mother's sister. I learned that the Ngóbe kin term for a man's mother-in-law (me) also refers to her sisters. In other words, a man's wife's mother and her mother's sisters are all considered mothers-in-law by the Ngóbe.

In discussions with Jacinto and others I learned about the Ngóbe practice of mother-in-law avoidance, whereby a son-in-law may never see the face of his mother-in-law nor enter a house where she is present, unless she is appropriately shielded from view, nor speak directly to her. Suddenly Eduardo's seemingly irrational behavior of months before became clear to me. It was completely understandable within the Ngóbe cultural context. Eduardo could not enter the house because one of his mothers-in-law, Jacinto's mother, was present. Of course, he could have sought shelter elsewhere but then he would have been too far from Jacinto's house to participate in the conversation and catch up on the local gossip. All of this was, of course, perfectly obvious to the Ngóbe, and their problem on that rainy day long ago was that they couldn't understand why an apparently intelligent adult male like me would ask such a dumb question.

with setbacks and difficulties (hopefully none of them insurmountable), and interspersed with comic situations and those that may produce anger. Understanding is achieved slowly. Pieces of information may not fit together in patterns until many weeks or months of patient and often-tedious data collection have passed. However, when the patterns finally begin to emerge, when glimmers of understanding begin to shine through the darkness, it is an exciting, exhilarating, enlightening experience. As an example of the process of learning in the field, the "Eating in the Rain" case study presents one of Phil Young's experiences during his initial period of research with the Ngóbe of Panama.

RESEARCH METHODS

Ethnographers use a wide variety of methods, both qualitative and quantitative to collect data in the field. The most comprehensive and easiest to understand guide to methods in anthropology—both field methods and analytic methods, and qualitative and quantitative methods—as well as discussions of the realities of ethnographic research, is H. Russell Bernard's *Research Methods in Anthropology: Qualitative and Quantitative Approaches*, second edition (1995). We highly recommend this book to any student who is contemplating ethnographic research, whether short-term or long-term, and whether overseas or in their own community. Here we will only highlight some of the key aspects of fieldwork.

Literature Search There are two views about the value of a literature search. One view holds that reading the literature before going to the field will contaminate your own views of what you encounter, so you are better off learning everything on your own after arriving in your field location. While there may be some marginal utility in this *tabula rasa* ("clean slate") method for the seasoned professional, there is no benefit to it for the novice. The other view holds that a literature search prior to fieldwork is very important, and it is this view to which we subscribe. What you were planning to do may have already been done, and there is such a thing as history. There is no sense in spending weeks in the field in order to reinvent the wheel, and certain events may have occurred that are important to know. There is also little to be gained by trying to stick to a narrow review, and a lot to be gained by doing what H. Russell Bernard calls a "snowball sample" (Bernard 1995). Call someone who has an interest in your question, ask for a list of names of all those whom he or she knows, and network out from that list. Do the same with books and journal articles. Search the stacks on the region where you select a relevant book to find if there are other related topics or texts you could not predict.

The *Annual Review of Anthropology*, which has been published since 1972 (it was a biennial review from 1959–1971), is a good place to start. It contains several hundred review-articles on anthropological projects. There are similar reviews for other sciences and social sciences.

Articles in anthropology and related disciplines are published in hundreds of independent journals, some of which are quite obscure and hard to track down. There are many journals published in foreign countries; these can only be accessed at the libraries of large research universities. There are also reports published by government agencies and private research foundations that might give the disciplined researcher insights not otherwise available.

The task of running down articles from hundreds of journals around the world would be exhausting. Luckily, there is the *Abstracts in Anthropology*, which is found in most university libraries. More sophisticated are the publications of The Institute for Scientific Information in Philadelphia: *Science Citation Index, Social Science Citation Index*, and *Arts and Humanities Citation Index*. Using these indices, it is possible to look up an article published twenty years ago and to find the citations of all those articles that have used the article since then. Furthermore, most universities and colleges have computer terminals that allow on-line searches (the drawback to computer searches is expense; see Bernard 1995 for more information on literature searches).

Participant-Observation

Participant observation is the method, par excellence, of cultural anthropology. Whatever the other methods an ethnographer may employ in the field, participant observation will always be prominent. Observing and recording one's observations is something that one can do at the very beginning of field research, even though an understanding of what was observed may not come until much later, as illustrated by Young's experience with the Ngóbe (see the case study above). Of course observation continues throughout the time when active participation has become possible. To a certain extent, the participation part requires "going native," that is, doing what the local people do. This is no longer just an anthropological technique. Many researchers from other fields find it necessary to become members of the communities they are researching in order to gain access to information which otherwise is not forthcoming (Bernard 1995).

When I (SS) was in Jardin, Colombia, I worked hard to find some way to participate in the community. It is not as easy as it sounds. One day, talking to the mayor, I asked him if *"mingas"* still existed in Jardin. A minga is a cooperative work group traditional to Colombia that I had read about. He beamed and pointed to the church and then to the hospital explaining both had been built through the use of mingas. In great detail he described how the people of the community of Jardin in the 1930s had ascended a local mountain and quarried rock, which they carried down to the valley to build both a church and hospital. The mayor then asked if I would like to help work on a minga the following day. I most certainly would! The following morning, I rode up to the top of a mountain in a 1982 Dodge dump truck. I spent the day building a road to a building that housed a TV translator. The translator picked up the TV signal from Medellin and shot it down into the San Juan River valley.

The minga I worked in spent the day carrying rocks from the dump truck to create a small road. It was a very festive event, but it consisted of hard and muddy labor. The minga was made up of a cross-section of the community: rich and poor, young and old, men and women. I had a chance to experience the very democratic sense of equality in the mountain town of Jardin. When I returned to the town, it was as though I had passed an initiation rite. Thereafter, I could sit in the town square and interview farmers without feeling awkward. For the next several weeks, I was called on to work on other mingas. On one we cut down wild cane to build corrals for a yearly "county fair." In the evenings, I would sit around with the people I had worked with, sip *aguardiente* (a liquor made from sugar cane) and beer, and pass *cuentos* (stories) about the history of the town. I was particularly interested in the period from 1948 to 1953 when La Violencia occurred, a civil war that turned town against town throughout Colombia and brought on the dictatorship of Rojas Penilla (I remember Penilla's portrait on the wall of the boy's school I had attended in 1955).

There are limits to participation, however. Some limits will be imposed by the degree to which the people have accepted the anthropologist and by the rules of the culture under study. During my (PY) first few weeks in the field, I was never invited to participate in a collective work party; and when I asked about doing so, I was put off by one excuse or another. After good rapport was established with a number of Ngóbe families and I was incorporated into the kinship network, I had to figure out culturally acceptable ways to refuse such invitations as they became too numerous and began to interfere with my own work. These Ngóbe work parties are all male activities. Because of my integration into family life, I was not asked to accompany the women of nearby households when they went to harvest root crops or collect firewood. In most societies there are some activities in which only women participate and others in which only men participate. In addition to gender, age and status may determine the cultural appropriateness of participation.

Sometimes participation may be viewed as threatening. For example, when I (PY) began my research among the Ngóbe, many men asked me if I was or was intending to plant crops. I answered truthfully that I had no intention of farming (honesty is always the best policy), that I was there for other reasons, and I explained my purpose. My response was met with clear signs of relief which I learned later was due to the fact that Panamanians had for years been encroaching on Ngóbe lands. My fluency in Spanish caused most people to categorize me with the Panamanians until they got to know me well.

Finally, the ethnographer should impose some limits on participation. In part this may be to retain a certain degree of objectivity, in part it may be necessary in order to avoid unnecessary physical risks, and in part it may be necessary to spare the feelings of those you are living and working with. Although each field situation is different, sexual liaisons or marriage in the field are not normally recommended (though both have happened), even if they may be culturally appropriate. The field researcher must keep in mind that she or he is a temporary resident and will be going home after a few months. Intimate relationships can make departure difficult both for the researcher and for his or her local partner. At one point during my (PY) work with the Ngóbe, when visiting a nearby hamlet with some of my "brothers," one man, whom I had gotten to know well over the months, decided that I must be lonely (my family had remained in the U.S.) and so he offered me his daughter in marriage. I politely declined, pointing out that I had a wife in the United States. This response elicited a "so what" from the polygynous Ngóbe, and I had to figure another way out of this particular dilemma. I pointed out that I had no sister to exchange and no land and would thus make a poor son-in-law. Even this argument did not completely dissuade the man. My brothers came to my rescue at this point and gently turned the incident into a joking matter, thus giving both father and daughter a graceful way to drop the matter by pretending that the offer had not been a serious one and the joke was on me. I, of course, accepted this interpretation with considerable relief and laughed with the rest (although, so far as I know, the offer had been a serious one).

Learning the Language   In order to be a successful participant observer, to conduct interviews, and to attend to many of the ordinary tasks of daily life in the field, it is necessary to learn the local language. While in some cases and for some purposes it may be possible to get by using a *lingua franca*, a language that is mutually intelligible to you and the people you are working with, it is always preferable to learn the local native language. If an anthropologist is working with a subcultural group in his or her own society, this may involve no more than learning the special vocabulary of the subcultural dialect (and, of course, learning how to use it appropriately). In other cases an anthropologist may find it necessary to learn an unwritten language about which there is little or no prior information. Becoming even marginally fluent may take months of effort and requires that the ethnographer know the fundamentals of linguistics (see above). However, in the end the effort expended in learning the local language will return great dividends in terms of the rapport one establishes (people almost everywhere are flattered when an outsider makes the effort to learn their language) and in the richness of the cultural understanding that one achieves.

Interviewing   In this section on interviewing, we review some of the more formal data-collecting methods used by anthropologists in the field. (This section relies on the summary provided by Bernard 1995, 209–210.) It should be kept in mind, however, that there is a haphazard quality to anthropological research, dictated by the circumstances of the moment. You never know when you are going to learn something new, and it is important to be extremely attentive to small details. People are remarkably interested in providing details about their culture and their own lives to someone who expresses genuine interest and who doesn't cut them off with another question when they are just beginning to elaborate on the last one. It is important to remember: What the researcher may initially view as a digression from the topic, the informant may see as an integral part of the tale being told.

All ethnographers conduct interviews in the field. Interviews are of four basic types: informal, unstructured, semi-structured, and structured. Informal interviewing is simply conversations with informants where no attempt is made to structure or control the content of the conversations. While it can be a rich source of data and provide often unexpected insights and leads to new topics throughout the period of field research, its greatest utility is during the initial stages of participant observation when the researcher is trying to develop a general picture of what the culture is all about, what some of the local do's and don'ts are, and what might be some topics worthy of detailed and more systematic inquiry at a later date.

The unstructured interview is perhaps the most frequently used form of data collection in ethnographic research. It is not simply informal conversation. Both you and your informant know that an interview is being conducted. You provide the topic or theme (and some prompt questions if necessary), and you let your informant talk at his or her own pace. You exercise only minimal control over the responses. For example, you may wish to steer the informant back to the topic if he or she has gone too far off on a tangent. Unstructured interviewing is quite time-consuming. It is appropriate for long-term research and works well when you can interview the same people on many occasions.

In the semi-structured interview a guide is used to insure that a particular set of questions and topics is covered, usually in a specified order. While the interviewer still allows considerable flexibility for responses, as in the unstructured interview, the goal is to insure that responses to all topics and questions on the interview guide are elicited. This insures that the responses collected from several respondents can be compared. The semi-structured interview is a good method to use if you are unlikely to have additional opportunities to interview the same people, if you are using several assistants to conduct the interviews, or if your intent is to collect data that is quantifiable. Anthropologists near the end of a period of field research often use semi-structured interviews. The questions they contain are based on information obtained from informal and unstructured interviews and participant observation.

In structured interviewing all informants are asked to respond to identical stimuli. Usually these stimuli are very carefully worded and sequenced questions, but other stimuli include a variety of tasks that informants are asked to perform. Bernard provides a detailed account of structured interviewing (Bernard 1995, Chapter 11). The idea in structured interviewing is to carefully control both the stimuli and the circumstances under which they are presented to the respondents. This may be difficult to do under some field conditions. It is the equivalent of the controlled experiments performed by psychologists in laboratories.

Informal, unstructured, and semi-structured interviewing can be done with groups as well as individuals. However, to be effective and produce reliable and valid data, a highly skilled interviewer must conduct group interviews, often with one or more assistants.

Surveys

Surveys generally presume a random sample of respondents. They consist of a set of formal questions and are frequently used by sociologists, economists and political scientists to collect a wide variety of data that is then subjected to various techniques of quantitative analysis in order to derive either hypotheses or conclusions. Oftentimes when the questions are formulated and administered by members of one culture (or subculture) to members of another, it turns out that at least some of the questions are not culturally sensitive, or are meaningless to the respondents, or are simply not the right questions to ask; and thus the results of such questionnaire surveys may be highly suspect. For example, in a survey administered to the Ngóbe by the Panamanian Ministry of Education in the early 1970s, the Ngóbe respondents were asked what they normally ate for breakfast, lunch, and dinner. Since the Ngóbe do not structure their eating habits around the concept of three meals a day, the results of this attempt to determine what the Ngóbe usually eat were meaningless. Anthropologists who make use of survey questionnaires do so toward the end of their research after they have enough data from other sources to compose a list of meaningful, culturally appropriate questions. Survey questionnaires that must be administered by an interviewer are a form of structured interview.

Tools of the Trade

In the last several decades anthropologists and researchers have gained access to technologies that aid research. As the following will imply, however, research tools are no better than those using them.

Tape Recorders, Cameras, and Camcorders

New technologies have made many new strategies of research possible. Tape recorders have long been used to record interviews, but in the past they were so bulky and conspicuous that they often hindered rather than facilitated research. Now, with recorders that will fit in a shirt pocket and come equipped with voice activation, people are likely to forget quickly that they are being recorded and will respond with greater spontaneity. However, it is ALWAYS necessary to get permission before using any kind of recording device or camera. To do otherwise is unethical and unprofessional. Some people may feel quite uncomfortable about being recorded or having their picture taken, or not wish it for religious reasons. In the 1960s during research with the Ngóbe, I (PY) found that most Ngóbe did not mind having their picture taken but were totally intimidated by my twenty-two-pound, big-as-a-bread-box Butoba tape recorder (state-of-the-art at the time). While some people did timidly consent to be recorded, the usual reaction when I turned the recorder on was that all conversation stopped. When I returned to Ngóbe country in the mid-1970s, hand-held recorders were available. Many young Ngóbe owned them, and they were recording each other and me!

Hand-held camcorders with instant playback have replaced the old fashioned movie camera as the tool of choice in the field; and where there is electricity, television sets are becoming ubiquitous and VCRs quite common. Family and community celebrations and other events can now be easily recorded and then played back to the audience. It is not a bad idea to give a VCR to the community as a gift and leave copies of videotapes so people can watch themselves. One researcher on the Trobriand Islands brought videotapes of the old festivals (originally on film) recorded by Malinowski in the 1920s so that young people could watch their grandparents dancing and playing cricket! They could then record their own dancing and playing and compare the two time periods. Here the anthropologist is giving back to people some of their own culture, bits and pieces of which are being lost.

One research method that I (SS) have found to be very rewarding is event analysis, a technique developed by Warner, Kimball, and Arensberg to study celebrations (Arensberg and Kimball 1972). I used it to study festivals in the Upper Midwest and the day of Corpus Cristi (Body of Christ) in Colombia. The difficulty of most celebrations is that they include a great many people interacting over a short period of time.

Event analysis requires a good camera or camcorder (or both). In order to carry out the analysis you have to already be accepted as a member of the community and understand local symbolism. In the case of the study of festivals of the Upper Midwest (Smith 1985), I became interested in why there are so many festivals in the part of the country where I now live (La Crosse, Wisconsin). I began by doing library research and discovered most of the festivals did not occur until after the early 1970s. There is Oktoberfest in La Crosse, Wisconsin, Apple Fest across the Mississippi in La Crescent, Minnesota, Sunfish Days in Onalaska, Syttende Mai in several Norwegian towns, Pickle Days, Wadu Shadu, Funfest Days, Fire Department Dance, Black Powder Shoot, Steam Engine Days, and many other colorful celebrations.

I spent two years attending these celebrations, taking photographs of parades and reading the local newspapers. My analysis led to the conclusion that these were celebrations developed by Main Street businessmen trying to overcome the impact of malls and interstates (Smith 1985). The celebrations work out the hierarchy of the towns and the symbolism of parades tells people what the participants think is important about their communities. For example, in La Crosse's Oktoberfest (which is a pale imitation of the German model), local men and women are selected to be "Fest Masters." There is a Mister and Mrs. Oktoberfest, and there is real competition over who is selected. Reading a list of participants is like looking at the power structure of the city of La Crosse, but power is not the only thing symbolized. So is commitment to community, traditional values, and the search for answers to community problems. One float in 1985 had the sign "Parents Without Partners" (for divorced or unmarried mothers and fathers) and a second float announced "Oktoberfest Welcomes a New Decade for Sex Equality." On it a young man and woman sat in a pair of giant scales in equal balance symbolizing feminist aspirations at the local universities.

Still photographs remain a rich source of field data as well as great memory joggers after a researcher has returned home from field research. Photos also generally make much-appreciated gifts that can help the researcher establish rapport quickly. Modern automatic cameras take the guesswork out of shutter speeds, aperture openings (f-stops), and focal distance, making photography in the field all but foolproof. A good set of photos is an excellent supplement to field notes.

Portable Computers and Special Software

The most modern of the research tools now used by anthropologists in the field is the laptop computer. With appropriate software, which is easily available, the computer can be used not only to record field data but also to perform both qualitative and quantitative (statistical) analysis as well. For some, the laptop computer has become as much of a necessity as a pen or pencil and notebook once were in recording field data. A decade or so ago, the researcher would have to wait to return home in order to use a mainframe computer to analyze statistical data. Today the work can be done in the field. The researcher can now collect new data to answer questions raised by the previous day's field research.

Good Old Pencil (or Pen) and Paper   However, a caution is in order. The wisest course of action is still to have a hard copy of your field notes and your daily journal or diary. If you are relying on a computer to record field notes, print out a hard copy after every session. Make several backups of your files. Mail at least one set of disk files and hard copy to a friend or colleague back home as soon as possible. Computers have been known to crash easily in the field, especially in tropical climates. Losing several weeks or months worth of work is not a pleasant experience. Though it may be tedious, handwritten field notes on cards or in notebooks may still be the most reliable, if not the swiftest, way of preserving your hard won findings.

Quality and Quantity   Ethnographic research and writing is largely qualitative. This distinguishes anthropology from other social sciences that rely more heavily on quantitative data. While cultural anthropologists will use quantitative data when available, they find ethnography more useful. Why this is so will be obvious to anyone who has lived in a foreign culture. Quantitative data are often unintelligible to anyone who does not understand the local culture. To do that, the researcher must live among the people he or she studies. Ethnography, for us, is deep emersion in a culture, to the point where one begins to learn to think like a native. We have personally only done this for some Latin American cultures and would not presume to be able to understand African, Asian, or other world cultures in quite the same sense. For cultures that an anthropologist has not experienced personally, he or she must rely on the accounts of others. While training as a professional anthropologist helps in interpreting the descriptive accounts of others such as travelers, missionaries, and government officials, it is always preferable to experience the culture directly; second best is to have available the accounts of other professional anthropologists. The anthropologist who has become really proficient in understanding another culture can reach into him or herself and describe the culture for others.

Most anthropologists go beyond mere description of cultures and societies. Theories about human behavior require comparative analyses of different societies through the study of many ethnographies. The anthropologist at this level of the quest is seeking generalizations. Anthropologists do not seek general explanations about human behavior from the study of just one society or one ethnography. The search for generalizations about human behavior is called ethnology, and the anthropologist who engages in this quest is called an ethnologist. It is common for a cultural anthropologist to do ethnography in the field during a part of the year and ethnology during another part of the year while in his or her office reading and writing. Ethnological research is also called the comparative method.

Most anthropologists tend to focus their research efforts on the intensive study of one or more communities, or a distinct group of people within a community, more or less within the same world region. They will also develop relatively detailed knowledge about the sociocultural systems of one or more continents from the writings of other anthropologists. In this book we will use examples from Africa, Asia, and other world regions, relying almost entirely on the works of our colleagues.

■Margaret Mead emphasized the importance of gender as a variable in data collection, and researched women in South Pacific and Southeast Asian cultures. Anthropology has become one of the most sensitive disciplines for women trying to understand women's rights in other cultures around the world.

Gender and Fieldwork   In the 1930s, Margaret Mead made clear the importance of gender as a variable in data collection and took advantage of her femininity to do research on women. In the 1970s and 1980s, the issue of feminism attracted many women anthropologists into the study of gender and equality. Women's studies programs became common on campuses throughout the United States with women anthropologists playing a leading role, a topic discussed in the next chapter. In another, we will have the opportunity to understand the important contributions women make in Sharon E. Hutchinson's study of the Nuer of East Africa. This study, like many other recent works, has added a completely new perspective on the nature of culture that could not be realized when only men studied mostly male cultures. Another important example of women expanding the works of male anthropologists is Annette Wiener's restudy of the economy of the Trobriand Islanders. Bronislaw Malinowski originally carried out research among the Trobrianders over seventy years ago. Wiener's work shows the importance of women's roles in the feasts and trade networks, something that Malinowski had little to say about (Wiener 1988).

Anthropology has become one of the most sensitive disciplines for women trying to understand women's rights in other cultures around the world. A complex dialogue has been opened in ethnographies that express women's perspectives and voices. These are written and translated by both men and women anthropologists who let the women of other cultures speak for themselves. One example is the story of Elvia Alvarado, a Honduran woman, who has commented on the "macho" worldview of the males in her culture (Benjamin 1989, 51–52). Two other examples are *The Granddaughters of Ixmucane: Guatemalan Women Speak*, a narrative explaining women's roles in the revolt against the Guatemalan government (Smith-Ayala 1991), and *I, Rigoberta Menchu: An Indian Woman in Guatemala* (edited by Elizabeth Burgos-Debray and translated by Ann Wright (1984). Rigoberta Menchu is a Quiche Mayan woman who won the 1992 Nobel Peace Prize. She has become a spokes-

■In Margaret Mead's study of socialization of Samoan children, she found that Samoan children are raised to adulthood with greater freedom than American children; consequently, they did not go through the emotional turmoil of American teenagers.

woman for oppressed women in Guatemala, and her work is also presented in *The Legacy of Mesoamerica* (1996) by Robert M. Carmack, Janine Gasco, and Gary H. Gossen.

Both the work of women anthropologists to rectify male biased ethnographies of earlier generations and the work by both men and women to let women speak about themselves and their cultures have significantly altered the way we see ourselves and the members of other cultures. This opening to women, created by women and now understood by men, has created a whole new style of scholarship and a dynamic world view lacking in earlier male dominated works.

EMIC, ETIC, IDEAL, AND REAL IN THE FIELD

Recall the discussion in the Introduction chapter where we said that cultural ideals, or emic point of view, are what people think they ought to do, while what the ethnographer interprets is a real or etic view. Recall, also, that we noted that the matter is more complicated. Let us now take a closer look.

First, in addition to cultural ideals, there is another emic view that we may call emically perceived reality. This is what insiders think they and others actually do. It is based on casual observation (not on counting instances); it consists of qualitative statements such as "most (or many, or few) people do that." Such informed observations of insiders can be quite useful in giving the ethnographer clues to how people perceive the degree to which they conform to the rules and beliefs of their own culture, and in giving information on permissible alternatives to ideal behavior and the circumstances under which the alternatives are permissible. (Of course, you have to ask a lot of questions to get all this.) We must be aware that native statements about actual behavior may, in fact, not provide an accurate picture of what is really going on. As ethnographers we make our own qualitative observations. This is one kind of etic or outsider view—we could call it the anthropologist's perceived reality. These may coincide with what we are being told, but of course we must exercise caution because our observations may have been influenced by what we have been told. The other possibility is that we may find that people don't appear to be doing—at least not very often, or to the extent reported—what we were told they do. Here again we must exercise caution because our perception of others' behavior may be influenced by our own cultural biases. If we really want to know the extent to which the behavior in a culture conforms to the ideals of that culture, as well as the types and frequency of variation that occur, we must collect a quantitative sample. Such a sample (and its analysis) provides a second type of etic view of reality. For example, if everyone tells you, that because corn is the ideal food, half the fields are always planted in corn and all you see after several days' observation is a couple of small corn fields in the midst of a veritable sea of bean fields, then it is clear that something is amiss. Either people's perception of what they actually plant is way off the mark, or your observations are. Under these circumstances, you may wish to take a systematic sampling of fields. By collecting all four kinds of data, our ethnography will be enriched; by carefully distinguishing each type of data in our account, we make it reliably useable in that other kind of etic analysis that anthropologists engage in, cross-cultural comparison.

One reason it is important to make these distinctions is that people vary in how they view their own culture, depending on their gender and age. Mature adults in many cultures believe that the behavior of young adults does not conform to the cultural ideals they grew up with, and they believe equally strongly that conformity was far greater in their own generation. Among the Ngóbe of Panama in the 1960s most everyone agreed that symmetrical exchange marriage arranged between kin groups—phrased by men as an exchange of *ngwae*, siblings of the opposite sex—was the ideal form of marriage; likewise there was general agreement among members of the older generations that the youngsters of marriageable age were conforming much less to this ideal than had those of their own generation. Men and women also differed on how they viewed conformity; women generally thought of themselves as sticking closer to tradition. Which perception was accurate?

The etic view, that of the ethnographer, may differ from both generational and gender views. It is often to be found in an ethnography along with the insider views. On the basis of observations over a period of time, the ethnographer may develop a sense of what people are doing and make a qualitative judgment about the extent to which his or her observations coincide with what people say they do. Now, in a case like Ngóbe marriage customs, it is not possible by just observing a man and woman living together to know if their marriage was or was not part of a symmetrical exchange (or for that matter, in some societies, to even know if they are married). In the Ngóbe marriage case, this is what I did (although the sample I obtained was not random in the statistical sense). From a sample of 254 marriages spread over four generations, I found that there had been no significant change in the ratio of exchange to non-exchange marriages in the four generations. The perception of older adults, male or female, with respect to the marriage behavior of younger adults was faulty, a result perhaps of the "generation gap" phenomenon.

Why is this observation important? It shows that while older members of Ngóbe society assume that younger members are acting like outsiders, both generations and genders respect tradition and attempt to conform to the ideals of the society.

This, then, is quantitative reality—a numerical sample of behaviors that tells us how many people, on average, conform to the cultural ideals and how many do not, and what the variations are. As in the Ngóbe case, the picture provided by quantitative data may differ substantially from what insiders think they do.

HAZARDS OF FIELD RESEARCH

It is easy to get carried away with the romance of anthropology (which is very real) in an introduction to anthropology, but there is a down side of which all students should be aware. Nancy Howell has written a book with the title of *Surviving Fieldwork.* She surveyed 204 anthropologists about illness and accidents in the field. In the forward, Rappaport notes the maxim "anthropologists are otherwise sensible people who don't believe in the germ theory of disease" (quoted in Bernard 1995, 157). One hundred percent of anthropologists doing work in South Asia report being exposed to malaria and 41 percent contract the disease. Thirteen percent report having hepatitis A. Accidents kill and injure researchers. Michelle Zimbalist Rosaldo died when she fell from a steep mountain trail in the Philippines in 1981. Thomas Zwickler, a University of Pennsylvania graduate student, was killed by a bus in India in 1985 (Bernard 1995). One of us cannot recall a single instance in his own research when he has not come down with dysentery in the field. The other, he of the cast iron constitution, can only recall two instances of being ill for more than a day or two while in the field; but he was beset by other hazards of the fieldwork enterprise: a broken arm, a cut that required stitches, two unsuccessful *coups d'etat* in two different countries and a successful one in a third.

Depression is common. One kind of depression is called "culture shock" and comes as the novelty of fieldwork wears off. Depression comes to be mixed with anxiety as the field worker is exposed to some of the negative aspects of fieldwork. Living conditions can be terrible. Smith's worst experience was living on the plantations of the south coast of Guatemala. There, violence was endemic and many of the people he worked with lived in squalor. The only way he coped with the situation was a weekly trip to Guatemala City to eat in a Chinese restaurant where the food was always safe. Even when living conditions are delightful (Smith's visit to Jardin), the loneliness of living in a strange culture can bring about intense depression and often a certain amount of paranoia. Often the fieldworker will pause and wonder if his or her work is worth the psychological pain.

When Young was living with the Ngóbe, he became convinced, after about four months of fieldwork, that his informants were deliberately lying to him when they said, "I don't know" in response to some of his questions. This suspicion turned out to be completely unfounded and a result of people genuinely not knowing some things, the anthro-

■Anthropology field-work can require living in terrible conditions for periods of time, such as this indian slum, in order to do research.

pologist asking questions that were not well understood because he did not yet know enough about Ngóbe culture, and the irrational interpretations that people suffering from culture shock often place on events.

Does culture shock cease to be a problem after several field trips? The answer is no, although if one returns repeatedly to work with the same group of people, the condition becomes more benign, and you more quickly recognize the symptoms for what they are. Working in a new culture is likely to produce culture shock as severe as during that first fateful field trip, but the experienced anthropologist will recognize the symptoms more readily and be able to cope more effectively with this endemic fieldwork "disease" than will the novice.

Do tourists get culture shock? Sometimes, yes, if they stay in a place long enough and actually involve themselves in the everyday life of the local culture. However, most tourists are usually in a place far too short a time or are involved only superficially, if at all, in the local culture to suffer more than a very mild case of culture shock.

Most anthropologists who conduct long-term field research also experience a phenomenon known as reverse culture shock. Having finally adapted to a foreign culture, the return home can be a trial in reverse. One often grows fond of the strange culture and comfortable in it. The other culture's sights, sounds, smells, and tastes cease to be exotic and become familiar. Living in a remote village with no telephone, no television, unpredictable electricity, gas lanterns, and without the daily demands of modern American culture can be very pleasant, particularly if the researcher has been successfully incorporated into the community. The return home to interstate highways, malls, and the constant bombardment from the electronic media is a shock to the senses and may make the researcher wish he or she were back "home" in the field.

Two other hazards of the field worth mentioning are those of food and drink, and here we are not referring to the potential health hazards of consumption. Rather, we refer to the difficulties of fulfilling cultural expectations and the need to learn how to circumvent them in a culturally appropriate way.

In Ngóbe culture, for example, visitors to a household are always offered food. This is the way hospitality is expressed. To refuse to eat the food is insulting. This is true in many cultures. Sometimes it is only a token amount but often the portion is generous and more than the guest can consume, especially if the guest is an ethnographer who has just eaten at two or three other houses where he was also conducting interviews. My (PY) first few attempts at house-to-house data collection were disastrous and ended well before midday, but observation paid off. I noted that there are two culturally acceptable ways to accept food, and then dispose of most of it after a few token mouthfuls without insulting the giver. One is to give most of it to the children in the household. They are always hungry. The other is to make sure you have something with you to wrap it up in and take it home.

In many cultures, offering guests alcoholic beverages is the means of displaying hospitality. Numerous anthropologists have gone through the experience of being offered alcohol in one form or another at every house they visit. One needs to learn quickly the culturally appropriate ways of refusal if one is to remain sober enough to do any research. While claiming to be a teetotaler may seem an easy way out, as Bernard (1995) points out, this may have the undesirable effect of having people mistakenly associate you with missionaries that may be in the area.

■   ■   ■

Chapter
Summary

Studying Cultures

Anthropologists generally try to avoid studying individuals, the topic of psychology. Even psychologists try to avoid studying individuals. The reason is misunderstandings that always arise when the human personality is central to research: people are annoyed to be asked personal questions, but are often very cooperative about their knowledge of culture, community, religion, or other topics on which they have opinions (though religions must be handled carefully). Perspectives on cultures are special ways of looking at some of the features that all cultures have. John Bennett focuses much of his work on the adaptive or coping strategies of cultures, not on individuals. He views cultures as dynamic systems interacting with their environments and with other cultures. Arensberg and Kimball, two famous researchers, also avoid studying the individual by focusing on communities, an important unit of all cultures, that allows them to study people through organizations, and not directly. Edward Hall and his wife also avoid the individual by examining in detail the different ways in which cultures organize, regulate, and utilize space and time. This allows them to study the mind without getting into the study of the individual. The mechanisms by which our mind processes information are called cognitive processes. While all normal humans are endowed with these cognitive processes, distinct cultural patterns come into being and are perpetuated through a general phenomenon known as enculturation. We do not fully understand how the mind interacts with its surroundings to produce these patterns, but studying cultural processes allow us to study culture without involving ourselves in the study of people. The study of cultural processes can be done by studying how language is used. While the ability to use human language is biologically based, the ability to communicate in a particular language is learned. Scholars are not in agreement about whether the language capacity is localized and distinct from other cognitive processes or generalized and part of a network of such processes. Language is, however, one of the most important ways in which humans store, process, and retrieve information and communicate with one another. It is one channel through which we learn our culture; other important channels are observation and participation (imitation).

All human languages share several characteristics that are not found in the known communication systems of any other forms of life. An unsettled issue is the nature of the interaction between language and culture.

Anthropologists gather information about different cultures by conducting field research. The process begins with a search of the existing literature about the society or community to be studied and the region in which it is located. Anthropologists then usually spend several months in the field living with the people, learning their language, participating in and at the same time observing their daily lives and activities and special events. Casual conversation provides general information about the culture and leads that may be followed up using more formal interviewing techniques. While much of the data ethnographers collect is qualitative, survey questionnaires and other means of collecting quantitative data are frequently used as well. Despite the hazards that are often encountered in field research, most ethnographers find the experience very rewarding, and survive to produce an account of the people they studied, called an ethnography. Comparative studies drawn from many ethnographies are called ethnologies, or a more popular name, *cultural anthropology*, the subject of this book. There are specialized ways of studying the individual that are found in writings on "culture and personality" which depend on projection techniques, such as Rorschach. These techniques work well but only when used by someone trained in anthropology and psychiatry. This book will stress both ecology and culture and personality; but unlike other similar books, it will stress political anthropology. Sometimes we will use the term political ecology in reference to our approach, which has parallels to Marxist anthropology; but we will try to avoid simplistic cause-effect relationships, such as personality depending on technological and ecological adaptations. In earlier writings we have found Marxist anthropology attractive, but over time it appears simplistic.

Chapter Terms

Term	Page	Term	Page
allophone	53	infix	53
bound morphemes	53	morphemes	53
descriptive linguistics	53	phone	53
enculturation	48	phonemes	53
ethnographer	58	phonology	53
ethnographic present	42	semantics	54
ethnography	58	socialization	48
free morpheme	53	syntactics	54

Check out our website
www.BVTLab.com
for flashcards,
chapter summaries,
and more.

Chapter 2

Human Biological and Cultural Evolution

Introduction: Anthropology and Evolution

Anthropology is based on two significant and intertwined concepts. One is biological evolution due to genetic changes; and the second is the evolution of culture, which is due to changes in symbols. Culture is the major adaptation that humans make to their habitats, and it depends on a specialized human organ: the brain. We know a great deal about technological change, changes to the brain, and changes to culture over the last three million years. However, we don't know how changes in the three are related. We know that technology, culture, and the biology of the brain are linked, but we do not know how.

The topic of evolution is controversial, and not everyone believes in it. Not only do many Americans deny theories on biological evolution in favor of religious ones, so do most people around the world. The story of creation is a cosmological worldview originally belonging to the Jews, who viewed themselves as a select people for whom God created the world—a view that came to be adopted by Christians and Moslems, who derived their beliefs from the same Old Testament but then went separate ways.

These people are known as "the People of the Book." They were often in conflict with each other, but they also shared many of their beliefs with each other and with most other people of the Middle East. A close study of pre-Biblical writings shows that the Jews, as well as most people of the Middle East, originally thought God was El, the god of the mountains. With the Jews, El became God who spoke to Moses on Mt. Sinai. Stories about the Garden of Eden, Adam and Eve, the catastrophic flood, the salvation of Noah and his family aboard the ark, and the dispersal of Noah's family by God were found in Babylonian creation stories, some of which were shared with Greek and Roman stories of the beginning of the world. In Greek and Roman myths of creation, important philosophic points of view, such as Thales' theory that all mammals were originally fish and Aristotle's notions of how life evolved from single celled animals to complex life forms, were combined with stories from the Bible.

■Noah, his family, and two of each creature on earth board the great the ark to escape the catastrophic flood. The story is traditionally taught in the Christian faith and many believe it to be historically accurate.

Many of the translators of the Bible were Romans and Greeks, whose surprisingly modern ideas later became incorporated into the theory of evolution in the nineteenth century. Thales argued that all life originated in the sea and that humans were originally like fish, while Aristotle argued that life had started from simple lower forms, such as single-celled amoebas and evolved into complex higher forms. While Darwin is considered the creator of evolutionary theory, biology textbooks often fail to present the ideas of Thales and Aristotle. Darwin's theory of evolution was not as radical as many think today.

What Darwin did was to flesh out Aristotle's and Thales' versions of evolution by adding evidence from fossils and artifacts discovered by road builders and in the construction of industrial buildings. The nineteenth century was a great age of construction and of the discovery of the past. Why did Darwin so dominate that century? While Darwin was a great scientist, he was also a great writer who combined the theories and discoveries of others to produce one of the great books of Western Civilization. It is important to realize that Darwin's theory of evolution adopted the contribution of many other naturalists' theories and facts. What Darwin contributed was the conceptualization of the story of biological life on earth, and he put it down on paper.

Darwin's Theory of Evolution

The debate between creationists and evolutionists is central to education, but few people believe exclusively in only a religious or a scientific point of view. Most people believe in both evolution and religion. More or less 93 percent of all scientists believe the universe had a divine creation but not necessarily by a Christian God. Recently, a few physicists have put forward the idea that a being did not create the universe—it has existed forever. The idea that the universe was not created by a metaphysical being but has always existed is difficult for most people to grasp, let alone accept.

Because of the conflict the two points of view generate, it is useful to view science and religion from the point of view of philosophy of science, which begins with careful definitions. According to this perspective, science and religion are not opposed to each other: they are two different kinds of statements. A **scientific statement** *is a logically related set of propositions that attempt to explain the relationships between certain observable facts.* A **religious statement**, on the other hand, is *an attempt to explain non-observable phenomena.* In short, a religious belief does not depend on observable phenomena, while a scientific theory does. Scientific and religious propositions do not oppose each other, and a person can hold both a scientific and a religious point of view because they are about different phenomena: observable and non-observable facts.

The distinctions between the two points of view need elaboration. Darwin's theory of evolution is an attempt to explain the fossil record, which is made up of bones and fossils. Bones and fossils can be picked up and studied, observed and measured. Cre-

scientific statement

A logically related set of propositions that attempt to explain the relationships between certain observable facts

religious statement

An attempt to explain non-observable phenomena

ation of the universe, on the other hand, cannot be observed or measured, but it can be believed or disbelieved. Thus it lends itself to religion. Furthermore, a scientific theory differs from a belief in that it can be tested to prove that it is false (but it cannot be proved to be true; nothing can be proved to be true). A belief, on the other hand, cannot be tested to be true or false. A belief can only be "verified" by going to a "higher authority" such as the Bible, the Koran, the sayings of Buddha, or a priest or minister of a religious order. Scientific theories are fairly narrow and limited, and not always satisfying. People often fall back on religion when science does not satisfy them.

A religious belief is always broader than a scientific statement, while a scientific statement must be narrower than a religious belief. Why this is so belongs to the philosophy of science and metaphysics and cannot be pursued here. Neither will we go into debates between religious leaders and scientists or secular philosophers, except to remind the reader that belief plays a central role in any ideology; and science is an ideology. Ultimately both religion and science depend on belief. Religion depends on the belief in a higher being, while science depends on the predictability of matter. There is no way to prove a scientific statement, only to disprove it. Evolutionists are often scornful of religion, but the universe and its origins are, indeed, a mystery. For that reason, many scientists hold on to a religious explanation of the creation of the universe as well as scientific ones.

Darwin, like many, was torn between religion and science. Darwin's theory of evolution was but one of many such theories on the origins of life that can be found in the first half of the nineteenth century. One of Darwin's contemporaries was Alfred Russel Wallace, who came up with the same theory of evolution at the same time and who also tried to hold on to both religious and scientific points of view. Although they were doing similar research, Wallace was a "spiritualist" while Darwin was torn between religious belief and atheism, becoming an agnostic in later life. While Darwin is often depicted as an atheist, he was not. In fact, he found it very difficult to abandon religion. The entire idea that evolutionists are atheists is a popular misinterpretation of the history of evolutionary theory. The theory was a dramatically new idea, but many who adopted it also believed in supernatural origins to the universe and tried to reconcile the two points of view. The early nineteenth century was a period of intellectual ferment in many fields not just in biology but also in physics, chemistry, and psychology. Few believed only in science or only in religion. An important question: why did Darwin's views predominate over many other theories?

Darwin's theory was broadly accepted because it was easy to understand. It has the power of great simplicity composed of two important concepts: variation and natural selection, neither of which is difficult to understand. The observation that life is varied is all around us and leads directly to natural selection. Variations in plants and animals were observed in the nineteenth century, in part because scientists were involved in breeding plants and animals for commercial food production and in part because explorers were discovering new life forms around the world. The same is true for natural selection. It was not difficult to observe that as modern hunting technology spread, many species of animals were exterminated. Rifles and other hunting tools helped to destroy the passenger pigeon, the great auk (which is related to the modern auk), and many other life forms that have ceased to exist. The disappearance of species led to challenges to creationism. According to creationists, once God made a life form, it could never disappear. In the eighteenth and nineteenth centuries, however, the disappearance of life forms was commonly observed as hunters the world over killed all kinds of animals in order to harvest their products. The protection of living species, such as the Right Whale, and other easy-going sea mammals was a major political movement in England and the United States in the nineteenth century.

Darwin was one among many naturalists (students of nature) who were trying to understand how plant and animals species had come into existence, and how they might be destroyed. Researchers had to focus on relatively narrow forms of evidence in order to shed light on evolution because nature was their laboratory, and nature is hugely complicated. The works of Darwin and Wallace are a good example of the narrowness of research, as well as the ethics of science. Most of Darwin's work focused on studying the variation in beaks belonging to certain species of finches found only on the Galápagos Islands off the west coast of Ecuador, while Alfred Russel Wallace worked on monkeys in the Amazon and frogs in Indonesia. Despite the differences in animals studied, Darwin and Wallace expressed identical theories of evolution. Wallace could have claimed the theory of evolution for himself, but ethics intervened. He thought Darwin should claim responsibility for the theory of evolution instead of himself because Darwin was better known and because Darwin had held his theory longer. While Darwin received recognition for his discovery, he insisted on sharing recognition for the theory of evolution with Wallace, giving us a picture of how these two idealists valued their ethics more than the public attention.

Darwin used the term "descent with modification" to discuss what modern biologists call natural selection. Darwin did not mean to suggest or imply that there was a direction to evolution, although even the choice of the word "evolution" suggests direction. What Darwin meant in using the phrase "descent with modification" was that nature is a neutral mechanism that "selects out" the least fit variants, while "selecting in" those that are most fit, thus modifying life forms to fit their environments. The English scientist Herbert Spencer had used the same phrase of natural selection five years before the publication of Darwin's book. For Darwin natural selection meant that an individual survived to the age of reproduction, for whatever reason, not that he or she did so due to strength, speed, intelligence, or because of having certain "superior" or "moral" characteristics, which is what Spencer meant. Spencer's theory of evolution was applied to human institutions and became very popular. It was Spencer's meaning of superiority phrased as "survival of the fittest" (a term Darwin never used) that came to dominate the popular literature in biology. It came to be applied to the superiority of the White race and inferiority of other races. It was Spencer's use of the term that appeared in the novels of Jack London, such as *Call of the Wild* and *White Fang*. Spencer's version of natural selection lasted well into the early twentieth century before Darwin's theory became popular. Darwin's theory only came to be accepted when Mendel's Laws of Inheritance were added, producing what is called the synthetic theory of evolution (synthetic meaning Darwin plus Mendel).

MENDEL'S CONTRIBUTIONS TO EVOLUTIONARY THEORY

Mendel's Laws of Inheritance were published after Darwin's theory. Mendel's observations on pea plants, which were carried out just before the publication of Darwin's great

■According to English scientist Herbert Spencer, natural selection meant that an individual survived to the age of reproduction due to having inherited superior characteristics. It was Spencer who coined the phrase "survival of the fittest."

work, were not accessible to Darwin and were not understood by many of his contemporaries. Mendel's laws would have added clarity to Darwin's theory. Darwin died in 1882, twelve years after Gregor Mendel had presented his paper on plant hybridization; but Mendel's Laws of Inheritance were poorly understood for almost a quarter of a century after the experiments that produced them. Why was Mendel's work not understood? It is tempting to think that Mendel's experiments were published in some obscure journal, but he sent copies of his research paper to 120 scientific organizations around the world. Apparently, scientists were not prepared to understand his explanation or the significance of his research. It was not until 1901 that two biologists independently ran across his paper, just as they were going to publish their findings. Again, these nineteenth century scientists, like Wallace, expressed their ethics. They gave Mendel credit for his discovery, which even today is not clearly understood (Eiseley 1958). Mendel not only discovered the laws of inheritance, he also explained how variation and natural selection worked, ideas that Darwin could not adequately understand in 1864 because Mendel's paper had not yet become popular reading. The combination of Darwin and Mendel's theories is known as the synthetic theory of evolution (meaning the synthesis of two theories). To Mendel's work is usually added modern population genetics, which requires such contemporary tools as the electron microscope.

Why is Mendel's work so important to Darwin's theory of evolution? During Darwin's lifetime, species characteristics were thought to meld or mix when the parents of an offspring mated. Detractors of Darwin's theory thought that over time any new characteristic would tend to lose its distinctive quality, and they attacked Darwin's theory on that basis. An alternative to Darwin's theory was Lamarck's popular notion that a species changes its characteristics through use. Many assumed it was Lamarck's theory that was correct, and that the environment molded the characteristics of a species over time. It was this assumption that Mendel was able to change, independent of Darwin's theory. He demonstrated the "particulate" nature of any characteristic. That is, he was able to demonstrate that the characteristics of a species do not blend or mix or meld, but rather they maintain their integrity generation after generation. They are either there, or are they are not there. What is only vaguely understood is how Mendel used his knowledge of mathematics to grasp this principle, for he did not know about the mechanisms of reproduction. It was not until 1876 that Oskar Hertwig, using a microscope, saw the eggs of sea urchins being fertilized by spermatozoa. He noted that the eggs of the female and the spermatozoa of the male are very unlike externally, but they have similar internal parts. What he saw are today called "chromosomes" and "genes," terms that were not in the vocabularies of Darwin or Mendel.

These terms are from population genetics, knowledge that did not belong to Darwin or Mendel. The term chromosome refers to the rod-like bodies in sperm and somatic cells that carry the genetic code. "Allele" means a variant. A gene is a position on a chromosome that controls a set of variations or alleles—such as the allele for distinct eye colors (black, brown, blue); hair structures (straight, wavy, kinky); the ability to taste certain chemicals; or to be passive or aggressive. A chromosome, as is commonly understood today, is made up of a single complex strand of the information molecule, deoxyribonucleic acid or DNA. A single chromosome of DNA will have different arrangements and patterns depending on which stage of mitosis or meiosis it is in. Ribonucleic acid, or messenger RNA, carries the code from DNA to the controlling mechanism of the enzyme, which then determines what the code means to the cell.

Mendel's two laws are the well-known law of segregation and the law of independent assortment. Both laws were based originally on the statistical analysis of characteristics of pea plants, which have relatively few chromosomes. Mendel contrasted size, color, and shape. He used his knowledge of mathematics to infer the meaning of the laws of inheritance by contrasting sets of pairs: tall/small, yellow/green, and round/wrinkled. We will not go into the statistics behind Mendel's reasoning since that would take us beyond the scope of this book. However some explanation is important, so we will try to be brief.

The law of independent assortment is derived from the law of segregation. While the law of segregation refers to the behavior of alleles on the same locus of a set of paired chromosomes, the law of independent assortment (or recombination) refers to multiple traits on the same set or sets of chromosomes. Again, using statistical probability, Mendel was able to show that certain statistical ratios appeared over and over again (combining size, color, and shape).

If characteristics are discreet, and are not changed through mating or by the environment, then how do they change? Here, again, we have access to knowledge not available to Darwin or Mendel. They were both aware that new variations appeared spontaneously in populations, often in the form of non-adaptive traits that led to the demise of those individuals with the traits. They also knew that the breeders of plants and animals were constantly looking for new traits that might benefit farm animals or their profits. Examples are thicker eggs for chickens, more powerful legs in horses, lovelier colors in flowers, and more tasty meat for consumption. Breeders were constantly looking for ways to improve their stock, but it would not be until the manufacture of electron microscopes in the mid-twentieth century that would allow scientists to understand the nature of mutations.

■Through his characteristic analysis of pea plants, Mendel was able to show that certain statistical ratios appeared over and over again (combining size, color, and shape).

THE BIG BANG: PHYSICS AND CHEMISTRY EXPLAIN ORIGINS

Most of evolutionary theory is focused on the origins and development of various life forms. However, the scientific understanding of the origins of the universe come primarily from physics, astronomy, and chemistry and tell us that the universe began with a "big bang" that lasted just a few seconds between 15 to 20 billion years ago. The earth began 4.555 billion years ago, and the first evidence for living organisms dates back to 3.5 billion years ago in the form of amino acids. These amino acids, better known as DNA and RNA, were described for the first time by James Watson and Francis Crick in 1953. The model they presented was that of a double helix, the strands of which were made up of four acids: adenine (A), guanine (G), thymine (T), and cytosine (C). Different combinations of adenine, guanine, cytosine, and thymine create the codes or blocks of information known as "genes."

Once the DNA molecule was described, evolutionary biologists explained that variations were due to any of a variety of changes to DNA: mechanical, chemical, or electrical. The most common way for scientists to duplicate nature is to beam an electronic charge through the DNA macromolecule, causing changes in the structure of the four acids or their paired relationships to each other. Electronic charges can duplicate changes produced by the most common source of mutations: solar radiation. Molecular and evolutionary biologists think that the rate of changes in different species due to mutations have changed through time due to changes in solar and other forms of radiation.

The changes produced by radiation are thought to be quite small. More dramatic are the changes produced when chromosomes break down and are reorganized in a variety of ways, which can happen as a consequence of heat or radiation. Chromosomes can break and reattach in a variety of ways, or paired chromosomes can break and then crossover to what was once a partner. These gross rearrangements create biological abnormalities that are so great that most mutant creatures do not survive past birth, and it is doubtful they have played much of a role in human evolution. However, in the case of certain plants—such as corn, wheat, barley, and other domesticated plants—we know that polyploidy (the multiplication and joining of chromosomes) may have created many of the plants we depend on for survival.

Evolution of the Primate Order

The geological subdivisions of time are studied by specialists interested in various aspects of the evolution of the planet. Geologic time is subdivided into eons, eras, and epochs or periods. We are primarily interested in the Cenozoic Era, during which time the class of mammals evolved. The primate order, to which humans belong, is among the oldest of the mammals beginning about 63 million years ago. In the following, we will follow the evolution of the primate order through the Cenozoic Era.

Geological time periods have been organized by major geological and paleontological events—such as the dividing of the world into continents, the appearance and disappearance of mountains and oceans, and the appearance and disappearance of major life forms—such as primitive and modern fishes, dinosaurs, birds, and mammals. The Cenozoic divides into the epochs of the Paleocene, Eocene, Oligocene, Miocene, Pliocene, and Pleistocene. When we come to the final geological era, we will shift from major geological and biological changes to

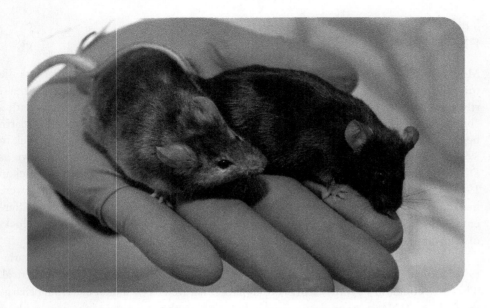

■ Since 2003 we have been able to genetically engineer mutations in what are called *knock out rats*. These rats will have a particular gene knocked out, or turned off, to produce a mutation, and then studied. The rat shown on the left has had a gene knocked out that affects its hair growth and is being compared to a genetically normal rat.

changes in culture known as the Paleolithic, Mesolithic, and Neolithic, which occurred during the geological period known as the Holocene.

The Primate Order, to which humans belong, is surprisingly ancient. Its origins can be traced back to the beginning of the Cenozoic 65.5 MYA in the shape of small insectivores or insect eaters, resembling the modern tree shrew or *Tupaiidae*. Tree shrews are not biologically related to the primate order and belong to the *Scandentia Order*, but their modern representatives give us some idea of the earliest evolutionary adaptations of primitive primates. The Cenozoic began with widespread extinctions, which occurred at the end of the Mesozoic. During this episode, the dinosaurs seem to have almost disappeared, probably due to asteroids striking the earth. This event was disastrous for the dinosaurs. Mammals on land and modern fish in the sea replaced dinosaurs. The Cenozoic was also marked by the appearance of flowering plants and trees, which were high-energy plants. While many argue that it was asteroids that destroyed the dinosaurs, others think that in addition to the impact of asteroids, mammals were better able to take advantage of flowering plants. This idea seems to fit the primate order particularly well. The insectivores, which form the base of the primate order, were small, comparatively large-brained, and active mammals with high metabolic rates that adapted to the new high-energy habitats and then radiated out as high-energy insect and fruit eaters.

The oldest insectivores have been discovered in Mongolia in the form of tree or bush dwelling primitive mammals that were contemporaneous with the last dinosaurs. Later, during the Paleocene Epoch (65.5–55.8 million years ago), mammals evolved from these forms to fill the niches that had been occupied by dinosaurs. Two forms appeared replacing land dwelling reptiles, one with carnivorous teeth that became mammalian predators such as hyenas, lions, cats, dogs, and wolves, while others developed herbivorous teeth for crushing and chewing and became herbivorous ungulates (such as cattle, horses, and sheep). The primate order began to radiate before this split occurred when small insectivores moved into environments that had not been occupied by dinosaurs or other mammals or birds: bushes and tree canopies of forests. Both birds and primates began their radiation about the same time and may be considered among the most successful of all animals.

■As the Ceno-
zoic era began,
mammals on
land and modern
fish in the sea
began to replace
the dinosaurs.

CLASSIFICATION AND EVOLUTION OF THE PRIMATE ORDER

Our knowledge of the evolution of the primate order depends on the fossil record. However, the fossil record is very uneven, with some species having high representation and others low representation. The low representation of primate fossils is probably the consequence of early primates having adapted to the tropics, where heat and humidity prevent fossilization. For that reason, we have to depend on contemporary primates to draw a picture of the evolution of the primate order (horses, which evolved on the dry grasslands of Mongolia are surprisingly well represented in the fossil record). The few primate fossils that have been discovered can be used to help us understand primate evolutionary history, but remember these are very few and far between (unlike horses).

The Primate Order divides into two suborders, the Prosimians, or pre-monkeys, and Anthropoidea, which includes New and Old World monkeys, apes, and humans. The suborder Anthropoidea, or anthropoids, divides into three superfamilies: Ceboidea or New World monkeys, Cercopithecoidea or Old World monkeys, and Hominoidea made up of apes and humans. The superfamily Hominoidea, in turn, divides into two families, the Pongidae (pongids) that includes the chimpanzees and gorillas and the Hominidae (hominids), or humans and their direct ancestors. These terms are useful to us in understanding the fossil record. The term **anthropoid** can be used for the ancestors or the characteristics of monkeys, apes, and humans; the term **hominoid** can mean ancestors or characteristics of apes and humans. **Pongid** can refer to ancestral or modern apes, and **hominids** can refer to ancestral or modern humans.

The success of primates is largely due to the development of characteristics that allowed small insect eaters to adapt to varying forested habitats, which were empty 63 MYA. The earliest insect eaters were mammals but were not primates. The ancestors of the anthropoids probably emerged about 36 MYA.

Here we wish briefly to examine the success of the primate order, followed by an overview of how it evolved. George Gaylord Simpson, the most influential paleontologist of the twentieth century, argued that the ancestors of anthropoid primates differ from other life forms in the development of generalized rather than specialized characteristics, which he associated with their high intelligence. The primates generalized characteristics were due to adaptations to tree life (Simpson 1949, 62–77). Anthropologists argue that many of the evolutionary adaptations which occurred in adapting to an arboreal existence gave the anthropoids certain advantages over ground dwellers, such as the development of very fine hand-eye coordination, stereoscopic and color vision. In addition, the orthograde (vertical) adaptation to tree living brought about a head that sits on the torso and can be turned easily from side to side for great visual acuity.

anthropoid

A term that can be used for the ancestors or characteristics of monkeys, apes, and humans

hominoid

A term that can mean ancestors or characteristics of apes and humans

pongid

A term that can refer to ancestral or modern apes

hominid

A term that can refer to ancestral or modern humans

These characteristics gave primates a three-dimensional sensing system in which smell and hearing became secondary to sight. The eyes of primates differ from ground dwelling mammals in their location looking forward instead of towards the side. Forward-looking vision produces an overlap of the fields of vision causing three-dimensional (stereoscopic) sight. The ancestors of the anthropoids were also able to distinguish color, particularly the color red. It is important for tree dwellers to be able to distinguish depth and color when moving through trees, unlike ground dwellers for which hearing and smell are more important sensing devices than vision. Many fruits have red coloration, allowing primates to see them from great distances, which explains why visual acuity for red was so important to primates. In addition, fine hand and eye coordination, when added to visual acuity, gave primates the ability to throw rocks and sticks with amazing accuracy.

It is the brain, however, that went through the most dramatic series of changes, a topic that will be very important when we get to the subject of culture. As we follow the evolutionary line from prosimians to monkeys, chimpanzees, and gorillas to the *hominids*, the brain becomes larger and more complex. Tree shrews and prosimians have small and almost smooth brains, while New World and Old World monkeys are more complex and larger. The brains of apes are even larger and more complex than those of monkeys. There are four ape lines: orangutan, gibbon, chimpanzee, and gorilla. All four share similar brains that are remarkably similar to humans in complexity, but are about half their size (average about 700 ccs, compared to 1450 ccs for humans).

There are many other important changes that distinguish tree-adapted primates from ground dwelling mammals, usually in clusters of linked characteristics. Just beneath the head is the upper torso that is capable of brachiation or hand over hand locomotion using tree limbs. One important bone allowing this movement is the clavicle, which is not found in most ground dwelling mammals, but is found in all primates. It separates the upper limbs from each other and allows movement of the arm in a 360-degree arc. In the lower body there are other specializations. In monkeys, chimpanzees, and apes, the foot is specialized, like the hand, for grasping tree limbs (unlike humans). When on the ground, chimpanzees and gorillas must use the upper limbs and are knuckle walkers. In humans, the foot and pelvis have specialized to allow bipedalism, or upright locomotion, without using the hands. The freeing of the hands for other tasks is central to human evolution.

The hand is of great evolutionary interest to paleontologists. Primates developed nails instead of claws, and moisturized pads with ridges (which in humans can be used to fingerprint an individual), and pentadactylism (five fingers or digits). The human hand has been freed from locomotion functions and has become extremely flexible. In humans, the thumb has developed the ability to oppose the other digits, leading to a "power grip" that can be used to grasp an object and throw it (such as a rock or javelin) or to sew a button on a shirt. While other primates are also able to throw, none has the ability to grasp the way humans do.

Much more difficult to ascertain, but no less important than biological changes, were changes to behavior and community organization. Reproduction is one trend that correlates with primate/hominid evolution. In general, there has been a reduction in the number of offspring born and an increase in the

■There are four ape lines: orangutan, gibbon, chimpanzee, and gorilla. All four species' brains are remarkably similar to humans in complexity.

amount of time needed to care for the young. Prosimian offspring are numerous and require comparatively little care, while chimpanzees and apes bear few young; and these have to be cared for by their mothers up to three and sometimes four years (most human children can walk at age two, and sometimes as early as age one).

Sexuality appears related to these changes, with the female having increased sexual receptivity as the need for a dependable mate increases. In monkeys, chimpanzees, and gorillas, one male tends to monopolize all females as they come into estrus, preventing other males from mating until the dominant one ages or become weak. Recent research suggests that bonobo chimpanzees differ in that they tend to use sexuality as a social mechanism to improve cooperation. Unlike other primates, bonobo males and females are similar in size, and there is little dominance by one male and more sharing by males of females. Many males and females pair off for life. A few anthropologists compare the bonobo to our ancestor, the australopithecine. The evidence is pretty speculative, but interesting (de Waal 1995, 82–88).

We do not know at what point in hominid evolution our human ancestors abandoned domination by a single male over several females and developed a ratio of one male to one female. Many argue that the change may have occurred as early as the australopithecines because of the lack of extreme sexual dimorphism (this refers to size differences between males and females). However, size is not the only variable. Also of some importance is how the sex act was carried out. In pronograde mammals, the male mounts the female from the rear. In chimpanzees, the pelvis is tilted towards the front and face to face intercourse is common. The pelvis of australopithecines is structured in such a way that intercourse probably occurred face-to-face. If female sexuality was not tied to an estrus cycle, and face-to-face intercourse was common, it has been argued that the male would be more apt to settle for a single mate. Such a change would have supported a human type family, but the evidence is very speculative. The fossil record really tells us little about behavior. However, the increased size of the human brain in offspring would have been associated with increased intelligence and less need for attention from parents, who would have had time for greater social interaction with other adults, leading to more efficient hunting and adaptations to their habitats.

In the 1960s, hunting became the primary explanatory feature to all of these changes; however, today a much more common explanation is the advantage of upright posture with all of the changes that are mentioned above as well as a significant change in diet from fruits to foods based on grasses, including shoots and roots. In addition, there is the change in locomotion from brachiation to running and jogging. These, along with some use of the hand for tool making and some hunting of small mammals, could have given our primate ancestors a Darwinian advantage leading to Australopithecus.

One noted change between lower and higher primates is the appearance of an incest taboo, which is an aversion to mating with close relatives. In the higher primates, incest becomes increasingly rare, and in humans is universally condemned between the father/mother and direct offspring, while in other relatives it becomes highly structured from society to society.

It has to be assumed that the incest taboo "evolved" as the primate order changed through time. In the following, we will trace what we know of the fossil record of the evolution of the primate order up the appearance of our hominid ancestors.

Paleocene   During the Paleocene (65.5–55.8 MYA), North America and Eurasia formed a single land mass. The fossil record indicates that the ancestors of modern primates first emerged in North America and Europe. A few fossils have been found in Africa.

The best known is Plesiapadis, a lemur-like creature found in North Dakota, which in the Paleocene had a climate similar to modern south Florida. Mrs. Ples, as the fossil is popularly known, fits neatly into a theoretical model of the evolution of the primates. It was a small and squirrel-like animal that had claws rather than nails. Its eyes were on the sides of the head, and it had a long, rodent-like jaw with gnawing incisors. It was able to climb and live in trees. As we might expect, it was more dependent on its sense of smell than its sense of sight. It was omnivorous and ate insects as well as fruits. While this form was probably not on a direct line of ascent to the primates, it has many similarities to modern prosimians such as lemurs, tarsiers, lorises, and galigos. At one time the Prosimians were considered a typology of life forms that fell inside of the primate order but today are classified outside into non-primate suborders, which we need not go into (Nickels, Hunter, and Whitten 1979, 165–170).

The Eocene   During the Eocene (54.8–33.7 MYA), the continents of the world were still connected, but the land bridge between Eurasia and North America was narrower. The climate was warm and mild, and landmasses were covered with forests presenting an environment into which Plesiapadis radiated producing many prosimian forms whose remains are found in both the New and Old World. George Cuvier first described, as early as 1821 for southern France, an early lemur-like creature called Adapis although he believed it represented a tree-adapted specie that had been destroyed by the Great Flood. Adapis is but one of many lemur-like creatures that appeared during the Eocene. Adapis had several cousins in North America, such as Northarctus and Smilodectes.

In the 1920s, and in recent years, fossil evidence has been discovered for the appearance of forms ancestral to apes and monkeys in Myanmar (Burma) called Amphipithecus and Pondaungia.

Oligocene   The Oligocene (33.7–23.8 MYA) was an age of cooling, with North America and Eurasia separating while the African landmass drifted into Asia. Many modern mammals—such as horses, deer, camels, elephants, dogs, and cats—took on modern forms during this time period. During this epoch the ancestral forms of the South American monkeys made their appearance, while in Europe and Asia cooling caused the disappearance of many primate forms. Ancestral primate forms crossed into Africa, where further radiation appears to have occurred (Nickels, Hunter, Whitten 1979, 173–177).

The best evidence for primate evolution is found in a fairly restricted region called the Fayum near modern Cairo, which was lush and tropical during the Oligocene. The site has yielded the hundreds of fossils of two genera of monkeys and four genera of apes. Oligocene fossils' monkeys and apes had a modern appearance and were fruit eaters, but they moved through trees on all fours and did not brachiate (hand over hand locomotion). David Pilbeam, a paleoanthropologist at Harvard University, thinks that the primate fossils of the Oligocene represent a diverse group of unspecialized tree dwellers that had begun to reach the status of true monkeys by 30 million years ago but were clearly not as specialized as apes. The ancestors of modern apes were adapting to life in trees, where the most important senses are those having to do with sight and grasping. Over time, three-dimensional, color vision and a thumb that could grasp gave rise to the modern primates: chimpanzees, gorillas, orangutans, and gibbons.

Miocene   The Miocene (23.03–5.33 MYA) could be called the "epoch of the apes" because of the success of these forms in the Old World, particularly Africa and Asia. In the

Miocene, the geology of the earth had taken the form it has today. India, which had been a large island similar to Australia, had drifted against southern Eurasia, pushing up the Himalayan Mountains. The Mediterranean Ocean was dry, facilitating migration between Europe and Asia; and there were land bridges between Alaska and Siberia, southern Europe and north Africa. The cooling trend that began in the Oligocene continued. As mountains rose, they pushed up landmasses producing cooler and drier conditions. In certain regions, such as Asia and Africa, the consequence was the appearance of grasslands, mixed woods, and forests, which further enabled the evolution of apes, monkeys, and the ancestors of humans.

The term Dryopithecines has been given to descendants of Adapis which evolved into the ancestors of chimpanzees and gorillas. Dryopithecus africanus, a comparatively small form was adapted to trees and was about half the size of a modern chimpanzee, and was probably its ancestor. A larger form, Dryopithecus major, was ancestral to gorillas, but was about a third their size (gorillas weigh up to 700 pounds, while Dryopithecus major weighed about 150 lbs.). The success of the Miocene apes can be measured through their wide diversification. In addition to Dryopithecus africans and Dryopethecus major, there was a very large form called Dryopithecus indicus that may have been the ancestor of a form called Gigantopithecus, a giant ape known only from one huge molar. G.H.R. von Koeningswald discovered the molar in an apothecary shop in the 1930s. The Chinese believed the tooth belonged to ancient dragons. They also believed that once the teeth were ground up they had the power to restore sexuality to aging men. Chinese manuscripts about the tooth indicate a giant ape form existed as far back as the eleventh century in southwest China (Nickels, Hunter, Whitten 1979, 177–183).

In addition to the above fossil forms, there was a marsh dwelling ape called Oreopithecus, whose remains were found in Italy and East Africa. Its small incisors misled paleontologists in the mid-twentieth century, who thought it might be an ancestor of humans but later it was found to be a brachiating, leaf eating ape adapted to marshy environments, similar to oreopithecus. Dryopthecines probably also evolved into gibbons and orangutans; however, the fossils for these are extremely rare, and the evolutionary connections are sketchy.

The Pliocene
During the Pliocene (5.33 and 1.8 MYA) conditions became optimal for tree dwelling primate ancestors to diversify into pongids and hominids, as tropical forests became woodlands interspersed with grasslands. *Dryopithecus major* and *minor* evolved into the gorillas and chimpanzees, which specialized in woodland habitats. The ancestors of hominids, in the form of Australopithecus, diversified into grassland bipeds. Fossil research shows that the ancestor of pongids and hominids may have begun to diverge from an as of yet unknown ancestor, similar to *dryopithecus minor*, between 5 to 6 million years ago. There has been some considerable luck in the discovery of fossils representing overall hominid evolution, but very few fossils representing the pongid line have been found. Due to the lack of fossil pongids, paleontologists and paleoanthropologists are forced to rely on contemporary apes, particularly chimpanzees, to understand the evolution from pongids to hominids.

Modern Chimpanzees represent our ancestors of about five million years ago. They are remarkably intelligent and have a wide range of vocalizations that allow them to form complex, hierarchical groups based on dominance hierarchies similar to those that must have occurred in the Pliocene. According to the study of hominoid genes at the Chimpanzee Genome Project, humans and chimpanzees share 98 percent of their genes. There are two types of chimpanzees, the common chimpanzee *(Pan troglodytes)* and bonobos *(Pan paniscus)*. Both live in tropical forests and depend on fruits and nuts (thus they are *frugivorous)*. Both are brachiators whose arms are longer than their legs, have large protruding lower faces with large canines, and a face that has ridges over the eyes. The back of the skull has a large ridge of bone for the insertion of the neck muscles, but it lacks a sagital crest (which is found on gorillas and in certain fossil hominids). Brain size ranges from 150 to 200 cc in adults, who tend to be between three to three and a half feet tall, and weigh between 100 to 200 pounds (males are larger and heavier than females).

Our ancestors, as well as chimpanzees and gorillas, probably descended from a genus of dryopithecine. Both chimpanzee and gorilla have 24 chromosomes, while humans have 23. (It is thought our ancestor had 24 chromosomes, but two of these combined into one.) The earliest hominids are called **australopithecines**. One of the first discoveries of a fossil Australopithecine was made by Dr. Raymond Dart, who was director of anatomy at the University of Witwatersand in South Africa. In 1924 he received a box containing fossils found in a limestone quarry. The box contained the remains of what has come to be known as the Taung's Child.

australo-pithecines

The earliest hominids

Today it is thought to be a young australopithecine that was about three years old when killed by a monkey-eating eagle. Dart published an article in the journal *Nature* in 1925 describing his amazing find which consisted of a fossilized brain, face, and lower jaw. Dart named the find *Australopithecus africanus*, or southern ape from Africa. Dart was trained in comparative anatomy. He drew the conclusion that given its size and complexity, the brain was that of a hominid rather than pongid, going against popular assumptions of the time period that the brain had evolved before the jaw. This reasoning was based on Piltdown Man, a forgery that combined fragments of human skull with part of the jaw of an orangutan excavated in 1912, a fake that was not exposed until 1953. Africanus was difficult for Dart to date since he did not have access to modern dating techniques. Australopithecus has been dated to 2.5 million years ago using potassium argon dating methods.

Further discoveries followed rapidly, particularly due to the work of Robert Broom. Broom was a Scottish geologist at the Transvaal Museum in Pretoria whose interests in Dart's discoveries led him to make other fossil discoveries and the distinction between two types of Australopithecines, a large and small one that he named Robustus and Gracilis, respectively. His own theory was the small one was the hunter and the large one the hunted. This theory was very popular in the 1960s, leading to a search for more hominid fossils. In 1973, Donald Johanson, an American anthropologist, focused research in the Afar region of Ethiopia, where among many similar fossils, he discovered almost 40 percent of the remains of a female australopithecine, who has come to be nicknamed "Lucy." The finds included an almost complete pelvis bone which showed that she was about half the size of a male australopithecine, weighing 75 pounds with a skull of 440 cubic centimeters (her skull would be twice the size of a modern chimpanzee). Her jaw and canines were smaller than those of a chimpanzee, but the molars were larger than modern humans. The rest of her body looked like that of a very muscular but bipedal hominid.

Further evidence gathered by Johanson's team indicates that australopithecines were not hunters or meat eaters but were vegetarians. The large and broad molars indicate that the teeth were used to grind foods found in grasslands, such as roots, grasses, nuts, and berries. Thus Johanson's evidence contradicted Broom's theory,

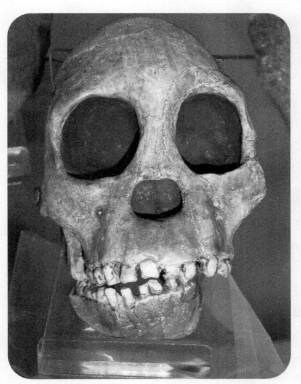

■The Taung's Child skull. It was Dr. Raymond Dart who realized the importance of the find that had been excavated from a limestone quarry in 1924.

leading to a downgrading of the entire theory of hunter australopithecines, and becoming a warning to avoid debates based on limited information. Recent fossil footprints discovered by Richard Hill at Laetoli, Tanzania, have been dated to 3.75 MYA. The prints show that australopithecines had feet that were very similar to modern humans. However, evidence from Lucy show that the great toe was more splayed than the modern foot and that the ankle was not modern, meaning that Australopithecus gracilis might have walked or jogged awkwardly but could not have run like a human (Pilbeam 1984, 94).

It was commonly accepted that Australopithecus dated to about 3 million years ago. Then in the 1995, Maeve Leaky, the wife of the famous paleontologist Richard Leaky, discovered fossil remains pushing the date back to 3.9–4.2 million years ago, which she named *Australopithecus anamensis*. In 1999, she discovered the skull and partial jaw of another fossil dated to the same time period, which she named *Kenyapithecus platyops*. Other discoveries have added to the complexity of the evolutionary record.

The Pleistocene Epoch

The Pliocene Epoch was followed the Pleistocene, which is dated to between 1.8 MYA to 10,000 years BP. While the Pliocene was an epoch of geological uplifting and drying, the Pleistocene was an epoch of repeated glaciations and pluvials (periods of rainfall). The glaciations occurred in the northern and southern landmasses. Glaciers occurred as far south as the 40th parallel in some places, while the pluvials occurred in regions that are directly north and south of the equator. It is estimated that at the glacial maximums, 30 percent of the Earth's surface was covered with ice while sea level dropped between 200 to 300 feet. In many regions, it became possible for our human ancestors to migrate from one continent to another, such as from Africa to Eurasia and from Eurasia to North America.

Glaciations and pluvials did not occur at the same time, but they were important geological events to which early hominids had to adapt, first biologically and then culturally. The Pleistocene was followed by the Holocene, or modern epoch, but most of the important biological changes to our species had taken place by ten thousand years ago. Most changes that occur from the end of the Ice Age to the present are due to changes in culture, not geology. The periods for the changes are known as the Paleolithic, Mesolithic, Neolithic, and Modern.

There were also four distinct glacial periods interspersed by warmer interglacial periods during the Pleistocene (the geological and cultural dates tend to confuse many; they should be kept separate). The glacial periods were cold but produced large game mammals that humans could have hunted during the last two glacial periods. Our ancestors remained in the warmer tropics during the first half of the Pleistocene primarily in the form of *Homo erectus*, an ancestor of ours that was between Australopithecus and modern Homo Sapiens.

■At the glacial maximums, 30 percent of the Earth's surface was covered with ice and the sea level dropped between 200 to 300 feet. In many areas, bridges formed of ice allowed humans to migrate from one continent to another, whereas today this would not be possible if traveling on foot.

Homo Erectus and the Lower Paleolithic

Many new fossils of Australopithecus and Homo erectus have been discovered over the last half-century in Africa. The story of human evolution in Africa is also the story of the Leakys, a remarkable family that has been responsible for many of paleoarchaeology's most exciting African discoveries. In the late 1940s and early 1950s, Louis and Mary Leaky, the famous husband and wife team, uncovered the complex picture of early Pleistocene evolution in Africa. In addition to dozens of australopithecines which they uncovered in the Olduvai Gorge of Tanzania and in Kenya, they made several controversial discoveries between 1962 and 1964 of another upright hominid which Louis called "Homo habilis," a term which means "handyman," "skillful person," and "man the toolmaker." *Homo habilis* lived between 2.5 to 1.6 million years ago occurring at the same time as the last australopithecines. *Homo habilis* had a brain size of 640 cc, one third larger than an average australopithecine. In 1972, Bernard Ngeneo discovered another fossil resembling *Homo habilis*, which has been named Homo rudolfensis (or KNM-ER 1470) which was assigned a date of 1.9 million years ago. Rudolfensis has a brain size of 510 cc and has been classified as a *Homo habilis*.

There is considerable controversy over *Homo habilis* that many anthropologists believe to be an early form of Homo erectus, while others believe the two forms were separate species. Louis Leakey's use of the term "man the tool maker" points our attention towards innovations in culture, and he gave the geological time period of the lower Pleistocene a term describing cultural findings: the Paleolithic.

The Paleolithic meant the Old Stone Age, and it coincided with humans as hunters. The tools of hunting and gathering brought about changes to the hands and face. The term *Paleolithic* was developed by John Lubbock in 1865 and combines two Greek words, *palios* or old and *lithos* or stone. The Paleolithic was divided into Lower, Middle, and Upper. Three distinct forms of hominid fit into these three periods. Homo Australopithecus and Homo erectus may have co-existed and took up the longest time period of the Lower Paleolithic, while Homo neanderthalensis took up the Middle Paleolithic and Homo sapiens emerged during the Upper Paleolithic and continues today. Each period is also associated with different stone tool-making traditions. The Lower Paleolithic is associated with hand-axe tools,

■A *Homo erectus* skull. *Homo erectus* existed as a biological species for close to a million years without significant change, making it a very successful hominid.

the Middle Paleolithic with flake tools, and the Upper Paleolithic with blade tools.

Australopithecus and Homo erectus spread from Africa through Europe and Asia. Australopithecus fossils are scattered and hard to generalize about, and it is unclear when the form ended. Homo erectus existed as a biological species for close to a million years without significant change, making it a very successful hominid. The face and head of *Homo erectus* are dramatically different from ours. The skull was long and low, sloping down from the center of the head to a low forehead, probably reflecting the small frontal lobes of the brain. It is the frontal lobe that went through the greatest expansion over a million years, and these changes were associated with changes in stone tool manufacturing discussed above. The skull has a heavy brow ridge, called the *supraorbital torus*, which is located across the eyes and over the root of a large nose. In certain forms, the brow ridges overlie the frontal sinuses, but in others the brow ridges are filled with spongy bone tissue.

The back of the skull, known as the *occiput*, is very different from *Homo sapiens* in that it is small vertically but very broad. There is a horizontal bar of bone crossing the occiput called the *occipital torus* which served as the anchor for powerful neck muscles needed to hold the head, with its massive face, erect. During the Lower Paleolithic, the brain increased from about 600 to 1400 cc. As the brain filled out, the face, with its massive jaw and teeth, shrank. The increase of the brain and decrease in the size of the face were probably related because as the one increased in size, the increasing use of efficient tools took pressure off the jaw in the process of masticating food.

It is difficult to discuss the relationship of postcranial features (those beneath the head) with cranial features because there have been few limb bones discovered. An exception is KNM-WT 15000, an almost complete skeleton of *Homo erectus* discovered by Richard Leakey and A. Walker at Nariokotome, Kenya. This and other less complete discoveries show Homo erectus' body was similar to modern humans, but had a much more powerful build. While the long bones were the same width, the outer walls are almost twice as thick as modern bones, while the inside cavity was narrower. The legs were not as angled in at the knees, and the acetabulum (the socket into which the femur fits) was larger than in modern humans. These and other features suggest that *Homo erectus* was substantially heavier than modern humans. The earliest *Homo erectus* males stood a little over 5 feet 2 inches, while the latest stood 5 feet 10½ inches, but sexual dimorphism (the difference between the size of male and female) was much greater in Homo erectus than modern humans. Fossil evidence for females is even worse than males; but on limited evidence it is estimated that female Homo erectus forms were about three-fourths the size of the male (which is about the size difference between female and male chimpanzees).

It has been suggested that the changes from *Homo erectus* to modern *Homo sapiens* was the consequence of the development of stone tools during the Lower Paleolithic. The earliest stone tools date back to the same time period as late Australopithecus and early Homo erectus. They are called Oldowan, or chopper-chopping tools, and date back 2.6 MYA to the beginning of the Lower Paleolithic. The tools have not been found in association with fossil forms, and it is possible both forms of early hominids used Oldowan tools.

While appearing primitive, Oldowan stone tools are more sophisticated than the earliest tools made by our human ancestors. Manufacturing required knowledge of how certain types of rocks, particularly river pebbles, will fragment when hit with another pebble, usually called a hammer stone. The rock type can be quartz, quartzite, basalt, obsidian, flint, or chert. These types of rock have a cryptocrystalline structure, which is also found in glass. When glass is struck a direct blow, a small circular piece will occur on the opposite side from the blow. A close examination of either the circular piece of glass or the scar it made (if the glass was not shattered) will reveal an s-shaped form. This is known as a conchoidal fracture. The physics of stone tool manufacturing is fairly complex and requires knowledge of how to hold the hammer stone, the angle at which to strike the platform of rock from which one wants to remove a flake, and so on. The tool manufacturer has to know a great deal and must be able to communicate that information to others. This makes us realize that as far back as the earliest Oldowan tools, their maker had a theory about how to make them, and the ability to communicate that theory to others, including his or her children. This evidence suggests Homo erectus had some form of language (the same reasoning applies to other ancestral forms associated with Oldowan type tools).

There appears to be a correlation between the appearance of stone tools, improvements in their efficiencies, and an increase in the size of the brain. One theory explains that Australopithecus, our first hominid ancestor, originated in a grassland environment. It probably developed simple Oldowan stone tools to harvest grains and food plants instead of using the teeth and muscles of the lower face. The tools brought about changes to teeth and jaws, which shrank while the brain almost doubled in size. Recent reports that fire may have been controlled as far back as 1.7 million years ago fit into an overall picture of a reduction in pressures for large teeth and jaw leading to a decrease in prognathism (prognathism is a term meaning a large lower face). The changes that began with Australopithecus led to the appearance of Homo erectus in the early Pleistocene.

Homo erectus was one of the most successful and long-lived species of the genus *Homo*. It lived much longer than its predecessor, Australopithecus, or us, Homo sapiens. As the population increased, communities hived off, with a few individuals leaving to set up new communities nearby. Over thousands of years, *Homo erectus* moved out of Africa and into Europe, Asia, and as far east as Indonesia (Java). As *Homo erectus* migrated, the body, face, and head adjusted to changing environmental conditions; and its tool manufacturing became more sophisticated, causing changes to the face, and so on.

Of particular importance is the appearance of *Acheulian* tools, which were no doubt made by the earliest *Homo erectus*, although the fossils and artifacts are not found in direct association. Acheulian stone tools clearly evolved out of the Oldowan technique described above but were more sophisticated. While Oldown tools can best be characterized as fist axes with only one sharp striking edge, Acheulian tools were worked completely around, taking on a characteristic almond shape. The manufacture of Acheulian tools appears to have taken a set of steps. The first step was to use a hammer stone to make a tool that looked much like an Oldowan handaxe. The second step, called the "baton technique," was to work the stone with an antler or horn to pressure flakes off of the prepared core. This technique was more efficient than the hammer stone technique used with Oldowan tools giving the Acheulean tool its almond shape. The consequence was to produce an even-cutting edge that would have been sharp enough for butchering game or to make other tools out of wood. The Acheulian tool was probably not used as a spearhead, but it was no doubt used to make such tools out of wood. The tools that were made by *Homo erectus* were used to hunt fairly large game mammals such as deer, elephant, and bear.

Acheulean hand axes have been found grouped together on cave floors and may have had some ritual use. They received much more attention in their manufacture than was necessary, giving anthropologists the idea that artistic beauty may have been an objective or that the tools had a religious use as well as a practical one. The idea that they may have had religious use sounds far fetched until one realizes that ancestor worship is commonly found in contemporary hunting and gathering societies throughout the world and is often associated with the burial of tools with the remains of a dead hunter. The tools may have symbolized the power of the eldest males, who were the leaders of the hunting bands. Recently, anthropologist Michael Winkelman (2000, 2008) has made a connection between the structure of the brain and religion in hunting and gathering societies. He thinks religion may have had adaptive advantages. A belief in the supernatural might have given our ancestors a common sense of identity that would have aided survival.

Acheulian tools, since they are made from stone, are difficult to date. Nonetheless, potassium-argon dating gives them a range of 1.6 MYA to 100,000 years ago, which is roughly the same time period as *Homo erectus* spread throughout the Old World. Both Acheulian tools and Homo erectus fossils are found in France, China, Africa, and Java in Indonesia. One such site called Terra Amata was a cave site where huts were built during the second or Mindel glaciation (450,000 to 380,000 years ago). While it is a cave site, it is found near the Mediterranean where, in addition to killing large mammals such as rhinoceros, oxen, wild horse, mammoth, and mastodon, *Homo erectus* also had access to turtles, rabbits, rodents, broom plants, hackberry, clams, oysters, and mussels. There is also evidence for cliff falls, where large numbers of animals were driven to their deaths.

At another French site called Lazeret, a cave was discovered which had sleeping rooms. The rooms can be identified because they had stone benches that were once covered with wild animal skins and cushioned with seaweed (Kennedy 1980). The excavator, H. de Lumley, also found the skull of a wolf that might have acted as a religious fetish. The brain had been removed, and the skull placed in the entrance of the cave possibly as a means by which to obtain its power.

Other excavations produce more evidence that *Homo erectus* could have been a significant predator. In excavations at Torralba, Spain, Clark Howell found that in a swampy valley, which was probably a migration route for large mammals, *Homo erectus* hunted elephants, horses, red deer, oxen, and rhinoceroses. One hunting technique was to light fires in the grassy uplands in order to drive large mammals into boggy areas where they could be easily killed. Initial butchering was managed with choppers and scrapers, while bifacial hand axes were used to batter open the skulls of elephants and other large mammals (Kennedy 1980, 343).

Another very important site is Choukoutien, a cave site located near Peking, China, found in the 1930s. Homo erectus inhabited the cave over a period of two hundred years, but the tools were only of a crude Oldowan type. These primitive tools, which originated in Africa, were common throughout Asia. As with a few European sites, there is evidence of cannibalism with the favorite food appearing to be the brains, which were accessed by breaking away the base of the skull. It has been suggested that *Homo erectus* may have practiced some form of endocannibalism, a type of ritual consumption of relatives documented on the islands of the Pacific. Aside from eating their relatives, which probably did not add many calories to their food consumption, their diet was varied with deer, pigs, horses, bears, rodents, hedgehogs, frogs, bats, hares, eggs, and hackberries (Kennedy 1980, 346).

The evidence from archaeology shows that by three hundred thousand years ago, Homo erectus was a widespread hominid which had migrated from Africa to Europe and

Asia, where it continued to evolve into modern Homo sapiens. In a few regions, such as Western Europe, Homo erectus adapted to cold conditions by developing some exaggerated characteristics that gave it a species designation: Homo Neanderthalensis or Neanderthal Man. A few writers argue that this form, which was once thought to be so primitive it could not compete with modern Homo sapiens, is a close relative and should be classified as belonging to our species and named Homo sapiens Neanderthalensis.

Neanderthal and the Middle Paleolithic

Here we take a look at Neanderthal man (and woman), who we now consider a close ancestor. The evidence for the closeness of Neanderthal man and Homo sapiens comes from research on DNA by Svante Pääbo of the Max Planck Institute for Evolutionary Anthropology in Leipzig, Germany. He chose Charles Darwin's two hundredth birthday to announce the outcome of research carried out by the Institute's Neanderthal Genome Project. DNA was extracted from four specimens of ancient man, including the original remains of Neanderthal discovered in the Neander Valley in 1856. Research was not unlike the recent Human Genome Project, which measured the size and nature of human DNA, except that Neanderthal material was found fragmented into tiny pieces and contaminated with bacteria and fungi that had to be purified. Once purified, the Neanderthal fragments were fed into DNA-sequencing machines and compared to modern Homo sapiens.

Dr. Pääbo has been able to show that Neanderthal and modern humans have very similar DNA and that both evolved out of Homo erectus. Our modern ancestors began to appear just as the last of the Neanderthal began to disappear. Exactly what happened between Homo erectus and the appearance of Neanderthal and modern Homo sapiens is not clear because the evidence is fragmentary and confusing. The Neanderthal Genome Project does show that there was little, if any, interbreeding between Neanderthal and modern humans but that both had speech and similar intellect. The most significant study is of a gene called FOXP2 that occurs in both Neanderthal and modern humans. FOXP2 is involved in the mechanics of speech production and implies that both forms had the same speech and mental abilities. These recent discoveries reinforce the point of view held by many anthropologists that Neanderthal is a cold-adapted version of Homo sapiens, who slightly preceded us and not a primitive hominid as once theorized, and that modern humans developed clothing and tools that allowed Homo sapiens sapiens to move into the same environment as Homo sapiens neanderthalensis. Then the two subspecies could have interbred, or one exterminated the other. We lean towards the first argument because it is very rare, despite human violence against humans, for one form to exterminate the other. The outstanding example is the extermination of a few native populations of Australia.

The significance of the Neanderthal Genome Project is that despite some very clear differences between Neanderthal and modern human, both are genetically identical. Neanderthal was a short, stocky hominid whose massive face and large teeth were probably adaptations to extreme cold. The most striking feature of the face is

■Svante Pääbo of the Max Planck Institute for Evolutionary Anthropology is a Swedish biologist who specializes in evolutionary genetics.

called facial prognathism, similar to Homo erectus. The face seems to jut out of the head. Part of the forward displacement of the face may be the consequence of greatly enlarged facial sinuses, which may have been an adaptation to severe cold.

The brain was as large or larger than most modern humans, and its body was quite similar to that of Homo erectus. Neanderthal produced a distinctive culture and tools called *Mousterian*. Mousterian culture is elaborate and impressive, dating back to two hundred thousand years ago, and is found in East Africa, Europe, the Middle East and Asia. Using bone, antler, or wood, Neanderthal chipped flakes off a specially prepared flint core. The core was discarded after it became too small, while the flakes were turned into a wide variety of tools. One of these tools, a flake that was used to scrape hides to remove flesh, may have been responsible for the reduction in the size of the teeth and face.

Evidence for religion associated with ancestor worship is found in many Neanderthal sites. One of the earliest burial sites is found at a cave site called the Grotte de Regourdou in France where a human was buried with the bones of deer and bear under a pile of ash and stone. The animal bones were probably offerings to the dead. Human burials have also been found at La Chappelle-aux-Saints, la Ferrassie, and Le Moustier in France. The burial at La Chappelle is of an old man who had lost many teeth and had arthritis. In addition, its face had been injured and one arm partially amputated. Marcel Boule, a French archaeologist, originally assembled the skeleton as bent over, giving the impression of ape-like primitiveness that would last from 1857 until recently when the skeleton was re-assembled showing that Neanderthal stood straight. Nearby was a burial of what may have been an entire family. In the cave site of Le Moustier, which is where the name of Mousterian comes from, was found the burial of a fifteen-year-old young man. He had been buried on his side with his head resting on his forearm and his legs drawn up to his chin. This type of burial is called the *fetal position* and can be considered a symbol of life and rebirth. He was buried with finely made Mousterian stone tools and joints of meat. Such burials are common among pre-modern people around the world.

Another cave site called Teshik-Tash in Afghanistan contains the burial of another young boy. His shallow grave was surrounded by the horns of Ibex sheep and stone tools. A similar site was discovered at Shanidar Cave in northern Iraq where the remains of eight individuals were excavated, four of which were simple burials and four were placed on top of each other. At one grave, pollen analysis revealed that the body of a middle aged man who had been covered with yarrow, cornflower, hyacinths, daisies, hollyhocks, and bachelor buttons. These flowers have healing properties and bloom in late spring or early summer, so it is possible to infer the season in which the person had died, and that the individual may have been a shaman or healer. This very human act of spreading flowers on a dead relative has many symbolic interpretations, including those of fertility and rebirth. Several of the bodies had been coated with red ochre, which is also associated with blood and rebirth among hunters and food gatherers. Another burial is of an elderly man in his late fifties whose left portion of his face had been badly injured and whose arm had been partially amputated. These burials suggest that Neanderthal must have had knowledge of some relatively advanced surgical techniques, as well as how to use drugs derived from plants. It is also probable that the injured man could not have aided in hunting, and therefore found other ways to achieve recognition by learning to be a shaman, story teller, or keeper of clan lore.

Yet another important site is Monte Circeo, Italy. Here was located a human skull with the base facing up within a circle of stones; the evidence indicates human sacrifice and possible cannibalism. Other sites have been discovered with Neanderthal burials and cave bear skulls placed in nearby holes and covered with rocks. These cave bear burials suggest some kind of cave bear worship. The evidence has received mixed interpretations, from the opinion that most of the evidence is circumstantial or accidental to that Neanderthal had religion and art, and was very human. The most recent evidence on DNA tips classification in the direction of placing Neanderthal next to us, as a Homo sapiens variant. A liberal interpretation of these discoveries would be that the structure of the human brain, as far back as Neanderthal, and earlier, has given our ancestors many of our qualities, and that these were products of natural selection. Art, symbolism, and religion may have occurred hundreds of thousands of years before the appearance of Homo sapiens, a subject we turn to next.

Homo Sapiens and the Upper Paleolithic

Neanderthal began to disappear from the scene in Europe and to be replaced by modern Homo sapiens between thirty thousand to twenty thousand years ago. The relationship between Neanderthal and Homo sapiens is not clear. There are two contrasting theories regarding the evidence. The first is the multiregional, evolutionary model which suggests that Homo erectus evolved into modern Homo sapiens in various regions of the Old World. The second is called "the replacement model" and suggests that modern Homo sapiens appeared in just one place, Africa, and then migrated to the rest of the Old World replacing other earlier forms, such as Neanderthal. A recent version of the replacement hypothesis is based primarily on genetic evidence called mitochondrial DNA (mtDNA) drawn from women around the world and is known as the "Eve hypothesis." MtDNA is inherited only by women, and the sample showed that humans originated in Africa about two hundred thousand years ago and spread from there to the rest of the Old World. The most recent evidence supporting this view shows that Africa has the greatest genetic variation, which would be expected if Africa were where humans originated. However, many question research that depends almost totally on genetic information from one gender and discards thousands of fossils and cultural evidence.

■Sites have been discovered with Neanderthal burials and cave bear skulls placed in nearby holes and covered with rocks. These cave bear burials may suggest some kind of cave bear worship.

An example of such fossil evidence is the remains of "archaic sapiens" found in South Africa and Israel, which reinforces the replacement model. It suggests that a Homo sapiens variant may have existed in the Middle East at the same time that Neanderthal lived in Europe. This interpretation suggests that Neanderthal was adapted to glacial conditions in Western Europe while modern humans first appeared in the climatic warmer Middle East much earlier and then migrated to Europe thirty thousand years ago, interbreeding with the cold adapted Neanderthal (earlier theories had Homo sapiens killing off Neanderthal). While it was once thought that Neanderthal and Homo sapiens were genetically very different, DNA studies cited above show they were extremely similar. Given thousands of years of interaction, modern humans may have bred with Neanderthal and brought about the disappearance of cold adapted features since these were no longer necessary given cold adapted clothing and the new tools of the Upper Paleolithic.

Let's take a closer looks at the Upper Paleolithic. The earliest stage of the Upper Paleolithic is known as the Lower Perigordian (sometimes it is called Chatelperronian). The tools are very similar to African Dabban blades. The following phase is much better known and is called the Aurignacian. The fossils are well known and conform to the characteristics of Cro-magnon (or Cromagnon). Like Neanderthal, the people of Aurignon culture were cave dwellers, but they had established highly successful hunting and gathering cultures based on the atlatl (throwing board) or spear thrower. This tool is still used in Australia by its aboriginal population, and the Aztec and Maya used it as recently as a few hundred years ago. During the Upper Paleolithic, because of the rich animal and vegetable resources available, human population densities expanded. Aurignacians or Cro-magnon are particularly famous for their paintings which were found in the very deepest recesses of the caves in which they lived. Drawings found on cave shelters resemble those of Australian hunters, who used their art to call up a mythological age called the "dreaming." It has been theorized that Aurignacians and Australians both believe in "mana," a type of supernatural forcefield found in the bodies of humans or specially trained humans (think of Yoda and "the force" in the movie *Star Wars)*.

The Aurignacian was followed by the Gravettian and dates from twenty-two thousand to eighteen thousand years ago. The Gravettian is named after the "gravet point" which has been compared to a multi-purpose penknife. Blades were fragmented into smaller "microliths" that may have served as points for arrows. The blades are too small for use in spears, but could have been used in arrows propelled by bows for small mammals and fish. Gravettian people are particularly well known for carved mammoth ivory of considerable sophistication made in the shape of horses, mammoths, camels, and many other mammals that were hunted. They were also able to manufacture eyed-needles out of bone, which suggests they made tailored clothing. A few scoop-like items made from mammoth rib might have been used for beating snow off fur (Clark and Piggott 1961, 64–97).

On the plains of Eastern Europe lived a Gravettian people who relied almost entirely on mammoths. While they also hunted horse, reindeer, fox, wolverine, and grouse, they used mammoth for food, fuel, and shelter. They constructed pit houses by digging four to five foot holes, which they roofed over with ribs and other bones from mammoths. Some of these structures were quite large and may have held several families related through males (patrilineal) or females (matrilineal). As with the Perigordian and Aurignacian people, the dead were given special treatment. In the west they were buried in caves, while in the eastern plains they were buried under the floors of their pit houses (perhaps because the outside ground was frozen). Bodies were contracted into the fetal position, and men and women were often buried next to each other. In many burials, the bodies were covered with the two shoulder blades of mammoths.

The dead were often decorated, giving us some idea of how the living dressed. Both wore pendants of fired clay or of deer teeth, snail shells, dentalium shells, and disks made of mother of pearl or fish vertebrae. It appears many of these items were traded between villages. Archaeologists Graham Clark and Stuart Piggot have written about the Gravettian people in that they demonstrated considerable aesthetic sensibility by carving objects from wood, bone, and ivory. They created patterns by boring small pits, alternating them with criss-cross pattern, herring bone forms, linear chevrons, and meandering lines (Clark and Piggott 1961, 64–97).

As mentioned, the form of hominid closest to ourselves is called Cro-magnon; and his tools were originally similar to the Mousterian of Neanderthal. Essentially flake tools, these evolved into more sophisticated forms over time. The Dabban, dated to between thirty-five thousand to forty thousand years ago, had "backed blades." These were very sharp blades, removed from a prepared core, and then trimmed so that blades removed had only one sharp edge. The blade might be further trimmed so it could be held in the hand without injury. Handles, in the shape of wild animals, might have been carved to further insure safety. The people of the Dabban culture lived along the Mediterranean coast where the terrain was lush. Similar cave sites occur in the Middle East at the Shanidar Cave site (the earliest levels of which were occupied by Neanderthal).

Cro-magnon and his/her Upper Paleolithic culture was not just a small improvement over Neanderthal—it was an entirely new design. We have mentioned the atlatl (an Aztec word) that was made of carved wood, antler, or bone in the shape of an animal with a hook fit into one end. The hook would be placed into the end of a spear, which could then be cast with great force giving Cro-magnon special biomechanical strength while hunting. Not unlike the use of the repeating rifle to hunt buffalo in the late nineteenth century, many animals in a herd could be killed without alarming the rest, thus increasing the success of the hunt geometrically over Neanderthal. Whereas Neanderthal might have killed one or two large mammals, Cro-magnon may have killed several hundred, particularly with the use of deadfalls and other traps (Clark and Piggott 1961, 64–97). These tools would have allowed the growth of the population, which is exactly what we see during the Upper Paleolithic.

There was also an improvement in artistic self-expression in the form of carved wood, mammoth ivory and stone figurines, and cave paintings. Some objects were made of fire-hardened clay. The most common carved figurines were mammoths, the primary victims of Upper Paleolithic hunters. Carvings were also made of bear, wolf, rhinoceros, ibex, and felines. The art work is no doubt associated with hunting, which in turn indicates shamanism and religion were linked not unlike that produced by American Indians. Human beings are rarely represented in cave art; but when they are, it is obvious that they are associated with hunting or fertility magic. The humans shown in cave art are always male, usually dancing and wearing the head of an animal with its pelt draping the dancer. Particularly impressive is the engraving of a dancer wearing a bison mask from the Cave of the Three Brothers (les Trois Freres) from Ariege, France. In another painting, a dancer wears a mask of a deer's head. In both paintings, the artists managed to portray the rhythmic motions of dancing.

There are also many enigmatic signs, such as pentagons, and other forms which are thought to represent traps but that may have had sexual meanings. There are also drawings of hands, made much as children still do in grade school art classes by blowing paint through a tube and across the hand. Many such hands have missing fingers cut off at the first or second joint, possibly sacrificial offerings to animals or to the sun as were once common among American Indians.

The most famous cave paintings are found in France and Spain, although there have been recent discoveries in the Ural Mountains of Russia. The paintings occur deep in the recesses of caves, far from light, and are difficult to access. Archaeologists argue that the difficult access added to the mystery of the paintings as, no doubt, did the flickering quality caused by primitive lamps.

Carved human figurines are found scattered throughout a vast region. Most are naturalistic, but the emphasis was undeniably sexual, unlike cave paintings. The figurines are always nude and female. Pregnancy is common, and sexuality is highly symbolized by exaggerated enlargement of breasts, buttocks, and thighs. According to most archaeologists, it is difficult to imagine that they could have had any other function than that of ritualized fertility and reproduction (Clark and Piggott 1961, 64–97).

Migration, Race, and Variation

By one hundred thousand years ago, modern humans or their direct ancestors had migrated throughout Africa and the Middle East, Europe, as well as Asia. While some of our ancestors stayed in one place, others continuously moved carrying genes from one region to the other. Over thousands of years, our ancestors had taken on the distinct forms they have today; but because of continuous migration, human varieties did not become separate species. By sixty thousand years ago they had spread to Australia. Between twenty thousand to thirteen thousand years ago, they migrated into the New World and evolved into the American Indian and Arctic Eskimo.

The fossil record does not tell us if the variations we refer to as "race" today were present at the time of Homo erectus, Neanderthal, or Cro-magnon. We also do not know if there was a specific sequence running from Homo erectus to Neanderthal and Cro-magnon in all regions of the Old World. Neanderthal is primarily found in Europe but may have been an intermediate form elsewhere. However, the evidence is lacking—to do any more would be to guess. For example, both in Australia and the New World, there is no solid evidence for Homo erectus or Neanderthal, so the evidence suggests fairly modern forms of hominid populated these regions. On the other hand, Western Europe shows evidence for Homo erectus, Neanderthal, and Cro-magnon; while China and Indonesia show Homo erectus and modern, but no Neanderthal. These patterns of evolution may be accidental and the consequence of the accidental discovery of only certain fossil forms. Changes to the picture will no doubt occur as fossil hunting continues.

The evidence from Choukoutien near Peking, China, mentioned above, appears to show a full range of changes from Homo erectus to modern Homo sapiens in the same region (but with no sign of Neanderthal). Carleton Coon used the evidence from Choukoutien to argue a controversial point of view: humans spread throughout the Old World by the late Paleolithic and evolved into five basic regional races separately (Coon 1962). One of the reasons his theory was controversial is that the definition of race was in the process of going through dramatic change when he published *The Origin of Races* in 1962.

The primary problem with the concept of race, used by biologists from the time of Darwin and through the first half of the twentieth century, was the tendency to look at race as pre-species. According to this perspective, the members of a race were becoming so different that one day they would not be able to mate, at which point they would have become distinct species. This point of view supported the perspective of racists who argued for the separation of the various variants of hominid (which was not the point of view advocated by Coon). According to one of Coon's antagonists, Ashley Montague, the term race had long since been replaced by other words such as "population," "biological group," "variant," or "deme" in the fields of biology and zoology. Montague argued anthropology should abandon the term entirely because it was no longer used in the biological sciences; but he also argued that humans adapt to their environments through culture and not biology, a point of view he popularized in the mid-1960s. Montague argued that there is no reason to think human differences would lead to speciation. He argued that the real reason why the word race continued to be used was the racist assumption that different "races" were biologically superior or inferior to each other, an idea that had long been abandoned by most anthropologists, but not by psychologists and sociologists who continued to test for differences in intelligence between races, either to challenge that such differences existed or to support them. They continued to use the R… word, either to support ideas of intellectual superiority, or to refute it.

By the 1970s, many anthropologists argued that there was no such thing as race, but that there are biological differences between people, and that these need to be explained. They argued that for almost ten thousand years, or from the end of the Paleolithic to about two thousand years ago, most populations did not travel far; and natural selection helped to create biological variations, many of which come down to us today, as human populations adapted to their physical habitats. Some regions of the world have been populated for longer time periods than others; and where they have, human adaptations stand out clearly. Africa has had the longest period of occupation with hunters and food gatherers using blade tools that were adapted to dense forest, open woodlands, savannahs, and deserts. In all these regions, there are small variations in Africans. Populations spread to Europe, the Middle East, and Asia.

While anthropologists argued the case that the word race should be abandoned, the civil rights movement tried to support the idea that all races are equal. Because the history of anthropology had included a period around the Civil War when the discipline tried to prove the inferiority of dark skinned populations, modern anthropologists were often accused of racism. Yet by the 1960s, most anthropologists had joined the fray arguing that all races were equal; and the attempt to abandon the word "race" became a historical footnote, but one worth making. Most anthropologists today argue that what they mean by race is variation and not speciation, and they continue to try to understand how the many biological variations came into existence. As we will learn, the most important variations between human populations are the consequence of adaptations to sunlight, heat and cold, agriculture, and urbanization. There appear to be no clear intellectual differences between populations that are biological in nature, and most differences that can be measured appear to be the consequence of successful and not so-successful strategies of education.

We will discuss the functions of most human biological traits after a short excursion to explain what we know about human migration. Our origins, of course, lie in Africa where Australopithecus evolved into Homo erectus, which then migrated into the Middle

East, Europe, and Asia. The first migrations occurred during one of the warm interglacial periods. In Western Europe where glacial conditions became extreme, cold adapted Neanderthal forms emerged, while elsewhere, warmer conditions and the development of sophisticated tools led to the appearance of modern looking hominids. Such regions as Northern Asia were not populated until late in the Upper Paleolithic, when modern but cold-adapted humans migrated into the Gobi desert, which was much warmer and damper during late Paleolithic, and rhinoceros, elephant, horses, deer, wild goats, and ostriches were hunted. From there, people with high cheekbones and shovel shaped teeth spread to Southeast Asia about thirty thousand years ago (these features, it is argued, are adaptations to cold). Ocean levels were low, and Japan was connected to mainland Asia during the Upper Paleolithic. People migrated across a land bridge; they hunted and fished using small canoes, lived in shallow pit houses, and produced primitive pottery (Nickels, Hunter, Whitten, 255–256).

During Upper Paleolithic, the Arctic was a cold tundra desert inhabited by herds of bison, mammoth, horse, and antelope that were hunted with the atlatl. People harvested sea life as far back as 16,500 years ago. Thirty thousand years ago modern humans that managed to cross over the Java Trench, over sixty-five miles of open ocean, inhabited Australia. The climate was drier than today, and there were no carnivorous predators. Stone tools were crude and reflect the poor quality of stone found there. Spearheads were made of wood or bone that were cast with an atlatl. A recent exciting find in the south is Koonalda Cavern that has a wall engraving. The other islands of the Pacific were settled more recently, two to four thousand years ago, by people who had agriculture, outrigger sailing canoes, and advanced knowledge of stellar navigation (Nickels, Hunter, Whitten 1979, 259).

The origin of the American Indian is controversial. Many Native Americans believe they have always been in the Americas, while Europeans of two centuries ago believed Native Americans were descendants of Ham, one of Noah's sons who formed "the lost tribe of Israel." Interestingly, as early as 1590, the Spanish Jesuit, José de Acosta, hypothesized that the American Indian came over a land bridge connecting Asia and the Americas. Thomas Jefferson, in 1781, published similar views, which are generally accepted today. Studies by physical anthropologists show that the American Indian shares many characteristics with peoples living in Siberia. The distance between Siberia and Alaska is about 90 km., which can be crossed by boat; or the distance might have been connected by a Bering Strait land bridge 1500 to 3000 kilometers wide. The ancestors of the American Indian may have crossed the land bridge while they were hunting mammoth, moose, caribou, bison, camel, bear, fox, and other animals that migrated back and forth between eastern Asia and Alaska. The date of crossing is about thirteen thousand years ago, which is the age of Clovis mammoth hunters, who are named after a hunting tool in the form of a long blade that had single flake removed down its length. These points are called fluted points and were preceded by smaller Folsom points used for hunting Pleistocene bison. Both the mammoth and giant bison were hunted to extinction about ten thousand years ago.

The dates for the peopling of Latin America are also controversial; for some are exceptionally early, such as twenty-two thousand years ago for Peru, and even earlier for Pali Aki cave in southern Chile which has radio carbon dates of thirty-five thousand years ago. Artifacts ranging in age from ten thousand to forty thousand years ago are found in North, Central, and South Americas; however, they are not found with skeletal material and are in the form of pre-projectile points, primitive hand axes that are cruder than the hand axes of Homo erectus. The question as to why such primitive

tools are found in the Americas has never been answered. The lack of fossil evidence for Homo sapiens is also a mystery. As the reader can deduce, the subject of ancient man in the New World is very controversial; it can only be touched on here. The most important point is that modern *Homo sapiens* or the tools he/she made had spread throughout the world between twenty thousand and ten thousand years ago. In the following, we wish to sketch out what is known about how modern human varieties came into being.

The populations we have been describing were hunters and gatherers. In general, the men did the hunting and fishing; and women gathered seeds, fruits, berries—but they also contributed to fishing and hunting. While it was once thought that there was a strict division of labor between the sexes with men doing all the hunting and women doing all of the gathering, in the 1960s, the topic of women's activities in hunting societies became more important to both male and female anthropologists. Research showed that the division of labor was actually very blurred, and that men sometimes gathered while women sometimes hunted. Both had considerable knowledge of hunting and gathering. The early point of view was associated with a theory that women "invented agriculture" due to their gathering experiences. However, we know today that men and women were equally involved in the activities that slowly led to the agricultural transformation with both genders involved.

The region where the agricultural transformation occurred is known as the **Fertile Crescent.** It is a 1500-mile region stretching from the mouth of the Tigris-Euphrates Rivers, down through the Levant, and southeast through Mesopotamia or modern Iraq. The Levant is a region of great geological complexity and lies just to the east of the Mediterranean. Winds tracking towards the east flow over the coast of the Levant and over the Pontic Mountains, which run north and south along the coast of the Levant. Rains fall in the mountains and to the east producing a region known as the "hilly flanks" of the Middle East. Further east, a rain shadow produces the desert of the Arabian Peninsula. The topography of the rivers and foothills of this region was important to the development of agriculture (Redman 1978, 20).

Vere Gordon Childe invented the term **Neolithic Revolution** based on the assumption that people moved to the lowland oases along the Tigris and Euphrates Rivers because of the desiccation of the climate, and that they developed agriculture after they came into close proximity with plants, animals, and water (Childe 1936). The discovery of the site of Jericho by Kathleen Kenyon in the 1930s seemed to confirm Childe's theory. However, Robert Braidwood, an archaeologist from Chicago's Oriental Institute, thought that it was more likely agriculture would be developed in a region where the wild ancestors of food plants occurred naturally. He carried out excavations in the hilly flanks at the site of Qalat Jarmo in 1948 where he found evidence that seemed to support his hypothesis. His point of view is called the **hilly flanks theory** and was popular through the middle 1960s.

Childe, Kenyon, and Braidwood were working on hypotheses that explained the origins of agriculture beginning in one local and spreading from there. However, in the 1960s, excavations showed that the beginnings of agriculture lay as far back as ten to eight thousand years ago and was widespread, practiced by people who were semi-nomadic and lived part of the time in substantial communities. Excavations showed semi-nomadic foragers were widespread throughout Iraq, Iran, Israel, Turkey, and into the mountains of southern Europe. Many theorists began to shift focus from agriculture as the cause of the Neolithic to demographic, climatic, and environmental factors.

Fertile Crescent

A 1500-mile region that stretches from the mouth of the Tigris and Euphrates rivers down through the Levant and through Mesopotamia (modern Iraq)

Neolithic Revolution

A term coined by Vere Gordon Childe to describe his assumption that people moved to the lowland oases along the Tigris and Euphrates rivers because of the desiccation of the climate and that they developed agriculture when they came into close proximity with plants, animals, and water

hilly flanks theory

The theory developed
by Robert Braidwood
that agriculture was
developed in a region
where the wild
ancestors of food
plants occurred
naturally, as
apparently supported
by excavations in the
hilly flanks of the Qalat
Jarmo site in 1948

**broad spectrum
hypothesis**

A hypothesis by Kent
Flannery that argued
that domestication
and village life were
part of a complex of
factors

Kent Flannery argued that domestication and village life were part of a complex of factors he called the **broad spectrum hypothesis.** He thought the changes took place in response to changes in population pressure that took place after the last Ice Age. His broad spectrum hypothesis theory stressed a shift in dependence from large, cold adapted mammals to foraging for a wide range of wild grains and small animals that might require considerable effort, but allowed the survival of larger families.

Excavations in the Middle East showed that by 9,000 BC a gradual change to farming was well underway, but that people depended on such wild plants as einkorn wheat, wild barley, and wild rye. The evidence seems to show that increased population densities pushed the development of agriculture rather than the other way around. Attempts to keep family size small were abandoned as techniques of food acquisition and shelter construction improved. Larger village populations were useful for all the work that agriculture required. As populations increased in size, new villages spread from those that were already settled. It has also been suggested that it was the brewing of beer that motivated people to spend time domesticating food plants.

By 6,000 BC the Levant was characterized by settled villages dependent on agriculture. Some villages such as Jericho were very large with several thousand people involved in manufacturing and trade, and with a specialized but relatively small component of full time farmers and herders raising a full range of crops, sheep, goats, cattle, and pigs. A Neolithic way of life spread throughout the Middle East to Europe, Africa, and Asia.

SKIN COLOR

There is probably no other single more visible human characteristic used to classify separate human populations from each other than the color of the skin. The term "race," for most people, means skin color. At one time it was commonly accepted that there were the following races: red or copper (American Indian), white (European), black (African and Melanesians), and yellow (Chinese and Japanese). For the last thirty years there has been a movement by anthropologists to drop the word race from the scientific literature. Not only has the word race been dropped, but also we now know that the mechanics of skin coloration is exceptionally complicated, and that there are many more skin colors than there are "races." While it is our most visible characteristic, it is due to only tiny differences in the human genome, possibly as small as less than a tenth of one percent.

Skin color is easy to understand. It is a genetically based response to the amount of solar radiation in the form of ultraviolet rays coming through the atmosphere from the sun. It should not be confused with heat. Ultraviolet rays are at the extreme of the light spectrum and can age skin, produce skin cancer, and break down folate, an essential element of Vitamin B necessary for reproduction. The skin responds to radiation through the creation of melanin by *melanocytes*, which are specialized skin cells. Melanin determines skin coloration. Populations along the equator are dark because they have to process high levels of ultraviolet rays, as well as absorb Vitamin B.

Color of skin is almost directly conditioned by distance from the equator because ultraviolet rays lose their potency as one goes north or south from the equator. In order to continue capturing Vitamin B (and D), skin color becomes lighter away from the equator. This explains why the closer a population is to the equator, the darker it will be and the less it needs to tan (examples are Africans, Australians, and Melanesians) to absorb ultraviolet rays. People who are further away will also have darker skin pigmentation (Greeks, Italians, and other people from southern Europe) and will darken a great deal more without burning when exposed to sun. Populations yet further away from the equator tend to be very light skinned and are sensitive to sun. They will tend to become sunburned when exposed and may be susceptible to skin cancer (Swedes, Norwegians, northern Russians, and Laplanders). This is not because there is so little sun but because the regions are often cloudy. Further east, in the latitudes of the steppes of Russia, Mongolia, and Tibet that are mountainous and where there is greater exposure to sun, people darken to a copper tone when exposed to sunlight (and it is these populations from which the American Indian may have originally spread).

There are a few significant exceptions to these generalizations. American Indians may have migrated into the Americas only thirteen thousand years ago and spread south, but have not fully adapted to solar radiation. American Indians living near the equator have much lighter skin than Africans, Australians, or Melanesians. Those living further north and south look remarkably similar (United States and Argentina), but are much darker in skin color than Europeans from the same latitude.

While people living in the lower latitudes absorb vitamin D from the sun, they must supplement what they receive through food plants, milk, and fish in order to avoid rickets or other skeletal problems.

COLD AND HEAT ADAPTATION

Human physiology responds to heat and cold in a variety of ways also found in other animals. Studies done on members of the American military reveal several interesting responses to cold that are specific to certain populations. Eskimos can place their hands in near freezing water and still continue to manipulate objects like marbles far longer than can European Americans, who are, in turn, more cold tolerant than African Americans. Eskimos have the capacity to stimulate the flow of blood through surface capillaries of the skin in hands and fingers at higher rates than other populations. This ability would, of course, be highly adaptive in Arctic environments. Australian Aborigines, who sleep nude on the deserts of Australia where it gets cold at night, have developed a quite different adaptation to cold. When the air is cold, surface capillaries contract and force blood to flow at deeper levels, thus making the surface of the body less sensitive to cold. It has also been demonstrated that Norwegians control cold by shivering more intensely, a function which is controlled by the hypothalamus.

There are general laws of physics that apply to people and animals. In general, people and animals living around the equator tend to be small and slender with relatively long and slender arms and legs, while those living in colder climates tend to be larger and heavier with short but large arms and legs. These populations are responding to two rules derived from physics: Bergmann's rule and Allen's rule. The two laws are derived from physics and solid geometry, and are determined by the relationships between lines, areas or planes, and volumes of solid objects. Bergmann's rule is an ecological one that correlates latitude with body mass in animals. Within a species, the body mass increases with latitude and colder climate. This is because larger animals have a lower surface volume to area ratio so that they radiate less body heat per unit mass. However, cultural factors—such as diet, clothing, and recent migration—may make the rule less applicable for only some people. Allen's rule is similar to

Bergmann's rule but applies to the appendages of arms and legs. People living in cold climates may have large bodies, as do the Eskimo, but they have short and thick legs and feet in order to retain heat. By the same token, people living in hot places may have small bodies but relatively very long legs and arms, such as the Nuer and Watusi, in order to quickly dissipate heat.

There are other adaptations to heat and cold. Populations moving to equatorial climates must adapt to heat by sweating. Sweating causes body heat to dissipate to the surrounding air. While all people have the same number of sweat glands, people moving to tropical climates increase their output of liquid and have a decrease in heart rates. Those populations that are biologically adapted to tropical environments are able to process greater amounts of liquid than those who are not. It is thought dark skin color is an adaptation to heat because it causes people to sweat more, and thus cool more efficiently.

While all populations can adapt to heat, people adjust more easily to warm and humid conditions than to hot and dry conditions found in deserts. Arab populations of the Middle East, Nilotic Africans (Watusi, Nuer, Dinka), and native Australians have adapted by developing genetic dispositions towards slenderness.

These generalizations are also true for other mammals, such as bears that are smaller towards the equator than towards the North Pole. Brown bears found in North America are considerably larger than those found in southern Mexico and Central America, while Kodiak and polar bears are extremely large and are adapted to the Arctic and Subarctic. Many animals that no longer exist may have been adapted to cold environments, such as wooly mammoth, dire wolf, and many other large Pleistocene mammals.

There are several other features of the human body that respond to climate, both directly and indirectly, and have been used to define race in the past. Hair color—including the hair of the face, scalp, and body—is directly related to melanin pigmentation. People with dark skin coloration will tend to have dark hair color, and populations with light skin coloration will have light hair color. Of course, in modern populations where there has been a great deal of genetic mixing, and migration, climatic generalizations no longer apply.

The color of the eye is also determined by adaptation to solar radiation. The highest incidence of light eye color tends to come from a relatively small region of Western Europe that has cloudy winters and mildly cloudy summers. It is in this region where blue eye color is found in up to 80 percent of the population. Melanin is found in the iris of the eye, the membrane that expands and contracts to let in more or less light. The iris is structured into a set of concentric circles, and color will range from almost black to very light blue depending on the amount of melanin. In people with very little melanin, the color blue is the color of the muscles that contract and expand the iris. The varying colors of the human eye, from light blue to green, hazel, light brown, brown and brown-black, are the result of mixes of melanin in the iris and oxygen in the blood.

The structure of the hair is also related to environmental adaptations determined by heat or solar radiation. In general, northerly populations tend to have straight hair, whatever the color is. As one proceeds south to the equator, hair becomes increasingly more wavy until in regions of Africa and Melanesia, they become so wavy that hair follicles tend to separate from each other to let heat escape and give a kinky look. Straight hair is an adaptation to cold climates since hair follicles tend to lie together, keeping heat in.

There are two more heat adaptations that help create the appearance of the face and were once used in determining race. The first is the structure of the nose. In frigid climates, it is important for air to be heated before reaching delicate lung tissue. This explains Neanderthals very large nose, which shoved out the face creating a prognathic appearance (and may apply to *Homo erectus* found in northern climates). Nordic and other Scandinavian populations have long and narrow noses, as do people from northern Asia, although shapes look very different. Instead of the nose being narrow, it is flat. The opposite is true of populations living in hot climates where it is important not to heat the air going to the lungs. This is accomplished by making the nostrils very wide and to shorten the distance to the lungs.

Lips also adapt to heat and cold since they are temperature and moisture sensitive. They act to dissipate heat; this is accomplished through their aversion or widening, which is typical of people in hot climates such as West Africa and Melanesia. Thin lips, such as found in northern populations, are meant to preserve heat and are typical of north Europeans as well as north Asians.

Two populations that are genetically not related show how parallel adaptations can give people very similar appearances. Black populations from West Africa are extremely similar to black populations from Melanesia. A century ago, many physical anthropologists wanted to classify them together because they have dark skin, frizzy hair, wide lips, broad but shallow noses, and slender torsos but long arms and legs. However, these populations are not genetically related. Their similarities are due not to historical connections but to genetic adaptations.

HIGH ALTITUDE ADAPTATIONS

Some human populations must adapt to high altitude where oxygen is thin, and they do so in similar ways. People who are not adapted to thin air such as found in Denver, Colorado, or La Paz, Bolivia, may find rapid movement difficult. Only after several months will they adapt to their habitats at altitudes higher than thirteen thousand feet. While they can become acclimated as their hearts learn to beat faster, and lungs may increase a little in size, they will not be able to compete with native populations. For example, in the Peruvian Andes, Native Aymara speakers have up to 30 percent more red blood cells than similar populations living at sea levels. The right ventrical of the heart is also often larger in order to pump a greater volume of blood into the lungs. It was once theorized that high altitude populations would be less fertile than those at sea level, but recent research has shown this is not true. However, respiratory ailments among infants do lead to higher mortality rates; and highland populations tend to have lower birth rates, larger placenta, slower rates of maturation, and delayed sexual maturity that may be adaptations to higher altitudes.

Populations coming from high altitudes are prone to problems at sea level because they are not adjusted to higher levels of oxygen. They may be prone to dizziness and nausea, which are temporary and they must adjust slowly to the new climate.

NUTRITION

Human beings must also adapt to the kinds of foods that they eat and to increased population densities. The agricultural revolution, which began about ten thousand years ago in the Middle East, had a profound effect on nutrition. Not only was there more food for a larger population, but also agriculture allowed women to bear more children in a lifetime than when they were hunter-gatherers. Hunter-gatherers are generally limited to two to three children that live to survival, in part because women have to nurse young children until they are old enough to consume cooked food (about three years old). Once animals, such as cows, sheep, or goats, and grains were domesticated, children could be fed cooked and pre-masticated grains with milk. The domestication of plants and animals led to women bearing and caring for many more children each generation, which explains the sudden increase in populations with the Neolithic (although exact estimates are not available).

While the Neolithic may have stimulated increased populations, it also led to other problems. While larger populations could be supported, the impact of infectious diseases increased geometrically as populations became more urbanized. The plagues that visited ancient Europe and Asia can be explained in terms of crowding and unsanitary living conditions. As generation followed generation, and many people died from diseases, people developed immunities to certain diseases such as measles, tuberculosis, chicken pox, and small pox. There were other side effects to the introduction of agriculture. As people shifted from diets dependent on animal proteins, they became increasingly vegetarian and dependent on carbohydrates. While there are food plants that are high in protein, such as many nuts and berries, they are also more difficult to grow and process than are grains or root crops. Calcium, which is needed for bone building, was often not available. Populations adjusted to the lack of calcium, diseases, and poor nutrition by becoming smaller with narrower chest cavities. Often, there were class differences in nutrition because meat and milk were available to the upper classes, bringing about differences in size. Upper class knights were often taller and heavier than lower class peasant soldiers.

The degree to which populations genetically adapted to various diseases over eons can be understood when examining the response of American Indian populations to diseases brought to the New World. One of the world's most horrific demographic experiences was the decrease of American Indians in the sixteenth century. The continental population of the Americas suffered a population reduction of 90 percent, while the people of the Caribbean, mostly speakers of Carib, were totally annihilated. Tribal populations living on the interior of South America still suffer from exposure to European diseases.

Changes in diet due to improvement of foods were common in the nineteenth century to Europeans, and many regions of the world today are responding to dietary changes. However, serious dietary problems are also widespread throughout the world. It has been estimated that between 16 percent to 63 percent of the world's population is undernourished. As Lappe and Collins (1982) have pointed out, the problem is not one of food. At the heart of the problem are political and economic structures that distort the distribution of resources. China, which was once undernourished, went through changes in land ownership and in the distribution of food; today few are hungry. India, Pakistan, and many Latin American countries continue to have land misused by elites when land is put into the production of certain products meant for export: tobacco, cotton, sugar cane, hemp, bananas, and coffee. In certain countries, such as Brazil and Argentina, vast tracts of land are used to raise livestock, which local populations cannot afford to buy (although both countries have gone through political changes that have led to more equitable distributions of food). Export commodities are usually sent from high debt countries to countries that own those debts. The debts in question are often several decades old and are the consequence of policies that allow the elites of poor countries to import manufactured goods in exchange for export commodities. This relationship has been given the name of "dependency" by world system theorists, a topic we will examine later.

Malnutrition means more than being hungry. Malnutrition causes problems in reproduction and in infant survival. Mothers who are not adequately nourished have more difficulty with labor, more premature births, more children who have birth defects, and more children who are smaller than they should be and often do not live beyond five years. Those who survive often suffer from other diseases, including brain damage.

It is clear to researchers that the solutions to world food problems lie in the realm of political and economic organization.

■   ■   ■

Chapter
Summary

Human Biological and Cultural Evolution

Evolutionary anthropology rests on two key concepts that emerged in the late nineteenth century as Darwin's theory of evolution and the anthropological concept of culture became popular. Darwin's theory differed from other speculative and religious theories in that it rested (and rests) on science. Science explains relationships between observable and measurable objects, unlike religion which explains the non-observable and non-measurable. Once these key concepts are accepted, everything else about Darwinism and culture are easily understood. Darwin himself had to move between religious and scientific concepts and the idea that he was an atheist is not true. The theory of evolution is based on 1) variation and 2) natural selection. Variation is based on the now known fact that DNA tends to become varied due to solar radiation, while natural selection refers to the way nature selects certain of those variations to survive. As is well known, it was Mendel whose Laws of Inheritance explained the mathematical relations between dominant and recessive alleles and helped make sense of Darwin's theory as applied to animals.

Changes in human evolution had to wait for an understanding of culture, largely explained in the twentieth century by cultural anthropology, covered in the text. This rests on an explanation of the evolution of the Primate Order, which began 63 million years ago with the first mammals. Much of our understanding of those changes rests on changes in the structure of the hand from an organ used to grasp tree limbs to the manufacture of tools. Australopithecus is understood to be the first tool-making apelike hominid that evolved into our upright ancestor Homo erectus. Homo erectus is the form that spread stone tools and culture throughout Africa, then Europe and Asia, and then became Homo sapiens sapiens, who spread to the New World about ten thousand years ago.

Chapter
Terms

anthropoid	84	**hominoid**	84
australopithecines	89	**Neolithic Revolution**	103
broad spectrum hypothesis	104	**pongid**	84
Fertile Crescent	103	**religious statement**	77
hilly flanks theory	104	**scientific statement**	77
hominid	84		

Check out our website
www.BVTLab.com
for flashcards,
chapter summaries,
and more.

Chapter 3
Development of Anthropological Theory

Introduction: The Idea of Paradigm in Anthropology

In the Introduction chapter, we described anthropology as "the study of humankind and all its manifestations in all times and places." We went on to explain that anthropology is made up of four subdisciplines: biological anthropology, linguistics, archaeology or prehistoric studies, and cultural anthropology. Some elements of anthropology are very close to science, others resemble natural history, and other elements are more similar to the humanities. Many anthropologists define the discipline as a science, but such definitions ignore the importance of natural history and humanities topics in anthropology. For that reason we are more comfortable using the term "paradigm" when referring to anthropology or other social sciences.

Philosophers of science have adopted the term paradigm to distinguish true science from other disciplines that are like science, but are not as rigorous, such as natural history and social science. The term is found in Thomas Kuhn's *Structure of the Scientific Revolutions* (1962). The *American Heritage Dictionary* defines a paradigm as "a set of assumptions, concepts, and practices that constitute a way of viewing reality for the community that share them, particularly in an intellectual discipline." The term paradigm is a useful concept for anthropology, the other social sciences, and natural history.

All approaches to knowledge have their strengths and weaknesses, and there are many distinct paradigms. Science, Kuhn argues, is one type of paradigm based on three criteria: quantitative analysis, the testing of hypotheses, and the use of experimental controls. However, while allowing great control and rigor, science is much more narrowly focused than the social sciences (including anthropology) or natural history. The social sciences and natural history, in turn, have the advantage of breadth and in studies of the context of behavior. The natural historian, for example, has the advantage of studying chimpanzees and elephants in their wild settings using approaches not usually available to a scientific methodology that must isolate behavior in laboratory settings.

The same is true of cultural anthropology, which a few anthropologists have defined as a type of natural history. History and anthropology share the need to interpret certain facts. For the historian, the facts often come in the shape of text, while for the anthropologist the facts come in the form of interviews and observations of how cultures operate. The subject of cultural anthropology is culture. Culture is symbolic and cannot be studied experimentally nor can symbols be observed, counted, or weighed; thus it cannot be a science as Kuhn defines it. The study of culture is both the strength and weakness of anthropology. As we explained in Chapter 1, culture is humankind's most striking adaptation to nature; however, it can only be understood by getting into the mind of a native informant. Cultural anthropologists, or ethnographers, have developed techniques that allow them considerable rigor, but the discipline cannot be like the paradigm set up by Kuhn.

What is particularly difficult is achieving the objectivity of science. While the objectivity of science is the goal for cultural anthropology it is best understood as a type of natural history, not true science. That is, it is based on observation but not testing. The fact that anthropology is not a true science bothers many analysts of human society; but history, law, most of social science, and most observations about human behavior also belong to the realm of natural history, not science. The nature of cultural anthropology has led anthropologists to explain it as a very difficult science and not a non-science. Most human knowledge falls into the realm of natural history.

Cultural anthropologists who are trained in the holistic, four-discipline approach of the discipline are often trained in scientific disciplines as well as more humanistic ethnographic techniques. For example, techniques used to date fossils and artifacts require training in chemistry and physics. Research in physical anthropology or archaeology also requires knowledge of botany, zoology, and paleontology. Similarly, cultural anthropologists, depending on their interests, may receive training in comparative literature, philosophy, political science, and history. Many are also trained in folklore, folk music, and folk dancing. Applied and medical anthropologists may find themselves depending on knowledge in business or health methodologies. While anthropology may approach science in its objectives, it is a paradigm of science and not a true science. The meaning of paradigm may be murky, but its use will become clear as we look into the origins of anthropology. The history of anthropology means the study of changing paradigms through time, going back to the very first ideas about science.

Shifting Paradigms: Aristotle, Plato, and the *Scala Naturae*

The history of paradigms in western history is useful for an understanding of the history of science, as well as an understanding of other paradigms in the history of Western Civilization. Anthropological paradigms based on the ideas of science are generally assumed to have developed in the nineteenth century, but many scholars argue that their antecedents are found in the ideas of Greek philosophers who lived during the "Golden Age of Greece." It was during this period that Greece produced its most famous philosophers, among whom three are considered to be instrumental to the development of logic, the natural history approach, and, finally, modern science. First was Socrates (469–399 BC), who believed it was important to see through cultural conventions and not just to manipulate them or to be manipulated by them. Second came his most famous student Plato (427–347 BC); and third was Aristotle (384–322), who in turn was Plato's most famous student (Erickson and Murphy 2003, 23–25). The knowledge acquired and created by Aristotle, which included the writings of Plato and other Greek philosophers, was practiced by Alexander the Great, who was not only one of the great military leaders of history but was also a brilliant scholar. It was he who combined the great ideas of other philosophers in his work and became one of the creators of Western Civilization.

On Alexander's death in 323 BC, the ideas of the Greek philosophers were spread throughout the then civilized world of that time, and then were adopted by political and scientific thinkers during the rise of the Roman Empire. Many Greek ideas regarding the universe became central to the Hellenic Religion, including Plato's ideas of divine beings and universal laws, while Aristotle's philosophic writings supplied the ideas of natural science and what became the ***Scala Naturae,*** or **natural ladder of life**. The natural ladder of life is the taxonomy of animal and plant species developed by Greek and Roman thinkers, originally organized into a religious overview, but which gradually became an evolutionary paradigm. As one can imagine, the *Scala Naturae* has gone through many changes from Greek and Roman times. Cultural, political, demographic, and economic changes have profoundly influenced the *Scala Naturae.*

One of the greatest changes occurred towards the end of the Roman Empire when social conditions deteriorated and Christianity attracted oppressed social classes. While early Christians were persecuted by the Roman state, the religion became central to the organization of what was left of the Roman Empire, absorbing Hellenism, the state religion of Rome based on the worship of Jupiter, Apollo, and other gods. Christianity emerged as scholars made the religion historically acceptable to the masses, but elements of Greek and Roman religion remained, particularly its structure. God, Christ, and the disciples replaced Jupiter, Apollo, and other Greek and Roman gods. Christianity, based on Jewish history, was transformed into the Catholic Church and became the state religion. Many Greek and Roman temples were transformed into Christian cathedrals. The most important Church Father was the Bishop of Hippo in northern Africa, also known as Saint Augustine (354–430), whose two books, *Confessions* (AD 397) and *The City of God* (c. 425), fused the gospels with Plato's theory of the universe.

What did the new religion look like? It combined much Roman, Greek, and Jewish theology with another based on the life of Jesus Christ. Remember that there was much more to religion than the Old Testament and the New Testament. There was much written on religious history, the history of the universe, and natural history based on Aristotle's *Scala*

■Socrates (469–399 BC) believed it was important to see through cultural conventions and not just to manipulate them or to be manipulated by them.

Scala Naturae

Also called natural ladder of life, the taxonomy of animal and plant species developed by Greek and Roman thinkers, which gradually became an evolutionary paradigm

Naturae. While we have the tendency to view the Middle Ages as not scientific, Aristotle's *Scala Naturae* supplied many crucial ideas that would later become central to natural history. This worldview organized all known minerals, vegetables, primitive and advanced animals, and humans into a pyramid with humankind on top. This was the *Scala Naturae*, which is still with us but much modified by modern science.

The *Scala Naturae* was familiar to the Greek and Romans of antiquity; however, Saint Augustine added the Platonic idea of a creator being, God, at the top, with Christ, Joseph, and Mary just a level beneath and the mass of humankind just under. This magical worldview became theology and was not conducive to science. According to Saint Augustine, God was all-powerful, all knowing, and unknowable; therefore it was pointless to study God or nature. The paradigm that emerged from the fusion of Aristotelian and Platonic philosophy is known as Scholasticism, which became the basis for knowledge in the Middle Ages. According to the Scholastics, everything to be known about humanity, nature, or God was revealed in Scripture. However, there was still room for some questioning because Aristotle had been an empiricist and he had not collected and described everything in the world, a task that was taken up by many Scholastics whose methods became the basis of natural history (Erickson and Murphy 2003, 25). Anthropology emerged from the empirical dimension of the *Scala Naturae* that focused on human evolution in the eighteenth and nineteenth centuries.

In order to keep the then known world in intellectual order, Scholasticism had to ensure that natural history and the Word of God remained consistent with one another. This was accomplished through the work of scholarly commentators, but cracks began to appear in St. Augustine's universe. New challenges to the *Scala Naturae* appeared that allowed anthropology to emerge, along with many other scientific and natural science disciplines. Scholasticism, a natural history theology slowly became converted to natural science. One of the key figures in the conversion of Scholasticism to science was Thomas Aquinas. According to Erickson and Murphy, when Islamic Moors invaded Christian Spain they carried with them the original writings of Plato and Aristotle before they had become adulterated. Thomas Aquinas (c. AD 1225–1274) acquired these writings and thus developed a very different vision of God than that of St. Augustine. Aquinas produced a new theology that was based on a rational universe, and not a magical kingdom created by God in six days. This new paradigm considered it acceptable for human reason to bear on theology. The Christianity of Aquinas was a kind of "medieval synthesis," which brought together natural history, the study of people (humanism), and God (religion). However, two centuries after Aquinas had opened Scholasticism to internal

■A new Christianity emerged as scholars made the religion historically acceptable to the masses; basing the faith on the life of Jesus Christ but maintaining some elements of Greek and Roman religion.

debates, new discoveries around the world by explorers and the excavations by amateur archaeologists, not to mention the studies of the skies by astronomers, caused the Thomistic synthesis to unravel (Erickson and Murphy 2003, 27). The events that dissolved the synthesis became known as the Enlightenment: the voyages of discovery, archaeological excavations, and the Scientific Revolution. The challenges did not occur in any single order, but happened almost simultaneously.

Above all, while these changes were occurring, the Great Chain of Being, in the form of natural history, continued to be accepted by most thinkers as the dominant paradigm. It was difficult for anyone to imagine any other universal framework, but each critical thinker would chip away at its vast edifice until, as Loren Eiseley has suggested, it was radically transformed into Darwin's theory of evolution (Eiseley 1958). The subject of evolution is contentious, but for many modern intellectuals evolutionary theory has replaced the Great Chain of Being as the most acceptable way to view the history of the world. Many would argue it is as much a mistake to completely ignore religion as it was for St. Augustine to ignore science.

The Voyages of Discovery and the Enlightenment

One reason for the emergence of the Enlightenment was the discovery of the New World, as well as other unknown lands and people. Moslem Arabs cut off trade between Europe and Asia in the tenth century, forcing explorers to find new trade routes for several hundred years. In the thirteenth century, Marco Polo (c. 1254–1324) spent seventeen years at the court of Kublai Khan, the Mongolian ruler of China. The information he collected and the goods he brought home spurred explorers to discover new routes to the Orient. Prince Henry of Portugal (also known as Prince Henry the Navigator, 1394–1460) is recognized for helping finance many of the early explorations and discoveries leading to those made by Columbus. Prince Henry died in 1460, a full thirty-two years before Christopher Columbus (c. 1446–1506) discovered the "New World" in 1492. During this period, many explorers discovered new lands and described them, particularly around coastal Africa. Columbus' discoveries stimulated explorations by others once the King and Queen of Spain, who published his exploits in newsletters, circulated the stories of his travels. Among the more famous explorers were Vasco da Gama (c. 1444–1506) who in 1499 navigated around Africa and India, Vasco Núñez de Balboa (c. 1475–1517) who discovered the Pacific Ocean in 1513, and Ferdinand Magellan who circumnavigated the world in 1522 (Erickson and Murphy 2003, 30).

The discovery of new lands, people, plants, and animals forced geographers, zoologists, and botanists to rethink the form the world was in and to revise the sacred *Scala Naturae*; but while there were challenges to this world view, it was not abandoned. The attempt to fit new forms of life into Aristotle's vision of the universe produced many challenges to Scholasticism, but they were met by appeals to the Bible (c. 1444–1506) and other theological works. According to Thomistic reasoning, newly discovered people around the world were "natural slaves" because they were imperfect human beings and needed the protection of the Church; however, contradictions with the idea of natural slaves soon arose within Scholastic philosophy. For example, if natural slaves were imperfect humans, then they could not have souls, thus making the work of missionaries meaningless. Yet much of the rationale for the Spanish and Portuguese colonization of the New World was exactly the need to save the souls of indigenous peoples. The proposition that

■It was initially believed that the souls of Africans and other dark skinned peoples could not be saved because they did not fit into the Biblical story of Noah and the lost tribes of Israel.

half the world could not be incorporated into the Catholic Church forced missionaries, such as Bartalomé de Las Casas (1474–1566) and José de Acosta (c. 1539–1600), to redefine these peoples as "natural children" instead of "natural slaves" creating a rationale for their salvation. This logic produced the argument that the people of the New World were members of the human family, and church scholars searched how this could be so. They found their answer in the story of the dispersal of the sons of Noah and their tribes upon the destruction of the Tower of Babel. The Indians, it was decided, were natural children because they were the descendants of Israelis who had migrated to the New World (Erickson and Murphy 2003, 33). Once it was possible to think of newly discovered peoples as human, the door was open to legal debates over whether they could be enslaved, a topic the Thomistic Father Las Casas would try to remedy with the New Laws of 1542, which made it against the law to use Indians as slaves (Nuccetelli 2002, 93–129).

While the souls of the indigenous peoples of the New World and Asia could be saved, those of Africans and other dark skinned peoples could not because they did not fit into the Biblical story of Noah and the lost tribes of Israel. Thus they could not be considered natural children, and they could be made slaves. While New World Indians could not be enslaved, other means were created to force the children of God to work like slaves.

Another interpretation on the origins of the Indians was that they were descendants of the survivors of the sunken continent of Atlantis, written about by Plato in his dialogues *Timaeus and Critias*. While Plato invented the story for allegorical purposes, many used this story to explain how the American Indian had degenerated from a great race of Mound Builders that lived thousands of years ago. Those who colonized the new lands could not believe that it was the people who lived there that were responsible for the ancient civilizations, some of which were not ancient at all. Documents showing that the cities of the Aztecs, Maya, and Inca were inhabited by their builders when they were colonized by Spaniards in the sixteenth century and whose existence was ignored for two centuries.

The profession of anthropology emerged as those trained in human-oriented natural history took opposed sides on the debate about human origins. Central to the debate was the topic of slavery. The debate between slaveholders and abolitionists in the United States looked to the newly developing discipline of anthropology for evidence supporting both sides. Research uncovered many languages and physical types that were previously unknown, leading to two schools of thought. One was the **monogenesis** school which argued the existence of a single "mound builder" race that had degenerated into many races over time, while a second school, called the **polygenesis** school, argued that God had created many distinct races to fit into the distinct environments of the world (Erickson and Murphy 2003, 33).

These two points of view played important roles in the period leading up to the American Civil War and after in struggles for civil rights by both American Indians

monogenesis

A theory of human origin that argues the existence of a single "mound builder" race that degenerated into many races over time

polygenesis

A theory of human origin that argues that God created many distinct races to fit into the distinct environments of the world

and African Americans. While the origins and development of the native peoples of the New World were debated, the primary topic would become the origins of Africans and the relationships of blacks to whites. Confusion over the nature of race was due to a lack of understanding of culture and how it related to biology. It was assumed, for example, that what we know today to be the languages and cultures of Asians were superior to those of Indians, that Indians and their cultures and languages were superior to Africans, and that all three were inferior to whites. These debates took place in spite of the fact that the Africans in question spoke American English, which had replaced their native languages. While early in the nineteenth century the arguments of anthropologists often supported racist positions, they became great supporters of the values of the Enlightenment as E. B. Tylor's definition of culture (explained in Chapter 1) came to be widely accepted. After the 1870s, anthropology can be regarded as an intellectual achievement of the Enlightenment whose humanistic point of view continues into the present.

Formative Anthropology

The formative period of anthropology is its earliest phase, belonging to the seventeenth century with the writings of the philosophers of the Enlightenment and lasting until late in the nineteenth century when Darwin's theory of evolution became dominant in scientific thinking. Anthropology emerged as a distinct discipline with its focus on the origin and distribution of *Homo sapiens*. While the Enlightenment is generally considered the age for the origins of humanistic thinking, democracy, and ideas of human rights, it was intellectually limited. Most Enlightenment thinkers tended towards racist ideas that dominated the period until the beginning of the twentieth century (and continues in many places into the twenty-first century). Anthropology is one of many disciplines that appeared during the Enlightenment adopting Darwinian evolutionary theory. It was one of the few disciplines to challenge racist ideas with empirical research. Its most important contribution was the development of the concept of culture, and its separation from the concept of race that Franz Boas used to challenge racist theory.

The basic problem facing Boas and other anthropologists was the use of the conceptual framework of the *Scala Naturae*, which was a typology of plants and animals that used the concept of race. Many discoveries shed light on the antiquity of human beings, but these did not fit into the commonly accepted ideas on creation theory. Glynn Daniel, a writer on the intellectual history of anthropology, has explained how the early archaeologists used language that fit in with their Biblical point of view—calling ancient spear and arrowheads "thunderbolts, fairy arrows, and elfshot." Some scientists and amateur archaeologists were truly creative. For example, Ulisses Aldrovandi, a seventeenth century zoologist, explained ancient stone tools as "due to an admixture of certain exhalations of thunder and lightening with metallic matter, chiefly in dark clouds, which is conglutinated into a mass (like flour with water) and subsequently indurated by heat, like brick." Tollius, a zoologist from Antiquity, claimed that chipped flints were "generated in the sky by a fulgurous exhalation conglobed in a cloud by the circumposed humor." Another typical explanation favored by clerics of various religions was that the objects found in the ground were placed there by God to test the beliefs of Christians in the authenticity of the Bible (Daniel 1962, 19).

Despite the discovery of ancient fossils and artifacts, it was difficult for writers to abandon the dates of the Bible. It should be kept in mind that the Bible acted as the charter for Western

Civilization, and it was taken literally along with the *Scala Naturae*. In 1648, James Ussher, the Anglican Archbishop of Armagh, published *Annals of the Ancient and New Testaments*, in which he counted the "begats" in the Bible and estimated the day of creation as 4004 BC. Not to be outdone, John Lightfoot, one of Ussher's contemporaries, fine-tuned Ussher's date to October 23 at 9:00 A.M, which was thought to have occurred before the Great Flood. This led a few researchers to coin the term "antediluvian" for objects that must have been deposited in the soil before that event. However, there were problems with such dates: the objects that were found in the soil appeared very old. A few analysts of fossils and artifacts grew skeptical about dates derived from the Bible. For example, Sir William Dugdale in his *History of War-wickshire*, published in 1650, declared that stone tools he had found were "Weapons used by the Britons before the making arms of brass or iron was known"; and De la Peyerere, another amateur archaeologist, declared that stone tools were made by some race existing before the time of Adam and Eve (Daniel 1964, 19–25). There were many researchers who could not believe what they saw and tried to find other explanations, such as chance. For example, in 1771, Johann Friedrich Esper, a priest, dug a cave site near Bamberg, Germany, where he found an extinct cave bear associated with human bones. His comment reflects the problems many had in the restricted time framework with which they dealt:

> I dare not presume without any sufficient reason these human members be of the same age as the other animals petrifications (fossils). They must have got there by chance…. (Daniel 1962, 42).

Daniel reports another amateur archaeologist in France that found seven human skulls associated with mammoth bones, but could get no one to believe him. Fossil hunters could not escape the Bible. For example, Father J. MacEnery, who had to dig through a ceiling of solid stalagmites to access fossils and artifacts, had the same trouble. Dean Buckland, one of MacEnry's detractors, discovered a similar site and decided the bones had to be intrusive, perhaps due to a burial. MacEnry gave his discovery a date only going back to Greco-Roman times (Daniel 1962, 43).

The Bible and *Scala Naturae*, despite all kinds of challenges, were difficult to abandon. Among those who could not abandon the theological explanation for the creation of the universe was the famous "namer," Carolus Linneaus (1707–1778). It was he who first modified Aristotle's *Scala Naturae* into a hierarchy of taxonomic categories using a system of *binomial nomenclature* familiar to every student of zoology and biology, which included the concept of race at the bottom of his hierarchy. Linneaus' system of naming and taxonomy building took him a lifetime. He thought it reflected "the secret cabinet of God." However, many theoreticians were approaching a modern theory of evolution. Loren Eiseley in *The Age of Darwin* thought that Linneaus' formulation (which stayed inside of dates of the Bible) predicted the outline of evolution described by Darwin (Eiseley 1958, 69–75).

Despite Linneaus' care to stay inside Biblically acceptable dates, evidence continued to accumulate that such reasoning led to dogmatic and unrealistic thinking. In order to salvage Ussher's dates, but make sense of the evidence, some scientists adopted "catastrophic doctrines" according to which the world had been made over many times due to floods, glaciers, volcanoes, earthquakes, and other catastrophes. The disasters were God's creations, replacing the single flood of Noah. Among the most famous was George Cuvier (1769–1832), the French founder of vertebrate pale-ontology. One of his students estimated that there had been twenty-seven catastrophes at the end of which God had recreated the world as we know it, coming tantalizing close to the idea of evolutionary change (Eiseley 1958, 69–75).

A more familiar name is Jean-Baptiste Pierre Antoine de Monet Lamarck (1744–1802) who tried to develop an alternative to Cuvier's catastrophic doctrine through his theory on the "inheritance of acquired characteristics." According to this doctrine, animals could pass on characteristics acquired during a lifetime by passing tiny changes to themselves on to their off-spring, thus speeding up evolution to fit within Ussher's six thousand-year time period. The most famous example of this theory was that of the giraffe, who stretched its long neck each generation to gain access to the tops of trees and passed its increasingly longer neck on down through the millennia (Erickson and Murphy 2003, 63).

The difficulty of rejecting Ussher's dates helps to explain why Louis Agassiz, one of the founders of paleontology in the United States, insisted on Cuvier's catastrophic doctrine in his own work. Agassiz became very famous for replacing dates based on Biblical floods with evidence on dates due to the expansion and contraction of European glaciers. Due to his work on glaciers in Western Europe, which he used to date fossils, he was appointed to Harvard University in 1848 and became one of the university's luminaries. He created its Museum of Comparative Zoology in 1860, only a year after the publication of Charles Darwin's *Origin of Species* (1859). Despite Agassiz' profound understanding of comparative vertebrate and invertebrate anatomy, particularly of fishes, he became a fierce anti-evolutionist, after the appearance of Darwin's theory, and remained so until his death in 1873. Despite his own knowledge of fossils, he was unable to abandon the influence of the Bible (Menand 2001, 97–140).

Agassiz was not alone. After the appearance of Darwin's theory, many well known scientists rejected evolutionary theory, but not because of a lack of knowledge. The knowledge held by natural historians in the late eighteenth and early nineteenth century of fossils and their relationship to modern life forms was extensive. Their inability to view these as having dates that preceded 4004 BC shows us how difficult it must have been to challenge the theological view of the universe that dominated their time period. The problems of the late nineteenth century help shed light on our own time, when people of great knowledge find it difficult to give up their religious views of the universe for Darwinian evolution.

However, with hard work the earth yielded up evidence for a new point of view on the part of researchers. Three-quarters of a century before Agassiz was appointed to Harvard, in 1785, James Hutton (1726–97), an evolutionary geologist published his *Theory of the Earth: or an Investigation of the Laws Observable in the Composition, Dissolution, and Restoration of Land Upon the Globe* which claimed greater antiquity for the earth than 4004 BC. Another geologist, William ("Strata") Smith, a hydraulic engineer concerned with reclaiming land from the sea, traced fossils found in coal mines throughout Great Britain that he called the "thread of life." He argued the history of fossils could only be explained by accepting a great antiquity for the earliest geological levels (Peacock and Kirsch 1980, 38). Also challenging Cuvier and Agassiz was one of the most important publications of the nineteenth century, Charles Lyell's *Principles of Geology* published

■ According to the inheritance of acquired characteristics theory, the giraffe stretched its long neck each generation to gain access to the tops of trees and passed its increasingly longer neck on down through the millennia.

in 1830. Lyell's work basically explained Hutton's original thesis. Hutton's publication was notoriously difficult to read, and Lyell's clearly expressed a "theory of uniformitarianism" which was the opposite of catastrophism. Lyell's much more clearly written book was widely read and received public support. One young reader was Charles Darwin, who adopted Lyell's work into his own. Lyell, following Hutton, explained that most of the dramatic physical changes that had occurred to the world could be explained in terms of natural, everyday events: rainfall, snowstorms, volcanism, flooding, and so on. He argued, as had Hutton, against the idea of worldwide catastrophes. It was Lyell's concept of uniformitarianism that would be one of the building blocks of Darwin's 1859 theory of evolution in *Origin of Species* (Eiseley 1958, 75–81).

EVOLUTIONARY THEORY AND RACISM IN FORMATIVE ANTHROPOLOGY

Darwin's theory of evolution offered an alternative to the *Scala Naturae* that came to be adopted by the scientific community. It would be another century before astronomy, chemistry, and physics developed dating techniques to accurately gauge the age of the earth and the universe, such as Potassium-Argon and Radiocarbon-14 dating. However, well before the middle twentieth century, most writers on evolution had adopted much earlier dates for human origins than those based on the Bible. While Darwin's theory replaced the *Scala Naturae* with a new and novel worldview, the theory brought about a new problem with old roots: the concept of race reared its very ugly head and came to dominate the new discipline of anthropology.

Before Darwin's theory of evolution, the term "race" was just as apt to be applied to characteristics that today are known to be learned, along with physical variations of distinct forms of *Homo sapiens*. Another term that might be used as an alternative was "civilization." It was not at all unusual for people to talk and to write about distinctions between the Irish race or civilization and the English race or civilization, which would sound peculiar today. Yet whether people talked or wrote about race or civilization, they assumed that people with light colored skin were superior to those with dark colored skin.

The term race is extremely controversial today, and many anthropologists have disputed its existence for a half-century. Other anthropologists adopt the idea that there is such a thing as race, but that it should only be used to refer to human physical or biological variability, and not to behavior. After Darwin's theory became popular, anthropologists and biologists continued to confused culture and biology. It was only when Franz Boas made his point of view central to the creation of classic anthropology that the myth of race begin to dissipate, but that would not happen until the beginning of the twentieth century.

Anthropological and ethnological societies were founded beginning in the middle of the nineteenth century in Europe and the United States as theories of cultural evolution became popular. With a few exceptions, they dealt with general, comparative, and evolutionary themes adopting the racial mythology of the age. Among the better known works were Gustav Klemm's *Allgemein Kulturgeschischte des Menshheit (Universal History of Man)*, a seven volume work published between 1843–1851; Johann Bachofen's *Das Mutterrecht (The Mother-right)* published in 1861; John McLennan's *Primitive Marriage: An Inquiry into the Origins of the Form of Capture in Marriage Ceremonies;* Sir Henry Maine's *Ancient Law, Its Connection with the Early History of Society and its Relation to Modern Ideas*, both published in 1861; Lewis Henry Morgan's *Systems of Consanguinity and Affinity of the Human Family* in 1871, and his *Ancient Society, or Researches into the Lines of Human Progress* in

1877; Sir James Frazer's *Golden Bough*, a multivolume series appearing in the 1890s; and Alfred Haddon's *The Study of Man* in 1889, which continued to develop evolutionary thinking but without abandoning Biblical dates (Peacock and Kirsch 1980, 40). The major topics covered in these works were kinship, forms of "primitive marriage," the origin of the state, and religion. There was little stress given economics, technology, or ecology, with the exception of Lewis Henry Morgan whose writings were surprisingly advanced for the age but trapped by the myth of race.

Loren Eiseley, the noted science writer, calls the nineteenth century the Age of Darwin due to the importance of evolutionary theories (Eiseley 1958). Anthropology emerged as a distinct evolutionary worldview by the 1850s. According to James Peacock and Thomas Kirsch, these works compared the similarities and differences of the people of the world, developing such methods as comparative history and coining key terms such as "endogamy," "exogamy," "couvade," and "totemism" (Peacock and Kirsch 1980, 40). The writers agreed that the subject of anthropology was all of humankind in all times and places, and that their approach to this vast subject "should be holistic—including biological, psychological, social, cultural, linguistic, and historical dimensions." In addition, the approach should be naturalistic and inductive, not speculative or deductive: and it should lack the theological presuppositions typical of earlier works (Peacock and Kirsch 1980, 41).

The approach of the writers of the middle nineteenth century sound very modern, but behind this scholarly scientific façade was the implicit assumption that modern, white, European peoples were superior to all other peoples. Race was a key word; however, racist explanation did not belong to God or the Bible, which say nothing about race. The important phrase is the term "natural selection," developed by evolutionary theorists in the eighteenth and nineteenth centuries. The popular argument was not that God made races but that superior and inferior races had emerged through a "struggle for survival." The idea of a "struggle for survival" is not found in the Bible. It meant competition between different variants of humans that led to whites being able to create world empires, while non-whites were meant to serve them. There were many debates on how certain races had appeared, succeeded, and then failed to compete with Europeans.

There were two schools of evolutionary thinking: *unilinear evolution* and *diffusionism*. However, according to Marvin Harris, these two schools of thought continued to confuse biology and culture until well into the twentieth century (Harris 1968). Throughout the world of science in the nineteenth century, there was no clear idea of the difference between biology and culture, culture and behavior, or behavior and biology. The ideas of civilization, progress, and evolution were also confused. The science of anthropology was closer to a type of "folk taxonomy" of societies around the world based on armchair speculation by an intellectual community that depended more on myth than any objective science. What they created looked like science, but it was really pseudo-science. The acceptance of evolutionary race-based thinking was not only that of anthropologists but belonged to most "sciences" that dealt with human beings—such as sociology, psychology, and economics. Mid-nineteenth century economists argued, for, example, that Africans should be slaves because of their innate inferiority, which led them to be slaves. This is a good example of circular thinking.

Unilinear evolution assumed that all of the most advanced cultures had passed through the same stages called savagery, barbarism, and civilization, or had stopped at one of the first two stages. Evolution was explained as due to a "struggle for survival" or "survival of the fittest" not a design by God. **Diffusion theory**, which appears the opposite of evolutionary theory, was really a form of evolutionary theory that stressed

unilinear evolution

The idea that all of the most advanced cultures had passed through the same stages—savagery, barbarism, and civilization—or had stopped at one of the first two stages

diffusion theory

The idea that cultures have devolved or degenerated from earlier, advanced civilization(s), such as ancient Egypt

space rather than time. There were two schools of diffusion theory, a British version associated with G. Elliot Smith and William Perry, and a German version associated with Father Wilhelm Schmidt. British diffusionism speculated that the most important characteristics of modern civilization could be traced back to ancient Egypt, the first civilization to be created, or so it was thought. We know today that there were yet more ancient civilizations. Diffusionists thought those cultures, which no longer had Egyptian traits, were "degenerate" (in a biological as well as a cultural sense) with their peoples having forgotten Egyptian culture, or "devolved." The German school argued that there were several early centers for civilization, a point of view that was called Kulturkreise (culture circles). It, too, argued that those cultures that did not fall within the definition of civilization had degenerated (devolved) from earlier civilizations.

Cultural evolution, whatever school it belonged to, was viewed as a process of mental improvement based on race. Those who belonged to "superior" cultures had obviously evolved to a higher level of intelligence or race (a theory which is repeated today in the "Bell curve theory" of Richard Herrnstein and Charles Murray 1994). While Darwinian evolution replaced Biblical ideas of origins, race became the dominant term in evolutionary theory. This theory was based on Darwin's principle of survival of the fittest; evolution came to mean natural selection for people of increasingly higher intelligence. When coupled to the belief in the superiority of certain races, these evolutionary and diffusionist explanations came to be tantamount to a rationalization for racism and imperialism throughout the world. This was made explicit in the works of Lewis Henry Morgan, August Comte, and Herbert Spencer, where the superior races were English, French, Spanish, and German. These categories today mean distinct and closely related languages, not biology.

One of the most famous theoreticians of the age of formative anthropology was Lewis Henry Morgan (1818–1881). A lawyer and banker, Morgan worked directly with the Iroquois of New York state. His ethnographic descriptions of the Iroquois are still used by contemporary scholars. After American anthropologists had abandoned Morgan's writings, Karl Marx and Fredrik Engels adopted them; they became a part of Communist ideology in the twentieth century. Although Morgan admired the Iroquois and American Indians in general, his own theory blinded him to challenge evolution; and he placed American Indian culture in an intermediate stage (he didn't realize that the advanced Aztec and Maya were biologically American Indians).

In his *Ancient Society* (1876), Morgan set out a speculative theory of cultural evolution. Unlike many of his generation, Morgan's research data were not totally based on armchair speculation but on research he did for an earlier work, *Systems of Consanguinity and Affinity in the Human Family* (1870). For that study, he sent questionnaires to people around the world he thought would report honestly on what they observed: missionaries, businessmen, colonial administrators, and diplomats (people whose ideas would be considered biased today). Once he received their replies, however, he tended to associate the descriptions with commonly accepted evolutionary stages of savagery, barbarism, and civilization. There were many other speculative theories, such as those of Henry Maine and E. B. Tylor. While these theoreticians had some valuable insights about the distribution of cultural traits, their general theories are seen today as being ethnocentric, racist, and contradictory. Diffusionists and evolutionists misunderstood newly emerging facts of cultural evolution and linked culture to biology through the concept of race. Today, we have come to realize that cultural differences are not a measure of biologically inherited intellectual capacity. In Morgan's day, however, the category of race did not mean a taxonomic category based on learning but biology.

Biology, behavior, and culture were confused together (we still struggle with the distinctions between biology and behavior).

Evolutionary thinking was just as important in Europe, where the idea of race underlay almost all ideas of cultural evolution. Two important writers were August Comte (1798–1857) and Herbert Spencer (1820–1903). Both can be considered conservative theoreticians for very different reasons. Comte's work is called "positivism" and was a reaction against the excesses of the French Revolution and the bloody wars produced by Napoleon Bonaparte (1769–1821). Comte's views are found in his multi-volume work *Course of Positive Philosophy* (1830–42), where he hammered at the idea that all branches of knowledge had passed or one day would pass through three stages: theological, metaphysical, and positive. His "theological" stage referred to explanation based on deities, his concept of metaphysical explained evolutionary stages in terms of abstract concepts, and positivism explained phenomena in terms of evolutionary phenomena and was Comte's word for science (Erickson and Murphy 2003, 40–41). In many ways, Comte belonged to his age. Even if his ideas on evolutionary stages were insightful, and we will be able to use them in our section on religion, nonetheless he insisted that a modern age must be based on a science based on human motivations. His thought was not very different from the Victorians we have just examined. Comte was called "pope of positivism." Comte did not belong to our modern age of science. For him, democracy was a dangerous institution, and a few knowledgeable "sociologists" that studied society, as a science, should guide society: a meritocracy of sociologists would rule society. Thought like his came to be the basis for race-based sociology in the early twentieth century leading to two world wars.

Paralleling Comte in England was Herbert Spencer who developed a theory of cultural evolution that came to be called Social Darwinism. Both Comte and Spencer developed their ideas before the publication of *The Origin of Species*. Many who read Spencer's work thought he showed that Darwin's theory could be applied to culture. However, his thinking was much closer to Lamarck's theory of acquired characteristics than Darwin's survival of the fittest. Spencer thought there was selection for activities that gave some few people superior advantage through a lifetime, and these superior characteristics were biologically passed on down through the generations. Evolutionary and diffusionist ideas, along with those of Morgan, Comte, and Spencer, were widespread in the nineteenth century and were interpreted to support European colonialism. It was these ideas that were the major challenges for the classic phase of anthropological thought (Erickson and Murphy 2003, 70).

Anthropology did not explain these early racist concepts. The age of formative (early) anthropology was a transition phase between a search for the origins and the meaning of human life based on the *Scala Naturae* to the acceptance of the paradigm of Darwinian evolution. However, the mythology of race continued to exist, and it became even more important. The concept of race was an ancient idea, but was originally thought to be a divine creation. With Darwinian evolution, the idea of race became a taxonomic unit created by the forces of nature, not God; it confused human biology and culture. During the age of classic anthropology the concept of race was separated from the idea of culture, and its importance was reduced or abandoned. At the same time that the idea of race was dropped from anthropological discourse, the entire idea of evolution shifted radically from the overview of changes in biology and intelligence to changes in culture due to innovations in technology and increases in the amount of energy used. Despite the importance of evolution to anthropology, many non-scientists deny its validity, creating one of the debates of the modern world.

The Classic Phase of Anthropological Thought, 1900–1970

The period covering the age of classic anthropology begins roughly in 1900, which is about the time that Franz Boas began training graduate students at Columbia University (1907). The date is arbitrarily selected, as is the date for its end, 1970. The age of classic anthropology was one in which the concept of race was replaced with the concept of culture. Most research was carried out in small scale and non-western societies. John W. Bennett has given that period the name of classic anthropology because much of the work produced during that time period is regarded as the "most typical or perhaps the finest the discipline ever produced" (Bennett 1993). What holds together classic anthropology? Bennett thinks four things: 1) a running commentary on the concept of culture; 2) dependence on reports from tribal society, by which he means relatively isolated "folk" removed from modern urban-industrial civilization; 3) a tendency to report on people who were vulnerable to exploitation; and 4) a tendency to report about them as though they were "timeless."

ethnographic relativism

Also called cultural relativism, the tendency to write about people as though they had always existed, and to do so with a sense of moral ambiguity

ethnocentrism

The common feature of all people to think their own culture is superior to others

Not only was there a tendency to write about people as though they had always existed but to do so with a sense of moral ambiguity, which was called **ethnographic** or **cultural relativism.** The opposite was **ethnocentrism,** the common feature of all people to think their own culture as superior to others. For Boas, the idea emerged that no one can impose the values of one society on another—that all forms of cultural behavior are equally acceptable and ethical. In recent years, anthropologists have argued that it is unethical to use a strong version of cultural relativism in which any and all behaviors are acceptable. As we will learn in a later chapter, the creation of the United Nations is associated with a search for universal human values which can be used to protect people against such extreme cultural behaviors as racism, rape, torture, extra-legal executions, the mistreatment of either men or women by the opposite gender, and genocide. The anthropologist would argue that it is one thing to try to understand the academic or theoretical reason for a cultural practice, but it is quite another to accept or condone it. Finding a universal standard of values has been difficult because what is acceptable or ethically neutral to one person may not be so to someone else. One example is the treatment of women or gay men in Islamic societies. Sexual behavior treated lightly in modern, western cultures can lead to "honor killings" by a near relative in Islamic societies. Interference by outsiders to protect people who are considered innocent by the standards of the modern United States can lead to accusations of colonialism. What appears, on the face of it, to be a simple humanitarian assumption about rights becomes much more complicated when attempting to find a universal standard acceptable to all.

Boas viewed culture holistically, but he also viewed it as ahistorical, as though it lacked history. Anthropologists today argue they can't view culture holistically and historically at the same time. Historians enjoy attacking anthropology for this odd contradiction, one which anthropologists find difficult to defend. Philosophy of science would argue that the problem lies in trying to grasp two abstractions at the same time. History is one abstraction, while holism is another. One can grasp the history of a culture as one abstraction, but to grasp the same culture holistically, and to refer the two abstractions to each other is intellectually a feat beyond most people's ability. The problem is the amount of detail in the two abstractions. Try it and see how far you can go!

John Bennett notes another characteristic of classic anthropology: ethnographers wrote episodically, almost as though they were telling short stories, which makes comparing their observations difficult. What part of which story does one compare? According to Bennett, this approach was not necessarily a bad thing because it introduced a type

■What is ethically acceptable or unacceptable in some cultures may be vastly different in others. One example is the treatment of gay men in Islamic societies. Treated lightly in western cultures, these lifestyles can lead to "honor killings" in Islamic societies.

historical particularism

The name given to early anthropological approaches in which ethnographers would omit fine details in their writings

of novelty that made the anthropologist, as opposed to the sociologist, something of a romantic, but less of a scientist.

The early phase of cultural anthropology was also non-evolutionary in order to concentrate attention on the details described by ethnographers. A few writers, such as Alfred Kroeber, attempted evolutionary approaches; however, they ignored fine details. For this reason, early classic anthropology has been given the name of **historical particularism** (Bennett 1998, 1, also see Erickson and Murphy 2003, 75). Bennett quotes Boas' student Ruth Bunzel as best capturing the meaning of *historical particularism* by stating that customs should be studied "as a phenomena in their own right," and not merely to explain the "museum-type problem of the origins and distribution of cultural traits." That is, anthropologists should concentrate on describing cultures, and not on creating evolutionary or diffusionist models, which are entirely speculative (Bennett 1998, 2, Mead and Bunzel 1960, 574).

Kroeber attempted to avoid the problem of the high detail of ethnographic descriptions through his definition of culture as a "superorganic" (1917). Instead of looking at detailed descriptions, he viewed the whole of culture as operating according to its own laws, which he thought were operating according to laws that were psychological or linguistic, and even mathematical. He thought cultures and languages were so complex they could not be compared. Similar ideas were expressed in Great Britain in a school of thought called British Structure Functionalism, which was influenced by the French sociologist, Durkheim. Durkheim and his followers thought society operated according to its own laws, and that the laws are sociological, making comparative analysis difficult (the differences between the concepts "psychological" and "sociological" were never made clear). One classic paper on the subject was Bronislaw Malinowski's "Baloma" monograph, based on research in New Guinea where descent was matrilineal instead of patrilineal. Malinowski was able to show how difficult it is to compare two kinds of societies, patrilineal and matrilineal, found on a single island. He challenged all comparative research until George Peter Murdock's statistical work of 1948 (Malinowski 1917).

As mentioned above, classic anthropology did not study the past, except as archaeology. American historical particularism and British structural functionalism dealt with the present, not on human origins or the past. It was felt that information on evolution was too speculative for a science of human beings. For these reasons, both American and British research in the 1930s tended to claim that they were "functionalist" but not "evolutionary." Functionalist sociology or anthropology viewed all elements of culture as related to each other, or as having a function of each other; writers did not try to understand origins. While earliest anthropology had dwelt on the origins of "civilization," writers thought each separate institution had its own separate and distinct evolutionary sequences, which could not be compared. Thus, family, marriage, economic activities, politics, and religion were thought to have evolved independently from each other and to have diffused elsewhere independently. It set the task of formative anthropology to the origins of culture, but not how institutions had evolved together (Bennett 1998, 63).

Franz Boas was the first to supply an alternative term to the concept of civilization, one that did not imply superiority, but relativity. He did this by separating the term "culture" from civilization as early as 1887 (Menand 2001, 384). Edward B. Tylor first defined culture in 1871, but his definition equated culture with civilization (see the Introduction chapter). Boas' use of the term culture was new, and quite unlike its original usage in the nineteenth century or Tylor's definition. In certain languages, such as Spanish, French, and Portuguese, the term culture is similar to its original American and British meaning as used by Tylor. In languages with a Latin root it is common to equate culture and civilization (in Spanish, *cultura* means high civilization, unless defined anthropologically). Yet Boas came to the idea of culture not from the Latin language but from the surprising direction of human physiology—it was his attempt to separate culture, race, and civilization. He migrated to North America from Germany in 1881 because his Jewish ethnicity made life difficult: and many have thought European anti-Semitism, as well as racism in the United States, influenced his perspective. He had received a PhD from the University of Kiel in 1881, hoping to do post-graduate studies at John Hopkins University, but was refused a fellowship. Instead, he used his time to do further studies among the Eskimo of Baffin Island. His dissertation had the title of *Beiträge zur Erkenntniss der Farbe des Wassers* ("Contribution to the Understanding of the Color of Water"). He tried to answer the question: how much does light have to increase or decrease in brightness before we perceive a change in its color? (Menand 2001, 384). His answer was that there could be no general law of sensory thresholds because differences in perception are not innate, an answer that went against popular theory. According to Boas, different observers have different responses depending on experience, and these differences are not innate; they are, consciously and unconsciously, learned, to which he gave the term "culture," as we would today. This tiny crack in the assumption of the relationship between biology and behavior led Boas to question the entire edifice of cultural evolution laid down by formative anthropology. He and his followers thought it was meaningless to argue that paganism evolved to barbarism and barbarism to civilization on the basis of race because human biology and culture were mutable. Culture and race could be defined clearly to be unlike one another; by doing so, Boas uncoupled any cultural evolutionary changes from the concept of race (or civilization). Social Darwinism, as racial or cultural evolution due to natural selection, was clearly not tenable.

He would do further work with the Kwakiutl and other Indians of the Northwest Coast before accepting a position as assistant curator at the American Museum of Natural History followed by an appointment at Columbia University in New York City, where he remained the rest of his life. While his life led to many achievements, his biggest battle and success was to destroy the concept of race as an equivalent to civilization or culture (Menand 2001, 384). Later in the twentieth century, the concept of race would be defined in terms of biological variation, called clines, particularly by Ashley Montague whose position was similar to Boas' in that race and culture were not to be confused. Boas thought that the most important concept for the study of humans was culture, and that culture existed only in the mind and could only be approached through communication between people (Bennett 1998, 403–406).

In 1902, a second piece of evidence gave Boas evidence to challenge the notion of the relationship between biology and superiority (race, civilization). Boas received funding from the Dillingham Commission of the United States Senate to study changes in the body shape of immigrants. To his own amazement, he discovered that Sicilian and Jewish immigrants and their children had different shaped heads. He concluded the reason for the changes was improved nutrition, not race or "culture," and certainly not "civilization."

Boas' research occurred at a point in time when Darwin's theory was unfortunately being applied to race, and when race was becoming the chief factor explaining culture or behavior. His pronouncement had a severe impact on polygenism (the idea that God had created many races that were stable and could not change form, an argument that continued to be made long after the end of the Civil War and into the mid-twentieth century). In fact, he delivered an address to the American Association for the Advancement of Science in which he bravely "dismissed as utterly unreliable virtually all nineteenth century research on racial difference" (Menand 2001, 386).

Boas also grasped the evil of colonialism directly. He pointed out that all of the vaunted superiority of Europeans over colonized peoples was the consequence of colonial institutions. Colonial institutions robbed colonized people from ruling and advancing themselves. He went further to accuse scientists of supporting racism and slavery on the basis of research by evolutionary anthropologists that was scientifically spurious and based on race or culture, the criticisms of which he published in his blockbuster book *The Mind of Primitive Man*, which became the basis for classic anthropology. Great care must be taken here: Boas did not say there was no such thing as race or that there was no such thing as culture, but that there could be no relationship between the two.

Unfortunately, while Boas had a great deal of impact on the world of science, he had little influence on public policy. At the time of Boas' scientific presentations, the United States was going through a hysterical reaction against immigration. The Dillingham Commission, despite Boas' research and publications, issued a forty-two-volume report that concluded that immigration must be reduced, for immigrants were racially inferior (the opposite of what Boas' research proved). This report was followed in 1915 by D. W. Griffith's racist movie *Birth of a Nation*, the revival of the Ku Klux Klan, and a return to racist xenophobia (Menand 2001, 387). Thus, classic anthropology, with Boas as its leader, can be understood as the reaction by anthropologists against evolutionary theories based on race, a position that was diametrically the opposite of formative anthropology.

For formative anthropology, the key word had been race; for classic anthropologists, the key word was culture, a word that Boas' students and their students would spend over fifty years clarifying and making so important to the English language that it has been incorporated into all of the human sciences and humanities.

While many racist theoreticians used Darwin's theory of natural selection to support the notion that races were, once formed, immutable and inferior to whites, Darwin himself did not support such arguments. Instead, many racial theorists turned to Herbert Spencer's *Social Darwinism*, a theory that was not endorsed by Darwin but which tied Lamarckian inheritance of acquired characteristics to Adam Smith's *Wealth of Nations*, also without Adam Smith's support, in which "survival of the fittest" was tied to capitalism; and both explained the origins of Victorian England where "might" made "right" (Erickson and Murphy 2003, 70).

It is generally acknowledged that Franz Boas went on the attack against evolutionary theory; and it can also be said that at the beginning of the twenty-first century, while the word "race" is still in use, most people prefer to talk about the reason for differences in behavior as having something to do with culture, not race. More precisely, it can be said that his attack was against racism, and that he succeeded. At Colombia University, he trained a cadre of anthropologists who created classic anthropology. That period came to be the essence of anthropology, shifting focus from race to culture. He was not able to completely do away with the concept of race, but today it is meant to be applied to biological variation, and not learned behavior. In that goal, he has succeeded.

However, while the concept of culture came to be broadly accepted by classic anthropologists, its meaning has never been clear. Boas' idea of culture was a very philosophical one, based on Kantian metaphysics. Boas' concept of culture was not based on the notion of a statistical average or mathematical average but of an intellectual ideal. A great deal was written about culture as a world view, somewhat along the lines of Kant's idea of Weltanschauung; but many thought the idea was vague and obscure. One of the most successful American philosophers to use the cultural concept was F. S. C. Northrop, who appears to have understood Kant as well as he did Boas and his followers in looking at culture as an ideal (1946). In *The Meeting of East and West*, Northrup used the approach of classic anthropology to explain World War II. He hoped that by getting people to understand each other's cultures as ideals future conflict could be avoided. Yet neither Boas, nor Northrop, nor any classic anthropologist was ever able to clearly explain what they meant by culture. Kroeber, his student, added to the confusion by first arguing that culture was like language, and then that it was like a mathematical equation. Many sociologists or sociologically trained anthropologists thought that culture might be some kind of statistical mean, but that was not what Boas meant either. Boas' idealistic concept of culture was to play a crucial role during the period of psychological anthropology, which became a key element of classic anthropology up until the period directly after World War II. While much still continues to be written about culture, its meaning remains illusive. We have, in our own definition, tried to stress that culture is both an idea and a concrete phenomena. Like many things that are human, culture is baffling; and it has stirred Boas' students, and students of his students, to continuously clarify what culture means.

The list of anthropologists trained by Boas, or by Boas' students is a virtual *Who's Who* of dominant theoreticians of the generation of classic anthropology. Among the most well known personalities were Melville Herskovits, E. Adamson Hoebel, Alfred Louis Kroeber, Robert Lowie, Ruth Benedict, Margaret Mead, Alexander Goldenweiser, Paul Radin, Clark Wissler, and Edward Sapir. A full list would run several pages, but these were the most imminent (and there would be many more disagreements on which of these were the most important). In addition, there would have to be added an equally long list of British structure functionalists that shared many of the same points, but a discussion of similarities and differences would themselves fill volumes. These eminent anthropologists would in turn create schools of their own, but none would achieve Boas' eminence. It is unfortunate that only a few of their names can be brought up here. In the chapters that follow, we will have a closer look at our "intellectual ancestors" or "founding fathers and mothers" (Erickson and Murphy 2003, 13), and their descendants. Many ideas created in the age of classic anthropology have become such essential building blocks of anthropology, modern social science, and contemporary culture that it is difficult to grasp how narrow the intellectual world once was. In the following, we examine just a handful of the most important anthropologists of the twentieth century.

ROBERT LOWIE AND ALFRED LOUIS KROEBER

The first two students to earn doctoral degrees under Boas were Robert Lowie and Alfred L. Kroeber. Lowie (1883–1957), like Boas, was of German/Jewish ancestry and moved to the United States when he was just ten. Like Boas, he was influenced by Kantian idealist philosophy, and supported ethnographic relativism. In 1917, he joined the faculty at the University of California at Berkeley, where he worked with Alfred Kroeber. Lowie became famous for his highly detailed studies of American Indians, particularly the Crow, among whom he worked for several decades. His most famous work is *History of Ethnographic Theory*, which took evolutionary anthropology to task and argued that there was no single explanation to culture (1937). After his retirement, he studied the German people after World War II, making him one of the first anthropologists to study a modern and complex society (Erickson and Murphy 2003, 76).

Alfred Louis Kroeber (1876–1960) began his scholarly interests in literature, but changed his profession to anthropology after meeting Franz Boas, under whom he wrote his dissertation. In 1911, Alfred Kroeber published a famous paper on kinship in which he argued that the laws of culture were largely psychological, which fit Boas' neo-Kantian paradigm of the importance of mind. He argued that culture was an entity *sui generis*, a thing onto itself, with its own internal laws, but he developed an idea that went beyond Boas called the concept of the superorganic, mentioned above (1917). He argued that culture operated according to its own laws, and that events occur in spite of "great men," an idea that was picked up in 1949 by Leslie White, a neo-evolutionist we will discuss. Kroeber's paradigm of culture was very popular, but also abstract and difficult to apply. According to Kroeber, culture operated according to its own laws. Sometimes he argued the laws governing culture were like those governing language and sometimes he argued that they were like mathematical formulas, but he was never to explain those laws. One of his most illusive arguments was an attempt to explain style, particularly the fashion features of women's dresses. While style is one of the subjects that appeared least susceptible to statistical trends, he argued that such capricious patterns as hem length, lapel change, and the placement of buttons are creatures of cultural cycles, which form statistical trends. Kroeber spent most of his life shifting back and forth between the highly detailed ethnographies of historical particularism, or highly abstract essays on the nature of culture as a superorganic.

His approach to culture, much as that of Boas, avoided causal arguments of any type, such as technological, biological, or environmental explanations for culture. Explanations that argued that certain physical entities "caused" culture were labeled "deterministic" or "materialistic." Culture should be explained idealistically, but Kroeber and his followers usually fell back on vague psychological explanations that help us understand why culture and personality, or psychological anthropology, came to be very popular in the middle of the twentieth century.

The need to avoid "materialistic" explanations was a response to nineteenth century excesses, which explained "civilizations" either through race or environment. Kroeber often ignored the obvious. For example, in 1939, he published *Cultural and Natural Areas of Native America*, which showed that distribution maps of Native American cultural traits fit into natural realms, suggesting a materialistic connection between ecology and culture; however, his book all but ignored ecological features. The idea of ecology interacting with culture would become the hallmark of anthropology several decades later.

Alfred Kroeber established a West Coast version of The American School of Anthropology at the University of California at Berkeley. Kroeber, like his teacher, Boas, sent students around the world to collect information on its peoples, including research on complex American culture. Kroeber was particularly influential on a generation of anthropology researchers and writers, keeping Boas' idealistic vision of culture central to the discipline.

MARGARET MEAD AND RUTH BENEDICT

One direction that became very popular in the twentieth century was psychological anthropology. Of particular importance was developing research to test the psychoanalytic ideas of Freud. Of particular importance were Margaret Mead and Ruth Benedict. The key word to their approach is *enculturation*, and it has influenced all of the social sciences and history. Enculturation is the complex process whereby culture contributes to shaping the personality of the individual. Because we will spend an entire chapter on psychological anthropology, it is sufficient to write here that Margaret Mead focused on the question of whether adolescent sexuality was biologically determined; and as a student of Boas, it should come as no surprise that her research showed that sexuality was, and is, broadly conditioned by culture. More controversially, Ruth Benedict showed that cultures themselves had personalities, a topic that helped create *national character studies* directly after World War II, and were vital to the American war effort. Both she and Mead pioneered a series of studies called "culture-at-a-distance" that gave both women opportunities to exercise their considerable literary talents (Erickson and Murphy 2003, 82–83).

LESLIE WHITE: UNIVERSAL CULTURAL EVOLUTION

Boas, Kroeber, Mead, and Benedict's work tended to stress psychological aspects of culture. However, there were also many attempts to explain culture as a response to evolutionary, ecological, or materialistic forces. One classic anthropologist who offered an alternative approach was Leslie White. He almost single-handedly resurrected the evolutionary approaches of the twentieth century; but he ignored the idea of race, and instead stressed the concepts of technology and energy. His approach offered an alternative to Boas and Kroeber's idealistic concepts of culture. One reason for White's evolutionism is the vast increase in evidence around the world for similarities in how civilizations changed through time. The discipline of archaeology was raising questions that had evolutionary implications. Kroeber conducted some of the research in Peru, where he used new methods to date ceramic sequences of pottery. Others trained by Boas in Mexico and the Middle East uncovered evidence that was hard to ignore, though Boas and Kroeber did just that to justify their psychological points of view. Parallels in the apparent cultural evolution of Mesopotamia (the Middle East) and Mexico and Peru (some carried out by Kroeber) were becoming clear by the late 1930s. White asked the question: how could many prehistoric regions of the world have parallel evolutionary patterns (or so it appeared)? Other questions were being raised by ethnographers, which were also raised by White, as they discovered great similarities in the kinship systems of peoples in very different parts of the world. They, like White, asked questions of how people in places as far apart as Central America, South America, Asia and Central Africa have identical named categories for relatives even though they were not connected by diffusion.

Leslie White, who established the Department of Anthropology at the University of Michigan, did his original graduate work in the Southwest on the Pueblo Indians and developed an interest on the relationship between technology and social structure. As a young professor of anthropology, he traveled to Russia and came under the influence of Marxist theoreticians. While his own work cannot be judged Marxist, some aspects were sufficiently Marxist so that he had a great deal of trouble getting his ideas accepted by the scientific community in the United States. This was especially true in the 1950s with its McCarthyism, a time when many evolutionary and ecologically oriented anthropologists got into trouble for their ideas—ideas which resembled Marxist technological explanations (and often were).

There are several components of White's work that are worth looking over and were published for the first time in 1959 in *The Evolution of Culture*, one of the landmarks of classical anthropology. The importance of the First and Second Laws of Thermodynamics, issues that are re-emerging in our environmental age, provided one core component in White's thinking. White began with the laws of physics, not psychology or race (a challenge to formative anthropology). For White, culture, like everything else, has to respond to the laws of physics. For White, culture was "an extrasomatic, temporal continuum of things and events dependent upon symboling" and he adopted Kroeber's concept of culture as superorganic phenomena (White 1959, 3). But while Kroeber (following Boas) was an idealist, White's notion of culture was materialistic, following a Marxist model.

While both White and Kroeber agreed that culture was a symbolic phenomenon, White could argue that culture was an energy using system. His axiom C = E (culture equals energy), underlay his argument that the evolution of culture was the result of cultural systems drawing greater and greater amounts of energy from the environment through increasingly more efficient technologies (T).

White's concepts of energy and adaptation are common today in anthropological human ecology. White represented a set of ideas that were diametrically the opposite of the psychological ideas of Boas, Mead, and Benedict. For White, culture is an energy capturing system whose survival depends on a continuous battle against disorganization. It is this battle to capture energy, to move in the direction of greater organization, which White defined as cultural evolution.

For White, any culture is both a symbolic system and a thermodynamic system. White placed a great deal of emphasis on energy, tools, and their products (going the opposite direction from Boas). Energy meant "the ability to do work." Work and energy were almost interchangeable. Because of this "interchangeability," culture should be measurable in caloric units. White and his followers attempted to measure the relationship between "culture" and "energy" with some degree of success as long as gross differences are used between relatively broad evolutionary stages. Thus, hunting and gathering bands derive much less energy in the form of calories from their environments than do modern societies, about one-twentieth of a horsepower per capita in contrast to modern societies which generate hundreds of horsepower per capita (White 1959, 42). For White, energy capture should be directly translatable to distinct evolutionary stages; energy capture (not ideas) was the cause of cultural evolution (the contrast with Boas' ideas raised considerable controversy in anthropology). Thus, a contrast between hunting and gathering societies and our own would show that while we consume hundreds of thousands of calories every day in the form of fossil fuels which drive our machines, less technologically advanced

■Hunting and gathering bands derive much less energy in the form of calories from their environments than do modern societies.

societies would consume much less. A male hunter-gatherer might only consume the amount of energy he/she personally put out each day, about two thousand calories.

White's theory is very systematic with culture having four key components: technology, economy, society, and ideology. He symbolized them: T, E, S, and I, and perceived them as layers, much in opposition to Boas "holistic" view of culture. For him, T was the driving mechanism, the component by which humankind derived energy from the environment, with the other layers laying over the first one. Another characteristic of White's theory was that he treated the environment as having little to do with cultural evolution; he thought it was a neutral system (this point of view is odd given White's materialism). He saw culture as a self driven, self-evolving system driven by the laws of physics, instead of the laws of psychology or linguistics.

While White's theory was published almost a half century ago, it remains very modern. White's contributions are similar to what is known today as "complexity theory." Complexity theory is used to examine the operation of large computers, the solar system, markets and trade, and culture as a self evolving set of systems and subsystems which are part of the universal tendency towards the growth of complexity (see Waldrop 1992, Lewin 1992). White's theory is much more acceptable today; however, during the 1940s and 1950s, he was accused of spreading Marxist dogma not only conservative politicians but also by fellow academics.

While White's technological determinism has never been popular, the thermodynamic (the importance of energy) part of his argument was ahead of its time. We accept the idea of culture as a symbolic system; like White, we think it must also be viewed as an energy-using phenomenon. This point of view is implicit in this text. Today we know we are in danger of destroying world *ecosystems* through an excessive use of energy (in White's time, the world appeared to have superabundant amounts of oil, and pollution was not a problem). We would argue that it is important to develop technologies that can do more with less energy, and that the planet is as important as its cultures.

While the thermodynamic basis of culture is valuable, the adoption of technological determinism is problematic. John W. Bennett adopts the idea that what drives change is "anticipation" and "coping" (both of which are psychological concepts, thus returning to Boas; Bennett 1976). For Bennett, adaptation is a form of decision-making, and that includes the choice of tools and innovations in technology. In addressing our ecological problems, we may turn to new technologies; we are also likely to modify institutions of economic organization, political systems, or ideologies to fit our needs. These changes may modify our technologies, as well as how we think. Modern anthropologists continue to dismiss the notion that culture change is driven by any one force or system (White's technological determinism or any other determinism). We argue further that culture change cannot be understood as a series of simple cause-effect events. At best, a cultural system is a dynamic system consisting of numerous interacting variables and feedback loops, an idea developed by Julian Steward.

JULIAN STEWARD: PARALLEL OR MULTILINEAL CULTURAL EVOLUTION

Julian Steward critiqued much of White's work through a more sophisticated and non-Marxist paradigm. Like White, Julian Steward had a grand view of cultural change; he avoided technological determinism, however, opting for an approach that was called "multilineal" evolution. According to Steward, the same adaptation might produce different evolutionary directions (pastoral nomadism in Africa produced quite different states than in Asia). On the other hand, many distinct adaptations might converge in similar evolutionary directions (modern technology is bringing about many parallel urban societies, Steward 1955).

Steward was trained at the University of California under Alfred Kroeber and Robert Lowie, and was thus under Boas' non-deterministic influence. He worked in the western Andes on the ancient civilizations of Peru and Ecuador, as well as in the American southwest. He also did ethnographic research among the Ute and Paiute of Nevada and Utah, and like White became interested in the relationship between technology and social organization in hunting and food gathering societies. In the 1940s, he was appointed by the Smithsonian Institute of Washington, D.C., to put together the *Handbook of South American Indians.* This book was compiled of studies that ethnographers had carried out on the Indians of Central and South America over the previous century as well as descriptions of the ancient Inca made by writers of the sixteenth, seventeenth, and eighteenth centuries. While the format of the *Handbook* itself is a modified culture area arrangement, similar to Kroeber's, Steward developed a cultural type that not only explored ecology and evolutionary levels but also integrated concepts based on sociopolitical and religious organization. These categories are found in the fifth volume of his "South American Cultures: An Interpretive Summary" (1949a). His categories, with care, are still useful today. His approach was further elaborated in a publication "Levels of Sociocultural Integration: An Operational Concept" (1951). We will be using Steward's evolutionary taxonomy in this book as developed by Marshall Sahlins and Elman Service, two classic anthropologists (1960).

Sahlins and Service, like Steward, were critical of White and considered him a unilineal theorist, much like Morgan. Their criticism targeted White's view that there was only one world culture to which all other cultures belonged. While White's unilineal theory was not acceptable, Steward, Sahlins, and Service adopted much of White's other ideas in what has come to be known as "cultural ecology" or multilinear evolution. They argued that many distinct cultures have evolved in parallel to each other due to the working of the same scientific laws. Steward made it his life work to find the laws. He was extremely interested in the fact that in various parts of the world, such as the Mideast, Mesoamerica, and Peru, there appeared to be parallel developments in cultural evolution (See his 1949 paper, "Cultural Causality and Law: A Trial Formulation).

Steward differed most greatly from White in how he viewed adaptation to the environment. While White viewed the primary adaptation to nature to be technology, Steward thought there were two important components involved: the cultural core and the superstructure. The core was made up of technology and subsistence activities—very close to what Marvin Harris means by infrastructure (the use of technology to derive subsistence from the environment) while the super structure was everything else. While White viewed culture as evolving due to technological change, Steward thought cultural change came about due to the interaction between core and environment, though Steward was vague about how this occurred. He was unable to come up with a more specific theory of this interaction complex and died without ever having become more specific. Some of his students and followers borrowed a natural selection argument from Darwin whereby innovations in behavior were selected in respect to the environment, if they gave the society adaptive advantage. This approach has been named "cultural materialism" by Marvin Harris, who has turned it into a major school of thought. While many of Steward's followers have adopted Harris' cultural materialism, many others have not because of the problematic history of Darwinian reasoning when applied to race.

■Pictured are Brazilian Indian chieftains, Kaiapos tribe. Cultures may evolve and change due to shifts in religion or ideology, as well as technology.

While there are many disagreements, there has been an adoption of Sahlins and Service's concepts of consecutive evolutionary stages of band, tribe, chiefdom, and state, mostly along the lines of Steward's techno-ecological theory of culture. Most anthropologists have adopted these evolutionary stages today. However, there is growing awareness that cultures may evolve and change due to shifts in religion or ideology, as well as technology, and that state policies can determine the development of new or changed technologies. The relationships among environment, technology, economic, and political systems, as well as ideologies are viewed as having much more complex interconnections than in White's or Steward's time.

Steward and his associates, to their credit, did foresee these complexities in a set of publications edited by Steward that have stood the test of time: *The Peoples of Puerto Rico* (1956) and *Traditional Societies and Modern Change* (1967). Anthropologists do acknowledge that a critical variable in culture change is technology. Only a moment's pause to reflect over the changes in American culture over the last four decades due to changes in automobiles, road building, communications, aerospace, and computers will convince the reader of the dramatic role technology and social organization play in culture change. At the same time we are aware of the importance of ideology, and in the need to make changes in how we treat our world.

French Structural Anthropology and British Social Anthropology

European writers, and particularly British "Structure-Functionalism" and French structuralism, influenced classic anthropology. Structure-functionalism is known today primarily due to the writings of Alfred Reginald Radcliffe-Brown and Bronislaw Malinowski. They, in turn, were influenced by the French sociologist Emile Durkheim (1858–1917), particularly his *Division of Labor in Society* (1893), *The Rules of the Sociological Method* (1895), *Suicide* (1897), and *The Elementary Forms of the Religious Life* (1912). Of particular importance was Durkheim's idea that "primitive" societies were less diversified than "modern" societies and had little division of labor, a term to which he applied the term **mechanical solidarity.** According to Durkheim, modern societies were more heterogeneous and cohered because people played many different roles, which required them to cooperate: he applied the term **organic solidarity** to modern societies.

Karl Marx was also influential on writers of the period of classic anthropology. In many ways Marx and Durkheim set out theories that are in strong contrast to each other. While Marx and Durkheim agreed on the nature of pre-modern society, they disagreed on the nature of modern societies. Marx was considered a radical theoretician, while Durkheim was considered conservative. For Marx, industrialization brought about class conflict due to the differences in peoples' interests. The bourgeoisie gained control over the sources of production in industry. The working class opposed the bourgeoise, and Marx predicted the conflict between owners and workers would lead to revolution and the emergence of a state based on the collective ownership of property. Durkheim (and Comte before him) had a very different view. For Durkheim, industrialization created heterogeneity. Organic solidarity was the means by which society could cohere through the invention of the state, which was viewed positively.

For Marx, the state represented the interests of the elite and should wither away after revolution (Erickson and Murphy 2003, 90–91). Durkheim explained that the *structures* (some would call them "institutions") of society (e.g., kinship structures, political structures, economic structures, religious structures) could best be explained in terms of their functions in adding to the solidarity of the society (either mechanical or organic solidarity, depending on the complexity of the society). Durkheim and Kroeber resemble each other, except that instead of the term superorganic, Durkheim used the terms *collective representation, collective consciousness,* or *group mind.*

Durkheim's theories were highly influential in the creation of A. R. Radcliffe-Brown's structure-functionalist anthropology in Great Britain. He brought his theory to the University of Chicago for a short period of time. While Durkheim's and Marx's theories were attractive to American classic anthropology, the most important achievement of British structural-functionalism was thought to be in methodology, particularly the research of Bronislaw Malinowski, Radcliffe-Brown's foremost student. While most American classic anthropologists followed Kroeber and Boas' psychological anthropology, explained above, a small minority followed Radcliffe-Brown and Malinowski developing a school of thought known as *social anthropology.* Malinowski was particularly influential and spent several years at Yale University training American anthropologists.

Malinowski's approach depended on explaining theory through research, which required living in a foreign culture for an extensive period of time. In Malinowski's writing, and the writing from the students he trained, ethnography and theory were two terms for the same thing. Thus we can explain the meaning of the term "structure-functionalism" in that the ethnographer explained the structure of society by writing about its function in an ethnographic case study. Most social science writers have a section on theory that applies to summaries of their research. However, structure-functionalist writers put their theory into their writing. Theory was built into the style of writing, an approach that is difficult to use comparatively.

Malinowski's research had been carried out in Oceania, a region that attracted many classic anthropologists in the middle of the twentieth century. Two of Malinowski's students became particularly important to classic anthropology. One was Raymond Firth who became very well known for his research on economics in Oceania, while the second was Darryl Forde who made his reputation studying the relationship between ecology and

---

mechanical solidarity

Durkheim's idea that "primitive" societies were less diversified than "modern" societies and had little division of labor

organic solidarity

Durkheim's idea that modern societies are more heterogeneous and cohered than earlier societies because people play many different roles that require them to cooperate

social systems in Africa. A. R. Radcliffe-Brown developed a school of thought known as British structure-functionalism and became well known for his work on the political and kinships systems of African tribes and chiefdoms, a region that now drew the interest of American researchers. In the 1960s, classic anthropology shifted directions from the broad study of the psychological nature of culture, an amorphous topic, to narrower but more intensely researched studies of different kinds of systems which form cultures or societies: kinship systems, political systems, social systems, religious systems, and so on.

British structure functionalism and American anthropology of the 1940s did not work well together, and there were many conflicts between advocates of the two approaches. For those who followed Boas and Kroeber, the idea continued to be to get into the mind of a few informants (emic anthropology). Those who were attracted to A. R. Radcliffe-Brown's school of social anthropology (structural-functionalists) insisted on much more detailed ethnographies based on interviews and censuses in order to create models of systems (etic anthropology). The 1960s was a period of radical social movements, and both approaches came to be viewed as conservative towards the end of the age of classic anthropology. Both were viewed as not being critical enough of capitalism and the class nature of American society. At the same time that anthropologists became influenced by Marxist and feminist anthropological studies of large-scale societies, small and rural societies began to disappear as they became incorporated into global political and economic systems. The entire idea of studying isolated societies was challenged, and at the same time those types of societies disappeared.

In addition, many young anthropologists found the academic world was not for them and developed applied approaches to anthropology. One positive feature of structure-functionalism that could be adapted into contemporary research and writing was the fieldwork of British writers. These had the impact of improving the fieldwork of applied researchers and were applied to education, nutrition, culture contact, migration, land tenure, and many other topics of culture that had been ignored during the formative phase of anthropological research. The New Deal drew a large number of anthropologists into applied work for the federal government. John Collier, who had been appointed Commissioner of Indian Affairs and was responsible for the rapid expansion of federally employed anthropologists, created the Applied Anthropology Unit of the Office of Indian Affairs. Applied anthropology drew both on American classic anthropology and British structure-functionalism.

American government agencies carried out projects relating to economic and resource development on various Indian reservations. The involvement of anthropologists in the study of policy questions in American communities also expanded well into the war years. For example, some anthropologists contributed to the U.S. Department of Agriculture's Rural Life Studies, which provided six community studies that focused on change in contemporary and complex rural communities. Walter Goldschmidt's classic *As You Sow: Three Studies of the Consequences of Agribusiness* documented economic exploitation by large corporate landowners and led to his vilification by California's agribusiness (Van Willigen 1993).

One of the most significant projects to come out of this time period was organized by the Committee on Human Relations in Industry at the University of Chicago. Included among the anthropologists were W. Lloyd Warner and Burleigh B. Gardner. This project produced the classic Western Electric or Hawthorn Works study of the relationships between working conditions and productivity, which is still used in modern business-management texts (Van Willigen 1993). These applied research projects fed back into academic anthropology.

British structure functionalism came to be unusually strong at the University of Chicago, where Radcliffe-Brown spent several years. Several anthropologists trained at the University of Chicago, such as John W. Bennett, worked on materials from modern industrial societies, such as Japan (Bennett 1958). Bennett's work on forestry management in postwar Japan, showing how Japanese institutions influenced the way that forests were managed, was years ahead of its time. These many strands of anthropological research continued on into the present, while others merged into global anthropology.

Paradigms of Global Anthropology

After the 1970s, globalization opened anthropology to the study of global forces, but it had an unanticipated consequence: the discipline began to lose its sense of identity. The small, patch quilt studies of rural cultures that had characterized anthropology began to disappear. Classic anthropology had been based on the study of culture in many distinct and unrelated pre-industrial societies, each cited for the proof it made towards a writer's sometimes esoteric point or points. With globalization, however, the collective term "culture" was replaced with more specialized concepts. These divided anthropology into many new subdisciplines with connections to other social science and history disciplines, such as development anthropology, economic anthropology, environmental anthropology, feminist anthropology, medical anthropology, political anthropology, and so on. Other disciplines that adapted themselves into anthropology were migration, gerontology, pediatrics, and demography, to mention just a few. These new disciplines also tended to cross-cut one another, sometimes in ways that were confusing to writers or readers who wanted to present simple classification systems such as kinship and marriage categories (Bennett 1998).

The distinction between micro and macro (local and global) began to disappear, not only for anthropology but for other disciplines as well. An overall folding of micro- into macro-levels of analysis brought about the disappearance of many traditional subdisciplines in anthropology. Just about all that could be clearly defined were the connections of social science disciplines to Enlightenment humanistic values. Global anthropology may have roots in past interests, but it is even more dispersed than classic anthropology. The concept of culture continued, and continues to be used, but its original meaning was almost entirely derived from the contemplation of shared mental products and customs derived from ethnographies like Malinowski's or Margaret Mead's studies on remote Pacific islands (Bennett 1998, 75). As Wolf pointed out in 1982, such remote cultures may have been invented by researchers and never existed as isolated communities. Recent research shows that almost all cultures in the world were connected to each other through trade or warfare, and the traditional concept of culture has become less useful. As anthropology has become more global, it has also grown more complex. While there are many paradigms going in the direction of "global anthropology," three categories stand out. One is Julian Steward's cultural ecology approach stressing culture and environmental interrelationships, which is called cultural materialism. Clifford Geertz expresses the second in interpretivist, or symbolic anthropology, which is highly humanistic and comes closest to classic anthropology. A third approach, one particularly well expressed by Eric Wolf, links Marxist anthropology to the impact of globalization.

CULTURAL MATERIALISM

We have explained the bases for Leslie White and Julian Steward's materialistic approaches. Here we would like to explain how their ideas have been brought into the age of global anthropology. The leading proponents of cultural materialism were Marvin Harris, Andrew Vayda, and Roy Rappaport. Materialistic explanations are those that reduce complex cause-effect relationships to physical, mechanical, or biological laws (laws of physics, laws of mechanics, laws of genetics, and laws of evolution). Cultural materialists excelled at arguing how seemingly nonrational practices—warfare, pig sacrifices, potlatches (redistribution feasts), the ritual sanctification of cows in India, human sacrifice among the Aztecs—have positive (though usually unrecognized) consequences in that they regulate population density, the availability of protein in the diet, the redistribution of food from areas of surplus to areas of shortage, and so forth.

Cultural materialism makes use of *cybernetic theory* with its emphasis on feedback relationships within and between various systems of adaptation. **Cybernetic theory** is the basis of computer technology and focuses on information processing. According to Harris, Vayda, and Rappaport, the environment or habitat selects for "traits," such as pig sacrifice and ancestor worship (the theory is based on population genetics in biology). According to Harris, parallels can be drawn between this type of "environmental selection" and Darwinian natural selection (Harris 1979, 60). Individuals living in a society produce new variants of behavior, some of which are more effective than others in withstanding environmental selection; and these new variants survive while the less well-adapted variants tend to disappear. According to Marvin Harris, the foremost proponent of cultural materialism:

> … selection processes responsible for the divergent and convergent evolutionary trajectories of sociocultural systems operate mainly on the individual level; individuals follow one rather than another course of action, and as a result the aggregate pattern [of culture] changes (Harris 1979, 60).

cybernetic theory

The interdisciplinary study of the structure of regulatory systems

■In India, cows are considered sacred and blessed. Sometimes, seemingly nonrational practices such as the ritual sanctification of cows in India, have positive (though usually unrecognized) consequences within cultures.

The cultural materialist explanation, which continues White's emphasis on technology as the driving force at the individual level, is very widely accepted as both a logical model and as one that has received considerable scientific support primarily from archaeology. However, we must remember that the archaeological record produces very little more than a record of material culture, that is, technology. The cultural materialist position is so all-pervasive that most sociology and history texts present the rise of capitalism as a consequence of the development of certain technologies such as the steam engine, McCormick's reaping machine, the cotton gin, and other familiar technologies.

Many who adopt a cultural materialist model prefer Marx to the idea of natural selection at the individual level. They argue such an approach can lead either to Social Darwinism or environmental determinism. Instead of selection at the level of the individual, Marxist anthropologists prefer to stress the idea of *modes of production* for each distinct level of history. For example, Wolf refers to a kinship mode of production, a mercantile mode of production, and a capitalist mode of production. These would subdivide into categories based on economic adaptations, but there is no reason to present them here since they occur elsewhere in the book.

Culture change, according to Marxist logic, is determined by dialectical forces, which are in opposition to each other, such as various forces of history and social classes of elites and masses that have differential access to the sources of production, such as feudal landlords and peasants or modern capitalists and factory workers. Tensions between the elites and masses (the dialectic) are such that transformations in social structures occur (through revolution) which in turn have their own internal contradictions (bringing about yet other revolutions). Marxism attempts to explain revolution and rapid culture change as being due to the internal contradictions between the haves and the have-nots. In capitalist societies, change is driven by the interests of those who own the sources of production and those who do not (capital versus labor). Marxism tends to emphasize the internal sources of conflict (Harris 1979, 141).

The weakness of Marxist and neo Marxist models is that it is extremely difficult to analyze what exactly is meant by the "dialectic." There are so many oppositional forces at any point in history that analysis often gets bogged down or the analyst arbitrarily selects only the most obvious forces. In addition, there are many assumptions about the nature of class relationships that have not turned out to be true. In American society, working class and capitalist classes have often had the same conservative interests, and there has been little in the form of revolution.

While Marxist theory and research strategies can be questioned, Marxist contributions to history and social science are indisputable. Of particular significance was the attention paid to the importance of economic factors in helping to form the social fabric. At a time when all other theories of cultural evolution were based on racial differences, Karl Marx's contribution to science is really remarkable.

Marxism, evolutionary anthropology, and cultural materialism tend to rely on "deterministic" explanations, that is, simple cause-effect models (also called linear-causal models). These approaches have lost their appeal in recent decades due to the movements of interpretivism and postmodernism. However, cultural materialism is useful for analyzing very extended time periods, such as those brought about during the Paleolithic, Mesolithic, Neolithic, and the Industrial Revolution.

POSTMODERNISM AND INTERPRETIVISM

Postmodernism and interpretivism are two recent paradigms of thought, which are often in opposition to materialistic explanations as well as each other. Postmodernism is principally a critique of conventional ethnography rather than a theory of culture. Post-modernists contend that the construction of cultural reality should not be limited to the members of a culture but should also include the ethnographer writing about culture: he or she is bound to interpret that culture according to his or her own experiences as a culture bearing human being. Postmodernists go so far as to argue that a scientific and objective ethnography is impossible. Postmodernism, a movement with origins in architecture and literary criticism, has permeated fields such as philosophy, history, sociology, political science, and women's studies, as well as anthropology. Within anthropology, James Clifford, George Marcus, and Michael Fischer argue there can be no such thing as scientific ethnography. Marcus argues that postmodernist anthropology should be a "deconstruction" of ethnographic texts (showing how they are biased by the culture of the writer) or "experimentalist ethnography," creating new methodologies of ethnographic writing. One form of experimentalism is a dialogue between ethnographer and informant where the process of communication becomes the object of study. Postmodernists look at writing about cultures as "text" and not as reality. At best, the postmodernist critique has opened the door to new kinds of ethnography, poetry for example, and highly inventive writing that resembles novels. When done well and with sensitivity, these explorations open new vistas to understanding other cultures, or that of the ethnographer. When done poorly and with little regard for scientific standards, postmodern ethnography degenerates into any-person's commentary on another culture and on the ethnographer.

More pertinent to the points of view adopted in this text is **symbolic anthropology**. This is a subdiscipline of anthropology that has been the hallmark of Clifford Geertz and his followers, who defend their style of ethnographic writing against the criticisms of postmodernists. Geertz's approach to ethnography is to emphasize the interpretation of the meaning and values of symbols in a culture. For this reason, his approach is sometimes referred to as **interpretivism**. Symbolic anthropologists argue that they have never thought of their ethnographies as pure science or pure reality and that they have always understood the problem of bias, but that techniques can be used which reduce bias. Clifford Geertz has developed a *thick description* model, which attempts a rather Boasian understanding of culture from the point of view of the members of the society. This Geertz does by writing about an ethnographic event, such as a funeral or a dance or a theatrical presentation, in intense detail. These events are interpreted in light of the cultural setting and require an extensive understanding of the subject culture and its history.

Geertz's writing is particularly rich and has become important to the Indonesian peoples whom he has been studying for many decades. He has been able to show how Indonesians respond to culture change by emphasizing their own symbolic world, despite the pressures to abandon traditions. His approach is a continuation of the American school of historical anthropology and, in the right hands, can offer brilliant insights into other cultures. It is, to use a term introduced earlier, a fine example of emic analysis in anthropology.

Postmodernism and symbolic anthropology are both humanistic approaches to ethnography, and both are rich in descriptive complexity; however, only symbolic anthropology really addresses cultural change through study of how people respond to outside pressures by developing pride in their ethnic heritage. Another set of approaches depends on models—simplifications or abstractions of reality—which seek an understanding of how sociocultural systems work, adapt, and change.

symbolic anthropology

A subdiscipline of anthropology that emphasizes the interpretation of the meaning and values of symbols in a culture; also called interpretivism

interpretivism

An approach to ethnography that emphasizes the interpretation of the meaning and values of a culture's symbols

■Malaysian school children. Clifford Geertz's writing has been able to show how Indonesians respond to culture change by emphasizing their own symbolic world, despite the pressures to abandon traditions.

POLITICAL ECONOMY

The third paradigm of global anthropology is political economy, which also has clear roots in classic anthropology. Political economy became very popular in anthropology during the 1960s and 1970s, particularly ideas of modernization, dependency, and world-system theory and globalization. Political economy has great historical depth and has influenced all of the social science disciplines. It began in the Enlightenment in the investigation of the origins of capitalism and colonialism and was first defined by Jean Jacques Rousseau (1712–1778) in *Discourse on Political Economy* (1994 [1755]). Rousseau pointed out that nation states manipulated their economic institutions through politics. Thus, capitalist institutions have characteristics based on the use of power by those who control the state, unlike the way they were portrayed by Adam Smith in *The Wealth of Nations*.

Particularly important to a political economy approach was Eric Wolf, who was trained by Julian Steward along with a cohort of like-minded graduate students at Columbia University in the late 1940s and 1950s. Wolf began to lay down research parameters that differed from classic anthropology in the mid-1950s (Mintz and Wolf 1957). Eric Wolf modified Immanuel Wallerstein's modern world system theory with the concept of globalization. Wallerstein's model was based on the idea of a world divided between a capitalist core, and poor and exploited periphery and a semi-periphery, which was between the core and periphery. While Wallerstein's model was based on the exploitation of periphery and semi-periphery by a capitalist core, Wolf offered an alternative perspective of interactive global networks of economic and political power in which many countries blocked the capitalist core through the development of state intervention in economic development. Wolf's influence brought to anthropology the discovery of what historians and sociologists had known for a long time: that social forms of communities were not created *in situ* but evolved in complex relationship to the institutions of larger societies, often in colonial settings (Bennett 1998, 74).

The Interaction of Global Anthropology Models

Global anthropology is a far cry from classic anthropology, yet most of its paradigms are rooted in that time period. One pioneer of global anthropology whose roots are in the classic is the applied anthropologist John W. Bennett. His book *The Ecological Transition* published in 1976, contained most of the basic element of global anthropology. In that precedent-breaking book, Bennett argued that the interactions among ecosystems, cultural institutions, and political economy play a fundamental role in globalization and adaptation but that they cannot be taken apart. However, he shows how they can be understood as analytically distinct systems, which have complex feedback connections to one another. He introduced the concept of **socionatural systems** (Bennett 1976, 1993). This view differs from cultural materialism in its consideration of the institutional arrangements that mediate between human beings and the natural environment. Bennett's approach further diverges from the cultural materialists in that he conceptualizes humans as adapting to local ecosystems through human decision making, not through natural selection. Bennett refers to this process as "minding," "anticipation," and "coping." (Bennett 1993). In Bennett's approach, local ecosystems become part of institutional change at the local level.

socionatural systems

The relationship among ecosystems, cultural institutions, and political economy

Bennett's groundbreaking work was also unusual in that it focused on a large part of southern Canada. He showed how the Upper Middle West of North America has been transformed by American farming and has transformed the original frontier cultures to such an extent that it is quite impossible to separate nature from culture. Finally, Bennett's globalization approach did not accept either a materialist or symbolic anthropology point of view but combined both.

In later work, he introduced the distinction between micro and macro models to facilitate global analyses. In his work, the macro-systems of the world interact at the local level through what he refers to as the "micro-macro nexus," the interaction of ecologies and institutions at the local level influenced by macro forces such as international trade and global financial patterns (Bennett 1985). Bennett's work on the globalization of modern southern Saskatchewan, Canada, shows how the people of the town of Jasper—farmers, ranchers, Cree Indians, and Mennonites—all respond to each other and to national, global, and local ecological pressures in a continuous process of adaptation and change (Bennett 1969).

In a series of papers dependent on Bennett's approach, globalization scholars described a series of complex models which included regional ecosystems, hierarchical market and administrative forces, pressure groups, and other forms of quasi-organized social and political interests, that is, institutions (Smith and Reeves, eds. 1989). A major achievement of Bennett's globalization perspective is that it combines a concern for studying complex socioeconomic processes with a flexibility of analysis that takes into account micro and macro level decision-making, as well as institutional pressures and facilities (Smith and Reeves 1989, Stonich 1993, Black and Young 1992).

Global anthropology models study the complex interrelationships among ecosystems, institutions, and political economy forces at the local level (Stonich 1993, 25) The approach is interdisciplinary, not just anthropological, for it is also used by geographers, economists, political scientists, and sociologists.

Global anthropology is very productive, particularly right now. In this time of environmental challenges and financial meltdowns, we must not only look at relationships between institutions but also at how the transitions in one system influence transitions in the others. Most significantly, the tide of global capitalism and the ineffectiveness of socialist command economies or protective state socialist economies are forcing transitions in economic systems to transitions in political systems.

The change to open economies can be called a global economic transition, and it is what most people mean by globalization. There have been many such economic

■Russian Prime Minister Vladamir Putin

transitions in the past, and they make up the discipline of economic history. However, most economic transitions in the past were restricted only to Western Europe and North America. Globalization has opened almost every country in the world to international trade and finance. Often, globalization produces very rocky and unstable political situations that can only be resolved through a political transition to representative political systems.

Thus, in some parts of the world globalization is having a significant effect on the political systems in the countries. In the process of privatizing property and businesses, previous totalitarian, authoritarian, or communist systems are forced to relinquish some power and control. In Western Europe and North America, this change has been ascribed to a growth in the middle class. The same change appears to be happening in some of the countries of the world effected by globalization, particularly in Eastern Europe, Asia, and Latin America, but less so in the Middle East and a few countries such as North Korea and Iran. The transition to open political systems can be called the political transition. Thus, we see that the economic transition forces a more democratic, or at least, a more representative form of government in several (but not all) nation states.

There are many examples of the linkages between these two systems (the economic and political transitions) found throughout this text. A critical example is Russia where Boris Yeltsin first tried to force his country through the economic and political transitions a decade ago. Prime Minister Vladamir Putin and President Medvedvev have blocked these, but it may only be a matter of time before a growing middle class increases its control of the government. Another example is modern Mexico where four successive presidents have been attempting a very similar operation, introducing free markets into a one party-state controlled by a corrupt government. Mexico's economy and political systems are opening, but the recent financial crises may limit success.

The current financial crisis may force a modification of globalization. The current downturn in the economy of the United States is forcing leaders of other countries, officers of the World Bank and the International Monetary Fund, outside investors, or various interest groups (international institutions) to slow down globalization. There are many examples that we will examine in the chapters to follow. Globalization has produced a rapid increase in the wealth of many nations, but critics argue it has also brought about increased class stratification as the rich get richer and the poor get poorer. As we will learn, there are others who argue that increased wealth has actually been much more evenly spread around and that statistics of developing economies are not reliable.

The third system that is intricately related to the political and economic transitions is the ecological transition to sustained development. The human concern with the environment is paramount in societies that live close to the land, such as most hunting/gathering and pastoral societies. With the advent of agriculture, humans began to shape the land to satisfy human needs, and populations swelled, putting more and more demands on the land. With industrialization, the link between humans and the land became even more tenuous; and for decades, our environment was abused and our natural resources depleted.

J. W. Bennett has called this process the ecological transition. His original meaning was quite different from ours, more pessimistic, with the transition from sustained yield societies (societies which live off nature's bounty) to modern societies characterized by non-sustainable growth (Bennett 1976). Non-sustainable growth is economic expansion that consumes the very resources needed for survival. Before discussing how we might approach a more optimistic model of the ecological transition, we need to understand a fourth transition to which it is intimately linked called the demographic transition.

The fourth global model is called the demographic transition. H. Leibenstein in *Economic Backwardness and Economic Growth* first described this in 1957. Leibenstein provided the first consistent theoretical framework explaining why families were getting smaller in prosperous societies. Previous theories had worked primarily on the basis of ethnocentric and naive, if not outright racist, assumptions about the nature of human sexual behavior. "Malthusianists" quoted Thomas A. Malthus and tended to believe in the natural sexuality of humans, which cannot be controlled without state-imposed policy. According to Malthus, populations grow by geometric progression while agricultural production only grows arithmetically. Thus, according to Malthusianists, the world is doomed unless states pass laws preventing population growth.

Leibenstein argued that Malthus was wrong and that family growth is not determined by natural sexuality. Leibenstein distinguished between three types of utility that children yield to their parents. First, for most parents, children are a source of pleasure and can be considered like consumption goods. Second, children have value as productive agents, especially in more traditional and rural situations. Third, children can provide insurance for old age or illness. The costs of the added child include the direct costs of food and shelter. Opportunity costs, or opportunities foregone, are the indirect costs. An example would be income which could have been earned by a woman had she not had to take care of a child, or a vacation trip that was foregone to pay for college tuition.

Leibenstein drew attention to what happens with prosperity and modernization. There is a higher survival rate for children and new occupational environments characterized by greater specialization and increased mobility. There is also an increased need for expensive educations. Even with rising incomes per head, the cost of an added child goes up whereas his/her contribution to family income goes down because he/she must support his/her own family in modern societies. It becomes rational to have fewer children, and this is what happens.

This is the ideal model. But what has happened in the periphery? We should take a closer look at the demographic transition. John Bennett points out that demographic transition has the following three stages:

1. The first stage is defined as the typical stage of affairs for most human beings: high birthrates balanced by high death rates with slowly growing or fluctuating population. This describes India, China, and most of the countries of Latin America and Africa until recently, when modernizing institutions altered the picture.

2. The second stage, considered to be the true transition, occurs when improved nutrition and medical care, associated with early stages of industrialization and modernization, results in a lowered death rate while birthrates remain high; this results in rapid population growth. Europe and North America went through this stage from about 1860 to 1950. This process has been operating to a greater or lesser degree in non-Western countries for the past century.

3. The third stage is associated with low birth and death rates, and a low rate of population increase. This comes about as levels of living rise, education spreads, and people begin to "trade off" fewer children for a better way of life (Bennett 1976, 113).

It is the second stage that is a problem in the periphery. For various reasons, the transition from the second to the third stage is "blocked." Population growth is interwoven with other feedback cycles. For example, the drop in mortality rates in the periphery is due largely to improved disease control, which has been introduced quickly and cheaply, and has greatly outpaced significant economic change. The resulting population increases tend to cancel out small increases in wealth and goods due to economic growth. Given current high population growth rates and low economic growth rates in most countries of the periphery, the issue is whether these countries will ever reach the theoretical point of economic prosperity at which people opt for small families.

Having discussed the demographic transition, we would like to propose a three-stage ecological transition: 1) the transition from hunting and food gathering (food extraction) to food production; 2) a shift from pre-industrial to industrial production, which is highly damaging to natural ecosystems; and 3) a shift, which is occurring now, from societies which are totally committed to industrial production to societies which are committed to sustainable resource management. This last phase is not to be regarded as a shift back to phase one in any sense but rather is an outgrowth of the contemporary interest in trying to protect natural resources and wild habitats. Sustainable resource management is a commitment towards managing nature's resources (primarily extractive components of the economy: forests, seas, grazing lands, farms, mines) to do the least possible destruction to ecosystems. The control of policies that govern ecosystem misuse is usually in the hands of local, state, and federal governments. These attempt to minimize the impact of privately owned businesses. However, in democratic societies, there is a balance that has to be worked out between those who wish to preserve ecosystems and those who wish to expand the economy.

Now notice the links between the transitions. It appears that an economic transition leads to a political transition, and this leads to a demographic transition that, in turn, leads to an ecological transition to sustained development. That there are links between these four systems is clear, but why and how they are linked is not clear. In many instances, the process begins quite the other way, with a cultural and value shift in the direction of an ecological transition. In the United States, the value shift towards an ecological transition began in the 1960s. Modern Mexico, even with its blocked political transition, is trying to bring about an ecological transition; and this is true in many poor countries. One must be careful here because this is only an apparent link between "systems" without the study of institutional choice. Societies must make choices through their (changing) institutions as to how they are going to chose which of these transitions will be followed and how far. A democratic society may not choose to protect its habitats but rather may choose to emphasize employment instead. This was true, until quite

■Sustainable resource management is a commitment towards managing nature's resources (such as the tropical rainforests) to do the least possible destruction to ecosystems.

recently, of fairly democratic communities on the Northwest Coast of the United States that chose to cut down forests in order to give loggers jobs. Of course, the lumber corporations had much to gain from this choice and put pressure on communities to choose in an anti-environmental direction. The Federal Government, with pressure from other American communities, forced the protection of habitats; and many logging communities felt that their interests and democratic rights were being overridden by a powerful government.

The connections between the transitions, then, are mediated by institutions that are part of the transition process. There is nothing mechanical or really predictable about the connections between "systems." We return here to the link between a postulated ecological transition and an economic transition. It may be easier to protect habitats when societies are wealthy. Again, to many this will sound like a complete contradiction: doesn't the creation of wealth destroy ecosystems? Yes. The evidence around the world for the last three hundred years is very clear. Yet the odd contradiction is that once societies have become economically prosperous, an ecological transition is possible and it is necessary. Why? Because one must invest wealth to protect habitats, and it takes wealthy societies to insure the protection of nature. Furthermore we have no choice; we have to protect the planet we live on.

It is not possible in this text to articulate all the interactions between the systems and to show the adjustments that have been, and are being, made in the transitional periods of rapid change. Instead, we only wish to point in the direction of institutional analysis. One cannot study only how humans adapt directly to their habitats; we must also examine how institutions intervene in making choices. Before getting caught up in overly optimistic predictions, we should end here by pointing out that transitions can be blocked. Blocked transitions may be more common in our experience of the last century than positive passage.

A blocked transition is the lack of ability to pass through one of the four transitions because of a failure along one or more of the other transitions. As an example, the ecological transition is blocked in China because its authoritarian central government has chosen to support short-term economic development over habitats. Plans to build the Three Gorges Dam on the Yangtze River are opposed by every ecological group in China—but to little avail. The lack of democratic process blocks the possibility of people making choices that would facilitate an ecological transition. In India, a huge and growing population acts as a block on both the economic and political transition; these blocked transitions act, in turn, to block either a demographic or ecological transition. Another example of how a lack of movement in one transition can act to block movements in other transitions comes from modern Mexico. Attempts to protect habitats there are blocked by poor people whose values are locked into day to day survival.

In the following chapters, students will have the opportunity to understand how these various transitions and blocked transitions operate without we, the writers, trying to explain every link, a task that would be monotonous to read and write. The study of the linkages between transitions appears to us to be the greatest challenge facing anthropologists in the twenty-first century.

■ ■ ■

Chapter Summary

Development of Anthropological Theory

Nineteenth century ideas about cultural change were unilineal evolutionary theories postulating that all cultures progress inexorably from simple to complex. One of the most famous of these theories was that of Lewis Henry Morgan who argued that cultures progress from a state of savagery to barbarism to civilization. Another set of theories to explain culture change and differences were those of the British and German diffusionists who believed that the development of civilization occurred in only one or a few centers and differentially diffused outward from these centers.

During the classic phase of anthropological thought, from 1900 to 1970, which began with a reaction against the speculative evolutionary theories of the nineteenth century, Franz Boas and his students in the United States developed historical particularism as a school of thought. Structural-functionalism (also known as British social anthropology) developed in Great Britain with two different emphases, those of Radcliffe-Brown and Malinowski. Both were to influence American anthropology in the 1940s and 1950s.

Three prominent theoreticians of the 1950s, Leslie White, Julian Steward, and Homer Barnett, held different ideas about culture change and evolution. White resurrected some of Morgan's ideas and postulated a form of unilinear or universal cultural evolution based on human control and use of different forms of energy. Steward focused on the relationship between cultures and their environments and argued for a theory of multilinear or parallel evolution. In Steward's view, cultures that began as very similar would evolve in different directions if subjected to different forces, and those that began looking very different would end up looking very much the same if subjected to the same forces. Steward is considered to be the father of cultural ecology. Barnett, with his theory of innovation, located the source of all culture change in the human mind.

Contemporary theory in cultural anthropology is divided among four views, each with its variations: materialism, Marxism, interpretivism, and postmodernism. Cultural materialism is an outgrowth both of Steward's emphasis on environmental factors and White's heavy stress on technology as the basis of cultural evolution. Marxist explanations also emphasize the role of technology but tend to ignore environmental factors. Interpretivism, a continuation of historical particularism, focuses on the symbolic side of culture, looking to understand the meanings and values of symbols through the eyes of a culture's members. Postmodernism has its origins in literary criticism and is more a critique of ethnography than a theory of anything. Postmodernists argue that ethnography is a type of fiction constructed by the ethnographer. We argue that by combining materialism with interpretivism it is possible to create a more satisfactory approach to the kinds of complex questions created by globalization. In seeking to find a name for this approach, we have chosen *political ecology*. Because a few cultural materialists for a Marxist approach to ecological issues have adopted this same term, we are not entirely happy with it. There seems to be little to be gained by arguing over the categories for academic points of view; and having explained that we are happy combining materialism and interpretivism, we will concentrate on substance rather than definitions and proceed.

Chapter Terms

cybernetic theory	139	monogenesis	117
diffusion theory	122	organic solidarity	136
ethnocentrism	125	polygenesis	117
ethnographic relativism	125	*Scala Naturae*	114
historical particularism	126	socionatural systems	143
interpretivism	141	symbolic anthropology	141
mechanical solidarity	136	unilinear evolution	122

Check out our website
www.BVTLab.com
for flashcards,
chapter summaries,
and more.

Chapter 4

Bands and Tribes:
Remote Peripheries

As we begin this discussion of bands and tribes, we must note that modern bands and tribes do not necessarily bear much resemblance to their paleolithic and neolithic ancestors. Only to a limited degree can we understand the bands and tribes of the distant past through the study of historic survivals on the peripheries of modern civilizations. A combination of archaeological evidence, historical accounts, and ethnographic descriptions allows us to make inferences about the economy, sociopolitical organization, and material culture of bands and tribes that existed prior to the development of chiefdoms and states. In doing so, however, we should remember two important points: First, the classification we use (band, tribe, chiefdom, state) is itself an arbitrary categorization of a continuum of culture types. Second, all of our historic and ethnographic, and much of our archaeological, data come from cultures that are the products of complex cultural evolutionary processes, not pristine paleolithic and neolithic forms. Bands of hunters and gatherers and tribes with a variety of different subsistence techniques exist or co-exist on the periphery of the modern world system. In the past, they were present on the peripheries of archaic empires. They generally lack forms of hierarchy. All other things being equal, which they never are, it is the remoteness from archaic or modern cores that best explains the lack of hierarchy in bands and tribes. The closer they are to trade routes, the more likely they are to develop hierarchical forms of organization.

Hunter-Gatherer Bands: Existing Outside of Civilization

Hunting and food gathering bands are the most remote societies both in time and space. Almost every region of the world still supports a handful of these societies, and they are extremely important to modern anthropology because they can teach us something about how societies once "lived lightly on the land." They also teach us that hunters and food gatherers are radically different from ourselves in ways we would not expect. While they hunt animals, they are generally peaceable. The relationships between men and women tend toward egalitarian; and while they worship nature, their attitudes toward day-to-day events are pragmatic and optimistic. (Tribal societies, on the other hand, whether pastoral or agricultural, tend to be warlike; and their treatment of women is highly variable.)

The family level of sociocultural integration, which is the only enduring level of organization, typifies band societies. The family is the unit of production, consumption, and decision-making par excellence. Forms of organization beyond the family level exist but are temporary and flexible in membership.

For most of human history, hunters and food gatherers, as well as tribal people, have gone about their lives largely unaware of civilizations, and when aware, unflinchingly unimpressed with what civilizations had or have to offer. One writer has described the economies of tribes and hunters and food gatherers as anti-civilization. Their economies are based on **reciprocity** or gift giving, rejecting the profit-based maxim of modern society. One develops the impression that hunters and food gatherers are not to be pitied but admired. And so it has been for thousands of years.

At the moment before the discovery of the New World in 1492, there were ancient civilizations around the globe that controlled regional trade empires. We know of their presence in Mesoamerica, the Andes, along the Great Silk Road of North Africa and Asia, a few running south into the Rift Valley of Africa, the Asiatic civilizations of China and India, and minor theater states in Southeast Asia. In Western Europe, small feudal states fought wars with each other to gain control over long distance trade.

reciprocity

Economic transactions between individuals or groups where exchange is based on trust that the person to whom something is given will be equally willing to give in return (moral relationships)

■Hunter-gatherer tribe in Ethiopia

More remote from these centralized and bureaucratic states were chiefdoms, societies too far away to be brought under central control, but participating directly in long distance trade. These will be examined in the following chapter. Examples are the chiefdoms of the Hawaiian Islands, the Northwest Coast, the Mississippi Valley, the eastern slopes of the Andes, possibly along the Amazon, in the southern parts of the Rift Valley of Africa, and in the mountainous regions of Asia away from the central valleys. Yet more remote were tribal societies, too numerous to summarize here, and most remote were hunting and gathering bands. While they were remote, however, research by anthropologists over the last several decades challenges our immediate notions of what the lives of hunters/food gatherers were like.

From earliest times, we find that humans organized themselves within a variety of biomes into hunting and food gathering societies which anthropologists call **bands**. Bands are highly homogenous despite considerable differences in environments. More than thirty thousand years ago, during the **Late or Upper Paleolithic**, hunting and gathering societies' levels of technological sophistication in the art of hunting and food gathering were only superseded, perhaps, by the traditional Inuit (Eskimo). In many parts of the world where agriculture and other ecological adaptations are impossible, hunting and food gathering continues today in forms similar to that of the past, except that the encroachments of modern "civilization" have made traditional survival difficult.

Ten thousand years ago, all societies were hunters and food gathers, although some of these may have achieved tribal levels of organization in parts of Southwest Asia where agriculture was developed. The same may have occurred a few thousand years later in the New World hearths of agriculture in Mesoamerica and South America. By the time of Christ, only half of the societies of the world were hunters and food gatherers. When the New World was discovered, hunters and food gatherers occupied only 15 percent of the earth's land surface (Murdock 1967, 13–14).

The older literature in anthropology tended to give the picture that "the specter of starvation" stalked the hunter and food gatherer. Marshall Sahlins argues that this was far from the case and that hunting bands were the "original affluent" societies (Sahlins 1972). Sahlins argues that the perception of hunters and food gatherers as societies of scarcity is an ethnocentric bias of peoples living in civilizations. Hunters and food gatherers had no one to compare themselves to and did not feel deprived. Richard Lee's work among the Dobe !Kung of the Kalahari Desert in southern Africa is an example of modern hunter/gatherers who survived comfortably on their traditional resources. Elman Service (1966) points out that during a good season a single hunter may not work more than three to four hours a day. Studies show that hunters tend to be healthier, on an average, than modern industrial populations. Slowly we have learned that hunters and food gatherers suffer few of the diseases and pressures of modern society, are healthy, and as we will see in the case study at the end of the chapter, eat very well.

Only a few isolated pockets of hunter/gatherer folk survive today. Among them are 45,000 Bushmen of southwest Africa. Most are attached to the Tswana tribe as serfs, but 5,000 of them pursue their aboriginal nomadic mode of life. One of these populations, the !Kung, has been studied extensively by the ethnologist Richard Lee. His studies give a sense of the "ethnographic present" of band society (see case study that follows later). The Koroca of southwestern Angola appear to resemble the Bushmen in culture and physique. About 170,000 Pygmies still live in the tropical forests of central Africa. Many of these are partially agricultural. In the Ituri Forest of the Congo basin, however, the Aka, Efe, and Mbuti still preserve an aboriginal way of life.

---

bands

Peoples on the peripheries of ancient and modern states and chiefdoms who practiced hunting and food gathering, had egalitarian societies, and were largely nomadic

Late or Upper Paleolithic

The last phase of the "Stone Age," coinciding with the appearance of biologically modern humans *(Homo sapiens sapiens)* and lasting from 40,000 to 9000 BC

In East Africa, the Dorobo and the Hadza have been recently studied. There are half a dozen groups of hunters in central Ethiopia. In India there are a number of hunting societies, but these are dependent on agricultural villages and are often treated as specialized castes. Australia still has havens of a few hunter and gatherer Aborigines. Many Inuit in North America still carry on their hunting/fishing way of life (Murdock 1967, 13–20). In South America there are still some small groups who depend heavily on hunting or fishing and gathering, but the non-agricultural groups of far southern South America such as the Yámana (Yahgan) and Selk'nam (Ona) of Tierra del Fuego and the Alacaluf of the Chilean archipelago have disappeared in this century.

There are many other hunter/gatherer populations who no longer practice their traditional economies but who have been of great importance in anthropological research. Among these are the Shoshones and Yumans of the Great Basin, the Paiute of Nevada, the Apache of the Southwest, and the Siriono of eastern Bolivia. The societies of the Great Basin are thought to be very similar to the hunting and gathering societies of pre-agricultural Mesoamerica, which we will be examining in a later chapter.

Generally speaking, there are broad similarities between hunting and gathering bands despite drastic differences in environments. However, even those remaining groups listed above have changed and become increasingly dependent on the outside world economy, often to the point where it is not clear whether they are still hunters and food gatherers. Many have been placed in settlements much like reservations. Sadly, many live in a state of welfare dependency; and alcoholism and suicide are common. The observations made in this chapter are based on studies carried out on the above and other now extinct groups in the nineteenth and early twentieth centuries.

When making comparisons between ancient and modern hunters and gatherers, one must exercise extreme care, as we noted at the beginning of this chapter. Modern forms of adaptation are comparable only in the most general of terms. There is little doubt, for example, that hunting and food gathering during the Late Paleolithic was a much richer form of adaptation than it is today. On the other hand, today many hunters and gatherers have access to high-powered rifles and sophisticated traps, which make the job of hunting somewhat less onerous than it once was, but can rapidly deplete resources. Resource depletion and the destruction of local ecosystems often leads hunters to become dependent on the resources of powerful and modern nation states such as Canada and the United States. The remaining native populations of the Arctic are particularly dependent on the resources of advanced industrial societies and are increasingly vulnerable due to habitat loss from logging and oil exploitation.

However, if we keep our perspective, recent and modern hunters and food gatherers can tell us much about the past and about how they adapt to their environments in the present.

■Many hunting and gathering tribes have been placed in reservations. Sadly, many live in a state of welfare dependency; and alcoholism and suicide are common. Margaret Washington holds a portrait of her granddaughter, Elyxis Gardner, thirteen, who was found dead in June 2008 from suicide on Wind River Indian Reservation in Wyoming.

DEMOGRAPHY, TECHNOLOGY, AND SUBSISTENCE

The remote societies referred to here as hunters and food gatherers, like other societies in this text, should not be understood as a primitive stage or as "the first stage in cultural evolution." We should look at them as dynamic forms of adaptation to either geographic or historical necessity. Hunters and food gatherers exist in areas quite remote from the trade routes of powerful civilizations. Once brought into those trade routes, as Aleutian Islanders were brought into the trade networks of the powerful Russian state of the nineteenth century, their ways of life tend to be destroyed and they end up on the bottom of the state hierarchy.

Hunters and food gatherers are not really "primitive," although that may be one's first impression because they live by strategies of adaptation that depend almost entirely on human energy. The variations in strategies show us how social organization can be used to make effective use of energy systems. The technologies of people like the Inuit are remarkably advanced in both their sophistication and complexity, as were those of the hunters of the Upper Paleolithic. On the other hand, the tools of some agriculturalists, such as the simple digging stick combined with fire to burn down trees, may be considered primitive; yet it was a highly efficient way to farm. To assume that there is an evolutionary progression from simple to complex in sociocultural organization caused by technological change is simplistic.

While technology is most certainly important to adaptation, we usually find that human technologies tend to be as complex as the jobs that need to be done, given the environment and sociocultural level of adaptation that the society has achieved. In the Arctic, survival requires complicated and sophisticated tools, which probably represent thousands of years of experimentation. Take, for example, the method that Inuit use to dispose of wolves. They take a sliver of sharp bone and soak it in urine until it is soft. Then they bend it into a semicircle and shove it into a piece of blubber, which they then throw out on the snow, where it dries and freezes. A wolf will usually swallow the blubber whole because it is hard to chew in a frozen condition. The blubber thaws in the wolf's stomach, the sliver of bone springs open, and the wolf is stabbed from the inside, hemorrhages, and dies. Ingenious, although hard on the wolf.

On the other hand, life in a tropical forest does not require complex tools and sophisticated clothing (actually, the less the better); but it does require an appreciable knowledge of the environment. The same is, of course, true of the Arctic. Here we see that one of the biggest problems with generalizations about hunting and food-gathering bands is technological determinism. It is easy to assume that the simplicity of band social structure is the result of simple low energy technologies. However, knowledge of the environment may require much greater sophistication than the knowledge of tools. In fact, tool systems, as among the Inuit, may be extremely complex. It will become apparent that hunter/gatherer social organization is not an adaptation to tools but to environments.

The Shoshone of the Basin-Plateau area of the United States are an example of a technologically simple society. A quantitative analysis of their technology showed that if one breaks down their culture into details such as basket weaves and shapes, religious beliefs, social practice, and other details, that the total includes three thousand items. In contrast, the U.S. forces landing at Casa Blanca in World War II unloaded five hundred thousand items of material equipment alone (Steward 1968, 69).

One concomitant of a hunting and gathering existence is the need to follow after migratory animals. A nomadic existence, in turn, places limitations on material culture. Generally, weapons and utensils must be kept at a minimum. An exception is the Inuit. They have harpoons with detachable heads, compound bows, stone blubber lamps, the igloo, kayaks (men's boats), umiaks (women's boats), and dog sleds, to mention just a few items of their material culture. However, it is also true that the Inuit are not all that nomadic. They focus their attention on sea going mammals and place their hunting sites on the migration routes of a variety of animals. The greatest change occurs between summer and winter when they move away from the coast inland to hunt caribou and other land mammals.

The single greatest problem for the hunter is the storage of food because, with the exception of the Arctic where food can be frozen, meat simply does not last long—there is no way to store it. This means that it is foolish to spend more than a certain minimum of time hunting. A surplus of meat is wasted meat. Because of this basic fact, meat is usually shared with all members of the band through reciprocity. Reciprocity is a type of economic relationship between individuals (not groups) where transactions are based on the idea of gift giving. If I have been lucky enough to kill an animal, I give the surplus meat to my close relatives as gifts, expecting gifts in return when they have equal luck. This type of sharing and return sharing is the *sine qua non* of a hunter's existence. It is not to be confused with barter, which will happen between groups. One is expected to be generous within the band; between bands one can negotiate an advantage.

One of the most persistent stereotypes of the subsistence techniques of hunters and food gatherers that has been overcome in recent studies is the role played by the animals hunted. Recent research shows that plant (and sometimes marine) resources are often much more important than animals in the diet. As Richard Lee (1984) points out, the hunter-gatherer subsistence base is surprisingly dependent on plant foods.

While the technologies of hunters and food gatherers are highly variable, with some (e.g., the Inuit) being as complicated as those of peasant agriculturalists, the ecosystems yield roughly the same calories per individual. Population densities are kept down through a variety of means—including abortion, infanticide, and reduced sexual activity due to taboos. Also, women who depend on high protein diets will tend to have lower fertility rates than those with diets high in carbohydrates.

These variables tend to support a cultural materialist interpretation of life in hunting and gathering societies. Limited calories means limited population densities, and limited population densities determine or influence the other "systems."

GENDER ROLES IN BAND SOCIETY

Among hunting and gathering peoples, there is little division of labor except by age and sex. All men are hunters, produce their own tools, build their own shelters (with considerable help from their female friends), and so on. It is usually reported in ethnographies that the men do the hunting and the women do the gathering, but that may be partially a result of the way that male ethnographers have collected their data. When one examines ethnographies about hunter-gatherer societies, a woman picking up the eggs from a bird's nest is called "gathering"; if a man does it, it is called "hunting." If a man gathers crawfish, it is fishing; if the woman does, that is gathering. Such a built-in bias may have affected the way that we see the division of labor between men and women in hunting and food gathering societies. In the final analysis, we will probably find that while men do most of the hunting and women do most of the gathering, the boundary between these two activities is less than clear.

The relationship between men and women in band societies tends to be fairly equal. However, the degree of equality in a marriage is directly tied to the economic productivity of the women. As a general rule, the more women contribute to the "public economy" the greater equality exists between the sexes and the less tenuous is the contract between men and women in marriage. The public economy is the visible economy, which is that which contributes to subsistence, i.e., gathering food. In a hunting and gathering society, as is shown in the case study on the !Kung (see below), women contribute very obviously to the food quest. This dynamic of gender equality is similar to that in the contemporary United States where there tends to be more equality in marriages when both men and women are wage earners. The more a woman earns, the more power she has in the relationship. The consequence, in both the United States and among the !Kung, is that women can abandon the marriage and survive on their own if the male becomes oppressive; and it often appears as though the male needs the economic talents of the female more than she needs him. These observations about the !Kung were made twenty years ago when Richard Lee made his first studies and are changing today as !Kung society becomes less based on hunting and gathering and increasingly on the ability of the male to market his skills (although the overall picture is very ambiguous, the tradition of female equality is powerful).

SOCIAL STRUCTURE: FAMILY, MACROBAND, AND MICROBAND

While band economies are extremely different from our own, kinship relations in band societies show some remarkable parallels at the family level to the kinship relations of modern industrial societies, at least for certain hunting/gathering populations (both the Eskimo and the !Kung). Hunter/gatherer and modern industrial societies have **bilateral networks**, informal kinship systems in which kinship is traced out from a man or woman to relatives on both sides of the family. The kinship relations diminish in importance as the relations become more distant. **Social structure** consists of the rules by which social organization is determined. In societies with bilateral networks, social structure ensures flexible social relations of kinsmen. One of the basic determinants of social structure in both band societies and modern industrial societies is the need for economic and ecological flexibility. Economic reciprocity (transactions) is tied to egalitarian networks. Bands must take advantage of changing and not always predictable resources scattered over large territories. Likewise, working families in modern corporate societies have to move several times during a lifetime to take advantage of different job opportunities. As with the band, the modern family cannot develop an extensive and centralized organization of kinsmen, such as lineages, clans, or other large and stable networks of kinsmen. In both kinds of societies the nuclear family and a close network of kinsmen are the major building blocks of social organization. However, there is an important difference in that the family in hunting/gathering societies cannot survive without the help of other families, while it is not at all uncommon for families to survive today without cooperation from other families (but not without the help of the state or corporate entities).

Band population densities may only be one person per square mile or less, and a band's territory may include several hundred square miles. This is true whether one is examining the Inuit of the Arctic, the Athapaskans of subarctic interior Canada, the Australian aborigines, or the Mbuti or Hazda of Africa. Such low densities are a response to resource distribution and availability. Hunting and gathering bands do not have highly structured memberships. They

Case
Study

Subsistence and Division of Labor Among the !Kung

Lee wanted to know how much of an effort was involved in hunting and food gathering, and how much the women contributed to the public economy. He carried out a series of experiments ranging from driving some !Kung to a place where food was easily available, to following them on the food quest. What he discovered was surprising to those who had assumed that the majority of a hunter/gatherer's time would be put into the food quest or that male hunting would be the dominant economic activity. The following describes Lee's first experience after he drove some !Kung men and women to gather Mongongo nuts, their major food.

> Without ceremony, the women fanned out and started to pick. Grabbing my camera, stopwatch, and notebook, I hastened to follow them. They bent from the waist with a smooth and effortless motion and picked 5 or 6 nuts each time and popped them in their *karosses*, one piece garments-*cum* carrying bags. Every ten minutes or so, each would return to the truck to spill out her load on the spot she had picked out. The individual piles began to accumulate rapidly. The men were collecting too, using smaller bags than those of the women. I sampled how rapidly the women were able to pick. They were gathering at a rate of 40 to 60 nuts per minute, or 2,000 to 3,000 nuts per hour. By two o'clock everyone was finished; they dumped their final few onto the piles, which looked enormous to me (Lee 1984, 35).

Lee calculated that each woman had gathered enough food to feed a person for ten days and each man enough for five days.

Lee's studies revealed that the !Kung enjoy a good diet and that they do not work very hard to get it. He determined that this was partly attributable to the fact that they depend primarily on vegetable food, which was gathered by women. Meat brought in by the men contributed only 30 percent of the calories. In addition to the mongongo nuts, the !Kung have an inventory of over one hundred edible plants; and the availability of plant foods made it possible for them to subsist on less than twenty hours a week of work. Not bad when one considers that the average industrial worker in this country puts in forty hours a week or more!

The tools of the !Kung are relatively simple, consisting primarily of the digging stick and the kaross, which serves not only to carry vegetable foods in but as a blanket as well. It is primarily their vast knowledge of the growth, ripeness, and location of local plants upon which they depend for survival. However, they are selective of the foods they eat, just as we are, depending on the mongongo nut as a primary food. Lee evaluated their "food hierarchy" and found that they tended to eat their way out of a camp—first eating the foods they desired, while walking further and further out, and later eating foods which were less desirable but closer to camp.

Despite the lesser contribution to the overall nutrition of the !Kung, Lee points out that meat has a great social value. When a large animal is killed, great cauldrons are used to cook and people gather to celebrate. The distribution of meat is done with great care, according to traditional sets of rules; for example, the wife's mother always gets the superior cut of meat. Successful distributions are remembered with pleasure, while improper distributions cause wrangling for weeks (Lee 1984, 45).

Hunting depends on the bow and poison-tip arrow, the knife, a springhare hook, and rope snares. Guns are almost entirely absent. While the !Kung hunt by tracking and killing, most of the successful hunting is done with dogs or by following burrowing animals underground or by snaring. The !Kung are superb trackers and can make accurate deductions from the faintest marks in the sand. They can identify an individual person merely by the sight of a footprint in the sand. They can deduce species, sex, age, speed, and physical condition from an animal's tracks. They can also deduce the number of hours or minutes elapsed since an animal passed by.

Once a man has successfully killed an animal, he does not receive the kinds of social rewards we would expect. Instead, the hunter's game is insulted during a ritual which Lee calls "insulting the meat." The successful hunter must be modest; here is a quote from the hunter Guago:

■ !Kung are superb trackers and can make accurate deductions from the faintest marks in the sand. They can determine species, sex, age, speed, and physical condition from an animal's tracks.

Say that a man has been hunting. He must not come home and announce like a braggart, "I have killed a big one in the bush!" He must first sit down in silence until I or someone else comes up to his fire and asks, "What did you see today?" He replies quietly, "Ah, I am no good for hunting. I saw nothing at all ... maybe just a tiny one." Then I smile to myself because I know he has killed something big (Lee 1984, 49)

The hunter who has killed "something big" can expect the following razzing from fellow hunters who go out to help him butcher the animal:

You mean you have dragged us all the way out here to make us cart home your pile of bones? Oh, if I had only known it was this thin I wouldn't have come. Peo-

ple, to think I gave up a nice day in the shade for this. At home we may be hungry, but at least we have cool water to drink (Lee 1984, 49).

The proper response to the insult is the following:

You're right, this one is not worth the effort; let's just cook the liver for strength and leave the rest for the hyenas. It's not too late to hunt today, and even a duiker or a steenbok would be better than this mess (Lee 1984, 49).

Insulting the meat, as Lee points out, is a means of maintaining equality in the group. Even Lee was not free from insults, as he found out one Christmas when he had an ox butchered for the group among whom he had lived and had to endure the teasing and insults that all hunters had coming to them.

---

tend to grow into macro-bands or break up into small micro-bands according to the availability and concentration of resources. A micro-band may consist of one to a few families, while a macro-band may contain up to a hundred or more individuals. The micro-band/macro-band social structure reflects the availability of resources (the micro-environment) and the attempt to control resources. Interestingly, similar features are found in modern industrial societies with elites which have resources often using their extended kin (macro-band) relationships to control wealth, although living in single family dwellings (micro-band), while in the poorest social classes many families (micro-bands) may attempt to pool their economic resources and live in the same apartment structure (macro-band).

Van Stone has described the shift from micro- to macro-band in his study of the Athapaskan Indians of western Canada, while Richard Lee has documented the same for the Dobe !Kung. The smallest unit would consist of a few families depending on restricted resources. With increased food supplies, the number of people would increase to two hundred or so. However, formal leadership was minimal—if it existed at all. Band size depended on resources; and many of the populations in the interior of Canada and southeast Africa, where resources were limited, tended to stay in micro-bands unless something unusual happened, such as a large kill from a herd of migrating caribou (Athapaskan) or the occurrence of a large number of Mongongo nuts (!Kung). The populations along the major rivers (Canada) or around waterholes (Africa), where resources were (are) richer, tended to form macro-bands and to stay relatively large unless resources dropped; then the macro-band would break up into micro-bands. It was only when macro-bands formed that ceremony became important:

By the time the ice had broken up and the river was clear and high, the Peel River Kutchin were gathered at three or four fishing camps along the lower river. This was a time of year when games and ceremonies were held and when raiding and warfare with the neighboring Mackenzie Eskimos took place. In summer, following a season of fishing and leisurely life, the larger groups in the fish camps would break up and return once more to the mountainous areas of the upper river (Van Stone 1974, 41).

sodality

A form of social group that cuts across kin groups and unites people on the basis of mutual interests

Writers describing hunting and gathering societies stress the lack of centralized authority and political structure. Van Stone describes the Athapaskan bands as composed of close kinsmen who regularly changed membership. Any particular band might be in existence only one or two generations. Even so, cooperative working groups were important, as were religious **sodalities** in ceremonial performances on ritual occasions (a sodality is a unit of social organization which cross cuts the band but is not based on kinship). The shift from micro-band to macro-band was an important occasion for the exchange of women in marriage, which was always associated with the exchange of ceremonial gifts. The exchange of gifts for women between micro or macrobands was a critical economic and ceremonial event, possibly related to the origins of trade.

MARRIAGE IN BAND SOCIETIES

Marriage is a form of recruitment of persons to band societies, and marriage was one of the key rituals of the life cycle, along with birth and death. Generally, women left the micro-bands into which they were born and married men of other micro-bands (but usually within the macro-band). This allowed bands to form alliances with each other, which of course helps expand the kinship network. In band societies, women usually married out of their **families of orientation** (the families into which they were born), but their **families of procreation** were often formed with men of their own macro-bands. It was and is important that the husbands were not close kinsmen (a practice called **exogamy**). Studies of modern hunters and gatherers show that the emphasis on women leaving their own macro-band has been overstated. That is, residence after marriage was not always patrilocal. Men might move out of their bands in search of a mate or might be attracted to a woman in a band where resources were richer. This practice is called matrilocal post-marital residence. In band societies, much depends on resource availability and much less on ideal rules. This flexibility diminishes among tribal societies where post-marital residence is usually more structured.

In hunting and gathering societies, as in our own today, marriage is often a matter of individual choice, although parental advice is not uncommon. Unlike our own society, however, marriage is more of a matter of economic necessity than a romantic event. A man without a wife or a woman without a husband is often miserable. The average man and the average woman cannot survive well without a mate. Steward says of the Shoshone:

> The irreducible minimum of Shoshonean society was the nuclear or biological family. Isolated individuals could not well survive in this cultural, environmental or ecological situation, and unmarried or widowed persons generally attached themselves to a nuclear family. This family was able to carry out most activities necessary to existence, for husband and wife complimented each other in food-getting and together they procreated, reared, and socialized their children. Women gathered vegetable foods, made baskets needed for this purpose, and prepared all food. Men devoted most of their time to hunting, which, though not very rewarding, was extremely important and time consuming (Steward 1968, 78).

Steward's observations about the Shoshone can be extended to the Hazda, the !Kung, the Athapaskans, and the Inuit. In all of these societies, many events might break up a marriage in addition to the death of a spouse. Either mate might become attracted to someone else or one of the two spouses might not be a good provider. Whatever the reason, marriage was not very stable and most men and women married at least twice during their lifetimes. This does not mean that marriage was taken lightly or casually. Jealousies tend to be just as serious as in our society and often resulted in homicide or suicide.

RELIGION IN BAND SOCIETIES: EXISTENTIAL IDEOLOGIES

Religion and ritual refer to those organized social relationships, practices, and beliefs that mediate the relationship of the members of a group to the deity or deities associated with

family of orientation

The family into which one is born

family of procreation

The family one creates

exogamy

Marriage outside of some specified group like a lineage or clan

that group (Rappaport 1979). The mediation ultimately connects humans to nature; and in hunting/gathering societies where religion is integral to all aspects of life, religion helps to maintain a balance between humans and the resources of the habitat.

Elman Service writes that the religions of hunters and food gatherers are "existential ideologies" and tend to reflect adaptations to their environments. They tend to be "naturalistic" rather than "supernaturalistic." That is, their worlds tend to be populated by forces and powers that are derived from the forces of nature rather than something that goes beyond nature. Often, a power not too unlike George Lucas' *Star Wars* concept of "The Force" is thought to pervade the world. Anthropologists call this non human "force" by the Polynesian word **mana**. Mana has been likened to an electrical force field. Humans and animals can gain access to mana through proper observation of certain rituals. As an example, within the Washo of California, a sorcerer, who controlled mana, might "shoot" a foreign body into a victim because he/she had violated some taboo, such as mistreating wildlife. Inviting a shaman, also with mana, who would pray, smoke tobacco, and sing special songs, would carry out a cure. These rituals would pull out the evil influence from the victim (Downs 1971, 188). Both the sorcerer and the shaman used "mana" but in directly opposite ways, one for bad magic and one for good magic. The curing rituals themselves usually have something to do with fertility or hunting magic. The man or woman of power is one who has learned how to handle mana; and often, if he or she is very successful at the manipulation of mana, he or she may become a shaman. While anyone can acquire some mana, and most persons know some of the rituals involved in being a shaman, the job implies danger and is avoided by many. This is because mana is often thought to "backfire" on the person using it (sometimes turning the user into a sorcerer). Mana is treated with healthy respect, and not all believe in their abilities to control it.

Mana pervades the forces of hunting and gathering societies, many of which have clear animal origins. The wind, rain, stars, and other forces of nature are also often personified. Animals are often "changelings," like the werewolf, and can and do change into human form; by the same token, humans can often transform themselves into animals.

The ties of the members of the band to the land is often reinforced by the personification of outstanding features of the landscape such as huge rocks, caves, tall trees, and water holes. These may be conceived as the abodes of the ancestors or other spirits. Territoriality blends into religion. One might say that the hunting band often worships its habitat.

Humans and animals are perceived to have souls, although hunters and gatherers ideas of "soul" differ considerably from our own. Instead of just one soul, a person may have several, some of which have an animal basis. Illness is often thought to be based on soul loss where one of the souls or a part of a soul may fly away or is captured by an evil shaman. Good Inuit shamans are famous for the trances they go into during which their own souls fly out of their bodies and recapture someone's lost soul.

A variety of taboos on the hunting of certain species or over-hunting a given habitat are obviously connected to the preservation of habitat. Other taboos, such as taboos on sex before the hunt and ritual occasions, may act to lower the birth rate; but other practices such as infanticide and the purposeful limitation of children may have a more significant adaptive impact. An example of a taboo which may have an ecological impact is the Inuit belief in Sedna, the goddess of the deep. Sedna protected animals from overhunting by setting out very specific totemic laws. An Inuit could not hunt more than three male red foxes in any one day. He had to place his knife on the body of any fox trapped so that its soul could take the soul of the knife back to the village of fox souls. If the hunter disobeyed these edicts, Sedna would sneak up and tip over his kayak, drowning him in freezing Arctic waters. Art and dance tend to reflect the naturalistic religions of hunters and food gatherers.

mana

A Polynesian word that is used in anthropology to refer to a powerful magical force, which can be manipulated by humans who have the appropriate ritual knowledge.

Artistic expression, while differing in terms of style, is usually an expression of hunting and fertility magic. Drawings that depict humans and animals involved in the hunt may be designed to magically encourage fertility. Dances are often tied to rituals of fertility and the hunt, with men and women dancing in imitation of the animals they have hunted or personifying the wind and the rain.

A **deity** is omnipresent and a source of ultimate power. A deity can be a force of nature or a force that is beyond nature (supernatural). Both magic and religious actions or thoughts involve supernatural phenomena. They differ in that religion assumes supernatural intervention for human benefit (or harm) while magic assumes cause and effect relationships that humans attempt to manipulate directly for good or evil. Both religion and magic help explain that which cannot otherwise be understood. People at a distance from ideologically driven states (e.g., China, the Mexica, the Inca) are attracted to religions which explain events as due to magical or nature based forces. Particularly in hunting and gathering societies, those activities touching on life threatening experiences—such as birth, illness, and death—tend to be the center of shamanic rituals based on nature and nature's forces. **Shamans** are persons who have access to power that appears to come from nature, such as a spirit helper in the form of a bear or wolf who intercedes on behalf of humans to protect them. The closer a society is to one of the ideologically driven states, the greater the mix will be between naturalistic beliefs and those based on supernatural forms and forces. As an example, hunting and gathering societies in Southeast Asia tend always to have elements of Buddhist or Hindu religion mixed in with the natural religions, while those on the periphery of the ancient Mexica states had elements of sun worship.

We have noted that in hunting and food gathering societies, every person is politically and legally autonomous. It is also true that in such societies, every person is his and her own religious functionary. No third party is designated to act permanently as minister or priest and to mediate with the deities. Religious roles are just as undifferentiated as the others we have looked at. Some people do take on the role of shaman, but this is a part-time, and sometimes temporary, occupation.

deity

A supernatural being, a god; that is, a being with powers which are beyond those of nature

shaman

A religious specialist, male or female, who is able to communicate with and control natural and supernatural forces and mediate between humans and these non-human forces

The Tribes of the Periphery

Tribal societies were generally closer geographically to archaic core states than bands, but they were far enough away that trade and warfare seldom resulted in hierarchical structures. However, they were too far from the core states for those states to dominate them. For example, the Inca empire of the highland Andes often attempted to dominate the tribes of the eastern Andean piedmont, but the distances were so great that the cost in food alone made warfare and domination too expensive. In addition, many tribal societies fiercely resisted and states paid great prices trying to subdue them. It was usually cheaper to leave tribes alone. This is no longer true, and in the modern age many tribal societies, which maintained their independence from the pre-European states of the Americas have been subjugated by modern core states such as Argentina and Chile.

At the most, tribal societies may be stratified in two tiers, nobility and a commoner class; more usually, however, there are no strong class differences. Individuals may be ranked on the basis of kinship for some purposes, but most social interaction is egalitarian. Prestige is usually achieved through personal ability rather than ascribed at birth. For example, among the eighteenth century Cherokee, a young man would join his first war party in his teenage years and between ages twenty-five to thirty would receive a war rank based on his success as a warrior. Between ages fifty to sixty, he would cease being a warrior and would become a "beloved man." Young men were expected to defer to the judgments of beloved men (Gearing 1970, 154). Tribal societies have more highly structured social systems than do hunter/gatherer societies, but at times it is difficult to make the distinction between the two. In reality, all societies form a continuum from simple to complex with respect to social structure, technology, and other features. The difficulty of distinguishing between tribes and hunter/gatherer bands is often the result of our arbitrary scheme of classification. This does not mean that the classification is not useful for analytic purposes. It does mean that some societies in terms of social structure and level of technology, for example, straddle the boundary between band and tribe or between tribe and chiefdom.

THE SHIFT TO FOOD PRODUCTION AND ANIMAL DOMESTICATION

One general distinction between hunting/gathering societies and tribal societies is that tribal societies produce food, either growing it as crops or as domesticated animals. There are, however, tribes that depend on wild food plants, such the Indians of California, and many who practice hunting, such as the buffalo hunters of the American Great Plains, whose resources are great enough to support large populations and a tribal social structure but who do not rely on domesticated plants or animals.

There were at least four major regions in which food production independently originated: the hilly flanks of Mesopotamia, the Tehuacan Valley of Mesoamerica, the northern part of the Amazon-Orinoco basin in South America, and Southeast Asia. In Mesopotamia, the beginnings of food production occurred directly after the last stages of

Figure 4.1

❑ Map of Hunters and Gatherers

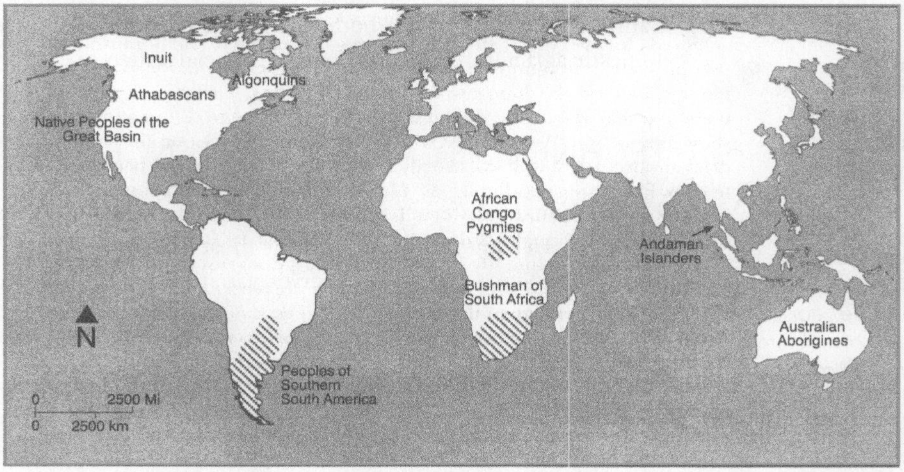

microblade

A type of implement found in European Mesolithic cultures and formed by snapping a blade into smaller pieces and forming those pieces into composite tools; also called a microlith

Mesolithic

The Middle Stone Age, the period during which the domestication of plants and animals took place, generally characterized by microlithic tools, dating from about 9000 to 7000 BC

ladang

The term used in Indonesia to refer to swidden plots (see Swidden)

milpa

The term used in Mesoamerica to refer to swidden plots (see Swidden)

swidden

Shifting between agriculture dependent on cutting down and burning a small patch of forest, planting crops on the plot for two or three years, and then allowing the plot to lie fallow (remain unused) for a number of years until the forest has grown back

the Upper Paleolithic. During the Lower and Middle Paleolithic, hunters ate whatever they could find. In the Upper Paleolithic (Stone Age), beginning about eighteen thousand years ago, they were able to concentrate on a single species of animal, cattle (Redman 1978, 58). Organized bands would have best hunted cattle, which are large and travel in herds. Tools were carefully worked blades like those found in western Europe during what is known as the Aurignacian. As time went by, the blades became more specialized and smaller, and are referred to as **microblades**. These are considered diagnostic of the shift from the Paleolithic to **Mesolithic** (Middle Stone Age), a term given to the period when humans made the shift from hunting and food gathering to food production. Some of the microblades were used to cut wild grasses, the ancestors of modern wheat and barley. Other important discoveries were mortars and pestles used to grind grains. In the area just north of the Tigris and Euphrates Rivers, in the foothills of the Tauros and Zagros mountains, it is clear that hunters and food gatherers began to rely on domesticated grains and cattle, and that they began to settle in villages. Charles Redman, the archaeologist, has argued that at the site of Malaha in the Upper Jordan Rift Valley people had become tribal between 11,000 and 9,000 BC, living in a large village (fifty houses) of semi-subterranean structures with floors of flag stones (Redman 1978, 73).

A similar model can be applied to the shift from hunting and food gathering in the New World. This happened in the Tehuacan Valley of the southern part of the state of Puebla, Mexico; however, it happened later in time than in the Old World (between 7000 and 2000 BC), and there were no domesticated animals involved. The early domesticates were maize (corn), beans, squash, and chili peppers. The first three became known as the triadic staff of life for the peoples of Mesoamerica, but the chili pepper was also important as an appetite stimulus and for the vitamins and minerals it provided. Settled villages, implying tribal social structure, can be traced to 2000 BC for the highlands of Mexico (Kehoe 1981).

Marshall Sahlins points out that in western California, southern Alaska, the American Northwest, parts of new Guinea, and other world regions (eastern Australia and the hilly flanks of the Tauros-Zagros mountains of Iran in prehistoric times), there were exceptionally abundant food resources and high population densities, and yet no need for the production of domesticated plants or animals. In the Northwest it was salmon, in California it was acorns, and in New Guinea it was sago (Sahlins 1968, 39). Sahlins refers to these seasonally available resources as a "natural agriculture." Important skills were developed to deal with the poisons in acorns, the storing of salmon, and the processing of sago. The California populations had both matrilineal and patrilineal descent; and despite the lack of domestic agriculture, they were tribal in social structure.

TECHNOLOGY AND SUBSISTENCE PRACTICES

There are many different types of subsistence practices associated with tribal society. The following is a summary of a few of the most important ones. The variations of subsistence practices produce a great number of variations in the types of sociocultural adaptations found in tribal societies.

Forest Agriculturalists Most tribes of the modern world are forest dwelling, agricultural societies distinguished by slash-and-burn cultivation, also known as **ladang**, **milpa**, or **swidden** horticulture. Once practiced in temperate as well as tropical zones, the spread of intensive agriculture has eliminated slash-and-burn horticulture from temperate zone countries, along with most of the tribes that formerly practiced it. A 1957 FAO report estimated that 200 million slash-and-burn cultivators (not all of whom are tribal peoples) inhabit some 14 million square miles of the tropics. (Conklin 1961, 27). Today it is likely that even more swidden cultivators occupy even less land area.

In swidden horticulture, the trees in a small plot of forestland are cut down, as is the undergrowth. Very large trees may be "slashed," meaning that a strip of bark is cut away from the tree exposing the cambium layer and effectively killing the tree. Toward the end of the dry season, using care to prevent forest fires, the cut over area is burned. The plot is planted for from two to four years, at the end of which time it is abandoned (except for the tree crops) and another plot is opened. While plot abandonment after just a few years has been regularly attributed in the literature to declining soil fertility, Robert Carneiro long ago presented evidence to show that this conclusion is in most cases unwarranted. The rapid growth of weeds appears to be the main reason for abandonment of swidden plots (Carneiro 1961). It used to be thought that swidden horticulture was detrimental to the fertility of tropical soils. However, Betty Meggers has shown that planters of swidden plots imitate the layered structure of the forest itself by planting tree crops—such as bananas, plantains, and certain palms—interspersed with a large variety of different root and seed crops. Tropical forests tend to be made up of thousands of different species of plants and trees. According to Meggers, garden trees and forest trees have the function of breaking up the force of tropical rains so that soils are not irreparably damaged (Meggers 1971). Having many species of plants within a small area also reduces the possibilities of crop destruction due to disease and insect pests. Most important, by moving their subsistence plot every few years, the cultivator and his family allow the tropical forest to regenerate.

Slash-and-burn horticulture, depending on soils and climates, can often support fairly dense populations with complex tribal and even chiefdom social structures. In the Southeastern United States, in pre-Columbian times, slash and burn horticulture supported large and dense tribal societies, such as the Creek and Natchez nations. The Natchez, who had a matrilineal descent system, may have been at the chiefdom or incipient state level. Today, the Natchez are thought to have been responsible for the development of chiefdom or state level societies in the Southeastern part of the United States and as far up the Mississippi river as St. Louis, Missouri. One of the most spectacular archaeological sites along the Mississippi is Cahokia, with its giant Monk's Mound complex, located in East St. Louis, Illinois. Monk's mound, the central temple, is one hundred feet high, covers sixteen acres, and may have taken two hundred years to build. Archaeologists have compared Cahokia and other southeast temple complexes favorably with structures of the politically sophisticated societies of Mesoamerica. The Maya groups of the lowlands of Central America, most with patrilineal descent, were organized socio-politically, at different times, in structures that ranged from tribes to chiefdoms to city-states with attached peasant populations.

Equestrian Hunters   A highly specialized type of tribal society developed on the American Plains during the frontier phase of American history. This is the period when land-owning eastern woodland Indians that had moved onto the plains and Indians from the dry southwest adopted the horse and the gun to hunt buffalo on the high plains. The Indians migrating from woodland to plains abandoned their agricultural way of life. A similar kind of culture appears to have emerged in southern Argentina and Chile and the Gran Chaco of Paraguay due to similar circumstances: the availability of the horse, the rifle, and herds of large game animals. The animals were the rhea (an ostrich-like flightless bird) and the guanaco, an American cameloid like the more familiar llama, although unlike the llama, never domesticated. Descendants of some of these populations became the gauchos of the plains of Argentina. Among the more famous of these equestrian hunters, noted for their resistance to subjugation and incessant raids on Spanish settlements, were the Abipón and the Mbayá.

The stereotypical image of the American Indian is that of the Plains tribes: the Sioux, Cheyenne, Comanche, and Arapaho. They are better known than the Creek or Chippewa, woodland Indians of the Eastern United States. However, Plains culture was an extremely brief episode that lasted only about three hundred years after horses were introduced into Florida and migrated into the Plains region in the sixteenth century. The tribal culture of the Plains Indians may have been fading towards a band type social structure as they shifted away from woodland agriculture to the hunting of buffalo (Oliver 1962).

Pastoral Nomadism   Another major form of adaptation of tribal societies is pastoral nomadism. Pastoral nomads tend to be highly independent and warlike. Historically, anthropologists have underrated their importance in trade. It is very likely that at least some pastoral nomads had reached the chiefdom level of organization in ancient times. Pastoral nomadism is the ecological converse of forest agriculture with a commitment to animal husbandry rather than growing crops in a tropical rainforest (Sahlins 1968, 33), and pastoral nomadism is thought to be as old as agriculture (Redman 1978, 135–140). Pastoral nomads traded milk, meat, and hides to agriculturalists in exchange for grain and manufactured goods after the domestication of the horse and camel made pastoral nomadism possible, which may have been six thousand years ago (Sahlins 1968, 33).

Case Study

The Natchez

That slash-and-burn horticulture can support fairly sizeable populations with complex social structures is supported by the case of the Natchez. The social system of the Natchez was particularly complex, with a dual division and aristocratic classes. The Natchez, who lived near Natchez, Mississippi, and were described by early Spanish explorers, may have been responsible for large temple complexes found throughout the southeastern United States. The Natchez people were sun worshippers, much like the Aztecs to the south in Mexico. They built pyramids to the sun, usually one at each end of a large plaza. Upon each mound was the dwelling of a priest chief, the Sun of Suns, brother of the celestial sun. He greeted his illustrious relative before the Sun temple while a perpetual sacred fire was tended in another temple.

The Natchez, typical of the Southeast Woodland peoples, were divided into moieties or dual divisions. Each village or town was organized into two groups that exchanged wives with one another, but the Natchez had an unusual marriage rule. There was a moiety of common-

ers and a moiety of aristocrats; the aristocratic moiety was divided into Suns, Nobles, and Honored People. The commoner or lower class moiety was referred to as Stinkers. The Natchez were matrilineal, with status traced through women. The unusual rule was that Aristocrats had to marry Stinkers, which elevated the children of male Stinkers to the status of their aristocratic mothers who could be Suns, Nobles, or Honored People. However, the children of male Aristocrats who married Stinker women dropped in status. Anthropologists have questioned how such a social system could survive because the children of male Aristocrats would be Stinkers, and in every generation, children of the successful male members of the ruling class would drop in status. Yet the emerging archaeology of the Southeast now shows that these horticultural people were hegemonic, conquering the surrounding peoples. Stinker warriors took wives from conquered towns, so there was a continued inflow of tribute in the form of women who would receive Stinker status.

The classic region for nomadism is the dry belt which crosses the Sahara Desert and East Africa, runs up through the Persian plateau and inner Asia, through Manchuria, Mongolia, Tibet, and into China (Sahlins 1968, 33, Wolf 1982). The most famous pastoral nomads are the "Noble Bedouin" of Arabia and the "Turkic" hordes of Inner Asia. Pastoral nomadism is also found in attenuated form in the north Eurasian forests and tundra, practiced by Sami (Laplanders) and various groups of reindeer herders of the Kamchatka Peninsula. In Africa, there is a great arc of grassland north, east, and south of the forested Congo where the Fulani of West Africa, the Turkana and Masai of East Africa, and the Hottentot and Herrero in Southwestern Africa are found (Sahlins 1968, 33). These are all societies that rely heavily, if not exclusively, on pastoralism.

TRIBAL SOCIAL STRUCTURE

Social organization in tribes is usually based on corporate descent group membership and not solely on the loosely structured bilateral networks commonly found in bands. However, there are tribal groups whose social structure is so lacking in hierarchy as to be very similar to bands, and some tribal groups are so hierarchical as to be confused with chiefdoms (and, indeed, may be chiefdoms). Tribes occur on the peripheries of states or chiefdoms. They had much more varied kinship systems than hunters and food gatherers, and we will only be able to sample a few here. While social structure is influenced by subsistence practices, it is also influenced by nearby chiefdoms and states. Any attempt to find a one-to-one relationship between subsistence practices and social structure has foundered except at the most general level. In general, tribes are less hierarchical than chiefdoms, and their social structures tend to be more direct expressions of adaptation to local ecosystems. Those tribes directly involved in trade tend to have greater hierarchy than those that do not, and often are considered chiefdoms. For example, the peoples of the Trobriand Islands tend to be classified as tribes by some writers and chiefdoms by others.

Bilateral Kinship   Strictly speaking, **bilateral kinship** is not a means of reckoning descent from an ancestor; it is a means of acknowledging who your relatives are by tracing links from yourself through your mother and father. Because bilateral kinship is traced from an individual (known as Ego in the anthropological literature), the networks of kinspersons thus recognized will be the same only for full siblings. These bilateral kin networks do not form corporate groups, although the kin relationships themselves may be socially important. Such networks may be the only basis of social relations in band societies. They can, and often do, exist alongside groups based on principles of descent in tribal and chiefdom level societies. In a bilateral kinship network, the entitlements and the responsibilities of an individual are established directly and only by links to others through one's parents and not by virtue of descent from some ancestor. Bilateral kinship networks are also called personal kindreds.

Types of Descent Systems   Tribal societies tend to be of two basic types. In those with **cognatic descent**, there is little gender inequality and little hierarchy. In societies with **unilineal descent**, gender inequality and hierarchy are usually more pronounced. We will examine here cognatic descent and the two common types of unilineal descent, matrilineal descent and patrilineal descent.

Cognatic Descent   The important difference between a bilateral kinship network and a cognatic descent group is that the latter is ancestor-oriented rather than ego-centered. In

bilateral kinship

Relationship to others (relatives) traced from an individual through his/her parents

cognatic descent

Descent traced through any combination of male and female links to a common ancestor

unilineal descent

Descent that is traced from a founding ancestor through either a line of females (matrilineal descent) or a line of males (patrilineal descent) to determine one's membership in a unilineal descent group

other words, membership in a cognatic descent group is determined by virtue of being able to trace one's ancestry back to the group founder. The most important feature of cognatic descent, and the one that makes it most confusing to those of us who do not use it as a form of organization, is that ancestry may be traced back to the group founder *through any combination of male and female links.* Tracing descent in this way has two important consequences for the individual. First it means that he or she can potentially belong to any of several cognatic descent groups—often eight because the group founder is rarely more distant than a great-grandparent. Second, societies with cognatic descent systems normally have rules about activation of membership, and this means that an individual will have to make some strategic choices during his/her life. In other words, choosing to be a member of one or two cognatic descent groups may preclude membership in others. With the Ngóbe of Panama, for example, cognatic descent groups own land and individual members have use rights. A man or a woman may claim membership in a group and farm the land belonging to that group, if either a parent or grandparent has exercised such rights. If neither a parent nor a grandparent has used the land, then an individual can no longer claim use rights, even though the individuals who do use the land are considered to be relatives through bilateral kinship reckoning. Availability of land is a major factor in the choices made by the Ngóbe.

The strategic or adaptive advantages of cognatic descent are flexibility and choice (although not as much flexibility as provided by bilateral kinship networks). Among many of the tribes of the Great Plains, cognatic descent provided the flexibility needed to balance populations and resources. Cognatic descent groups are also found among Amazonian peoples, such as the Kalapalo and the Xinguana, and among many of the peoples of the Pacific islands.

An important feature of most tribes with cognatic descent is that they generally have low population densities and live in remote regions. Their trade connections appear to be undeveloped, and they tend to be more self-sufficient than other tribal societies. Men and women tend to regard each other with a fair degree of equality, but men control public leadership posts, as they do in tribal societies with unilineal descent systems.

Unilineal descent   The other major type of tribal social structure is unilineal descent. In unilineal descent systems, membership in a descent group is determined by birth and an individual belongs to only one group, that to which his mother or his father belongs. If descent is traced back to a founding female ancestor through a line of females, the group of living members is called a **matrilineal descent** group. If descent is traced back to a common founding male ancestor, the living members constitute a **patrilineal descent** group. Descent groups that collectively own land or other property are considered to be corporate groups. Such groups are usually referred to as matrilineages if membership is determined through a line of females and patrilineages if descent is determined through a line of males. Unilocal, post-marital residence rules are common in societies with unilineal descent. If a man must live with his wife's relatives, this is called matrilocal residence. If a woman must go to live with her husband's relatives after marriage, this is called patrilocal residence.

Lineages may in some societies be associated into larger groups know as clans. Lineage members can usually trace descent back to a genealogically known common ancestor; clan members also believe themselves to be affiliated by descent from a common ancestor but this ancestor is often a mythical being or a heroic figure of the distant past to whom precise genealogical links cannot be traced. Usually lineages have many functions in both everyday life and ritual. Clans, on the other hand, rarely have other than ritual functions although they at times have served as the basis for units of warfare as among the ancient Scots. However, it is more common for warrior groups to be organized as sodalities that

matrilineal descent

Descent traced through a line of females (Both women and men acquire membership in a matrilineal descent group from their mothers, but only women can pass membership in the group on to their children.)

patrilineal descent

Descent traced through a line of males (Both men and women acquire membership in a patrilineal descent group from their fathers, but only men can pass membership in the group on to their children.)

crosscut unilineal descent groups. Such warrior associations were found among the Plains Indians and in many African tribes such as the Maasai.

dispersed clan

A clan whose members live in many communities throughout a tribal area

territorial clan

A clan that claims ownership of a territory in which its members are concentrated

endogamy

Marriage within a specified group like a clan or a lineage (Clan endogamy is more common than lineage endogamy.)

moiety

A division of society into two social groups, usually based on a rule of unilineal descent

phratry

A grouping of two or more lineages or clans into a larger group based on a belief in common descent, like a moiety except that the lineages or clans form more than two groups, called phratries

Clans may be **dispersed** or **territorial**. Dispersed clans have members in many communities throughout a tribal area. This results from a rule of clan exogamy, that is, a rule which says that a person must marry someone who is not a member of his or her own clan, combined with a rule of either patrilocal or matrilocal residence. Dispersed clans are common among the indigenous peoples of Southeast Asia such as the Hmong who live in the highlands of Laos, Cambodia, and Vietnam. Territorial clans are found in places like the densely populated highlands of New Guinea and among some groups in the Amazon basin, and they were found among the ancient Scots. While not all of the members of a territorial clan live in a particular village or territory, the majority does; and these dominate politically the few members of other clans that may reside in the area.

Territorial clans may result from a rule of clan **endogamy**, a rule that specifies that a person must marry a member of his or her own clan. Territorial clans seem, by and large, to have more strongly developed trade connections with other clans, tribes, chiefdoms, and states. In territorial clans, patrilineal descent tends to predominate although there are exceptions. Marriage to women of other clans is a means by which alliances can be developed with neighboring clans. The clan claims and defends a territory, which is the core of the clan's land.

Clans themselves may affiliate into larger groupings, usually on the basis of descent from a putative common ancestor. If the clans of a society divide themselves into only two such groups, the groups are called **moieties** and the society is said to have a moiety system. In societies where such a dual division occurs, a concept of dualism is usually manifest in many other aspects of social organization and symbolic thought. Dualism is a pervasive concept in the traditional organization of the Gê speaking peoples of Brazil such as the Sherente, Shavante, and Bororo. Sometimes clans will form higher-level groups, but there will be more than two such groups in the society. Such groups are called phratries (sing. **phratry**). Unilineal descent groups—whether lineages, clans, moieties, or phratries—are bound together not by the living but by the ancestors.

When tribes became chiefdoms and then states, as occurred in the Valley of Mexico, the underlying tribal structure was sometimes retained. The Aztecs of Tenochtitlan were organized into four major hue-calpullis or phratries (multi-clan forms of social structure) that quartered the city. These, in turn, were divided into calpullis or clans, which consisted of land-owning corporate lineages. The same was true with ancient Rome, which preserved its tribal social structure until quite late (many of the technical terms used by anthropologists to describe kinship were derived from Roman social organization).

Brian Schwimmer, an anthropologist at the University of Manitoba in Canada, has developed a World Wide Web site with an excellent set of tutorials covering the principles of kinship, descent, marriage, and post-marital residence. These tutorials contain quizzes at the end of each unit. Any student who is feeling even slightly confused by any of the above discussion should visit this site. The address (URL) is

http://www.umanitoba.ca/anthropology/kintitle.html.

Functions of Descent Systems   Descent systems appear to have had several distinct regulatory functions. These are regulation of food production and distribution, property rights, warfare, population, and trade. Anthropologists generally agree that food production allows tribal societies to maintain larger and denser populations than bands, but disagree as to why larger populations would pressure the development of corporate descent groups. Ecological and evolutionary explanations favor the idea that food production leads to population increase, and *larger populations need greater regulation* than hunter/gatherers. Larger aggregates of people need more formal means of social control. This means law must be more formalized, and there must be those who enforce the laws. This leads to increase in hierarchy and stratification, although most social control mechanisms remain informal. The most formal procedures emerge when there is conflict between groups, such as lineages or clans, which must be resolved by an intermediary.

It is also theorized that cooperation among groups larger than the family is needed to produce the food to feed a larger population. Lineage and clan groupings emerge in order to handle the more complex tasks of planting and weeding, and in the manufacture of household goods. The distribution end of the economy, it is thought, may have brought about the development of a "big man," a central figure who could gather surplus production from families and distribute it back within clans or villages, *particularly if the families are producing different kinds of foods and other goods due to ecological variation* in the tribe's habitat. It has also been argued that as food production and distribution become more complex, it is possible for authority figures to gain access to power and to use their positions to expand authority and control beyond what is needed by the local group. Yet all these theories are problematic: the difficulty of measuring the relationship among such variables as power, technology, population, calorie production, social structure, climate, and resource scarcity makes it difficult for any theory on the origins of tribal social structure to gain prominence.

To explain tribal organization as a simple function of plant or animal domestication and food production would ignore the many subsistence-based food-producing societies that do not have lineages and clans and closely resemble hunters and food gatherers in organizational simplicity. It would also not account for hunters and gatherers and fisherfolk, such as those of the Northwest Coast of North America, who have highly developed corporate lineages and are clearly tribal, if not chiefly, in their level of organization. The key does not appear to be agriculture by itself, but pressures on resources. If population densities are low, it would not be economically worthwhile to spend a lot of time and energy on the maintenance of descent systems. People practicing agriculture in regions with relatively low population densities tend not to have unilineal descent systems. Instead, they have cognatic descent groups or simple bilateral kinship networks. Both provide options in terms of group affiliation. Unilineal descent systems, in theory, do not; however, it should be pointed out that, in reality, *ad hoc* adjustments are common in unilineal descent systems to take account of such things as demographic fluctuations in relation to land availability.

In hunting and food gathering societies it does not make much sense for a band of people, whatever their internal organization, to own territory, whether they hunt land or sea animals. What would be wiser is to have an agreement (a verbal treaty) between people living in a region that everyone has equal access to all resources, as long as no one overexploits them. This is **public ownership** of resources, and differs significantly from **corporate ownership** typical of tribes. As we saw, the Dobe !Kung dole out permission to use the resources around their various waterholes freely, which is a form of generalized reciprocity or public access, as long as no one abuses the privilege. Hunting societies, then, would tend toward bilateral kinship networks because these are the most elementary of all systems and require the least amount of organizational effort and there is no ownership of

public ownership
Rights to the use of a resource are public to anyone

corporate ownership
Rights to the use of a resource are limited to those who are members of a group and are much more specific, in contrast to public ownership. In tribal societies, lineages or clans or other groups based on a principle of descent may be corporate owners of property.

natural resources. This would also be true for food producing societies in which the pressure on resources is so low as to not make the ownership of resources important. In societies with low resource pressure, whether hunter/gatherers or food producers, the ownership of resources would be public.

With increasing population pressure, resources become scarcer and control becomes more important for survival. Thus, a shift from public ownership of resources to corporate ownership by tribal lineages or clans is to be expected. The "bounded" quality of tribal units of social structure is then easily explained by the corporate ownership of resources by lineages and clans within which rights are collectively defined by birth. Such rights are **ascribed**; that is, they accrue to an individual by virtue of birth into a given lineage or clan.

It would seem that once intensive use of resources begins to produce scarcity, open access is no longer advisable. Now labor investments intensify, and it makes sense to restrict the sharing of the land and other resources to the group that is putting in the effort. *Ownership of resources now matters.* There are legal and cognitive reasons for the increasingly corporate or collective nature of resource ownership. It is necessary to find a very simple mechanism by which to determine rights. Because these are not societies with complex courts and legal systems like our own, the simplest way to structure rights is by birth. A child is born and his/her rights are determined by whether the society wishes the rights to run from mother to child (matrilineal descent) or father to child (patrilineal descent).

At the tribal level of organization, descent groups, not individuals, usually hold land, pastures, crops, and animals. Families have use rights to property because of their membership in these larger corporate groups. That is, the individual has the right to use land and other property through his family, and his family has a right to use land through the lineage, and the lineage has ownership by virtue of the relationship of its members to a common ancestor. Unlike modern capitalistic societies, every person has an inalienable guarantee of a livelihood. No household can be excluded from direct access to the means of its own survival.

One popular theory developed by cultural materialists and human ecologists, particularly Marvin Harris and William Divale, was that tribal social structure, religion, and warfare were means of controlling population, and that types of descent were the products of different forms of warfare. This theory is illustrated in the following case study.

Warfare, whether local or long distance, is found among both matrilineal and patrilineal tribes. It is a universal characteristic of tribes (but not of hunter/gatherers). Harris and Divale argue that warfare can be interpreted as a means of population control, but not through the death of men. They argue that the male war complex tends to give males high status and females low status among both matrilineal and patrilineal societies, leading to the practice of **female infanticide**, the practice of putting female children to death. Harris and Divale show that, statistically, tribal warfare leads to a lowering of fertility rates among tribal peoples by lowering the number of women who survive each generation.

Harris and Divale's theory about the relationship among descent, warfare, and population control is controversial; however, it does suggest why bilateral hunters/food gatherers and food producers with low population densities have very low levels of warfare, and why tribes with high population densities have unilineal descent (both matrilineal and patrilineal) and high levels of warfare. The kind of warfare found among tribes is what we would call a type of feuding. It is sporadic and small-scale and, in the view of the new institutional economics, it produces high transaction costs; that is, it makes trade very expensive.

ascribed status

Status in a society that is determined by birth

female infanticide

Causing the death of a female infant either through ritual murder or through neglect (In societies where this occurs, it is usually permitted because sons are considered more valuable than daughters.)

Case Study

Yanomamo Descent and the Male War Complex

In 1968, Napoleon A. Chagnon published a description of his initial contact with the tribal Yanomamo. The Yanomamo, who occupy the border country between Venezuela and Brazil, have subsequently come to represent the violence of men in tribal societies. Chagnon described how the men blow green powder up each other's noses through hollow tubes, which then causes green mucus to flow from their nostrils. After ingesting the drug, the men sit half-naked and shout at and pound each other, first with fists and then with their clubs. The patrilineal Yanomamo engage in local warfare. Sneak raids on their neighbors account for 33 percent of all deaths (Chagnon, 1968, 1974). Similar levels of violence are reported for other patrilineal tribal peoples around the world, including the Dani and Tsembega Maring of New Guinea. This led anthropologists to the initial idea that patrilocal residence, patrilineal descent, and warfare might be tied to each other as a means of reducing population. However, Marvin Harris pointed out two findings:

First, the deaths of the men did not reduce population increases because women bear the children, not men. Second, matrilineal societies are equally warlike. Marvin Harris expanded the theory into what he called "the male war complex." It not only explains warfare but also descent.

Patrilineal descent tends to be associated with patrilocal post-marital residence (the woman goes to live with her husband) and matrilineal descent with matrilocal post-marital residence (the man goes to live with his wife). Residency, in turn, appears to be determined by a complex of variables. According to Marvin Harris and his associate William Divale, patrilocal societies, which are statistically dominant in tribal societies, occur when it is advantageous for the society to be patrilocal; this would occur whenever men are dominant in the food quest and when *warfare is local*. On the other hand, when women are dominant in the food quest and *warfare or trade are long distance*, it is advantageous for the society to organize itself around women because the men are gone much of the time. Matrilocality structures the family around a core of mothers, daughters, and sisters, but it does not produce peace. In such societies, groups of men from neighboring villages go on long distance trade or warfare quests. The example given of matrilineal-matrilocal societies practicing long distance warfare and trade is the Iroquois of New York, who preyed upon the Huron, and vice versa. Other examples are the Nayar, a soldier caste in the state of Malabar (India), which specialized in long distance warfare, and the Mundurucu of the Amazon (Divale and Harris 1976).

The Political Economies of Tribes: The Impact of Trade on Tribes

Fredrik Barth, a student of Persian nomads (Iran) has described how pastoral nomads achieve "fictive chiefdoms." Their conical clans have a chief or chiefs at the top, which makes them appear like true chiefdoms. They are almost always patrilineal with descent traced through the male line from a founding ancestor, usually the mythical founder of a clan, down to the present day "chief" (Barth 1969). However, as Barth's close analysis of the Basseri nomads shows, the chief is really first among equals. He can only initiate an activity after the other adult males of the clan agree to his decision. According to Barth, the reason for the apparent but not real political centralization is the need for there to be a leader who can "appear" to make complex decisions about which way the herd of animals should go. This is so in order that outsiders are given the impression of great consolidation of power in the hands of one man. A second reason for the fictive chief is the need to have one individual represent the tribe when dealing with city dwellers, who are accustomed to the idea of centralized authority. However, back on the desert, the exigencies of a nomadic existence make every family an independent decision-making unit in most things.

The nomadic societies described by Barth were adapted not only to their arid environments but also to trade relations to other like tribes and to settled town and city dwellers. They operated within and between evolved states, and they had done so for literally thousands of years. The ancestors of people like the Basseri nomads appear to have operated in chiefdoms that were components of ancient states, such as the Persian Empire (AD 226–641), which dominated trade routes for several centuries in the Middle East.

Instead of "fictive chiefdoms," at least some pastoral nomads may have been, and others today certainly are, true chiefdom social systems in which the ranking of relations between clans and settled "khans" represent hierarchical connections determining complex trade relationships. A settled Khan, who may be linked by marriage to members of a state, cannot be considered as "first among equals" or as a fictional chief but as a paramount chief who acts to negotiate trade relationships with settled villagers and trade brokers. This brings us to the topic of the impact of trade on tribal societies, and the relationship of trade to social structure.

Trade is more important to tribal societies than traditionally thought, and trade relationships helped produce corporate property ownership and redistribution economies. This model is derived from *Eric Wolf's Europeans and the People Without History* (1982). Wolf suggests that before the rise of the European-American world system, elaborate trade routes existed around the world. He describes several of these trade routes including those of Mesoamerica, the Andes, Africa, Central Asia, Southeast Asia, and Europe. He goes on to describe how these trade systems were displaced and destroyed by the trade systems put into place by European civilizations in the centuries after 1600 (Wolf 1982).

The model presented here is also reminiscent of an earlier ethnographic model presented by Edmund Leach in *Political Systems of Highland Burma* (1954). Leach conducted research among the Kachin of Burma as best he could while serving in the British military during World War II. The region of Rangoon, a port of trade, was organized into an Asiatic style state. Further up river, which was the path of trade, existed Shan chiefdoms. These were intermediate nodes on the way to the "periphery." The periphery, the region of the Kachin, was tribal, but not an isolated sphere of human activity. Rather, it was integrated into the economy of the whole of Burma; and even today, under a socialist dictatorship, the "hill tribes" maintain much of their tribal independence and trade opium for Western goods.

It is possible to make the following generalizations about the relationship of tribal societies to distant states:

a) Ethnographically described tribes are not the self-sufficient, autonomous representatives of an earlier evolutionary stage they were once thought to be. They are, rather, the remains of societies that, while peripheral to states and chiefdoms, were nonetheless connected to them and to other tribes through trade.

b) Tribes, prior to the rise of Western Civilization, had goods worthy of state attention but not usually of sufficient importance or quantity to energize the state into conquest.

c) The relationship of state to tribe also was mediated by geography—the remoteness of the tribe. Distance makes the transportation of goods expensive (it raises transaction costs). Thus, it is not economically efficient to conquer distant tribes because of the costs not just of conquest but also of maintaining control; but such tribes can be integrated into the trade network of the state. Distant tribes remained for thousands of years warlike and non-hierarchical at the edges, but increasing in hierarchy where trade was of increased importance.

d)   The principal unit of production in a tribe is the household. Kinship is the chief means of organizing the economy; yet goods may be amassed by a big man, traded, and the returns redistributed in the more hierarchically organized tribes.

e)   Corporate ownership of resources prevents individuals from trading away the group's resources.

Interestingly, hunting and gathering bands of Canada and New England were transformed into tribes and from tribes into chiefdoms when English and French traders offered money and guns for furs. Warfare between previously peaceful bands of hunters escalated overnight, and internal hierarchy and ranking became common. Similar processes occurred when the slave trade in Africa transformed bands into tribes and tribes into chiefdoms or statelets (Wolf 1982).

Tribal social structure, that is, the kinship and descent system, is a response to a number of factors including two features of political ecology. First, there is a need to control local resources for the production of goods for trade (as well as consumption). This would intensify the need for collective ownership of resources by the group. Second, there is a need to respond to the complexity of trade. As the number of people and the number of goods increases, trade relations become more complex. It is one thing for two to twenty persons to exchange a few goods with each other, but quite another when several hundred exchanges of many different types of goods take place. The complexity of transactions increases exponentially as the number of people and goods involved goes up. As the complexity of trade increases, it becomes more efficient to select representatives to act as traders, thus creating hierarchy (here the role of big men as intermediaries and traders becomes clear). At this point, the logic of tribal society fades, and the rationale for chiefdoms becomes clear. The complex interaction of resource control and trade produces hierarchy. Thus, tribes with minimal hierarchy are those with the least developed trade connections and mechanisms of resource control.

EMBEDDED ECONOMIES

Neoclassical economists tend to look at an economy as an institutional component of society, which can be treated as a unique and separate system, distinct from other societal institutions and operating according to its own laws. Many anthropologists argue to the contrary: in tribal societies economies are "embedded" in the social matrix.

Karl Polanyi, an economic historian, argued that an economic exchange is no more than a temporary episode in a continuous series of social transactions. In tribal society, the value of a good is determined not by anything intrinsic to the good but by the relationship of the two persons exchanging the good. That is, social relationships take primacy to economic ones. In tribal societies, those things that an economist would not consider "economic," such as kinship and politics, are the very heart of the economy. Tribal economic systems resemble, yet are quite different from, the band systems of hunters and food gatherers. Like band systems, economic relations are familial, and the foci of economic exchanges are extended families. Production, for the most part, is a domestic function, as is consumption. According to current theory, production is geared to family needs, not to the demands of "consumers." However, unlike band societies, household production is not self-sufficient, and there must be exchanges between extended families, villages, or tribes.

A tension exists between the tendency toward hierarchy brought on by trade and the tendency toward egalitarian values based on the equal access to resources. When trade gets the upper hand, the tribe becomes increasingly hierarchical, with certain families gaining monopolistic control over trade. These families often act like petty aristocrats. If this process continues far enough, the egalitarian tribal structure is transformed into a chiefdom with hierarchical structure and status distinctions—and later, class distinctions (such as we found with the Natchez). The process of hierarchy creation helps to explain the big man complex and its transformation into the chiefdom. The collapse of trade networks can reverse this process—thus, the non-directionality of adaptive evolutionary change.

THE BIG MAN COMPLEX: REDISTRIBUTION OR TRADE?

potlatch

A redistribution feast, traditional among some Native peoples of Northwestern North America, in which an individual gives away wealth in order to achieve prestige or higher status

Tribal societies tend to be characterized by what Sahlins has referred to as the "big man complex." A variety of this complex called the **potlatch** is found among the indigenous groups of the American Northwest Coast. It is a widespread institution, and many attempts have been made to explain it. Sahlins sees the big man as the center of an egalitarian redistribution system, which assures equality and surplus (Sahlins 1965). At the heart of the potlatch is the "big man" who acquires privileges and ritual recognition for himself and his group through his generosity. One ecological explanation is that the big man acquires vast quantities of wealth, usually in the form of food, in order to give it away during feasts, thereby overcoming short term and local food shortages. A competing interpretation, we propose, is that the big man complex is not an egalitarian give away at all; rather it is a means of distributing trade goods within a regional trade network.

The big man complex, like other economic aspects of tribal society, tends to fit snugly into the social structure. In tribes with little hierarchy, feasts tend to be local and include only close kinsmen. As we examine more hierarchical tribes, the big man complex increasingly resembles a pyramid. When we cross the fuzzy line from a tribe to a chiefdom, we find that feasting tends to be focused on a single chief, who is the center of a large political and ceremonial system, such as is found in Hawaii. In a chiefdom, as Sahlins puts it, the political order is underwritten by a centralized circulation of goods, flowing toward the top of the social pyramid and down again instead of laterally. Furthermore, in a chiefdom each presentation implies a relationship of rank. This pyramid is a redistribution system; and as we will see later, with some modification, it becomes the basis for early state type societies.

TRADE AND RITUAL IN TRIBAL SOCIETY

Why would tribes trade? One good reason would be to overcome ecological differences in resource availability. According to modern ethnographic studies, tribal societies had elaborate sets of trade networks, which developed both within a geographically widespread tribe and between tribal groups that were adapted to distinct ecological zones. For example, there was a large trade center at the Dalles in eastern Oregon situated between two different tribal groups, the Chinook Indians of the lower Columbia River and the Umatilla Indians of the upper Columbia River. The two Indian tribes were adapted to different ecological conditions; west of the Dalles is rain forest country, and east of the Dalles is grassland desert. The two tribes met at the Dalles and traded goods from the two distinct ecological zones. The Chinook traded dried salmon up-river and the Umatilla traded deer meat down river. Lewis and Clark, who visited the trade center, described it as controlled by aristocratic families, as were the trade routes. Other trade partners of the Chinook carried on trade further west, down the coast of Oregon.

Because some of these tribes were hostile toward each other, certain individuals had ritual relationships with specific members of other tribes with whom they were "blood brothers." Blood brothers were sworn to protect each other and were supposed to avenge attacks on trade partners by members of their own tribes. Such ritual networks crisscrossed North America far back in time so that archeological artifacts from as far south as Florida are found in the Midwest along with goods from the Northwest. There is much evidence of prehistoric trade between Mesoamerica and the southwestern, southeastern, and midwestern regions of the U.S., as well. Archaeological evidence also hints at extensive trade networks throughout South and Central America and between Mesoamerica and the Andean region.

■   ■   ■

Chapter
Summary

Bands and Tribes: Remote Peripheries

In this chapter, we have examined two levels of sociocultural integration: bands and tribes. Hunting and gathering bands currently exist only on the remotest peripheries of modern states, and they have become dependent to varying degrees on the economies of state systems. Prior to the domestication of plants and animals, hunting and gathering was the only game in town, in habitats resource rich and resource poor. We cannot know exactly what these early hunting and gathering societies might have been like, although we can be sure there was variety in their adaptations. The family was, and is, the only enduring unit of social organization within the band. Larger units were flexible and temporary. Beyond a less than rigid division of labor based on sex and age, egalitarianism carried the day in band societies. Generalized reciprocity (gift giving) serves as the principal—sometimes the only—means of resource distribution. We base our inferences about the life and times of ancient hunters and gatherers on archaeological evidence, historical accounts, and ethnographic descriptions, as we do for the tribes of old.

Modern tribes exist on the peripheries of states and are partially dependent on them. In tribal societies egalitarianism still predominates, and the family is still an important decision-making body as well as a primary unit of production and consumption. However, larger and denser populations intensify resource use and result in the need to develop controls over resources. Trade brings access to a wider range of resources but exacerbates the need for resource control in the process. Collective ownership of property vested in corporate descent groups with use rights available to individual members and families is a common tribal solution to the problem of control over resources and trade. In the tribal level of organization, we see the beginnings of unequal access to resources and of rank and hierarchy, preconditions for the development of full-blown systems of social stratification at the chiefdom level.

Chapter
Terms

Check out our website
www.BVTLab.com
for flashcards,
chapter summaries,
and more.

Chapter 5
Chiefdoms and Pre-Modern States: Core-Periphery Relations

During the pre-industrial period, cores were occupied by chiefdoms. Chiefdoms formed an evolutionary stage between tribes and states. They had greater centralized authority than tribes but less than states. In general, chiefdoms occupied a greater number of distinct ecosystems than tribes, and their chiefs had much greater power than tribal leaders (who should not be called chiefs). States resemble chiefdoms, but their kings can initiate wars and they can occupy many more distinct ecosystems. A key to the difference between tribes, chiefdoms, and states is power. In tribes, power is diffused between clans; in chiefdoms, it is centralized into a single chiefdom, and in states it is centralized into a king.

Characteristics of Chiefdoms and States

States are hegemonic political entities, but chiefdoms are not. Aside from hegemonic control of territory, chiefdoms and states greatly resemble each other; it is often difficult to distinguish the two. Archaeologists often have trouble distinguishing whether the remains they dig up are chiefdoms or states. While they are organized like miniature states, chiefdoms do not have the capacity to control territories the size of states, a characteristic that may not be visible to archaeologists. Both states and chiefdoms are hierarchical. However, in states the division between the rulers and ruled is sharp, while in chiefdoms such a division is not clear-cut. Kings that have the ability to start wars without the support of those who are ruled rule states. In chiefdoms, chiefs cannot begin wars without the support of their followers.

CHIEFDOMS

There are many chiefdoms that still exist or existed until recently, and they give us some idea of what the ancient chiefdoms may have been like. For example, many of the Hawaiian Islands were ruled by chiefs up until the turn of the twentieth century, although a few retained tribal characteristics on poorer islands. In addition to the Hawaiian Islands, the Indians of the Northwest Coast and parts of California were organized into chiefdoms. Chiefdoms often occur next to tribes; however, the populations of chiefdoms were larger than tribes, ranging from five to fifty thousand depending on the carrying capacity of the habitat. Moreover, while all chiefdoms have large populations, their adaptations are quite varied. We can use our knowledge of Hawaiian chiefdoms to apply to European and American chiefdoms that have disappeared.

Chiefdoms have varying types of social structures. Some societies evolved into chiefdoms with matrilineal descent (Northwest Coast), others with patrilineal descent (Mesoamerica), and still others with cognatic or bilateral descent (Polynesia). Europeans appear to have evolved chiefdoms that were patridominant with extended family systems, possibly at the clan level. Various localized adaptations contributed to transformations from tribes to chiefdoms in certain regions, but recent theory suggests that outside pressures (other societies, trade, war) were also key factors in the shift from tribal organization to chiefdoms, and from chiefdoms to states (Wallerstein 1976, Wolf 1982).

paramount chief
The single chief at the top of a pyramidal hierarchy

Where they occurred, chiefdoms were ranked and stratified societies with a single **paramount chief** at the top of a pyramidal hierarchy. Unlike states, everyone in a chiefdom believed that they were descended from a single, founding ancestor. A myth of common descent unified all. In fact, the elites were usually endogamously separate from commoners (endogamy occurs when members of a group or class marry one another, as opposed to exogamy where members marry out of a group or class). The male elites were usually free to take women from commoner ranks as wives or concubines, but the reverse was never true. Chiefdoms were stratified into at least two classes: nobles and commoners. Sometimes a third class of slaves occurred at the bottom, and sometimes a class of warriors or artisans was present and intermediate between nobles and commoners. The paramount chief was considered sacred, like a god. His close relatives formed an elite bureaucracy and were supported by taxes and tribute (in part derived from the control of trade). The tribute payers were commoners, sometimes other chiefdoms, and nearby tribes which had been subjugated by the chiefdom. The aristocracy manipulated trade, warfare, and religion—the three major sources of power within these societies.

■Many of the Hawaiian Islands were ruled by chiefs up until the turn of the twentieth century.

As mentioned, chiefdom adaptations were highly varied. The chiefdoms of the Northwest Coast (Kwakiutl, Haida, Tlingit, Tsimshian, Bella Coola) were hunters and food gatherers depending on the rich coastal fisheries of salmon and trout; sea mammals such as porpoises, sea lions, and whales; and land animals such as bear, deer, duck, and geese that occurred in such profusion as to allow large human populations to flourish. There were also riches in berries, roots, and other plants; and the forests supplied cedar and fir for their long houses. The traders and warriors of the Northwest Coast plied the waters between Alaska and northern California.

The chiefdoms of Africa—the Kpelle of Liberia, the Bemba of Zambia, the Lozi of Zimbabwe, the Ngoni of Tanzania, and the Zulu of South Africa, to name a few—practiced intensive hoe cultivation (with very little irrigation) of sorghum, millet, maize, and cassava, sometimes combined with cattle herding.

The chiefdoms of the Pacific such as Samoa, Tahiti, Tonga, and Hawaii, like the peoples of the Northwest Coast, depended on the bounty of the Pacific, but also grew taro, coconut palms, and breadfruit using irrigation, hoes, and hillside terraces. In North America, chiefdoms were found in the middle and lower Mississippi valley (some of these were possibly states). The most famous of which built the temple mounds at Cahokia (near East Saint Louis) and had an economy extremely similar to the earlier chiefdoms of Mesoamerica: pot irrigation of maize, beans, and squash and the hunting of deer and turkey.

Earlier evolutionary/ecological theory on the emergence of chiefdoms argued that chiefdoms overcame ecological specialization through the use of redistribution mechanisms, such as ritual feasts. The classic example was the high islands of Hawaii where it was theorized villages and kinship units had specialized in the production of different goods found in distinct ecological zones on the large islands. However, ethnohistorical research by Timothy Earle now shows that neither villages nor kinship units specialized in the exploitation of distinct ecosystems. Earle found that kinship units tended to generalize their adaptations by including production in many separate ecological zones (Earl 1987). Recent research on state organized societies in the Andes, such as the Inca and their predecessors, shows that they too did not specialize in production by ecological zones. As in Hawaii, however, families tended to organize their kinship units to exploit many distinct ecosystems (Moseley 1992, Van Buren 1996). Since trade was an extremely common feature of Polynesian society, with giant canoes plying their wares between the high islands, redistribution may have been a way of exchanging goods between different chiefdoms in order to facilitate trade. The genesis of chiefdoms, then, lies not in overcoming ecological specialization and uncertainty but in the monopolization of trade by powerful chiefdoms. Trade is also a key feature of chiefdoms in the Andes and in other regions of the world. Evidence for trade was particularly well demonstrated for the early chiefdoms of Mesoamerica, such as the Olmec of La Venta.

On the Northwest Coast that also had well developed trade, connecting Alaska with northern California, goods were distributed by means of a potlatch, a feast where chiefs would ceremonialize their rank, status, and privileges by giving away goods. The rank of the chief was determined by the wealth he/she gave away, and the status of a commoner was symbolized by the gifts that were received. The potlatch or ritual feast of the American Northwest Coast chiefdoms was one mechanism for the redistribution of trade goods. According to Johnson and Earl, it was also a means by which the elite in Hawaii could control trade and actually tax commoners. As Johnson and Earl point out, "redistribution is simply an elementary form of taxation" (1987, 235). Similar redistribution economies based on feasting and distribution are found in most chiefdoms, as is trade.

Case Study

The Olmec Chiefdom of La Venta

In the 1950s and 1960s, archaeological investigations on the island site of La Venta in eastern Mexico revealed a temple/pyramid center dating to about 1500 BC, with no antecedent settlement and no surrounding homes or farms. It was thought to be a temple complex where slash-and-burn farmers came from afar to worship local gods. Trade and warfare were not considered important. Archaeologists assumed the Olmec were a peaceable people who spent their time worshipping stars and numbers. The site was re-excavated in 1986 by Robert Sharer and William Rust (Rust and Sharer 1988). Rust and Sharer discovered that there were several antecedent settlements and that the site of La Venta in 1500 was a temple complex surrounded by a large village or town. They also discovered that warfare and trade were important elements to Olmec society. The site was much older than originally thought. One hundred and seven occupation sites were located, mostly along a river levee (Rust and Sharer 1988).

A flood destroyed the site in 1780 BC; and then between 1750 and 1150 BC it was reoccupied. In this later phase, pottery was more elaborate and was an object of trade. There was more of it, and it was better made. Grinding stones were discovered along with obsidian, which had to have been imported, *indicating long distance trade*. Marine species decreased, fresh water species increased, and a mangrove swamp disappeared. This implies that the region was being drained through the construction of drainage/irrigation systems, and that agriculture was much more complicated than slash-and-burn (possibly the Olmecs had irrigation agriculture). Research showed that the river was silting up, and the Atlantic was becoming more distant. The irrigation works imply organized human labor, and that implies hierarchy.

Sometime during 1150–800 BC, an elaborate pyramid in the shape of a volcano was constructed. There was an increase in pottery, and it was more elaborate. Forests were being cleared, and polished green stone celts were manufactured or traded in. Social stratification increased and the site may have been the center of a chiefdom or simple state. La Venta is a spectacular site. A plaza flanked a large pyramid, which has never been fully excavated. Large basalt columns surrounded special precincts and platforms. Excavations uncovered tombs; and "offerings" of serpentine and jade celts, ceramics, and jade beads were buried along a line running through the center of the plaza. Underlying the plaza floor and small platforms were mosaic pavements and massive offerings of serpentine (Grove 1981, 378–379). By 900 BC, La Venta was abandoned and its monuments ritually shattered.

Nearby San Lorenzo and Tres Zapotes show similar if not more elaborate constructions. The pattern of trade and the emergence of chiefdoms are found in highland Oaxaca, Morelos, and in the Valley of Mexico. Similar sites occur throughout Mesoamerica at about the same time period, and archaeologists have noted the connections between chiefdom social structure and trade (Flannery and Marcus 1983).

Figure 5A

☐ Diagram of La Venta from Coe, Snow, and Beson, *Atlas of Ancient Americas*

La Venta

STATES

In states the central authority figure (king, emperor) can initiate a political act while in chiefdoms the central political figure does not have the authority to act without the support of his/her direct kinsmen and subsidiary chiefs, whose authority ramifies down through lower levels of hierarchy (subchiefs or clan heads). This distinction between chiefdoms and states depends on the idea that in a true state, the authority of the people to act is vested in a central leader. Here the state is an abstraction, a contract between the ruler and the ruled, usually mediated by religion. The king may represent a god, or he/she may be god; this is not true of a chief.

States are **stratified** into one or more social classes. The very upper class, the aristocracy, was endogamous, but did not pretend to be related to the commoner class. In fact, the elites usually ritually separated themselves from commoners on special occasions and in their dress. Rules, called **sumptuary rules**, were often passed preventing commoners from dressing or behaving like the aristocrats. The elites might also be stratified according to kinship connections to the ruler. The clearest line of separation was between the elites and commoners. The commoner class could also subdivide into other class divisions. One common distinction was between urban dwellers and the peasants living on the land. In addition, there was often a final distinction between all of the above and a caste of slaves, or of people with no rights, such as the **untouchable** caste of India. The more powerful the state, the greater the levels of hierarchy that tended to occur between the king and his close kinsmen and the bottom caste. The distinction between **class** and **caste** is that members of different classes can marry each other while members of distinct castes cannot. Thus, in the above, the aristocrats, commoners, and slave groups were often organized into distinct castes, while inside of the commoner caste there might be many levels of social class.

One of the most difficult problems in analyzing the differences between states and chiefdoms is that chiefdoms were sometimes incorporated into states when states had the resources to become highly centralized. However, those states then might become independent chiefdoms when the state contracted, a feature very common to Asiatic states and chiefdoms.

Early states resemble chiefdoms in that their economies were also based on redistribution; but the act of distribution by the state had the political function of securing the support of the commoner class, particularly of those specializing in military activities and household manufacturing. Commoner classes specializing in the manufacture of goods (potters, weavers) depended on the largesse of the state to feed them, and the state depended on specialists for the ceremonial goods it needed to set itself apart. Peasants, who grew food for the state, were usually outside of this welfare redistribution system.

Another feature setting states and chiefdoms apart from tribes, and from each other, is warfare. One of the characteristics of chiefdoms, which sets them apart from tribes, is *the occurrence of ritualized warfare*. Among the peoples of Mesoamerica at the chiefdom level, warfare was part of a ritual complex in which warriors were captured for sacrifice (something like an elaborate football game between chiefdoms). Warriors initiated warfare in tribes to gain personal status, while the chief controlled warfare in chiefdoms. In both chiefdoms and states, warfare was not local, but long distance, and was part of the process of gaining tribute from other societies. Chiefdoms and states, with their long distance warfare, *reduced the costs of trade transactions* by preventing local warfare. In both states and chiefdoms, peace was usually sanctified by the development of a ceremonial center, often the focus of pilgrimage. While pilgrimages were found in state level societies, peace was

---

stratification

The separation of a society into one or more social classes

sumptuary rules

Laws that specify privileges of the elite or nobility while simultaneously prohibiting commoners from exercising the same privileges

untouchable

In the Indian caste system, a fifth category outside the social system that is made up of those people whose occupations are considered ritually unclean

class

A social category that refers to the rank and social status of its members

caste

An inherited rank and status distinction, members of which are expected to marry others of the same caste

■The Olmec of Mesoamerica were a people of ritual warfare. Shown here is a jaguar-shaped cuauhxicalli in the National Museum of Anthropology. This altar-like stone vessel was used to hold the hearts of sacrificial victims.

maintained not by sanctuaries but *by the force of the state through the use of armies.* These were trained for the purpose of imposing rule throughout a large territory. In exchange, soldiers were supported by the state, a characteristic not found in chiefdoms where the warriors were never full time, but were the kinsmen and retinue of the chief.

The Rise of Chiefdoms and States

Several theories have been proposed to explain the appearance of chiefdoms and their transformations into states. Particularly important have been ecological and evolutionary explanations. Several factors are thought to have been important in the transformation of tribes to chiefdoms and chiefdoms to states: increasing energy consumption, changes in technology, increasing population densities, irrigation agriculture, and ecological circumscription (White 1959, Sahlins and Service 1960, Steward 1955, Harris 1979). More recently, trade has become a very important factor in explaining the transitions. However, none of these theories is adequate by itself, and some regions require explanations which place a greater weight on ecology and other regions on trade.

ECOLOGICAL EXPLANATIONS

ecological circumscription

A theory by Robert Carneiro who argues that agricultural societies evolve when growing populations are prevented from migrating due to the ecological features around them

The most common explanation for the shift from tribes to chiefdoms and then to states is an ecological one based on **ecological circumscription.** This ecological theory, developed by Robert Carneiro (1970), begins with the introduction of simple irrigation technology within a tribal setting. As irrigation technology improves, the population grows until it reaches the boundaries of its ecological setting (usually rich alluvial soils set in arid habitats or bounded by mountains). Populations ramify into different ecological zones and expand in numbers at the same time, introducing needs for social control, redistribution, and further improvements to irrigation technology. These three features—social control, redistribution, and irrigation agriculture—it was theorized, interacted to transform tribes into chiefdoms, and chiefdoms into states.

While the theory of ecological circumscription works for regions with alluvial valleys and arid habitats (Mesopotamia) or mountains (the Andean states), it does not work at all well for regions like the Hawaiian Islands or the Northwest Coast of North America. In both cases, chiefdoms developed, but they either had no agriculture at all (Northwest Coast) or had very little irrigation (Hawaii). Similar problems emerge with states described in this text arising in East Africa with pastoral nomadism (and no irrigation) or many states in Mesoamerica, which lacked complex irrigation systems, or at least systems that could only be built by states. There is also the problem that some peoples with complex irrigation agriculture, such as the Ifugao of the Philippines, remained tribal.

TRADE FACTORS

As early as 1974, a special seminar brought together archaeologists and economic anthropologists who emphasized the importance of trade in the emergence of complex societies. K. C. Chang, Robert McAdams, Jeremy Sabloff, and others suggested that involvement in trade can bring rapid, massive changes in the structure and technology of society, as well as in patterns of motivation, mobility, and leadership.

The recognition that trade was a factor in these sociopolitical changes altered the traditional view of bands, tribes, chiefdoms, and states as independent evolving social units. A new perspective that places states in the center of trade networks—with chiefdoms, tribes, and bands progressively more peripheral—owes much to Eric Wolf's book *Europeans and the Peoples Without History* (1982). Wolf argued that anthropologists should stop trying to understand bands, tribes, chiefdoms, and states as autonomous and isolated social systems evolving toward some equilibrium endpoint justified by local resources. More recently, Gary Feinman and Richard Blanton have been studying the rise and fall of the civilizations of Mesoamerica (Mexico and northern Central America) in terms of interacting networks of trade rather than a series of independently evolving "empires" or "states" which replace each other through time. Other anthropologists are responding to Feinman's theory by describing other regions of the world as "world systems," such as Darrell E. La Lone's study of "An Andean World System" (La Lone 1994), but the phrase world system is a problem because Emmanuel Wallerstein used the term *modern* world system to describe the world's economy since its emergence in the sixteenth century (1974). What we are looking at is not modern, and it is not capitalist in the same sense as defined in the next chapter. Wallerstein described the modern world system as composed of a core of wealthy and capitalist states in western Europe, a periphery made up of societies which contributed wealth to the core and became poor, and a semi-periphery of societies which emerged in the twentieth century which were intermediate between core and periphery (e.g., Mexico and Brazil).

While Wallerstein's terms are useful, they should be modified for a pre-modern world. The term **tributary empire** is used here to refer to those world systems that existed prior to 1492. Within these, **hegemonic cores** dominated tributary states. **Tributary states** supplied tribute to the cores (the centers of empire). Outside of the empires, chiefdoms, tribes, and hunting and gathering bands were in contact with each other, warred and traded with each other. Sometimes the chiefdoms were turned into tributary states when the empire spread, and at other times they were independent of the core. This expanding and contracting model characterizes many of the regions of the world, such as the Valley of Mexico or the Tigris and Euphrates river valley. The periphery would be the regions of bands and tribes. The semi-periphery would correspond to chiefdoms.

Chiefdoms of the semi-periphery were found in places that were less able to monopolize trade than hegemonic cores, but where resources would support large populations

---

tributary empire

Pre-modern world systems based on hegemonic cores controlling trade and warfare and receiving tribute from the societies in the periphery, which they dominate

hegemonic core

The center of a tributary empire, usually a tribute-taking state controlling a periphery of tributary states

tributary state

A state found in the periphery of a hegemonic empire that pays tribute to the empire's core

■Two bushmen kindle a fire in Namibia, in the Kalahari Desert.

(such as the high islands of Hawaii or the North-west Coast of North America). Tribes of the periphery were more remote still. From time to time, tribes responded to trade and warfare by transforming into chiefdoms, and chiefdoms into states, as happened in Central Asia with the Mongols under the leadership of Genghis Khan.

If the forces producing hierarchy were not maintained, the states or chiefdoms would collapse back into tribes. This happened to many empires in Asia, and it also appears to have happened in Central America and Colombia after the Conquest by Spain. Hunters and gatherers continued to occupy places that would not sustain large populations. In this new perspective, trade and warfare are viewed as dynamic components of political ecology, not as independent economic or cultural variables, and not really "causes."

The transaction cost model of Douglas North can be applied to the origins of chiefdoms and ancient states. North uses the concept of transaction costs to explain how trade affects human institutions. There are two types of transaction costs: the cost of transportation and the cost of gathering information to make trade predictable. The first type of cost is easily understood. It takes energy to move goods over a landscape, and that energy is the cost of transportation. Making transportation easier can lower transportation costs (inventing the wheel, carrying goods by horse, using a boat). The second meaning is not as clear but is easily understood. Any economic transaction, whether between individuals or groups, requires information. The following are examples of information needed: What is the distance to be traveled? How many men and women will it take to carry the goods or how many pack animals? How many boats? What are the dangers involved? Who will have to be paid off (toll booths, regional warlords)? What will the trader receive for his/her goods? How many battles will have to be fought, and how much will it cost to pay your protectors? It takes work to find the answers to these questions, and that work (also energy) is the information costs of a transaction. If a way can be found to reduce information costs, trade (or war) is more efficient. Those societies that can lower the costs of trade (or war) are more efficient and will have the greater opportunity to survive, all other things being equal. We have seen that there are other variables probably at work, so trade and its costs do not provide a full explanation for the origins of chiefdoms and states; however, they are important factors.

If this sounds too abstract, think for a moment what happens when you go shopping. The work put into shopping is a transaction cost. You lower the cost of transaction by studying newspaper advertisements. For example, think of buying a used car. You would never think of driving all over a large city to check the costs of a used car since the transaction costs (gasoline, time) would be very high. By reading a newspaper, you drop your transaction costs and your trade relations become more efficient. Think of a city with no newspapers, where every good has to be checked on by every buyer each time there is a transaction. This is an example of high transaction costs. Introduce newspapers and other types of advertising and transaction costs drop, making economic transactions more efficient. This is an example of reduced transaction costs.

Carla Sinopoli has described hegemonic empires, cores, and tributary states in her studies of the Vijayanagara Empire of India, and the model applied to precapitalist states

(1994a, 1995). Applying North's idea of transaction costs, we can connect hierarchy to trade and warfare through the idea of transaction costs. Hierarchy, in the form of bureaucracy, is one way to reduce transaction costs; it is a means of organizing complex events to make a transaction more efficient. Bureaucracies can aid in improving transportation by directing the building of roads and their maintenance and developing armies to protect the roads, but they are also a means of reducing information costs by collecting information on future transactions (spying?). At the same time, however, bureaucracies can be expensive because it takes work and specialists (who have to be fed) to staff them. A bureaucracy or hierarchy will expand as long as it increases the efficiency of a growing political system, but may collapse if it overextends itself and becomes unprofitable (as appears to have happened over and over in human history).

In societies where the ownership of resources is in collectives (clans), transaction costs can be reduced by centralizing decision making into a chiefdom. In such societies, traders benefit because the demands of kinsmen from clans and lineages are reduced; and they are better able to cooperate with the evolving authority system in the development of monopolies of trade (and may themselves be a part of the evolving state or independent). Further centralization into states can reduce transaction costs further. The ownership of resources will shift from collective ownership in clans and lineages to the ownership of major resources by the state. It makes no sense to develop hierarchy and bureaucracy where there are no gains (profits) to be made, so only those societies which are in the paths of trade will benefit by greater hierarchy. Shifts in trade routes can bring about the development of chiefdoms and states, but can also bring about their collapse.

The emergence of ritual warfare may be connected to decreasing transaction costs. Among the first patterns that appear with chiefdoms is the ritualization of warfare. The classic feuding style of warfare found among tribes, which makes violence against the traveler unpredictable, was transformed into ritual war. Ritual war is predictable, almost like a weekly football game between two cities, and can reduce the costs of transactions (allowing trade) when societies wish to exchange goods since the center of violence can be avoided. Among the Olmec of Mesoamerica, we find evidence for ritual warfare in the form of capturing warriors of other chiefdoms for human sacrifice. This appears to have been a well-organized, ritual event, and from time to time took *the form of a ritual ball game* played in ball courts. The losers of either wars or ball games were sacrificed.

Another feature that appears in chiefdoms and states is the religious pilgrimage. Pilgrimages resulted in a substantial number of travelers going to a sacred ceremonial center where they not only worshipped their gods but also exchanged goods. The evidence for pilgrimages occurs in the archaeology of La Venta, and also for most of the early chiefdom sites in Mesoamerica such as San Jose Mogote and Chalcatzingo in the Central Mexican highlands. Similar types of developments have been mentioned for the Shan chiefdoms of Burma, and a few archaeologists have argued that the cores of the first chiefdoms were pilgrimage centers (Flannery and Marcus 1983, Drennan 1976). The pilgrimage-trade connection is still common in the Andes today among the Aymara and Quechua who organize pilgrimages to carry the images of Christ and the Virgin Mary to Catholic cathedrals, where markets are established and goods are bought and sold. It is suggested that sacred pilgrimages were one way of reducing transaction costs by producing a safe zone where economic transactions could occur without fear of war. Both institutions, ritual warfare and pilgrimages, reduce transaction costs by making trade predictable and possible.

The type of trade that occurred between chiefdoms was primarily stimulated by differential access to resources between neighboring societies (not differences within societies). This is particularly evident in Mesoamerica where highland/lowland trade appears to have stimulated the development of La Venta, San Lorenzo, and Tres Zapotes in the lowlands of Mexico, and Chalcatzingo, San Jose Mogote, and Cuicuilco in the highlands. The peoples of the lowlands traded such goods as feathers, shells, stingray spines, and other products from the Pacific littoral for such highland products as obsidian, jade, mica, and other minerals.

The essential difference between trade among tribes and trade between chiefdoms is that in chiefdoms trade is organized by a central authority (the paramount chief), while in tribes it is not (and transaction costs are very high in trade between tribes ... a lot of work is involved because trade is between individuals). The centralization and the control of production in chiefdoms for purposes of trade and redistribution would increase efficiency. The same is true for ritual warfare. Through increased levels of hierarchy both long distance trade and long distance ritual warfare benefit.

Chiefdoms evolved as populations increased, as resources were worked more intensively to support them, and as trade increased in volume and distance. The institutions of chiefdoms became those of states. Ritual warfare became tributary warfare as it intensified, increasing the need for hierarchy and improving the efficiencies of organization, which in turn expanded the success of both trade and warfare. In tributary warfare, states are subjugated to the power of a core and forced to pay tribute in food or other forms of wealth. It is no longer enough to count coup by touching another warrior with a stick or sacrificing him during a ceremony; now it pays to demand tribute from the defeated warriors. While the Olmec had ritual warfare, by the time of the Aztecs war was for tribute. Throughout the highlands of Mexico, the Aztec state gathered tribute from hundreds of other cities, towns, and villages that were in subsidiary ritual relationship to it; this was also true of other imperial states. The wars were similar to those of the chiefdom level and were formalized; but the losers now became a part of empires and paid tribute in many forms, including women, quills filled with gold, mantles of fine feathers, jade, and gold (Gasco and Vorhies 1989).

Gradually, local alliances or warfare allowed a few chiefdoms to gain access and control over the resources of the surrounding tribes, incorporating them into the core chiefdom. Over time, these systems became hegemonic empires. Societies which were too far away or too warlike, or whose resources were poor, would be left alone and retained their tribal social structures. An important point to remember is a hierarchical bureaucracy is costly to maintain and is, itself, a type of transaction cost. It will not survive unless there are strong incentives. When the expense of maintaining hierarchy becomes too great, hierarchies collapse (North 1990).

Successful incorporation of other chiefdoms led to the transformation of land ownership from the independent clan or lineage of the tribe to the paramount chief. When this process continued, chiefdoms were converted into states. Where the process could not continue, chiefdoms retained their structure for hundreds of years until the emergence of the modern world system after 1492 caused their collapse.

Why did not all chiefdoms evolve into states? There was a limit on the expansion of certain chiefdoms where resources were limited, such as Polynesia or the Northwest Coast. Trade and warfare are expensive, and are associated with growing tax and tributary rates. As chiefdoms grew larger, their armies and traders had to go further afield. The demand for greater taxes from commoners and tributary fiefs had their limits and

■A view of the Mesoamerican city of Teotihuacan which flourished as a hegemonic empire from approximately 200 AD to 600 AD

alienated the commoner class. Societies located in regions where trade could not be monopolized could not transform themselves into states. Such would occur in oceanic situations where chiefdoms could not monopolize sea trade or where there are few natural boundaries, such as mountains, forcing trade through narrow river valleys.

The Dynamics of Archaic States and Empires

The picture usually drawn for the evolution of the state is that it was a slow, incremental process, during which people passed from a relatively egalitarian tribe/chiefdom social system to a bureaucratically organized and hierarchical state. The changes are explained technologically through the introduction of intensive irrigation-based agriculture, over which the elites first gained control, and then used it to control commoners, peasants, and slaves. So much time passed in the process that when the state came into existence, the average commoner had no memory of the garden of tribal or chiefdom Eden. Yet this picture is inaccurate. In the two regions of the world where good data are available, Mesopotamia and Mesoamerica, the shift from chiefdoms to states was dramatic and very rapid. In Mesopotamia, the shift from multi-village, desert chiefdoms to the state of Uruk took only a few hundred years, and the population going through the transition must have been aware of what was happening and participated in the transition. In Mesoamerica, the shift from the chiefdom of Teotihuacan (pop. 35,000) to the state of Teotihuacan (pop. 150,000) happened with the same speed and drama, literally overnight. There is no evidence of force being used to coerce commoners to accept the authority of the emerging state.

As noted earlier, societies do not evolve independently within an ecological setting which limits their final stage of sociocultural organization. Rather, societies are interconnected in networks extending over natural regions, and it is the interconnections that facilitate change. In Mesopotamia, between 4500 and 4000 BC, several Ubaidian desert chiefdoms were transformed into the Mesopotamian state system of Uruk (Algaze 1993). In Mesoamerica, chiefdoms at Teotihuacan, Cholula, and Monte Alban in the highlands and Tikal, Bonampok, and Palenque shifted from chiefdom to state status between 1100 and 700 BC. Between the same years, there emerged an Andean hegemonic system in South America, the core of which was ultimately dominated by the Inca state in the fifteenth century AD, before it fell to the Spanish invaders.

The model that emerges at the state level is the same as the one described for chiefdoms, but bigger and paradoxically less complex at the level of decision making. While chiefdoms are similar to each other, the institutions of core states at the center of hegemonic systems share even greater similarity. Philip Curtin, a historian, argues that after a certain point the institutions promoting cross-cultural trade become the same, even though they operate inside of very different cultures. Why this is so brings us back to the relationship among trade, tributary warfare, and hierarchy. Distance and volume of trade or war makes these activities expensive and complicated. To lower expenses, societies become increasingly hierarchical and bureaucratic. The ownership of resources is taken over by the state (the king), and large bureaucracies are created manned by aristocrats who can show kinship connections to the king or who pledge unwavering allegiance. The bureaucracies take over the decision making process; fewer people make more of the decisions for the society. In a sense complexity has been resolved through simplicity (there are fewer people running the show; commoners obey elites, they do not make their own decisions). The paradox: complexity creates simplicity.

Elizabeth Brumfiel writes: States are powerful, complex, institutionalized hierarchies of public decision-making and control. They are created to implement the relations of production in stratified societies and to mediate conflict between diverse economic interest groups (1994, 1).

Let us look briefly at some of the pre-industrial state systems (or empires) that existed prior to the development of the "modern" world system.

THE EARLY MESOPOTAMIAN EMPIRES

The prehistory of Mesopotamia is exceedingly complex. City-states and empires rose and fell. Beginning about 4000 BC, widespread trade came into existence and was extensive throughout the area and beyond. Economic and political allegiances shifted and changed, and cross-cultural communications were probably extensive. Despite considerable archaeological research, the record is still lacking in detail and precision. Following we provide only a brief account.

Core temple communities, implying a chiefdom level of organization, begin to appear as early as 6000–5000 BC in southwest Asia. In the Levant, which is located just on the margin of the eastern Mediterranean, fairly substantial agricultural chiefdoms existed at 6000 BC. Jericho, a town with a high wall and several thousand people, has the features we expect of chiefdoms. Further east, on the "hilly flanks" of the Taurus and Zagros mountains, economies based on herding sheep, goats, pigs, and cattle and growing wheat and barley were well developed. Agriculture began its spread from this region into Europe and transformed hunting and gathering societies into tribal agriculturalists over the following millennia (Renfrew 1979).

Some of the upland villages grew large and had well-designed temples, implying chiefdom social structures. One of the most remarkable was Catal Huyuk in south central Turkey, which was thirty-two acres in size at 6000 BC. Further east in the highlands of Iran and Iraq were other similar temple communities such as Jarmo, Sawwan, and Choga Mami. The temple centers apparently also served as storage centers for surplus foods, which were needed by the tributary villages during periods of drought (Frankfort 1956).

The chief of the core community would probably have been first on a line of descent from an originator god or an earlier chief (Krader 1968, 56–57). Like chiefs in many chiefdom societies, he would have been also a reservoir of religious knowledge; and he would have been able to control the community because he was the conduit of communication—the crucial link—between the people and their deities. Since one of the primary threats to the community in Southwest Asia would have been drought, there is good reason to think he would have also been a "water wizard." That is, there may have been a strong belief that the chief's relationship to the supernatural forces was responsible for bringing water. (We find a similar belief in Mesoamerica.) Few would be tempted to challenge such power because the result might be a dry spell brought on by angry gods through the medium of an angry chief. There is evidence from one chiefdom, Eridu, that the temple community worshiped Enlil, a water god represented by a fish (Eridu is one of the many sites classified as Ubaidian, discussed below).

At about 3400 BC in Southwest Asia, and somewhat later in Egypt and China, we find the chiefdom structured temple community with its probable collective ownership of property under a single chief shifting in social structure to become the city state, the core of an archaic empire. Growing populations, increasingly more complex water works, trade relations with other growing states, and, probably of greatest importance, the subjugation of weaker peripheral chiefdoms and tribal societies to the status of tribute paying members of the core state—all are significant factors that brought the city-state into existence. Thus, Uruk, the first of a series of city-states in this region, came into being.

This change occurred not in the fertile hilly flanks region but south on the dry Mesopotamian plain. For most of its length, the Mesopotamian plain of the Tigris and Euphrates rivers is less than two hundred miles wide. It is arid, a rain shadow region of the Pontic mountains to the west, and was originally best suited to pastoral nomadism. Anthropologists once theorized that the development of irrigation agriculture stimulated state development, but it is now clear that trade down the two river systems was the stimulus (Algaze 1993). The first known city-state was Uruk. Emerging out of the Ubaid chiefdom level cultures, it became the core of the first hegemonic empire (4000–3100 BC).

The Ubaidian cultures, and those of Uruk which followed, belong to the region of Sumerian language and culture. Uruk first became a core city-state dominating outlying villages and towns, and then spread into the highlands to control trade and tribute over a vast region. The shift from the latest Ubaid phase (known as Ubaid 4) to the city of Uruk was dramatic. First there were just a few villages; and then during the Early Uruk phase the population suddenly tripled in size going from 800 to 2,400 people and the population of the region jumped from 6,000 in sixteen villages to 20,000 in forty-five villages (Johnson 1973). Many of the sites contained workshops where artisans produced high quality ceramics, which were traded throughout a vast region. Within a few hundred years accounting devices were produced which used styluses to mark soft clay tablets. These were fired in ovens. The tablets indicate that bureaucrats in the core were concerned with production, trade, tribute, and control over a periphery of lesser states and chiefdoms. Often a chiefdom would become transformed into a hegemonic state, only to become the tributary state of another core. As an example, one of the first cores was at Kish, an early kingdom; however, its ruler came into conflict with the then ruler of Warka, Gilgamesh. Gilgamesh

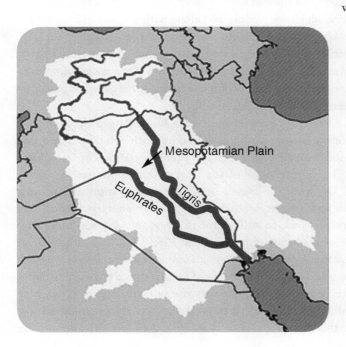

conquered Kish and turned it into a tributary state of Warka. During this early period, it was common for the core of power to shift from one city-state to another.

The city continued to expand in the Middle Uruk period during which time monumental architecture appeared suggesting the increasing importance of state and religious activities. Elite government administrators were appointed to the outlying peripheral states as ambassadors or consuls and kept track of tribute owed and paid by using small clay counting devices kept in hollow clay balls. Early theories held that these urban systems came into existence because of irrigation agriculture, but the Uruk irrigation systems were not large enough to feed the city dwellers. Much food was probably received as tribute from the periphery (as was the case for the city of Tenochtitlan in highland Mexico, and probably for the earlier Teotihuacan).

In the following millennium, from 3000 to 2000 BC, the Uruk core acquired the characteristics of true urban society with 70 to 80 percent of the population living in urban centers of one thousand people or more. The city of Uruk grew to forty thousand people or more. Each city belonged to a founding god, drawn from the complex Sumerian pantheon to which a large temple was dedicated. These temples, called *ziggurats*, were giant stepped pyramids made of clay bricks. A temple bureaucracy controlled the urban centers.

Uruk collapsed when it was unable to sustain control over Mesopotamia. It was followed by Ur at 2800 BC, which grew to be even larger than Uruk. Archaeologists believe that Ur had larger armies and more efficient bureaucracies than Uruk. The bureaucracies were means of decreasing transaction costs, but were themselves an expense. The bureaucracies were also involved in the development of waterworks, particularly irrigation systems, the building of roads, and the protection of cities. The economies were centralized, and goods were distributed to the various social classes according to status. During the development of Ur, true writing evolved out of the recordkeeping clay tablets, and this may explain how it became more efficient and able to control a larger area. Writing, bureaucracies, and trade were all linked. As trade expanded in volume and distance, writing became more efficient and the state more bureaucratic. With the growth of the state, the power of the ruler grew. In death, the ruler of Ur and other royalty were accompanied by sacrificed soldiers and retainers, which were entombed along with wagons and oxen. One tomb of the later core city of Ur contained seventy-four people, of which sixty-four were women of the court in ceremonial dress. Human sacrifice is common in the period of early states, both in the Old World and the New World. Human sacrifice is a means of symbolizing the power of the state and the sacred quality of the king; it not only confers power on the king but also may have been a means of social control.

The core-periphery set of relationships in Southwest Asia changed through time for reasons that are very poorly understood. Later, new core states would emerge, and in turn collapse, as they abused their ecosystems or lost their efficiencies of war and/or trade and became corrupt. Today, the floor of the Tigris and Euphrates has many examples, including that of Ur, which collapsed because of salinization, the process where irrigation cannot clear away the accumulation of salts, or where poor planning led to waterlogged fields, problems which still plague this region today and make irrigation an important feature of state planning (Spooner 1982). Babylon followed Ur and, in turn, was followed by the Assyrian and Persian empires in Southwest Asia. All of these inland empires were based on the monopoly of long distance trade, redistribution economies (markets are very rare), and the construction of massive cities with gigantic architecture symbolizing the power of the state and its rulers and absolutist religions. It is easy to argue that the religions of these inland empires are personality cults based on the power of the king and his queen. The massive quality of these early inland states, the control of trade by the state, and the absolutist qualities of religion continued up through the time of the Persian Empire, and then gradually ceased as economic and political power shifted to the empires of the inland sea.

After the seventh century AD, the rise of Islam led ultimately to the rise of the Ottoman Empire in Turkey. World War I and the monopolization of trade by Western Europe and North America transformed the Mesopotamian hegemonic system into a periphery of the modern world system. Its primary function became that of supplying oil to the Western industrial core. In recent years, Iran and Iraq have warred with each other to reclaim control of the region where ancient civilizations once flourished. The Persian Gulf War can be understood as the attempt by Saddam Hussein to give birth to a new and powerful Mesopotamian civilization (potentially dangerous from the viewpoint of the Western nations).

EMPIRES OF THE INLAND SEA: THE MEDITERRANEAN

The empires of Mesopotamia were primarily based on overland trade following river systems. Overland trade made these empires rich, as long as they could monopolize the regional economies. Irrigation supported large populations, but to it was added the taxes paid by tributary states up-river and downriver. Boats were used where possible, but trade relied heavily on wheeled vehicles pulled by draft animals (horses, asses, and oxen). Transaction costs were high in these geographically massive inland empires. West of Mesopotamia, a very different series of tributary states evolved based on waterborne trade, which pushed down transaction costs. Here were found Hissarlike (Troy in western Turkey) and Kultepe, whose building styles were the basis for those of the later Greek and Roman empires of the Mediterranean.

Troy was a port city on the Aegean Sea. The rich royal tombs of Troy, excavated by Heinrik Schliemann in the late nineteenth century, contained the bodies of men and their wives accompanied by fine ornaments made of copper and gold. Troy and other city-states of the Aegean and eastern Mediterranean were involved in long distance trade that slowly turned to the use of small sailing ships, which were able to sail further and further from shore. Contact with Mesopotamia increased and trading centers called *karums* emerged with marketplaces. The karums were neutral entrepots, or commercial centers, where the authorities regulated prices, but it appears that the giant trade monopolies of the inland empires were not characteristic of the city-states of the inland sea.

Mainland Greece had been inhabited as far back as 6500 BC. The people first lived in stone and mud houses connected by courtyards and passages (Fagan 1985). Similar villages are found on the island of Crete as far back as 5500 BC. After 3500 BC, southern Greece developed the cultivation of olives and grape vines interspersed with cereal crops. There was a tremendous increase in village crafts as well as the manufacturing of painted pottery, marble vessels, and magnificent stone axes. Copper and bronze were introduced and were tied to the rapid increase of trade throughout the Aegean (Renfrew and Wagstaff 1982).

According to Brian Fagan, the Aegean is well endowed with comfortable ports, which allowed water borne trade and easy communication between the various islands. Sailing vessels are depicted on Cretan seals as early as 2000 BC. Trade in olive oil, wine, metal tools and ores, marble vessels, and pottery flourished. With the shift from overland to sea-based trade, transaction costs plummeted; and there began an inexorable shift away from massive, theocratic states with the architectural emblems of empire to trade empires which depended less on complete hegemony for survival. Could it be that ships killed the giant pyramids? The building styles that emerge in the Aegean are much less massive than what preceded them in Mesopotamia or Egypt. (Egypt is covered in the chapter on the Middle East.) Might it not be that the shift from overland trade to sea trade was tied to a shift in energy used from monument building to energy for building ships? This is an interesting, but speculative idea. However, as Leslie White argued almost fifty years ago, societies at any given time have access to only limited amounts of energy and must make choices about how to use it.

The Minoans   The Minoans were famous shipbuilders. While their palaces at Knossos on the island of Crete are fascinating, the monuments are nothing like the massive constructions of Mesopotamia and Egypt. On the other hand, their ships were huge and magnificent, transporting gold, silver, ivory, wine and olive oil, in exchange for ornaments from Central Europe, the Aegean, and the Near East. Even ostrich eggs were traded in from North Africa.

At least nine periods of Minoan civilization have been uncovered. Greece and the mainland of Italy had Minoan colonies and formed the periphery of the sea-based civilization. Even in the earliest periods, trade occurred with ancient Egypt. At 3730 BC, signs of long distance trading increased. In 1700 BC, an earthquake leveled the palaces, and building began anew. The palace at Knossos reached its greatest size between 1700 and 1450 BC. (The palace at Knossos has been replicated in a fine restaurant found on the wharf in Tarpon Springs, Florida.) These buildings, made of limestone blocks and wood columns, are noted for the fine art work on the walls, which tells us a lot about life on Crete. The buildings themselves are not spectacular. Among the scenes depicted are acrobats leaping across the backs of bulls and pictures of aristocratic courts.

The Cretans were renowned mariners, and paintings of their sea exploits are found on the walls of the palaces at Knossos. Their religion included human sacrifice and the worship of Zeus, as a bull, and an Earth Mother complex. The exact nature of their social and political structures are not well understood because their writing system, called linear A and also used by the mainland culture of Mycenae, has not yet been completely decoded. However, the gods of the people of Minoa are very similar to those of the Greeks who follow. One tantalizing piece of the jigsaw puzzle was the story of the Minotaur, a mythological creature who was quartered in a labyrinth under the central palace of Knossos. A thousand years later, the Greeks told the story of Ariadne, who used a string to find her way in the and out of the labyrinth; but the meaning of the legend is puzzling. Was the Minotaur evidence for a fertility cult? Did it have something to do with the cult of bull acrobatics where young men and women grabbed the horns of onrushing bulls and leapt over their backs? These legends and the archaeology of the palace yield thin clues, and there is much guesswork. It is fairly obvious that the power of elite differs significantly from Egyptian or Mesopotamian kings. Religion is not a personality cult, and it is difficult to identify specific kings and their queens. Religion has shifted, possibly in the direction of Greece with its mysteries and oracles, from a centralized and totalistic religion linked to a massive bureaucracy, to something very different where the gods have more human dimensions. In 1473 BC, a volcanic explosion destroyed Minoan Crete, and the core of power shifted in the direction of the Aegean mainland.

Ancient Greece   European civilization traces its roots back to Greece, which itself was preceded by Mycenaean civilization. Mycenaean kings ruled over walled fortresses and were buried in spectacular shaft graves. The lives of the kings were immortalized in the epics of the poet Homer. Mycenaeans refined a writing system originally developed by the Minoans. Mycenae dominated Mediterranean trade until northern barbarians destroyed it. After the fall of Mycenae in 1200 BC, small town merchants on the Greek mainland continued to trade. By the seventh and eighth centuries BC, small colonies of Greek settlers lived on the northern and western shores of the Black Sea and along the north coast of Anatolia.

In Greece ranges of mountains separate many fertile agricultural areas. Traders formed networks of small city-states that competed with each other for trade and political power. Athens was one of the larger and more prosperous states rivaled by Sparta. Greek city-states only unified in times of political stress, such as when the Persian King Xerxes tried to dominate Greece. His defeat at Marathon (490 BC) and again ten years later in a naval battle at Salamis brought the Greek city states together and produced the age of Classical Greek civilization (Fagan 1985).

Athens was the foremost of the Greek city-states and became the head of a league of maritime cities, which were transformed into an empire. Athens attracted wealthy immigrants, built the Parthenon, and produced philosophers and playwrights whose works come down to us today: Plato, Socrates, Sophocles, Aeschylus, and many others. Classical Greek civilization only flourished for fifty years, yet during this brief time produced the idea of a democratic civilization.

The lowered transaction costs of sea trade made a thriving economy possible without theocratic bureaucracies. Athens produced a democratic civilization with a religion that was much less totalistic than anything that came before. Reading Greek mythology one has the feeling that the gods and goddesses were much less frightening beings than those which preceded them. They demanded much less of people and acted a lot more like humans than powerful gods. Even the Minoans practiced human sacrifice, but with the Greeks that ritual ended. Is there a relationship between reduced transaction costs, democracy, and a flourishing maritime economy? This is an interesting question, and one which cannot be answered with the limited data; however, the relationships are provocative and worth mentioning.

Athenian supremacy was not to last, however. Bickering with Sparta never abated, and there were deep animosities between the two cities. Sparta's government was based on military discipline and a rigid class structure, while Athens was more mobile and democratic. Rivalries led to the disastrous Peloponnesian War (431–404 BC) that left Sparta dominant and Greece in disarray. Greece soon fell under the control of Philip of Macedonia, who ruled between 359 and 336 BC. His son, Alexander the Great, then created an empire that embraced the entire eastern Mediterranean as far as Mesopotamia, uniting the entire ancient world. His empire, too, was not to last and fell apart within a generation.

One other state worth mentioning arose where Lebanon is today. Known as the Phoenician Empire, it resembled the Greek city-states but was less of an empire than a network of trading cities with their anchor in Lebanon. The Phoenicians set up cities throughout North Africa, the most famous of which was Carthage, which was to challenge the power of the Roman Empire.

The Roman Empire   None of the civilizations that we have examined in the Mediterranean dominated the surrounding region as totally as the ancient societies which preceded them. This is not true of Rome, which developed into a massive trade based empire. The Roman Empire developed out of earlier, small Etruscan democratic city-states, not unlike those of the Greeks. Some of the Etruscan buildings were substantial, and the architecture and art evolved into Roman building and art styles.

The Etruscans were the first people to fortify the famous Seven Hills of Rome. In 509 BC, the last Etruscan king was expelled by native Romans, who began to develop their own city-state. Influenced by classical Greek civilization, the Romans created their own distinctive culture. By 295 BC, Rome dominated the whole of central Italy, and by 280 BC the entire Italian Peninsula (Freeman 1993). At this time, Rome was democratic, governed by a delicate balance of aristocratic and popular authority (Fagan 1995, 457). After two hard fought wars with Carthage, the Romans achieved mastery over the western Mediterranean by 200 BC. By 133 BC, much of Asia Minor was under Roman domination. As Rome expanded, civil strife led to autocratic rule, first under the dictator Julius Caesar and followed by his great-nephew and heir, Octavian, also called Augustus (Freeman 1993). Under Caesar, the Mediterranean and much of Europe was brought under Roman rule. Roman legions campaigned in Egypt, Mesopotamia, India, and as far as western Europe and Britain.

The Emperor Augustus reorganized the civil service and established a Pax Romana over a vast region. There followed a period of great material prosperity and peace, but in the second and third centuries Roman rule began to founder. Shortage of land for farming and increasing disrespect for Rome led Germanic tribes at the periphery of the Roman core to challenge Rome's hegemony. In AD 395, when Emperor Theodosius died, the Roman Empire split into a western and eastern division. Tribal and chiefdom organized societies to the north continued to attack and finally sacked Rome itself. The European provinces were overrun by warrior chiefdoms, and Rome collapsed.

What were these warrior chiefdoms? The Romans have left descriptions of the Celtic and Germanic tribes and chiefdoms, and they are essentially like the tribes and chiefdoms we have discussed. They were organized into matrilineal (Celtic) or patrilineal (Germanic) clans, under chiefs who had control of mana and who relied on magicians for their power (think of Merlin the magician in the court of King Arthur). Roman rule was never able to completely dominate the chiefdoms of the northern fringe, and descriptions of these people come down to us in Roman writing and European mythology. Among the best known are the Celtic tribes of what are today Scotland, Wales, and Ireland. These, and their Germanic neighbors to the east, constantly challenged Roman authority. Roman towns were found in the lowland valleys along rivers, but Roman rule did not control the tribes and chiefdoms of the periphery, fitting the model we have described (core-periphery). Rome overextended itself, and it is not that the barbarians of the periphery became stronger than Rome but that Rome itself lost its capacity to control its bureaucracy and army. For example, the Roman government sent consuls to rule the provinces, often granting them land. The representatives from Rome often married into the local chiefly aristocracy, and their children lost their loyalty to the central core. Later, when the Roman armies tried to subject rebellious chiefs on the fringe of their empire, they faced fighters trained in Roman techniques of war.

After the collapse of Rome, the tribes and chiefdoms of the periphery, over time, became the European states, particularly as they assimilated the new Christian religion, which spread from Rome as it disintegrated. We will pick up on these peoples in the next section, particularly in western Europe where the manorial system, established by the Romans originally, became coupled to medieval Christianity and emerged as feudalism.

Brian Fagan points out that Rome left an impressive legacy:

> Its material legacy can be seen in the road system, which still provides a basis for many of Europe's and the Near East's communications, and in the towns, like London, which are still flourishing modern cities. In cultural terms, its principal legacy was the legal system, which lies at the core of most western law codes. Roman literature and art dominated European culture for centuries after the Renaissance (1995, 458).

The collapse of the Roman Empire created a vacuum in the Mediterranean that was filled by the development of the north African Islamic empires. These sat on the Great Silk road and made inroads as far as central France and most of Spain, controlling all trade for centuries. These new cores, mostly city-states, monopolized the overland trade routes east to China and the sea routes of the Mediterranean. The lack of access to trade was one of the most important factors pushing the European states into the Dark Ages. The European states were not to emerge from the Dark Ages until after the Spanish drove the Moors out of Spain, united under the Catholic monarchs, Ferdinand of Aragon and Isabel of Castile, and sponsored the discovery of the New World, thus opening new trade routes west over the Atlantic Ocean, and later across the Pacific.

The Origin of Feudalism in Ancient Europe

Until 1985, the world was dominated by the modern world system made up of a Euro-American core with peripheries in Africa, Asia, and Latin America. Today the modern world system is being transformed into a global system in which the core is fragmenting and segments of the periphery are taking on core characteristics (open markets, capitalism, private property rights, democratic reform), in ways that are very surprising to traditional anthropology. The origins of the modern world system are inauspicious and lie in cultural adaptations of west European states. In order to understand their origins, we have to delve into their prehistories.

While chiefdoms emerged in Western Europe quite early, there was a lack of stimulus for their transformation into states until very late. Explanations for this supposed backwardness range from primitive technologies to mythic religions. However, Western Europe simply did not lend itself to the development of irrigation style civilizations with large populations, such as found in other parts of the world; and trade was not a major stimulus to development. There are two reasons for this. First, in Europe, mountains and deserts do not circumscribe fertile regions. Western Europe, for the most part, is a region of vast plains and woodlands. The populations of the region used a form of slash and burn agriculture from about 5000 BC to about 1500 BC when the Bell-Beaker people (named for the shape of a pottery bowl) introduced the iron tipped plow and oxen. Even the introduction of this new technology, however, did not give rise to any dramatic changes. The lack of circumscribed environments meant that people were free to migrate to new locations whenever population densities began to produce unacceptable social and economic pressures. There was little to tie people to specific regions. As late as the fourteenth and fifteenth centuries there was a lot of unoccupied land, particularly in northern Europe. Population pressures resulted in migration, not hierarchy. While trade was important it remained local and limited in scope. Trade was limited because first Greece and then Rome dominated trade in the Mediterranean. Later, Islamic empires were to control the same trade routes. It was not until Europe spread to monopolize those routes that trade stimulated the rise of states in Western Europe.

A second factor is the prevalence of rain-fed agriculture. Irrigation agriculture is both a means of sustaining large populations and a means of controlling them. Irrigation systems were not needed in Western Europe. Rainfall was adequate for productive agriculture. Without irrigation or trade, there was little stimulus to restrict settlement to river valleys, develop large communities, or develop the management complexes needed by early irrigation-based societies (such as the Chinese mandarins). The introduction of agriculture does not seem to have had the same impact on the region of Western Europe as it did in other world regions where civilizations evolved. Even after the spread of Bronze Age cultures through the Central Aegean (Crete, Greece) into parts of Southeastern Europe between 4000 BC and 500 BC, little dramatic change in the level of sociocultural integration occurred in Western Europe.

Colin Renfrew, one of the foremost archaeologists working on European prehistory, thinks that most of Western Europe was occupied by clan-based chiefdoms (Renfrew 1979) until the period of Roman domination. These chiefdoms would never number more than a few thousand people. They would be tied to local nature gods, to whom the people would make sacrifices. Very little of this ancient time comes down to us. We do know that the people spoke various Celtic dialects, some of which became Scot, Irish, Welsh, and Cornish in later history. Like other chiefdoms, they were warlike, with the men painting their naked bodies blue before going into war, which they fought in the nude. Their religions we can only speculate about. The religious celebrations centered on burial vaults where the great chiefs and ancestors were buried. These burial vaults are scattered throughout most of Western Europe as massive standing rocks called **menhirs, dolmens,** and **passage graves.** What mythology we have of the time period implies some form of matrilineal descent (for Celtic peoples), which was also practiced on the other side of the ocean, in Eastern North America, until the European Conquest. We also know very little about trade during the prehistoric period. Agricultural states were relatively late on the scene in West European history, coming into existence only in the seventh century, and these European states differed from other archaic world systems in that they were highly decentralized and comparatively weak. The story of the development of city-states and peasant societies in Western Europe begins and then, for a while, ends with the rise and fall of the Roman Empire. The chiefdom societies that existed in pre-Roman Western Europe are poorly understood today, despite extensive archeological remains. The remains range from such impressive structures as Stonehenge on the Salisbury Plain in southern England to burial shafts known as dolmens which are found as far north as Denmark and as far south as Spain.

> **menhir, dolmen, passage grave**
>
> Burial monuments from the Mesolithic or Neolithic eras found in Western Europe, which usually consist of three vertical rocks supporting a fourth roof rock and are thought to be burial sites of chiefs

THE IMPACT OF ROMAN RULE

The imposition of Roman rule changed the chiefdom social structures significantly in some regions, but not in others. The strongest changes were in West Central Europe where Germany and France are today. Portions of eastern Great Britain were also substantially changed, and many Roman ruins are found there today. However, the regions of Wales, Ireland, Cornwall, and Scotland retained much of their ancient forms of organization, continuing to operate in decentralized chiefdom social structures until after the Middle Ages. The major organizational shift in all of these regions was the development of the Roman administrative town, strategically placed in important military and trade locations. These towns were primarily garrison towns, but they also had important trade and tribute functions as Rome traded its manufactured goods and wines up into the northern provinces of its empire in exchange for grains and timber. Soldiers, who were garrisoned in the towns, protected traders against thieves and bandits. Certain of these towns, such as London and Paris, achieved the status of city-states although it is doubtful that they controlled much of the countryside or developed a peasantry until the seventh or eighth centuries.

The relationship of the town to the rural countryside is fuzzy. It does not appear that the rulers of the garrison towns and city-states originally had direct control over the rural peasantry. Rather, it appears that while "consuls" appointed by Rome often ruled the towns from the regions where they lived, the countrymen were still organized into clans under the rule of chiefs. These chiefs, in turn, paid homage to the towns and city-states and were responsible for the actions of their kinsmen. The Romans looked down on the countrymen and referred to them as "barbarians" (Cunliffe 1979).

It is extremely difficult to pinpoint when this social structure began to shift. However, with Roman rule, which lasted almost five hundred years, population densities began to climb. Land became increasingly scarce, and it would appear that the rural chiefdoms were slowly converted into fortified manors as the competition for land intensified. By AD 700, which marked the end of Roman rule and the beginning of the Middle Ages, the social structures of Europe were made up of key towns, most of which survive today, usually established on the banks of major rivers, and a rural countryside made up of fortified manorial estates. The manors were originally occupied by representatives of the Roman state and may have been the origin of the manorial system (to be described later). The manors fed the towns and were administratively tied to them, but were not part of the distant chiefdoms. The riverain towns monopolized trade along the river valleys. When Roman rule ended, the administrative power of the towns waned. A class of manorial lords found themselves in control of a rural countryside, but then lost control to rural chiefs. The disintegration of Roman rule resulted in a period of extensive, although not always intensive, conflict, as manorial lords vied with one another to expand their rural holdings. In many instances, the local chiefs replaced the manorial lords, but in many other instances the manorial lords shifted their allegiances to the chiefs and became part of the manorial system (the exact series of events are not clear).

While AD 700 more or less marked the end of Roman rule in Western Europe, it also marked the beginnings of the spread of Christianity, trade, and the growth of tributary states. At the heart of the newly emerging economy was the manor and the river-based town. The manors were agricultural, while the towns depended on trade. Christianity differed from the traditional nature religions of the ancient Celts and Germans in being "universalistic"—that is, Christianity was a religion that could appeal to anyone, not just a person from a specific locale. The lords of the manors adopted the new religion as missionary priests migrated from Rome into northern Europe. The new religion served the political function of uniting people within the **manorial system.**

The manorial system, as a distinct rural economy, emerged from Roman imposed rule after the seventh century. It was based on agriculture. The manor was an estate, the patron of which was a chief who controlled many manors. The occupant of the manor had the right to use the estate in exchange for tribute paid to the chief, but did not really own the land. As in chiefdom systems, the chief controlled the land, and in traditional society, before the introduction of Roman rule, was magically identified with it. The introduction of Christianity reduced the connection between religion, a

manorial system

An economy system consisting of large landed estates ruled by lords under the tributary control of a single king or queen

specific chief, and a specific territory controlled by a single clan (the leader of which was the chief). Religion and trade produced greater centralization, and small manors were brought under the control of more powerful chiefs. War and the centralization of authority continued in a familiar pattern. In England, the invasion by William the Conqueror in 1066 brought about the further centralization of rule and the appearance of the state. The new Anglo-Saxon state was never to be at peace with itself, and the familiar conflict between the ruler and his chiefly supporters became one of the themes of English history. With William the Conqueror, feudalism had emerged.

The economy of the rural manorial system is called **feudalism**, a word derived from *fee*, an estate in land. It was based on tenancy, not ownership, of land (manorial system and feudalism amount to the same concept). The king was the owner, and from him the tenants-in-chief held their estates in return for military service. At the bottom of the scale was the serf or **villein** who paid the rent to his lord who occupied a middle position between serf and king (Halliday 1989, 40). The power of the king was dependent on the Christian church, much as the power of the chief was dependent on magical religions.

The Christian church, in effect, replaced Roman rule. It also had profound influence on the next thousand years in the organization of the manorial states and the weak city-states. These arose along the river systems of Western Europe where trade moved on rowboats, sailboats, and rafts. In the following, we will pay some attention to the organization of the feudal societies of Europe from which capitalism sprang. It is important to keep in mind that while our stereotype of the Middle or Feudal Ages is that of authoritarian and despotic regimes, the political systems of Western Europe were extremely weak in contrast to many other despotic systems, such as India or imperial China. Trade was very local in Europe during the Middle Ages. Fairs were held within trade towns, tying in several manors and their lords. Trade flowed on the rivers of Western Europe; and the manorial lords, who placed barriers in the path of trade by demanding taxes from traders, increased the costs of trade so that trade could not expand until the states expanded in size. In the tenth century, a manorial estate was the size of a small county and became the base of that political unit in British history. Blocking any further development of trade, however, was the monopoly over trade by North African states along the Mediterranean and Mongol states in Inner Asia.

feudalism

The economy of the rural manorial system in which land the king owned was occupied by tenants who held estates in the land in return for military service

villein

A peasant living and working on a manor who resided at the bottom of the manorial status pyramid

■William the Conqueror

EUROPEAN FEUDAL SOCIETY

Most agrarian states throughout the history of the world have had feudalistic social structures, but there is considerable variation in these structures. Scholars that generalize from European historical models outward to Asiatic systems such as found in India and China make a grave error; the reverse is also true. There are also places in today's "Third World" countries that, because of similarities of the human experience (poverty, despotism), scholars describe as feudalistic. One of these world regions is Latin America, but the similarities are superficial and Latin American countries are not feudal but centrist. During the colonial period they were elements in a highly centralized state bureaucracy run by Spain and Portugal.

European feudal systems never achieved the level of integration of China or, for that matter, the level of any other major pre-modern imperial state. Europe, for a long time, was made up of a series of small, regional, manorial systems that paid tribute to a central but relatively weak authority. Such principalities might, in turn, pay tribute to a yet more central authority, such as a king or queen of a relatively large territory, such as France. However, the authority of that final level depended on the cooperation of the middle level tribute givers and takers. These were weak feudal systems in which the rights to property, people (labor), their inventions, and productivity rested primarily in the hands of the barons in the middle range and only secondarily in the hands of the members of the highest "ruling" level. Kings and queens ruled only at the mercy of the middle level. This appears to have been particularly true of England, and somewhat less true in Spain or France. These two countries became highly centralized in the period from the tenth to the fifteenth centuries. The reason England had the least centralized of the feudal estates may lie in the diminished influence of Rome on the far off English domains, particularly the "western fringe": Wales, Scotland, Cornwall, and Ireland. It was also true, however, that the western fringe was a trade periphery. This would change radically with the development of shipping technology during the sixteenth century when new world-wide trade routes opened up.

It was the lack of an overall integrating force that set apart the European states from other regions between AD 700 and AD 1700. It also helps to explain the rise of capitalism in the West instead of the East. No one would have predicted the vast growth in the wealth and power of England and the Netherlands, and the failure of China to keep up with the West, had he or she compared England and China in the tenth or eleventh centuries.

It is argued that capitalism emerged first in Western Europe precisely because of the weak feudal social structure. France and Spain were much more centralized and resisted the capitalist transformation that England went through. Once England was transformed, it came to dominate the world through its much more efficient forms of political and economic organization, which insured (for a time) its domination of the seas, and thus the major routes of oceanic trade.

The chief landowner during the Middle Ages was the Roman Catholic Church. It was the repository of learning, and its top heavy bureaucracy amassed wealth in the form of land in exchange for salvation. In the Middle Ages, when a man or a woman died, their place in heaven would be secured if they turned over their estates to the Church. In many respects, the Church had the trappings of a state (North 1981, 125). Western Europe was the region where classic European feudalism emerged.

In tenth century Western Europe, law and order existed only within settled regions where the manorial system dominated and where the Catholic faith pulled cultures together. Beyond these settled regions banditry interfered with trade and commerce, raising transaction costs so that trade was minimal. It cost more to move goods than to move labor, and so we say that goods had a higher "transaction" cost. On the other hand, there was a lot of surplus land available, so laborers were brought to the manor where they could farm the land and receive protection from the lord of the manor. Manors appear to have had limits in size. There were economies of scale in production; that is, the larger the manor was, the more it could produce—up to a point. As the number of inhabitants protected by the lord of the manor grew and the distance of farmed lands from the castle increased, the costs of protection went up and

■The local castle and the knights of the manor were the protection that was needed for the manor to function.

the efficiency of the manor dropped. This means there were limits placed on the efficient size of a manor, which in turn limited political centralization.

The local castle and the knights of the manor were the protection that was needed for the manor to function. The local lord was, in turn, linked to overlords in a series of linkages that ran up to a king. Between the king and the local lords, there might be several intermediate levels. At each level, the lord provided knight service for his superiors (North 1981, 127).

Property rights in the feudal states of Western Europe were grants of tenure in return for military service, but a feudal lord could flout the demand of his king for that service. However, the lord of the manor did not own his land—the land belonged to the king. The lord and his knights were both a warrior class and a ruling class whose survival depended on militarism. Douglas North, an economic historian, writes,

> The ideological gloss overlying this class was chivalry, a term that brings to mind King Arthur, the Round Table, knight service, and courtly love, but in practice was more a rationale for a class that lived by violence (North 1981, 127).

Property rights of peasants and freeholders were conditional grants of tenure in exchange for services, goods, and rent. The social structure established on the economic base of a tributary peasantry and a manorial elite has been described for England by George Homans, a sociologist (1941) and is summarized in the following:

> In most villages there were two social classes. The more substantial villagers were called the *husbonds*. They had houses instead of cottages. Poorer farmers were called *cotters* or *cotmen* and they lived in cottages; the husbonds were substantial farmers and it is from this social class that we get the word husbandry (and husband). The local two-class system appears to have been common throughout Europe. The husbonds had control of units of land called *yards or yardlands* (in northern England they were called *oxgangs*), usually about thirty acres in size (Homans 1941, 339). The smaller fields, usually about five acres in size were called the cotlands and were held by the cotters, or cotmen. Oxgangs and yardlands were fixed parts of larger units called plowlands in the north and hides in the south; both were about 120 acres in size. Homans thought the most important circumstance explaining size was that 120 acres was the amount of land which one plow team could manage in one year's work (Homans 1941, 340). It was a unit for assessment of taxes and other

charges. The farmers who worked these tracts usually combined their efforts working collectively for the lord of the manor. The exact size of plowlands and hides, of course, actually differed depending on environmental and climatic conditions, and so the number of individuals working the land would also tend to differ from region to region.

Homans described one English manor of the thirteenth century, which he argues was not necessarily typical, but was well described. His analysis gives us insights into the social structure of Medieval Europe.

According to Homans, in 1279, Angareta de Beauchamp held the manor of Spelsbury as her dower of the inheritance of the Earl of Warenne and Surrey; and at her death, the manor reverted to the earl. *She did not own the manor.* As was typical at the time, she had a right to tribute from those who worked the land, but the land itself belonged, ultimately, to the king. The Bishop of Worcester, who was over the Earl of Warenne and Surrey, held the Earl of Warenne and Surrey's lands, and the bishop, in turn, "held of the king" (Homans 1941, 344).

Three plowlands of the manor were in *demesne*, which means they were tilled under the management of the officers of the manor; the rest of the land was in the hands of her tenants. There were three kinds of tenants: freeholders, *villeins* (serfs or peasants), and cotters. There were six freeholders (a freeholder did not have to work, but paid rent, and had a higher rank than a villein). The wealthiest rented a mill and six acres of land, which freed him from almost all services. Thirty-three villeins held one yardland each in villeinage; but too poor to pay rent, they were required to till and harvest the lady's plowlands. The villeins also had to collect nuts in the lady's wood and to give her wheat from their own plot of land. In addition, once a year, she took whatever portion she pleased of the money and goods of her villeins (Homans 1941, 344).

The poorest class was that of the cotters of whom there were six, three men and three women. They also tilled the lady's land, but they did fewer hours of work and got less land. The differences in status of the three groups were class-based and reflected rank, often determined by military service to the lord of the manor. Homans writes of the structure of the manor:

> There were two parts of the manor, a greater part, which was in the hands of tenants, and a lesser part, the demesne, which was managed by officers of the lady of the manor and tilled by her servants and her villeins. On this demesne there was probably a manor house and court, with farm buildings, and in the hall of the manor house the hallmotes [meetings] would be held. According to the amounts of land they held and the rents and services they rendered in return for their land, the tenants were divided into classes, which were also called by special names. Among the tenants also were men who held particular positions in the economy of the manor: the miller, the smith, the reeve [overseer], and the bedell [messenger and arranger of events]. Lastly, besides having her rents and services from her tenants, the lady exercised certain other rights over them, especially the right of holding a manorial court. They had to attend it, and she took the profits of its justice (Homans 1941, 345).

Such was the structure of the English manor in the thirteenth century. The relationship of the lord of the manor and his tenants was permanent. As long as he or she lived, the lord would have the same families of tenants and vice versa. The two were perpetually bound together in a patron-client relationship, but the relationship was seldom face-to-face; many lords held many manors. However, while the relationship between the lord and his tenants was based on tradition and appears rigid, the lord could only make so many demands on the tenants; and the king could only make so many demands on his vassals. If the lord became too exacting, the tenant would run away and find another lord. If the king made too many demands on his vassals, they might revolt. Here we see a definite limit to oppression, and there is also a limit on hierarchy and centralization. While the tenant had good reason to stay in the lord's good graces, there was much mutual loyalty and understanding (Homans 1941, 347).

THE CATHOLIC RELIGION

Integrating the feudal social structure was religion. The Catholic religion dominated Europe until the Protestant Reformation in the sixteenth century. The universe was organized hierarchically based on the six days of creation. Lower ordered things were farther down the hierarchy and were created within the first days of creation. Man was conceived as standing on top of the pyramid because he was created last. Woman was perceived as having lower status than man because she was created out of man. Woman was the vessel for the "seed" of the man, his children. The hierarchy of creation had several mirror hierarchies that explained to people the nature of the social, ecclesiastical, and supernatural universe. The religious universe was a projection of this world's social structure.

In the social model of the feudal world, the king represented God on earth and ruled by divine right. Beneath him came his direct relatives, who formed the nobility. Beneath the nobility was an aristocracy, which was also ranked according to the relationship of the individual to members of the nobility, their wealth, and military ability. The aristocracy basically formed the manorial elite. Beneath the landed aristocracy were the peasants, who were also arranged according to rank.

The ecclesiastical model of the world was composed of a semi-divine pope on top and a hierarchy of cardinals, archbishops, bishops, and priests. There were also a large number of monasteries and nunneries inhabited by members of the aristocracy, who ruled, and peasants, who toiled. Most families, from the peasant classes on up, won recognition for giving at least one son or daughter to the mother Church. Behind the ecclesiastical model, there was the supernatural model composed of God the Father, his Son, and the Holy Ghost, forming a triumvirate. In addition, and often equal in importance, was the Virgin Mary. Joseph, her husband, was also prayed to and perceived as a god that could intervene on behalf of humans. There was also a vast pantheon of saints, both men and women, who were ranked according to their importance to humans. While Christians like to state that Christianity is monotheistic, in fact, from a non-Christian viewpoint, it looks quite polytheistic. Villages and individuals were named for saints, and the saints were treated as lesser gods.

The individual was born into this world as a component of one or several of the social pyramids. His status, like that of the Chinese or Indian peasant, was fixed at birth and was not questioned. Fate determined all. State religions imposed upon peasants, generally, explain reality in terms of the acceptance of one's fate and role in life.

While the religious beliefs and social structures of the peasants in the early feudal period were relatively stable, the social structures of the European chiefdom-like states were weak in contrast to those of the conquest states which emerged in Mesopotamia, the Mediterranean, and elsewhere. There was lack of a stimulus to bring about the early development of such tributary empires in Europe.

■ ■ ~ ■

Chapter
Summary

Chiefdoms and Pre-Modern States: Core-Periphery Relations

On the eve of the discovery of the New World, there were a set of empires around the world based on agriculture and the control of trade over vast regions: an Asiatic empire centered in China and India; a north African-Southwest Asian empire connected to China along the Great Silk Road, made up of Islamic states which shifted in core status; an Andean empire with the Inca at its core; and a Mesoamerican empire, controlled by the Aztecs. While productive agriculture was a general characteristic of chiefdoms and states, control of trade best explains the status of the cores of these hegemonic systems. Several of the most powerful early Muslim states, which based their cores in desert regions such as Saudi Arabia, had no agriculture to speak of but depended on tribute for food. The core states of these systems rose and fell and shifted, depending on success in trade and warfare. Other lesser states were either tribute payers to the cores or stood as semi-independent societies, in either case collecting tribute (or booty) in turn from the smaller societies that they dominated. Examples are the Tarascans of western Mexico and the Tlaxcalans of central Mexico, neither of which were ever completely dominated by the core states of the central valley. On the peripheries of the core were many chiefdoms. A short list of chiefdoms would include the American Northwest Coast, Polynesia, the lower Mississippi valley, the Great Rift Valley of Africa, and the Western Isles of Europe. Several of these regions became states; several, such as Polynesia and the Northwest Coast, did not. More peripheral yet were tribes, and bands of hunters and food gatherers. All of these systems operated in symbiotic relationship with each other, connected through trade and warfare. These regional economic systems were semi-autonomous, on their margins trading with each other. Processes of expansion and contraction were continuous in these empires.

In this chapter, we have focused on the emergence of chiefdoms, city-states, and empires; and we have argued that population increase and demand for additional resources provided the stimulus in some core areas for the intensification of patterns of trade and warfare. In the process, tribal forms of organization were transformed into chiefdoms; and some of these, perhaps due to a combination of technological, political, and economic innovations, came to dominate their neighbors. These became the early city-states and archaic trade and tribute empires.

We have sketched a trade-tribute-redistribution model of chiefdom expansion, and we have shown how this model presaged the development of early states and empires. We have drawn upon data from ancient Mesopotamia and the Mediterranean to illustrate the process of early state formation. Finally, we have sketched a picture of feudal Europe and examined some ideas about why state formation in this region occurred so much later than in other regions and why, for a long time, European states remained weak and decentralized. When a trade empire finally begins to emerge in Europe at the end of the sixteenth century, its worldwide impact goes far beyond anything we have examined so far. It is out of west European feudal societies that the modern world system emerges.

In 1492, with the discovery of the New World by Columbus, all of the world's regional trade systems were rapidly connected to each other. A new core in western Europe, which was in the form of chiefdoms in the seventh century had become the states of Spain and Portugal by the fifteenth century; these then monopolized all the trade networks of the world and transformed the archaic empires into a single world system, the one Wallerstein calls the "modern world system." By the early seventeenth century, Spain and Portugal gave up their core status to England and Holland; and later the other west European countries became members of the core of the modern world system. The modern world system survived until 1985. We examine all this in the next chapter. We are currently in the throes of another transformation into a "global world system" with post-industrial societies rapidly taking the place of industrial societies. This will be covered in later chapters.

Chapter Terms

caste	186	paramount chief	183
class	186	stratification	186
ecological circumscription	187	sumptuary rules	186
feudalism	203	tributary empire	188
hegemonic core	188	tributary state	188
manorial system	202	untouchable	186
menhir, dolmen, passage grave	201	villein	203

Check out our website
www.BVTLab.com
for flashcards,
chapter summaries,
and more.

Chapter 6

The Modern World: Capitalism, World Systems, and Globalization

In the year 1492, and for the next decade, West European civilization made exploratory connections with the other hegemonic empires of the world. The New World was discovered, Africa explored, and Asia opened to trade. China's core and peripheries were already well known due to the travels two centuries before by Niccolo Polo and his son Marco. These merchants from Venice represented the newly developing commercial viewpoint of West European societies. These societies, as we learned in the last chapter, were predominantly feudal and agricultural. However, changes were occurring in Venice and northern Italy where the new viewpoint of mercantilism was evolving, a philosophy that forced Europeans to look beyond the limited structures of feudalism and to world trade. Venice and other northern Italian city-states represented the high point of the **Renaissance**, marking the transition from the medieval to the modern world. The Renaissance, or rebirth, was the consequence of the increased importance of the older Roman and Greek ideas of science and philosophy over the predominantly religious ideas of the Middle Ages.

England was still mired in feudal philosophies and legal structures. Its day in the sun was yet centuries in the future, and the Venetian adventurers of the waning fifteenth century would have been surprised to find how the world would be structured three hundred years later in 1792. For these adventurers, the world was a closed place that they were helping to open. In the year that Columbus set sail to the New World, China and India dominated and controlled trade and power in the Orient. The Mediterranean was still in the hands of

Renaissance

The period marking the transition from the medieval to the modern world, roughly from the fourteenth through the sixteenth centuries, when the arts and philosophies of the ancient world were rediscovered and made the basis for a new birth of European culture

the followers of Muhammad in Egypt and Damascus, Syria. These Islamic states had bottled up trade in a monopoly. Later, the Islamic core would be moved to Turkey as the center of the new Ottoman Empire. The Europeans began nibbling at the control of the Islamic states in North Africa. Spain, in the same year of 1492, drove the Moors (Arabs) out of Spain and the western Mediterranean. Japan, at the time, was an island wrapped in feudal duties and social structures, just like England.

To the north of Italy, inland along the Rus, Volga, and Dniepper rivers, Slavic chiefdoms accepted Christianity and were transformed into a state with its core at Kiev in modern Ukraine (Krader 1968). The new state was influenced by the Eastern Orthodox religion with roots in the Byzantine Empire. Not unlike the peoples of Great Britain, the Russian state began with a weak feudal system; however, in the centuries that followed, Russia took a distinct turn toward a highly centralized state. In the eighteenth century, its new empire would be dominated by Peter the Great, who would expand its borders to the east (a topic to which we will return at the end of this chapter).

The Mercantilist Roots of Capitalism

The ideas of modern capitalism would have appeared absurd to people in 1492, and the centuries immediately to follow. Modern capitalism is founded, in part, on the idea that trade leads to wealth, and that wealth itself can be unlimited. In the fifteenth century, the dominant philosophy of political economy was **mercantilism.** Mercantilism rested on the basic and simple assumption that all wealth was limited. One nation's gain was another nation's loss. One nation could only become wealthy if another country became poor. This philosophy underwrote the expansion of the countries of Western Europe and explains their constant wars (Boorstin 1983, 653). Besides being large, a country had to balance its trade relations by constantly increasing its source of gold and silver. Monopolies were granted to special government authorized companies to search for, and control, wealth. Many private adventurers sought riches in the lands discovered by the explorers searching for trade routes.

Spain and Portugal were very successful at expanding their empire states, but there were threats of war over how to divide the lands discovered by Christopher Columbus. A rivalry between King John of Portugal and King Ferdinand of Spain was settled by Pope Alexander VI, who at the Treaty of Tordesillas divided the world in two, with the line splitting the two running north and south 1,200 nautical miles west from the Cape Verde Islands. Lands west of the line belonged to Spain and those east of the line belonged to Portugal (Boorstin 1983, 174).

The new empires were based on mercantilism. However, in imposing their theory of mercantilism, the adventurers, traders, and representatives of Spain and Portugal destroyed the old hegemonic empires and created peripheries of destitute societies everywhere their policies prevailed. The Aztec and Inca empires, as well as the societies of the West Indies (Caribbean) and the East Indies (Indian Ocean), were soon poverty-stricken backwaters as internal trade was destroyed or monopolized by Spain and Portugal, and later by other European states.

mercantilism

The dominant philosophy of political economy, which is based on the idea that all wealth is limited and can only be divided, not created

THE AGE OF EXPLORATION

The search for wealth, the competition for colonies, and the constant need for expansion coincided with the Age of Exploration. The Portuguese crossed over to North Africa in 1415 and captured Cuenta, reaching Madeira in 1419 and the Canary islands shortly after. The Azores were colonized between 1439–53. The Portuguese worked their way down the west coast of Africa. In 1488, Bartholomeu Diaz rounded the Cape of Good Hope, putting the Portuguese in East Africa, the Persian Gulf, Indian Ocean, China, and the islands beyond. In 1493, Columbus returned to Spain to describe his discoveries of the New World. Vasco da Gama, under the flag of Portugal, reached India in 1498. Ferdinand Magellan, a Portuguese, discovered the Philippines, where he died in 1521. In 1528 De Soto landed in Florida, discovered the Mississippi River, and traveled as far north as Kansas (Hughes 1987, 8).

The knowledge we have of the events of this period and the consequences for the peoples of the periphery has paled the halos of the heroes of exploration. One example is Vasco Nuñez de Balboa. An adventurer born of obscure parents, Balboa discovered the Pacific in 1513 in western Panama. Originally, he was more interested in the discovery of gold than unknown seas, an interest for which the son of a Panamanian chief (cacique) criticized him:

> What is the matter, you Christian men, that you so greatly esteeme so little portion of gold more than your own quietnesse … If your hunger of gold, bee so insatiable, that onely for the desire you have … I will shewe you a region flowing with golde, where you may satisfy your ravening appetites (Boorstin 1983, 257).

The son of the cacique went on to describe how to find a sea where they would discover ships carrying gold. While searching for gold and accidentally discovering the Pacific, Balboa

Figure 6.1

❑ Map of Voyages of Discovery

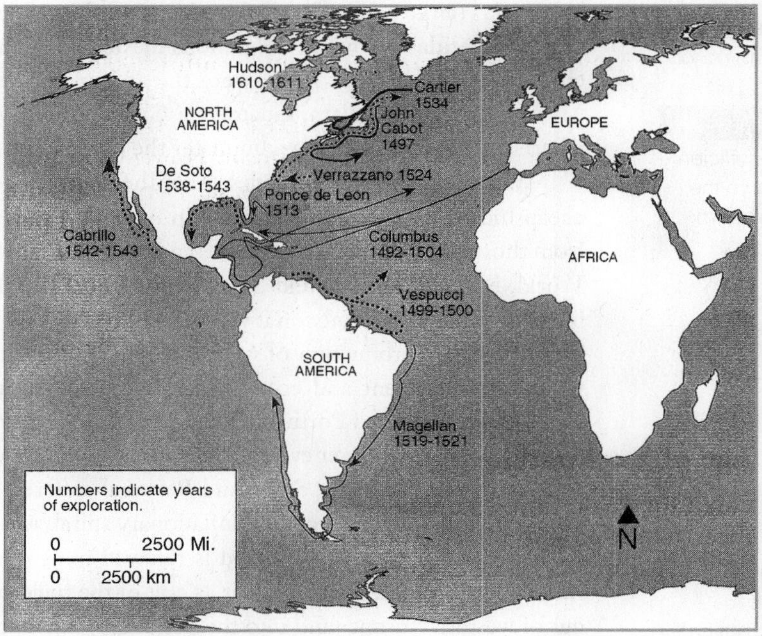

encountered the village of the Quarequa, whose customs so incensed the Spaniards that they set their hunting dogs to tear these people apart. Six hundred people were slain. Similar incidents can be reported for most of the explorers. However, it is much too easy to pass judgment on their accomplishments. Any student of the histories of this age knows that the explorers and conquerors were both heroic and anti-heroic. Columbus did have the will to keep his crews together, as most students have read, but he also was responsible for acts of genocide against the Indians of the Antilles. The explorers were not working to expand the knowledge of the Old World, as children have been taught for centuries, but to gain access to new lands and to dominate trade with those lands. Heroism and exploitation went hand in hand. There is the incredible heroism of Hernando Cortez in his fight to save his men from ritual sacrifice by the Aztecs, but then there is also his role as the conqueror of the peoples of Mexico, for which he received royal titles, land, and the free labor of the people he enslaved.

The events of discovery are difficult to tie to the events that followed discovery. The descriptions of adventure are usually not coupled to the spread of disease and population collapse, but there are those connections. The explorers, and the Europeans who followed on their heels, introduced diseases. Also, the impact of mercantilist trade philosophy was devastating to the people of the non-European regions of the world. The collapse of regional trade led to the wholesale collapse of economies, and often to the incentive to live.

THE IMPACT OF SPAIN AND PORTUGAL ON LATIN AMERICA

The colonial period in Latin America begins in the early sixteenth century with the conquest of the Aztec in Mexico by Hernando Cortez in 1521 and the conquest by Pizarro in 1533 of the Inca Empire centered in the Peruvian Andes. The Spanish explorers and the conquistadores followed the philosophy of mercantilism to the letter. The **conquistadores** discovered wealth in the form of silver in Mexico and gold in Peru and Bolivia. Very quickly, they established a new economy in their colonies based on mining and large **haciendas** (large and self-sufficient farms). Labor was provided by the Indians in the form of **encomiendas**, tributary obligations to the new nobility (discussed in Chapter 11). New cities, built with Indian labor, were the administrative centers of the mining economies: Mexico City, Guadalajara, Guatemala City, and on down to the tip end of remote Chile, where Santiago was built to administer the domains of the southern Andes.

Within the next four decades, all of the major cities of Latin America were founded on cheap Indian labor. The cities of Latin America had a very different institutional structure from those of Puritan New England, and preceded them by a century. The cities of the New World, both Portuguese and Spanish, were administrative cities with large and expensive bureaucracies whose function it was to supervise the extraction of wealth from the landscape, rather than the production of wealth (Portes and Walton 1976). Economic theory had no place for investment and economic development. Trade was a form of plunder. Wealth poured into Spain and Portugal. The myth of El Dorado (the gilded one) drove such explorers as De Soto to discover even more wealth; the consequences, however, were not those predicted. Instead of wealth, Spain and Portugal suffered from inflation; prices for bread and shoes quadrupled during a great inflationary spiral, which lasted throughout the last part of the sixteenth century. This period is referred to as the crisis of the sixteenth century, and Immanuel Wallerstein identifies it as one of the major causes for the movements of people out of western Europe (and into the periphery) due to growing poverty. This spiral was not limited to Spain and Portugal but spread throughout Europe producing economic panics,

conquistador

A Spanish term meaning "conqueror" that refers to the first wave of colonists to the New World, whose actions were based on mercantilist beliefs

hacienda

A large, self-sufficient estate similar to the manors of Western Europe that was granted to the conquistadores in exchange for their loyalties to the Hispanic and Portuguese crowns

encomienda

A right given to the conquistadores and their immediate descendants to Indian labor, but not to their lands

which in turn spurred more exploration and further expansionism, and more inflation (Boorstin 1983, 653). While Europe suffered economic deprivation due to massive inflation, the New World suffered from population collapse.

During the period from 1560 to 1580, much of the Indian population of the Americas collapsed in "the great dying" (Wolf 1982). The population collapse was the consequence of diseases and brutal treatment at the hands of the Spanish and Portuguese. After the collapse, which has been estimated to be between 60 and 90 percent of the entire population, vast lands were left wide open. The children of Indian and Spanish unions, the *mestizos*, as well as many Spaniards, took over the lands and transformed them into haciendas (Mintz and Wolf 1957). By 1700, the economies of the Americas were composed of large cities run by extensive but inefficient bureaucracies, giant haciendas, and gold and silver mines. These three institutions, taken together, accounted for up to 80 percent of the productive wealth of Latin American societies. The bureaucrats, mostly from Spain, formed the upper levels of aristocracy, both secular and religious. Beneath them came a lesser nobility of locally born Creole elites, many of them the owners of extensive hacienda lands. Beneath these, in turn, were mestizos. Some of the mestizos had come into control of large haciendas and had considerable status, but not as much as the Spanish and Creole aristocrats who controlled the offices of the bureaucracies. Beneath the mestizo landowners came poorer mestizos, Indians, and black slaves.

The impact of Spain and Portugal on the New World is usually described in terms of the benefits of new European technologies. However, the collapse of regional trade networks and the monopoly of trade by the new elites brought famine and population collapse not economic development. It was not until four centuries later that the population began to make a comeback, but the region has continued to be troubled by the institutions of mercantilism and its philosophies.

THE IMPACT OF WESTERN EUROPE ON AFRICA

The story for Africa is a mirror reflection of Latin America. When the populations of the New World collapsed, slaves were taken from Africa to do the work of the settlers of the New World, thus robbing Africa of its young. While silver, gold, and sugar were the wealth drawn out of Latin America, in Africa the exploited commodity was "black ivory"—human beings captured and then sold into slavery (Wolf 1982, 195).

Initially, the demand for slaves came from South and Central America after the collapse of Indian populations in the sixteenth century. Slaves were imported to work sugar, coffee, and cotton plantations. Later, the growth of cotton and tobacco plantations in the southern United States added to the demand (Wolf 1982, 197–198). Europeans radically transformed African societies when they brought in metal, hardware, firearms, gunpowder, textiles, rum, and tobacco to exchange for slaves. Generally, Europeans did not hunt for slaves but created politically powerful elites to obtain slaves for them. Many of the slave hunter societies became centralized states with kings, courts, and bureaucracies. Shillington writes about the extent of the slave trade:

Figure 6.2

☐ Early Global Economies Based on Slave Trade

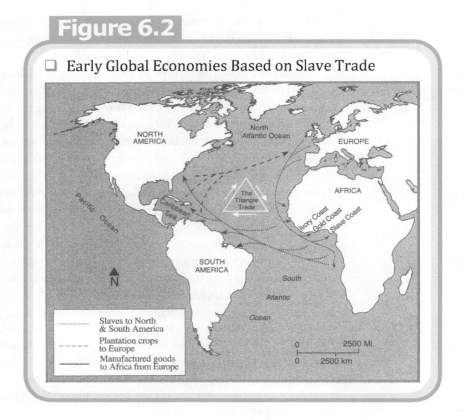

With the rapid expansion of slave exports in the eighteenth century virtually every part of the Atlantic coastline from Senegal to southern Angola became involved in the human traffic. The greatest concentration of European trading forts was along the so-called "Gold Coast," the coastline of the modern state of Ghana (Shillington 1989, 174).

The slave trade increased the level of warfare along the western interior of Africa, and it caused a serious loss to the productive potential of the region. All regions of western Africa were seriously affected by a loss of manpower. The incalculable suffering of the slaves is probably impossible to understand. The impact on African society was immense since the slave trade went on for over three hundred years.

African slaving states rose and fell as they received support or lost support from European slavers. Slave tribute-paying tribes and slave-taking states came to hate each other; as their relations with Europeans changed, so did their relations with each other (Wolf 1982, 228–229). Many of these hatreds remain with the modern tribal societies in Africa. Generally speaking, in the post colonial or modern period, one of the greatest single political problems facing Africans centers on these age-old tribal feuds based on the slave trade. These hatreds were especially fueled in the late nineteenth and early twentieth centuries when colonial authorities administratively grouped together ethnic groups that were enemies (to be discussed in Chapter 7).

THE EMERGENCE OF GREAT BRITAIN AS A TRADE EMPIRE AND THE COLLAPSE OF FEUDALISM

We have examined world history from roughly ten thousand years ago to the symbolic date of 1492. Since the development of the first hegemonic states, roughly in the time between 4000 and 3000 BC, the long view of human history has been a story of unrelieved poverty for the masses of peasants and urban dwellers. It is only in the last two hundred years that just a few places in the world have enjoyed prosperity: Western Europe, the United States, Canada, Australia, and Japan. In the nineteenth century, it became apparent that the members of these societies were eating better, living longer, and were more secure than the peoples who had lived in the hegemonic empires we discussed earlier (Rosenberg & Birdzell 1986).

Between the sixteenth and nineteenth centuries, this prosperous industrial core emerged with a dependent periphery, the former hegemonic empires we read about in the last chapter. There has been a great deal of research done in attempting to explain the rise of the West. The explanations range from outright racist theories on the superiority of West European societies (which do not explain Japan), to Marxist theories which explain prosperity in the core as a consequence of the poverty of the periphery, to ideas about the impact of the Protestant religion on West European economic ideology. More recently, a theory is emerging which explains the origins of capitalism as the consequence decreasing transaction costs for trade on the part of Great Britain, a point of view consistent with how we viewed the changes in social structures in traditional social systems in the last two chapters. Here, we wish to explain other theories first, and then to discuss how trade theory applies to social structure.

Two theoreticians who attempted to explain the rise of capitalism were Karl Marx in *Capital* (1936) and Max Weber in his *The Protestant Ethic and the Spirit of Capitalism* (1958a). For Karl Marx, the explanation for the rise of capitalism was largely materialistic. To put his argument simply: the invention of new technologies brought about new relationships between human beings as workers and as producers. The new relationships of production changed class structures. For Marx, capitalism was largely the same as the emergence of a profit-making class of people, the capitalists, the producers who dominate society. Marx explained the rise of wealthy social classes as a consequence of the exploitation of laboring populations in Western Europe. Emmanuel Wallerstein has taken Marx' analysis and made it the basis for a description of the modern world system. According to Wallerstein's more global perspective, the wealth of the core is due to the plundering of the poor societies of the periphery. The positions of both Marx and Wallerstein are distinctly materialistic and rest on the origins of the new technologies of the west as the means for exploiting cheap labor.

Max Weber, while not denying the materialistic base of capitalism, saw the impetus for change as coming from a new geist, a new spirit, which was to be found in a new attitude toward productivity based on the Protestant religion ethic of competition. Yet Weber's thesis does not explain the rise of Japan in the nineteenth century, nor does it explain the impact of globalism in our age.

A third position examines the changing institutions of British society to explain why Great Britain, and not some other society, became the core of the new world system. The economic historian, Douglas North, has shown that there were crucial changes to British economic institutions, particularly private property rights and the organization of trade, which help explain the rise of capitalism. We examined in the last chapter how, in pre-capitalist societies, property belonged to the state, particularly the most productive property: land. North's perspective is that the state of Great Britain abandoned the control of land and that a landed elite emerged whose point of view was entrepreneurial and who sought to make profits by investing in land. These changes led to the rise of industrial entrepreneurs in the major urban areas of Great Britain. Only once these changes were in place could Great Britain shoulder aside the mercantilist states of Western Europe; for its institutions had become more efficient and able to dominate world trade.

Douglas North's explanation of capitalism does not begin with Great Britain as a core dominating a periphery, but with the question of how Great Britain's institutions became more efficient than those of Portugal and Spain. The transformation of British institutions occurred at the time that Spain and Portugal dominated the world, in the sixteenth and seventeen centuries. By the eighteenth century, Great Britain had replaced Portugal and Spain as the new core of the modern world system. How did that happen?

While the answer is not simple, we attempt to summarize it. North argues that the manorial system in England led, very gradually, to an expansion of population, a process which happened all over western Europe in the thirteenth and fourteenth centuries. The consequence of population growth was overpopulation. The Black Plague in the second half of the fourteenth century, a biological disaster of immense proportions, resulted in the death of between one-half to three-quarters of Europe's population. Land became cheap and labor dear, giving peasants economic leverage in demanding higher wages. In Great Britain, the change in labor value occurred just as new merchant towns were growing, and the peasants were able to bargain for higher wages, threatening the structure of feudalism.

The challenges to feudalism were met throughout Europe through the assertion of authority by centralizing states. The kings and courts of Great Britain, realizing the threats to national survival by the other states of Europe (France, Spain), followed the flow of the challenge to feudalism by *abandoning land tenure based on tribute*, turning over the ownership of property to the aristocratic classes. The state ceased to own the land and invested more heavily in trade, supporting the construction of ships and port cities. It is important to emphasize here that the feudal system of Great Britain was never strong. It was better to give up feudalism for a distinct type of political economy, one based on trade and the private ownership of property, rather than attempt to emulate the more centralized and bureaucratic economies of, for example, France and Spain.

With the innovation of private property rights and a growing emphasis on trade, new trade towns evolved in Great Britain. The development of trade towns in Great Britain produced new wealth; and it became possible for kings to hire mercenaries instead of relying on a knight's tribute of forty days of service per year, further eroding the tributary system. The size of a king's army no longer depended on tributary relationships to the lower nobility but on the size of his purse, which expanded as taxes were paid on private property. This was another factor in the shift from tributary rights to private property rights, as the king sought to base his power on the taxation of private property and trade, not on tribute. North argues that the demand by the newly landed elites that they have some control over the taxes they paid to the king led to the founding of the British Parliament. While early parliamentary politics can hardly be called democratic, here was the origin of democracy, as we know it today. It began with private property rights, the need to protect those rights against a hungry state, and the slow increases of prosperity to the entire population, a process that took the better part of three centuries.

The story of politics in Great Britain is basically the struggle between a king wanting to increase his/her hegemony over world trade through a powerful military, particularly a navy, against the interests of an aristocracy whose growing wealth depended on investments in land and industry. Over time, a new social class emerged as former feudal peasants moved from the countryside to the city, became factory workers, and then formed the ranks of an urban-based middle class, whose interests lay in directions opposite both those of the king and the aristocracy. These middle class entrepreneurs used their growing wealth and numbers to support either the king or the aristocracy as they bid to increase their own powers.

The emergence of private property, the growth in the expense of the military, and the success of trade towns led to the destruction of feudalism and the development of capitalism. In Chapter 3, we examined the development of democratic capitalism in North America. At this point, remember that while Great Britain was going through the changes described in these pages, America was developing a powerful trade society that did not have to worry about the conflicts between a king and his aristocracy, and therefore was able to build a society based on lower transaction costs for trade.

The Industrial Revolution and the Rise of Capitalism

According to Eric Wolf, the major engine of the transition to capitalism was the development of the textile industry in eighteenth century England. Karl Marx would agree with his analysis, with an emphasis on human greed, the new capitalists, and exploitation of an urban **proletariat** (a social class without property). Max Weber, on the other hand, would explain the development of capitalism as due to the rationalist values of Protestantism. According to Weber, this new religion taught the idea that success in this world rested on good works, and good works depended on entrepreneurial investment and competition in this world, not the next.

The alternative argument, presented by Douglas North, points out that before any of these changes occurred, new legal relationships to land and property had evolved and were stimulating productivity. North points out that economic relationships were being reorganized from peasant based tributary agriculture to a society based on private property rights, and that changes in those rights kicked off the industrial revolution. He believes that capitalism has less to do with making profits than in changing property rights. Changes in landownership stimulated the production of food, which became cheaper. At the same time, the idea of private property rights was extended to the ownership of rights in ideas. The protection of ideas led to new inventions, and these led to the industrial revolution. North argues that the real basis of the industrial revolution was in the innovation in law, in developing a state that protected people's ideas. Innovations in sea trade occurred at the same time. The invention of clocks, **astrolabes** (optical instruments used to navigate by the stars at sea), and other innovations made British ships highly competitive.

These three theories (changes in the forms of production, new competitive values, and changing private property rights) are often presented as opposing each other; instead, they are all different parts of the same story. A growing supply of agricultural goods in the countryside and the development of industrial technology in the urban sectors led to a stimulus-response relationship between urban and rural areas. Technological innovation in industry led to a demand for labor in urban areas, while the same technological change had the opposite effect in the countryside. These were the consequence of new institutions, but they did lead to human exploitation as well as a transition to capitalism. England became the core of an economic system based on a new type of economy. Mercantilism was being replaced with capitalism; peasant tributary economies were disappearing in favor of urban-based workers in factories.

Capitalism differs from mercantilism in several respects. One, it defines wealth as unlimited; new forms of production and trade lead to new levels of prosperity. Second, the ownership of resources is not by the state but in the form of

proletariat

A social class consisting of those without property (The rural proleteriat are those without land, and the urban proleteriat are those without wealth or the opportunity to acquire wealth.)

astrolabe

An instrument used to measure the altitude of the sun or stars used in navigation

corporation

A legal fiction that gives a group or association of people the private property rights of a single individual in order to protect the rights of any one member by distributing liabilities to all

economic liberalization

The transformation of state capitalist or state socialist societies into democratic capitalist societies, and in general, refers to the introduction of free or open markets to societies that have closed markets

private property. Third, production is no longer in agriculture but in an urban-based industry. The new industries were not organized by feudal ties but by **corporations**, which are legal fictions giving groups of men and women the rights of individuals (private property rights are extended to corporations and protected by the state).

The earliest changes toward modern capitalism were carried out in their most extensive forms in Great Britain and in its North American colonies. These two economies, along with the Netherlands, abandoned mercantilism. The other countries of Western Europe soon began to modify their economies in the direction of capitalism, a procedure that is called **economic liberalization.** Most west European countries, by the middle of the eighteenth century, were complex mixes of capitalism and mercantilism. Economic liberalization was a threat, as much as it was a promise, and had the potential of destroying aristocratic classes where these did not have the economic resources to take advantage of the changes.

Two examples of societies that were slow to liberalize are France and Russia. Both had state dominated economies, powerful aristocracies who benefited from tributary economies, and the domination of old mercantilist ideas, not entrepreneurial capitalism. Despite these generalizations, both countries possessed economic interests that were able to imitate the industrial technologies of England and quickly developed urban working classes. In both countries, the urban and rural poor often allied with each other, and in the end destroyed the aristocracies of both countries—first in 1789 with the French Revolution, and then in 1917 with the Russian Revolution. Peter the Great (Czar of Russia from 1682–1725) was to utilize the philosophy of mercantilism to expand Russia's colonial base from the west to the east; and the expansions continued under Catherine the Great (1762–1796) and her dynastic offspring until the abdication and execution of Nicholas Romanov in 1917. Eric Wolf has shown how the feudal social structures of both France and Russia led to these two most famous revolutions (Wolf 1969). The remarkable lack of similar class revolutions in Great Britain (although there were civil wars, such as the war leading to the beheading of King Charles I in 1649) underlines the point that while capitalism exploited the working classes, in Great Britain innovations stayed ahead of radical demands for the redistribution of wealth while the opposite happened in those societies which failed to liberalize their economies. The lack of epic class struggles in Great Britain was due to the slow and incremental shifts in human rights policies, which benefitted the urban working class.

INDUSTRIALIZATION AND POLITICAL CHANGE IN ENGLAND

The development of industry and the slow gains on behalf of the working classes have been well documented for England. It is always obvious that the wealthy benefited at the cost of the poor under capitalism, but it is also fair to observe that the working classes were not without their own political talents and were able to demand and receive a share of the growing prosperity.

In the 1780s, Thomas Coke of Norfolk began scientific farming on his estates and in 1784 published his new techniques in his *Annals of Agriculture.* This period is a classic demonstration of capitalism and the demand for efficiency. Coke's improved efficiencies led to far greater yields, but it also led to the enclosure of estates as wealthy landowners bought out smallholders and deprived cottagers of their pasture rights on the commons. The enclosure of lands led to higher rates of wool production, and these were the consequences of greater efficiencies of land use. However, the cost to the rural cottagers was enormous. It meant that wealthy landowners were able to buy out small landholders, who had previously been protected by the tributary economies, which gave them rights in land. Peasants were reduced to becoming landless laborers, and many were forced to migrate to the growing urban centers (Halliday 1989, 154).

Mechanical innovations transformed the cotton and woolen industries, pulling the landless poor to the cities, while at the same time destroying cottage industries. A spinning machine, developed in 1769, could do the work of a dozen women and led to the growth of textile factories in Lancashire and Yorkshire. Edmund Cartwright invented a power loom in 1785, although it was not perfected for thirty years, forcing weavers, their wives and children to become factory employees. James Watt developed the steam engine in 1769, leading to further efficiencies of scale in industry and a revolution in transportation. After 1780, large-scale production of food and manufactured goods began to supersede small-scale farming (Halliday 1989, 154–156).

The publication of Adam Smith's *Wealth of Nations* led to a *laissez-faire* (French for leave it be, or leave it alone) philosophy of political economy. While the wealth of the few was multiplied, poverty and misery became common among the masses that were not protected by the state. Peasants and former textile producers were driven into the slums and forced to work long hours for appallingly low wages. England became split into a country of rich and poor. Political movements appeared and were repressed. The Habeas Corpus Act was suspended, allowing people to be imprisoned without trial. Many were shipped to Australia as convicts. Yet fears grew among the ruling classes as similar pressures in France led to the French Revolution in 1789 and the rise of the French Republic. This same period coincided with a series of wars with France that lasted until 1815, the year that Napoleon was defeated by the Duke of Wellington at Waterloo.

The defeat of France was followed by a period of extreme repression on the European Continent and in England. Technological change continued apace; and in 1830, Stephenson's train, Rocket, achieved a speed of thirty-five miles an hour. Further technological innovations were introduced to the factory system, but new revolutions brewed in Europe and fear grew among the British elite that they might lose all. There was great distress in England with strikes in towns and riots in the countryside. In 1833, Parliament passed a series of measures to help the poor. The first Factory Act was passed prohibiting the use of children below the age nine in cotton factories. The state assumed greater responsibilities for the poor, and the Poor Act of 1834 offered some relief but was still essentially harsh. Charles Dickens' novels made their appearance describing the inhumanity of the Poor Law. A People's Charter was drawn up demanding universal suffrage; its rejection was followed by riots, and the conditions of the working class continued to deteriorate. The repeal of the Corn Laws, which had prevented the importation of cheap food from abroad, led to an improvement of living conditions. However, it was not until the 1870s that the lives of the British working class finally improved through reforms, particularly the Education Act of 1870 that established primary schools. In the 1880s, new reforms made employers responsible for accidents in the workplace, children had to go to school, wives could keep property separate from their husbands, and the third Reform Act gave the vote to agricultural laborers.

Yet England's economic success in the nineteenth century was the consequence, to a great extent, of other countries' failures. While Europe and the United States had suffered from war and revolution, England had remained politically stable. A free trade policy, inaugurated in the 1840s, allowed her to import cheap raw materials; and her foreign policy and merchant fleet carried goods around the world. The slow growth of wealth in England and the improvement in the lives of the working class were directly linked to Britain's markets around the world for its inexpensive goods. In turn, these successes were the consequence of Great Britain being the center of a near monopoly on world trade—the core of the modern world system—whose growth and success held the promise, not yet fully realized, of solving many of the problems of the poor.

The period from the middle of the nineteenth century to World War I was one of nationalism, competition for control of world trade, and the creation of colonies in the peripheries (Great Britain, France, Italy, Germany, and the Netherlands were the dominant countries of the core). The United States was not greatly involved in competition except in its own backyard of Latin America. Great Britain maintained its dominance throughout this period; however, each core country developed its own trade periphery, often loaning money, as Great Britain did to Argentina, to develop railroads, mines, and farm systems.

Britain's efficiencies of trade were due to continuous internal changes in the institutions of political economy, reducing the frictions between social classes and keeping transaction costs low. All the West European countries in these years went through significant internal change, as they vied for external advantage; but they were not as successful, overall, as was Great Britain, which became the model of liberal political economy. The success of internal change led to greater nationalist sentiments, external competition for world markets, and friction—and finally to World War I.

COLONIALISM: THE BRITISH IN NORTH AMERICA

According to Immanuel Wallerstein, the modern world system began to form in Western Europe in the sixteenth century. The core consisted of those countries that controlled trade and production (So 1990, 186–187, Wallerstein 1988). As England gained control of the world system, its economy shifted in the direction of capitalism, as described above.

Wallerstein, and other world system theorists, have worked out a pattern of "waves" of colonialism, some of which date back to pre-capitalist times. The waves were connected to the economies of the core. The world system expanded in a series of waves beginning in the sixteenth century. Wallerstein's explanation for the waves is that they were responses by the world system to economic events in the core. We have read about the crisis of the sixteenth century. For Wallerstein, that period of inflation was the primary reason for the expansion of European colonialism to the periphery. Two facts are clear for the sixteenth century: Inflation created a class of paupers who sought to improve their lives by migrating, and capitalists in Western Europe tried to soften the impact of inflation by investing in the periphery (Wallerstein 1979).

Population growth, indeed, explains a great deal about the cycles of colonization. We have learned that population growth in Europe was cyclical. From the middle of the tenth century to the early fourteenth, there was strong growth with great economic investments in such structures as the Gothic cathedrals of the time. This episode of growth ended with the Black Death of 1347–1348, when from one third to one half of the population may have perished. Recovery took generations; estimates of English population show a total of 3.7 million in 1348, followed by a loss of 600,000 by 1350, with only 2.25 million remaining by 1374. As we learned, recovery from that catastrophe occurred as Britain was evolving new institutions, and may be a partial cause of cultural change. By 1545, Britain had 3.2 million, but rural depopulation had already begun as the economy shifted from feudalism to early forms of capitalism (Hughes 1987, 8).

English colonial expansion in North America, Australia, and New Zealand had its origins in the nation-building process in Great Britain. The Spanish and Portuguese had split the world between them, as we learned earlier. The other European countries were soon in competition to either find other unknown lands or to take lands away from the Spanish and Portuguese. In 1496, Henry VII issued letters of patent to the Genoese adventurer Giovanni Caboto (John Cabot) to find new lands; and on the 24th of June 1497, he reached Cape Breton (Nova Scotia), which he claimed for Henry VII. His discovery, and those made by his sons, established the English claim to the New World. The first permanent English settlement was made in Virginia in 1607 with a charter from James I. The Pilgrims (English dissenters) landed in 1620 at Plymouth, and the British began to expand into other possessions in the New World, followed quickly by expansion into Australia and New Zealand (Hughes 1987).

The English immigrants brought a form of adaptation that differed considerably from the originating model of sixteenth and seventeenth centuries England. In 1606, the Virginia Company was chartered to launch a colonization venture at Plymouth (where it was known as the Massachusetts Bay Colony), organized through joint stock companies. Shares had been sold to individual investors, and many of these became colonists of the Pilgrim religion. Each family participated equally in running the townships. The cost of government was very low. In addition, every citizen in the new colonies were expected to read the Bible, producing a 100 percent literate society, very different from what had been left behind in England. Out of this early New England culture a new political economy, democratic capitalism, emerged in the nineteenth and early twentieth centuries.

While the British had to support the cost of royalty and aristocracy, and a large and expensive bureaucracy as well, a leaner, more efficient, model emerged in the United States. For example, as late as Theodore Roosevelt's presidency (1901–1908), the American government only absorbed 7 percent of the gross national product. That figure did not change significantly until the New Deal (1933–1938), under Franklin D. Roosevelt, when it jumped to just over 30 percent. The transaction costs of European governments have always been higher. The consequence was the rise of a new and very prosperous form of democratic capitalism.

THE CAPITALIST LEGACY: DESTRUCTION OF INDIGENOUS WORLDS

Europeans monopolized the trade of the various hegemonic cores: Egypt, China, India, Mexico, and Peru. The internal trade networks maintaining these empires collapsed, as well as those maintaining chiefdoms. European traders and explorers did not reach most of the chiefdoms until the seventeenth and eighteenth centuries. By that time the vast regional trade networks had vanished, but the remains of temples and towns in Hawaii, Mesoamerica, Mesopotamia, China, India and the Andes bore mute testimony to these vanished systems. European imperialism further destroyed the natural adaptations that the peoples of these regions had worked out over thousands of years. In their place Europeans introduced strange practices that were poorly adapted to the habitats and further eroded human adaptive responses, until fairly recent times when populations began to make a comeback. While the decline of native populations in the New World ceased in the late eighteenth century and began to recover at the beginning of the nineteenth century, increase was very slow until the early twentieth century when many native populations in Latin America, for example, began to increase at rates comparable to those of the general population in the nations where they lived.

Capitalism has been a continual threat to the indigenous peoples of the world. Some, such as the various Native American groups and the Maori of New Zealand, survive

Case Study

Triangles of Trade in the Caribbean

The British, in competition with Spanish, Dutch, and French interests, initiated plantation agriculture in the Caribbean in the sixteenth century. Many of the islands changed hands several times. The British colonial model in the Caribbean is very different from those of North America, but it formed a part of a larger economic system in the form of triangles of trade, which included North America. Thus developed one of the most inhumane forms of trade based on three points: First, rum produced in New England was shipped to Africa for use in the slave trade (rum was used to pay for slaves). Second, slaves were sold to the Caribbean to be used on sugar plantations. Third, sugar was shipped to New England to produce rum. All the Caribbean islands began as properties of Spain. However, by the eighteenth century Trinidad, the Bahamas, and

Jamaica were in British hands, and Haiti and Martinique were in French hands. Most of the other islands remained in Spanish hands (Mintz 1985).

The social structures of the Caribbean islands—whether British, Dutch, French, or Spanish—were based on racial stratification: social structure depended on the ownership of land and the color of skin. Blacks were poor and power-less; whites were rich and powerful. Cuba, Puerto Rico, Haiti, Jamaica, Trinidad, the Bahamas, Curacao, and parts of coastal Central America came to be a part of the Caribbean plantation system, and part of the triangle of trade. Not until well after World War II did the British and other countries begin to abandon plantation economies; but the heritage of sugar wealth, racism, and power politics based on trade still dominate the region.

today. Others—such as the Puelche of Argentina, the Yahgan of the island of Tierra del Fuego in Chile, and the natives of the island of Tasmania—did not. The people of the peripheries have suffered many adverse experiences at the hands of the colonizers. Some were placed on reservations. Many suffered genocide (biological destruction) or ethnocide (destruction of their cultures). Those who survived the onslaught of Western Civilization have managed to adapt to the modern world without completely giving up their cultural heritage and ecological adaptations. Many are trying to live in both our world and in theirs, an extremely difficult task.

John Bodley has described the phase of migration of people from the evolving core into the tribal periphery as the uncontrolled frontier. Governments around the world allowed their citizens into tribal regions but did not protect the tribal populations from the inevitable attacks by civilized people on uncivilized barbarians. The pattern of tribal destruction in Latin America is remarkably similar to that described for the United States. In the 1820s, the Mapuche (Araucanians) and Tehuelche, who held back the frontiers of civilization, occupied most of central Chile and the Argentine pampas. Settlers moved on to their lands and inevitably attacked the natives, who counter-attacked. The military was called in; and by 1883 they were finally defeated, and vast regions of rich agricultural land were opened for white settlers (Bodley 1982, 50).

Originally used as penal colonies, Australia, New Zealand, and the island of Tasmania were opened for migration from Great Britain in the late eighteenth and nineteenth centuries. The large, British owned islands were used to reduce prison populations in Great Britain and specialize in sheep production, whose wool was shipped to England. As with North America, these Pacific regions were used to relieve the pressure valve of a growing population. The native populations of the island of Tasmania were decimated by the middle of the nineteenth century as their island was taken over for sheep herding.

A similar story is told for the Australian Aborigines, although many more survived than in Tasmania because the interior of Australia was not very inviting and continued to support hunters and food gatherers well into the early part of the twentieth century.

The Maori of New Zealand fared a little better, perhaps, because they were able to counter European aggression with some of their own. Immigrants from the British islands settled New Zealand; and by 1840 thousands of settlers, traders, and missionaries shared the island with about one hundred thousand Maori who tolerated and even aided foreigners. By 1858, due to the usual frontier pattern of white exploitation and diseases, the Maori population had fallen to fifty-six thousand and the white population had risen to forty thousand. The government pursued a vigorous policy of land alienation. The colonists demanded the best lands, drawing the resentment of the Maori. The Maori began to resist, and in 1858 elected their own king and organized troops. Social revitalization movements arose and the Maori returned to their customs, such as tattooing. A war broke out which lasted twelve years and killed thousands on both sides. Today, as in the United States with the Native Americans, the Maori and the European New Zealanders are trying to come to terms with a painful past.

A similar, but not as well known, story occurred on the Pampas of Argentina. As Europeans developed refrigerated shipping, the grasslands of Argentina became specialized in growing beef on lands once occupied by Puelche and Tehuelche Indians. Where these native populations did not die off, they were integrated into rural Argentine life as **gauchos**, South American cowboys. The gauchos became a rural lower class lorded over by the light skinned masters in Buenos Aires, distinctions which are yet today reflected in rural folk songs. Often when one listens closely, the rural cousin mocks his rich relatives from Buenos Aires and their civilized ways.

In other parts of the world, such as highland Bolivia and Peru, colonizers encountered mostly peasant farmers who were already the subjects of state systems, not independent tribal peoples. We have discussed the colonial systems imposed on the peoples of Latin America and will examine them more closely again in Chapter 11. While initial contact brought high death rates due to the introduction of diseases and the collapse of trade, most of these populations today have been incorporated into modern nation states and have been politically very active in protesting their own abuse for the last half century.

NORTH AMERICAN INDIANS: THE EFFECTS OF THE FUR TRADE

Eric Wolf links the genocidal attack on the Native peoples of North America to the fur trade. Until the British conquest of Canada, the Dutch West Indies Company (also active in the Caribbean) controlled the international fur trade, and Amsterdam received a large percentage of furs obtained in North America. The earliest target of the fur trade was beaver; and after its biological collapse due to over trapping, it was replaced with sea otter. Beaver and otter furs were primarily used for hats as Europeans tastes shifted from wool to fur. Only in the nineteenth century did furs go out of favor to be replaced with hats made of

---

gaucho

An Argentine cowboy, usually of Indian descent (Araucanian), who specialized in cattle herding on the great cattle haciendas

◼ A young Maori man performs a cultural dance. Traditional tattoos adorn his face and legs.

■Argentine gaucho, or South American cowboy

silk and other materials. As early as 1608, the British established trading posts at Jamestown, Virginia, followed by posts at Fort Nassau at Albany in 1614, New Amsterdam in 1624, New Plymouth in 1620, and Massachusetts Bay in 1630 (Wolf 1982, 163).

Each post, which soon became a fortress town, was located on a major trade route to the inland riches of the fur country. The French controlled the trade on the St. Lawrence River, which led to the Great Lakes, allowing them to monopolize northern trade in furs, while the English controlled the southern access to trade along the Hudson River. The fur trade disrupted customary Indian adaptations. Traders demanded fur from one group after another, paying them with European artifacts and forcing Native American groups to compete for new hunting grounds, thus intensifying warfare. Entire populations were decimated. Frenchmen and Englishmen supported different tribes and supplied them with guns and powder to attack each other. European diseases further decimated the same populations. Disease and warfare combined brought on population collapse. For example, the Eastern Abenaki of the Maine coast had a population of ten thousand in 1600, but by 1611 only three thousand survived. The survivors gave up their traditions of coastal fishing and hunting waterfowl and established small family hunting territories inland, causing larger kin groups to lose their social integrity.

The Wendar (Huron), a confederation of between twenty thousand to thirty thousand people committed to horticulture, entered into the fur trade in the early seventeenth century. They and the Iroquois developed a warring relationship with each other. The English supported the Iroquois, and the French supported the Wendar. The Iroquois, a confederacy of six—Mohawk, Oneida, Onondaga, Cayuga, Seneca, and Tuscarora—did not have many beaver in their territory. According to Seneca traditions, the League of Five Nations—Mohawk, Oneida, Onondaga, Cayuga, and Seneca—was in existence by about AD 200. The Tuscarora became a part of the league in the early eighteenth century. In 1648, the Iroquois destroyed the Wendar for their beaver lands. In 1656, they destroyed the Erie and the Neutral Nation and opened war on the Illinois in 1680. Iroquois success was aided by the superior firepower of their English allies.

The fur trade and warfare fed on one another and changed the ecological adaptations of the northeastern tribes. The men abandoned agriculture for warfare and trade. Women continued to grow crops, and it is possible the new ecological relationship reinforced already existing patterns of matrilineal descent. Continuous warfare forced many tribes to migrate west. Thus, the Potawatomi, Sauk, Fox, Kickapoo, Mascouten, and Illinois were driven west from Lower Michigan and Ohio. Many tribes combined to form new groupings as populations declined. Fusion and alliance led to the loss of old rituals and the development of new ones.

For example, the Midewiwin replaced the collective Feast of the Dead practiced among Huron and Iroquoian speakers. The Feast of the Dead, as Eric Wolf explains, was a celebration of local villages that, once every ten to twelve years, would bring together the bones of the dead to a central location. All of the bones would be mixed together symbolizing the solidarity of the entire tribe (say the Huron nation). While the Feast of the Dead celebrated local group identity and the succession of local leadership, the Midewiwin was directed towards the individual and his integration into a hierarchical association that transcended both locality and descent group (Wolf 1982, 172). The association was translocal, integrating local tribes into the fur trade through identification with a Mide lodge, an association of warriors. Entry and advance into the higher grades of the Mide lodge required wealth, and the fur trade was a source of that wealth. Each member of a Mide lodge owned a medicine bag of religious artifacts, including a shell. The new member was shot with rays from the shell and was then reborn as a member of the lodge (the influence of Christianity was strong). In this way, local descent groups yielded to the development of a translocal church, connecting local groups to outside forces, including traders, government officials, and missionaries (Wolf 1982, 172).

In 1830, President Andrew Jackson pushed the Indian Removal Act through the U.S. Congress. The act called for the removal of all eastern tribes to reservations in the Great American Desert west of the Mississippi. Federal government policies, competition, and warfare drove tribes west. Many adapted to horse nomadism on the Great Plains and became buffalo hunters. Traders established trading posts and purchased buffalo hides, and the competition was renewed until the buffalo were practically destroyed. By 1840, a frontier had been organized beyond which the Native Americans were supposed to live, and a string of forts was established running from Texas to Canada (Bodley 1982, 87). However, when Texas, Oregon country, and the Southwest passed into American control in the 1840s, settlers began to stream across the plains; conflict was inevitable. Coercion was used to dispossess the Indians of their western lands. In 1890, Native Americans owned over 137 million acres of land. By 1934, those holdings had been reduced to just 56 million acres. Most of the lands were not suitable for agriculture. Reservations grew smaller, and their resource bases were insufficient to support their populations. Native Americans revolted constantly against the system that was destroying them. In the end, many Native cultures were destroyed. Alcoholism, depression, and suicide became a common part of reservation life, with few exceptions.

The Rise of Modern Democratic Capitalism

The story of the peripheries of the world, however, is not the story of the core countries; these have experienced a very different world, which we will try to describe in the next section. The political economies that emerged in Great Britain and North America are called **democratic capitalist.** These were novel systems that emerged between 1700 and 1850 from mercantilism. The capitalist system, as a distinct system, was only described for the first time by Adam Smith in *The Wealth of Nations* in 1776. At the outset, it is important to point out that not all capitalist societies are democratic, but all democratic societies are capitalistic. The relationship between democracy and capitalism is an important attribute of this type of political economy, but why the two work well together has never been clearly spelled out; and the topic is very controversial. Since the middle of the 1980s, a number of Latin American countries have attempted to democratize, going from authoritarian states to democratic states; and the Soviet Union has attempted to introduce both free markets and democracy. China has also attempted to adopt capitalism, but without democracy. Other regions in Eastern Europe, Asia, Africa, and the Middle East have experimented with various mixes of capitalism and democracy; but all these regions are troubled because it is very hard to keep the two transitions (the transition to democracy and the transition to capitalism)

democratic capitalist

The term for the political economies that emerged out of mercantilism in Great Britain and North America between 1700 and 1850 in balance with one another. Recent consequences have been an upsurge in ethnic nationalism and regional violence instead of peace and prosperity.

It is important to understand that capitalism is a powerful machine, which can do much damage to people and environments unless carefully monitored by democratically elected officials. Joseph Schumpeter, one of the twentieth century's chief economists, was an extreme pessimist about the potential survival of democratic capitalism during the 1930s because of the Great Depression and the looming war in Europe. Karl Marx made similar predictions in the nineteenth century about the demise of capitalism. Both predicted the replacement of democratic capitalism with totalitarian dictatorships of the right, called **state capitalist** (Schumpeter), or the left, called **state socialist** (Marx). The histories of the political economies of the core since World War II have been very different from what was predicted for them. At the end of the twentieth century, the majority of state capitalist and state socialist governments are moving in the direction of democratic capitalism, even with all of its ups and downs. For example, since 1985, every Latin American country, except Cuba, has had democratic elections. Many, including ourselves, would question just how democratic many of these countries really are, particularly in Central America, but the direction of change is clear.

The differences between state capitalist, state socialist, and democratic capitalist are not always clear, often shading into each other. State capitalism is a type of political economy which operates according to market forces but lacks democracy, and in which state intervention in the economy benefits those who already have wealth (and who control the state). Mexico and most other Latin American republics have used the rhetoric of socialism or capitalism to gain the support of the working or capitalist classes, but have been predominantly state capitalist since the 1940s. The introduction of reforms to sell off state run industries and introduce democracy over the last decade has been rocky, at best. State socialism lacks true markets and should operate as a redistribution economy benefiting the working classes. Such were the ideal goals of the Soviet Union, China, and many African republics. Instead, the state grew extremely rigid and bureaucratic and was unable to compete in world trade, and in each region has gradually collapsed. Attempts to introduce democratic capitalism in all these regions have had very mixed results, the consequence of **structural power** (the tendency for the old elites to retain control of the political economy). We will deal with the problems of how the various regions of the world react to the twin transitions to capitalism and democracy after getting a basic understanding of democratic capitalism.

CHARACTERISTICS OF DEMOCRATIC CAPITALISM

The chief attributes of modern capitalism (not democracy) are entrepreneurialism; competition; the search for profits; the operation of land, labor, and capital in "free" markets; and cycles of expansion and recession along with continuous technological innovation.

Entrepreneurialism   Schumpeter described *entrepreneurialism* as one of the chief features of modern capitalism. Entrepreneurs are individuals who can recognize a market for a good and can organize capital, land, and labor to produce that good. Schumpeter recognized that there is a pattern to entrepreneurial activity. First, there is the success of the single entrepreneur, say Henry Ford, who invents either a new good or a new way to produce a good. This is followed by the second characteristic: competition.

---

state capitalism

A political economy characterized by state ownership of industrial capital other than land, the restriction of private property rights to the wealthy classes, and markets controlled by the elite to their advantage

state socialism

A political economy characterized by state ownership of industrial capital and land and by centrally controlled and managed economies

structural power

Control over the political process by the elites who control state capitalist or state socialist economies; also the residual control over power by former elites once economic systems no longer exists

Competition   The entrepreneur's success is followed by a *swarm* of competitors, which causes prices to drop and demand for a good to increase. Sooner or later, all of the competition floods the market, and the demand for a good goes down. The activities of the swarm more or less describe a business cycle that begins with expansion and ends with contraction. It is the business cycle that is the most dangerous feature of capitalism since the cycle can be either moderate (soft-landing in a recession) or extreme (such as the Great Depression). Extreme cycles can produce powerful social movements such as fascism or socialism, which threaten the institutions of democratic capitalism.

The Search for Profits   Driving the activities of the entrepreneur is the search for profits. In order to increase personal profits and those of shareholders, the entrepreneur constantly searches for ways to decrease costs. This can be done in two ways: increase efficiency or decrease labor costs. Increases in efficiency are possible only by investing more capital in improving technology, which may also reduce the amount of labor required for a task. The reduction of labor costs puts the working class and entrepreneurs into conflict with one another. As noted for Great Britain, a continual drop in wages brings political violence on the part of the working class. Under favorable circumstances, democratic reforms are the result.

Free Markets for Land, Labor, and Capital   One of the most controversial characteristics of capitalist societies is the free market for land, labor, and capital (one reason why wages fall). The histories of the core countries describe the rise and fall of governments, which come into existence to protect one of the three components of capitalist markets, particularly labor. The conflicts between the entrepreneurs and the politicians protecting land, labor, and capital have been continuous. As long as countries were more or less autonomous and could survive on the sale of goods within national markets, competition between countries for markets had little effect on labor and labor unions. In the last two decades, globalization has had a particularly severe impact on labor in the core. Investments by transnationals in the former periphery are causing radical job losses that, in turn, are causing changes in American social structure and decreases in the power of labor unions. Part of the lower middle class has dropped into the working class and part of the working class has dropped below the poverty datum line, which is the amount the United States government has decided one must earn to support a family without undue hardship (about $15,500 in 1995 for a family of two adults and two children).

The drop in the demand for labor and the increase in capital investments have produced third world conditions within the core. It has become common today for people to be without homes and jobs, social and economic characteristics that were once only found in places like Mexico or Tanzania. Families are suffering from these changes, and so are the relationships between men and women, which we will discuss in another chapter. Tensions between different ethnic groups have gone up significantly. Core and peripheries are merging to look more like each other with problems in common. As an example, the kind of urban poverty once found in squatter settlements around Mexico and other Latin American cities is beginning to characterize the inner cities of the countries of the core. On the other hand, the suburbs of Mexico City look increasingly like the suburbs of American cities across the border in the United States. Automobiles, air pollution, and long drives between the central city and the suburbs are no longer an American prerogative.

Expansion, Contraction, and Technological Change   Important features of democratic capitalism, which grow out of the first four characteristics, are continuous technological change and the expansion and contraction of the economy (our business cycles: recession and depression). Entrepreneurs come up with new goods (for example, computers and software), which require workers to learn new tasks. The new goods cause changes in the culture (you may be able to work at home on a computer instead of driving to a job). Competition, expansion, and contraction of the economy cause a great deal of pain (you may not be able to find any job).

This kind of constant innovation, expansion, contraction, and the push for continuous change has now been a characteristic of the core countries since World War I, if not before. International competition, beginning in the 1970s, has reached the point where no region of the world is safe from the demands of capitalism. While all cultures undergo more or less continuous change, the changes are often so slow in non-industrial societies as to be almost imperceptible. It is the *rate* of change that is so remarkable in industrial (and post-industrial) societies today. For example, from the turn of the century until the 1950s, the two cities of Puebla, Mexico, and Medellin, Columbia, were relatively small, with little in the form of modern technology. In the 1960s, their populations expanded to half a million and today are well over two million. Once predominantly rural, urban sprawl spreads from both cities and the countryside is rapidly disappearing as it is industrialized.

This has been a century of incredible change within the core countries. Many writers attribute the growth in the wealth of the core countries to the theft of the wealth of the periphery. In the early period of modernization, in the sixteenth and seventeenth centuries, there is reason for the argument since the wealth of Mexico, Egypt, and India ended up in the coffers of British capitalists (Hobsbawm 1962). The wealth of the United States is explained by continuous investment in poor countries and the removal of profits from those countries. However, most of the recent wealth of the core has been due to investments by core countries in core countries. About 96 percent of all economic investment is by core countries in core countries. Only about 4 percent of all Wall Street investments go to the periphery, which is part of the reason for the poverty found there. Core investment in the periphery was somehow thought to produce dependency and poverty by robbing these regions of their natural wealth, but recent increases in investment are accompanied by increasing prosperity. The percentage of people in absolute poverty in Chile, for example, has dropped from 36 to 26 percent in the last five years. Even so, patterns of exploitation of periphery by core still exist, but they are shifting from raw materials to cheap labor.

Writing in the 1960s, modernization theorists, such as Marion Levy, viewed **modernization** in a positive way (modernization was idea that the introduction of modern technologies would lead to the transformation of traditional institutions to democratic capitalism). However, challenging their writings were those who feared that capitalism would not work in the periphery. Dependency theorists argued that instead of improving the lot of the average worker, capitalism had the opposite effect—causing increasing disparities between rich and poor. The answer proposed was state intervention in the economy to protect people and natural resources. In the middle of the 1980s, the debate became confused as the Soviet Union began its transition to capitalism and democracy. In the United States, economic theoreticians nervously eyed the apparent growth in the power of international capital interests and the lack of ability of the American political system to control capital flow. By the late 1980s, the impact of what is now known as globalization began to threaten the political economies of the West European countries due to the loss of jobs to the countries of the periphery. The job loss led to many in the middle class dropping into the working class, while the working

modernization

The idea that the introduction of modern technologies would lead to the transformation of traditional institutions to democratic capitalism

classes suffered steady erosion in earning power. These economic shifts gradually led, in the 1990s, to a general lack of support for elected governments. This phenomenon is growing in the United States in the form of anti-government political movements such as private militias in the western states, which threaten a once reasonably stable political economy. To the extent that governments can no longer insure the economic well-being of their citizens, they are increasingly viewed with suspicion.

BLOCKED TRANSITIONS TO CAPITALISM: ARTICULATION, DISARTICULATION AND STRUCTURAL POWER

■A Mexican vacation resort (top) and a shanty (bottom) in a slum area of Tiajuana, Mexico. Theorists argue that instead of improving the lot of the average worker, capitalism has the opposite effect, causing increasing disparities between rich and poor.

Since 1985, many countries that introduced socialist or state capitalist economies earlier in the century began to attempt the transitions to capitalism and democracy. Countries that go through the economic transition to capitalism successfully are said to have **articulated** economies; those that do not are **disarticulated**. In articulated economies, the characteristics of capitalism described above lead to an increasingly more efficient work force, which is rewarded by higher wages. In short, the working class is more or less integrated into the capitalist economic sector, usually because of the growing importance of democracy. Examples would be South Korea or Taiwan; both countries were state capitalist and anti-democratic until very recently.

In disarticulated economies, which are much more common, wages and productivity are not linked, a historical problem in the countries of the periphery. Disarticulation is a term meant to describe the *disconnection between the increasing efficiencies of the work force, as more efficient technologies are introduced, and the rewards to workers.* Nation states that are predominantly non-democratic tend to have great difficulties in overcoming disarticulation. Both Mexico and Russia are examples. In addition, if the economies are based on international trade, with the cost of labor being determined by forces outside the control of a nation state, disarticulation will be hard to overcome. Thus, when international economic forces cause capitalists to lower wages in order to compete, then disarticulation occurs. The United States has gone from having a highly articulated economy to one that is increasingly disarticulated. The economies of the peripheral countries, in certain instances, may be moving in just the opposite direction: from disarticulated to articulated. However, successful articulation requires democratic reform so that growth in the economic sector is distributed more or less evenly among social classes, and government corruption is avoided.

The transition to capitalism, without democratic reform, will founder due to disarticulation. However, the transition to democracy is difficult in formerly authoritarian and

articulated economy

An economy in which the increasing efficiencies of the work force due to more efficient technologies leads to higher wages

disarticulated economy

An economy characterized by a disconnect between the increasing efficiencies of the work force due to more efficient technologies and the rewards to the workers

authoritarian government

A political system composed of economic elites such as industrialists, planters, and military men

totalitarian government

A political system controlled by a single party

totalitarian countries. In early sixteenth century England, property rights came first, followed by political rights to a very limited aristocratic class. To a great extent, what we call representative democracy in the United States is the consequence of the extension and recognition of political rights to the individual by the state after first protecting property rights. In early English society, the transition came from the top down with the British aristocracy being granted property rights by the Crown in the fourteenth century, and later political rights (North 1981). Several centuries went by before those rights were extended to the mass of the population. In the United States, similar rights were extended first to white, male property holders and then only slowly to the rest of the population.

The anthropologist Eric Wolf argues that the organizational possibilities for democracy are limited by structural power. Structural power refers to political forces created by state capitalism and state socialism, which continue to dominate after the collapse of these political economies. As an example, the dinosaurs of Mexico's archaic state capitalist system are holding back democratic reform through the assassinations of reformers. Similarly, in Russia, the old communist politicians try to hold back President Yeltsin's reforms. Structures of power block the transitions to democracy. State capitalist and state socialist societies bog down because of authoritarian and totalitarian forms of structural power, old elites who refuse to give up. Attempts by countries to democratize as they go through the economic transition to capitalism are often blocked by the very models of economic organization they are trying to overcome.

Since World War II, **authoritarian** governments have associated with state capitalism, and **totalitarian** one-party states with state socialism. The two political systems mirror the economies they manage. Authoritarian systems are composed of the various economic elites of the countries in question. Thus, in Central America where plantation economies dominate, the elites tend to be planters and military men. In Argentina, Brazil, and Chile, which have more complex economies, they tend to be industrialists, planters, bureaucrats, and military men. Authoritarian political systems often have multi-party forms of organization, but no one can mistake them for true democracies. For the most part, authoritarian systems are anti-labor and function to reduce the wages of the working class leading to economic disarticulation (de Janvry 1981).

Anti-Capitalist Revolutions

The second part of the great transformation, from colonialism to independence (the first part was from feudalism to capitalism, mentioned earlier), was accompanied by peasant revolutions in those societies outside of Great Britain but in the core. In traditional societies, peasants may have been exploited by elites but certain minimal rights were also protected. With the introduction of private property rights and the disappearance of tributary rights, exploitation of the peasants increased. A wave of revolutions occurred in the nineteenth century in western and eastern Europe. Most of these early revolutions have been called "peasant revolutions" (Wolf 1969, 1982). Two major examples are the French Revolution of 1789 and the German Revolution of 1848 (Hobsbawm 1962, Wolf 1969).

Karl Marx's theory of capitalism was explained earlier. It was meant to explain the revolutionary violence in the west European countries in the nineteenth century, not violent social movements in the periphery. Nonetheless, in the middle of the twentieth century and in the decades to follow, his theory on the exploitative tendencies of capitalism was applied to violent political movements outside of Europe by such writers as Peter Worsley (1957), A. G. Frank (1969, 1978), and Immanuel Wallerstein (1974). Basically, the predominant view was that the development of prosperity in the core produced poverty in the periphery, and that violent social movements were the natural results of exploitation. These theories, culminating in Wallerstein's world system theory, were attempts to explain a second wave of violent peasant social movements in the countries of the periphery. While capitalism and democracy were the key driving forces behind the transformation of the core, these were blocked by the core in the periphery through such mechanisms as protecting corrupt dictators and preventing the redistribution of wealth.

Applying Marxist theory to the periphery, the anger of the peasant classes led to violent revolutionary transformations. In general, socialism and state capitalism were viewed as means of redistributing wealth, and challenging the capitalism of the core (Wallerstein called these anti-system revolts). Anti-system revolutions occurred in the twentieth century: in Mexico in 1910, in Guatemala from 1946 to 1954, in El Salvador from 1946 to 1949, in Nicaragua from 1979 to 1990, and in Bolivia from 1937 to 1940. With the sole exceptions of Cuba and Nicaragua, socialism did not succeed, but state capitalism did. State capitalism, seen most clearly in Mexico, depends on **corporatism,** a form of political economy in which the state owns and controls most of the factors of production but does so with theoretically open markets (i.e., markets that respond perfectly to supply and demand). Corporatism envisions the state as a giant corporation protecting the rights of the various classes and preventing them from exploiting each other. Unfortunately, the long run experience of state capitalism in Latin America has been largely negative, with industrial elites developing who use the power of the state to advance their own ends, as we will examine in Chapter 11.

In the same years that Mexico went through its radical revolution against industrial capitalism, roughly from 1910 to 1917, the country of Russia went through similar crises, but the resolution was *socialism* not state capitalism. *Communism*, or socialism (the two terms are usually interchangeable) where introduced, abandoned the use of open markets in favor of a centrally organized state, which made private property illegal (unlike state capitalism in Latin America). Many of the countries that emerged in Asia, such as India and Pakistan, never went so far and more resemble state capitalist models, but used the term socialist, all of which is confusing. Common features of state capitalist, state socialist, and communist models are *a lack of trust in private property and a high level of optimism that the state would solve economic and political problems.*

The Russian Revolution of 1918 created the Soviet Union, and a communist state was brought into being in China in 1949. The American war in Vietnam ended in 1975 with that country becoming socialist, along with its neighbors, Laos and Cambodia. In the 1960s, anti-capitalist transformations also occurred in much of Africa, leaving it with a majority of socialist style governments by the 1980s. The same is true for much of the Middle East and Asia. Former colonies of core capitalist nations chose socialist or state capitalist political economies, at least initially.

THE SOVIET EXPERIENCE: REVOLUTION, REFORM, AND BLOCKED TRANSITIONS

The last decade of the twentieth century experienced a dramatic series of transformations, primarily in formerly socialist states in Asia and Africa, but also in state capitalist societies such as those found predominantly in Latin America. These movements were largely non-violent,

corporatism

A form of political economy in which the state owns and controls most of the factors of production, with theoretically open markets

but the transition from either socialism or state capitalism is turning out to be more difficult than many anticipated, primarily because of the resistant structures of power. Russia's difficulties underline the problems of transition to open markets and democratic politics. One of the primary problems, in addition to the structure of power, is disarticulation.

Before Russia became the Soviet Union, it had brought much of the region east of Russia itself under its control. Russia at the turn of the twentieth century was a curious amalgam of imperialism, capitalism and feudalism. It was a semi-peripheral and medieval society with an advanced capitalist urban economy coupled to a feudal rural society controlled by an authoritarian Czar (Goldman 1992, 5). During World War I, much of the military and the peasants began to rebel against a war which seemed to have the primary aim of adding to the status of a French speaking aristocracy, and little to do with the interests of the working classes which fought the war.

On November 17, 1917, the Bolsheviks seized control of the key centers of administration and communication, and the Czarist government collapsed. According to the historian Paul Johnson, Vladimir Lenin, the architect of the future Soviet Union, had no real power base in Russia and never sought to create one. He concentrated exclusively on building up a small organization of "intellectual and sub-intellectual desperados" which he could completely dominate (Johnson 1992, 59). Lenin's Bolshevik elite had little support from peasants or workers; skilled workers tended to support the opposition Menshevik camp.

While industrial workers, peasants, and soldiers fought the Russian revolution, it was Lenin who had the final say in the reconstruction of Russian society. In early 1917, the first All Russian Congress of Soviets (worker unions) met with 822 delegates, which Lenin attempted to dominate, but instead alienated. He was forced to escape to Finland, but returned to challenge the provisional Kerensky government. On October 25, 1917, he seized the city of Petrograd and in the following months imposed Soviet rule on Russia. In the initial stages of his takeover, Lenin depended entirely on armed bands (Johnson 1992, 65). Thus began the great terror that was to be continued by Joseph Stalin after Lenin's death.

Under Stalin, state terrorism came to be the common modality of rule. Both Lenin and Stalin carried out purges of the Communist Party and genocide against those ethnic populations of the Soviet Union that resisted the demands of the new socialist state. There is no accurate figure on the number of people who died, but estimates are that 30 million people may have been sacrificed to this experiment in socialism, which ultimately failed (Goldman 1992, 11).

■Joseph Stalin (far left) and Vladamir Lenin (near right)

Marvin Harris, a leading American anthropologist, attributes the collapse of the Soviet Union to the "structural incompatibilities" of Soviet institutions (Harris 1992). A prime source of infrastructure malfunctioning derived from the inherent limitations of the bureaucratically top-heavy, centrally planned and administered command economy. At the enterprise level, managers were watched by bureau chiefs in order to assure conformity with a massive list of rules and regulations that had various unintended consequences. The number of workers an enterprise employed determined money for incentive bonuses, and this led to the hiring of large numbers of unneeded workers. Crude quantitative quotas resulted in the production of poor quality goods and invited falsification. "Since salaries, bonuses, and promotions depend on achieving the plan, the temptation, indeed the pressure of the centrally planned system is to fake output" (Armstrong 1989, 24 cited in Harris 1992).

When there is no connection between worker productivity and reward to the worker, the incentive to be productive is lost. This is a form of disarticulation common in socialist economies. Perhaps the true genius of Mikhail Gorbachev was his ability to see through the myth of socialism as a means of saving Russia from the outside imperialist powers and realize the extent to which it was producing economic disarticulation. Gorbachev realized that it was no longer possible to close Russia off from participation in the evolving global economic enterprise. For Russia to survive, it had to link with international capitalism and link worker productivity with economic incentives.

Gorbachev's attempt to do this began with a reform plan called *perestroika* or restructuring, which was introduced in 1986. This plan loosened state control over the economy and attempted to stimulate individual initiative. *Glasnost*, or openness and candor, introduced in the political sector, relaxed the political environment. Perestroika also had a large impact on foreign policy, changing the Soviet Union's relationship to the core. This was only the beginning of a five-year period of turmoil which resulted in Gorbachev's replacement by Boris Yeltsin in 1991.

Boris Yeltsin became responsible for taking a much-reduced Russian state through the transitions to open markets and democracy. Two fundamental institutional reforms are critical to achieving a capitalist market economy. Russia had to release price controls and privatize the economy. When Yeltsin tried to get political support from the parliament (the Duma), members of the old power structure blocked him. In order to force the Duma to his will, he had to order the army to attack the Russian Parliament building. On October 3, 1993, tanks under his control pounded the parliament into a blackened shell. This act made Yeltsin appear to be "anti-democratic," and many accused him of acting like one of the old Czars. Thus, the very process of attempting reform of the socialist economy forced Yeltsin into non-democratic methods.

Yeltsin's next move was to abandon the old Parliamentary leaders and to call for a new election, which ratified a new constitution giving him greater powers. In the election on December 12, 1993, Russians ratified a new constitution; however, they also elected both the upper and lower houses of a "new parliament." In the election, many of the old communist leaders were re-elected along with anti-democratic nationalists. Within two hours of the opening of the State Duma, a debate about procedure turned into a shouting match; the communists and nationalists were soon at each other's throats.

Yeltsin attempted to bypass the parliament by ruling by decree, appointing free market reform advocates to his cabinet. The blocked political system prevented the new laws from having much effect, however, except in the central urban areas such as Moscow and St. Petersburg. Yeltsin was given advice by Jeffrey Sachs of Harvard University, who urged him to push through a rapid reform package in order to escape disarticulation. His message failed. There is a lesson here about the connections between the economic and political transitions. Jeffrey Sachs may have been correct about the need for immediate and radical economic reform back in 1991–1992, but his advice to Yeltsin may not have been realistic. This underscores Eric Wolf's warning about structures of power. By pursuing reforms, which were too dramatic and not understood by the Russian people, Yeltsin lost the very support he needed for reform. Now, having slowed down the pace of reform, he is able to gain greater political support and so can pursue a somewhat more conservative direction of reform, but reform nonetheless. However, democratic reforms were to be blocked on another front as well.

In 1995, Boris Yeltsin was forced to deal with the breakaway republic of Chechnya, an ethnic republic of Chechen speakers who have long sought independence. The Russian army invaded Chechnya and bombarded its capital, Grozny. Russian women tried to get their young men back from the front, embarrassing Boris Yeltsin on television with an image of a less than effective military. Close scrutiny of the military led to allegations of corruption and further undermined Yeltsin's regime.

In the election of December 1995, the Peasant Party and Communist Party made strong inroads against reform minded parties. Yeltsin scrapped his pro-western foreign minister in favor of one who is not as strongly western; but by 1995, he had pushed reforms to the point where real markets began to emerge. In 1991, most forms of private business were illegal. Russia now has about 2,500 licensed commercial banks, 600 investment funds and 40 million shareholders. Prices have been set free since 1992, and over 16,000 medium and large state firms have been privatized so that now 62 percent of the economy is privatized. Russia's state owned sector is now smaller than Italy's (*The Economist* May 1995).

There were many fears that the new market economy was going to produce such deprivation that the communists and nationalists would win the election of 1996. Yeltsin, in fact, began weakly against challenges from former communists and nationalists' blocks. However, in the last days of the campaign, Russian voters appeared to realize that they did not want to return to a socialist system, and Yeltsin won a closely contested election. However, he is a physically weakened person and suffers from a heart condition. In the meantime, many argue that the free market has created a new wealthy class in the central cities, while those working for state enterprises and living in rural areas remain poor and potential sources of support for the socialists and nationalists.

The difficulty of keeping the transitions to open markets and democracy on an even keel is dramatically spelled out in the recent history of Russia. However, many other countries have also experienced the difficulties of balancing the two processes, including most of the countries of Eastern Europe and Latin America, and a few countries in Africa and Asia. While the details differ from region to region, the difficulties of moving from closed to open economies and reforming the political process towards democracy are among the most complex problems of the end of the twentieth century and the beginning of the twenty-first century.

The Globalization of the World System

The elections in Russia in the summer of 1996 began with an initial success by the left-of-center parties sympathetic with the restoration of the old Soviet Union. As structures of power began to win the election, support increased for Boris Yeltsin, leading to his reelection. The 1996 Russian elections tend to support the argument that the transitions to democracy and capitalism are still attractive to Russians, despite all of the pain. Similar arguments can be mustered for most world regions: despite the pains of reform, few regions are willing to return to either socialism or state capitalism if voters have a choice.

Globalization is forcing many countries into reforms supported by the International Monetary Fund and the World Bank, and by the countries of the core, but the final consequences of change are impossible to measure at this time. Immanuel Wallerstein, looking at the crises of the 1980s, predicted that core nations would look for cheaper labor rates. This is happening; however, the opening of markets, the abandonment of socialist style closed economies, and the innovation of new forms of participatory democracy were not predicted. These new models, such as found in Russia and Eastern Europe, may not be the familiar ones of North American style political economies but they are a far cry from the old anti-system answers of the middle of the twentieth century. In addition, many economists are currently arguing that the attraction of cheap labor rates is more than offset by the lack of education in formerly third world countries. Initial investments tend not to lead to profits but to poorly made goods. These discoveries are affirming the need to improve education in the United States and other core countries in order to compete in the international trade arena. In the American election, economic nationalism in the form of protected trade was beaten back and non-isolationists views prevailed.

We are now witnessing the emergence of a new world system called the "post-modern" or "global" world system. The final phase of the modern world system lasted from the end of World War II until approximately 1985. The world is currently going through a process of economic reorganization due to a shift in the core countries from economies dominated by the industrial sector to those dominated by the service sector and by investment capital rather than industrial capital (Helms 1994: 11). Investment capital is capital that is invested in projects strictly for profits, not for social welfare or national needs. Industrial capital is capital that is used to generate an industrial sector in a modernizing society. The motivation on the part of state officials and investors is to create a stable society by expanding the industrial sector creating jobs. For example, in the period from World War I until the early 1970s, Detroit's automobile manufacturing was central to American productivity and was a key industry producing jobs. In the 1980s, automobile manufacturing became highly computerized, and jobs were lost. In the 1990s, the key sector of economy is in the software industry, in jobs which are no longer central to the industrial economy, particularly in such service occupations as communications and finance. An industrial core and a largely agricultural periphery characterized the modern world system and semi-periphery to which the core exported finished industrial products. The institutional policies of the states of the core supported the growth and development of privately owned transnational corporations and large military complexes. These two systems were intricately tied together into "military-industrial complexes." The policies of the core countries were designed to make the military-industrial complexes successful, if not always efficient. The success of the private sector and the military was thought necessary to compete with the state socialist block as it gained allies in the countries of the periphery and semi-periphery. From 1950 to 1985, the capitalist core and the socialist block competed around the world during the Cold War. With the collapse of the Soviet Union, there has been a shift from industrial to investment capital strategies. One consequence is that industrial occupations, the mainstay of core workers, moved to the periphery and semi-periphery. Educated and efficient workers have become street people. (There is the perception that "jobs are being lost" to poorer countries.) The developing countries may be the beneficiaries of "post-modernism," as the period of globalization is called by American

Case Study

Soviet Socialism and Environmental Destruction

The collapse of socialism in the former Soviet Union and Eastern Europe has brought to light environmental destruction due to socialist industrial development beyond the worst nightmares or fears of environmentalists. It also underlines the desperate need for market connections to the global economy at the international level to succeed, while at the same time democratic reform at the national level gives people power to protect their habitats. Both of these must be accomplished in order to pass through the ecological transition to sustained development.

Documenting the damage alone is a monumental task. Boris Yeltsin ordered the Geography Institute of the USSR Academy of Science to collect statistical data and to map the dimensions of the Soviet Union's environmental mess. Much of the following is derived from that study (Sneider 1992).

As an example, a gigantic steel works known as the Magnitogrosk Works was a showcase for socialist progress. Begun by Stalin in 1929, it grew to a sprawling combination of ten gigantic blast furnaces, thirty-four open-hearth ovens, and dozens of rolling and finishing mills. The Institute reported that the Works produced 800,000 tons of waste a year, which were pumped into the air. Nearby, another steel center pumped an additional 350,000 tons into the air. Soil samples twenty-four kilometers away (fifteen miles) found concentrations of metal five to ten times the natural rate. More than a third of the adult population and two-thirds of the children suffer from respiratory diseases in the city of Chelyabinsk (Sneider 1992).

The region of Chelyabinsk is also the site of several once-secret nuclear facilities, including Chelyabinsk-65, the largest secret nuclear waste-reprocessing site in the former Soviet Union. Several major accidents, beginning in the late 1940s, spread nuclear radiation over the area. Huge amounts of unprocessed nuclear waste are stored there with seepage going into ground water and Siberian rivers (Sneider 1992).

Other statistics about environmental damage to the landscape of the former Soviet Union are numbing. To compensate for agricultural inefficiencies of the collectives, the Soviets used massive and uncontrolled amounts of pesticides and chemical fertilizers. As a consequence, 30 percent of all produce is contaminated and should not be eaten; 42 percent of all baby food has unacceptable levels of nitrates and other pesticides (Sneider 1992). Industrial growth has put 70 million of the 190 million people living in 103 cities in danger of respiratory and other diseases from air, which has five times the U.S. allowed limits of pollutants. Almost three-quarters of the surface water is polluted, and one-fourth is completely untreated. Wastes are killing many important bodies of water including the Aral Sea, the Sea of Azoz, the Black Sea, and Lake Baykal, the deepest lake in the world (Sneider 1992).

A radiation map, never released to the Russian public but made available to *U.S. News and World Report*, pinpoints more than 130 nuclear explosions, mostly in European Russia that were conducted for geophysical research, to create underground pressure in oil and gas fields, or simply to move earth for dams. No one has any idea how much they have contaminated land, water, people, and wildlife. The map has red triangles marking spots near the large island of Novaya Zemlya where nuclear reactors and other radioactive wastes were dumped into the sea. A nuclear submarine reportedly sank there (Goldman 1992, 224).

The once pristine region of Siberia is no longer pristine. Some 920,000 barrels of oil are spilled every day in Russian Siberia—the equivalent of one Exxon Valdez spill every six hours. One pool of spilled oil in Siberia is six feet deep, four miles wide, and seven miles long (Goldman 1992, 224). Thousands of gas flares in Siberia create the largest pool of light in the Eurasian land mass. Sulphur dioxide from the flares has created acid rain, which has destroyed 1,500 miles of timber, a region half the size of Rhode Island. The forests of Siberia are being cut down at the rate of 5 million acres a year, posing a bigger threat than the destruction of the Brazilian rainforest (Goldman 1992, 224).

Much of the damage surveyed above just touches on the ecological disasters of the Soviet Union. These disasters were the consequence of a "growth-at-any-cost mentality" and reflect the Soviet Union's obsession with gigantism and its ability to twist science into a tool of politics. Everyone has heard of Chernobyl because it happened at a time when the Soviet Union had initiated glasnost. Yet another disaster was not reported until recently: In 1957, a nuclear storage facility near Chelyabinsk exploded sending eighty tons of radioactive waste into the air and forcing the evacuation of ten thousand people (Goldman 1992, 225). The extent of deaths and destruction is unknown.

Stewardship of the environment appears to have been remote from the minds of the central planners of the Soviet Union. We will close the topic of the environment with a short survey of the impact of Soviet thinking on the Aral Sea, one of the largest inland lakes in the world. Water use is one form of energy consumption, and world use of water for irrigation grows every year. China plans to build the largest dam in the world to control its river systems in central China. It might pay close attention to what the Soviet Union did to its ecosystems with similar plans.

In the 1930s, economic planners decided to construct extensive irrigation canals in order to create cotton farms in the dry lands of Soviet Central Asia. The irrigation ditches fed off two rivers, the Amu Daria and the Syr Daria. These flow into the Aral Sea, a body of water about the size of Lake Huron. By 1989, the sea received only one-eighth the level of water it had in 1960. Its water level had fallen forty-seven feet, more than a quarter, and its volume had shrunk by two-thirds. Its total area diminished by 44 percent (Sneider 1992). Fishing villages lost their livelihoods as the shoreline moved ten miles. A new desert was created on the open beaches of the old sea, creating vast dust storms. In addition, the central planners saturated the cotton fields with fertilizers, insecticides, and pesticides contaminating all water resources. The populations of the region were deprived of clean drinking water and their soils were poisoned. Diseases and child mortality shot up.

The problems of the Aral Sea have been dumped into the laps of the new rulers of the five Soviet Central Asian states that form the Aral Sea's water basin. In the meantime, the people of the region feel as though imperialists had exploited them. Their lands have been destroyed while the lone cotton crop was the only thing the bureaucrats in Moscow wanted (Sneider 1992).

academics. Finance capital is responding by "fleeing" to where the profits are highest, and that often means where labor costs are relatively low.

Many economists, such as Robert Heilbroner, argue that multinational corporations and international financial institutions have accumulated such vast power and influence at the expense of national capitalism and state agencies that multinationals will soon control more than 50 percent of the world's economic production. Alvin Wolfe, an anthropologist, has long theorized that supranational organizations are stronger than nation states (Wolfe 1977).

Yet there is another view. Several recent surveys of the world economy published in *The Economist* show that there has, indeed, been a dramatic change in the world's economy between 1979 and 1995, but not one favoring the rich transnationals. The boundaries between national financial markets have dissolved; and a truly global financial market has emerged along with a tremendous increase in international trade, the growth of multinational businesses, and a rise in international joint ventures. However, the strength and importance of specific multinational corporations have diminished since the 1970s when between two to three hundred transnational corporations dominated the world economy. Today there are more than thirty-five thousand transnationals competing for the same limited capital. These companies do not have the same capacity to control economic events as their predecessors, and many have had to decrease in size or break up into separate companies (IBM recently broke up into thirteen different companies).

Instead of Wolfe's nation state being at the mercy of transnational corporations, *both transnationals and nation states have limited control over the flow of international capital.* Who, then, controls the flow of capital? According to *The Economist*:

> It is run by outlandishly well paid specialists, back room technicians and rows of computer screens. It deals in meaninglessly large sums of money. It seems to have little connection with the "real" world of factories and fast-food-restaurants. Yet at times such as October 1987, when all over the world stock markets crashed, it seems to hold the fate of economies in its grasp. The capital market is a mystery and thus a threat (*Economist* 10/19/92).

The integration of this vast economic powerhouse is not due to a conspiracy by a few wealthy transnational capitalists but is the by-product of the decision making of hundreds of thousands of investors who use their computers and instant electronic information super highways to assess the profitability of an investment. Financial investments are now being made by individuals whose computers give them access to world markets, and choices are being made in the transfer of capital entirely on the basis of profitability rather than the development of nation states or the creation of jobs or the survival of specific transnational corporations. In short, the state, corporations, and labor unions have all lost the ability to regulate investments in favor of their own interests. While this transformation was occurring in core countries, in developing regions, the same forces brought about the collapse of state capitalism and socialism, for roughly the same reason. It became impossible for states to control the movement of capital.

One consequence of this worldwide economic transformation is that efficiency and performance of corporations have become the definitions of success. Poor efficiency leads to reductions in employment both in labor and management. Job loss is no longer only a threat to the lowly employee but to middle and high level managers as well. This means that if someone can organize an efficient plant in Mexico or Indonesia, capital will flow to it.

How can these changes be measured? One measure is the increase in the rate of capital flow around the world. The international business of banks in 1965 was $55 billion. By 1980, the stock of "international" bank lending was $324 billion. By 1991, the figure had risen to $7.5 trillion. In the meantime, Japan and the countries of the Pacific Rim became a part of the core at a time when the Soviet socialist experiment began to founder. In 1985, Mikhail Gorbachev came to power in the Soviet Union. First, he attempted to reform the Soviet Union under the twin banners of glasnost (the idea of political openness, opening to democratic reform) and peristroika (restructuring: privatizing state run industries and introducing open markets). By 1990, it was apparent that the new openness had led to such political instability that the Soviet Union was dissolving. In 1991, it dissolved itself and the Cold War officially came to an end. The end of the cold war radically changed the relationship of the United States to Latin America, the Middle East, Africa, and Asia, as well as the Newly Independent States (NIS) of the former U.S.S.R. Basically, the United States reduced its interest in the politics of developing countries, and these then began to move in directions that were ideologically the opposites of what they had been during the cold war (ideologically, they were generally anti-American).

A new core that consists of the United States, Western Europe, Japan, and the "Asian Tigers" characterizes the emerging postmodern or global world system. The socialist "counter-core" has evaporated. Certain countries of the semi-periphery, such as Mexico and South Korea, are beginning to resemble the core in the highrise buildings of their central cities. On the other hand, the inner cities of the United States are beginning to resemble the crumbling old mega-cities of the periphery. In addition, many former socialist societies are slipping into the poverty of the periphery. June Nash, an anthropologist who specializes in the study of southern Mexico and Guatemala, argues that there is a global crisis in the making as capital flees the core and is invested in the periphery (Nash 1994). Entire industries, which once belonged to the core, are migrating to the semi-periphery and periphery. Jobs are being lost in the core, which is also experiencing homelessness and illiteracy. She argues that capital invested in the periphery is creating ecological wastelands due to the abuse of environments (Nash 1994), an issue we will explore further in later chapters. There is under way an economic transition in the countries of the periphery towards capitalism. The transformation is more or less universal. Many argue that this transition is also marked by an increasing gap between the rich and the poor, and greater absolute poverty among the lowest.

■   ■   ■

Chapter
Summary

The Modern World: Capitalism, World Systems, and Globalization

This chapter has covered the emergence of modern capitalism, the modern world system, the expansion of both, and the destruction of tribal societies. We have also examined the problems of economic disarticulation and the difficulties of the transition to capitalism and democracy. We looked closely at Russia to see just how difficult it is to introduce both market reform and democracy under pressures from a globalizing economy. One of the biggest questions is whether countries trying to reform themselves can do so, or if the burden of moving from economic disarticulation to economic articulation is too difficult to achieve within a democratic form of government.

In the following chapters, we will examine globalization more closely. Globalization depends on new economies, which depend on the control of information and its dissemination. Globalization holds new promises, particularly to the countries of the former periphery, many which are finding themselves released from their dependent relationships on the core. Yet, it remains to be seen if the processes of globalization can successfully address the interrelated challenges of reducing poverty and managing resources sustainably.

Chapter
Terms

articulated economy	233	gaucho	226
astrolabe	220	hacienda	215
authoritarian government	233	mercantilism	213
conquistador	215	modernization	231
corporation	221	proletariat	220
corporatism	234	Renaissance	213
democratic capitalist	228	state capitalism	229
disarticulated economy	233	state socialism	229
economic liberalization	221	structural power	229
encomienda	215	totalitarian government	233

Check out our website
▶ www.BVTLab.com
for flashcards,
chapter summaries,
and more.

Chapter 7
Ethnicity, Ethnic Conflict, and Social Movements

Globalism led to the collapse of socialism and state capitalism in the former Soviet Union, in Eastern Europe, in Africa, and Asia, and has destabilized working class groups in countries with democratic capitalism. These changes have produced new social environments that, in turn, have produced new social movements. Social movements are a fact of history and have ranged from peaceful political and religious reforms to violent revolutions. However, in the latter part of the twentieth century and beginning decades of the twenty-first, these social movements are more explicitly based on ethnicity, surfacing in a myriad of forms ranging from **civil rights movements** in countries practicing democratic capitalism, to ethnonationalism in formerly socialist countries, to movements aimed at protecting the rights of indigenous peoples around the world in all types of countries. Some of the movements are peaceful, attempting to work within the system to gain equal recognition before the law (civil rights movements). Other movements are violent, seeking to change the system with one group vying for power and political control over other groups (ethnonationalism). Yet other movements are composed of people who simply want to be able to retain their own traditions, who want to leave others alone, and want to be left to themselves (indigenous movements). To understand these movements that have so much to do with ethnicity and ethnic identity, we must first explore the concept of ethnicity.

We begin this chapter with the topic of ethnicity. What is it? We then examine how ethnic societies are changed through assimilation and acculturation around the world, and later focus specifically on American society. We consider social movements in the twentieth century, some of which have been ethnic movements and many of which have not. We study five types of movements: transformative, reformative, redemptive, alterative, and ethnonationalist. We examine the reformative movements towards multiculturalism and indigenous rights movements, radical ethnonationalist movements, revolutionary transformative peasant revolutions; we end with a discussion of the current reformative trends around the world towards capitalism.

Ethnicity and Ethnic Identity

What is **ethnicity**? Technically, it can be defined as regional or national identity based on language, religion, or heritage. But what does that mean exactly? Is the label American an ethnic or multi-ethnic concept? The same question can be applied to German identity, to French identity, or Lithuanian identity. Each of these countries is also made up of people with distinct regional identities, which are sometimes more important to them than their national identity. In addition, these countries were in turn cobbled together from smaller entities, many of which have ethnic identities today. For example, many Parisians do not like to be confused or identified with people from the region of Lorrain because of its proximity to Germany. Germans, too, often think of themselves more in terms of the urban region from which they come rather than having a German identity. (Thus John F. Kennedy's famous comment, *Ich bin ein Berliner*, by which he intended to say 'I am a Berliner,' but which means 'I am a jelly doughnut,' is remembered from a speech in Berlin). However, when either France or Germany has been at war with each other, the regional distinctions evaporate; the national identities suddenly appear exceptionally important.

David Maybury-Lewis, one of the creators of Cultural Survival, Inc., has commented that "ethnicity is one of the obscurest issues of all" (Maybury-Lewis 1997).

> In spite of the fact that there is much talk nowadays about ethnicity and ethnic groups, it is not always clear exactly what that means or why ethnicity should have such a powerful hold on human imagination and behavior. Ethnic conflict has supplanted communism as the specter that is haunting the world. Writers, commentators, and newspapers are currently telling us that people are everywhere giving in to the primordial urge to band together with others like themselves and to harass or kill those who are different (Maybury-Lewis 1997, ix).

Social scientists have tried to define ethnicity by establishing categories of behavior, identity, and symbols called ethnic markers, but such ambitious research projects have usually resulted in more confusion than clarity. The reason is that ethnicity really means the same thing as social or group identity, and such identity can be remarkably vague and difficult to define. Ethnicity is the identity an individual ascribes to him or herself that is generally accepted by others. Ethnic markers, then, can be religious, regional, matters of national origins, or language-based, and usually depend on how a person views him or herself. Often the view changes with time. I (SS) am of Spanish-American (my mother) and Scot-Irish (my father) ancestry. However, I grew up in Bolivia, Colombia, and Mexico; so while I look Anglo (blonde, blue eyed, ruddy complexion), I feel Latin American and I speak a Colombian dialect of Spanish. I am really Spanish-Scot Irish American. Since my background is rather complicated to explain, I usually call myself American. When making out the census form, I check the category for White, but I often wonder why I don't check Hispanic. These categories are arbitrary. Affirmative action programs

civil rights movement

A reformative social movement designed to ensure the rights of minorities (including women) and to create an egalitarian social order

ethnicity

Regional or national identity based on language, religion, or heritage, with ethnic identities usually identifiable by self defined "ethnic markers," such as flags, speech patterns, costumes, beliefs, or other criteria which separate one ethnic group from another

have probably prompted many to mark an ethnic or minority category in order to gain some advantage. I must admit to having thought of adding my mother's Spanish surname to my own as Sheldon Smith-Montez, at times, because of my pride in my Spanish heritage and curiosity to see what would happen; but I have grown children and the name business would become too complex, so I stick to my American heritage. How many of us can change our ethnic identity more or less at will? Also, when I lived in Latin America, and when I travel there, I tend to think of myself as an American; when I am in the United States, my ethnic identity tends to shift in the direction of Latin American, particularly when I am around people from Latin America. My ethnic identity, as is true for many people, is not static.

Societies tend to simplify reality, and I mark myself as White because I have been taught to think of myself that way. My actual background, like most other human beings, is far too complex to categorize by any one ethnic marker. Much depends on the situation. Is a particular identity important? When looking at all my choices (markers), I realize ethnicity is a way of simplifying reality and gaining an identity as a member of a group, most of the members of which share enough features in common to provide a common identity. Yet the groups I've belonged to have changed over my lifetime. We often shop around for the most obvious means of giving ourselves an identity (and an advantage). Usually, people tend to accept these differences in each other, bond within a larger definition of national identity, and get along. However, it is apparent that such a bonding pattern is not the case in some parts of the world, as illustrated by the Israelis and Palestinians in the Middle East, the Guatemalan Ladinos and Maya, the Muslims, Croats, and Serbs in Bosnia, the Irish and British in Northern Ireland, the Basques and Spaniards in Spain, and so on. How do we approach an explanation of why ethnic violence has surfaced at the beginning of the twenty-first century? Many scholars are currently arguing that the reason for ethnic violence is the disintegration of the modern state due to globalism. Others are offering the argument that ethnicity has always been important but that social science theories on the development of states prevented ethnicity from being a subject of study. When ethnicity is studied, it turns out that when societies discriminate against ethnic groups, those ethnic groups tend to become antagonistic in the preservation of identity.

Why has ethnicity received so little attention until recently? According to Manning Nash, an anthropologist at the University of Chicago, the modern nation-state was supposed to replace ethnicity "as the most potent, maximal, and perduring form of social and political organization"; thus social scientists paid little attention to the category (Nash 1989, 1). The modern nation-state was founded on the idea of citizenship, which has overtones of voluntary allegiance, loyalty, and of exclusivity, while ethnicity was viewed sometimes in romantic terms like volk (meaning *folk* or *people*), a vestigial, colorful remnant of earlier times—soon to be swamped by the inexorable tide of the nation-state, that most rational, efficient, modern, and natural form of social and cultural being. The old assumption of the importance of the modern nation-state and the disappearance of ethnic identity was tied to a drive to create an all-encompassing social science theory, which drove out the category of ethnicity all together (functionalism, discussed in Chapter 2). As Nash points out, a universal theory of social science never came about, however; and we are forced to try to grasp ethnicity not as an arcane feature of pre-industrial society but as a feature of modern life. Today, however, something else is happening. It now appears that far from being unimportant, perhaps ethnicity has always been with us and always will be (Nash 1989, 2). The question remains, why are some ethnic groups suddenly violent?

Samuel Huntington, a political scientist, argues that ethnic wars are cultural wars and that these are inevitable in the new century (Huntington 1996). He argues that ethnonationalist wars, such as that in Bosnia, are the form of conflict in the future. Because of globalism, the state is threatened everywhere; and ethnic groups, which were previously separated, are now brought directly into confrontation with each other: cultures of China, Russia, India, and Moslem will be in conflict. In short, for Huntington, the disappearance of the state is tied to the appearance of ethnic conflict, which is pretty much the opposite idea of the appearance of the modern state bringing about the disappearance of ethnicity altogether.

It is argued in this chapter that ethnic conflict is not the consequence of the collapse of the state. Rather, a peculiar kind of state is collapsing—the socialist state organized around ethnic identity. While all societies appear to experience ethnic conflict, few experience cultural wars. When examining the various nation-states of the world, the lack of attention to ethnicity due to the idea of the emergence of the modern state is surprising. It is not possible to drive through any country without running into ethnic variations, which range from mild to dramatic. A drive through any large American city will show dramatic differences, but so would a similar drive through European, African, Asian, Middle Eastern, or Latin American countries. Such variations are often not apparent to the tourist, however. For example, in Mexico, there are language and value differences between those from northern Mexico and southern Mexico, sufficient that locals often refer to other Mexicans from elsewhere as gringos. Poblanos from the highland city of Puebla distinguish themselves from the coastal natives of Veracruz. Very similar distinctions are made between those from the region of Antioquia, Colombia, the state in which Medellin is located, who are called paisa, and those who come from the northern coastal cities of Cartegena and Baranquilla. The paisa will often hold him or herself aloof as a speaker of pure Castilian (Castellano) and will mock the lowlander for his or her dialect of coastal Creole. Most of these differences are in fun, but recently the paisas have warned of creating a separate state of Antioquia in order to maintain their ethnic purity.

A drive inland from Lagos, Nigeria, astonishes the traveler with the range of ethnic variation in just a short distance: Ibos, Hausa, and Fulani, all dressed in their own tribal outfit. A similar tour of Adis Adaba in Ethiopia, Tehran in Iran, or of the Chinese or Russian countryside reveals extensive ethnic and regional variations. These differences are rarely, if ever, commented on. People live with differences. For the most part people of different ethnic identity are left to their own devices; they manage their languages, their religions, and go about their tasks while participating in a national culture that may require them to speak a second language (Nigerian English, Ethiopian Italian, Farsi, Chinese, or Russian). Yet in many regions of the world, politically dominant groups outlawed ethnic identity and heritage; and where this has been true, ethnicity stands out as extremely important, as something to be achieved and expressed.

Several regions of the world, including the United States, have attempted **ethnocide**, the destruction of the ethnic identities of subordinate cultures. There are many examples, including American Indian groups that have largely lost their identity because their languages and customs were made unlawful, much as has been true for southern Mexico for a variety of ethnic groups. In recent years, many Mexican Indian populations, particularly the Maya, are retrieving their ancient identities, as the following case study demonstrates.

ethnocide

The destruction of the ethnic markers, ethnic identity, or culture of an ethnic group or groups

Case
Study

Sna Jtz'ibajom, the House of the Writer

Ethnologists have been working for several decades among the Maya of the Mexican state of Chiapas and across the border in Guatemala. The Maya of Chiapas have been at odds with the Mexican state for several hundred years. The Maya are among the many minority peoples around the world who have been persecuted, not just in the form of economic exploitation, but also cultural exploitation. For example, the Mexican Balet Folklorico, held at many Mexican universities, is a series of ethnic dances from throughout Mexico, all but one of which portray Mexican regional and ethnic groups as heroic and proud. The dance of the Maya occurs last and mocks the Indian who is portrayed in a drunken and debauched state, barely able to stand, making lewd gestures to his mate. This racist dance has nothing to do with traditional Maya, but it does show how many Mexicans think of the Maya Indian.

The dynamic culture of the Maya is thousands of years old. In the last decade, much like Indonesian theater made famous by Clifford Geertz, a rebirth of native pride is bringing native Maya back to an appreciation of their own cultures. Robert M. Laughton, an ethnologist with the Smithsonian Institute of Washington, D.C., has recently described the role that anthropologists played in a cultural renaissance of the Maya (Laughlin 1994). Up until the 1950s, Maya Indians of Chiapas were held in debt peonage (like slavery) on coffee *fincas* (farms, ranches, and haciendas). The Mexican government introduced the National Indian Institute (INI) to San Cristobal las Casas, the major city of Chiapas, with the mission to civilize and assimilate the Indian. Originally, the program was designed to give anthropologists knowledge about the Maya of Chiapas, but in 1982, representatives of the Maya told Robert Laughton:

> You have published many studies, but always in other countries where we never see the results. Our people are now literate in Spanish but they don't know a quarter of what their fathers or grandfathers know about our culture. When the elders go to the grave they take their knowledge with them. We would like, at least, to put on paper our customs for the sake of our children and grandchildren (1994, 13).

Cultural Survival was organized in 1973 by David Maybury-Lewis to help preserve threatened peoples and cultures around the world. Laughlin approached Cultural Survival and received seed money to help the Maya achieve their goals. So was born Sna Jtz'ibajom, the house of the writer.

INI gave office space and Maya Tzeltal speakers, with the help of linguistically trained ethnologists, organized to preserve their heritage. The Mexican government published their bilingual (Spanish and Tzeltal) booklets. The new booklets gave the Tzeltal the earliest Spanish descriptions of their encounters with the ancestors of the modern Maya. They recorded folktales and described customs which are now of the past. However, these books were only taught in local schools using the Spanish version because the instructors did not know how to teach any of the Mayan dialects.

In 1988, Laughlin and his associates tackled this problem by training the Maya to read and write their own dialects. They offered a six-month course to be taught in Mayan homes. To their surprise, men, women, and children lined up for the classes. In three and a half years, 1500 diplomas were awarded. Laughton writes of the school, "Every one of its teachers wants to teach and every one of its students wants to learn" (Laughlin 1994, 14).

In 1992, twenty teachers in the federal school system of Chamula asked for the same training. It has been a major breakthrough to have teachers admit that they are not doing a good job teaching; half of the instructors received diplomas. Literacy in the native dialect has stimulated confidence and ability to learn Spanish.

The success of Sna Jtz'ibajom has moved beyond the classroom. The Bread and Butter Puppet Theater was invited to help the Maya learn how to put on skits using their texts. Thus was created the Teatro Lo'il Maxil, Monkey Business Theater. There followed the rebirth of Maya theater in Chiapas.

> Their latest play, *The Jaguar Dynasty*, closes the circle. For the first time in a thousand years the Mayans are witnessing on the stage the lives of the forgotten kings of Yaxchilan and their royal wives (Laughlin 1994).

The theater of the Maya has gained much prestige and has traveled to Mexico City, Guatemala, Honduras, Canada, and the United States. Mayan culture is recovering its centrality, and Mexicans are picking up an image of the Maya very different from that of the drunken dancer and his mate.

ASSIMILATION, ACCULTURATION, AND MULTICULTURALISM

As is well known, many cultures in American history have been forced to submit to domination by the ethnically dominant white groups but have been kept apart and have retained separate cultures: American Indians, African Americans, and Hispanic-Americans. Yet the histories of most ethnic groups in North America have not been stories of segregation but rather of **assimilation**. Many groups were assimilated to American culture, at least in the early history of the Republic, because that was the only alternative. The Anglo-Saxon elite expected newcomers to adopt their customs and values. John Quincy Adams expressed it this way:

> To one thing they [immigrants to the United States] must make up their minds, or they will be disappointed in every expectation of happiness as Americans. They must cast off the European skin, never to resume it. They must look forward to their posterity rather than backward to their ancestors; they must be sure that whatever their own feelings may be, those of their children will cling to the prejudices of this country (quoted in Calhoun 1994, 250).

Early immigrants were expected to surrender their ethnic identities to that of American culture, and the American public school system was created in order to ensure the enculturation of non-Americans. The assimilationist model was clearly the one that dominated American life prior to the middle of this century. Schoolbooks were written to enculturate children to the norms of American culture, but the United States was not alone in this model. It was typical for countries like Mexico, Chile, Brazil, and Argentina that, before the turn of the last century, opened their doors to immigration from Western Europe with the expectation that the new immigrants would assimilate to the national characteristics of these countries. It is not at all unusual to meet blue-eyed, blond, European-looking individuals in cities like Puebla, Mexico, who speak and act totally Mexican and whose parents have only dim memories of German or Polish ancestors.

Assimilation is an asymmetrical form of social interaction: the dominant group expects the subordinate group to adapt to its standards, or else it cannot progress economically. Despite the socialization tools of the public schools, by the early twentieth century it became apparent that some cultures would not assimilate; but they would adopt some of the values of the dominant culture. When one culture adapts to the culture of another society, the process is **acculturation**. The following is a classic definition of acculturation:

> … those phenomena which result when groups of individuals come into continuous firsthand contact, with subsequent changes in the original cultural patterns of either or both groups (Redfield, Linton, and Herskovitz 1936, 149).

Why have some groups been totally assimilated to American culture while others remain only partially acculturated? Probably the simplest explanation is that some of the immigrants to the United States (or to Brazil, Chile, Argentina, etc.) came in large colonies of several thousand and managed to retain some of the markers of their ethnic identities while others came in small groups of only a few hundred and were culturally swamped by the dominant culture. An example of the second type is my mother's Spanish community of La Farma, a settlement in Moundsville, West Virginia, at the turn of the last century. The first generation spoke Spanish and practiced the Catholic faith; however, by the second generation, the language had been forgotten, and the Spanish com-

assimilation

The surrender of ethnic markers or identity (or culture) to a dominant ethnic group, which may be forced or voluntary

acculturation

The adaptation of one culture to the culture of another society

munity had dispersed. An example of the first type is the case for the town of Westby near La Crosse, Wisconsin, which was settled by Norwegians in the mid-nineteenth century but still actively retains its traditional Norwegian values. Several thousand Norwegians, not by a few hundred, settled Westby. The size of the community, then, has a lot of influence on whether an ethnic group is assimilated or acculturated.

Assimilation is obviously a political tool in the hands of elites to impose cultural control on others. Acculturation is a more neutral, less political process that will occur to any cultural group moving into a new culture. I (SS) had the experience of being a member of very small American communities throughout Latin America because my father was a Foreign Service Officer, and it was far easier to learn Spanish and adapt to Latin American culture than to expect others to speak my language or understand my ways. However, there was little pressure placed on me to assimilate; instead I chose to live in two cultures, and have done so most of my adult life.

Fredrik Barth developed one explanation behind the survival of ethnic identity in the 1969. He proposed that ethnicity is tied to ecological adaptation when people occupy a distinct niche (Barth 1969, 19). We will see many examples of the way in which ecology reinforces ethnicity in the chapters to come. For example, the distinctions between pastoral nomadism and farming have always been of primary importance in establishing ethnic distinctions in the Middle East and parts of Africa. However, as shown in the following case study of the Greek community in Tarpon Springs, Florida, such a relationship is far from one-on-one.

multiculturalism

A reformative social movement that seeks to grant distinct ethnic groups the right to retain some or all of their heritage

A third political model, **multiculturalism**, appeared in the latter part of the twentieth century in the United States, Canada, and Western Europe. This model is based on the increased political power of various ethnic groups. Multiculturalism is really a social movement and will be discussed later in this chapter. It is a movement that demands a certain degree of cultural autonomy and recognition.

While multiculturalism has gained prominence in American society, the rights of one group to maintain its customs often runs into the demands by other groups that it change behavior. There are several examples here, one from Muslim and one from Hmong immigrants, both of which have cultural practices that allow men to control women. An extreme version of male dominance is expressed among a very limited number of Muslims who practice clitoridectomy, a form of genital mutilation of young girls that Americans find repugnant and which has been made illegal in many communities. Among the Hmong, there is the practice of the future husband kidnapping a future bride, who is often only ten or eleven years old. Several Hmong men in the Minneapolis–St. Paul region have been arrested and jailed on kidnapping and rape charges, often with pressure from feminist groups to impose harsh punishments on the perpetrators. Judges, who are sensitive to both multiculturalism and women's rights, have been torn between the demands of the two groups.

■The Hmong culture encourages dominance over women. Cultural practices maintain this mindset, such as the future husband kidnapping a future bride who is often only ten or eleven years old, not unlike the young girls shown above.

ETHNICITY IN THE UNITED STATES

Many minority ethnic groups in the United States believe that our society, like others, is plagued by ethnic strife. Populist writers often argue that ethnic differences lead to conflict. Others argue that ethnic conflict is the consequence of discrimination and that American society has a long ways to go to achieve promises to the poor and minorities, but that conflict can be erased. Attempts to address discrimination resulted in affirmative action programs and multiculturalism since the 1960s, not just in the United States but in Western Europe as well. In Chapter 3, we examined several cases of ethnic conflict in the United States. The growing anti-minority and anti-ethnic rights sentiments of extreme right wing movements in the United States, Great Britain, France, and Germany have left social scientists puzzled. A few support the idea that it is peoples' differences that produce conflict. Others explain the current and ominous conflict between ethnic groups as the consequence of economic deprivation. They argue that globalization, with its impact on jobs in the countries of the core, is why skinhead and neo-Nazi groups are attracted to extreme nationalist movements. Recent attacks against Turkish immigrants in Germany are blamed on young people whose jobs are being threatened by immigrants. In Chapter 3, similar problems were described for African-Americans and Koreans in Los Angeles.

The civil rights movement in the United States can be traced to the abolitionist movement, which grew in the period directly before the American Civil War. In 1970, Daniel Patrick Moynihan (more currently a Liberal Democratic senior senator from New York, but then an eminent sociologist) and Nathan Glazer published a book called *Beyond the Melting Pot.* Until their book was published, it was commonly assumed that all ethnic groups in the United States were in a melting pot and that ethnic cultural values were disappearing due to the dominant American culture. Melting pot theory assumed that schools, which had been organized to force children to forget their traditional languages and ethnic values, had succeeded. Glazer and Moynihan surprised American society by showing that, in fact, ethnic groups were not disappearing but were a part of American life. They summarized statistics on the survival of ethnic groups and ethnicity for New York City that are surprising. As of 1970, New York had 859,000 Italians, 564,000 Russian Jews, 389,000 Poles, 312,000 Irish, 220,000 Austrians, 175,000 British, 100,000 Hungarians, 50,000 Greeks, Czechs, and Rumanians, 50,000 Yugoslavians, 5,000 Mexicans, and over 1,000,000 Afro-Americans. The statistics have changed since then. Today there are many more Mexicans, and in addition there are thousands of Vietnamese and Hmong.

Five years after their 1970 book, Glazer and Moynihan published a theoretical text, *Ethnicity: Theory and Experience* (1975), in which they tried to explain why ethnic populations survived in American society. One explanation was that the development of the welfare state promoted the interest of ethnic groups; and secondly, inequality prevents ethnic groups from being assimilated. However, this is only part of the picture. In the early 1970s, the radio storyteller, Garrison Keillor, invented the community of Lake Wobegon, Minnesota, made up of Norwegian Lutherans and German Catholics. This community has become a mainstay of his popular *Prairie Home Companion* telecast on Saturday nights by National Public Radio. There are Scottish folk in Virginia who stay home Saturday nights to learn about events in Lake Wobegon, with its war memorial to the Lost Norwegian (the community "which time has not forgot nor can the decades improve ... where all the women are strong, the men good looking, and the children above average"). While Lake Wobegon may be Keillor's invention, the town is not really very different from the Norwegian community of Westby,

Wisconsin, just thirty miles from La Crosse. The Norwegian spoken in Westby is purer than that spoken in Norway; and Norwegian linguists have been known to visit the region in order to study the earlier versions of their language, which is no longer spoken in Norway.

Keillor's ethnic Germans and Norwegians were not products of welfare economics, and they certainly cannot be regarded as members of unequal castes or classes, not in Minnesota and not in Wisconsin. The answer seems to lie in quite a different direction: ethnic groups currently survive in the United States because no one tries to make them illegal. American society is multi-cultural because that is the way it now defines itself. Most studies of modern ethnic groups focus on minority populations and discrimination against them. It is not very difficult to understand that those groups, which are discriminated against, will tend to persist because they are not accepted into the larger American community. Yet the discoveries of Glazer and Moynihan remind us that there are many ethnic groups which survive and persist despite the fact that they are not currently discriminated against.

In 1981, the conservative historian and writer, Thomas Sowell, who is also an African-American, wrote a book which also details the ethnic variations in American society. Irish, Germans, Jews, Italians, Chinese, Japanese, Blacks, Puerto Ricans, and Mexicans form the American mosaic, as Sowell calls American society. He makes an interesting point: the mosaic of American society cannot be discussed as minority versus majority because there is no majority. The largest single strain that can be ethnically distinguished is people of British ancestry, and they make up only 15 percent of the American population (Sowell 1981, 4). Sowell also points out that no ethnic group has been wholly unique, and no two are completely alike. Each shares a different history, its own geographic distribution, and even has distinct age differences reflecting distinct fertility patterns. Incomes, occupations, and unemployment rates differ significantly; there is no simple explanation for all of the variations. Discrimination has influenced the prosperity of distinct groups, particularly those with dark skin pigmentation; but some have succeeded despite extreme discrimination such as Chinese communities on the West Coast. In Chapter 3, we examined several ethnic groups—all of which have been discriminated against—which appears to be a common thread in Sowell's descriptions of the histories of ethnic communities. Inter-ethnic violence, of the kind emerging around the world, is extremely rare, however; and it cannot be explained solely by examining American ethnic history. For explanations, we have to step outside of the United States because our own definition of American ethnicity is multi-cultural and multi-ethnic.

Contemporary Social Movements

The collapse of the Soviet Union has led to the sudden explosion of ethnic revolutions and regional wars throughout the old socialist periphery of Eastern Europe where terrorism and genocide are common. In the 1980s and 1990s, there were many ethnically based wars raging in both capitalist and socialist countries. Examples are Azerbaijan, Iraq, Guatemala, Peru, Ethiopia, Angola, South Africa, Sri Lanka, and Mozambique. The Philippines is involved in a war with communists and Moslem insurgents. As we look around the world, it is hard to avoid the impression that almost every other country outside the core is either ruled by extremists or just barely able to maintain a democratic government.

Case Study

The Greek Community of Tarpon Springs, Florida

An example of one ethnic group surviving in a multicultural society is the Greek community of Tarpon Springs, Florida. This fairly large community has adopted many of the characteristics of American culture while holding on to many of its own, a common process in acculturation. One of the reasons the original community never let go of its Greek ethnic identity is the size of the original population. Like many other ethnic groups, the Greeks of Tarpon Springs were first discriminated against for their dark skins and foreign language. Yet they managed to find niches for their economic specializations—sponge diving, fishing, and, today, tourism—which brought them up the economic ladder. The occupations the Greeks tended to adopt also allowed Greek men to express *philotimo*, a sense of manliness, which was very attractive in the early part of the twentieth century to other Americans in South Florida. A tour of Tarpon Springs in the mid-1990s shows that the acculturated Greeks are proud of both their American and their Greek identities, whereas an older anthropological theory, one that dismissed the importance of ethnic culture and heritage, had predicted the demise of this and other ethnic communities.

In 1966, anthropologist Edwin Buxbaum, who had made a study of the Greek community of Tarpon Springs, Florida, declared that it would disappear in twenty years. He theorized that it had lost its specialized occupation of sponge diving and could not survive another two decades. In 1996, articles continued to appear in newspapers about the Greeks of Tarpon Springs and their sponge diving culture. In 1979, the city planner of Tarpon Springs told me (SS), "The Greeks are stronger than ever." She argued that rather than disappearing, the Greeks of Tarpon Springs have given the city its particular political identity such that the city is continuously asserting its autonomy, authority, and independence against the county within which it is located and against its sister cities.

Buxbaum, working with 1960s social science models of community, had predicted the demise of Greek culture because he viewed the community of Tarpon Springs as a closed organic model in which various institutional features were functionally adapted to each other (structural-functionalism). He argued that when one or more such feature disappeared (sponge diving), so would the community. The current theory about the growing importance of ethnicity in a secularizing world helps explain the continued survival of Greek ethnicity. The role of political identity and the need to maintain identity against the hegemony of outside forces does a lot to

explain why, a century after their arrival, the Greeks of Tarpon Springs continue to survive.

Tarpon Springs was originally established as a spa for wealthy Philadelphians, and between 1882 and 1885 catered to wealthy Northerners. In 1899, John K. Cheyney, a wealthy banker from Philadelphia, had his yacht in the area and learned about the large sponge beds of the Gulf of Mexico. He used his influence to interest sponge merchants in New York City, most of them of Greek and Jewish background, to initiate sponge diving in the area outside the harbor of Tarpon Springs. In the following decades, the Greeks of Tarpon Springs effectively organized themselves into a political community within which Greek symbols have great rhetorical power against other groups.

Between 1891 and 1900, there was a large migration of sponge divers to Tarpon Springs led by John Cocoris and his brothers (Buxbaum 1967). The early Greeks of Tarpon Springs are described by John Campbell, an anthropologist, in his study of Greeks on mainland Greece (1964). They were highly individualistic, characterized by *philotimo* (spiritually strong), *kumbaros* (the godfather of a child), and a highly democratic civic culture. Immigration to Tarpon Springs was mostly from the island of Halki, north of Rhodos. By 1905, there were five hundred sponge divers, and by 1940, over a thousand. Typically, males would live alone for several years and then return to Greece to obtain a Greek wife. The sponge diving industry brought its own support system: Greek boat builders, ship chandlers, provisioners, marine mechanics, financiers, and wholesalers, called packers, who sold the sponges up north. In 1907, the Greek community constructed an impressive Greek Orthodox Church with a gold dome, which later became a shrine for Greeks throughout the United States. The church was organized through The Community, a fourteen-member council representing the various islands. The American Hellenic Educational Progressive Assocation (AHEPA), a national Greek association, was highly active in the community.

Between 1900 and 1948, the sponge industry grew dramatically along with the Greek community of Tarpon Springs. The spa culture of Philadelphia died out due to the Depression and in reaction to the success of the Greek community. The Greeks were very industrious and acquired real estate and material goods, becoming middle class Greco-Americans. They were described as highly aggressive; some gravitated into banking and politics. The Greeks came to be represented in the city's political system. Several became mayors, police chiefs, fire chiefs, commissioners, and so on. However, while their combined population was greater than any other group, internal competition and contentiousness prevented stronger alliances. As Buxbaum put it, "Where there are three Greeks, there are five parties" (Buxbaum 1967, 42).

In 1947, at the height of the sponge diving industry, a red tide struck, eliminating sponges along the Gulf of Mexico (the red tide is a bacteria which attacks sponges and other sea life). Panic hit the Greek community of Tarpon Springs, and many predicted the end of the community. In 1946 there were four hundred sponge boats operating out of the port. In 1967, there were only seven, and by 1979 there were three. A few remain today for tourists. In addition to the red tide, in the late 1940s, the Dupont Company introduced synthetic sponges that were much cheaper than organic sponges. The boat crews dispersed and the skills were lost. Many of the younger men left the community and went to work in the steel mills of Youngstown, Ohio, and Gary, Indiana, where new Greek communities were formed. Many predicted that with the disappearance of sponge diving, which was considered the Greeks' ecological niche, the Greek community would disappear.

There were acculturative changes. Patriarchal family structure has practically disappeared, and the status of women reflects changes in American society. Arranged marriages have completely disappeared, as has philotimo

and kumbaros. The animosities of the early settlers towards each other no longer exist, and the community is still strong, though few children learn Greek. The most important and significant event is a three-day event, the Epiphany Celebration, beginning January 6, when the Archbishop of the Greek Orthodox Church of North and South America throws a gold cross into the bayou. Boys from the Greek community dive into the bayou to retrieve the cross, an event that is reported in the *Tarpon Springs Leader*. The newspaper has always printed the names of all the boys who have ever found the cross, back to the 1920s. The paper congratulates the Greek community for its celebration, and all of the industries and commercial enterprises of the region print large ads congratulating the Greek community.

A close study of the history of the Greek community in Tarpon Springs shows that it has survived because it had the political skills to do so, and it continues to exist because it is a relatively large community of Greeks. Smaller communities have not survived as well, as Greeks find mates who are of different ethnic backgrounds. However, it is also important to note that American political theory has built into it the idea of equality. Such is not the case, surprisingly, for the former Soviet Union and the former socialist societies of Eastern Europe, which we turn to later in this chapter.

EXPLAINING SOCIAL MOVEMENTS

There have been several attempts to explain the explosion of ethnic violence around the world. An example is Samuel Huntington's new book which argues that these are cultural wars and that they are an inevitable response to globalism. He argues that the process of globalism is bringing together cultures of very different types, which were previously separate, and which respond to each other with violence. Hebrews, Palestinians, Chinese, Tibetans, Russians, Croats, and Serbs—all at each other's throats; the communist menace has been replaced with the menace of cultural wars. Huntington's point of view represents the view of many who believe that the state as in a process of free fall, and that with its disappearance, ethnic groups will go at each other's throats. Civilization will disappear. Yet there is an alternative explanation: ethnonationalist conflicts are social movements produced by **relative deprivation** and have limited scope and world impact (a theory of history). Other less violent social movements are movements toward indigenous rights, civil rights, and multicultural movements. Social movement analysis depends on two major variables: theories of history and the theory of relative deprivation. An analysis of ethnonationalism and other ethnic rights movements, given these two variables, produces the image of a less explosive world, but still not a pretty one.

Theories of History   There have been many attempts to explain moderate social movements, revolutionary violence, terrorism, and genocide. Earlier theories explaining social movements tended to look at the relationship between imperialism and social movements. It was relatively easy to understand that the Mexican Revolution, which began in 1910, was a revolt against the dictator Porfirio Diaz who had attempted to modernize Mexico by allowing foreign capitalists to gain an economic stranglehold over much of the

relative deprivation

A social science theory that explains the motivation of people involved in social movements and found in the feeling of alienation by a people who feel that they are illegitimately deprived of status, property, power, or worth

Mexican landscape. The same is true for the revolt of Fidel Castro against the dictator Juan Batista in Cuba in 1959 or the revolt of the Sandinistas in Nicaragua against the dictator Somoza in 1979. How do we begin to explain current ethnic genocide in former Yugoslavia and other East European countries, however, or the terrorist activities of Palestinian Arabs and Iranians? How do we come to grips with the often extremely complex play of events in socialistic and mixed capitalist/socialist countries in Africa, such as Uganda? How do we come to understand the grassroots Moslem fundamentalist movements in Iran and the Sudan? As we move into the latter part of the twentieth century, explanations that seemed sufficient at mid-century no longer pertain. The argument, so popular for the last thirty years, that capitalism and modernization is the root of all violence no longer works. Theories of history, that is, explanations about why history operates as it does, are a feature of all analytical approaches to social movements.

Theories of history are generally teleological; that is, the ends of the social movement are viewed as somehow destined (Aberle 1991, 318). The goals of the leaders of the movements can be explained as follows: willed by God (Muslim fundamentalists); the product of secular forces such as cultural evolution (cultural materialism) or dialectical processes (Marxism); the long course of history (political economy); the destiny of the ethnic group (ethnic nationalism); or the destiny of a particular minority group (liberation of American minority groups). As Manning Nash (1989) has noted, the theory of history that dominated social science until the early 1980s was the inevitability of the nation-state and the disappearance of ethnic identity. Now, we find ourselves working towards a more realistic assessment of the relationship between states and ethnic groups.

The spokespersons for social movements are usually charismatic and regard themselves or are regarded as in touch with superior forces, or as having superior knowledge about the forces of destiny (this generalization would also apply to the theorists of history such as Max Weber, Karl Marx, Talcott Parsons, C. Wright Mills, etc.). The charismatic leader is a prophet who explains to his/her followers what is about to happen. An example of a recent American prophet involved in our moderate civil rights movement would be Martin Luther King. An example of a prophet of radical revolution would be Cuban leader Fidel Castro. An example of a prophet of ethnonationalist change would be the Ayatollah Khomeini of Iran. The three prophets cannot be separated from their messages, which are three very different readings of history.

Theories of history serve to mediate, channel, and constrain the actions of individuals and groups; and the three prophets mentioned were successful in channeling new forms of behavior. King structured his message within the ideology of American political economy: reformist messages of change. Fidel Castro structured his within a Marxist theory of history; his was a radical message advocating the destruction of capitalist social structures. The Ayatollah Khomeini offered a vision of Islamic fundamentalism: God would replace the satanic capitalist state. When politicians and other power brokers attempt to mobilize (manipulate the behavior of) the masses, they often combine raw emotions with racist theories of history. An example would be Serbian President Slobodan Milosovic's vision of history based on the myth of Serbian greatness coupled to socialist ideology, which drove many of his followers to commit genocide in the Bosnian civil war. Certainly another example would be Hitler's theory about the Germans as a master race, which led to the genocide of European Jewry. These theories combine the manipulation of emotions (patriotism) with the creation of a scapegoat (Jews and Muslims) that is used to explain why the heroes (Germans and Serbs) have not succeeded.

The existing institutions of a society constrain the extent to which the message changes society, producing relative deprivation (explained next). If conflict itself is a part of the theory of history, then deprivation may produce a strong likelihood of periodic violence (Cuba and Iran). To the extent that violence is not a part of the theory of history, it will play a lesser role; but given extreme deprivation, it is always a possibility (USA).

Relative Deprivation   One explanation for social movements is based upon the assumption that relative deprivation provides the motivation for action. According to the theory of relative deprivation, all people consider themselves deprived of something—status, wealth, power, or acceptance. Obviously, and objectively, some people are more deprived than others. However, some people don't feel deprived while others do. Social movements develop when a large number of people feel deprived and are frustrated at their inability to overcome their deprivations and achieve status, prosperity, power, or acceptance by others. Many different types of movements arise as a result of this frustration. Some are violent and some are non-violent; some demand total change and immediate gratification. Others demand only partial change and moderate improvement in life style.

Social movements in this and other centuries were, and are, movements by people who organize themselves to effect change in the face of resistance (Aberle 1991). In this century, the single most constant factor producing social movements has been the desire of certain groups to improve their economic and political success. Movements early in this century were largely secular, while more recent movements are spurred ahead by religious and ethnic beliefs. One interpretation is that the demands by people early in this century were basically economic and political, but that social changes did not add meaning to life, whereas ethnic and religious movements appeal as much to inner feelings of self-worth and well being as to economic and political desires.

In the histories of the nineteenth and twentieth centuries, core countries have largely stayed ahead of feelings of relative deprivation and have experienced a largely peaceful existence. While the prosperity of elite classes grew, so did the prosperity of the middle classes and the working classes. Working class occupations in the first two-thirds of the twentieth century grew to the point where it has become difficult to distinguish middle and working classes. However, in the 1980s, the living wage of working class and many middle class groups fell in the United States. This has produced a spiritual malaise and has led to relatively peaceful multicultural movements and also a rise of fundamentalism.

Resource Mobilization   Deprivation, alone, cannot explain social movements because it is too universal a characteristic. Some discontent can always be found, but social movements are infrequent. One suggestion is to examine **resource mobilization**, that is, how a group is able to mobilize resources on its behalf. Without sufficient resources, which include the ability to organize, even the most angry cannot launch a social movement. What are the resources needed to produce a social movement? They are tangible assets such as money, channels of communication—such as leaflets, newspapers, radio, and television—and human skills such as leadership, organizational talents, personal prestige, and knowledge of the people and institutions the movement hopes to change. Also critical are the time to devote to the movement and the commitment of followers to their cause (Calhoun, Light, and Keller 1994, 555).

Patterns of peaceful accommodation have not been followed in the countries of the periphery. While total wealth has increased, the rate of increase for elites has been extremely high. The standard of living of the rural classes has actually decreased in a great many countries over the last thirty years. Many of the rural poor have fled to the cities and become the urban poor. The middle classes have generally expanded and enjoyed some of

**resource
mobilization**

The ability of a group
to control resources
on its behalf in order
to achieve its goals

the wealth—at the expense of the working class, some would argue. As the distinction between rich and poor grew early in the century, there were increasing numbers of social revolutions, particularly as the poor gained access to modern forms of communication (resource mobilization). Today, where socialist models have not worked, people are turning to ethnonationalist and religious movements to address their feelings of deprivation.

In addition to resources, the social environment must be conducive to change. Structural power, as explained earlier, is a factor in allowing change; totalitarian or authoritarian governments will not allow change. Thus, the general prosperity and the open political system of the United States in the 1950s and 1960s were factors behind the rise of various social movements, including civil rights, women's, and environmental movements. There must also be *cognitive liberation*, that is, the belief that one can succeed against superior forces and powers. Cognitive liberation is usually tied to a theory of history, which stimulates a group to act because it believes it can succeed. Examples are the peasant revolutions examined at the end of this chapter (Calhoun, Light, and Keller 1994, 556).

TYPES OF SOCIAL MOVEMENTS

Among the more sophisticated studies of social movements is David F. Aberle's study of Navajo reaction to their deprivations. Aberle showed that many Navajo turned to a *nativistic* religion (this means to return to the traditions of one's native ancestors), the worship of Peyote as a means of coping with poverty and powerlessness on their reservation (1991). Today, Moslem populations in the Middle East are turning to fundamentalism for much the same reason; and in Eastern Europe and the former Soviet Union, people are turning to ethnic identity, as well as religion.

social movement

An organized effort by a group of people to achieve goals and effect change in the face of resistance

According to Aberle, a **social movement** is an organized effort by a group of human beings to achieve goals in the face of resistance by other human beings. Social movements are organized and differ from individual acts, such as that of a mugger knocking down an elderly woman and stealing her purse or a psychopath who randomly kills people in a McDonald's restaurant. Such pathologically aberrant persons are not to be confused with revolutionaries or terrorists, although they are at times recruited to such movements.

reference group

A group with whom one can contrast the status, power, success, and worth of one's own group

Aberle points out that social movements are always associated with some notion of distress due to deprivation, dysphoria, or discontent with the current state of affairs. The concept of relative deprivation requires the existence of a **reference group**, that is, a group with whom one can contrast the status, power, success, and worth of one's own group and that of people living in the same vicinity who have higher degrees of wealth and/or power. The spread of television to almost all areas of the world, even the most isolated village in the Amazon rainforest, has suddenly provided an immediate and wealthy reference group, the people and cultures of the core. People around the world who are not in the core respond to the blocked transitions to prosperity and democracy with frustration and anger, which often translates into social movements. Aberle classifies social movements into four types, the first four are discussed below. The fifth was not in evidence when Aberle wrote.

transformative movement

A social movement whose goal is total change of the current social order

Transformative Movements **Transformative movements** aim at total change in the social order. The Mexican, Russian, and Chinese Revolutions, Marxist revolts in Africa and Asia, as well as activities by the Palestinian Liberation Organization and modern, Marxist revolutionary movements, the Black Power Movement (which had a violent and transformative ideology distinct from the reformative civil rights movement) of the 1960s are a few examples. These are true revolutions. Such movements usually have secular theories of history; that is, they are rarely religious. In the first half of this century, most major revolutionary movements were predominantly secular, but not democratic. Many were decisively anti-religious such as the Mexican Revolution and the Russian Revolution, both of which outlawed religions. (Mexico outlawed the Catholic religion, particularly in the 1930s, but then legalized it once more in the 1950s). These movements are always violent and have the aim of over-throwing the ruling class, which by definition will require violence. Certain movements that were once transformative have themselves changed through time, as Aberle points out. For example, the African National Congress (ANC) began as a transformative social movement in South Africa; but with the release of Nelson Mandela and democratic changes in the social environment, it became a reformative movement moving away from a radical ideology. Some movements begin as reformative but become transformative or redemptive when they do not succeed.

Reformative Movements **Reformative movements** target certain aspects of society for change. Examples are the many civil rights movements on behalf of racial and ethnic minorities, women, homosexuals, etc. Today we can see two examples of these movements, which will be discussed later: multiculturalism in the United States and the indigenous rights movements, predominantly in Latin America and Africa. In former socialist countries, such as Russia and in many developing countries such as Mexico and Brazil, current reformative social movements favor capitalism and democracy. Like transformative movements, these movements also tend to be secular. However, these movements are reformative rather than transformative because the illusion that society can be transformed overnight has vanished. The people in these societies are not like their predecessors who rejected their own societies and tried to dramatically transform them. The reformers accept the social order as basically okay. They have come to realize that the millenarian dream is not to be achieved. Now it is acknowledged that the only path open is one of slow reform, the attempt to pass through the political and the economic transitions, both of which have to be carefully balanced. That is, the aim is not to throw out the social system but to insure that it distributes benefits fairly and democratically.

While these movements are reformative, they can be quite violent. The Zapatista revolt in Chiapas has claimed several hundred lives; however, its aims are relatively moderate, mostly the demand that the Maya participate in the political process, not that the world be changed to a Marxist dream state. Violent protests in Bulgaria shook up the capital city of Sophia, and next door the Serbs served President Slobodan Milosevic his walking papers.

Democratic reform movements appear, by their nature, to occur whenever modernizing societies attempt to introduce free market reforms. This is because free market systems tend to exacerbate the worst features of corrupt, non-democratic governments, making the rich richer and the poor poorer. Democracy is viewed as a means of combating corruption and allowing everyone to participate in the developing capitalist economies.

One of the most difficult problems today in achieving the transition from totalitarian or authoritarian governments, whether these are state capitalist or state socialist governments, is the danger of opening the door to ethnonationalist movements. These movements, as will be described, are both transformative and redemptive; but they are also violent and non-democratic.

reformative movement

A social movement that targets certain aspects of society for change

■A young Navajo boy and his horse. David F. Aberle's study of Navajo reaction to their deprivations showed that many Navajo turned to a nativistic religion, as a means of coping with poverty and powerlessness on their reservation.

redemptive movement

A social movement that attempts to change individuals but not society

sectarian movement

A religious type of redemptive movement that finds the world to be evil and seeks to help the individual expel evil from his own soul

alterative movement

A social movement that calls for a change in some aspect of the individual

Redemptive Movements

Redemptive movements attempt to change individuals, not society. According to Aberle, the defining characteristic of redemptive movements is the search for a new inner state of grace. Changes in behavior are sought to achieve that state of grace. Virtually all such movements reject at least some aspects of current society. They find the world to be evil, and they aim to help the individual expel evil from his own soul. **Sectarian (religious) movements**, such as the born again Christian movement and the Moonies are American examples. The Peyote religion, the Ghost Dance of the Plains, and the millenarian movements (cargo cults) of indigenous peoples in Oceania are examples.

The Peyote religion is a movement occurring on American Indian reservations. Peyote was originally used by Mescalero and Lipan Apaches in the 1770s, then diffused to the Plains tribes where it was adopted, and then spread to Canada. The use of peyote was organized into the Native American Church. Aberle's classic study showed how the Navajo Indians of the American Southwest, who had suffered economic deprivations, such as the loss of sheep (wealth) when the U.S. government decided to cut the herds, turned to curing ceremonies within the Native American Church. At first legalized, the movement has been recently made illegal, and it has gone underground. Another very famous redemptive movement is the Ghost Dance religion of the Plains Indians.

Alterative Movements

Alterative movements, which call for a partial change in the individual, are quite familiar to all of us. Birth control movements, movements aimed at teaching sex education, and movements aimed both for and against abortion (family planning versus right to life), anti-smoking, and "just say no" are examples (we will not be dealing with alterative movements here). These movements vary; some are secular and some deeply religious.

Aberle differs from many social scientists that use relative deprivation theory by pointing out the importance of the directing ideology and program of the movement. He also points out that many movements succeed and become the establishment. A group that once aimed at revolutionary change may turn to trying to maintain its own existence as a successful revolutionary elite instead of proceeding to deliver on its original promises, such as in present day Cuba. It is also not unusual for an organized movement, once having gained success, to largely disband and join the establishment. Such is largely what happened to the anti-war movement of the 1960s, and it is also true for the civil rights movements. Success often leads to disintegration of a movement, as the ideology of the group becomes difficult to support in light of the disappearance of the anti reference group (the young become older, have children, and the reference group of the "older establishment" disappears, and with it an anti-establishment ideology). In addition to the four types of movements described above, we now see a fifth type emerging, which combines the characteristics of reformative and redemptive movements.

Case Study

The Ghost Dance of the Plains

In 1869, a Paiute prophet named Wodziwob had religious visions that foretold the end of the existing world, the ousting of whites, the return of dead relatives, and the restoration of Indian lands and integrity. These doctrines spread rapidly among Plains tribes whose way of life had disintegrated under white pressure and the extermination of the buffalo. Though attempts at military resistance generated by cult doctrines were smashed, the cult spread widely and diversified into local versions. Then in 1890, a second

Ghost Dance cult inspired by another Paiute prophet, Wovoka, spread eastward across the Plains and even to some Eastern Woodlands tribes. Again the cult stressed return to the traditional ways of life that had broken down. If the patterns of traditional culture were purified and restored, the vanishing buffalo would return, the dead ancestors would come back, and the Indians could drive out the whites with magical protection against the power of bullets (from Keesing 1981, 407–408).

ethnonationalism

A social movement that is both transformative and redemptive and whose goal is ethnic and religious separation from the larger social system

Ethnonationalist Movements　**Ethnonationalism**, with the goals of achieving ethnic and religious separation from the larger social system, of the kind we see in former socialist and developing regions, combines the characteristics of transformative and redemptive movements. They tend to be anti-democratic, volatile, and violent. An example is the Iranian Revolution of 1979, which brought to power the charismatic Ayatollah Khomeini and established a Moslem theocracy (discussed in Chapter 9). Other examples are the attempt to establish a separate Sikh state in India (described in Chapter 10), and the various Moslem fundamentalist movements in the Middle East (described in Chapter 9). In such a context, to the extent that cultural differences, ethnic identities, and religious affiliations cross-cut one another to produce myriad diverse combinations, the likelihood of violence will increase, particularly if a motivating factor is a belief in the superiority of one group over another, or a history of subjugation by one group over another. Likewise, if a region contains several groups with distinct cultural or ethnic identities who are accustomed to an autonomous or semi-autonomous existence, then any attempt by a territorial state to deprive these groups of their autonomy and their identities, to homogenize them, or to insist that a national democratic identity take precedence over ethnic or religious based identities is likely to produce resistance, possibly in the form of violence against the state. In Russia, ethnonationalists such as Vladamir Zhirinovsky, promise a return to the glory days of the Soviet Union, including the recapturing of Alaska. In Algeria (North Africa), a former socialist government is attempting to introduce democracy, but it is destabilized by Moslem fundamentalist movements. We will, in this chapter, closely examine the case for Bosnia in the former country of Yugoslavia.

There are many other examples of ethnonationalism discussed in the chapters to come, but not all of them have clear goals. For example, there are the conflicts in the African countries of Rwanda and Burundi between Tutsi and Hutu (Chapter 8) and in Bosnia between Serbs, Croats, and Muslims (this chapter), and other ethnic groups in the former country of Yugoslavia. The savage attacks, ethnic cleansing, and mass rape occur between people who have lived as neighbors for generations, of whom most suffer from the same economic deprivations; and from most points of view, these ethnic groups are not

Case
Study

The Vailala Madness

Other millenarian movements were the cargo cults of Melanesia. These were similar to the Ghost Dance religion in the importance ascribed to the ancestors, for whom the native populations marched hoping for the delivery of cargos. Early in the movement, the ancestors would deliver the cargos in sailing ships, but after World War II, expectations were high that the deliveries would occur in Flying Boxcars.

As of 1919, the Elema of coastal New Guinea had experienced waves of European influence: missionary teachings, early experience as plantation laborers, introduction of the few items of European hardware the Elema could afford, and pacification. In that year, a movement broke out among the Elema that for a time set whole villages into collective "head he go round," a psychophysical state reminiscent of the dancing mania of plague-ridden medieval Europe. People lost control of their limbs, reeled drunkenly,

and eventually lost consciousness. Who formulated the ideology is not clear. Central in it was a belief that the dead would return, bringing with them a fabulous cargo of European material—knives, cloth, canned goods, axes, and so on. Sacred bullroarers and other ritual objects were destroyed in a wave of iconoclasm, in communities where dramatic rituals and spectacular men's houses had been focal points of life. The Elema abandoned normal gardening projects and devoted their efforts to elaborate preparations for the return of the dead (From Keesing 1981, 409).

The upsurge of Moslem fundamentalism in the Near East is a contemporary example of a redemptive movement which has global implications because of its impact on national political systems, such as in Iran, and also in Algeria, Egypt, Turkey, and other cultures of the Middle East discussed in Chapter 9.

---

really competing for the same jobs. Why, at this point in time, are ethnic conflicts so common, particularly in former socialist states? To the argument of economic deprivation must be added the point that ethnic groups in these regions are trying to dominate the levers of newly emerging states.

The nineteenth and twentieth century have experienced great change; and in the process of world modernization, many people have suffered at the hands of others. Reference fields are constantly changing for many peoples throughout the world, for modern communications brings the world to people in once isolated towns and villages. As Aberle points out, the changes that result in alterations in relationships are multifarious. For example, Mexicans can follow events in Poland on national television as that government goes through the political and economic transitions. Guatemalans are highly aware of changes in modernizing Russia, and so on.

In the following, we wish to examine several modern social movements, all of which have very different characteristics. We begin with the largely reformative civil rights and multiculturalist movements in the United States, movements that have secular reformist ideologies. Then we look at indigenous rights movements, ethnonationalist movements, peasant wars of the twentieth century, and finally, at current reform movements towards democracy and capitalism.

Four chapters follow this chapter on distinct regions of the world: Africa, the Middle East, Asia, and Latin America. Each chapter details the secular transformational movements (peasant wars) of the early and middle twentieth century, discusses the democratic reform movements, and then touches on a few of the ethnonationalist movements which occur in each region. This chapter is intended as a theoretical overview of these movements to provide a context for understanding.

■Matata Ihigihugo, whose husband, three children, and sister were killed by Rwandan Tutsi soldiers in a 1996 massacre of three hundred Hutu civilians. Such acts are motivated by the desire for ethnic cleansing.

Multiculturalism and Indigenous Rights: The Legacy of the Civil Rights Movement

The development of human rights movements around the world dates back to the period directly after World War I, a period when idealistic political movements arose to insure that ethnic strife would not block the transitions to democratic reform around the world. The goals were achieved, largely, in the core but failed in the periphery. In Latin America, a movement called **Indigenismo** developed in the countries of the Andes, particularly Peru, Ecuador, and Bolivia, sponsored by Raul Haya de La Torre, the creator of the Peruvian political party American Popular Revolutionary Alliance (APRA). APRA, which began as a radical and transformative movement, lost its force when its leaders were incorporated into state capitalism, a political movement described in Chapter 11. Very similar movements developed in Mexico and Central America. The Indian rights movement ran into grave problems in Guatemala and Central America, resurfacing as a violent transformative movement in the 1970s and 1980s. The Shining Path Movement and Tupac Amaru are two violent transformative movements that rose out of the failure of the largely reformative indigenous rights movements in Peru.

Many human rights movements in Africa were transformed into anti-colonial transformative movements in the 1960s, and we will discuss what happened to them in Chapter 8. In South Africa, the African National Congress began as a reformative movement and then changed to radical transformative in the 1960s, 1970s, and 1980s when it appeared that a peaceful approach would not work. Recently, it converted back to its original reformist ideals.

Human rights movements in Asia in the 1930s, largely due to a lack of success, became radically transformative in the 1940s, although Ghandi's reformist approach to the rights of the Indian people succeeded. However, in China human rights and civil rights movements became radically transformative in the creation of the Chinese communist state; and similar changes occurred in Burma, Vietnam, and Cambodia, topics covered in Chapter 10. Today, these radically transformative movements have shifted to a reformative mode, attempting the transitions to capitalism and democracy.

indigenismo

A transformative movement in Latin America in the early twentieth century whose goal was the liberation of Indian communities, but later became a means of co-opting Indian communities within conservative and state capitalist political parties

In the United States, the cross-fertilization of anti-colonial movements in the periphery combined with minority rights movements on behalf of African Americans during the Depression years. However, in the period after World War II, these movements were, in turn, transformed into reformative movements towards granting equal rights to women, as well as gays and other groups. Included in these movements were environmental and animal rights movements that strove to grant nature its rights.

What began as the movements to grant former slaves equal rights in the United States blossomed into multicultural movements to preserve the ethnic identity and civil rights of many other ethnic groups as well, many of which did not fit into the label of minority. Many "liberation for minorities" concepts were broadly expanded, as mentioned above, to include women, gays, and recent immigrants. The rights of humans were also extended to the rights of nature (Nash 1989), resulting in environmental movements.

Multicultural Movements in the United States

Multiculturalism in the United States has its parallels in other prosperous countries, including most of those in Western Europe. An example is Switzerland where people of German, French, Italian, and Romansch heritage preserve their distinctive cultures in integrated communities. Switzerland is currently studied as an ideal model for multiculturalism because it has long used open markets and an extremely open democratic style, with a federated political economy permitting a great deal of flexibility in allowing ethnic identity to be a major factor in community political organization. The Swiss model is one that should be closely examined by people in other countries suffering ethnic conflict, such as Canada with its French minorities or Spain with its Basque minorities. Those countries that have tried to impose rigid centralized political states are the ones which are suffering from ethnic conflict.

Multiculturalism is a matter of policy in countries like Switzerland and the Netherlands, but in the United States it has become a reformative political movement that has attempted to use affirmative action programs as a tool to distribute jobs and power more equitably to a variety of groups. As members of various ethnic groups have expanded their ability to mobilize resources, they have attempted to use affirmative action programs to ensure themselves government funding for academic positions, training, and special consideration in minority hiring in small businesses. The use of affirmative action is an excellent example of resource mobilization because American culture was open to the demands for equality at the same time that the groups demanding reform were achieving some degree of control over the political process.

While in the period of the 1960s, 1970s, and 1980s, Americans accepted the argument that ethnic and minority groups, which were not politically represented, should be given special help through affirmative action programs, such a theory of history is losing support. Affirmative action programs were meant to provide jobs to members of minority groups and the disadvantaged; however, globalization, which now threatens the jobs of many middle class voters who once supported these programs, has brought a shift in national ideology. It is difficult to predict at this point whether affirmative action will be kept in its original form. Referendum 209 in the state of California recently sought to end race or gender-based preferences in state and local-government hiring, contracts, and education. Just over 54 percent of the voters supported the measure, while 46 percent opposed it; a federal judge blocked the measure as unconstitutional.

The history of the American civil rights movement is a study in changes in the theory of history that drives social movements in the United States. Beginning with a strongly reformist movement in the 1960s, which attempted to aid groups through affirmative action and other programs, globalization has decreased the strength of the movement. The current change in theory appears to argue that it is more important for the American economy to create jobs for all, rather than to selectively help those who are disadvantaged by discrimination.

INDIGENOUS RIGHTS MOVEMENTS

Here we come to another type of social movement that is becoming more common throughout the world. It is a type of civil rights movement common in the countries of the periphery. It is the plea by the people who first occupied many world regions that they be allowed to protect their lands and dignity. The term ethnic has been used here to refer primarily to populations in modern and modernizing countries who view themselves to have a common heritage, often including language and religion, and who believe they are distinct from other similar groups. Yet whether they are minorities or majorities, they have been living in modern nation states of one type or another for several generations. The term **indigenous** is a special category used for ethnic groups who are not accustomed to being members of modern states, but who have primary claims on lands that have been taken from them, or their cultures are threatened by members of the evolving states in which they live.

This may be a little confusing. Are ethnic groups different from indigenous groups? Yes and no. In terms of cultural configurations, there may not be a great deal of difference in the phenomena called culture. However, indigenous peoples are those who were the original inhabitants of a territory and whose claims to the ownership of the land are based on the lands having belonged to them before belonging to anyone else. It is this particular claim, and its denial by those who control the state, which makes it important to add the term indigenous to our list of concepts.

According to Maybury-Lewis, indigenous peoples "were there first and are still there and so have rights of prior occupancy to their lands" (Maybury-Lewis 1997, 7). These criteria work well in the New World to distinguish Native Americans from those who came after 1492. There is also little trouble in distinguishing the Aborigines of Australia or the Maoris of New Zealand as indigenous from European settlers who came later (Maybury-Lewis 1997, 8). On the other hand in Europe, Asia, or Africa, the distinction between indigenous and ethnic groupings falls apart. In these regions, mosaics of different peoples who have lived next to each other for thousands of years make the labels ethnic and indigenous difficult to apply, and the distinction is probably not important in such cases.

Another important characteristic distinguishing indigenous peoples as a distinct type of ethnic grouping is their marginalization or subordination to others, usually members of nation states. Indigenous group have usually been:

> ... conquered by peoples racially, ethnically, or culturally different from themselves. They have thus been subordinated by or incorporated in alien states which treat them as outsiders and, usually, inferiors. Isolated or marginal groups that have not yet been conquered by a state are also considered indigenous, because it is only a matter of time before they are subordinated (Maybury-Lewis 1997, 8).

indigenous

A special category used for ethnic groups that are not accustomed to being members of modern states but that have claims on lands taken from them or whose cultures are threatened by members of the evolving states in which they live

■Indigenous Australian Father and Daughter. There is also little trouble in distinguishing the Aborigines of Australia or other "indigenous" peoples from Caucasian European settlers who came later.

Case Study

Maya Land Tenure in Guatemala and Mexico

The loss of land and the re-establishment of traditional forms of land tenure have been central themes in indigenous movements, particularly in southern Mexico, Central America, and the Andes of South America. The Maya and other Indian groups lost much of their land to large ranchers and coffee growers during the period of the 1880s. Most of the revolutions in southern Mexico and Central America were produced by the relative deprivation of the loss of land, which was, and is, the only economic source of survival. While many groups have used revolutionary violence, there has also been a long term legal movement by Indian and poor rural peasants to reclaim their land rights by legal petition in Mexico and Guatemala (Smith 1982). Often groups fight off the encroachment of large plantations, such as occur in the state of Escuintla on the coast of Guatemala, by hiring lawyers who have worked with the government to create

cadastral maps which show exactly who owns what. However, these attempts have largely failed.

In countries like Mexico, Guatemala, Peru, Ecuador, and Bolivia, and much of the periphery, the state provides little protection of private property rights for any social classes. Property is defended with power. The elites in southern Mexico, Central America, and the Andes hire small armies to protect their rights; and the poor fight back, producing civil war. Even when the dust finally clears and groups reduce their violence, property rights are unclear. Often after conflict has ended, it begins again because of the lack of clarity of rights. As one Peruvian economist put it, people cannot be prosperous without owning property; and as long as states cannot guarantee property rights, conflict continues. An excellent example of the problem with property rights and conflict is found with the Maya of southern Mexico in the state of Chiapas.

Land Ownership   Why don't states create private property rights? In part they don't because wealthy elites find it against their interests, but so do indigenous groups. The problem is that indigenous peoples face a dilemma when it comes to land ownership, as is classically portrayed by the Maya. If indigenous peoples have economies which are traditionally based on collective rights so that basic economic forms such as reciprocity and redistribution are based on those rights, and these rights underlie collective identities and collective social structures, what happens when governments argue in favor of private property rights and various groups sue to develop those rights? Should the traditional forms of land ownership continue, or should they be replaced by private property rights?

In many instances around the world, indigenous peoples have lost their land rights to others more powerful than themselves. When development anthropologists work with newly democratizing governments on behalf of indigenous peoples to reclaim stolen lands, collective forms of property are hard to protect. This is because of the lack of title to specific plots of land by individuals. When a village, a clan, or lineage collectively owns land, it is difficult to protect that land with laws designed for individual ownership. When large tracts of land in remote regions are involved, it is doubly difficult for governments to intercede on behalf of someone whose lands are being used by others. For example, a tribal group in Malaysia may petition a government to protect its lands against lumber cutters. However, by the time action is taken, the trees have been cut and removed and the loggers are long gone.

Land Tenure and the Zapatista Revolution   The complexity of this issue has been brought to light recently in the Zapatista Revolution in the state of Chiapas in modern Mexico. On January 1, 1994, several thousand Mayan Indians attacked the provincial capital of San Cristobal Las Casas calling themselves *Zapatistas* after the revolutionaries who were active in the period from 1910 to 1923 to the north in the states of Puebla and Morelos. The Mexican army counter-attacked and forced the Zapatistas back into the lowland jungles. Their spokesman, the enigmatic, pipe smoking sub-commander Marcos, declared that the attack was a response by the Mayan people to the North American Free Trade Agreement (NAFTA) and to attempts by the Mexican government to privatize their collective plots of land, which are called *ejidos*. American academics sympathetic to the Maya promptly appeared on American television to describe how the treaty and privatization would destroy the collective lands of the Maya Indians. They argued that the NAFTA would lower tariffs between Mexico and the United States, allowing American farmers to flood Mexican markets with cheap food. The anthropologists further argued that government privatization would lead to the ejido land of the Indians being taken over by local ranchers. Yet several anthropologists, in reports published in *Cultural Survival Quarterly*, presented a somewhat different picture, one that is much more complex than at first understood but which underscored the complexity of politics and collective land tenure.

The Zapatista movement was first assumed to be a radical, Marxist, transformative movement. Very quickly, however, comments from Subcomandante Marcos made it obvious that Zapatista interests were reformative, not transformative. What the Zapatistas wanted was fair democratic representation in a region that had long put power into the hands of old elites: both ranchers who owned their lands as private property and Mayan coffee farmers who owned their lands in collectives, both of whom supported the Institutional Revolutionary Party of Mexico.

George Collier, professor and Chair of the Department of Anthropology at Stanford University, who has been studying agrarian politics in Chiapas since the 1960s, argued that the aim of the Zapatistas was not to overthrow Mexico, or the state of Chiapas, but to reform the corrupt political system that had controlled Mexico since 1926, and which has abandoned the Maya in Chiapas. Collier points out that the Partido Revolucionario Institucional (PRI) redistribution of lands in Chiapas in the 1930s had favored those peasants who could be co-opted by the state.

■Mayan coffee picker holding fresh crop.

Instead of freely giving lands to landless Mayan peasants, the PRI helped to create an elite of coffee growing Indian communities in highland Chiapas, particularly in the community of Chamula.

A closer examination revealed other complexities. The Zapatistas came from the eastern part of lowland Chiapas, where poor migrants from the overpopulated western highlands had moved following trails blazed by loggers in the 1950s. These people were originally Mayan Catholics, like their brethren in the collective coffee lands of the highlands; but in the 1980s, these people abandoned Catholicism in favor of evangelical Protestantism. According to Collier, the Maya of the eastern lowlands shucked ethnic origin for more generic peasant identities (Collier 1994, 15). The reason for converting to Protestantism was in order to escape the demands of the cargo system, described in Chapter 11. Basically, this traditional Catholic ceremonial system puts enormous pressures on Mayan peasants to expend large amounts of money and other wealth on Catholic folk religious celebrations. This practice shores up the collective identity of the Mayan towns, but at the cost of investment in land. The new evangelicals, as the Catholics call them, also became opposed to the PRI; and the PRI responded by dismantling subsidies for the farmers of eastern Chiapas. These populations did, indeed, feel threatened by the opening of markets that were forcing the peasants to compete against falling international prices for their agricultural goods. Maya Indians in the traditional highlands continued to support the PRI and continued to receive subsidies, while in eastern Chiapas, the PRI used harsh tactics to keep peasants in line. Protestants were expelled from highland villages. According to Collier, the government accepted the expulsions as consistent with the rights of natives to prescribe customs in their communities, but he believes this was a justification for supporting "henchmen who wanted to rid themselves of opposition at the local level" (Collier 1994, 17).

Gary Gossen, director of the Institute for Mesoamerican Studies at the State University of New York at Albany, adds further detail. He points out that Chiapas is not ethnically homogenous and that the Maya are many different Maya. Of particular importance in recent years has been the conversion of Maya Indians from the town of San Juan Chamula to Protestantism. Converts were driven out at gunpoint in the 1970s, for Chamula's highly centralized, cacique-controlled municipal government correctly perceived them to be a threat to its authority" (Gossen 1994, 19). Gossen argues:

> The rebels are indeed Maya in origin, ethnicity, and language, yet they are, in a sense, twice-cursed and (perhaps twice politicized), for most of them are both Indians and displaced persons—individuals who have been obliged to seek their destiny as de facto refugees from their Indian communities of origin (Gossen 1994, 19).

Gossen agrees with Collier that it is the NAFTA's threat to small farmers which prompted these Maya to revolt, but that it was not the Indians of the collectively owned lands who were in the Zapatista army. It was unhappiness on the part of Protestant Maya with the authoritarian structure of the predominantly Indian **municipios** that really prompted the attack against highland towns.

> It is ostensibly for this reason that thousands of Maya Protestant converts have lost their landholdings in certain Indian communities since 1965. They have been forcibly expelled as disruptive non-traditional cultural influences. In fact, the Protestant converts have been the most likely to challenge traditional cacique authority, and the caciques have hidden behind state protection of traditional religion to get rid of threats to their political monopoly (Gossen 1994, 20).

Gossen's and other studies show that there has already been a great deal of change in the direction of open markets and that many peasants are no longer real peasants. What is most surprising is that the cargo system and the elders, which have been positively described by many writers, turn out to be linked to the PRI and the source of the alienation of Protestant Maya who form the core of the revolt.

This brings us back to the issue of land tenure among the Maya and other indigenous groups. The issue of land tenure is a complex one that has no simple resolution. In the 1930s, collective ejidos were created in part to gain support for the PRI, but a close examination of the factors leading to the Zapatista Revolution shows that a simple "return to the ejido" is not quite the benevolent option many assume will reinforce Mayan values. Neither does the privatization of older ejidos appear to produce anything other than more conflict.

The complexity of this problem cannot be solved by the simple choice between supporting collective or private property rights. The assumption that the Zapatistas were protesting only threats against the collective ownership of land is not accurate. What is the case is that the Zapatistas were protesting the lack of democratic alternatives between their exploitation at the hands of the ranchers or their alienation from the old collective lands. Their protest underscores the value of the transition to democracy in regions of the world that have been dominated by one-party-states.

ETHNONATIONALIST MOVEMENTS

Not long ago, writers like ourselves (see Smith 1994), were optimistic that the democratic transition and the capitalist transition would be passed through relatively quickly. However, at the same time that democratic reforms were beginning, new anti-democratic movements appeared. Unlike the reformative movements we have just examined, many of the new movements were neither peaceful nor reformative but were, and are, violently transformative and redemptive. They are given the name ethnonationalist. Ethnonationalist movements, unlike the transformative peasant wars such as the Mexi-

---

municipio

Spanish term for a political division that is the equivalent of a township

can, Russian, or Cuban revolutions, are not secular movements. Rather they are movements pushed by those that wish to impose their religions and ethnic values on others, or to carve out separate nation states for themselves. These movements are largely based on terrorism, genocide, and a very different theory of history than the theories that drove peasant revolutions or the civil rights style movements in the United States or the current democratic reform movements discussed below and in the chapters to follow. Examples of these movements are found in the upcoming chapters. In the chapter on Africa, we discuss the genocide in Rwanda and Burundi. In the chapter on the Middle East, we present the rise of Iran, the Moslem fundamentalist movements in Turkey, and the Israeli-Palestinian controversy; and in the chapter on Asia, the conflict between Sikhs and Indians is presented. In this section, we will closely examine the conflict in Bosnia, a state of the former country of Yugoslavia.

One explanation for modern ethnonationalism is that as authoritarian countries begin to democratize; ethnic groups that were never allowed self-expression find a new possibility of grabbing control of the state. Deprivation of ethnic identity, due to its suppression by the state, emerges in the form of ethnonationalism. That is, when old authoritarian or totalitarian states attempt to become democratic, ethnic and religious groups that have been suppressed try to gain control over state policies. This point of view is diametrically the opposite of what social science theory of history originally predicted in theories of modernization (Esman and Rabinovich 1988, 11). Modernization theorists anticipated that democratic reform would lead to secularization and the demise of ethno-religious identity entirely, not its re-emergence. Thus, until recently, the assumption made by social scientists was that democracy leads to secular societies. Social scientists tended to pay scant attention to ethnicity or religion except as background or history to their anti-ethnic theories.

However, democracy and secularism appear to have parted company in certain world regions. The abandonment of socialism has produced violent ethnic and nationalist movements in Eastern Europe and in the Republics of the former Soviet Union. The best-known conflicts are between Armenians and Azerbaijanis in the southwestern part of the Commonwealth of Independent States and between Croats, Muslims, and

■The body of a man is carried away after being killed in a massive suicide bombing of the Ministry of Justice in Baghdad, Iraq. The explosions shook downtown Baghdad during the morning rush hour as people headed to work. Suicide bombing is a form of violent ethnonational warfare.

Serbians in Yugoslavia (particularly in Bosnia). However, these are just two of many nationalist/ethnic conflicts that are occurring throughout Eastern Europe and the Commonwealth. Among the other ethno-nationalist conflicts are those of Bashkirs, Chechen-Ingush, Gagauz, Abkhazians, South Ossetians, Meskhetians, Tatars, Georgians, and Moldovans. The Serb/Croat conflicts will be examined in some detail. The others will not because they are too historically complex to be dealt with in this text and the conflicts are highly similar to each other.

There are several interpretations for the root causes of ethnic violence and genocide, which are very popular right now. One popular argument that is made about ethnic nationalism and conflict in Eastern Europe and the former Soviet Union is that it is very old, in some cases dating back hundreds of years. A second explanation is that ethnic conflict is usually rooted in religious differences, particularly Moslems versus Christians, but also Catholics versus Protestants, and Christian versus Jews. A third point of view is that the two world wars have exacerbated ethnic hatreds as various ethnic populations systematically practiced genocide against one another. Yet another point of view is that the ethnic groups in question identify with specific territories and are fighting for ancient lands.

These arguments, on the surface, make sense. Most of the ethnic conflicts at the present time are, in fact, territorial. Ethnic groups are either trying to gain back control over old lands, or they are trying to expand the lands they control. Religious differences, age-old animosities, conflict over language usage, and cultural differences are all ammunition for nationalist fighters. At the present time there appears to be little that outsiders can do to bring peace. It is as though first there must be a sacrifice of thousands of innocent human beings and a general destruction of the economies of these regions before the fighters will come to their senses. However, these pessimistic views of history may already be challenged by events in regions of the world that are predicted to collapse in paroxysms of ethnic violence.

David Maybury-Lewis argues that such theories about the future of ethnic warfare are too extreme. He argues that ethnic violence depends on the social environment, that it is a response to the policies of states:

> A closer look at ethnicity shows that is not an innate attribute of human behavior, but rather a potential which all of us have and which may or may not be activated. Nor do feelings of ethnic solidarity inevitably lead to conflict when they are activated. It all depends on the context.

He goes on to argue that it is the state "which has to decide whether to recognize their distinctiveness, if so how to accommodate it, and if not how to suppress it" (Maybury-Lewis 1997, xi).

Stanley J. Tambiah of Harvard follows the direction expressed by Maybury-Lewis. He theorizes that these ethnonationalist movements are due to political deprivation imposed on ethnic populations by former socialist states. According to Tambiah, ethnic conflict is the consequence of the perceived political deprivation of certain ethnic groups who have been deprived of power, wealth, or status by other ethnic groups. The Russian anthropologist Valery A. Tishkov gives a similar and interesting interpretation to ethnicity arguing that the real culprit is a theory of history that produced ethno-nationalist policies in socialist states. This theory of history argues that socialist states were organized according to ethnic identity, not democratic equality. Socialist states thus set ethnic groups against ethnic groups. Today, as democratic reforms open these societies, those ethnic groups that had a monopoly on regional control or were discriminated against by socialist states attempt to capture state control; ethnonationalist war ensues.

Soviet Policies and Ethnonationalism

Tishkov, who is director of the Institute of Ethnography and Anthropology of the Russian Academy of Sciences and former Minister of Nationalities in Boris Yeltsin's government, argues that Soviet and East European policies created ethnonationalism. He explains that most East European and Soviet scholars tend to view ethnicity as heavily "primordialistic," based on an academic theory of "ethnos" which overlaps with Marxist-Leninist theory. In Eastern Europe and in the Soviet Union, where most of the ethnic conflict is occurring,

> Anthropological and historical writings provide dominant groups in particular regions with their own cultural heroes, roots (reaching back even into upper paleolithic times), and sense of pride as "indigenous nations" (Tishkov 1994, 444).

This view of ethnicity was tied to the Marxist-Leninist ideology of ethnonationalism that dominated the Soviet state, a state in which ethnic groups legitimated their borders and statuses by forming administrative units or republics:

> The scholarly taxonomic classification of "types of ethnic entities" (tribe, *narodnost*, and nation)—involving such conceptual categories as "ESO" (ethno-social organization) and "ETHNIKOS" (people of the same nationality living outside of their "own" state territories)—justified the administrative statehood granted to what I call titular nationalities (i.e., those which gave titles to republics) (Tishkov 1994, 444).

Ethnonationalism, rather than being a remote and unimportant category of identity, in Eastern Europe and the former Soviet Union was legitimated by Soviet academic studies, which produced policies that shaped the definitions and arguments "of politicians, intellectuals, and the common man" regarding ethnicity. Even recently, Soviet specialists continue to argue in support of ethnic rights—elaborating lists of grievances against others; justifying territorial, political, and cultural rights; and finding people and cultures to blame. The scholars "explain events in terms of materialistic, economic, and social class analyses: a simplistic, culturally based, we-they dichotomy" (Tishkov 1994, 445). In short, scholars in the former Soviet Union and Eastern Europe, by using socialist theories of ethnic identity, may be part of the problem rather than the solution.

Tishkov goes on to explain that ethnonationalism was extremely popular among European social democrats in the nineteenth and early twentieth century, and was used to form a new political map of Eastern Europe after World War I. During and after the Revolution of 1917, Lenin and the Bolsheviks used the slogan of ethnic self-determination to win non-Russians to their side; ethnonationalism became the basis on which socialist federalism was based. All Soviet constitutions embodied the principle of a right to self-determination for ethno-nations:

> But it should be stressed that this "brave" social experiment arose within the context of one-party, totalitarian rule and strict centralization enforced from Moscow (Tishkov 1994, 447).

The principle of ethno-nationhood was not equally applied, however; and in each territory one ethnic group or another was recognized as having superior rights, often given the power to be the governing group. In other words, the socialism of the Soviet Union and Eastern Europe was not egalitarian socialism with all persons having equality before the state but rather the purposeful creation of ethnic republics ruled by dominant ethnic groups within a socialist national framework, in turn ruled by Russians. Relative deprivation was the inevitable consequence of such discrimination, and ethnonationalist warfare is the current consequence.

Tishkov believes that such a social system has made it extremely difficult to create even the most rudimentary civil institutions in Eastern Europe and in the former Soviet Union:

> Ethno-nationalism became prominent as an alternative to a strong, centralized state with ineffective representation at the local level. It called on romantic, emotional images for a new form of solidarity without necessarily resolving the problems of democratic representation at the local level. If and how these are to be resolved under ethnonationalism remains to be seen.... After decades of literary and practical nation building, ethno-nationalism has become entwined in a wide spectrum of public ideologies and political mentalities. It has won considerable social support. And peristroika greatly facilitated the process (Tishov 1994, 448).

David Maybury-Lewis presents a similar argument in his book *Indigenous Peoples, Ethnic Groups, and the State* (1997). He points out that after the Russian revolution, Lenin wrote a constitution in which Russians would be one of a number of equal peoples within the Soviet state. After Lenin's death, Stalin went on to organize the Soviet Union along ethnic lines, but not in any egalitarian sense. Instead, he organized Soviet states into administrative hierarchies. At the apex were the Soviet Socialist Republics, each conceptualized as the domain of a particular ethnic group. In addition, there were autonomous republics and autonomous districts and national regions, each also defined in terms of an ethnic nationality. Stalin, and Lenin before him, assumed that ethnicity and nationalism would fade as socialism became dominant; but in practice, certain ethnic groups always gained greater rights than others, and Russians formed the upper echelon of government everywhere. People who were given special rights could use their own language, publish their own books, and maintain their religions. At the same time other groups did not receive state recognition and were denied their cultural heritage. Thus, from the beginning of Soviet rule, certain ethnic groups were relatively deprived as opposed to others (Maybury-Lewis 1997).

This same model was used in Yugoslavia and in other East European socialist states. The dissolution of socialism brought about the collapse of the Soviet Union, but it also brought about the collapse or near collapse of other socialist countries, such as Yugoslavia. Powerful armies had suppressed ethnic conflict in "socialist" ethno-states for the better part of this century. With the collapse of socialism, various ethnic populations have demanded the right to rule themselves and to create their own countries, no matter how tiny.

From Anti-Capitalist to Pro-Capitalist Movements

Theories of history have championed distinct kinds of movements throughout this century. Radical transformative movements of a largely secular, socialist type drove movements around the world outside of the core countries until very recently. These movements will be examined in the chapters which follow, largely tied to the disintegration of colonialism around the world. The revolutionary movements described were, for the most part, anti-systemic (anti-capitalist), but they were not based on ethnicity. They were anti-capitalist and non-democratic, although they may have had the patina of democracy. They were anti-systemic because the system, global capitalism,

Case
Study

Ethnonationalist Movements in Bosnia

Particularly troubling in the 1990s were the civil wars in the disintegrating country of Yugoslavia, particularly in Bosnia, a state of former Yugoslavia. The civil wars, which started in the summer of 1991 with federal military action to suppress separatist movements in the Yugoslavian states of Slovenia, Croatia, and in the spring of 1992, Bosnia-Herzegovina, killed more than two hundred thousand soldiers and civilians, wrecked the economy of central Yugoslavia, and created a half-million refugees. As a result, Yugoslavia no longer exists.

The Communist order that held Yugoslavia together began to disintegrate as early as 1986, and entered a crisis in December of 1989, which the international community failed to recognize (Burg 1993, 363). Yugoslavia was a federation of the south Slavic peoples created in 1918. Yugoslavia united the unstable ethnic enclaves of Slovenia, Croatia, Bosnia-Herzegovina, Serbia, Montenegro, and Macedonia (from north to south). Yugoslavia was invaded and occupied by German and Italian forces in World War II. The Germans allied themselves with various ethnic groups with whom they had historical connections, such as Slovenes and Croats, and used these peoples to subjugate the region committing genocide, particularly against Serbs. When the war was over, the Yugoslav Communists (mostly Serbs), led by the Croatian

Joseph Broz Tito, were militarily dominant. Yugoslavia became a communist republic in 1946.

Conflict between all of these groups was continuous throughout history, although it subsided under Tito. However, in the 1980s, ethnic conflict emerged again due to economic differences (Goldman 1992, 171). Under Tito, a single ethnic group dominated each state of Yugoslavia. Serbia was under Serb control, and other ethnic groups had few rights. Croatia was under Croat control, etc. As the Yugoslav state began to disintegrate and democratic options opened up, and as the world stood back waiting for a new democracy to emerge, the various distinct ethnic groups attempted, instead, to wrest the control of each emerging state for themselves.

The ethnic conflict began when Albanians living in Kosovo province in southern Yugoslavia, which was under Serb control, attacked Serbs and Montenegrans. Albanians tried to terrorize the Serbs (Goldman 1992, 171). Serb resentment of Albanians mounted; and they looked for help in state and Serb party authorities, particularly Slobodan Milosevic, who became the President of Serbia and encouraged pro-Serb, anti-Albanian rallies throughout the republic. He attempted to establish Serb control of the political system by taking over the police, courts, and civil defense in southern Yugoslavia.

Serb nationalists gained control of the Yugoslavian military, particularly the air force, while Yugoslavia began to disintegrate into its constituent territories (Slovenia, Croatia, Bosnia-Herzegovina, Montenegro, and Macedonia). As Yugoslavia disintegrated, Serbs in Serbia and those living as ethnic enclaves in the other emerging states tried to increase the size of Serbia or tried to take control of the regions they lived in, causing civil war.

Of the former states of Yugoslavia, it is Bosnia-Herzegovina that came to suffer the most. Bosnia-Herzegovina is a multi-ethnic state composed of ethnic Muslims (44 percent), Serbs (31 percent), and Croats (17 percent); Yugoslavs form only 6 percent of the population. The three ethnic groups are separated, not so much by ethnic differences, but by their histories and religious beliefs. The Bosnian election of 1990 produced a polarized political situation between Croats, Serbs, and Muslims. This

Figure 7A

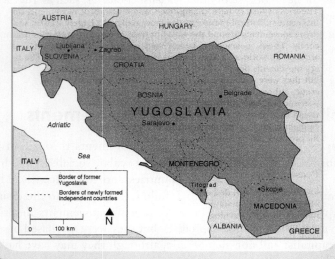

⬜ **Contemporary Map of Former Yugoslavia**

AUSTRIA
HUNGARY
ITALY
Ljubljana · Zagreb
SLOVENIA
CROATIA
ROMANIA
BOSNIA
· Belgrade
YUGOSLAVIA
Adriatic
Sarajevo ·
ITALY
Sea
MONTENEGRO
Titograd
· Skopje
MACEDONIA
ALBANIA
GREECE

— Border of former Yugoslavia
----- Borders of newly formed independent countries

0
0   100 km
▲ N

was resolved with a coalition government composed of representatives of the three ethnic groups. However, Croats and Serbs in Bosnia wanted to join a "greater Serbia" and "greater Croatia." Civil war ensued. The United Nations and NATO agreed to prevent the Muslims from arming themselves, and the civil war soon turned to a genocidal attack with Serbs and Croats carrying out "ethnic cleansing" of Muslims in their ethnic regions. Both tried to expand their territories.

Serbs were fighting Muslims and Croatians, and these two ethnic groups fought each other and the Serbs. Muslim women were forced into "rape camps." The city of Sarajevo (where World War I began with the assassination of Archduke Ferdinand, the heir to the throne of Austria and Hungary) was subject to continuous bombardment by Serb forces in the surrounding hills. The problem from hell was born. United Nations peace keeping forces, from time to time, had brought cease-fires to the fighting and opened the airport at Sarajevo so humanitarian supplies could get in to the population.

However, the fighting continued until 1995, with the Dayton Accords, when the United States and the United Nations forced peace on the three groups. This was followed by an imposition of peace when the United Nations, with a contingent of American forces, brought the fighting to an end by using the threat of force in Bosnia-Herzegovina.

The ethnonationalist theories of Croatian and Serb leaders produced civil war, and they led to an invasion by NATO, as well as an economic boycott by the United Nations, NATO, the United States, and Western Europe. Ultimately, the boycott led to economic suffering. In addition, a new type of relative deprivation evolved in the early months of 1997. Many had not supported the ethnonationalist ideas of Slobodan Milosevic and suffered the images of themselves as racists. In early 1997, these groups began massive protests. This new movement in Serbia resembled the democratic reform movements that brought an end to socialism in Poland, Hungary, and the rest of Eastern Europe.

was viewed as a danger which would destroy weak systems. Today, the anti-system systems, socialism and state capitalism, are being abandoned because they have not worked. Recently, peaceful pro-capitalist movements have emerged.

PEASANT WARS

Eric Wolf has shown that modernization had the initial impact of disturbing age-old ecological adaptations of peasants to their environments and their tributary relationship to governing elites (Wolf 1966, 1982). In traditional societies, peasants may be exploited by elites but certain minimal rights are also protected. With the introduction of colonial capitalism and the disappearance of tributary rights, peasants were exploited more than they had been before the introduction of capitalism (Wolf 1982). The new transformation set off violent revolutions in various core countries. The first wave of revolutions occurred in the nineteenth century in western and eastern Europe. Most of these early revolutions have been called "peasant revolutions" (Wolf 1969, 1982). Two major examples are the French Revolution of 1789 and the German Revolution of 1848 (Hobsbawm 1962, Wolf 1969).

A second wave of violent socialist movements began outside of the core in the periphery in the twentieth century as the destructive characteristics of capitalism spread through colonialism. Why was democratic capitalism successful in the core but destructive in the peripheries? While capitalism and democracy were key driving forces behind reformist movements in the core, the democratic component was blocked by the core and local elites in the periphery. This is because the elites in the periphery were put into power by the elites of the core, they were anti-democratic, and they wanted to retain power. The revolts were the consequence of relative deprivation, oppression by local elites, and blockages to modernization. Most of the revolts were radical, anti-core, revolutions with theories of history that were anti-capitalist. The consequence was the development of a series of radical, secular, communist/socialist societies, many of which were also anti-democratic and were often also against religion (Wolf 1969, 1982, Huntington 1993). A short list provided by Eric Wolf in his study of peasant revolutions in the twentieth century includes Mexico (1910–1917), Russia (1918–1921), Algeria (1958–1961), China (1946–1949), and Vietnam (1963–1975) (Wolf 1969). Indirect spin offs from these major revolutions occurred throughout Central America and South America, Africa, and Asia. All of these movements turned out to be against religion because religion was viewed as part of the old traditional social system, which exploited the peasant classes.

PRO-CAPITALIST REFORMATIVE MOVEMENTS

Each of the next four chapters ends by examining the emergence of new reformist movements. These largely democratic social movements began in the 1980s and are occurring now (Huntington 1993, 1996). Samuel Huntington refers to these movements as the "third wave" (the first wave was the nineteenth century European revolutions; the second was the transformative revolutions just discussed). This third wave appears to be tied to the process of globalization, which was explained in Chapter 6. The most recent social movements are difficult to classify because many of the movements have yet to consolidate into identifiable political forms. Most of these are reformist movements; they are largely anti socialist and favor free market systems and multi-party democracies.

These movements have so far not been violent (an exception is the Zapatista revolt in southern Mexico); they do not seek to overthrow the state. Instead, they are seeking to reform their institutions so they will provide incentives to escape poverty and create prosperity. However, and inevitably, as open market reforms begin to take effect, the reforms create distortions between haves and have nots. That is, those with wealth and power gain more wealth and power; and those without get less, producing relative deprivation and explosive political tensions (and an example here is the Zapatista Revolution). The only way to resolve these tensions is through democratic reform, the demands for which often follow directly after the introduction of capitalism making it difficult to separate the two transitions anywhere. These pro-capitalist, pro-democratic reform movements are occurring throughout eastern Europe and in parts of the Soviet Union, but are also occurring in Africa, Latin America, and other regions of the periphery. We will examine these movements in the chapters to come. These reformist movements are not transformative peasant revolts as were the earlier ones but are, instead, largely made up of urban and industrial peoples who have become disillusioned with the promises of socialism and communism (Huntington 1993). The movements can best be classified as reformative because they are gradualist, moving a step at a time to dismantle communism and socialism. While a few movements began as transformative, such as Russia in 1991, by 1996–1997, they had slowed down to move a step at a time because of the complexity of reform. The movements are also reformative rather than transformative because they are not utopian or millenarian; that is, the leaders do not believe that society can be magically transformed overnight, as did the revolutionary leaders of the early twentieth century.

■   ■   ■

Chapter
Summary

Ethnicity, Ethnic Conflict, and Social Movements

While the end of the Cold War was greeted with relief and the hope for the end of hostilities around the world, such has not happened. Hostilities have actually increased dramatically. While in the United States civil rights movements are losing their ideological vigor, ethnonationalism in former socialist countries threatens the regional stability of Eastern Europe and the Middle East. The capacity of the United States to bring about peace in former Yugoslavia is being tested by the complexity of the issue, and the same is true in the Middle East. At the same time, new democratic movements are occurring in formerly authoritarian and totalitarian parts of world. As part of this budding new democracy, indigenous groups are developing strategies to reclaim ancient lands and revitalize cultural heritages.

There are many complex transitions that we have to examine around the world which have to do with the creation of a new world, one that could not have been imagined just half a century ago. It does not rest on socialism, the promise of the past, but on the very democratic capitalism, which was once thought such a threat. However, the transitions to capitalism and democracy are not easy; they may undermine traditional ways of life. We will spend time in the next four chapters trying to grasp these complex issues. Anthropology has a claim to explanations regarding these complex issues, and in the following chapters we will gain a better understanding of the future role of this extraordinary discipline.

Chapter
Terms

acculturation	249	municipio	268
alterative movement	259	redemptive movement	259
assimilation	249	reference group	257
civil rights movement	245	reformative movement	258
ethnicity	245	relative deprivation	254
ethnocide	247	resource mobilization	256
ethnonationalism	260	sectarian movement	259
indigenismo	262	social movement	257
indigenous	264	transformative movement	257
multiculturalism	250		

Check out our website
www.BVTLab.com
for flashcards,
chapter summaries,
and more.

Chapter 8
Africa: Overcoming a Colonial Legacy

Modern Africa is a troubled land. Europeans substantially altered Africa's history through the dramatic expansion of slavery in West Africa and mineral exploitation in East and South Africa. In the late nineteenth century, Africa south of the Sahara was divided among European states; and then in the middle of this century it began a slow emergence into independent, but troubled African states. Hunger, disease and ethnic violence have replaced the once utopian hopes of social planners in the 1950s and 1960s. Africa enjoys geographic and geological riches that should be more than adequate to insure prosperity. However, Africa is a continent of great diversity containing vast deserts and rainforest. The problems of living in these extremes contribute to low population densities. The harsh nature of the environment makes transaction costs very high and has contributed to slow economic development, and even the best of intentions are blocked. Deserts and rainforests make the construction of roads and railroads in certain regions extremely expensive. In West Africa, an inhospitable climate supports dangerous endemic diseases such as malaria, river blindness (onchocerciasis), and African sleeping sickness (trypanosomiasis), borne by the tsetse fly and dangerous to both humans and cattle. Cholera is re-emerging as a ravaging disease in regions where it has not been seen for decades. Both cholera and the tsetse fly have had a devastating effect on the transitions to political and economic development. AIDS is also reducing the capacity of certain African countries to modernize, particularly Uganda and Zaire (Weeks 1992).

Drought along the Sahel region south of the Sahara has caused the deterioration of ecological conditions to the point where populations can no longer survive. In vast regions, certain problems of adaptation may be

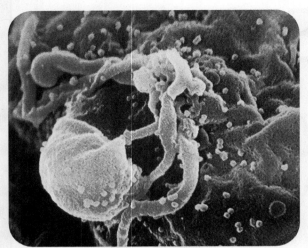

■An electron micrograph of HIV-1 budding from a cultured white blood cell. The AIDS virus is reducing the capacity of certain African countries' ability to modernize.

the consequence of ecological mismanagement, such as the misuse of water and the mismanagement of rangeland. European colonial intervention helps to explain some, but not all, of modern Africa's problems. Drought and brush fires in Ghana, Cote d'Ivoire, Togo, and Benin have transformed forests into deserts. These same forests are natural resources that could sustain logging; however, uncontrolled cutting has often led to deforestation and then to desertification (Sullivan 1989, 59). The *harmattan*, a dry wind that blows out of the Sahara in January and February, has exacerbated drought and helped the spread of desertification (Sullivan 1989, 15).

In pre-colonial times, sub-Saharan Africa was a land that spawned numerous chiefdoms and tributary states which were involved in extensive trade networks extending across the continent, linking with the trade routes of North Africa and the Mediterranean. This picture contradicts the one presented by the first anthropologists to venture into Africa, who portrayed pre-colonial Africa as a continent of isolated, autonomous tribes. A more balanced perspective on Africa's past and present may be gained by examining the human ecology and political economy of pre-colonial Africa.

Africa and Anthropology in the Twentieth Century

Africa has played a special role in the development of anthropology as a discipline and has acted as a giant mirror reflecting the excesses of anthropological theorizing (Moore 1994). The first theories showed Africa to be what European intellectuals wanted it to be: a land of primitive tribes remote from European civilization, a pre-capitalist cultural Eden which could show scholars what very ancient Europe must have looked at during the Stone Age.

In the 1930s, anthropologists turned away from evolutionary speculations and tried to move in two other directions. The first was to search modern Africa for its prehistoric tribal roots, a search for how pre-modern societies were functionally integrated into systems of social production, economy, clanship, and religion. This approach was called structural-functionalism as expressed in the writings of Bronislaw Malinowski, who had first written about tribal society in Melanesia, and whose theoretical perspective profoundly influenced African scholars when he was appointed the first chair in anthropology at the University of London (London School of Economics). Modernization was viewed as the destroyer of African tribal society.

During this period of anthropological research, roughly from the turn of the last century to the 1960s, Africa was under the control of European colonists. Europeans had monopolized long distance trade, particularly in East Africa, for well over a century. The Europeans had also pacified African societies, imposing European administrators and their courts on traditional African society. Tribal societies, it appeared, had little to no trade and were functionally integrated into small egalitarian communities. The anthropologists were often philosophically opposed to European rule, but only the very few dared to challenge colonial authorities. Overall, there was the unquestioning acceptance that a tribal Africa had preceded the colonial period, and that anthropologists' job was either to find out what

Figure 8.1

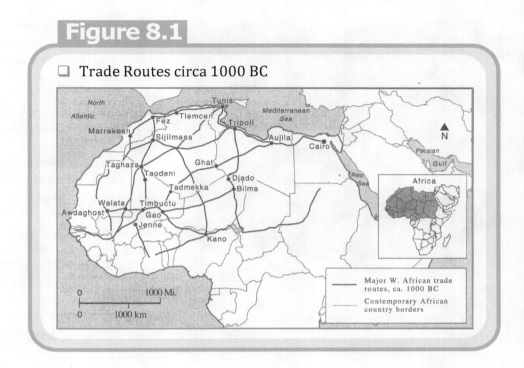

☐ Trade Routes circa 1000 BC

that tribal society was really like before the introduction of colonial rule or to describe the impact of modernization. The idea that pre-contact societies might have resembled European or Asiatic empires was not seriously considered. The anthropologists were searching for the exotic, the traditional, and/or the pre-modern. Exotic tribes were needed to substantiate the thesis of a pre-colonial tribal existence.

The structural-functionalism of Malinowski and Radcliffe-Brown and their students and colleagues resulted in numerous classic ethnographies containing detailed studies of kinship, social organization, economic organization, and religion and magic. Underlying most of these studies were two orienting assumptions: all aspects of culture were believed to be interrelated; and the societies themselves were considered to be highly static, essentially unchanging, and always tending toward, if not actually being in, a state of equilibrium. Characteristic of the African ethnographies of this period was a strong emphasis on cultural ideals often to the virtual exclusion of descriptions of real behavior that deviated from the ideals.

To researchers, Africa had become a place of urban moderns (those who had accepted western ways) versus rural tribes (those who had not become western). Those who worked on these two subjects (modern and tribal) had a tendency to keep the two topics separate, and a reader of their studies today would have the impression that urban Africans and tribal Africans lived into two different worlds.

In the 1950s and 1960s, Africans began to throw off the yoke of colonialism. African writers in the newly independent African states became critical of the theories of anthropologists. Africans felt that they had been pigeonholed as tribal others, which really had little to do with their own histories or experiences. At the same time, the structural-functional equation came to be replaced by a multiplicity of interests in archaeology, kinship, gender, economic development, political change, art, religion, and many other topics. The idea that societies were structurally bound into systems began to fade as the complexity of Africa replaced an assumed tribal simplicity.

■Maasai warrior in traditional dress. The Maasai are a well-known tribe and ethnic group of Kenya. Some view modernization as the destroyer of African tribal society.

In the past few decades, archaeologists have unearthed ancient civilizations in sub-Saharan Africa that have characteristics very similar to other ancient states we have examined. These characteristics include trade, war, empire building, the importance of hierarchy in the central place, and the existence of non-hierarchical societies at the peripheries. The notion of African society as tribal society has been replaced with that of an Africa which is no more traditional than any other world-region. Many writers are resolving the distinction between the urban modern and the "tribal other" by doing away with these simplistic and contrived distinctions. Does the term tribal still have meaning? Only if one realizes that tribe is not an evolutionary stage but rather an adaptive level of sociopolitical integration which frequently occurs at the peripheries of core states.

As to anthropology's early tendency to overtheorize, Sally Falk Moore writes,

> Anthropology is older and wiser now. It is clear that in all societies there are newly invented elements that are given legitimacy and prestige by being labeled traditional [tribal]. Local assertions of what is traditional are just that—assertions. They do not necessarily constitute an account of actual happenings in the historic past (Moore 1994, 128).

The Geography and Ethnography of Africa

When talking about Africa, what is most striking is the diversity of the cultures that exist on this continent, as well as the diversity of the environments in which they live. To begin, Africa is immense. It is fifty-two hundred miles from Tangier in North Africa to Capetown in the far south; and it is forty-six hundred miles from Dakar in the far west to Cape Guardafui, the easternmost point of the African horn (Bohannen and Curtin 1995). For the most part, this chapter focuses on the peoples south of the Sahara, primarily because the Middle East includes much of North Africa, which is discussed in the chapter to follow. However, the distinctions between geographic regions are Eurocentric; no assessment of Africa can exclude ancient Egypt, which will be included in the following.

Despite the distinction of Middle East and Africa, the Arabian Peninsula is part of the African continent. The Rift Valley, which cuts through Africa, begins in northern Turkey, forms the Jordan Valley, the Dead Sea, and the Red Sea, and cuts a vertical swathe down through to Lake Rudolf. The rift divides and spreads around Lake Victoria, joining again at the head of Lake Nyasa; and then it runs south to the Shire and Zambezi river valleys. The rift forms some of the deepest lakes on earth and is part of one of the most ancient trade routes (Bohannen and Curtin 1995, 19). Along the Nile, in the rift valley to the south, and into southern Africa were found chiefdoms and kingdoms from prior to the colonial period.

Some of the prominent rivers such as the Niger, the Nile, the Volta, the Zambezi, and the Congo end in basins that empty into the sea. However, most rivers fall off steep escarpments into the sea, limiting navigation from the sea for most of the continent. Not only is navigation difficult but also the environment seriously constrains the development of agriculture. While the northern and southern ends of Africa enjoy a Mediterranean-like climate and vegetation, just inland vast deserts and arid plains cover thousands of square miles. Humid forests straddle the equator producing gallery forests along major streams. These tropical forest zones have little topsoil and do not lend themselves easily to permanent field agriculture. Going south and north are found true deserts, the Kalahari and Sahara. Between the humid forests and deserts are extensive savannas, which occupy the greatest number of square miles in Africa. The savanna is made of stretches of tall grass, intermittent bush, and scattered trees; and it is this habitat that played the greatest role in the development of the human ecology of Africa in pre-colonial times. Of particular importance was the development of a combination of **settled farming** and **transhumance herding**. Settled farming tended to occur in those regions where rainfall resources or irrigation from rivers would support settled villages. An example would be the Nile River Valley, which has supported settled villages for well over four thousand years. Often viewed as an opposite form of adaptation, in fact, the herding of cattle, sheep, goats, or camels was often combined with settled villages. For example, the settled village and town populations along the Nile and elsewhere often also supported herders who had to find grasses to forage at some distance from home. Other peoples practiced true transhumance herding, going back and forth over the landscape as though it were a giant carpet, using the settled towns and villages for trade purposes. Often members of their families would settle in the villages and act as intermediaries between settled agriculturalists and transhumance herders. These should not be thought of as opposite poles of adaptation but rather as options or alternatives ranging from settled villages to transhumance herders with all combinations in between.

settled farming

Farming that occurs in regions where rainfall resources or irrigation from rivers supports settled villages

transhumance herding

The herding of cattle, sheep, goats, or camels by going back and forth over the landscape, using the settled towns and villages for trade purposes

Political Ecology, Trade, and Empire Building

One of the first observations coming from the study of Africa is that empires and states are not new but have an ancient history based on trade and human adaptations to natural habitats, and transhumance herding has been of great importance. The political ecology of Africa, before the period of European colonial domination, can be explained, at least in part, as hegemonic empire building to reduce transaction costs of trade following a tremendous arc running from Egypt in the north to the Zambezi River valley in the south.

The cores of empires shifted through time, primarily due to changes in the importance of trade routes and the rise of imperial states outside of Africa (Rome, Byzantium). However, with the colonial period, the collapse of trade and the imposition of European rule led to the destruction of indigenous institutions, particularly along the trade route running south of Egypt, through the Rift Valley, and down to what is now called the Lake Country of Central Africa (Ensminger 1992). In the modern period, attempts to create new institutional structures have been met with many frustrations, which will be described in this chapter.

VILLAGE AGRICULTURE

The evolution into a food-producing way of life occurred between 7000–8000 BC in Africa and the Middle East. There is more known about this transition in the Middle East than in Africa, particularly in the hilly flanks region just north of the Tigris and Euphrates Rivers (discussed in Chapter 4).

The evidence for a neolithic way of life is, however, strong in the Nile River Valley, particularly in the dry Fayum Depression just south of Sakkara and Memphis. The Fayum Depression was the site of a lake fed by the Nile River that supplied villagers with water for crops and herding. Houses were small, semisubterranean, oval houses with mud walls.

In both Southwest Asia and northeastern Africa, the first movement towards crop cultivation began with the gathering of wild grain. There were natural concentrations of heavy yielding grasses known as cereals. While wheat and barley were domesticated in Southwest Asia, the people of Egypt and Nubia (south of Egypt's first cataract) cultivated certain strains of wild barley perhaps as far back as 10,000 BC. Sorghum and millets originated in northeast Africa and were harvested in the Khartoum region of the upper Nile by 6000 BC. People decreased their reliance on hunting and increased their dependence on domesticated plants and also animals. With the development of farming, people began to settle down in permanent settlements, and populations increased in size. Women could bear more children and care for them, and more children meant more labor. These early communities, however, did not become completely dependent on agriculture for some time, continuing a partially hunting and gathering existence. The climate was wetter then and provided some vegetation west and east of the Nile. Gradually, the climate dried out to the point where there was no rainfall and the desert encroached the banks of the Nile. Between 5000 and 4000 BC, permanent settlements of full time farmers became established in the Nile and adapted their farming techniques to the river's annual flooding. By 3500 BC those north of the first cataract had combined to form the kingdoms of Upper and Lower Egypt.

Crop cultivation, based on barley and wheat, spread along the Mediterranean margins of North Africa. The region south of the Sahara was far wetter between 8000 and 4000 years ago than it is today. A belt of rivers and lakes stretched across the continent from the upper Niger delta in the west, through Lake Chad, to the upper Nile. Large settlements of fishing communities developed, but they turned to farming as the region became drier after 4000 BC. The Sahara Desert spread, rivers declined, and lakes disappeared. Between 3000 and 1000 BC, Neolithic farming spread throughout this growing savannah belt. (Shillington 1989, 30–31).

The new farming way of life spread to the tropical zones of West Africa, and new crops were domesticated for a distinct forested ecological zone. Considerable evidence from the Cameroons in West Africa depicts a way of life dependent on palm nuts, yams, fruits, and goats by 1000 BC. Most people south of the equator remained hunters and food gatherers until iron was introduced two thousand years ago, at which time tropical agriculture spread south and eastward through the forest zones, finally reaching the region of southern Zaire and northern Angola (Shillington 1989, 31).

Gold was mined and traded throughout West Africa, and it was an important factor in state evolution. Several trade empires flourished in West Africa before the colonial period. Islamic trade states also emerged, such as the Songhay Empire, the state of Kanem and Borno near Lake Chad, and the Hausa and Yoruba of Nigeria.

Divine Kings, Trade States, and African Art   These pre-colonial states shared certain characteristics. At the center was a divine king whose well-being and the well-being of his people were combined. If the divine king was healthy, so were his people. If he became sick, his people suffered. Towns were unusually large, and urbanization was tied to trade. Each region had its own king, usually a patrilineal kinsman of the divine king, whose powers were similar. These states were commercial emporiums (Smith 1988, 6). The divine king usually had a monopoly over all trade, and the most important single trade article was cloth. West African states offered security along the trade routes combined with specialization in agriculture and crafts and markets occurred here on a larger scale than anywhere else in Africa. Men and women had highly developed artistic skills for the production of objects made out of wood, stone, ivory, terracotta, or cast out of bronze, brass, and iron. Modern collectors of art around the world venerate many of these objects. One of the modern ethnic groups of West Africa with a reputation for the production of African art is the Yoruba, whose ancestors once formed the kingdom of Yoruba, a state level society.

PASTORALISM: THE CATTLE KEEPERS

Cattle were a source of wealth, prestige, and social status for many pastoralists in East Africa, and led to divisions between rich and poor and a domination of women by men. The importance of cattle has led writers to name this economy the cattle complex. Men were the keepers of the cattle; women grew food and processed it. The wealth of a man depended on the number of wives he had and their children. Cattle were traded for women, and alliances formed between elite cattle herders were based on the exchange of women for cattle (cattle cemented the marital union). As men grew older, they ceased to

Figure 8.2

❏ **West African States, AD 1000**

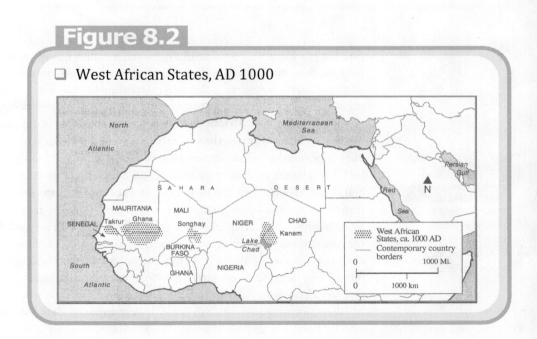

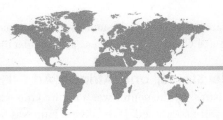

Case Study

The Yoruba

Settled village agriculture reached state levels of organization about a thousand years after the introduction of agriculture to West Africa. The Yoruba of modern Nigeria are the descendants of one of the many pre-colonial states of West Africa; they are typical of the tropical agricultural societies of the region. The homeland of the Yoruba is ecologically variable, stretching from swamps and lagoons of the coast across rainforests, and rises towards the oil palm bush and woodland savannah at the bend of the Niger. It is a fertile region, watered by many rivers and streams. The Yoruba kingdom depended on a form of food production common to West Africa: mixed crop agriculture, which included the common yam, the cocoyam, plantain, its close relative the banana, kola trees, and oil palm. In the sixteenth century, cassava and maize were introduced from South America (Smith 1988, 4).

While there was one major king, the Alafin, the society was organized into twenty or more kingdoms with some, but not all, ruled by members of the same patrilineage, often known as obas. In the extreme north was found the great capital city of Oyo, where the Alafin, or sacred king, lived; and a hundred miles to the south was Ile Ife, the spiritual center of the Yoruba people. The kingdom of the Yoruba at one time occupied a region as large as England. Today the Yoruba form one of the largest ethnic groups in Africa's most populous country of Nigeria. Many of the modern chiefs are descended from the obas and have the same title and sacred qualities. They often find themselves in conflict with the modern state of Nigeria. Because the formation of modern states is based on former colonial divisions, which were seldom congruent with the territories of ethnic groups, modern Yoruba are also found in the neighboring republics of Benin and Togo. When the Portuguese arrived in the fifteenth century, the Yoruba had already been organized into major and minor states for several hundred years.

Yoruba traditional religious ideas, with origins in the state and body of the divine king, were incorporated into the Islamic faith after the tenth century. Of particular importance to Yoruba religion was the idea of journey, particularly of the human spirit, through birth, death, and reincarnation. Yoruba men and women, as slaves, brought their religion to the New World where it became Candomble in Brazil and Santeria in Cuba and modern Miami and New York. Ritual parties occur in New York City led by priests of the Yoruba deity Obatala (Drewal 1992). In Brazil, Santa Barbara of the Thunder, a Catholic deity, is the reincarnation of Oba, the Yoruba goddess of the river Oba and the third wife of the god Xango; market vendor priests are obas, the ministers of Xango.

---

care for the cattle and became the managers of the work of women and of young cattle herders, their male children. The man who was successful in marriage, who expanded the size of his herd, whose male children married successfully, and who was successful in giving his daughters in marriage to other successful men became regarded as a chief.

Shillington, the African historian, points out that through a process of natural increase, a herd of fewer than twenty cattle could multiply to several thousand in one human generation, allowing men to accumulate wealth which their male offspring inherited. Cattle were used as bride wealth, and men with large herds could thus acquire several wives. Women were the main cultivators of the land, and **polygyny** (the marriage of a man to more than one woman) increased a man's ability to feed a large family and added to his wealth. Cattle could also be used in trade. Men with no cattle became dependent on the wealthy, and those with many head of cattle owned the material basis for the status of chief (Shillington 1989, 147). When cattle herders were able to monopolize trade and owned very large herds of cattle, they became an upper class, in some cases a kind of aristocracy. Those who failed as cattle keepers became tillers of the land or herded the cattle of others, forming a lower class. Alternatively, cattle herders dominated foreign groups of

polygyny

Marriage between one male and two or more females forming multi-family social structures

■In what came to be known as the Cattle Complex, stock were traded for women and through this exchange, alliances were formed. The number of cattle owned determined wealth, prestige, and social status.

subsistence agriculturalists. However, under normal circumstances, the constant movement of cattle kept the social structure fluid; and the rise to power of chiefs and the development of states was relatively rare.

Cattle were important in economic transactions and were used almost like money. They also had tremendous symbolic value. There was a whole system of beliefs surrounding cattle that prevented their regular slaughter for food. (However, there is also evidence that the prevalence of ritual occasions gave cattle subsistence value.). Thomas Barfield underlines the importance of cattle:

> The symbolic value of cattle among East African pastoralists was so high and their use in social transactions so critical that they literally defined the cultural order ... Raiding for cattle, lending them to friends, exchanging them in marriages, sacrificing them in rituals, decorating their bodies and singing their praises was an end in itself: pleasing to the mind and giving life a purpose (Barfield 1993, 36–37).

When successful and in the center of trade, these pastoral populations expanded and transformed into states ruled by kings whose control was reinforced by developed or borrowed myths that gave them divine status as god kings. When Europeans began to dominate the region, they often allowed the upper class aristocrats to continue ruling (as was true in Uganda, Rwanda, and Burundi).

In Chapter 4, we briefly examined pastoral nomadism as an ecological adaptation. The pastoral region of Africa lies south of the Sahara, running west to east in the Sahel across the whole of Africa, and north to south in the savanna grasslands of East Africa, following the line of the Great Rift Valley (Barfield 1993, 4–7). There are no true "nomadic" pastoralists in sub-Saharan Africa; most combine cattle with agriculture (Middleton 1995).

In some areas the maintenance of large mammals, particularly cattle, sheep, and goats, precedes agriculture. Sites in the northern African states of modern Algeria and Libya show very early pastoral societies, dating as far back as 7000 BC. The most important animals were sheep and goats, with cattle becoming most important after 4000 BC. Cave paintings show every aspect of domestic life: huge herds of long-horned cattle are cared for by people of Mediterranean and Negroid types who wear woven cloth, had elaborate ornaments and hairstyles, and used round pots to store milk and cattle blood.

The presence of grinding stones suggests that they harvested grain and were part time agriculturalists, not unlike the modern Maasai of Kenya. It is thought that cattle displaced other nomadic mammals, and that overgrazing may have led to rapid and final desiccation of the Sahara after 2500 BC.

Pastoralists south of the Sahel and throughout East Africa have very similar social structures. Patrilineal descent is combined with age set associations or sodalities. The age set determines the status of distinct generations, as well as privileges and responsibilities of a male through a lifetime. Herding is young men's work; they go off during the day and return to the compounds, called cattle kraals, in the late afternoon or evening.

These populations had a common adaptation, but also had distinct ethnic identities (which would include language and religion). They were migratory pastoralists who managed livestock through communal land tenure of pastures. This combined with the ownership and management of the herds by individuals (Bennett 1993, 293). That is, tribes or clans did not own cattle or other forms of livestock collectively. Producers moved with the herds, or they settled in villages. They combined semipermanent residence with transhumance in order to maximize the use of pasture. Pasture was seasonally variable. Since the herds moved at intervals, it was impossible to assign permanent ownership of land. Instead, a complex legal code evolved regarding use rights to land and water. A cattle owner's rights to graze his stock were derived from his membership in a grazing group, which was usually a tribal subsection holding customary rights in different regions.

Herd owners worked out mutual arrangements to prevent a tragedy of the commons from occurring. Negotiations, pushing, and shoving, armed resistance, and raiding were part of the adaptive response to pastoralism. Low intensity ethnic conflict was a common adaptation. According to Bennett, these and other techniques were reasonably effective in a region of low-fertility and low-density populations. However, with population expansion and the imposition of colonial and then modern states, changes in tenure and increases in population have fueled ethnic conflict in an arc that roughly corresponds to the traditional territories of pastoral populations.

Polity: The Segmentary Lineage

Evans-Pritchard and other structuralists were convinced that trade was essentially non-existent between the Nuer and other tribal societies of East Africa. They devised a powerful model to describe the Nuer social structure based strictly on pastoralism. This model, as pointed out earlier, became the model which anthropologists applied to African society in general, producing the impression that African societies lacked trade (or at least that it was singularly unimportant) and were egalitarian, politically and economically autonomous tribes. Evans-Pritchard, who estimated the Nuer to range between 250,000 to 300,000 people, viewed them as an isolated people who were tied morally to each other by a religion that valued cattle. In their isolation, they had no need for permanent chiefs or leaders, and so had devised an **acephalous political system** that lacked political office (acephalous means headless; the clans lacked chiefs at the very top and tended to depend on democratic alliances among family heads). Clans and lineages were neatly organized by means of descent through the male line (patrilineal descent). In his streamlined model, the maximum unit of organization was the patrilineal clan, which subdivided into maximal, major, minor, and minimal lineages. These sociological constructs were expressed on ritual occasions when people sacrificed cattle to their male ancestors. Minimal lineages would celebrate the deaths of immediate ancestors (they were the equivalent of extended families); minor lineages would include these and other

acephalous political system

A political system that lacks a permanent chief or leader

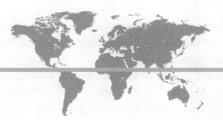

Case Study

The Nuer

One of anthropology's most celebrated people, the Nuer, are an excellent example of a pastoral nomadic people. The name "Nuer" is well established in the literature, and we will use it here. However, as with numerous groups of people throughout the world, the Nuer have their own name for themselves, *Naath*, which means 'human beings.' In the last two decades they have been caught up in a violent civil war in the southern Sudan (discussed later in this chapter). Sir Edwin E. Evans-Pritchard (1902–973) described these people in a timeless ethnography. Evans-Pritchard's ethnographic study of the Nuer (1940) is considered to be one of the great classics of anthropology, ranking with Bronislaw Malinowski's studies of the Trobriand Islanders. These two peoples have been the subject of countless lectures, papers, dissertations, and books. The Nuer, as lovingly described by Evans-Pritchard, appear outside of time as a relentlessly democratic pastoral people who love their cattle and have little interest in trade or the outside world, and who use controlled feuding as a form of social regulation.

In the early 1980s and 1990s, a young woman ethnographer, Sharon E. Hutchinson, tried to understand the forces which had transformed Nuer society since 1940, when the first Nuer study appeared in print. The picture Professor Hutchinson presents does not have the solid lines of Evans-Pritchard's classic study, and she was struck by the fluidity and violence of Nuer society fifty years after the classic picture was laid down. Evans-Pritchard's studies were based on the theories of British structural-functionalists, who dominated African studies in the middle of the twentieth century. These viewed all components of society as mutually and structurally connected with unity, equilibrium, and order as the explanations for the institutions of a society. The ethnographer's job was to explain how the various components reinforced and explained each other. The following section on polity sets out the logic of Evans-Pritchard's theory about the Nuer, which was extended to include most of the pastoralists of East Africa.

---

heads of the minor lineage, major clans would celebrate major clan heads, and so on to the top. However, this formal model appears only to have been a representation of ideal culture. Reality was much more flexible (Hutchinson 1996).

Rituals of Adulthood: Entrance to the Age Sets

Evans-Pritchard documented the initiation rites of young men and women. All male Nuer were initiated by a severe operation called *gar*, in a ceremony that occurs between the ages of fourteen and eighteen. Their foreheads were cut to the bone, with a small knife, in six long cuts. The ritual gave them membership in an age set. Nuer age sets are generational sodalities of warriors which crosscut (and thereby linked) the Nuer clans. The function of the ritual was to define the relationship of every male Nuer to every other male Nuer (Evans-Pritchard 1940, 257). The ritual of gar symbolized the passage from adolescence to manhood. Similar rituals are commonly found among all the Nilotic peoples of the Rift Valley. No ritual marks the passage to adulthood for Nuer girls. Rather, a girl was considered to be a woman after she had given birth to her first child (Hutchinson 1996, 190).

complementary opposition

A process whereby groups with distinct interests at a low level are tied to each other by common membership in a higher level category which draws their cooperation

Complementary Opposition

In the 1960s, Marshall Sahlins suggested that the Nuer were not at all isolated. What Evans-Pritchard had described could best be understood as a form of predatory expansion, the key feature of which was **complementary opposition** or the massing effect (Sahlins 1961, 1968). Individuals in low-level units of social structure (minimal lineages) would come into conflict with each other over women, cattle, and bride wealth, but would combine to face higher-level opposition. Thus individuals within minimal lineages would fight each other over local slights, but would collaborate to oppose the interests of men at the level of minor lineages; and these would combine to oppose major and maximal levels. At the very top, the Nuer people, as a whole, would unite against the neighboring Dinka. This model fit neatly into the raiding/feuding facts of life reported on the ground and helped to explain how a people, relentlessly feuding with each other, could cohere as an ethnic group, at the same time.

How could the Nuer prevent intra-ethnic conflict from tearing their society apart? There were two answers: one was the *Leopard-skin chief*, and the other was *ritual pollution*. The leopard-skin chief, also known as the earth priest, prevented conflict within Nuer society from getting out of hand through the use of mediation. Homicide was one of many ways of polluting society, or putting matter out of place (Douglas 1966). The sacrifice of cattle could restore order, and the function of the earth priest was to force men from different social units to sacrifice their precious cattle to restore order. Disorder or a lack of harmony with Kwoth, the over-arching god of the Nuer, could also be brought about through incest, through non-payment of bride wealth, and by not fulfilling the obligations of widow remarriage (also known as ghost marriage). Thus, feuding, cattle ownership, and obligations to Kwoth were drawn into marriage and kinship.

This description was applied to the Nuer, and by extension, to most pastoral nomads until recent times. We will return to an evaluation of the changes they are suffering through later in the chapter.

While the Nuer may have been tribal, and probably never had a centralized political system, other pastoral populations achieved chiefdom and state levels of hierarchy. This primarily appears to have occurred in ecological settings where rainfall determined a pastoral way of life, but trade opened the options of leading to hierarchy: herders created complex states. The history of North Africa and Southwest Asia is one of shifting dominance between these two modes of adaptation, settled villagers and herders, sometimes as tribe, sometimes as chiefdoms, and sometimes as states.

Transhumance pastoralism of cattle is particularly characteristic of the region of Eastern Africa; and today includes the countries of Sudan, Ethiopia, Somalia, Kenya, and Tanzania (Bennett 1993). Complex institutions, such as the belief in divine kings, evolved around pastoralism, and anthropologists have studied these extensively. However, these were not isolated, marginal, tribal peoples. Trade, not subsistence, was the powerful force impelling the transformation of tribal societies into chiefdoms and states, which have been common in East Africa since ancient Egypt. When trade was cut, as it was during the period of European domination and control, these societies did not disappear but shifted back to their primary adaptations; and they continued to survive in another form as dependent peasants or warlike tribes on the periphery or margins of other trade states (Ensminger 1992).

THE CAMEL NOMADS OF NORTH AFRICA

Arab

An ethnic label applied to all Arabic speaking peoples of the Middle East and North Africa

Bedouin

Nomadic, desert-dwelling, Arabic-speaking people

The Middle East and North Africa were characterized by a human ecology of camel nomadism. The term **Arab** used to be applied to those people who were desert dwellers and lived in black tents; however, over the past century, this term has been turned into an ethnic label for all Arabic speaking peoples of the Middle East and North Africa. The term **Bedouin** is now used to set aside desert dwellers from sedentary townspeople. The Bedouin produced many of the ruling dynasties that conquered sedentary kingdoms and formed the core of armies that spread Islam, transforming the desert from a barrier to an overland highway (Barfield 1993, 58).

■Desert dwelling Bedouins rely on camels for food and transportation across the vast arid deserts

Wild camels became extinct long ago, but two domesticated species survived: one-humped camels (dromedaries) that evolved in southern Arabia between 3000 and 2500 BC, and two humped camels (bactrian), which were domesticated in Central Asia between 2500 and 2000 BC (Barfield 1993, 58). It is the dromedaries that are the most numerous type of camel today and form the basis of human ecology in North Africa and the Middle East. They are well adapted to hot and dry lands; and using them, the Bedouins were able to exploit vast arid zones. These truly remarkable animals store fat (not water) in their hump and can go for long time periods without water. When they do drink, camels can consume up to 100 to 120 liters at a single watering.

Camels provide transportation and food, carrying loads of up to two hundred kilograms and supplying milk (they are rarely slaughtered for meat, only on ritual occasions). Camels became particularly important with the development of trade in incense from southern Arabia. Incense was used in the temples of the ancient world, and camels became the indispensable transporters over the desert highways. The nomads who raised them were politically unimportant until they found a way to fight from atop of one-humped camels without falling. Before this time, it was not possible to use the sword and lance because of the insecure seating. The breakthrough took the form of a special camel saddle, a wooden frame placed around the hump. While camels could never compete with horses in war, horses could not survive where camels could. For this reason, control of the desert caravans fell to the desert Bedouins, particularly after the development of Islam, a topic we pick up in the following chapter.

THE DEVELOPMENT OF TRADE ALONG THE NILE

The region of the Bedouin, North Africa and Southwest Asia, became the Islamic empires after the eighth century AD and are not dealt with here. Those empires unified the peoples of what is today known as the Near East or Middle East. Before that time period, Rome and or the Byzantine Empire controlled North Africa, including Egypt. Prior to the rise of Rome, the core of trade and control was Egypt. Egypt integrated trade throughout the Mediterranean for several thousand years, and its history is critical to understanding the rest of Africa.

Badarian

In predynastic Egypt, the era in which a culture of tribal people lived along the Nile around 5000 BC

Amratian

The era after the Badarian in which the societies of the tribal people who lived along the Egyptian Nile showed increasing stratification and trade

Gerzean

The era after the Amratian, around 4000 BC, during which the people living along the Egyptian Nile had theocratic chiefdoms, extensive trade, and highly developed agriculture

Egypt The civilizations of Southwest Asia overlap those of Egypt, and both were based on peasant agriculturalists, who had developed irrigation based villages and towns. Archaeologists first find evidence for tribal societies along the Nile about 5000 BC, which are referred to as the **Badarian**. People lived in small mud huts and paid a great deal of attention to the burial of the dead. The next phase was a continuation of a tribal type of society, but with increasing signs of stratification and trade called the **Amratian**. Burials were placed on top of Badarian burials, suggesting cultural continuity. Fine monochrome pottery was manufactured with geometric and naturalistic designs. Egyptians decorated themselves with green or gray eye makeup and used maces in warfare. At 4000 BC, new institutions emerged which reduced the transaction costs of trade, and theocratic chiefdoms appeared during the **Gerzean**. Gerzean craftsmen were highly accomplished, manufacturing beautiful pottery, stone bowls, stone mace heads, and jewelry, and showing the existence of a vast trading network. By late Gerzean times, the agricultural economy was highly developed supporting a class of wealthy people, many of whom were buried in **mastabas**, stone tombs that were to become the giant pyramids of the Old Kingdom (Redman 1978, 282–283).

There is evidence of trade connections between Mesopotamia and Egypt as far back as 3500 BC (Fagan 1995). Trade may have run from as far north as Turkey through overland routes to Egypt, and then far to the south transforming tribes into chiefdom type societies. Egypt, in North Africa, became ultimately transformed into one of the most powerful prehistoric states, its influence extending far to the south.

Of particular importance to traders were metals: first copper, then bronze, and of course gold. One of the earliest known sites for the mining of copper was Sinai, the small piece of land in northeastern Egypt that links Egypt to the Middle East. Early copper working in this region is thought to date as far back as 4000 BC; copper and bronze were widely used in both ancient Egypt and in Southwestern Asia.

Evidence for Egyptian religion is found in the early chiefdoms. Grave goods depict the peculiarly Egyptian preoccupation with death and the afterlife, which became the foundation for Egyptian ideology. It is clear that the religion of the Egyptians was based on tribal and chiefdom nature worship transformed into a state ideology. The pharaohs claimed to be earthly incarnations as gods, much as chiefs and kings of other African chiefdoms and states. The rulers of early farming communities are thought to have been religious leaders and rainmakers who controlled the floods of the Nile. As their power and authority grew, they came to claim direct descent from the gods themselves. The early animal gods were transfigured into beings with human bodies and the faces of hawks, cats, dogs, and crocodiles. These were to be found in the formation of the stars, thus producing a complex cosmogony that connected the earth with the sky. Anubis was the jackal headed god who collected the soul upon death. Osiris was the god behind the pharaoh and Isis, the lion headed mother goddess, while Set, the evil god who opposed Osiris, had a human head and the body of a serpent.

mastaba

A predynastic Egyptian stone tomb that later developed into the giant pyramids of the Old Kingdom

By 3250 BC, regional chiefs had been subjugated by kings, one ruling Upper Egypt (southern Egypt) and the other Lower Egypt (northern Egypt). The trend toward centralized power and social organization continued with King Narmer, Egypt's first pharaoh, who conquered Lower Egypt and built the first Egyptian city at Memphis. He made himself into a divine god, the head of a theocratic state. However, while Egypt had its famous temples and pyramids, it was not as urban as Mesopotamia, with most of the peasantry living in rural villages. Occupying the temple complexes were priests and the bureaucrats who ran the state. While the symbols of kinghood were different, based on a distinct culture with distinct gods, the singular statement of power very much resembled that of Ur but was also quite different (see Chapter 5 for a discussion of Ur). For example, the religion of Ur was based primarily on fertility, the fear of flooding, and angry or authoritarian gods (elements of Sumerian religion were incorporated into the Old Testament). Meanwhile Egypt, which had control over floods through its fine irrigation system, had a religion based on a pleasant afterlife. There were few human sacrifices in early Egyptian history, unlike Ur. Hieroglyphic writing on papyrus was also developed and, as with the clay tablet writing of early Sumeria, was a form of temple accounting for an evolving state. The peaceable theocratic state gave way to a conquest state with river-based cities vying for power to control trade up and down the Nile.

At 3100 BC, Egypt established a central government, initiating the first dynasty and became a historical entity. Inscriptions and monuments of the rulers of the early dynasties have been discovered and identified. The first dynasty is dated to the same time period as the Early Dynastic for Mesopotamia. By the beginning of the second dynasty, the capital was established at Memphis, a strategic location that unified Upper and Lower Egypt. Intermarriage and warfare were used to stabilize the Egyptian state, with kings from the south taking their brides from the north. These rulers fostered international trade. Wood and rare stones were brought in from the Levant (modern Lebanon), metal ore from Nubia, and ivory from farther south in Africa. The administration of long-distance trade and irrigation was controlled by a bureaucracy at Memphis, and were to characterize Egypt for three thousand years. A festival of royal power took place regularly, and a cult evolved centered on the person of the god-king whose death was ceremonialized by his burial in giant pyramids. Writing and science flourished, and hieroglyphic writing became common.

A modern symbol of ancient Egypt is the pyramid, the first of which was built at Saqqara and is dated to 2700 BC. This first structure is a step pyramid. The giant pyramid

■The great pyramids of Giza were built in 2600 BC for King Khufu. The pyramid has come to be recognized as a modern symbol of ancient Egypt.

at Giza, a true pyramid, was built at 2600 BC for King Khufu (Cheops). Thirty dynasties would follow, with pyramids characterizing the early periods; however, giant statues and burial temples, such as the rock tombs of the Valley of Kings (1500 BC), characterized the later dynasties. The final years of Egypt were dominated by Greece, and later Rome. One of the final dramatic episodes was the love affair between the Roman aristocrat Anthony and the Egyptian ruler Cleopatra. Their suicide deaths and the incorporation of Egypt within the Roman empire by Emperor Octavian is accepted as the final end of the Egyptian Empire (30 BC), but its power really continued into modern history.

Meroe　As far back as Old Kingdom times, Ancient Egypt had conducted trade with the Nubian region to the south. An elaborate chiefdom or kingdom known as the island of Meroe emerged near the fourth cataract, just to the north of where the Blue and White Nile come together. This region lent itself to rainfed agriculture, cattle, and other forms of livestock. With the help of iron tools, the people of **Meroe** developed a mixed economy, which combined agriculture with cattle. This pattern became typical in the savannah regions of tropical Africa and where agriculture was marginal pastoralism dominated.

Meroe was able to control trade into the Nile Valley; it could, and did, develop trade to the east to ports on the Red Sea. When relations with Egypt became strained, or when Egypt was under the control of Greeks or Romans, Meroe developed state level institutions and monopolized local trade. Trade connections extended far to the east to India and Indonesia. Meroe exported its traditional products of ivory, leopard skins, ostrich feathers, ebony, and gold. The cattle-herders and peasant cultivators were spread over a wide area and were ultimately under the control of a king and court. Yet Meroe was much less centralized than the Egyptian state, and minor chiefs and heads of family clans ruled most families. In very similar fashion, the people of Meroe moved over a wide arc to the east and west, and retained a great deal of political autonomy from Egypt and other empires.

Anthropologists a generation ago assumed that states evolved due to the development of irrigation agriculture and large populations. However, it is apparent that Meroe did not have irrigation or large populations. Complex chiefdoms and states arose as strategic adaptations to control trade and trade relations with surrounding populations. Other kingdoms, many based on pastoral nomadism, rose and fell in an arc just south of Egypt, until the Roman Empire challenged their hegemony, and trade and empire building shifted elsewhere.

THE DEVELOPMENT OF GOLD TRADE

Trans-Saharan trade, connecting East and West Africa with North Africa, stimulated the rise of other kingdoms, such as Great Zimbabwe, the Nok of Nigeria, the ancient empire of Mali located where modern Ghana is, and the more recent Kongo empire based in Zaire. The period in central Africa between AD 1000 and 1500 is generally called the **Later Iron Age**. It was once thought new peoples had come into East Africa and displaced people of the Early Iron Age because it was an age of great economic, social, and political development. It is now evident, however, that there were no great population migrations. Instead, local people had been stimulated to develop chiefdoms and states as a consequence of the external demand for African gold, copper, slaves, and ivory, which was especially important in India for bridal ornaments.

Meroe

A people that lived to the south of Egypt as far back as Old Kingdom times, which had an elaborate chiefdom, iron tools, and a mixed economy of agriculture and trade

Later Iron Age

A term used by anthropologists and historians for the region of Central Africa between AD 1000 and 1500

Figure 8.3

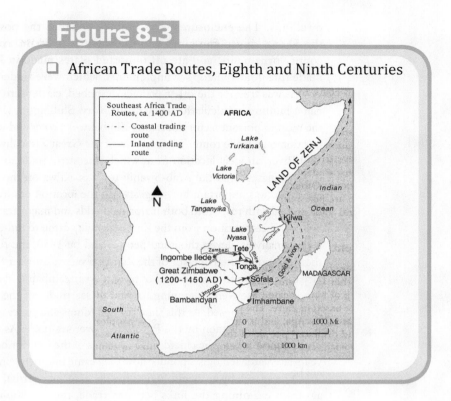

❑ African Trade Routes, Eighth and Ninth Centuries

Indian Ocean Trade Centers The east African coast was known to Greek and Roman traders, who referred to the region as Azania; and there are references from AD 100 to coastal market towns. The people of Azania were experienced fishermen and were very knowledgeable in the use of small coastal boats made of wooden planks, which were knotted together with lengths of coconut fiber (Shillington 1989, 124).

Trade in the Indian Ocean was given a great boost by the spread of Islam in the seventh and eighth centuries. The region came to be called the Land of Zenj. Arab sailing ships, known as dhows, were able to take advantage of the monsoon winds, which blow towards east Africa between November and March, and towards India and the Persian Gulf between April and October. As the demand for African ivory and gold rose, Muslim settled along the coast, developing trade towns speaking Swahili, a trade language based on Bantu grammar with many Arab words. The Swahili speaking towns, with their camel caravans, in turn, stimulated the rise of chiefdoms and states in the east African interior (Shillington 1989, 128). In addition, other camel caravans from Islamic states in North Africa crossed the Sahara and further added economic stimulation, which brought about new states in West Africa in Senegal, Mali, and Niger at about the same time.

Gold Trade in East and West Africa One of the east African states which holds great fascination for modern archaeologists is Great Zimbabwe. Between AD 1200 and 1450, this great city-state developed with a subsistence base on nomadic pastoralism. However, its wealth was based on trade in gold. The region to the west, known as Leopard's Kopje, was rich in gold bearing rock and was made into a tributary of Great Zimbabwe. The modern country of Zimbabwe (once known as Rhodesia) is named for this ancient empire, the center or capital of the larger Shona state. Elaborate stonewalls, probably not built for defensive purposes, encircled clay built dwellings. The enclosures were built to enhance the power, mystery, and prestige of the Shona kings. The kings and their courts lived in luxury, surrounded by gold and copper ornaments, and ate off imported plates made in Persia and China. Craftsmen made fine gold and copper implements, which were traded east.

As was true for the other peoples described, cattle were very important and so was big game hunting, particularly elephant for ivory. Shillington (1989) points out, however, that the most important factor governing Zimbabwe's power and wealth was the capital's strategic position on a trade route. The remains of the Great Zimbabwe capital are at the head of the Sabi River, an ideal location from which to control trade to and from the goldfields of the western plateau and the Arab-Swahili town of Kilwa on the coast. Fage (1995, 133) agrees that trade was important but suggests that the location of Great Zimbabwe was actually less than ideal with respect to both major goldfields and major trade routes. However, overpopulation and competition from the Zambezi valley came to influence survival. By 1400, the city had as many as eleven thousand people; and by 1450, the region could no longer support them as trade shifted in favor of the Zambezi valley. Another Shona state, Mutapa, used military domination to gain control of trade; Great Zimbabwe collapsed. However, by this time the Portuguese were beginning to control sea trade off the east coast of Africa, and soon Mutapa also collapsed. At this time the chiefdoms and states of Africa were being threatened by the monopolization by the Portuguese over sea trade. As the coastal cities were brought under alien control, the chiefdoms and states of the interior began to crumble. Five hundred years later, archaeologists ponder how they came into being in the first place.

The search by anthropologists for the essence of tribalism in Africa prevented scholars from examining the links between trade, the development of chiefdoms and states, and the relationship of these to less centralized tribal societies on the peripheries or margins. The model which emerges today for many world regions is not of an evolutionary set of successive stages (band, tribe, chiefdom, state) but rather a dynamic and replicated center-periphery model. (We use this classification with the specific meaning of levels of sociocultural (including political) integration. While in the long term there were bands before tribes, etc., once all levels were in existence a dynamic relationship came to exist among groups at different levels of integration. In addition, the level of integration of any given group could and did vary through time, depending on such major factors as population size, political economy, trade, property rights, and relations with neighboring groups.) This is the model that emerges from a careful look at the pre-colonial history and prehistory of sub-Saharan Africa. The center, either a true state or a chiefdom, responded to the need to reduce transaction costs by developing hierarchical social structures. In true states, a king could initiate a political action, but in a chiefdom his (or her) actions were limited by a need for support from close kinsmen and the leaders of supporting clans. The distinction between states and chiefdoms is probably impossible to really ascertain, and from our perspective, not particularly helpful. It is fairly apparent that the greater the importance of trade, the more important the state and its hierarchical structure.

The Emergence of Slave Trade Societies in the West

New and powerful states emerged in the period after the sixteenth century associated with the European slave trade, such as Oyo, Dahomey, and Asante (located where Ghana is today). Slavery had existed in Africa well before the colonial period, and as an institution had ancient roots. Slaves were used as wealth and for trade, but much depended on the nature of the political economy of the society. In tribes, slaves, for the most part, had the status of household workers. In chiefdoms and states, they formed a special category of labor and were used in exchange for goods. However, slaves could buy themselves out of slavery, or marry and join households The demand for slaves by industrializing European societies, particularly as plantation workers, escalated and transformed the slave trade in West Africa as some African rulers decided to trade one of their most precious resources—labor—for European trade goods.

Portuguese sailing ships first reached the West African coast in the 1470s in a search for gold, but slaves soon became more important than gold. We have seen in the last chapter how the demand for slaves in the New World had a severe impact on African social structure, robbing it of its young. Some 293,000 slaves landed in the Americas and Europe between 1451 and 1600; in the seventeenth century, slave exports quintupled to 1,494,000 in response to the growth of sugar plantations. In the eighteenth century, over six million people were exported from Africa; and although Britain abolished the slave trade in 1807, two million more slaves were transported from Africa to the Americas between 1810 and 1870 (Fage 1995, 254–255; Wolf 1982, 197–198).

Europeans radically transformed West African societies when they brought in harder metals, hardware, firearms, gunpowder, textiles, rum, and tobacco to exchange for slaves. Portuguese slavers stirred up war between the kingdoms of Kongo and Ndongo, which collapsed. The Asante state came into being as a slave state under the support of European slavers. Generally, Europeans did not hunt for slaves but relied upon politically powerful African elites and merchants to obtain slaves for them. Many of these slave-hunter societies became centralized states with kings, courts, and bureaucracies based on the West African divine kings, but with much greater importance granted to warfare. Tribute giving societies remained at a tribal level dependent on agriculture. Yet both the slave states and tributary tribes had very similar kinship systems, for the most part based on patrilineal clans. Shillington writes about the extent of the slave trade:

> With the rapid expansion of slave exports in the eighteenth century, virtually every part of the Atlantic coastline from Senegal to southern Angola became involved in the human traffic. The greatest concentration of European trading forts was along the so-called "Gold Coast," the coastline of the modern state of Ghana (1989, 174).

The main source of slaves was warfare, and the supply of captives at the coast was the result of local wars being fought in the interior. According to some, the prime motive of the wars was the formation and expansion of states based on the slave trade. Shillington argues that the slave trade was the prime motivation for warfare, leading to the total destruction of weaker societies by the stronger slave states (Shillington 1989, 176).

However, it seems unlikely that the African kingdoms would destroy the resource that was central to their own economic well-being. Fage (1995, 265–266) offers an alternative perspective, namely, that African rulers engaged in the slave trade with full regard for their own well-being, balancing labor needs against desire for European trade goods, and in fact controlling the export of slaves.

Slave tribute paying tribes and slave taking states came to hate each other; as their relations with Europeans changed, so did their relations with each other (Wolf 1982, 228–229). Many of these hatreds remain in modern societies in Africa, and form at least a part of the basis for ethnic conflict in countries such as modern Nigeria and Ghana. As an example, the Yoruba state collapsed and was followed by the slaving states of Oyo, Dahomey, and Asante that had very similar religions and social structures but greater access to slaves. The Asante were particularly known for the symbol of Asante kingship, the Gold Stool. These three states preyed on the people of the interior, who became slave givers, while Oyo, Dahomey, and Asante became slave takers.

The Heritage of Colonialism

In the late nineteenth and early twentieth centuries, particularly in the period beginning in 1884–85 with the Congress of Berlin to the period just before World War II, Europeans carved up Africa into colonies. One of the many contributing causes of World War II was the assumption by Europeans that they needed colonies to supplement their own diminishing resources. Europeans did not physically colonize West Africa, primarily due to climatic conditions. They did colonize East and South Africa, to a degree because of mineral riches, and a healthier climate. In all of Africa south of the Sahara, however, boundaries were imposed by European politicians and diplomats who were primarily concerned with gaining control over natural resources and who paid scant attention to the needs of native populations (Carter and O'Meara 1986) or ethnic group boundaries.

In many instances, previous slave raiding populations were organized within "countries" containing the tribes they had previously raided. During the colonial period, European administrators tended to favor certain tribes over others to administrate the new countries (such as the Ibo in Nigeria). Sometimes these "ruling" tribes were previous slave raiders or slave tribute givers, thus creating intractable tensions between rulers and ruled. The new governments of Africa have inherited geographic boundaries that are arbitrary and contain populations that sometimes are intensely antagonistic to each other. A major problem is uniting the various groups to function as one nation. This problem is compounded when ethnic distinctions and antagonisms are used by modern authoritarian regimes to maintain power.

The history of southern Africa needs special mention since it does not fit the overall history of Africa discussed so far. Cattle herding peoples from the late Iron Age times had settled in southern Africa. The societies were mostly self-sufficient tribes and chiefdoms, such as the Sotho-Tswana of Namibia, the Nguni of the region east of the Drakensberg Mountains, and the Xhosa and Khoisian speakers of the south. During the sixteenth century, European sailing-ships, especially Dutch and English, began using the southwestern cape as port of call in their long voyages around Africa. Europeans wanted cheap meat from cattle, and the natives were not always willing to sell at low prices. Europeans would seize the animals and sail off, causing the natives to attack traders.

The Dutch set up the Dutch East India Company to solve these problems and formed a permanent settlement at Table Bay in 1652. The Dutch hoped to monopolize the regional economy and control trade in food. Khoisian pastoralists managed to unite an opposition against the Dutch in 1659 but were decimated. The Dutch declared a right of conquest and took over the cape peninsula establishing the Cape Colony. The Dutch, today known as the Boer or Afrikaners, continued to immigrate into the region and formed a Dutch colony. The Afrikaners expanded the colony and came into conflict with other tribal and chiefdom societies, pushing them into what later, in the modern state of South Africa, would become their regional homelands or Bantustans, a topic we will return to later.

ADAPTATION TO THE STATE AND DEVELOPMENT

Traditional African societies did not passively accept the Europeans, and they responded politically to the expansion of European interests. In West Africa, a variety of distinct crops became the focus of European exploitation. Palm oil replaced slaves as slavery became illegal in Europe and America. Palm oil was important in soap making and as a lubricant. Eric Wolf explains that warrior elites and state organizations geared to the slave trade found it difficult to adapt to the new palm oil trade. The elites responded by using slaves on palm oil plantations. However, middlemen on the coast and small peasant cultivators undercut the elites, and soon European wholesalers began to deal directly with the new producers. Former slaves, educated in European religious missions, became the new commercial elites. The spread of European all-purpose money replaced iron, copper and cowrie currencies, further undermining the old economies (Wolf 1982, 330–332). The West African economies expanded and then contracted with the economic depressions of capitalist societies, particularly the Great Depression of 1873. Europeans and Africans struggled to control local supplies and to drive down prices, particularly the price of labor.

Conflict ensued, and Europeans called for law and order. Having abolished slavery in their own countries, Europeans used its continuance in Africa to justify wars with the old elites and the establishment of colonial rule (Fage 1995, 267). The kingdoms of Asante, Dahomey, Oyo, Benin, and Aro were conquered; and European control was imposed on West Africa.

THE TIDE OF LIBERATION

The exploitation of Africa was not received passively. By the end of World War II, African leaders had strong popular support in their efforts to return Africa to African rule. The ideas of independence were not new in Africa and were inspired by the same documents which led to democratic changes in western Europe in the late nineteenth century. As would be true in wars of liberation fought in Asia, the new leaders of Africa used the same arguments about human dignity and worth put out in the founding documents of Western Civilization: the French Rights of Man and the Bill of Rights in the Constitution of the United States. African scholars, such as Arnold Temu and Bonaventure Swai, searched and found arguments regarding ideas of freedom originating in African history (1981). Many of these ideas were incorporated into the political positions taken by the African National Congress and made more explicit in the recent election of Nelson Mandela as president of South Africa.

New political ideas were highly diverse, ranging from Islamic concepts about the equality of the faithful to American ideals of liberal democracy. In eastern Africa, the Kikuyu of Kenya, whose fertile lands had been enclosed by European farmers, had begun their protests as early as 1921 when the Young Kikuyu Association was formed. By 1929, many independent African churches claimed, "Africa for the Africans." After World War II, the forces for liberation accelerated. The war itself had created great demand for African goods, and rural peoples were attracted to the cities which doubled and tripled in size. Explosive political movements began to transform African society. In 1945, a gathering of the sixth Pan-African Congress in Manchester, England, brought together the new revolutionary leadership. Many leaders were the future presidents of free African states: Kwame Nkrumah of Ghana, Jomo Kenyatta of Kenya, and Nnamdi Azikiwe of Nigeria.

Sally Falk Moore, writing about the role of anthropology during this time period, sketches how African leaders came to question the way that European and American scholars had appropriated African history. Anthropologists "found themselves in an uncomfortable state of political self-consciousness" (1994, 76). They became critical of their own theories and substituted world system and dependency theories for their outworn evolutionary models (Moore 1994, 77). Many embraced Marxist interpretations of history, as did African leaders. By the 1990s, anthropologists, other African scholars, and African politicians were all searching for new models that were neither capitalist nor Marxist.

THE RISE OF SOCIALISM

In the 1960s, anthropologists and African intellectuals were optimistic about Africa's future. In the 1990s, the optimism has been replaced with anxiety. Very few of the newly independent countries of Africa managed to develop democratically elected governments, or to achieve economic stability. Within a decade of independence, colonial capitalism had given way to the rejection of democratic/capitalist norms and the adoption of blends of Marxist Leninist Maoist revolutionary thought in a majority of the developing countries of Africa (Sklar 1986, 13). Yet it was not only the experiences of African leaders which led them to choose socialism. Many leading western intellectuals, anthropologists, other social scientists, and historians vigorously supported socialism as the means to overcome dependency. One highly influential writer, Regis Debray, thought socialism was a natural form of political organization for African tribal societies.

Western "Marxism" was integrated into African political theory by western thinkers to produce "Negritude," a new ideology of African socialism that was supposed to break the bonds of slavery, capitalism, and imperialism, particularly in formerly French colonial countries. Revolutionary leaders in Africa adopted anti-western, anti-core ideologies based on Marxism, and used the language of socialism to develop one-party mass political movements. Often these political structures were Marxist in name only. A common theme developed: the countries of Africa, more so than any other developing region, should use socialism to achieve economic development because the pre-modern societies of Africa were socialist in nature due to their dependence on the collective ownership of resources. The confusion between collective ownership of property in tribal societies and centralized socialist governments has led to problems no one intended or predicted.

Conflict between ethnic and tribal groups played an important role in the selection of socialism since many African leaders did not believe democracy was possible in societies where inter-ethnic strife was high (Sullivan 1989, 4). To maintain order, many Africans chose military states with socialist style governments, such as Nigeria. Others attempted democratic capitalism, such as Liberia. Both approaches depended on heavy handed rulers. Financial policies emphasized economic investment in urban regions and disinvestment in rural regions, which often alienated rural ethnic groups and reinforced urban/rural splits. Where resources allowed, the political leaders borrowed money from international banks and distributed the largesse among their followers, leading to increasing political conflict. In the 1980s, international banks began calling back their debts due to internal economic pressures in capitalist countries, intensifying the demands for political change in Africa. Many of the once hopeful socialist governments were faced with rural violence and tried to meet violence with violence, adding to the spiral of ethnic and regional warfare. In the following, we will examine the region of East Africa to understand how human ecology and ethnic nationalism have fueled violence, often in the form of genocide.

Regional War and Ethnic Conflict

One of the most serious problems facing the African republics is the animosity between different ethnic groups. Some locate the source of modern ethnic conflict in rivalries that existed in pre-colonial times, while others see such conflict as largely a product of colonialism. There is some truth in both of these views. There is also evidence that modern African elites, in some countries, have used ethnic differences as a political tool. Warfare and feuding were clearly widespread in the pre-colonial societies of Africa, particularly

Figure 8.4

☐ Contemporary Map of Africa Showing Areas of Conflict

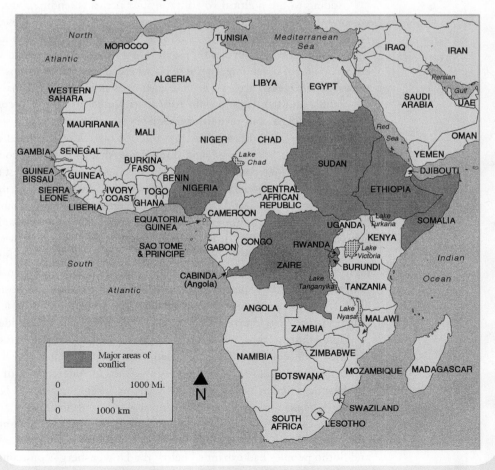

among pastoral groups. Even though most inter-group violence ceased during the colonial period, the memories of what one group did to another centuries before became part of the ideology of conflict between modern peoples. Many of the regional conflicts in Africa appear to have their origin in ideological disagreements, such as Marxism versus capitalism; but on closer scrutiny, it turns out that ancient animosities underlie the modern rhetoric. The breakdown of order and the extensive feuding, which destroyed Somalia from 1990–1992, is a case in point.

Among the many ethnic distinctions found in East Africa, of particular importance is the one between cattle-owners and tillers of the soil. This is more an ideological than pragmatic distinction, as no group is purely pastoral. Lucy Mair, writing in 1974, points out that these two groups go by different ethnic or tribal names in different regions. In Rwanda and Burundi, they are Tutsi and Hutu. In southern Uganda (Bunyoro), they are Huma and Iru. In the former kingdom of Ankole (also in Uganda), they are known as Hima and Iru (Mair 1974, 166–192). While in modern communities, the distinction between cattle owners and farmers seldom applies (many have other occupations), the aristocratic bias of these distinctions continues, and as we shall see in the section on Rwanda and Burundi, may be used as an excuse for genocide (though this is obviously not the only or even dominant basis of genocide). In the 1970s, Idi Amin and Dr. Milton Obote fought a war to determine which tribe would control the state, a war that decimated Uganda and made outsiders aware of the horrors of genocide.

Adding to the political volatility in East Africa is feuding, both within and between pastoral societies. Traditional feuds between clans and tribes have escalated with the introduction of modern weapons. Alex de Waal, an anthropologist who has worked on human rights issues in Sudan, makes the point that guns have exacerbated what was originally a controlled form of feuding, to the point where among some groups "people adorn themselves with images of firearms and use cartridges as jewelry" (de Waal 1996, 242).

Ethnic and tribal conflicts in Africa have often erupted into complex regional wars. Refugees, soldiers, and revolutionaries from several poor African states spill across each other's borders, at times attracting international attention and interference. These ethnic/regional conflicts are found throughout Africa and have become more intense over the past decade. As a consequence, Africa contains the world's largest number of refugees.

While modern populations of the states of the region are primarily sedentary, relatively significant proportions of the populations of Kenya (12 percent), Somalia (70 percent), and Sudan (22 percent), continue to follow this age-old adaptation to fragile arid and semi-arid lands (Bennett 1993, 297). J. W. Bennett argues, in a recent overview of migratory pastoralism, that while the slave trade and colonial repression were major forces affecting indigenous peoples, many of the disturbances of the region today—regional wars, genocide, and hunger—are the consequence of the collapse of a "man controlled ecological system" (1993, 303). Here, we focus on migratory pastoralism as a socio-natural adaptation in order to emphasize the close interrelationships among adaptation, ethnicity, identity, and conflict.

The ethnic groups, which are to be found in the arc from Ethiopia to South Africa, are tribal and chiefdom societies. Many became true states and have distinct political heritages despite similar human ecologies. They include peoples of Christian, Animistic and Islamic religions. They speak many languages and include the Karamojong of northeastern Uganda and the Maasai of central Kenya and northern Tanzania. Farther south along the east African coast, town-dwelling, Swahili-speaking Arabs were interspersed with cattle raisers of the same ethnic background; and far to the south, Tswana, Nguni, and Sotho peoples had expanded below the Drakensberg Mountains into modern South Africa by AD 1400.

In the following, we will examine some of the regional conflicts in East Africa, once a region of predominantly pastoral peoples. Over the last two decades, revolutionary conflicts have overwhelmed East Africa, particularly in the countries of Ethiopia, Somalia, Sudan, and most recently the twin countries of Rwanda and Burundi. The conflicts are impossible to contain within the countries where they begin. Ethnic groups who are in conflict with each other often live in more than one country; and warfare crosses borders, producing regional conflicts. Many of these people are migratory pastoralists for whom national borders mean little. Adding to ethnic tensions in the region is the migration of refugees across the borders of the countries they live in, to other countries where they can be cared for in refugee centers or where they can find protection living with members of their own ethnic groups. For example, during the war in Uganda, many Ugandans took up residence with relatives in the Sudan; and during the Sudanese civil war of 1955–1972, many southerners crossed into Uganda, Zaire, and the Central African Republic to live with relatives there (personal communication of PY with Zande in and around Yambio, southern Sudan in 1982).

ETHIOPIA: FAILURE OF CHEAP FOOD POLICIES

The Ethiopian Empire, headed by aristocratic king Haile Selassie, collapsed in 1974. The Soviet Union supported the new pseudo-socialist state, which nationalized foreign companies and the lands of the aristocracy. Political rivalries resulted in mass executions and disappearances. In 1978, Mengistu Heile Mariam came to power as the head of a Marxist one-party state allied to the Soviet Union (the party was named the Workers Party of Ethiopia).

Heile Mariam introduced policies that favored the urban working class and thereby alienated a number of ethnic groups, including peasant farmers and pastoralists of the rural regions. Farmers and cattle herders were paid low prices for their produce in order to keep food cheap for urban workers. Liberation movements in Eritrea, Tigray, and Welo provinces led Heile Mariam to use scarce funds to support his military, rather than to support rural economic development. Policies to keep food cheap for the urban population, coupled with excessive investment in the military, had the consequence of blocking economic development and virtually destroyed the economies of the three revolutionary provinces. Lack of significant investment in the economy and two civil wars led to widespread hunger and starvation, which received world-wide attention. In part, hunger was the consequence of cheap food policies that induced peasant farmers to abandon the land and pastoralists to convert cattle to grain; in part, hunger was the consequence of the several revolutions. The government refused to allow food to be transported by international relief agencies to Tigray and Welo provinces because of the belief that the food would be used to support the rebels.

The recent transformations in Russia and Eastern Europe, the general questioning of socialism as a means of escaping underdevelopment, and the abandonment of one-party states caused Heile Mariam to introduce reforms, including the re-introduction of market mechanisms. However, he was too late because the Eritrean People's Liberation Front defeated his army in Eritrea and declared their independence, while a second revolutionary army from Tigray province defeated what was left of his army in Ethiopia.

Ethiopia's new president (since 1991) is Meles Zenawi, the leader of the victorious Tigray guerrilla movement (Tigray is still a province of Ethiopia). He and his supporters have redrawn the country's borders along ethnic lines, arguing that they have

■Ethiopia's president (since 1991) Meles Zenawi.

learned from their communist predecessors not to force peoples of widely different ethnic backgrounds to conform to the same federal rules and regulations. The new Council of Representatives has agreed to let the regions have as much say as possible in their own governance, with their own representative assemblies, judiciaries, and police forces. The central government will control defense and foreign affairs. This has caused some to fear "regionalism run rampant," but the advocates of division along ethnic lines believe that the new democracy they are creating will ameliorate any resentment that might exist among ethnic populations (Smith 1995). Independent Eritrea's president, Issaias Afwerki, is cooperating with Zenawi as they attempt to put both houses in order.

SOMALIA: THE BREAKDOWN OF CLAN-BASED SOCIAL CONTROLS

Somalia sits on the eastern horn of Africa. An Islamic society, it acts as a link between Africa and Arabia. It is an arid to semiarid country the size of Texas and has a population of 8 million, mostly pastoralists. During the colonial period, the north was controlled by Great Britain while the south and east were controlled by Italy. The country became independent in 1960, but secessionist movements gave way to civil war in 1987 and 1988 (Sullivan 1989, 110–111).

Until recently, the Revolutionary Socialist Party (RSP) ruled Somalia. The RSP first allied itself with the Soviet Union until 1977. At that time, its head of state, Major Mohammed Siad Barre, felt threatened by Ethiopia's new socialist direction and its ties to the Soviet Union and allied himself with the United States (Bohannen and Curtin 1995, 266). He granted the United States naval facilities at the capital of Mogadishu and at Berbera. These bases have been used as staging areas for the U.S. Rapid Deployment Force. Somalia has also participated in the United States' organized war games and has received substantial economic aid. Despite a Marxist style dictatorship, the mismanagement of food aid, and a poor human rights record, the United States continued to support Barre until the civil war, when his violent attacks on civilian populations forced suspension of U.S. aid (Sullivan 1989, 110–111).

Before Barre imposed a socialist one-party state government on Somalia, subclans used Sharia law (the Islamic legal code derived from the Koran) in organized village courts. Each village had a subclan chief and village elders who maintained social control. Usually family heads were expected to maintain social control over the young, and punishment was family or subclan based. Once a dispute occurred between subclans, the elders would mediate the dispute, as is common among pastoral peoples. The clan elders of the most powerful subclan controlled each village and town. Barre imposed local governments controlled by young socialists who introduced secular law and challenged the rule of the elders. The power of the state alienated the traditional clan leaders.

Exiles formed rebel armies in the country and overthrew Barre in 1990. However, then clan-based factions began fighting with one another, primarily led by the young socialists, not the clan elders. The country was awash with weapons provided by the United States and the Soviet Union. Two warlords split the country into warring subclans. While Somalis should be less divided than many other African people since they share the same language and all belong to the Sunni branch of Islam, in fact they are split into warring clans and subclans. Mr. Barre suppressed clan warfare for twenty-one years. Yet with no central government and with the elders having been pushed aside, lawlessness reigned; and heavily armed gangs representing different clans, often of the same tribe, killed each other in the countryside and in the streets of Mogadishu. However, they usually kill even more innocent bystanders than each other (Smith 1995).

The major battle was between two warlords of the same clan, General Muhammed Farrah Aideed and Mr. Ali Mahdi Muhammad. General Aideed was angered when clan leaders gave the presidency to Ali Mahdi. The resulting fight between the two killed four thousand people. In December of 1992, the United States sent a 35,000-man army to back United Nations forces in pacifying the country. General Aideed and Ali Mahdi shook hands and agreed to put an end to violence. They also agreed to take their "technicals," heavily armed trucks, out of the major cities and to store them until agreement could be reached on the first step towards the political reconstruction of Somalia. In the process of searching for peace, however, the United States forces lost several men. Due to public pressure, the United States was forced to remove its forces as Americans became critical of the United Nations; and later the United Nations also left before any real peace had been achieved. General Aideed was killed on August 1, 1996. His Mogadishu-based rivals, Osman Ali Atto and Ali Mahdi Muhammad, called a cease-fire. Aideed's son and successor, Hussein Muhammad Aideed, did not cooperate. He renewed attacks, vowing to exterminate his father's enemies (*The Economist*, August 31, 1996, p. 7).

RWANDA AND BURUNDI: THE POLITICS OF ETHNIC VIOLENCE

Rwanda and Burundi are two small, densely populated countries with overlapping histories. They are located just north of Lake Tanganyika and northwest of Tanzania. In both countries, in pre-colonial times, a minority of pastoralists, called *Tutsi*, dominated a majority of agricultural peasants, called *Hutu*, (89 percent of the population in Rwanda and 85 percent in Burundi). The Tutsi, in both countries, were organized into aristocratic clans with kings and queens in control of the two distinct lands (there was a Tutsi king and queen for Rwanda and a Tutsi king and queen for Burundi). The kings controlled trade and extracted tribute from the Hutu, often in the form of labor. Tutsi dominance of Hutu in pre-colonial times does not appear to have involved any large-scale or systematic violence in either Rwanda or Burundi (Prunier 1995; Lemarchand 1994).

Lucy Mair, in her ethnohistory of the region, argues that the Tutsi established domination over the Hutu several centuries ago, creating a kingdom with petty states. A body of hereditary experts, who used a secret code and esoteric language to keep their faith secret from the Hutu, kept secrets of ritual and taboo. This council formed the advisors to the kings and were responsible for naming and installing successors, as well as distributing land and cattle to Tutsi overlords. Rwanda and Burundi kings appointed territorial subordinates, who acted as chiefs. Below the aristocratic cattle herders, the Hutu had their own chiefs, which were subordinate to the Tutsi. The Hutu could herd cattle for their owners

■Young children on a Rwandan farm. In pre-colonial times, a minority of pastoralists, called Tutsi, dominated a majority of agricultural peasants, called Hutu.

and did most of the work for them, but they could not own cattle and, thus, could not acquire wealth (Mair 1974, 174).

Alex de Waal does not agree with Mair's interpretation and says that in Rwanda the Hutu, Tutsi, and Twa (a small minority group) were "three different strata of the same group, differentiated by occupational and political status" (1994, 1). He likens the relationship to that of a caste system and says that individuals could, with difficulty, change categories. While he does not dispute Tutsi dominance in pre-colonial times, de Waal points out that Hutu and Tutsi shared the same language, culture, and religion and lived in the same communities.

Lemarchand presents a similar view of the pre-colonial Hutu-Tutsi relationship in Burundi. He argues that the concept of "tribe" is "patently inappropriate to describe communities that speak the same language (Kirundi), that share much the same type of social organization, and whose members lived peacefully side by side for centuries" (1994, 4). He further notes that the term "hutu" has the meaning of "social subordinate," as well as being an ethnic identity label (1994, 10).

During the late nineteenth century the two regions were a part of German East Africa. After World War I, Belgium became the protector of the two new countries of Rwanda and Burundi. After World War II, the two countries became United Nations mandated territories, and colonial authorities continued to rule through the Tutsi aristocracy. Scholars agree that the colonial governments enhanced Tutsi dominance. In both countries, Belgian authorities simplified the government bureaucracy and granted the Tutsi higher-level posts and special privileges. The Tutsi came to look at their power and privileges as natural rights (Des Forges 1994).

In both countries, independence has brought a sharpening of ethnic distinctions, with both Tutsi and Hutu politicians and intellectuals developing distinct versions of history to support their views of themselves and the other (Lemarchand 1994; Prunier 1995). While cattle have lost their importance in modern times, the Tutsi view themselves as the descendants of the true cattle-owning elite and believe that only they have connections to the true gods who originated the region. They identify with their herds of cattle and believe farming is lower class work. The Hutu view the Tutsi as exploiters—lazy and pretentious people of violence who use their status to exploit the poor Hutu. The Hutu view themselves as victims of

Tutsi exploitation, as hard workers, as peasants who understand and identify with the land, and as Catholics.

After the French and Belgian authorities turned Rwanda and Burundi back to their own peoples, both Tutsi and Hutu began to form political parties based on ethnic identity. Each had its own militant wing. In 1959, in Rwanda, a band of young Tutsi killed one of the few Hutu sub-chiefs, leading to a Hutu attack on Tutsis when many died. Chiefs on both sides organized attacks and counter attacks. In 1963, Hutu authorities executed all those Tutsi in positions of power, killing between ten to fifteen thousand Tutsis. There followed a Tutsi massacre of Hutus.

The popular press has taken a primordialist view in its reportage of the conflicts in Rwanda and Burundi (and, for that matter, elsewhere). In this view, cultural or ethnic identities are believed to have an essentialist character; that is, they have ancient, enduring features. An opposing view, one favored by many scholars, is that political processes play a fundamental role in the formation and consolidation of ethnic identities. This is called the instrumentalist view. The ethnic violence in both Rwanda and Burundi in the late twentieth century seems best explained not by ancient antagonisms from a bygone pre-colonial era, not by primordialism, but by deliberate manipulation on the part of radical politicians and military officers, by instrumentalism (Lemarchand 1994). De Waal points out that the coup in Burundi in 1993 received immediate international condemnation, which prevented extremists from holding on to power. He goes on to note that the genocide in Rwanda, in 1994, did not receive the same swift international condemnation because the killers succeeded in convincing the United Nations and the press that it was spontaneous ethnic violence (1994, 2). A small group of elites, both Tutsi and Hutu, has been responsible for mythologizing history, exaggerating ethnic differences into perceived hatred and engineering genocide for their own political ends. Yet the question remains: How can a small number of extremists convince a large number of people that they should carry out massive killing, mostly of their neighbors? Perhaps Mary Gore provided one answer when, at the Cairo World Population Conference in September 1994, she said, "Rwanda is a tragedy and a warning. It is a warning about the way in which extremists can manipulate the fears of a population threatened by its own numbers and by its massive poverty" (quoted in Prunier 1995, 353).

■Rwandan genocide victims. Upwards of eight hundred thousand people were killed in the massacre, which was an attempt to eliminate Tutsis completely—men, women, and children.

SUDAN: A CLASH OF CULTURES

The Republic of Sudan is one of the largest countries in Africa. With its rich agricultural and pasturelands and its trade potential, it could also be one of the most prosperous. Instead, it has had a history of famine, revolution, and regional war. The famine is partly the consequence of desertification, but it is also the consequence of the regional wars that have been consuming East Africa for the last decade. According to John W. Bennett, the Sahel has suffered desiccation due to overgrazing because pastoralists are being forced into smaller regions, the opening of marginal lands to cultivation, and drought cycles (Bennett 1993, 258–259). Spooner (1982) blames aridity on the increased number of tub wells, which attract more cattle than a region can absorb. The cattle crop the grasses and turn grassland to desert. The Nuer, an important pastoral group, live in the central Sudan (considered a part of the south) and presently form a part of the southern revolutionary army, the Sudanese Peoples Liberation Army (SPLA).

The region was under the rule of Egypt and Turkey in the nineteenth century until an Islamic revolt established an Islamic theocracy in 1881. The theocratic state of Sudan was overthrown by Great Britain and made into a British colony until 1956, when the country was granted independence. Until 1956, the British ruled the Arabic-speaking Muslim peoples of the north and the black African Christian and pagan south as separate territories. The Muslim north was based on agriculture, cattle raising, and trade centered in the ancient city of Khartoum, at the confluence of the Blue and White Niles, and Port Sudan on the Red Sea. Here, Muslim culture dominated. Transhumance herders, such as the Nuer and Dinka, and village agriculturalists such as the Zande (of anthropological fame) who had once been a part of the Zande tributary state that encompassed parts of the southern Sudan, Zaire, and the Central African Republic populated the southern region with the city of Juba as its capital and hub of trade. The southern groups were either pagan animists or had adopted Christianity. Both the Muslims and the Animists had histories of feud and war. The Nuer were on the margin of the ancient Islamic state in the north. Upon independence, northern and southern Sudan were merged into one country, an action many social scientists consider to have been a grave error (Shillington 1989, 385). Unlike the situation in Rwanda and Burundi, the cultural differences between northern and southern Sudan are striking.

The non-Muslim southerners considered rule by the Moslem northerners as no more acceptable than rule by the British. Civil war tore the country apart between 1955 and 1972. In 1969, socialist Jaafar Nimeiri came to power; and in 1972 the southern regions were granted semi-autonomy, southern military officers were integrated into the higher ranks of the military, and the fighting ceased but southern discontent did not disappear. The Nimeiri government sought to rebuild and modernize the war-torn country with aid from numerous international donors, including USAID and the Untied Nations Development Program (UNDP). However, the National Islamic Front, under the leadership of Dr. Hassan al Turabi, became increasingly influential and began to receive help from radical Iran after 1979.

In 1983, responding to the National Islamic Front, Nimeiri instituted Moslem Shari'a law to replace the penal code, and he purged the southern officers from his military. Southerners reacted by renewing armed civil conflict. Colonel John Garang led the southern-based Sudanese People's Liberation Army (SPLA) against the central government. His army was predominantly made up of Dinka and Nuer warriors who replaced their traditional spears with automatic weapons. The region around the southern city of Juba and the city of Wau in central Sudan became rallying points for SPLA forces. The fighting disrupted cattle herding and, combined with drought, drove people into the cities (which are held by the government). Both the rebels and the government have prevented food aid from reaching civilians (Sullivan 1989, 112–114).

Nemeri was overthrown in 1985; and in the election that followed in 1986, Sadiq Al Mahdi, the great grandson of the Mahdi, the leader of the theocratic state of the Sudan in the 1880s, was elected prime minister. While the new Prime Minister Sadiq Al-Mahdi wished to reduce the role of Shari'a law, Moslem fundamentalists in his regime prevented a return to secular law and attempted to make Shari'a even more extreme (Sullivan 1989, 112–114).

In June 1990, the Revolutionary Command Council for National Salvation, under the leadership of Lieutenant-General Omar al-Beshir, deposed Sadiq-Al-Mahdi in a military coup. The coup was masterminded by Dr. Hassan al-Turabi. The new military junta, headed by the Islamic Front, is racing to become the first regime in Africa to impose Shari'a law on a nation that is almost one-third Christian and Animist.

We examined the traditional Nuer in a previous case study. By 1983, the Nuer were caught in the complex civil war, which tore the Sudan apart, as the northern Sudan attempted to impose Shari'a law on the southern Sudan. In addition, the Nuer were also caught up in the ethnic wars in Ethiopia, and they tried to find refuge there, as well as in the ancient city of Khartoum, where Sharon Hutchinson was able to interview them in refugee camps. Many were no longer rural people but urban migrants trying to establish a foothold in a rapidly changing world, one that they understood quite well.

Most dramatic, in this society where cattle defined life, cattle, the repository of wealth in the age of their parents and grandparents, were replaced by guns, the bigger the better. The use of guns entered into the definition of women and bride wealth, as well as the power of families, chiefs, and courts. The new warrior association was a subsection of the SPLA, led by John Garang, and often fought other warrior associations of the SPLA and other Nuer families. The influx of guns from the outside world caused inflation in the cost of cattle and thereby in the bride wealth given for women. The world has been turned upside down, as recalled in the words of a fifty-year-old refugee:

> This is not the first time I have seen terrible destruction. I am old and the first [civil] war [1955–72] was there as well. This one began in 1983. Everything horrible you can imagine was done. Bentiu town was full of gun-toters. The Arabs lacked nothing: whatever they wanted from the people, they seized. They would beat you, steal your cattle, and then [try to] marry your daughter with cattle stolen from you! If you refused, they would just take her! So, we left with nothing because the soldiers took by force. If your son had a wife, they would just fall on her [and rape her] without a word—even in her husband's presence! Living conditions grew worse and worse until 1985. That's when our young men became strong and went to the bush to unite with the SPLA. They were fed up with being beaten! (Hutchinson 1996, 18).

NIGERIA: THE DISMAL TUNNEL

On November 10, 1995, Ken Saro-Wiwa and eight of his followers from the Movement for the Survival of the Ogoni People (an Igbo subgroup), an environmental movement attempting to preserve Nigeria's peoples and lands from the worst excesses of oil exploitation and military rule, were executed by the military government of General Sani Abacha. They were guilty of protesting the attacks against the Ogoni people and environmental destruction from the vast oil industry. In 1993, the political situation was promising: an open election appeared to put Moshood Abiola, a wealthy businessman, into the presidency and would have put Nigeria in the center of democratic reform in Africa. Instead Abiola was jailed; and in June of 1996, his wife was shot dead in her car. Many label Nigeria as the most corrupt country in the world, when it should be among the wealthiest.

Like many countries in Africa, Nigeria is a historical product of the colonial era. It was created by Lord Frederick Lugard, a British colonial governor-general, and named after the Niger River. Nigeria brought together three huge and highly developed ethnic groups: the Muslim Hausa and Fulani in the north, and the Yoruba in the west (about whom we read earlier). In addition, to the east were the tribal Igbo (also called Ibo), an egalitarian people who were famed for their works in bronze (Harden 1990). In the 1960s, these four ethnic peoples created political parties based on ethnic identity and then proceeded to slaughter each other in a genocidal civil war. The war ended with the defeat of the Igbo people, whose mineral rich country of Biafra was brought back within the boundaries of the Nigerian state. The end of the war also ended the ethnic conflict, but it did not bring democracy.

General Yakubu Gowon, the winner of the war, was overthrown in a palace coup in 1975. For the next twenty-four years, Nigeria suffered through a series of civilian or military dictatorships. Richard Joseph argued that Nigerians were caught in a dismal tunnel syndrome, a consequence of a theory of state called **prebendalism**. According to this theory, state offices are regarded as prebends (stipends, or political entitlements) that can be appropriated by officeholders, for themselves, to be used to generate material benefits for themselves, their constituents, and their ethnic and kin groups (Joseph 1996). The Abacha regime put the theory into practice to an extreme, having created more millionaires than any predecessor government. Over the past twelve years, however, Nigeria has seen democracy, beginning with the election of Olusegun Obasanjo in 1999. Aside from the election of 2007, which was condemned by outsiders as flawed, democracy in Nigeria continues today, most recently with the election of Goodluck Jonathan in April 2011. Other African countries, such as South Africa, Tanzania, Zambia, and many others, are transitioning to democracy as well.

> **prebendalism**
>
> A theory that holds that state offices are regarded as prebends or political entitlements that can be appropriated by officeholders for themselves to be used to generate material benefits for themselves, their constituents, and their ethnic and kin groups

The Democratic Transition of South Africa

Autocratic governments have given way to democratically elected ones in South Africa, Zambia, Cape Verde, Sao Tome, Benin, Madagascar, Lesotho, Niger, Mali, the Central African Republic, and Zaire. Many would argue that the movements are not indigenous and that the leaders are puppets of the Europeans and Americans, but a close analysis of the recent history of Africa's transitions to democracy and capitalism show otherwise.

Nowhere has the transition to democracy been more unexpected or more sudden than in South Africa. Also, no other country better demonstrates the interconnectedness of politics and markets, and the force of globalization in transforming a society. Yet many doubt the significance of the democratic transitions of the late twentieth century. John Comaroff, professor and chair of the Department of Anthropology at the University of Chicago quotes Gerlta Riviero, the ex-Hungarian ex-wife of the hero of Malcom Bradbury's *Doctor Criminale*, a futuristic novel:

> Democracy, the free market, she asks, "Do you really think they can save us? ... Marxism [was] a great idea, democracy just a small idea. It promises hope, and it gives you Kentucky Fried Chicken" (Comaroff 1994, 34).

Until 1994, South Africa was rigidly segregated by race according to the laws of apartheid. Apartheid, a formal system of segregation of the races, was adopted by South

Africa in 1948, although racism dates back to the origins of the Afrikaner colony in the seventeenth century. Apartheid was a legal code according to which every citizen was typed according to skin color and ancestry: White, Colored, Asian, and Bantu. Government policy regarding political rights, housing, education, and welfare in general were determined by the Apartheid code (Sullivan 1989). Many believe capitalism underlay apartheid, but South Africa has hardly been capitalist. Like many Latin American country, it was state capitalist; capitalism was compromised by the state for the rich whites. These now realize that their own prosperity depends on promises of prosperity for everyone (Comaroff 1994, 35).

Under apartheid, about 17 percent of the population is White and had full rights and access to resources. Every black person was a citizen of a tribal homeland, called a **bantustan**, but had no citizenship rights in the country of South Africa. A bantustan is like a country inside of South Africa, such as Siskei and Transkei. These are not to be confused with the black townships surrounding the industrial cities of South Africa. However, many of the workers in the townships have citizenship in the bantustans, which is one reason the government of South Africa claims that people living in the townships cannot also have South African citizenship. However, about a quarter

■ "For use by white persons"—sign from the apartheid era. Apartheid was a legal code according to which every citizen was typed according to skin color and ancestry.

bantustan

A tribal homeland to which every black person belonged under Apartheid

of the black African population of South Africa lives in or near one of the industrial cities in black townships. Until 1986, Blacks had to carry passes on which were stamped their work permits. Attempts to protest the lack of rights led to a series of attacks by the government on Black townships, including the Sharpeville massacre of 1960 during which more than sixty persons were killed. The Black Consciousness Movement during the early 1970s was led by Steve Biko, who was arrested after an uprising in the Johannesburg suburb of Soweto and beaten to death in jail (Sullivan 1989). Sanctions were imposed on South Africa by the United States, and by many members of the United Nations. By 1987, the pressure began to take its toll.

On September 6, 1989, White South Africa's reactionary approach to the race issue came to a sudden end with the election of a Nationalist leader from Transvaal Province, Frederik de Klerk. On December 13, within months of taking office, de Klerk broke with tradition by meeting with the leader of the African National Congress (ANC), Nelson Mandela, who had been in jail for twenty-seven years. In a surprising move, de Klerk lifted a thirty-year ban on the ANC on February 2, 1990; and on February 11, he released Mandela from jail. Mandela described de Klerk as "a man of integrity." While Mandela initially supported a Marxist state, soon after his release from jail and before the election, he abandoned Marxism and embraced the free market. Supporters of **Inkatha**, the conservative political movement led by Zulu Chief Mongosutho Buthelezi (Shubane 1992), attempted to block the election, as did White right-wingers, both of whom wanted to have their own homeland.

Inkatha

A conservative political movement led by Zulu Chief Mongosutho Buthelezi

On March 28, 1994, Inkatha supporters marched into Johannesburg to protest at the ANC headquarters. ANC and Inkatha gunmen shot at each other and into the crowd, killing several dozen and leading to fear that the April 27, 1994, election would be derailed.

Further meetings were held; Buthelezi and Zwelethini were given assurance by the ANC to important roles in the new government, no matter what the election results were. The final election was a stunning success for Mandela and the ANC. Comaroff captures the symbolism of the election:

> 1:15 p.m., Monday 2 May, a warm winter day in Cape Town. The Grand Parade, an old square redolent with the icons and echoes, the buildings and barricades, of South African colonial history. Nelson Mandela, formally elected President in Parliament just an hour earlier, is due to speak to an assembled mass—and the nation at large—from the balcony of City Hall. It is the same place where he gave his famous speech, in February 1990, after being released from prison. Perhaps two hundred thousand people clog the square, many of them holding aloft banners; an airplane, advertising a local radio station and trailing the sign "God Bless President Mandela," flies overhead. Hundreds of brightly colored new South African flags are draped all over City Hall. Alongside is an old Victorian commercial building. It too has flags flying from poles on its front balcony; eight in all, each one about three times the size of the national flag. These, however, are white and plain. They bear the visage of another old man; he is white. In large letters beneath his image are inscribed three words: KENTUCKY FRIED CHICKEN (Comaroff 1994, 38).

The election of April 26 had to be extended for two more days due to the huge throng of voters and the inexperience of the government in organizing the elections. Thousands of people stood in the sun in long lines, and with great patience, for the opportunity they never thought they would have: to vote. Black South Africans, who had been waiting for the vote since the birth of modern South Africa eighty-four years prior did not seem to mind the long wait. Violence did not take a holiday; bombs went off in KwaZulu Natal killing several dozen. Yet voters would not be deterred; some even suggested they would be glad to die to have the opportunity to vote.

Not surprisingly, the ANC won 63 percent of the vote, and the National Party came in second. Nelson Mandela took the oath of office on May 10, with Second Deputy President Frederik De Klerk. The First Deputy President Thabo Mbeki was a loyal supporter of President Mandela. Camoroff observed that the election in South Africa in 1994 was more than electoral process—it was a social movement, democracy with a large D: "It is striking how frequently the battle was described as a millennial, sacred gesture; how hardened atheists, alumni of the struggle, spoke of spilling tears in the polling booths" (Comaroff 1994, 37).

Mandela faced tremendous challenges in pushing through the political transition. He was a revolutionary used to giving commands, but now he had to act democratically. One of his first actions was to invite Chief Buthelezi into his cabinet. The ANC dominated the new government and had made many promises to Black South Africans to redistribute wealth (Cramer 1994, 208–212). At the same time, Mandela dared not decapitalize the economy in meeting his promises. Blacks lacked electricity, jobs, and education. Whether they would have the patience to achieve these slowly, and not to alienate the whites that dominated the economy, was an open question. An equally important question was whether whites would realize that they had to pull in their belts for a number of years to accept responsibility for imposing a heritage of apartheid on the blacks of South Africa?

The question boils down to the blocked transitions. Population growth among Blacks in South Africa is high; poverty is high. Environmental destruction has been high. Prosperity has to be achieved through the close balance between the political and economic transitions: jobs and education must be created. Yet, the ANC dare not implement the Marxist rhetoric of its revolutionary past if it is to create a democratic South Africa. To the north, there are many Marxist/socialist governments that have collapsed, many of which were based on Black one-party states based on rule by a single tribe. From Angola to Mozambique, from Somalia to Sudan, from Liberia to Rwanda and Burundi, the message is to proceed cautiously along the twin transitions to democracy and open markets and not to alienate any one of the various ethnic/minority groups in the new South Africa.

■   ■   ■

Ecological
Maladaptation

Famine in Africa

Much world attention has focused on the problems of hunger in Africa. In the 1980s, famine was widespread in twenty-two African nations. The Food and Agricultural Organization (FAO) estimated 70 percent of all Africans did not have enough to eat (Sullivan 1989, 2). While food supplies improved slightly in some African nations in the 1990s, this has been due largely to international food relief. Africa's population growth continues to outpace growth in agricultural production. In the 1990s, the FAO listed six sub-Saharan African countries with critical food security problems and sixteen with marginal food security. Although drought is frequently cited as the main factor, one cannot ignore the impact of misguided state agricultural policies of former colonial and modern African governments on food security. These policies have favored the transformation of peasant-based food production for local consumption to an industrially based agriculture favoring the production of exports. The consequence has been a steady decrease in food grown for human consumption and an increase in hunger.

During the seventy or more years of domination by Europeans, the economies of the African colonies were organized to benefit the colonists. Cash crops—such as cocoa, coffee, groundnuts (peanuts), cotton, and rubber—were substituted for food crops and exported to international markets (Sullivan 1989, 3). While some peasant farmers benefitted, in many regions large plantations were established and run by foreigners. Migrant labor was encouraged, leading to the decline of food production in the home villages of the laborers. European companies, using migrant African labor, also developed mining, further reducing the number of farmers in the countryside.

After independence was achieved, many of the plantations and mines continued to function as foreign "enclaves" within Africa or they were nationalized. Even when they were nationalized, they maintained their export orientation. Through this process, large masses of land were taken out of the production of food for local consumption and turned towards the production of export commodities.

By the late 1960s, with large plantations specializing in growing export commodities, most local food production depended on small peasant plots of land owned by households. With the introduction of modern farm practices in the late 1950s, small peasant and tribal farmers stayed ahead of the demand for food. However, with decolonialization and the movement towards socialist governments, new policies were initiated which had unintended consequences. Socialist governments, trying to get the support of urban workers, held down local food prices by forcing farmers to accept artificially low payments for the food they grew. On the other hand, artificially high prices were placed on export commodities to stimulate export agriculture, which generated foreign currency, needed to pay off foreign debts. (Reeves 1989, McCorkle 1989).

The consequence of these two policies has been devastating. Most rural populations are subsistence oriented and grow enough to feed themselves and their neighbors. They also grow a small surplus to sell at market to buy clothes, seed, fuel, and other amenities that families cannot produce. This small surplus has fed most of the urban populations for decades. By motivating farmers to grow only export commodities and by lowering their motivation to grow food for local consumption, there has been a continuous lowering of agricultural productivity in Africa. (Reeves, 1989)

At the same time that food production has been dropping, the population of Africa has increased dramatically. The evidence that is available points overwhelmingly in the direction of a serious and deepening agricultural crisis in Africa south of the Sahara. The most visible symptom of this malaise is declining per capita food production. Sub-Saharan Africa is the only region of the world where per capita food production declined over the last two decades. With a population growth rate of 3 percent per year, Africa managed only a 2 percent annual increase in food production during the 1960s, 1970s, and 1980s. By the end of the 1970s, per capita food production was only 80 percent of its 1961 level. Famine has rapidly become the most common symbol of African life at a time when Asia and Latin America managed to achieve per capita increases in food production (Lofchie 1986, 161).

In the mid 1980s, food riots in cities and starvation in the countryside, collapsing economic conditions, the disintegration of social services, increasing urban violence and reluctance on the part of international lending agencies to loan more money—all caused many Africans to question the totalitarian political economies which had evolved over the last three decades. Many African countries have begun to abandon socialist type governments and to move in the direction of democratization and privatization (Knight 1992).

Chapter
Summary

Africa: Overcoming a Colonial Legacy

Africa and its peoples have suffered tragically at the hands of European colonial governments. They are suffering again under the totalitarian regimes of their own leaders. Africans are becoming aware that simple European models of capitalism or Marxist socialism are not going to lead them out of ethnic conflict and regional war, nor help them achieve economic stability and sustained development. Awareness is growing. The answers may lie in the introduction of democracy, open market systems, a reduction in the growth of the population, and balancing African economic demands with the demands of the natural environment and human health. There is also a growing awareness of Africa's ancient heritages, of its many successes, its gifts to a world which once was.

The most critical understanding of all is that competing in the modern world trade system is not a matter of choice but a need that can only be met with peace and democratic reform. Many countries have begun the hard work, and in a later chapter we will spend time examining some of the most surprising changes to have taken place in Africa, particularly the election of Nelson Mandela in South Africa.

Chapter
Terms

acephalous political system	287	Inkatha	310
Amratian	291	Later Iron Age	293
Arab	289	mastaba	292
Badarian	291	Meroe	293
bantustan	310	polygyny	285
Bedouin	289	prebendalism	309
complementary opposition	288	settled farming	282
Gerzean	291	transhumance herding	282

Check out our website
www.BVTLab.com
for flashcards,
chapter summaries,
and more.

Chapter 9

The Middle East: Ethnicity, Oil, and Conflict

This chapter describes the changing political ecology of the Middle East. The Middle East is a region difficult to define because the term has been used in so many ways to include many different groups of countries. Today, Middle East refers to the region that includes northern Africa and southwestern Asia, including Turkey, once the heart of the great Ottoman Empire, which spread well into Eastern Europe. Going across the face of Africa from west to east, the following countries are currently considered to be a part of the Middle East: Morocco, Algeria, Tunisia, Libya, Egypt, Israel, Lebanon, Turkey, Syria, Jordan, Iraq, Iran, Saudi Arabia, Kuwait, Bahrain, Qatar, the United Arab Emirates, Oman, and Yemen. Today the peoples of this region use the terms "Middle East" and "Middle Eastern" to refer to their region and to themselves (Rassam 1995, xxxv). In the past, a distinction was made by some scholars between North Africa and the Middle East, with the latter including Egypt and all the rest of the non-African countries listed above. French scholars use the term "Near East" to refer to Egypt plus the non-African Arab countries.

In this region, Mesopotamia and Egypt were the first cores of civilization; here are found the earliest dates for the first cities of the world. It is one of the cradles of civilization, and it is the region in which Judaism, Christianity, and Islam evolved. These three religions are based on the first mythic religions of the first states of Ur, Sumer, Babylon, and ancient Persia. Egypt lent its early influence to the creation of these religions as well, and later Greece and Rome added their imprint. The interplay among ecological, political, and economic forces, many of which are from outside of the region, are not easy to sort out; nor can one discuss this region without some mention of the great passions involved.

The region is culturally complex and diverse. In addition to the three religions of Judaism, Christianity, and Islam, it contains four major cultural complexes, three ancient and one recent. The old culture complexes of this region are Arab, Iranian, and Turkish; the recent one is Israeli.

The tendency in the popular press is to stress the conflict between the religious differences of Jews in Israel and Palestinian Arabs living on the West Bank, or what is left of Palestine. However, there are many other conflicts due to distinctions of Islamic identity, whose nature is impossible to understand without knowledge of the culture history of the Middle East. Conflicts are also fueled by differences between radical (socialist) revolutionaries who espouse state control of resources, such as factions in the governments of Libya, Iraq, and Syria, and Sunni fundamentalists who wish a return to non-socialist, religiously based governments. The Sunnis, in turn, struggle with the Shiite factions who also wish for theocratic type states and that the Shiite government of Iran supports. Within Israel, there are factions that want to create a Jewish ethnic state and factions that want a modern and secular society.

The Middle East is a passionate place, one in which political ecology, the emotions of ethnic diversity, and the stages of history are so intricately combined as to not be separable. In the following, we combine these into a single story, which will then lead into the current conflicts and controversies of the Middle East.

Political Ecology and Cultural Diversity: A Historical Overview

Because the Middle East spills across North Africa, Southwest Asia, and parts of southern Europe, geography tends to be highly diverse. As with Africa, land tends to lend itself to either settled village agriculture (grain agriculture or tree and vine crops) or pastoral nomadism. In regions where there is no irrigation, the lack of land for agriculture is a serious problem because of the destruction of land over the centuries. Most of the forests have been cut down. A few areas, particularly around the Persian Gulf, have vast petroleum reserves; however, only a few countries have access to the oil, creating wealth in Saudi Arabia, Iran, Kuwait, Iraq, and the United Arab Emirates, but making other countries poor cousins. Yet oil did not become important to the region until after 1945. Before then, control over trade in a variety of goods (over many of the caravan routes of antiquity) tended to determine wealth. As discussed in the last chapter, trade was a constant feature of North Africa, tying together ancient city-states and civilizations up into Afghanistan.

Mountainous regions in eastern Turkey, northern Iraq, and southern Iran have considerable rainfall; but altitude and cold winters make them ill-suited to extensive agriculture. These regions are used to raise sheep and goats. There is considerable work being done to capture the highland water and pipe it into lowland regions, but this may cause conflict between different states whose water may be taken by others (e.g., Iraq and Syria are angry that Turkey is damming up the waters from the Tigris and Euphrates for its own use).

■The Middle East is a passionate place, one in which political ecology, the emotions of ethnic diversity, and the stages of history are inseperable.

Transportation has always been a problem because of deserts and mountains. However, as Bernard Lewis, a noted historian of the region, puts it, the sands of the deserts were major transportation links for pastoral nomads; the camel was like a ship adapted to sand. Trade formed the connectivities of the Great Silk Road on through the Sinai, up into present day Lebanon, Syria, through Turkey, Iran, and Afghanistan, then on to China. The goods which were exchanged are familiar: gold, silver, slaves, ivory, dates, palm oil, wine, pottery, spices, and, the creations of nomadic pastoralists: carpets (Wolf 1982). Most cities, which were the cores of imperial states, were located at junctures between bodies of water and overland trade routes through dry lands. The colonialism between 1830 and 1950, as well as subsequent ethnic warfare, seriously disrupted transportation and trade, impoverishing the urban populations who once depended on trade and manufacturing for a livelihood. During the colonial period and to modern times, transaction costs were raised by inter-ethnic violence. In earlier ages, transaction costs were reduced by those states that could control the violence between the members of distinct ethnic groupings.

The history of the Middle East has been one of conflict between local ethnic groups and powerful states, which imposed peace and attempted to monopolize trade. Often the ideology of the challenging ethnic groups was a type of populist egalitarianism based on pastoral nomadism. The story behind the conflict is the mythology of Cain and Abel: Cain, the agricultural townsman, slays Abel, the rural pastoral nomad, a conflict presented in all three major religions. This fable encapsulates the often-repeated conflict through the ages of the small sect of true believers, versus the state that binds all to a creed of toleration.

An early example is Manicheism, the creed of Mani, a blend of Christian and Zoroastrian beliefs that opposed the pagan Roman state. A second example was the heresy of Mazdak. Mazdak, who flourished during the early sixth century in Iran, espoused religious communism, which underlies modern Shiite ideology found in Iran and among Hizbollah radicals (the party of God). Another example is the Maccabees, a volatile Jewish sect that led resistance against the Syrians and then the Romans. The Roman state practiced a polytheistic form of

Figure 9.1

☐ Physiographic Map of the Middle East

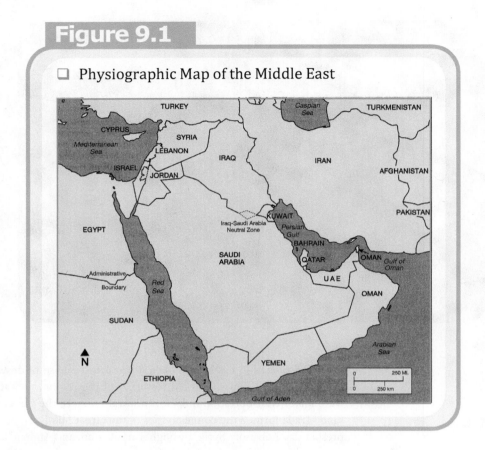

religion centering on Jupiter. The Maccabees refused to sacrifice animals to Jupiter, but were finally crushed in AD 70 after almost two centuries of guerrilla tactics against the state (Gilbert 1990, 36–37, Lewis 1995, 31).

The dialogue between advocates of populist egalitarianism and imperial authoritarianism has been continuous since ancient times. Peace and trade were never achieved without the smoldering resentment of Christian, Hebraic, or Islamic sects, each of which saw itself as the true follower of an egalitarian, but not democratic, faith. Today, religious and ethnic tensions continue between authoritarian states imposing order and radical movements and demanding populist forms of governance.

Much of the conflict and tension through time can be understood in terms of control of trade and competition for resources in a region of relative scarcity. The Middle East has always been a region of diverse ecological zones: deserts, foothills, mountains, plateaus, plains, river systems, and forests. Into these ecosystems distinct ethnic villages, with their varied cultures and religions, evolved over thousands of years, sometimes drawn into the control of states and sometimes remaining on the tribal margins of great civilizations. The earliest evidence for trade and the imposition of chiefdom social control dates back to 7000 BC at the site of Jericho. Jericho, at a crossing point on the Jordan River, was on a major trade route and may have been the first chiefdom or mini-state in ancient Mesopotamia. Its people lived in round, brick houses, had irrigation agriculture, and reared livestock. They also had a spectacular stonewall 1.6 meters thick and over 2 meters high, surrounded by a ditch 8.5 meters wide. On the interior of the wall was a stone tower over 8.5 meters high; both the wall and tower were probably defensive works. Trade during this early period was in salt, bitumen, and sulfur from the Dead Sea area, turquoise from the Sinai region, cowrie shells from the Red Sea, and obsidian and greenstones from Anatolia (Redman 1978, 78).

Brian Fagan makes the point that ecological differences would have produced distinct trade goods, and that states would draw otherwise antagonistic peoples into peaceful trade relations (Fagan 1995). Trade routes of camel herding nomads crisscrossed the region bringing in the goods the region lacked, such as fine woods and metals, for which grain and local goods were exchanged. Trade moved up and down the Tigris and Euphrates by boat and camel caravan to the highlands of Iran (Persia) and into the deserts of pharaonic Egypt. As trade expanded, city-states grew, competition for goods intensified, and city states fought for dominance. Distinct states had their day in the sun and then vanished as trade routes shifted, climates changed, or regimes fell apart. When they were successful, states became powerful and highly stratified. However, stratification based on ruthless administrators and increasing demands for tribute from diverse peoples produced poorly integrated, volatile empires. Nonetheless, the archaeology of the region, including a recent discovery of Bronze Age shipwrecks, shows that the Middle East has always been the cross-roads of the Old World, lying athwart the water route from the southern Ukraine to the Mediterranean via the Black Sea, the Bosporus, the Sea of Marmora, the Dardanelles and

Figure 9.2

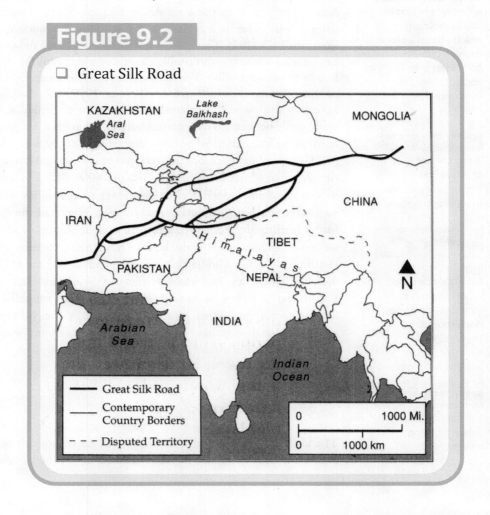

❑ Great Silk Road

the Aegean Sea. One-hump camels traversed the deserts of sand as far back as 3000 BC, while boats and rafts navigated rivers and seas (Goldschmidt 1983, 9).

Human Ecology

The human ecology of the Middle East parallels much written in the previous chapter, in part because North Africa is considered part of the Middle East. Southwest Asia, as discussed in Chapter 5, is the birthplace of agriculture and pastoral nomadism. Nature did not endow the Middle East lavishly. There are no grassy plains, and nine-tenths of the forests have been cut down. Water is scarce and precious; and while minerals have been mined since ancient times, they do not amount to much, except for oil. In addition to trade, the two other major adaptations have been irrigation agriculture (the oasis) and pastoral nomadism (which, of course, was an aspect of trade).

IRRIGATION AGRICULTURE

From the earliest settled towns and villages, irrigation agriculture has been an important facet of human ecology in the Middle East. The dates for the first irrigation in Southwest Asia are very close to those for Ancient Egypt. Simple family-based irrigation probably dates at least as far back as the site of Catal Huyuk in ancient Anatolia dated to 6000 BC (Redman 1978, 185). These early systems are still used today and are called **qanats**; they can be used whenever water-table elevations under a hillside are higher than the land surface in an adjacent valley. Vertical wells on the hillside are combined with horizontal wells to channel water fanwise into fields (Bennett 1993, 207). Another similar technology is the **kerese**, a shallow well combined with tunnels and manholes. Both of these technologies could easily be manned by a single clan and did not require great organization. These systems can be found in tribal and chiefdom villages throughout the modern Middle East.

Grander but more brittle were **perennial irrigation** works controlled by states, the oldest of which dates back to 3000 to 4000 BC. These required massive inputs of human labor and a great deal of knowledge of hydraulics. While these systems had the advantage of operating throughout the year, they had the disadvantage of flooding or losing fertility due to **salinization**, the accumulation of salts. The qanats and kerese were ecologically sustainable, but the perennial irrigation systems on which the great civilizations of the Middle East were dependent were not. Unlike Egypt, with its predictable hydraulics, the water systems of Southwest Asia (especially the Tigris and Euphrates) were apt to be influenced by sudden rainfall in the nearby Tauros and Zagros mountain chains, producing floods in the valleys (Spooner 1979). These unpredictable floods may explain the early needs for water wizards, shamans who could control rainfall and are a part of the mythology of the three religions, particularly the story of the Noah and the flood.

PASTORAL NOMADISM

The last chapter presented a description of camel nomads, which are also found in the desert lowlands of Southwest Asia. In addition to camels, various distinct ethnic groups

---

qanat

A simple family-based iirrigation system in which vertical wells on a hillside are combined with horizontal wells to channel water fanwise into fields

kerese

A shallow well combined with tunnels and manholes to provide irrigation

perennial irrigation

Irrigation works controlled by states, which operated throughout the year and required knowledge of hydraulics and massive human labor

salinization

The accumulation of salts in irrigation systems, which caused loss of fertility

Ecological
Maladaptation

Desertification in the Middle East

Desertification, the process of desert expansion as a result of human degradation of fragile semi arid environments, is a worldwide process. There are few regions that escape the problem, but it is particularly serious in the Middle East. With a high proportion of these marginal lands, the Middle East must support one of the highest populations living in this type of environment (Spooner 1979,15). To make matters worse, the population is growing rapidly, encouraged by Islamic state policies. Saudi Arabia, for example, has an annual population growth rate of 1.53 percent. Saudi Arabia's population in 1990 was 15 million; today it is 26 million.

According to Brian Spooner, a key researcher of Middle East problems, desertification constitutes a serious threat to food production (1982). Desertification occurs at two ends of an adaptive continuum in the Middle East and Africa: irrigation agriculture and pastoral nomadism. For centuries, these adaptations functioned very effectively until economically oriented development efforts upset the delicate ecological balance in this fragile environment. These two forms of adaptation were components of inter-related food production systems. For thousands of years, nomads traded meat and animal products to agricultural-ists for cereal grains, fruits, and vegetables.

Although irrigation can make an arid region productive, it can also destroy the soil if the process is mismanaged. Unfortunately, this seems to have been the case throughout the Middle East, according to Spooner. Huge development schemes have been intent on increasing the amount of water introduced into the soil, but have ignored the importance of the soil/water balance. Just as too little water can render a soil unproductive, so can too much water. Spooner estimates that almost half of the irrigated land of the region is no longer productive, due to salinization, waterlogging, and leaching, all attributable to inadequately regulated irrigation. Salinization is the accumulation of salts in the soil, which are toxic to most plants, caused by inadequate drainage and rapid evaporation. Poor drainage can also cause waterlogging, where water soaked soils become highly acidic and oxygen deprived. Leaching dissolves the nutrients in the topsoil and carries them down into the lower soil levels, thereby depleting the topsoil.

Irrigation mismanagement is found along the Nile in Egypt, the Tigris and Euphrates in Iraq, the Oxus and smaller rivers of Soviet Central Asia, and the Helmand of Afghanistan (Spooner 1979, 41). Engineering skills and hydraulic theory have been transferred to these regions, but institutions needed to manage massive irrigation systems in an environmentally sound manner are lacking.

The second major cause of desertification is the settling of pastoral nomads. The pastoral adaptation evolved in an environment that could not support intensive farming and functioned effectively for thousands of years. However, encouraged by state sponsored development schemes, scores of nomadic groups have either abandoned their herding to farm this arid land or have increased the size of their herds in order to be able to export meat, hides, and other animal products. Those who maintain their pastoral lifestyle are restricted to much smaller grazing areas, which result in overgrazing. This has caused long term deterioration of vegetation and soil erosion. Unfortunately, intensive use of these marginal lands is turning them into true deserts, which can support neither agriculture nor herding economies and is causing starvation among previously well adapted peoples.

According to Spooner, misguided policies have done very serious damage to formerly productive land, where desertification has affected almost 300 million of the 410 million acres in Iran, 135 million out of 161 million acres in Afghanistan, and only a slightly smaller proportion in Pakistan. These vast areas have been so poorly managed that they can no longer be used efficiently for any kind of food production.

Clearly these development policies have failed the people and abused a fragile ecological system. Spooner argues that development specialists should help transhumance herders to more effectively develop the traditional talents and techniques they already have and not to introduce non-adaptive forms of economic behavior. The technology of pastoralists has been generally assumed by development planners to be uncomplicated. The fact is that it is a fairly complex, highly effective, and ecologically sensitive adaptation that should be studied by planners, not dismissed as primitive and inefficient.

also herded sheep and goats on horseback, muleback, or by foot in the mountains and valleys of Iran and Anatolia. Sheep and goat economies were highly flexible and allowed tribal populations great independence from the states of the region.

Thomas Barfield shows how sheep and goat herders follow the concept of *il rah*, the tribal road, synchronized migrations by different tribes over the lands they exploited (1993, 93–104). Fredrik Barth has commented that it is as though the tribes were following gigantic carpets over the landscape. The **khans** or chiefs of these tribes controlled the maps of movements, often living in towns, offering their allegiance to the state. If times were bad, they led tribes in attacks on the same towns and states, demonstrating the two sides of the **trade/raid nexus**. When in his trade mode, the tribesman on horse, mule, or foot connected up with the townsman and formed linkages in the trade routes running east and west across the Middle East. When at war, the links broke down; the tribesman vindicated his honor, but suffered poverty. Whether a herder of camels, goats, or sheep, the tribal nomad could be the raider or trader. The cycle of the peaceful pastoralist versus the warlike nomad ties to the Cain/Able analogy offered earlier; and the cycle is also a part of the rise and fall of religious sects and states, which in turn connects to the political economy of the three religions of the Middle East: Judaism, Christianity, and Islam (the People of the Book).

Political Economy and Religion

The histories of ancient empires in the region of the Middle East go back, of course, to Mesopotamia and Egypt, and overlap many cores and peripheries, religions, state ideologies, political movements, and conflicts. There is no simple cake-like layering of history, with historic levels cutting from Gibraltar to Damascus. Instead, the closest analogy is conglomerate, the geological formation made of a complex mix of gravel, large stones, boulders, and a matrix of cement (time). States with their religions spread, encompassed ethnic groups, converted them, encouraged peace, imposed bureaucracies, and then gave way to new states and became their peripheries. New state religions rapidly became ancient legacies, and these in turn became incorporated within new states with new conversions. Every belief system in the Middle East has ancient roots, dating back to pre-Islamic empires and combining nature worship, ancestor worship, and **monotheism** (the belief in one god). The modern peoples of the Middle East are the descendants of ancient empires, and their beliefs correspond to one of three books: the Christian Bible, the Jewish Torah, or the Islamic Quran (Koran). However, still today on the peripheries are tribal peoples with beliefs, some of which probably go back to pharaonic Egypt and Ur.

The pagan religions that preceded and are partly incorporated in Judaism, Christianity, and Islam, were **polytheistic**, worshipping many gods; and they were **cosmic**, having to do with the natural powers of the cosmos. They grew out of

il rah

A tribal road over which synchronized migrations by different tribes occurs

khan

A tribal chief

trade/raid nexus

The cycle practiced by pastoral nomads: a tribe with successfully protected herds—and thus surplus animals—trades; an unsuccessful tribe raids

monotheism

The belief in one god

polytheism

The belief in many gods

■The Islamic Quran

cosmism

The belief that the natural powers of the cosmos are supernatural beings

a-cosmism

The belief that the natural powers of the cosmos are not supernatural beings themselves but are controlled by greater principles or forces

supernaturalism

The belief that controlling principles or forces supersede the natural universe

tribal and chiefdom religions, which they resemble; the animal headed gods of the Egyptians and the great interest in the connections of the gods to the stars is a good example of a polytheistic and cosmic religion. Judaism, Christianity, and Islam differed from pagan religions. For one, they are **a-cosmic**: they search for principles that go beyond the visible powers of our cosmos. Second, they are monotheistic, believing in one God. The powers that they seek to explain are not natural, but are **supernatural**. Scholars of religion have suggested that the origin of the three religions may be found in the monotheistic religion created by the Egyptian Pharaoh Amenhotep IV, also known as Akhnaton or Ikhnaton. Akhnaton developed a religious sect that ousted all of the gods of the Egyptian pantheon except one: Ra, symbolized by the Aton or sun disk. The Jewish historian Martin Gilbert finds the link between Judaism and Akhnaton's sun worship in the Hebrew word Adon, which means Lord (Gilbert 1993, 13). In a remarkable paper published in 1948, the anthropologist Leslie White wrote the following:

> In Egypt in the fourteenth century before the Christian era some remarkable events took place. Monotheism came to the fore and waged war on the old polytheism. All gods were abolished save one, and he was made Lord of all … What caused this upheaval that shook Egypt to its foundation and extended its influence even to us today? One of the answers has been: Ikhnaton (White 1949, 235).

However, White rejects the idea that one man changed history so profoundly, and instead presents the position that the monotheism of Akhnaton was a long term trend in Egyptian history, which Akhnaton exploited to gain power for himself, his supporters, and his deity, Ra, against the priesthoods of all the other gods. Akhnaton was discredited by his successor Rameses II, who came to the throne in 1292 BC. Martin Gilbert believes Rameses II was the pharaoh mentioned in the Bible who enslaved the Jews, but it is also thought that Moses and the captured Hebrews already had the concept of monotheism before they were brought to the court of Rameses II. However one looks at it, it is the religion that Moses inspires which becomes Judaism; and it is this religion that underlies both Christianity and Islam. The Jewish faith is more than a religion. In addition to faith in a single deity, it embraces a set of ethical and moral principles covering every aspect of life, from hygiene and behavior to justice and equality before God and the law.

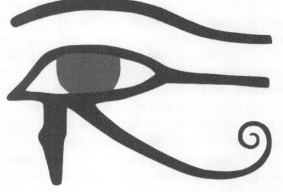

FROM UR TO BABYLON: THE ROOTS OF JUDAISM

Many aspects of Hebrew culture bear traces of the influence of Babylonian culture. The story of the flood, the sacrifice of a loved one (Isaac), and the finding of a child in the bulrushes who is really a prince are all Mesopotamian in origin (Gilbert 1990, 3). Abraham, the father of the Jews, is said to have come from Ur of the Babylonians, mentioned in earlier chapters. Abraham was of a Semitic tribe that became powerful in Babylon around 4000 BC, after migrating from the Syrian desert into the Mesopotamian delta, perhaps as traders. Semites controlled Ur until the Sumerians, a non–Semite population possibly from central Asia, conquered it. Sumer flowered, and the seeds of monotheism took root, originating as a reaction against polytheistic cosmic religions.

Abraham and his followers, about 2000 BC, wandered westward with his flocks of sheep, perhaps to Canaan (modern Palestine) where Abraham died. His followers continued across the Sinai into Egypt, where they settled about 1800 BC. This is about the time that the Hyksos, an Asiatic people, conquered Egypt and dominated it for the next two hundred years. The Hebrews, or Haibiru, appear to have formed a special social class with various functions and roles, of both low and high rank, within and outside the law in the Hyksos dominated society. As a tribe of sheepherders, they may have been looked down upon by the urban dwelling Egyptians and may even have been sacrificed to the Egyptian gods (a Biblical theme).

In about 1550 BC, the Egyptians revolted against the Hyksos, and it has been suggested that it is at this time that the Hebrews were enslaved by the Egyptians. Its priestly class strictly ordered Egyptian life, and it is during the apotheosis of Akhnaton that monotheism becomes a challenge to that class, appearing again with Moses a hundred years later. Moses, it has been theorized, was an Egyptian prince who converted to the religion of the untouchable Habiru. Others believe that Moses was a Hebrew who was adopted by a royal princess and raised as an aristocrat. Whether the Hebrews were expelled from Egypt, or they left of their own accord, is a matter of conjecture. The fact is Moses led his people from Egypt back to the land of his father, Abraham, in present day Palestine-Israel. There is much debate whether his followers were many or just a few, thousands or hundreds. Once in the land of Abraham, they linked up with a loose federation of nomadic tribes of Semitic origin, converted these to Judaism, and established the small state of Israel, which remained a federation of tribes for decades.

It is possibly during this time that the Jews developed their standards of hygiene. Records show that whenever the Jews have been forced to live in adverse conditions, it is the Jewish community that stays healthiest. Israel survived under a series of unstable dynasties until the death of Solomon in 930 BC, and then divided into two kingdoms: a northern kingdom called Israel and a southern kingdom called Judah, which held on to the temple of Jerusalem. Judah had the advantage of the sacred shrine, and it had the better rulers. In 722 BC, Israel fell to the Assyrians, who were in turn conquered by Babylon in 612 BC. In 597 BC, the king of Babylon, Nebuchadnezzar, captured the holy city of Jerusalem, and the kingdom of Judah was destroyed; its people sent into exile. The Hebrews survived their exile by returning to their nomadic existence called the **diaspora**. They dispersed carrying their religion with them in the form of three books that contained their laws and ethical codes. The new religion emphasized the importance of life in a region in which many of the cults—Roman and pagan religions—focused on death. The new code stressed that humans had to choose between good or evil. It was during the diaspora that the laws were codified and written down. The Biblical code of the Jews was not the first written law. The code of Hammurabi was much earlier and established the legal bases for such matters as sale, purchase, inheritance, theft, and manslaughter. However, Jewish law was the first set of laws based on an understanding of moral principles. The books of the Bible were also important in that they stressed the special relationship between religion and ethnicity: Judaism and the Hebrews. Judaism is the only one of the world religions to have this characteristic. It has been theorized that it was this exclusive connection between religion and ethnicity that led to the more inclusive religion of Christianity, which is not based on ethnic identity. The Jews have remained a separate people who refuse to assimilate to the religious belief of their conquerors. They have also always been among the primary traders and commercial people in any region of the world where they settle.

diaspora

The dispersed Jewish peoples who were expelled from their homeland at different times over the centuries; also refers to Palestinians expelled from their homeland in more recent times

Figure 9.3

❑ Map of the Jewish Exodus

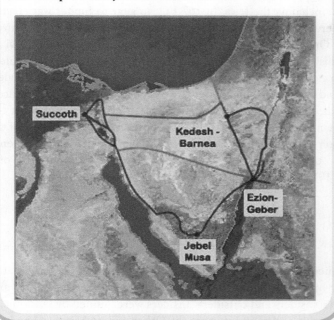

One of the most remarkable characteristics of the Jews, which goes back to their earliest origins and remains true today, is that the emphasis on reading and interpreting the Old Testament has meant that each man, and most women, are literate. This has meant that the Jews, in their wanderings, were often the chief scribes, the bureaucrats, the traders, the bankers, and have always been commercially successful. In a sense, they travelled as a group through the cradles of civilization and were always among the most sophisticated, often becoming the major advisors to kings. The Greeks referred to them as philosophers of race. It was not only the Jewish people that inspired others but also that their religion awed the peoples of these ancient civilizations; the ideas of the Jews underlay the major philosophies of others. Even at the high point of the Middle Ages, when Jews were relegated to the lowliest of occupations, that of moneylenders, they succeeded and became the focus of jealousies, which come down to the present age.

This brings us up to about two thousand years ago, when the region which we call the Middle East was divided between two powerful and contentious empires: Rome and Persia. The western half, including the countries of the eastern Mediterranean from Bosnia to southern Egypt, was part of the Roman Empire. The eastern half belonged to Persia, which had incorporated Babylon. The cultures and languages of these two empires were very different from today. While Egyptian culture was yet distinctive, it had been incorporated into the Roman Empire.

The Persian Empire was composed of the remnants of the earlier empires of Sumer, Akkadia, Assyria, and Babylonia. Cyrus the Mede, the founder the Persian empire, overthrew Babylon in 539 BC. Recognizing some commonality between the religion of the Jews and his own Zoroastrianism, a religion which also stressed the belief in a single god, good and evil, Cyrus released the Jews from captivity and ordered the rebuilding of the Temple at Jerusalem. The Hebraic religion came to be influenced by several Zoroastrian ideas, among them the cosmic struggle between the forces of good and evil, between God and the Devil, judgment after death with reward or damnation, and the coming of a savior (Lewis 1995, 28). The Jews rose to prominence under Persian rule, even though they had the option of returning to Israel, which many did.

The Persian Empire fell to Alexander the Great (336–23 BC), and the Jews adopted Greek dress and lifestyle. They also became familiar with the writings of Greek philosophers, but they did not adopt the pagan religion of the Greeks. Many Jews migrated west along the North coast of Africa, into Eastern Europe, and as far north as modern Russia. They were usually traders, developing firm reputations as experts in commerce.

The Jews were tolerated under the rule of the heirs of Alexander (Ptolemy I and Ptolemy II) but not under the Seleucids. The Seleucids, descended from Seleucus, one of Alexander's Macedonian generals, conquered Judea in 198 BC. One of the Seleucid rulers, Antiochos IV, attempted to impose Hellenism, the Greek religion based on the worship of Jupiter, on all his subjects, including the Jews. In 167 BC, an altar to Jupiter was erected inside of the Temple at Jerusalem. Underground resistance movements were organized against the Seleucid state. One band, the Maccabees, named after their leader Judas Maccabeus, began to win skirmishes against Seleucid forces and finally marched into Jerusalem in December of 164 BC to cleanse and purify the temple. Roman rule expanded into Judea, displacing the Seleucids, and at first allowing the Jews to continue their religious practices. However, like the Seleucids, the Romans came to expect that its citizens would adopt the Hellenic religion. Yet Roman religious persecution was no more acceptable than that of the Seleucids, and the Jews soon developed many distinct anti-Roman **messianic movements** (movements of revival and transformation which emphasize faith in the appearance of a messiah; Lanternari 1963, 19). One of these messianic movements became Christianity.

> **messianic movement**
>
> A movement of revival and transformation that emphasizes faith in the appearance of a messiah

THE BIRTH OF CHRISTIANITY AND THE RISE OF THE BYZANTINE EMPIRE

Bernard Lewis (1995) argues that during this age, in the Middle East and elsewhere, the universal custom was for human groups to draw a firm line between themselves and others: insiders and outsiders. Insiders were defined by kinship and ethnicity, and outsiders were the Other, the barbarians. The Jews and the Greeks introduced a new twist: one could become an insider by abandoning the religion and identity of Other, and accepting a Judaic God, or a Greek pantheon. The Romans expanded the ideas of the Greeks, to create a Roman state that incorporated all of its peoples within the Roman empire, but insisted that the Hellenic state religion be adopted by the newly incorporated folk. Judaism continued to preach that it was the religion of ethnic Hebrews. Christianity arose as one of several Jewish movements, but one with the Roman twist of accepting the state, *but not its religion*. The other Jewish movements ranged from the Pharisees who fought bitter civil wars against the Romans, to the Essenes who practiced the monastic worship of a future Messiah, and retreated into the desert.

The actual origins of Christianity are both lost in time and are points of serious theological disagreement. One popular perspective is that the Christian sect was one of several Jewish Messianic movements, but one which preached the acceptance of the Roman state, and a live and let live relationship between Caesar (the state) and God (the supernatural). Here is the fusion of the tolerant Hellenic philosophies of the Romans and Greeks, with their fascination in final cause and ultimate principles and the a-cosmic, monotheistic, supernaturalistic religion of the Jews, and the simple idea that religion should not be based on ethnic identity. Christianity, unlike Judaism, did not deny the Roman state but argued that Christianity was not of this world. The new religion appealed to

■Roman religious persecution led the Jews to develop many distinct anti-Roman messianic movements. It was from these movements that Christianity was born.

the lower classes of the Roman state. At first persecuted, it spread quickly; and within three hundred years after the death of Jesus Christ, it became the state religion of Rome and the Byzantine Empire.

Constantine I (AD 306–337), the first Christian emperor of the Roman Empire, established a second, eastern capital at Constantinople. At the end of the reign of Emperor Theodosius (AD 379–395), the Roman Empire was permanently split into a western part ruled from Rome and an eastern part ruled from Constantinople. The eastern part became known as the Byzantine Empire. The western empire was soon destroyed by barbarian invasions. The eastern empire survived for another thousand years, with Greek as the state language and Christianity as the state religion. The Byzantine Empire was controlled by a command economy, driven and planned by state authorities. This continued a tradition that can be traced back to Egypt: the Byzantine rulers tightly controlled the economy. The state intervened in industry, trade, manufacture, and in agriculture (Lewis 1995). Brian Fagan writes,

> What had begun as an adaptation to the realities of living in an arid, but fertile floodplain environments had developed into a web of economic and political interdependency that was far larger than anything the world had seen before—the remote forerunner of the vast global economic system of today (Fagan 1993, 201).

THE BIRTH OF ISLAM AND THE RISE AND FALL OF THE OTTOMAN EMPIRE

To the east, a new dynastic line, the Sasanids, came to power in the Persian Empire in AD 226, with its core in Iran to the north of the Tigris and Euphrates Rivers. Zoroastrianism was restored and became the state religion; Persian (Farsi) remained the state language. The Persian and Roman empires had fought endless wars with each other. The wars were based on competition for territory and control over the trade routes between East and West. The Sasanids were able to monopolize trade to the east because the most direct trade route ran through Persia. However, the southern part of the trade route ran through the lands of the Arabs of Yemen; neither Sasanids, Byzantines, nor Romans showed much interest in dominating these people on the periphery, who were described as warlike and savage. The costs of conquering these remote people would have been too great. Arabia, at AD 100, was free of any sort of authority but was surrounded by small states and made up of peoples who made their living from the trade routes, which crossed through Arabia to Yemen and then by sea to Africa and India (Lewis 1995, 41). This region would become the heart of the first Islamic state.

In AD 613, Muhammad, also called The Prophet, was an undistinguished native of Mecca, a ritual center and trade city in southern Saudi Arabia; he began to denounce the pagan polytheism of his fellow tribesmen. Mecca was an Arab town which held its power from trade, but it was and is important as the site of the Ka'bah, a cube-shaped structure of unknown antiquity, which originally housed the idols (360) of the various gods and goddesses venerated by Arab tribesmen (Goldschmidt 1983, 25). Travelers and scholars have long pondered why so many ritual centers of Judaism, Christianity, and Islam all occur in such proximity. One working hypothesis is that pilgrimage centers have always been important in regions where trade is a critical economic feature of state development, and that all of these ancient holy sites are on trade routes where tribal war was common.

Three years before, when Muhammad was forty years old, he had experienced a series of revelations from the angel Gabriel. These were later written and became the Quran, Islam's holy book. Within just two decades, Muhammad united nearly all of Arabia into a new religious and political community. Within twenty years after his death in AD 632, the followers of Muhammad had seized the Byzantine Empire and overwhelmed the Sasanian state, transforming both into an Islamic state. The speed and magnitude of conquest by a religious leader and his followers was unprecedented. Muhammad's utterances and personal example became the model for the behavior of millions, and a new organizational framework was established in the form of the Islamic state (McNiel 1963, 421).

The Islamic religion began with the teachings of Muhammad, who is believed to be the last of the prophets referred to in the Bible. Muslims, as well as Christians and Jews, believe that their traditions date back to Abraham, the first prophet. A basic difference between Christian and Muslim belief is that for Christians Christ was the son of (and an incarnation of) God, whereas for Muslims he was just another prophet like Muhammad. Muslims, however, believe that God revealed the text of the Quran or Koran to Muhammad; it is the Koran and its teachings that set the Islamic religions apart from Christianity or Judaism (Goldschmidt 1983).

■The angel Gabriel giving revelations to the prophet Muhammad.

five pillars

The core undertakings expected of everyone who practices Islam

Islam

The religious system of Allah according to his Prophet Muhammad

Quran

The revealed Word of God through Muhammad, the last of his prophets

At the heart of Islamic belief are the **five pillars**: 1) the declarations of faith, the term **Islam** itself means submission to the will of God (there is no other god but God); 2) the five daily ritual prayers, recited facing Mecca; 3) almsgiving; 4) fasting during Ramadan; and 5) the pilgrimage to Mecca, to the Ka'bah, at least once in a lifetime. Each of the pillars has its own series of rationalizing and validating stories. The **Quran** is the revealed word of God through Muhammad, the last of his prophets. The Quran cannot be a direct guide to human conduct; it must be interpreted. It is the interpretations that produce the many Islams. Two sects emerged after the death of Muhammad in AD 632: the Sunnis and Shia. The Sunni sect and the Shia sect are similar in most respects; however, they differ primarily in the Shia belief that the Islamic community should be led by an Imam (priest) who is a direct descendant of Muhammad through his daughter, Fatima, and her husband, Ali. Sunni leaders are drawn from descendants of Muhammad's brother-in-law, Abu Bakr. These disagreements have led to major conflicts. The Shia sect has a major religious celebration commemorating the massacre of Ali's son, Husayn, by Sunni warriors. Today, the Shia form the poorer classes of the Middle East, except in Iran where they are numerically dominant. The distinctions and animosities between the two sects have played an important role in the rise of conflict. Differences in wealth have been a source of relative deprivation for the Shia and are a root cause of many fundamentalist Islamic social movements.

The radical transformation of North Africa and Southwest Asia during and after the death of Muhammad has been partially explained by the benefits the new religion gave to the varying ethnic groups of the region, mostly Arab speakers, through the lowering of transaction costs in long distance trade. Abner Cohen has argued, "[Islam is a] blue-print of a political-economic organization which has overcome the many basic technical problems of the trade" (1971, quoted in Ensminger 1992, 59). Ensminger, an anthropologist, points to the well-researched connection between long distance trade the world over and conversions to Islam. It was the long distance traders who did much of the converting, and Islam tended to follow major overland trade routes. Of particular importance in trade were spices from the east. Islam offered commercial advantages that reduced transaction costs. Conversion to Islam provided a ready-made way to turn outsiders, with whom one might be in conflict, to insiders who shared a world view on the importance of honoring business contracts and other ethical obligations. True believers had a nonmaterial interest in holding to the terms of a contract. The new converts would be subject to commonly held sanctions for default on agreements. Beyond its religious appeal, Islam enhanced trade relationships by facilitating predictability in exchange and lowering transaction costs. That is, inter- and intra-societal feuding was reduced by a common religion making trade less expensive. However, when the religion was highly successful, bureaucracies and centralized authorities were not far behind, dooming many of the egalitarian ideas of Muhammad and his followers, and setting up the cycles of conflict between established states and true believers. These generalizations do not apply to Christianity, which cannot be connected as directly to trade, but, as we noted in Chapter 5, was of particular significance in helping to integrate the states of western Europe in the Middle Ages.

Conflict Between Islamic Sects

The simple message of the Prophet Muhammad became the basis for a new religion and the ideology for a series of new empires. The new religion accepted Jesus Christ, as a prophet, but not as the Son of God. Muhammad was the last prophet and did not aspire to sacred status. The first statement of doctrine had its beginning at Medina and at the ancient sanctuaries of Mecca and the Ka'bah. This first, **charismatic phase**, can be identified with the personality of Muhammad and included most of the present-day countries of the Arabian Peninsula (primarily Saudi Arabia, but also modern Yemen, Kuwait, and Oman). The charismatic phase was one of theological simplicity, which built upon existing traditions of both polytheistic religions and the monotheism of Christians, Jews, and Zoroastrians. Muhammad viewed the other religions as having tendencies towards corruption, stemming from the multiple schools of theological debate and interpretation; and he insisted on a very strong monotheism with but one law, that given to him by the angel Gabriel. An essential quality of Islam was and is the argument that it needs no interpretation because it is the word of God and should be read directly. However, much like the New Testament of the Christians, the Koran, written a generation after the death of Muhammad, gave rise to different schisms that not only gave their own interpretations to the Koran but also questioned the legitimacy of the traditions of other interpreters, laying the groundwork for the continuous conflict of the Islamic world.

The charismatic phase ends with Muhammad's death in AD 632 and is followed immediately by the development of several distinct traditions of interpretation, many leading to the development of powerful states that extend outside of the Arabian peninsula. Muhammad had succeeded in bringing the Arab tribes (those who spoke Arabic) together, but the union was shaky and threatened to dissolve. Muhammad's core followers chose Abu Bakr, his father-in-law and one of his earliest followers as their new leader. Bakr became the first **caliph** (derived from *khalifa*, an ambiguous Arab word which combines the meaning of successor and deputy) or successor; dissident tribal groups immediately challenged the legitimacy of his rule. Abu Bakr fought a series of wars to bring back the dissidents and reunite the confederation of tribes established on the basis of this new faith (Lapidus 1988). A small but disciplined core brought back the rebellious tribes until Arabia was once again unified at the death of Abu Bakr (AD 634).

charismatic phase

The first phase of a redemptive movement, such as Islam, when followers believe in their messianic or charismatic leader, such as Muhammad

caliph

A title for the head of a Moslem state

There followed a brief period of turmoil and political unrest until the Ummayad dynasty assimilated the previous Sasasnid Empire and ruled until AD 750. During the rule of the Ummayads, the Islamic faith spread as far as Spain in the west and India in the east. Arab followers of Muhammad, who maintained tightly knit garrisons of Islamic believers, primarily ruled this new empire. The Islamic faith was not imposed on the distinct ethnic groups under Islamic rule under the Ummayads.

Paralleling the expansion of the Islamic empire was the codification of the religion. The Quran was composed of the sayings of the Prophet, usually by length, added to the Old Testament of the Christians and Jews. Memories of the sayings and deeds of the Prophet Muhammad were studied along with the Quran. These **hadiths,** (authenticated accounts of Muhammad's sayings and actions) as they were called, were kept alive in oral tradition until the ninth century when they were compiled into an official codified version, which is recognized as Muslim scripture along with the Quran. Similarly, from the seventh century on, Muslim judges and scholars began to reform existing tribal laws to conform to the moral and ethical standards of Islam. This became *Shari'a*, the sacred law of Islam not strictly speaking, the word of God, but considered to be divinely inspired. A body of legal specialists, the **ulema** (men learned in Islamic doctrine, but not priests or judges), interpreted the Shari'a. Under the Ummayads' rule, other ethnic groups were controlled by their own laws, codes, and judges (Lapidus 1988). The Sunnis accepted the interpretations of the ulema, but the Shi'ites only accepted the ulema interpretations when led by the Imam, the true descendant of Muhammad.

While the caliphs of the Ummayad dynasty directed the Arab community, the Shi'a sect, who believed that only the ulema had sacred qualities, did not consider them sacred. The Shi'a believed in an *Imam* (sacred leader). According to Shi'a principles, there has been a succession of twelve Imams in Islamic history. Each, except the twelfth, was deprived of worldly rank and murdered by caliphs. The twelfth was divinely hidden by God and is the Hidden Imam, who has not been seen since 941, but who will one day return as the one guided by God (Pinault 1992). In the absence of the Hidden Imam, worldly authority devolves upon the ulema, who are ranked according to knowledge of the Quran and have true authority, even over the caliph. On the other hand, the dominant Sunni sect accepted the rule of the caliph in combination with the ulema (one way to view the distinction is the Sunnis were willing to cooperate with the state and the ulema as controlled by the caliph, whereas the Shi'ites were not). Early conflict between the two groups has lasted to the present.

In 744, a split between several factions led to the overthrow of the Ummayads and the rise of a new clan from Mecca, the Abbasids, whose empire was much more centralized and bureaucratized. The Moslem capital was moved to Baghdad, at an intersection of trade routes on the Tigris. The Abbasid Empire was distinct from that of the Ummayad in that the role of government became more important; and the office of the caliph was elevated, sanctified, and removed from public view. Instead of sitting with the ulema in the open, the caliph was housed in a royal palace. The new rulers chose consensus and continuity, rather than the rights of the religious warriors. The caliph was no longer one among equals ruling with consent, but an autocrat ruling a vast bureaucracy. With the move to Baghdad, Iranian warriors displaced Arab warriors and the distinction between Arab and other ethnic groups became less and less important as Islam was made a state religion by the Abbasid leadership. Arab ethnicity and the Islamic religion were no longer one and the same. The Arab monopoly of power had ended, and Iranian Moslems became part of the ruling elite. Stress was placed on Islamic rather than Arab identity. One interpretation of events is that the Abbasids

hadith

An authenticated account of Muhammad's actions and sayings

ulema

A body of men learned in Islamic doctrine, though not priests or judges

represented the reemergence of the Persian Empire, with the resurgence of Persian ethnicity over Arab ethnicity. Others argue that the new dynasty represents a political movement away from domination by an aristocracy of Arabs, but that the new dynasty was not specifically Persian (Goldschmidt 1983, 68).

Under the Abbasid Empire, the ulema became the legal court of all Islamic followers and not just the court of the Arab faithful. The ulema sat in the market place and expounded sacred law, applied it, and became the true heirs of the prophet. However, the caliph and his court also acquired sacred qualities to go with their new powers, a characteristic which was antithetical to early Islamic traditions, and added to the divergence between the Sunni and Shi'a sects.

Disputes between Sunni, Shi'ites, and other religious and secular groups led to the weakening of the Abbasid state, which was seized by Persian (AD 945) and then Turkish (AD 1055) adventurers (McNiel 1963). Before the year 1000, the breakdown of the Abbasid state was complete. In the eleventh and twelfth centuries, the forces of Christendom advanced in Spain and Sicily, Bedouin Arabs swept through Libya and Tunisia, and from the Asian steppes Turkish invaders came that were to create a new capital at Istanbul (Constantinople). In the fifteenth century, the Ottoman Empire of Turkey gained control over what was left of the Moslem Middle East and developed a new imperial order. Power shifted from Baghdad, Egypt, and Medina to Istanbul, and a hegemonic bureaucracy, which was highly centralized and was ruled by a sultan, controlled the powers of the state. The sultan controlled the extensive Ottoman bureaucracy through the ulema, which in turn became a bureaucracy of religious officials (Hourani 1991).

Jewish and Christian communities suffered persecution at the hands of these Islamic states, but no more so than any other ethnic groups. Judaism and Christianity were viewed as monotheistic religions, like Islam; and unless they challenged the Islamic state, they were left to their own devices in their own neighborhoods, towns, and villages.

European Expansion, Ethnic Conflict, and the Fall of the Ottoman Empire   Increasing control of world trade by the European core slowly brought about the decline of the Ottoman Empire. European attempts to stop the Moslem armies date back to the eighth century when the Franks (in what is now France) stopped the Moslem

■Sunrise over Baghdad. With the move to Baghdad, the distinction between Arab and other ethnic groups became less important as Islam was made a state religion. Arab ethnicity and the Islamic religion were no longer one and the same.

Crusades

Militaristic expeditions by Christians in medieval Europe to recover control of the Holy Land from various Islamic states

expansion at the Battle of Tours in AD 732. In the eleventh century, European leaders initiated the **Crusades** to beat back the Moslem armies and to return the Holy Land to Christian rule (McNiel 1963). The first crusades ended in the recapture of Jerusalem and the massacre of both Jewish and Muslim communities. The Christian crusaders were also interested in gaining control over the trade routes of the Middle East. By the sixteenth century, the Portuguese had taken control of port cities in the Middle East and into the Pacific as far as Malaysia, displacing Islamic rulers, and in turn being displaced by the Dutch and English (Wolf 1982).

Europeans slowly gained control over the Mediterranean and the Indian Ocean; and while the Ottoman emperor in earlier times could choose when and where to attack Christian Europe, his armies were at the mercy of Europeans, particularly the stronger forces of the Austrian Hapsburgs and the tsars of Russia. In 1699, the Ottomans signed the Treaty of Karlowitz, ceding Hungary to the Hapsburgs and the Aegean coast to the Venetians. In 1774, they lost the Crimea and allowed Russia to speak on behalf of Orthodox Christians. In 1798, Napoleon Bonaparte occupied Egypt and marched into Palestine. Other Muslim dynasties in India, Iran, and Morocco were also losing against the rising might of Europe in the eighteenth century (Goldschmidt 1983, 136).

Imperialist advances by the West tend to overshadow the internal problems of the Islamic states, particularly the Ottoman Empire. During the first thousand years of the struggle between the two world systems, the Muslims had the upper hand. Their state monopolies allowed trade to flow, and manufacturing was successful. The only serious advantage of the West was in military equipment, which was imported by the Ottomans. Although Moslem, the rulers of the Ottoman Empire originally allowed Byzantine Christians to continue to be governed by the Patriarch of Constantinople. In the sixteenth century, Jewish and Christian communities had lived in special quarters of the Muslim lands and were exempt from paying local taxes or obeying local laws and regulations. There were many other ethnic groups that were also semi-autonomous, such as the Kurds of Turkey, the Christians of Armenia, and the Greeks of the Greek mainland, which was under Ottoman rule. With the defeat of the armies of Sulayman the Magnificent at Vienna in 1529, Ottoman leaders recognized that their highly centralized political economy was not as efficient as the less centralized European states. Reforms were initiated, but it was too late.

■Peter the Hermit, as he was called, depicted showing the crusaders the way to the Holy Land (Jerusalem) during the First Crusade.

■Sulayman the Magnificent was the longest reigning sultan of the Ottoman Empire. However, his defeat at Vienna in 1529 began the decline of the Ottoman Empire.

In general, the Ottoman Empire allowed a great deal of ethnic autonomy, but when threatened could be extremely repressive. Rebellions in the provinces of the Ottoman Empire were met with extreme violence. It is reported that parts of Greece and Anatolia were depopulated during the period from 1623–1640 when Sultan Murad IV used extremely brutal means to impose order. Periods of repression continued well into the nineteenth century, and we read today about how the poet Lord Byron joined the revolutionary Greeks in their fight against the Turks (Ottomans). By the nineteenth century, the Ottoman Empire was much reduced in territory, mostly to what is today known as the Middle East, including the modern regions of Palestine, Egypt, Turkey, Iraq, and western Saudi Arabia. It soon lost Egypt to France.

During World War I, the Ottoman Empire joined the Austro-Hungarian Empire and Germany against England, France, and the United States, and was defeated. Great Britain led the Egyptian Expeditionary Force that conquered Palestine and coastal Syria in 1917–1918. The winning European powers split up what was left of the Ottoman Empire, but not before its infamous attack on the Christians of Armenia, who were almost destroyed as a people. The genocide of the Armenian people was the beginning of many of the horror stories of the twentieth century. Turkey also lost a great deal of territory to Russia in the middle of the nineteenth century, particularly in central Asia (Goldschmidt 1983) and, by the turn of the century, was "the sick man of Europe." By 1918, the partitioning of the Ottoman Empire was complete. France gained the countries of Lebanon and Syria, and the British took control of Egypt, Iraq, and Palestine. Eventually, the British and Russians divided Persian Iran; however, after World War I, with Russia weakened by its own revolution of 1917, the British took over Persia and imposed their own rulers (Keddie 1981). The British folk hero, Sir Lawrence of Arabia (Colonel T. O. Lawrence), helped Sheikh Faisal, a leader of the Saudi clan, to revolt successfully against the Turks. Later, the Saudis were to feel betrayed as Great Britain and France partitioned the Middle East, and the new country of Saudi Arabia was placed under British control (Lacey 1981).

Prior to World War I, the Ottoman Empire responded to increased European competition by allowing European businessmen free reign, and the local elites lost their control of trade and commerce except where they created alliances with the colonials. These converts to European ways were the **compradors** (commercial elites or upper classes), and their children and grandchildren would become the future elites of the Middle East in the twentieth century.

compradors

The commercial elites or upper classes of the Ottoman Empire who were enriched by links to European colonial governments

The Rise of Independent States in the Middle East

During the period before World War II, a series of nationalist movements in the Middle East shook the western powers. After World War II, beginning in the 1950s, nationalist movements became increasingly more violent. Leaders, such as Gamal Nasser in

Egypt, demanded complete independence and the establishment of a single pan-Arab socialist state, which would unify the entire Middle East, as it had been unified by the Ottoman Empire. Yet Egypt and Saudi Arabia were alone among the new states in having a strong sense of ethnic identity: both were Arab and Sunni. Such was not the case with most of the other newly created states, which were riven by inner rivalries and hatreds (Lewis 1995, 359).

In the period directly before and after World War II, royal houses that traced descent to Muhammad ruled the nation states of the Middle East; many had become corrupt in the eyes of the young members of the military. General Nasser would overthrow King Faruk in 1952, and his action would form a model for many other military leaders in the newly formed countries of the Middle East.

Nasser and other leaders of the Middle East failed to achieve their pan-Arab dream, but by the 1960s the British and French were pushed out of North Africa and Southwest Asia. Iran, however, continued to be dominated by the British, French, and the United States. In the 1960s, the United States began to play an increasingly greater role in the Middle East as the other powers retreated and as the influence of the Soviet Union grew (Lacey 1981).

One transformative movement became dominant in almost all countries of the Middle East: the Ba'thist Party. Ba'thist philosophy, first announced as a socialist movement in Syria, called for land reform, nationalization of basic industries, complete unification of the Arab world, and militant resistance to Israel and imperialism. The anti-Jewish, anti-imperialist philosophy appealed to many Arabs dismayed by the newly created state of Israel in 1948. A few scholars, such as Samir al-Khalil, have argued that Ba'thism was based on an amalgam of Nazi state socialism and Marxism (1989).

One-party bureaucratic states based on socialism emerged in all of the countries of the Middle East with the exception of the richest oil producers: Iran, Saudi Arabia, Kuwait, and the United Arab Emirates. These were ruled by more traditional kings and their families (who had been put into power by the British). By 1979, two types of political systems dominated the Middle East: secular socialist states, provisionally tied to the Islamic ulema, but with a secular public orientation; and royal-ulema, traditional kingdoms largely tied to Islamic ulema and ruled by shaykhs (often written 'sheiks' in English). Both types of countries were Islamic; however, the socialist secular states tried to reduce the power of the Islamic religion, while the royal kingdoms ruled through the Islamic ulema. Both systems depended on oil exports. Both redistributed wealth by selling oil and then giving the proceeds to the general populace through state bureaucracies in the form of subsidies and services. The old comprador class continued to dominate the new economic systems because of their knowledge of commerce. The only exception was Israel, a democracy which sided with the United States, and which became the only predictable ally in the region. The Soviet Union became an extremely influential ally to the new socialist societies; and an uneasy alliance developed between the United States, Israel, and the old oil kingdoms of Saudi Arabia, Kuwait, and the Arab Emirates against the Soviets and their allies.

In 1979, a Shi'ite revolution in Iran established a third type of authoritarian society, one based on a combination of a fundamentalist interpretation of Islamic shari'a law and the redistribution of oil wealth. Shari'a was interpreted by the ulema and headed by its highest authority, the Ayatollah Khomeini; a theocracy had been born. The new society was supposed to be based on the model of Islamic societies of a thousand years before, and its radical leaders began to use Iran's oil wealth to subvert neighboring socialist states and shaykhdoms by financing Shi'ite fundamentalist movements in Iraq, Saudi Arabia, Egypt, Algeria, Syria, and Jordan. Both socialists and royal houses were considered corrupt by the new Shi'ite elites of Iran.

■Drilling the first oil well in Kuwait on April 13, 1953. Both the socialist secular states and royal kingdoms came to depend on oil profits in order to give the proceeds to the general populace through state bureaucracies in the form of subsidies and services.

These three types of state systems, secular socialist (Jordan, Syria, Iraq, Yemen), theocratic, (Iran), and royal-ulema (Saudi Arabia, Arab Emirates, Kuwait, Oman) are, for the most part, one party states. Two exceptions are Egypt and Turkey, which are trying hard to borrow the European model of pluralistic democracy. Turkey is closest to the European model having rejected traditional models under the leadership of Kemal Ataturk in the period after 1917, and it is in deep trouble today. All societies of the Middle East, with the sole exception of Israel, have large one-party governments. Corruption and inefficiency are common, and state control of the economy has led to economies that are unable to compete outside of the borders of their own countries. High standards of living are only possible in those countries where the population densities are low and the rates of return from oil revenues are high (Saudi Arabia, Kuwait, Arab Emirates, Oman). It has become common for the secular socialist states, such as Iraq and Syria, to spend fortunes on military armament and to blame royal theocratic states for being stingy in giving them funds for the welfare of the poor. It is not difficult to understand that the secular socialist states tend to repress the political demands of their own peoples, squandering billions on their military and alienating the poor, who are drawn to their Islamic religions in protest. The Nasser-inspired idea of a Pan Arab socialist state no longer has the strength it did, in part because of the misuse of financial resources in squabbles between the leaders of those countries that would have formed the United Arab Republic.

The Oil Trade Countries: Conflict and Community

The topic of oil wealth must be added to those of trade, ethnic and religious conflict, and imperialism. Of the world's known oil reserves, 60 percent are found in the Middle East, and oil has revolutionized the twentieth century and made the Middle East central to all energy policies. While the globalization of the world economy due to computers and instant communication has created new forms of power and wealth not imagined two decades ago, the world still runs on oil.

According to Daniel Yergin, three great themes underlie the story of oil. The first is the rise and development of capitalism and modern business. Oil is still the biggest and most pervasive business, and Standard Oil of the United States was among the largest of all multinational corporations in the middle of the twentieth century. Oil deals underlie much of the history of twentieth century business transactions (Yergin 1991).

The second theme is global politics and power. World War I and II were fought to determine who controlled the access to oil. The strategic importance of oil did not begin with the automobile, but with the oil-powered battleship. Winston Churchill, who was the first lord of the Admiralty in the period just before World War I, realized that to beat the German navy, the British had to raze its old coal fired battleships and build new ones to run on oil. He realized that only oil could produce the great efficiency and speed needed in modern naval war, and Great Britain planned to be the master of the seas.

A third theme is the age of hydrocarbon man, the transformation of society due to the access to fossil fuels. Dependence on oil is a constant concern. Industrial countries are trying to find alternatives, such as electric cars and buses, as well as electric plants not based on oil. We are not apt to give up our dependence on oil until a better alternative is available. Looking back at the 1970s can highlight just how important oil is. An oil crisis was created in 1973–1981 when the Organization of Petroleum Producing Countries (OPEC), partly made up of Arab oil states, used an oil embargo to protest against the support by the United States for Israel in a 1973 conflict against several Arab states. By 1980, the price of oil had risen from $2.53 to $41.00 a barrel, fueling a period of world wide inflation.

A decade later, a coalition of the United States, Russia, Syria, Egypt, Great Britain, and France would fight the Persian Gulf War of 1991 against the dictator of Iraq. The war was fought, in part, due to a fear that Saddam Hussein might dominate Kuwait and Saudi Arabia, allowing him to gain control of over 20 percent of all world oil supplies. Saddam's invasion of Kuwait, on August 8, 1990, led to an American declaration of war on January 12, 1991. Within a month the war would be over with thousands of Iraqi casualties and one hundred American dead.

The strategy Saddam Hussein used, of gaining stature in the eyes of other Arabs by facing up to the invading Americans and their allies and causing as much damage to them as possible, was short-circuited by an American land invasion which lasted only a hundred hours and resulted in fewer than a hundred American dead. Saddam Hussein's efforts failed to produce anything other than agony for his own people. The air attacks by United Nations' forces destroyed Iraq's economic infrastructure and killed thousands of innocent victims. Hussein blamed the United States and its allies. Then, in the months that followed, he systematically repressed the Kurds in northeast Iraq and Shiite minorities in the southern marshes (called Marsh Arabs) who thought they could overthrow him.

However, the Persian Gulf War changed the dynamics of power politics in the Middle East. The new alliances between the United States and several old enemies of Israel, especially Russia and Syria, made it possible to work out a peace treaty between Israel and Palestinian Arabs. One interpretation of events after the Persian Gulf War would be that the generation of prosperity in the Middle East is dependent on an end to conflict between ethnic and religious groups, particularly between Israel and the Palestinian people. Conflict destroys the possibility of trade and trade relationships, and produces poverty even among the most oil rich people in the world.

Terrorism and Regional Conflict Between Palestinian Arabs and Israel

As control of Palestine shifted from Turkey, to Egypt, back to Turkey again, and then to Great Britain after World War I, the lot of the Palestinian peasants or *fellaheen* declined, producing a series of revolts, the first of which occurred in as early as 1834 against Egypt. Originally living in villages controlled by patrilineal collectives, which redistributed land to member families, Palestinians were displaced by wealthy Arab families, and after World War I, by Jewish communities (Kimmerling and Migdal 1994, 16–17). Kimmerling and Migdal argue that of particular importance was the force of the European market economy that put land in the hands of private landowners, both Arabs and Jews, and took it out of the ownership of the fellaheen. However, it is in the period after World War I that the lot of the Palestinians became particularly onerous. Peasants sank deeper and deeper into debt to moneylenders, who increasingly confiscated the land that had been used as collateral (Kimmerling and Migdal 1994, 18).

Jewish communities lived in Palestine during Ottoman rule and were tolerated by the ruling Turks. Wealthy Jewish philanthropists supported many of these communities, called the Yishuv. Tension between local Palestinians and Jews only became significant after World War I. Many Jews migrated out of the newly emerging Soviet Union due to anti-Semitic pogroms. Many also migrated from Romania, Bulgaria, and other East European countries where they lived in extreme poverty. They were attracted by the socialist ideology of early **Zionism** (Zionism was the movement to create a national home for the Jews). One of the most important innovations was the **kibbutz**, a communal form of land tenure, which was very successful in turning the desert into a garden.

The rise of anti-Semitism, between World War I and World War II, led to support for immigration by Jews into Palestine. However, Arab populations had grown as the economy of the region improved, and they had not only become accustomed to a degree of self-rule but also believed Palestine to be their own. During World War I, the British had promised the Emir of Mecca that he would be the monarch of an independent Arab state if he would lead a revolt against Ottoman rule, which he did. Palestine was placed into Arab hands, and Jewish migration was supposed to be restricted; it was not. In the period just before and during World War II, Nazis financed anti-Semitic Arab movements in Palestine. The ambiguous tenure of the Jewish people, the growing size of Jewish communities, anti-Semitism, and the promises to the Palestinian Arabs led to conflict.

After World War II, the United Nations voted to establish a state of Israel, but the plan was unworkable because one-fourth of the Jewish communities were outside of the lands set aside for the new state. This led to a civil war between Jews and Arabs, culminating in the establishment of the state of Israel in 1948. Approximately a million Palestinians fled to the surrounding states, and a state of conflict ensued between these two peoples despite the 1979 Sadat–Begin peace treaty between Egypt and Israel. A million were left behind to live in what was left of Palestine: the West Bank, administered by Jordan.

THE PALESTINIAN MOVEMENT

In 1967, volunteers from the West Bank combined with the armies of Egypt, Iraq, Syria, and Jordan to attack Israel. A well-organized Israeli Army defeated the Arab armies. This is called the **1967 Six Day War**. As a result, many of the non-Jewish Arabs who had been living within the state of Israel were forced into refugee camps on the West Bank, which was taken over by Israel. The image of the Palestinian Arab became that of a displaced person, a downtrodden refugee. About one-third of the Palestinian Arabs lived in dismal refugee camps operated by the United Nations. Within a decade, great improvements were made in the lives of the refugees, but not of those left behind on the West Bank, the remaining lands of Palestine. The young refugees quickly made the transition from illiterate rural to literate urban dwellers. Generally, more Palestinian Arabs refugees enrolled in higher education than other Arab groups, between 80 and 90 percent compared to 53 percent in the Arab world as a whole (Peretz 1977, 32).

Egypt, Jordan, Syria and Iraq competed in their use of the Palestinians for their own purposes. Each country had its own Palestinian "leaders" group that it backed. However,

Zionism

The movement to create a national home for the Jews

kibbutz

A communal form of land tenure by which Jews returning to Palestine were able to turn desert areas into gardens

1967 Six Day War

A war in 1967 in which the West Bank, Egypt, Iraq, Syria, and Jordan attacked Israel and were defeated within six days

these states could not cooperate until the crisis leading to the June 1967 war built to fever pitch. The Arabs, imagining a smashing success against Israel, were willing to cooperate with each other. Countries that had little interest in the Palestinian problem, such as Morocco, Tunisia, Algeria, Sudan, and the Persian Gulf states, became more involved (Peretz 1977, 42–43). Israel's defeat of Egypt, Iraq, Syria, and Jordan in the Six Day War had a traumatic impact on the Arabs of Palestine and on the unity of the Arab states. The Palestinian Arabs were no longer able to believe in the leadership of the Pan-Arab cause. Four hundred thousand Palestinians were displaced from their homes, many for the second time. Most of the refugees fled from the West Bank to Jordan. The West Bank was conquered by Israel, and Israelis began settling the region in 1968. Tens of thousands of Palestinian Arab refugees began life over again in tents. Nearly all had the common objectives of asserting Palestinian identity and avenging years of Arab defeat by eliminating Israel and Zionism. While Arab leaders continued to define Pan-Arab socialism as their objective, Palestinians created the Palestinian Liberation Organization (PLO) under the leadership of Yasser Arafat, with both right wing and left wing factions, to destroy Israel and liberate Palestine.

Created in 1968, the PLO became the formal political organization working for the Palestinian cause. Behind it were several organizations that used international terror: Fatah, al Sa'iqa "Thunderbolt," Palestinian commandos organized by Syria, and the Popular Front for the Liberation of Palestine (PFLP), led by George Habash. Fatah was the largest organization that carried out terrorist raids within Israeli occupied territories, while the PLO attempted to negotiate with the international community. Other commando groups engaged in sabotage operations against civilian installations within Israel and abroad. Both Fatah and the other groups drew strength from the deep misery of the Palestinian people and were financed by the oil states of the Middle East. The period of the 1960s catapulted Fatah and Arafat from obscurity to an overall leadership of the Palestinian people (Kimmerling and Migdal 1994, 214). Over the decade, a new ideology of Palestinian emergence as a people became dominant.

In the early 1990s, Arafat and the PLO emerged as the spokesperson and the key organization representing the Palestinian peoples. However, within the local Palestinian community, splits emerged between Fatah, supporting Arafat and the Palestinian Authority (the former PLO), and other more radical and militant organizations, such as Hamas (all mostly Sunni groups) and the even more radical Hizbollah, the Shi'ite party of God. The PLO continued to gain power, and their battle against Israel intensified until the United States, in 1991 directly after the Persian Gulf War, decided to become actively involved in brokering a peace agreement. After three years of delicate negotiations, which were almost derailed a number of times, an agreement was signed.

On May 5, 1994, delegates from Palestine and Israel signed the documents forging a peace treaty between the two sides. The agreement gave Palestinians in the Gaza Strip and West Bank town of Jericho limited self-rule. United States Secretary of State Warren Christopher brokered the intensive negotiations. The autonomy granted to Gaza and Jericho was later extended to the entire West Bank. Residents of the autonomous area carry their own passports, and Israeli soldiers were replaced with Palestinian policemen, mostly former Fatah fighters of the PLO.

There are many complex issues to be ironed out, such as the physical size of the security strips around the settlements into which Palestinians would not be allowed to go, and the extent to which Palestinians will have the right to navigate the Mediterranean waters off the Gaza coast. These and other details will take considerable time and effort to iron out. The Palestinian Authority is currently seeking recognition as a state from the United Nations General Assembly. Many states have already established diplomatic relations with Palestine, even though its statehood is controversial. The pact failed to address many of the most difficult issues, but the peace process itself was locked into place.

The most critical problems are maintaining continuity to the economic and political transitions, particularly in the Gaza Strip. The Gaza Strip is a roughly rectangular coastal area on the eastern Mediterranean, approximately twenty-eight miles long and five miles wide with a population of 1,657,155 people.

Descriptions of the West Bank are little better. The population of the West Bank is 2,568,555, making it, with the Gaza Strip, one of the fastest growing areas of the world. How does such a poor and highly populated region go through the economic transition successfully?

Case Study

Traditional Marriage and the Dilemma of Feminism in Gaza

The Gaza Strip, one of the segmented territories of the Palestinian Authority, is home to hundreds of thousands of Palestinian Arabs.

> The Gaza Strip is an area of extreme, almost impenetrable demographic, economic, social, political, and legal complexity. It has one of the highest population densities in the world; over two-thirds of the people who live there are refugees and nearly half are younger than age fourteen. The economy is weak and underdeveloped …. The visitor to Gaza is first struck by the dramatic juxtaposition of a serene Mediterranean coastline with teeming poverty and squalor (Roy 1994, 67).

Gaza contains many radical groups, such as Hamas and Hizbollah, which have been responsible for car bombings in Israel and attacks on the Palestinian Authority. However, it is also a close knit society, one in which there is a considerable survival of Arab traditions, particularly in respect to the status of women. Despite the secular political views of the majority of men and women, traditional male control of women and expectations for *bint 'amm* marriages continue and are supported by Islamic militants. Bint 'amm is the marriage of a man to his father's brother's daughter, technically known as a patrilateral parallel cousin marriage. Such marriages are usually associated with a bride wealth payment from the groom's family to that of the bride (from the father to the father's brother, which may amount to several thousand dollars). Research by Dale Eickelman shows that the actual category of father's brother's daughter is not as narrow as the term implies, because a father's male cousins can substitute for brothers, thus expanding the category of bint 'amm marriage to their daughters as well. Regardless of actual genealogical relationships, arranged marriage with

close family members is an expectation, especially among the upper classes in the Middle East. The young adults, however, often have their own ideas.

The expectations of radical leaders (members of Hamas and Hizbollah) who are committed to the traditions of Islamic culture are often contradicted by how young people interpret the idea of radical which often means pro-western, secular, and socialist. The contradictions between traditional Islamic society and feminist ideas from the west are often left ambiguously open. The young often do what they want, as described by Paul Cossali and Clive Robson in their ethnographic reports on Gaza society (1986). To show the contradictions in Gaza society, they describe the experiences of several young Arab women.

Maha, aged nineteen, is not a radical supporter of any movement. She represents the many poor young women whose western values clash with those of their parents and Islamic militants. Maha has one sister and ten brothers, and she grew up in a traditional Muslim family. In her description of her attempts to become an independent and modern western woman, she has to fight her own mother, who accepted and practiced the subordination of women, as well as her brothers, who were little help:

> This attitude encouraged my brothers to try and prove their manhood by controlling me. It was ridiculous sometimes. When my little brother Ahmed was six years old he used to demand that I make him tea. If I asked him why I should do that he used to say, "because I'm a boy and you're a girl." He doesn't even like tea! (Cossali and Robson 1986, 29).

Maha's mother believed that a woman's place is in the home, especially in the kitchen. She believed that nice girls should not go out. So Maha responded by saying, "I'm not a nice polite girl. I'm rude. Now will you let me go?" When Maha tried to get her brothers to clean up after themselves, the mother would get angry and denounce Maha saying, "I'm here to do these things."

Maha complained that there are only a few women in Gaza who studied medicine or engineering, which are men's fields. Men think a woman's role should be to bear and bring up children, and most women think the same. According to Maha, even in radical Gaza society, nearly all marriages are arranged.

> What happens is that women who have sons who want to get married visit families where they know there are young single women. The girls come and offer them something to drink, and all the time they're being sized up and asked questions to see if they're suitable.... One day, shortly after I'd finished school, my mother came to my room and said, "Maha, get dressed. You must meet some women." (Cossali and Robson 1986, 29)

But Maha refused bint 'amm marriage, telling her mother she would never marry anyone from her own family. Maha's negative attitude towards accepting the kitchen as her place followed her decision not to marry a kinsman. She felt that it was important that women work outside of the home because it was a way of being independent of the family. She discovered that it is very difficult to be independent.

> There is no social life for women—just visiting friends. Even that's difficult. I have to tell my mother where I'm going and who I'm going to see and exactly when I'll be back. If I'm not back on time, then I'll be forbidden to go out for a week. There are no clubs for women ... (Cossali and Robson 1986, 29).

While Maha is not interested in politics, many women are. One is Nabila, a radical activist supporting a secular state. Nabila makes an even more explicit statement of feminist views.

As a women's activist, I see my role as fighting for social change without which the Palestinian revolution can never achieve victory. Women's role in the revolution is as important as men's, and we must have freedom to move and express ourselves on an equal basis with men. This is difficult in Gaza because our society is much more religious and conservative and so we rely heavily on direction and lead from the outside. We take strength from the successes of Palestinian women in Lebanon where the revolution has brought about dramatic change. My aim is to strengthen women's confidence in their own ability to shape their lives and the future (Cossali and Robson 1986, 34).

These women represent the secular direction of Gaza society, found throughout the Middle East, particularly among the socialist and radical young. However, their point of view is not shared by Muslim fundamentalists, such as Majda, a second year student at the Islamic University of Gaza.

I owe a lot of thanks to the Islamic University here in Gaza for making religious books available to me so that I could read about Islam. I read about the proper Islamic dress, for example, and then I looked at my own clothes. I felt that I wasn't fully covered.... But we are surrounded by unbelievers. Some women are just ignorant, and it's our job as believers to show these women the way, step by step. Some have had ample opportunity to know Islam, Sharia Law and Islamic morals and dress. Yet they still stubbornly follow secularism... (Cossali and Robson 1986, 40).

Cossali and Robson go on to document the severity of the split between secular and Islamic points of view. Their book, *Stateless in Gaza*, was written well before the emergence of the new Palestinian Authority, Hamas, and Hizbollah; but it illustrates well the dilemmas of Gaza society, the support both for secular and Islamist points of view. This split is found in every country of the Middle East. Thus, one should be cautious in generalizing about women's roles, women's issues, and about broader trends in Middle Eastern societies.

Then there is the political transition. In recent decades there has been one formal center of power: the Israeli military administration, which is made up of military districts run by military governors. Replacing the Israeli military is the PLO, once terrorist organization, and once revolutionary movement. Chairman Yasser Arafat needed to be able to abandon the style of revolutionary leader and become a political leader who could help his people achieve the transition to democracy. Before chairman Arafat died, he was trying to abandon his style of autocratic leadership, but failed to do so. Arafat served as president through November 11, 2004, and Mahmoud Abbas has served from May 8, 2005, to the present.

Israeli Identity: Ethnic or Civic?

We have examined the origins of Judaism. In the twentieth century, the Jews of Israel wanted to both create an ethnic identity for themselves and a civic definition of a secular state. Joel S. Migdal, professor of international studies at the University of Washington, and co-author (with Kimmerling) of *The Palestinians: The Making of a People* (1994), writes that Israel is a society in flux, trying like its neighbors to choose between an ethnic or civic definition of the nation state. He outlines Clifford Geertz' early recognition of the split between these two directions: the first recognizing a primordial need for identity, and the second recognizing the need of economic progress, political order, and social justice. These two facets of society pull political groups in different directions, and represent modern Israel. The ethnic factor seeks to collapse the nation state and ethnic group into one, denying other groups certain rights, while the civic factor does the opposite, arguing for membership and full rights to all who take on the duties of citizenship (Migdal 1996, 183).

Palestine was a creation of the British Empire, originally intended as a multi-ethnic state and a homeland for the Jews, which became a historical contradiction. Zionism attempted to open the door to the immigration of Jews, who came from a wide variety of distinct ethnic groupings and were to receive equal representation at Knesset Israel, the Jewish parliament established in 1926. The question of creating a Jewish-Arab Palestinian society was elusive and tabled during the 1920s and 1930s. The British intent was the creation of a civil society, but the 1948 War led to the partition of Palestine between three states: Israel, Jordan, and Egypt (which claimed the Gaza Strip). A Jewish state was formed in Israel, with Arabs having only secondary rights. Zionist leaders in the leading Labor Party supported secular socialist values, and Israeli state institutions reflected a civic tendency although there were many contradictions (Migdal 1996, 193).

The 1967 Six Day War led to an expansion of the territory of Israel over the West Bank and Gaza, and also to a replacement of the civic concept with the claim of a common Jewish ancestry defending the Israeli state. "Society was not a civic construction of mortals but derived from the rights (especially, territorial rights) of the pre-existing nation, the Jews" (Migdal 1996, 195). The civic-oriented Labor Party lost control of the state in 1977 to Likud, also a Zionist party but representing many of the more religious Jewish communities and supporting the idea that Israel should be a Jewish state (Migdal 1996, 195). From 1977 to the present, these two parties have continued to support various forms of the civic-ethnic controversy.

Figure 9.4

❑ **Map of Israel and West Bank**

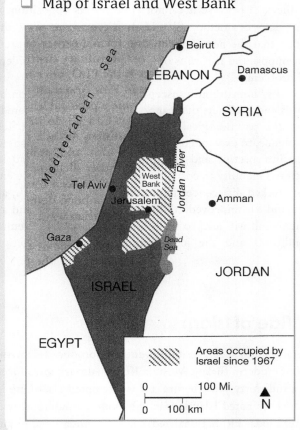

Areas occupied by Israel since 1967

One of the most important recent changes is Israel's recognition of the Palestinian Authority, which forms the beginnings of a new Palestinian state. However, the statelet is split between competing factions, as described in the case study on feminism in Gaza.

Modernization and Islamic Fundamentalism

Paul Magnarella, an anthropologist at the University of Florida, has documented the contradictions between modernization and Islamic religious movements in Turkey. Turkey's dilemma is found throughout the Middle East, from Algeria and Morocco to Iraq, Egypt, and Syria. It is also found in Jordan, in the newly emerging state of Palestine, and in the kingdoms of Saudi Arabia and Kuwait. The dilemma is near universal in the Islamic world. An example is Algeria. In the 1950s and 1960s, Algerians fought a war against colonial France. The National Liberation Front (NLF), a Marxist revolutionary party, successfully led them. After the war, the NLF organized Algeria as a secular socialist country. In 1989, the Algerian government legalized the Islamic Salvation Front (ISF) and offered free elections, which took place in December 1991. The ISF won the first round of the general election. The government, headed by the NLF, canceled the second round, outlawed the ISF, and jailed many of its leaders. The government and its NLF leaders fear an Islamic dominated government; many ISF leaders, in fact, call for a totalitarian Iran style government. Others argue against such a government. The government faces a dilemma because it cannot continue its opposition to democracy, yet leaders of the ISF deny democracy. Should the government allow the ISF to win elections with the hope that the new government will face the same pressures for democracy, or should it oppose the ISF, thus opposing democracy? President Mubarik of Egypt faces identical problems.

Magnarella looks at what he calls "humankind's susceptibility to indoctrination by ideologies that present faith worlds and faith acts that cannot be empirically validated" (Magnarella 1993, 5). He adopts the psychological theory of political scientist Ted Robert Gurr, a student of civil violence, to explain conflict in the Middle East, particularly in Turkey. He argues that interpretive and informational conditions lead to human discontent, and that a society's inability to correct such infrastructural deficiencies as rapid population growth, marked differences in the distribution of wealth, an insecure economic situation, demand for improved educational opportunities, and an inefficient and corrupt government—all will lead to support for ideologies condemning these conditions. The conditions and the ideologies lead to violent action (Magnarella 1993, 119).

Turkey: Resisting the Tide of Islam

Magnarella argues that modernization and secularization eventually produced deprivation, particularly in rural regions of modern Turkey. Mustafa Kemal Ataturk introduced a radical secular state to Turkey a full thirty years before it was attempted elsewhere in the Islamic world. In the 1920s, he eliminated Islamic teaching from the public schools and outlawed the Muslim brotherhoods. He nationalized Islamic foundations, eliminated the formal power of the ulema, and outlawed traditional Muslim headwear for men. He replaced Arab script with the Roman alphabet and replaced the Islamic calendar with the European.

In the 1930s, Ataturk moved even further, prohibiting religious education and converting many mosques to secular use, many of which were turned into museums. Ataturk's control of the government and the military allowed him to impose secularism on Muslim Turkish society. However, his goals of a secular society were achieved primarily among the urban elite, but not in the countryside where Islamic values were preserved. Devout Muslims attacked secularism. For them, Islam was the spiritual necessity of Turkish life. They valued Islam as a counter to atheistic leftist movements and ideologies, which gained ground after World War II (Magnarella 1993, 89).

Magnarella describes how Ataturk centralized the economy through state corporatism (a political economy very similar to that in Latin America during the same time period). In its pure form, state corporatism is a system in which the ruling elite has organized the society's interest groups into a limited number of singular, compulsory, noncompetitive, hierarchically ordered, and economically differentiated units, each with a monopoly of power in its own area of decision making.

Ataturk's desire was to create a state that was free of foreign capitalism and controlled by his associates. He died in 1938, on the eve of World War II. After the war, American and West European pressure forced the Turkish government to open its political system to opposition parties, but the state maintained control of the economy. Since 1985, Turkey has attempted to democratize itself. Under one recent leader, the government tried to abandon state corporatism in favor of capitalist democracy; however, it faces many dilemmas, not the least of which is civil violence and political terrorism.

Deprivation is particularly visible in the shanty towns that surround most every Middle Eastern city. In the 1970s, over half of the people of Ankara, Istanbul, and Izmir, the largest cities in Turkey, were shantytown residents.

> The all-pervading bureaucracy has not been able to enforce a minimum of town planning, and the majority of urban Turks live in Jerry-built concrete jungles, without parks or open spaces, with polluted air to breathe—often one large slum punctuated by oases of bearable living, which seem to those outside them, as havens of luxury. Rapid change … has produced a social as well as economic crisis. The sheer misery of living … has bred radicalism (Mango 1979, 130).

The rural populations, such as the Kurds of southeastern Turkey bordering Iran, have suffered economic deprivation as well. The urban situation led to urban guerrilla warfare, in support of Muslim fundamentalism, while the Kurdish situation has led to a civil war in the countryside for the last decade. In the last five years, a new political movement called the Refah (Welfare) Party, has challenged the traditional parties, both the Republican People's Party (RPP), founded by Ataturk, and the Democratic left, and also the conservative Motherland Party. Fresh elections in December of 1995 gave the Refah the biggest single share of the vote (21 percent), and made the secular leaders of Turkish societies very nervous. One of the fears was that the military, fearing an Islamist takeover, would once again take over the government. Because Turkey is a member of NATO, the growing power of Islamists makes American and European leaders nervous. The dilemma is that as the United States, NATO, and European leaders pressure Turkey to institute democratic reforms, the Islamist forces, such as Refah, grow in power. Very similar movements are to be found in Algeria and Egypt, where openings to democracy are filled with religious parties supporting Islamic states.

While fearing attacks by outsiders in World War I and World War II, Americans have not generally experienced attack against themselves until recently. The number 9/11 stands for the September 11, 2001, attacks on the World Trade Center in Manhattan and the Pentagon in Washington, D.C. The attack by Moslem radicals came as a total surprise and has caused the United States to focus its military attention on terrorism. The 9/11 attacks killed over three thousand people and introduced Americans to international

Case Study

The Kurds: An Ethnic Nation with No State

Most of the Kurdish population occupies an area of mountains and high plains in the contiguous border areas of Iran, Iraq, Syria, and Turkey and the adjacent border areas of the former USSR states of Georgia, Armenia, and Azerbaijan. The Kurds call their land Kurdistan, an area estimated to be between 500,000 and 520,000 square kilometers, and they have lived there for more than two thousand years. They believe themselves to be descended from the Medes who conquered Nineveh, the capital of the Assyrian empire, in 612 BC. For a variety of reasons, including their distribution in several nation-states with different census policies, it is difficult to estimate their total population. Estimates for the mid-1970s ranged from 13.5 to 21 million total for all countries mentioned. A 1980 estimate puts the total at 17.2 million.

Traditionally, the majority of Kurds were pastoral nomads who resided in groups related by lineage and clan ties. Some were agriculturalists that lived in permanent villages. Today, most live in settled villages, but many still derive much of their livelihood from pastoralism, sheep and goats being the principal animals raised. Wheat, barley, and lentils are the main crops in agricultural villages. Pasturelands are generally owned collectively by clans while agricultural lands are family-owned. Kurdish society consists of a small class of aristocrats and a larger class of commoners. Most aristocratic families today live in the urban centers of the region, as do many landless commoners who have moved to cities in search of wage labor.

Kurdish kin groups consist of patrilineages grouped into clans, several of which in turn form a tribe. Membership in clan and tribal units is fluid, permitting outsiders to attach themselves and become fully incorporated after several generations. Traditionally, marriages are arranged first by the women of the bride's and groom's families, and then finalized by the men when the bride wealth is agreed upon. The ideal marriage is one in which a man marries his father's brother's daughter (called patrilateral parallel cousin marriage). Interestingly, in the 1960s it was reported that the majority of marriages were of this type. Residence after marriage is patrilocal. Sons inherit equally from their father, but daughters do not inherit.

Conversion to Islam took place in the seventh century. Today, most Kurds are Sunni Muslims, but a few groups in southern and southeastern Kurdistan are Shi'ite or members of other lesser-known Islamic sects.

Rapid social change and recent events in the states occupied by the Kurds has had a differential, but in all cases profound, impact on all Kurdish groups; however, it is difficult to predict what the long-term outcomes might be. The Kurds continue their lengthy battle to gain some form of self-governance in the several states they occupy. Some would be content with autonomy within a state while others struggle for an independent territorial state of Kurdistan. Conflicting goals in this regard, coupled with differences between Sunni and Shi'ite groups, have sometimes been manipulated into intra-Kurd conflict, as happened most recently in Iraq in 1996. During the latter half of the twentieth century, the Kurds have been subjected to massive violence and human rights violations in most of the states in which they live. They have suffered repression and violence at the hands of both the Pahlavi and the Khomeini governments in Iran. The Iraqi government of Saddam Hussein forced the resettlement of several thousands of Kurds and later gas-bombed Kurdish communities. In Iraq, as well, the Kurds are split between the Kurdistan Democratic Party (KDP) and the Iraqi Patriotic Union of Kurdistan (PUK), which distrust one another (though they share the same political goals) and have sometimes engaged in open conflict. In addition, the Turkish government has long refused to recognize that the Kurds exist as a distinct group, although it has sent military forces against the Kurds in Iraqi Kurdistan and has been waging a civil war against the Kurds in the Turkish countryside for more than a decade. The UN has attempted to protect the Kurds from further aggression, as has the U.S. with its "no fly" zone, but to little avail.

The tactics that the various Kurdish groups have used, which often include violence, in their attempts to achieve some degree of autonomy within the territorial states in which they live, seem better adapted to success in the context of the earlier political systems of this region—the tributary states. Modern territorial states, even in the Middle East with the fairly recent legacy of the **millet** system of the Ottoman Empire (a system that provided some degree of religious-political autonomy to religious minorities), are unlikely to grant any meaningful autonomy to the minority Kurdish populations within their borders, or to any other minority. For, unlike the tributary state, the prime directive of the territorial state is to absorb into one nation all the minority nations within its borders.

In the Middle East, as we have seen, this is an adequate, if oversimplified, description of the situation. Dale Eickelman's perspective on the geographic spread and historical trajectory of Islam is illustrative.

(The information for this case study is derived from Busby (1995) and MacDonald (1989)).

millet

A religious and political unit under the Ottoman Empire that was defined by its adherence to a religion and to which certain rights and privileges were granted

terrorism, a form of violence that had become common in many parts of the world, but not in the American homeland. Since that date, there have been thousands of books written on the subject of terrorism. We have learned of a terrorist organization called al' Qaeda and its leader Osama bin Laden, who declared war on the United States. Osama bin Laden, a recently assassinated Islamic leader, was responsible for the destruction of the World Trade Center in New York City. The subject of the cultural friction between Islam and American values has become an important subject in modern anthropology.

Al' Qaeda is composed of Islamic extremists who are dedicated to the destruction of the United States. The Taliban was a religious movement that had taken over Afghanistan and which was supported by the government of Pakistan. Immediately after 9/11, the U.S. military, particularly the Marines, went into action. The Taliban government of Afghanistan was quickly overthrown by American forces and their allies. Elections were held with the help of the United Nations, and a new government formed that promised peace to the peoples of a country beleaguered by internal violence due to a several decade long civil war between traditional and radical Moslem factions. The new president, Hamid Karzai, who had fought against the Soviet domination of Afghanistan in the 1980s, seemed ideal to lead his country away from several decades of violence. He was an ethnic Pashtun, who appeared to have the backing of the people of Afghanistan. His new government appeared to represent most of the ethnic groups of the country. For many Americans, this was their first introduction to ethnic conflict in South Asia, a topic that had occupied many anthropologists over decades.

Much of what I have summarized above comes from the writings of academic anthropologists, and from interviews given by Middle East specialists on the *Lehr News Hour*. However, we have been surprised to learn that there is much more to anthropologists' activities than academic research. Readers of the *New York Times* and the *Christian Science Monitor* were surprised, in September of 2007, to read that a young woman anthropologist, who called herself Tracy, was working with the American military to reduce the power of the Taliban insurgencies. She was reported to operate with the Human Terrain Team, also made up of trained anthropologists. The *Times* reported that many academic anthropologists were outraged at the use of their discipline within what they considered a

■Immediately after 9/11, the U.S. military, particularly the Marines, went into action. The Taliban government of Afghanistan was quickly overthrown by American forces and their allies.

colonial war. Others were not so sure, particularly those with expertise in Afghanistan and Pakistan. Even more surprising to readers was the activity of one young Australian anthropologist, Lt. Col. David Kilcullen, working to improve the effectiveness of American counter-insurgency operations in Iraq under General David Petraeus. Dr. Kilcullen's work was reported on in the *New Yorker* magazine. According to Kilcullen, most of what Americans think of as terrorism is a global insurgency that cannot be met with traditional military approaches. When one reads about Tracy and Kilcullen's strategies, it is apparent that winning the war against terrorism has little to do with traditional warfare and has a great deal to do with alleviating distress brought on by certain aspects of globalization, including the perceived lack of legitimacy of secular leaning governments. In 2010, General David Petraeus, a student of insurgency from an anthropological perspective, was placed at the head of the American military in the Middle East.

Many Islams

Eickelman rejects emotional explanations of ethnic violence that depend on fears of Moslem fundamentalism and terrorism. He argues that the heart of conflict in the Middle East is the constant reinvention of Islam itself, and its attempt to come to grips with varied cultural traditions and now with modernization. Eickelman writes that the core of Islam transcends specific cultures, including its culture of origin. At the center of Islam is a set of ideals and expressions of religious truth; these are considered immutable. These core beliefs are subject to interpretation and reinterpretation, however, and produce sects, schisms, and challenges to belief. Islam is a remarkably varied religion, one which anthropologists once thought could be understood as the difference between Great (literate, urban) and Little (folk, rural, provincial) Traditions, following the ideas of Robert Redfield for folk Catholicism in Latin America. Yet Eickelman argues that there is a dynamic to Islam which goes fundamentally beyond contrasting written (Great) and folk (Little) traditions. He summarizes a series of recent anthropological studies of Islam, starting with Clifford Geertz (1968), to show that in virtually every community or locale studied over the years Islam is conceived of as a religion or world view which is fragmented, a language which is differentiated into many statements, not a singular and uniform world view (1981). According to Eickelman, these opposing conceptions of Islam are always co-present and form a dynamic tension with each other.

Eickelman argues that there has been a tendency to view Sunni and Shi'a Islam as though they are the major, if not the only, opposing Islamic doctrines. He points out that neither is homogenous and goes on to discuss other Islamic groups and religions such as Alevi, Sufism, Maraboutism. He argues that westerners tend to read their own very western tradition into the Islamic religion and into Islamic education. For Eickelman it is a mistake to view Islam as a single religion, or even many different religions, but that it is "more accurate to regard belief and practice as prismatic" (Eickelman 1981, 235). Westerners, he thinks, have a lack of understanding of the constant innovative quality of Islam; and they do not understand the nature of Islamic education, which we confuse with our own orthodox priesthoods or universities (with scholars delving into increasingly more boring information as they specialize in their respective disciplines).

Students of Islamic schools, rather than becoming priests, become politicians, soldiers, merchants, ministers of state, bankers, and others who move in the real world. The sense of religious versus secular knowledge is less fixed than in the West. Islam can incorporate science, medicine, and politics to the degree that such knowledge does not contradict Islamic laws. Islamic education provides a rigorous mental discipline, and much of the Quran is memorized, but without an intent of seeking explanation (Eickelman 1981). Poor as well as rich could sit in on lectures, and there was no faculty or administration in mosque universities. The relationship between the learned and the *umma* (community) was and is more porous than in our world of academic and non-academic. There are no rigorous, organized groups of scholars, administrators, bureaucrats, and other Western style educational apparatus.

The phrase Islamic fundamentalism tends to be used to incorporate the large number of distinct Islamic groups that are considered politically radical, but the term may be meaningless. The very process of state building in the Middle East appears to be tied to protests against the power of the state and the need to return to the original message of Muhammad. Each of the various sects of Islam (Sunni, Shi'ite, and Sufist) has built within itself a protest against corruption and power. The history of the development of states in the Middle East is also the history of Islamic protests against the centralization of authority.

Eickelman's analysis fits the view of this text: each region of the world has its own dynamic which must be understood on its own terms, and not in terms of a EuroAmerican cultural model. The picture of the Middle East is of many Islams. Add to this picture the diversity of cultures and derived ethnic identities, and one begins to appreciate the complexity of this vast region. Add the history of autonomous or semi-autonomous governance under the aegis of tributary states and empires until the advent of territorial states in the region in the late nineteenth and early twentieth centuries. Add the presence of two other major religious traditions, Judaism and Christianity, a recently created state (Israel), and peoples like the Kurds who claim shared identity but occupy parts of different territorial states and have no state of their own, but desire one in the current context. With each addition, the level of recent violence in the Middle East is perhaps more understandable, although hardly acceptable.

■   ■   ■

Chapter
Summary

The Middle East: Ethnicity, Oil, and Conflict

Geographic and cultural diversity are characteristics of the Middle East. Deserts and mountains have created isolated pockets where ancient cultural practices are preserved, while invasions have added layers of cultural diversity. While nine-tenths of the population is today Islamic, Islamic cultures overlay and share space with a great many ancient cultures and religions. A global culture spills over this diversity today, encouraging new forms of political participation—some democratic, some not—but also threatening many groups with a universal culture which has caused sects to turn to fundamental statements of their religious principles. Violence has often been the result. The modern Middle East is a region in transition from totalitarian rulers and populist egalitarians towards democratic tolerance on all sides. Yet the transition has not been smooth, has often been blocked by cross-cutting ethnic and religious conflicts, and remains incomplete. In this chapter we have focused on the origins and substance of various conflicts. We have tried to emphasize that a democratic balance is necessary in the choices people must have, if they are to support their governments through tough economic reforms, and that democracy is no panacea. Under certain circumstances, it may become a dead end, leading to totalitarian religious sects dominating the scene.

Chapter
Terms

1967 Six Day War	338	kibbutz	338
a-cosmism	324	messianic movement	327
caliph	330	millet	346
charismatic phase	330	monotheism	323
compradors	334	perennial irrigation	321
cosmism	324	polytheism	323
Crusades	333	qanat	321
diaspora	325	Quran	329
five pillars	329	salinization	321
hadith	331	supernaturalism	324
il rah	323	trade/raid nexus	323
Islam	329	ulema	331
kerese	321	Zionism	338
khan	323		

Check out our website
www.BVTLab.com
for flashcards,
chapter summaries,
and more.

Chapter 10

Asia: The Emerging Tigers

The vast region of Asia is divided into three subregions: South Asia, consisting of the nations (in alphabetical order) of Bangladesh, Bhutan, India, Maldives, Mauritius, Nepal, Pakistan, and Sri Lanka; Southeast Asia, which includes Brunei, Cambodia, Indonesia, Laos, Malaysia, Myanmar (formerly Burma), the Philippine Republic, Thailand, and Vietnam; and East Asia, which includes China, Japan, Korea, Singapore, and Taiwan. Tibet was formerly a South Asian nation but is currently administered by China. Four major world religions, each with many local variants, are prominent in the region: Buddhism, Christianity, Hinduism, and Islam. In addition, there remain many tribal religions, often called animistic religions because of their inclusion of beliefs in nature spirits. The religious diversity of Asia is surpassed considerably by its cultural diversity and the diversity of its landforms, climatic zones, and ecosystems. In short, Asia is a designation of convenience just as is its opposite, the West. In this chapter, we will devote attention to China, India, Indonesia, Vietnam, and Japan.

Asia has drawn the interests of philosophers, anthropologists, historians and other scholars since the Age of Enlightenment. For Georg Fredrik Hegel, the eighteenth century German philosopher, Asia is the beginning of history, and Europe is its end, just as the sun rises in the east and sets in the west. The East is a region of despotism, where political subjects are like children "who obey their parents without will or insight of their own" (Hegel 1956), while the West is where rationality and capitalism emerged in world history. This is clearly a very Eurocentric view of the vast diversity of cultures, nations, and religions that comprise Asia.

Changing Ideas About Asia

The alignment of rationality with European civilization neither began nor ended with Hegel, who was writing at the end of the eighteenth and beginning of the nineteenth century. The concept of rational choice was attached very early to the creation of European capitalism, while other political economies around the world were generally treated as lacking in rationality. The connections between capitalism, rationality, and the origins of science were elemental to the writings of Max Weber, for whom the Protestant religion was the basis for the origin of capitalism, double entry bookkeeping, even Western classical music (Weber 1958). Weber, who could read neither Chinese nor Hindi, wrote two treatises on the religions of the Orient: *The Religion of India* (1958a) and *The Religion of China* (1951). His book on China maintained that this region of the world lacked significant external trade relations and was a formidable feudal bureaucracy ideologically organized by Confucianism, with a predominantly agricultural economy. India was more rational due to its trade connections to the West, particularly when it was under the control of Islamic (Mughal) leaders; however, India's rationality lay somewhere between that of China and Europe. Religion, in the early twentieth century, was seen as having a key role in the evolution of society: oriental religions were viewed as naturalistic, originating in nature worship and supporting totalitarian regimes, while Christianity was world rejecting, supporting secular democratic states, science and capitalism (Larson 1995, 38).

Figure 10.1

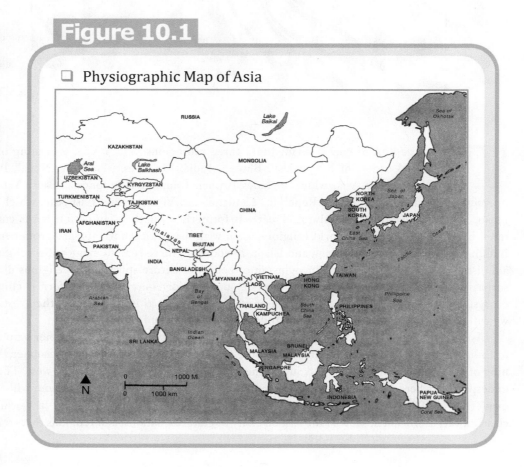

☐ Physiographic Map of Asia

Cultural materialists reversed the argument. They perceived human ecology to play a deterministic role behind political economy, and religion was merely a means by which the elite controlled the peasants. In the writings of Karl Marx, religion was the opiate that clouded the eyes of peasants and allowed society to be controlled by elites. According to Karl Wittfogel, Oriental despotism, rested on the ability of states to control the distribution of water in hydraulic empires. These were empires dependent on state run waterworks, such as dams, large drainage systems, and reservoirs. Hydraulic empires, such as China and India, were located largely in regions that were arid or suffered from aridity on a seasonal basis. Irrigation and population density have remained key factors in modern explanations for the rise of centralized bureaucratic states in Asia.

The opposition between a totalitarian orient and a democratic, capitalist Occident is implicit in much social science and historical theorizing in the twentieth century, including that of world system theorists, who treat India and China as semi-peripheral regions of the capitalist core. China and India adopted anti-system, socialist political regimes to escape the ravages of capitalism (Larson 1995, 40). While these theories remain important, a new focus on ideology and strategies of state formation is forcing revisions in the stereotype of Asiatic states. Three new and related propositions are emerging. The first is that trade, along with irrigation agriculture, was always important in state formation in Asia. The second is that religion was a means of reducing transaction costs over large regions, improving the possibilities of trade. These two factors, as we have seen, played a dominant role in the Middle East as well. The third proposition is that the association of modernization with the secularization of society, the disappearance of the family, and the importance of the individual applies in the West, but not in the Orient (another term for Asia).

The third proposition does not mean that family and religion are everywhere unchallenged in Asia, for castes, clans, and extended families do not have the cohesion and social significance they once had. Westernized young people often are indifferent to the religions of their parents. However, in Asiatic cultures, there is less infatuation with ideas of individual freedom, and the search for individual identity outside the family and community is not as appealing as in many Western cultures. Many of these observations apply as well to Africa, the Middle East, and as shown in the next chapter, Latin America. While the West wakes up to the importance of the family, these cultures remain family-centric and there is much to learn from them.

■Oriental despotism rested on the ability of states to control the distribution of water in hydraulic empires. These were empires dependent on state run waterworks, such as dams, large drainage systems, and reservoirs.

In addition, the core-periphery model of the world system theorists is being challenged with the emergence of different parts of Asia as either a new core or new cores (depending on the level of generalization), often challenging one another. Japan has long been an affluent and successful challenger to western core hegemony. South Korea has joined Japan, usually as a partner, and so has Taiwan. These three nations, often called the Asian Tigers, have, with varying levels of success, made the transition to democracy. China, on the other hand, is emerging as a commercial giant whose political direction may be a threat to the Asian democracies. Then there are the countries of Southeast Asia— Thailand, Vietnam, Malaysia, Indonesia, and the Philippines—all of which are changing with such speed as to make generalizations impossible. These five nations are currently becoming integrated into the global economy. As they do so, their political systems, for the most part, are becoming increasingly more democratic, or the need for democracy is becoming more obvious to their citizens. The successful combination of family enterprise, capitalism, and corruption-free governments are becoming models for the other countries of Asia. Yet these same countries are challenging the Western stereotype of Oriental, as a powerful work ethic combined with careful investments are drawing jobs away from Europe and the United States, particularly in the textile industry.

India, the geographic giant of South Asia, is a socialist democracy which is being challenged by religious parties whose basis is Hinduism and Indian ethnic identity (despite the fact that India contains hundreds of self-identified ethnic groups). Will India maintain its traditions of democracy, or will it become a Hindu style theocracy? What then of its common border with China? Will these giants threaten each other? What of volatile Pakistan? North of China and India are the former republics of the Soviet Union, many of them wealthy in natural resources but currently engaged in a shaky transition between authoritarianism and democracy. What role will they come to play?

The need for a balanced transition toward capitalism and democracy is nowhere more apparent than in the poverty-stricken country of Bangladesh (average income of $183.00/year), whose people are struggling to abandon a generation of autocratic rule. Bangladesh has a national average population density of 2,097 persons per square mile (twice that of New York City) and a population growth rate of 2.3 percent The population doubles every thirty years and is currently 120 million. A quick glance at a map of

◼A Bangladeshi woman sits at her roadside cigarette stall in Dhaka. Severely impoverished Bangladesh has a national average population density of 2,097 persons per square mile and an average income of $183.00/year.

Asia shows that Bangladesh occupies flat delta-lands into which flow rivers from Nepal, Assam, India, and China. These rivers receive rainwater from the Himalayas to the north. Most of the country is flat. Once a year monsoons flood the region, and the floods vary in severity. In 1988, 1989, and 1990, the floods were extensive. Those of 1990 killed over fifty thousand people (Baxter 1992, 135). Much of the flooding of Bangladesh is a consequence of deforestation to the north in the Himalayas, mostly controlled by China. Over the last decade, the Bangladesh government has met the problem by constructing large multi-storied concrete towers that people use as shelter from the floodwaters. Nonetheless, there are not enough of these structures to protect everyone, and in bad flood years thousands can be expected to perish.

Human Ecology and Cultural Diversity

The geography of Asia reveals endless variation. Mountain ranges and deserts cross and are crossed by political divisions which have changed through time. Parts of northern Asia, for example, were once regions of the Soviet Union, but are so no longer; however, their histories have been influenced by the rise and fall of that empire. The heart of Asia is a huge mountain massif with mile-high passes and radiating ranges lying to the east and west. The mountain ranges bisect Asia into northern tundra of pastoral nomads and southern and southeastern realms of monsoon rains and peasant agriculture. These last two regions lie within monsoon Asia, and incorporate the major civilizations of Asia, particularly China and India, but also Vietnam and Thailand. The cultures of the mountain regions surrounding the lowland civilization were culturally influenced by them, and from time to time have been incorporated into their empires. Mountain ranges isolate separate ecological and cultural units; and historic changes, migration, and the success and failure of empire building have produced great human and ecological diversity.

Very important to Asia's human ecology has been the history of its irrigation systems, of which there have been two distinct types. The first is found predominantly in China and is associated with the growing of paddy rice. Rice was first domesticated in the Yangtze Valley before 7000 BC, but paddy rice agriculture did not fully emerge until a thousand years ago. Such systems require the development of an artificial environment, a network of ponds and lakes in which the soil is flooded by irrigation systems. An impermeable soil pan is developed which is insulated from the direct action of rainfall by a layer of water and microorganisms that work without oxygen and contribute to the creation of a rich layer of black soil under water (Wolf 1969, 27). Such systems require predictable irrigation systems, which in turn require the harnessing of rivers, lakes, and other water systems by the state. Paddy rice agriculture allowed the support of very large populations, required the investment of large levies of workers, and led to the development of complex states.

The ecological zones outside paddy rice were used for the growing of oil-bearing seeds, cotton, tea, or pepper. Mulberry trees were grown for leaves, which fed silk worms and generated a whole industry of silk manufacturing. Oil, cotton, tea, pepper, and silk were all key ingredients in the export trade of China. The mutual reinforcement of state power, trade, and the support of large populations historically led to the highly centralized states which dominated China from the beginning of its history.

Less centralized are the tank irrigation systems of India, Ceylon, and Southeast Asia. These are quite similar to those described in the last chapter on the Middle East. However, tank irrigation systems depend on monsoon rainfall, and not on subterranean water sources. Such tanks date from the earliest Indian states of Harappa and Mohenjo Daro consisting of large reservoirs which were used in the irrigation of a variety of crops: rice, wheat, barley, or millet depending on the local environment. In association with the fabricated pools were high ramparts, platforms for houses, and drainages that allowed the control of monsoon floods for villages, towns, and cities. Scholars, such as E. Leach, have theorized that tank irrigation, since it requires local political centralization but not the integration of rivers and lakes, did not require the coordination of state bureaucracies such as found in China, but that it would have contributed to local hierarchies like the caste system found in India. Such systems, called **jajmani** systems, were redistribution economies in which foods and goods were distributed back to the laboring population by a jajman, a landlord of sorts, who dominated the political hierarchy of a valley. Goods were distributed back to people according to their level in the caste system. India, unlike China, consists of a hierarchy of local political elites and not a single imperial authority.

From earliest times, the mountain ranges, with their west to east river systems and passes, and the northern steppe, were used as trade routes which crossed Asia ending at port cities on the east coast of Asia. It was in these highland regions that pastoral nomadism formed natural adaptations. Pastoral nomadism was basically the same camel- (but of the two hump or Bactrian type) or sheep-based system described in the last two chapters. A little unusual were the Yak breeders of highland Tibet whose animals are adapted to the cold and arid highlands. All three types of nomads contributed to the trade networks which crisscrossed the Himalayan mountains, and still do so today. The mountainous country of Afghanistan is almost totally dependent on trade, sheep and goat herding, as is much of northern Pakistan. Just to the south of these regions, the Indus River and Ganges that connect north to south, carried that trade to the Indian Ocean. Where trade and productive agriculture combined, and where food could be grown to support urban populations, there evolved the ancient cores of China and India with their distinct irrigation systems. These trade and production systems are a continuation of that found in North Africa, the Great Silk Road, as it meandered toward the eastern terminus in the port cities of Asia: Shanghai, Macau, Saigon, Bangkok, Rangoon, Calcutta, Madras, Bombay, and Karachi.

jajmani

An economic redistribution system in which foods and goods were distributed back to the laboring population by a jajman or type of landlord

■Paddy rice agriculture provides jobs and leads to the development of complex states.

Unlike Hegel, Marx, and Weber's theories about the tradeless domination of subsistence agriculture on the histories of Asia, trade in fact played a powerful role and was intricately combined with irrigation and pastoral nomadic ecologies. The story of trade in Asia compares favorably with the story told in the chapters on Africa and the Middle East. However, with the domination of Europeans, the trade networks collapsed; and so did the critical nature of the human adaptations described, which then became primarily subsistence-based adaptations. Thus Hegel, Marx, and Weber were examining what was left of Asia after the Europeans had monopolized the trade connections, and most of the above named cities were in European hands. Today, the Asians are regaining their status in the ancient game of trade, and the core-periphery distinction is falling away.

China: From Confucianism to Communism

With four hundred million people a century and a half ago, and over a billion now, China has long been highly populated. It is a vast nation of 3,691,502 square miles, making it almost 670,000 square miles larger than the United States, with tropics to the south and the subarctic to the north (Cressey 1963). The western half of the country has high inhospitable mountain ranges, but these mountainous regions were important to China because through those passes were the trade connections to the west.

The core of ancient China lies along two great rivers: the Hwang Ho in the north (the Yellow River) and the Yangtze in the south, both regions of low-lying plains with yearly monsoon rain. This core region divides evenly at a line between the two rivers between a northern temperate zone and a southern subtropical zone (Cressey 1963).

THE EARLIEST CHINESE: ECOLOGY, TECHNOLOGY, AND TRADE

Yang-shao

A Neolithic tribal society that lived in ancient China between 6000 and 5000 BC

The alluvial soils of the fertile flood plains are constantly renewed through flooding and sedimentation and lend themselves to intensive agriculture, which is very old. Neolithic, tribal societies known as the ***Yang-shao*** emerged between 6000 and 5000 BC. These were dependent on rice, millet, pigs, dogs, chickens, and water buffalo and made stone sickles, mortars, pestles, and ceramics (Gernet 1996, 37). Early Yang-shao villagers practiced shifting agriculture, cultivating millet as their main crop; however, burials show evidence of status differences, and possibly some form of hierarchical clan organization. By 3000 BC, the *Yang-shao* were making very attractive pottery vessels for steaming food, which is the basis of most contemporary Chinese cooking (Fagan 1995, 298). *Yang-shao* pottery may have been an important trade item. Similar cultures were found along the Yangtze with evidence for weaving. These farming villages were followed by the Hsia dynasty between 2207 and 1766 BC, which showed significant advances in craftsmanship, including elegant jade and ceramic wares. The rammed or beaten earth construction of the Hsia, which was used for the bases of temples, possibly marks the beginning of the first Chinese dynasties (Gernet 1996, 38).

Lungshan

The first chiefdom-type society, which lived in northern China between 4000 and 2000 BC

The first chiefdom type social structures appeared during the ***Lungshan*** culture, which emerged between 4000 and 2000 BC, the organizational parallel of chiefdoms in North Africa and the Middle East. By 3000 BC, *Lungshan* farming culture spread throughout northern China in larger and more permanent villages than those of the *Yang-shao* people,

■Statue of philosopher Confucius at the Shanghai Confucian Temple. Confucius taught that social order was based on virtue

divination

The practice of attempting to foretell the future

scapulimancy

A divination method in which animal bones are painted with special symbols and heated in a fire to produce cracks that are then studied to determine the future

Ti

A superior being in the Chinese pantheon of gods during the Lungshan period

with irrigation and paddy rice cultivation. This clan-based culture had a religion based on shamanism and ancestor worship. **Divination** by means of animal bones (called **scapulimancy**) was practiced. The scapulae of various animals, which had been painted with special symbols, were heated in a fire. Cracks through the symbols were used to predict the future, particularly of the royal elite. Much later, these symbols became Chinese writing. The *Lungshan* also had highly sophisticated bronze metallurgy and elaborate fortifications of rammed earth.

THE RISE OF THE CHINESE DYNASTIES

Scholars believe that between 2000 and 1000 BC chiefdom social structures evolved into states with the appearance of the Shang Dynasty, and the center of Chinese civilization shifted further west to the region of modern An-Yang in northeast Honan province. Chinese writing, the chariot, divination, human sacrifice, and bronze manufacturing appeared or continued to evolve; and there was an upsurge in the number of sites of archaic civilizations (Gernet 1996, 41). Thirty monarchs ruled during the Shang, and there were six changes of the capital in the area of western Shantung, southern Hopei, western Honan, and northern Anhwei. In 1953, archaeologists uncovered a site in Honan province with a wall of rammed earth sixty feet thick and the remains of dwellings, workshops, furnaces, and molds for bronzes. At An-Yang, a royal cemetery contained the burials of the eleven kings, most of which had been looted. In 1976, the unlooted tomb of the wife of a Shang king was found with riches in bronze and jade, and with sixteen human sacrifices. Whole chariots with horses still in their harnesses were excavated. Another recent discovery revealed an army of seven thousand men made of terra cotta. The implication is that the chariot was used extensively in warfare. The Shang chariot was light and strong, with large wheels of many spokes. These chariots were not unlike chariots found in Syria in the seventeenth century BC. Warfare was combined with human sacrifice. In several graves, decapitated corpses were found, while in others were found heads without bodies. Many of these discoveries suggest the existence of rites requiring the sacrifice of prisoners of war (Gernet 1996, 42).

During the Shang, roads, staging posts, and extensive canals were used for trade. Silk weaving and the production of cotton textiles became highly sophisticated, as did the use of fire in the production of fine porcelains and bronzes. The production of cast iron became an important industry. China became a big exporter of luxury products: silks, bronzes, ceramics, cotton goods, tea, mirrors, lacquer ware, and furniture. China's traffic in fine trade goods extended to every major port city in the Old World. It was because of the success of Chinese trade throughout the next several thousand years that the maritime nations of Europe were drawn to that part of the world in the sixteenth century (Gernet 1996, 29).

Shang political economy rested on the idea of the king as a semi-divine being who interceded on behalf of his people with the high god **Ti** through the use of oracle bones for divination (made out of scapulae or tortoise shells). The royal palace was the center of

theocracy

A form of government in which a sacred deity is considered the supreme ruler

Chou dynasty

The first empire in China (1100 BC–AD 220), which formalized the rule of the king within a philosophical tradition outlined by Confucius

filial piety *(hsiao)*

A social order in which a son is subordinate to his father, who in turn is subordinate to his father and ultimately to the emperor, who is subordinate to Ti

activities for a cult of kings, a **theocracy**, and of an aristocratic society which was hierarchically organized through patrilineal clans. The heads of family were also the heads of family worship. The theocratic kings of China had religions that were very distinct from those of Egypt and Sumeria, but they were, nonetheless, magical beings: humans with supernatural attributes. The Shang domain extended to the Yangtze plain and beyond. The Shang was followed by the **Chou dynasty** which formalized the rule of the king within a philosophical tradition spelled out by K'ung Fu-tzu or Confucius (551–479 BC).

CONFUCIANISM AND CHINESE CULTURE

Confucianism was to serve China until this century, and is still a state legal tradition as well as a moral philosophy, backing the rule by elites in modern Taiwan and Shanghai. Confucius taught that social order was based on virtue, which came from ritual performance symbolizing **filial piety**, or *hsiao*. Filial piety demanded the subordination of the son to the father, the father to his father—all to the interests of **tsu** or patrilineal clan as determined by the gentry. The gentry paid homage to the emperor, and the emperor to Ti. Family harmony was based on the worship of the ancestors and acceptance of the hierarchy of aristocratic society. Ancestor worship helped bind the multilayered tsu into a functional whole under the proscriptions of the ideology of Confucianism.

At the root of Confucian philosophy was the traditional family. The traditional Chinese family structure existed until 1950—when it was outlawed by the Communist state. The family depended on the tsu. The tsu included all people with a common surname who traced descent from a common ancestor (Eschleman 1994). The tsu might be made up of several thousand people, often entire villages. The upper level of the tsu

Figure 10.2

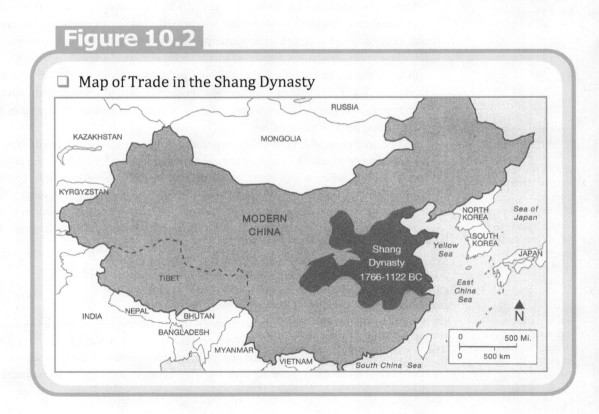

❏ Map of Trade in the Shang Dynasty

was the **gentry**, an intellectual class, which received income as landlords. Those gentry who were successful in passing a national exam based on Confucian philosophy became members of the **Mandarin** bureaucracy, which ruled China. The Mandarin bureaucracy was subdivided into nine status levels, each tied to comprehensive state exams, which formed the elites of the clans. At the lowest level of the tsu were the rural farmers, the **peasants**, who comprised the bulk of the poverty-stricken population. Poverty contributed to poor medical care, particularly for females (Chao 1977).

The outlines of clan social structure were set out in Confucius' codes of behavior. The traditional clan was important for a variety of functions, most of which have been lost today. The tsu loaned money to the peasant class for traditional, if extravagant, weddings and funerals. It established schools for clan members, exercised judicial authority, collected taxes for the government, and maintained the ancestral graves (Chao 1977). Confucianism spread from China to most of Southeast Asia during China's various conquests. It became the norm for upper class behavior in Vietnam, Cambodia, Laos, and in most regions that were not influenced by Islam or by Hinduism.

Males held a favorable position in Chinese society, and the Confucian code subordinated women. In the ideal Confucian family, women were supposed to be submissive and to learn from their husbands how to be pure and faithful. A woman should follow the three submissions: obey her father when a child, her husband when she is married, and her oldest son when she is a widow.

Confucianism is based on Chinese cosmology, which sees the world as composed of two complementary elements: the yin which is female, passive, dark, and weak; and the yang which is male, bright, strong, and active. In traditional China, female infanticide was common because boys were preferred to girls. Boys continued the lineage; girls did not. Marriages were not based on love and romance but were arranged. The Chinese practiced exogamy, which meant that the girl had to leave her village (the home of her patrilineal clan members) due to the rule of patriclan (tsu) exogamy; that is, she could not marry anyone with the same surname. She would be completely removed from her own family (known as the family of orientation) and would move in with her husband's family (to form a new family called the family of procreation). In the new family, she had to submit to her husband and to her new mother-in-law. She would only have power in her own right through her own son, when he was grown and married, and in her ability to dominate her daughter-in-law.

The traditional Chinese wife's responsibilities were to bear male children and work for her mother-in-law. The failure to bear male heirs gave the husband the right to take a concubine or other wives. One indication of female oppression was **foot binding**. Women's feet, bound from childhood, were reduced to three inches in length from toe to heel. This practice was found primarily among the gentry and was a means of restricting women's movement. Peasant women were not required to go through the procedure.

CHINESE FEUDALISM: PEASANTS AND ETHNIC MINORITIES

The basic pattern of Chinese civilization—multiethnic and expansionistic—was maintained for thousands of years. The ethnic group that has been dominant through time has been the Han Chinese. Other distinct ethnic groups have either retained their language or identity, or they have been **sinified** (have adopted the Han Chinese language and Confucian ethic). In the sixteenth century, Chinese Han social structure was feudal. However, Chinese feudalism was unusual in that patrilineal clans, not the state, owned most land and lands were rented to clan members by the Mandarin elites. Thus, most Chinese peasants were not landless but had access to land either through inheritance or through a complex set of leases or rents. Landlords and cultivators were linked not through hereditary rights but through business contracts and a bureaucratic elite (Wolf 1969, 106). Behind the throne, the ethic of Confucianism helped the state control its various peoples.

China, with its highly centralized state and the ownership of land through hereditary clans, stands in strong contrast to Western Europe in the sixteenth century. Remember that in Great Britain, a weak feudal system disintegrated; the king turned over land as private property to the aristocracy, and he then tried to keep the aristocracy weak by gaining the support of a developing industrial class. This led to the development of capitalism and the industrial revolution. The dynamics of culture change for China were very different. In China, the highly centralized state would go through cycles. These would begin with the invasion of a corrupt China by northern barbarians, who would establish a new dynasty. That dynasty would become corrupt, leading to the rise of secret societies, many with charismatic leaders, who attacked the state and weakened it. According to Eric Wolf, secret societies with names like the White Lotus, the Eight Tigrams, the Nien, the Great Knife, the Boxers, and the Society of the Faith were traditional to Chinese society. These challengers, often based on anti-Confucian Buddhist principles of egalitarianism and feminism (explained in the section on India), would fight among themselves, and either succeed in establishing a new state or an invasion would bring northern barbarians in to establish a new state.

This was the cycle that began in the seventeenth century when the Ming dynasty became corrupt and weakened, and was attacked by secret societies. The Manchu, *Sinified* (Chinese speaking) tribesmen from the north, found little difficulty in invading China and establishing a new dynasty, the Ch'ing, in 1644 (Wolf 1969, 104). The invaders seized North China without much fight, but this would not be true in South China where the southern Ming held out against the Manchu armies. The Manchu slowly extended their rule, consolidating their empire into the most extensive empire in the world. By 1759, the Ch'ing empire controlled territories covering thirteen million square kilometers. Modern China, by contrast, is only 9,736,000 square kilometers. The Ch'ing empire embraced Outer Mongolia, Taiwan, and regions since occupied by Russia. In addition, most of the Asian countries of Nepal, Burma, Thailand, the Philippines, and Korea recognized Ch'ing sovereignty and were dependent on it. In the eighteenth century, this empire entered a period of great prosperity due to an unprecedented upsurge in agriculture, manufacturing, and trade (Gernet 1996, 480–483).

This new dynasty was to survive until 1911, when it, too, became weakened by outsiders, collapsed when attacked by secret societies, and was replaced by a communist political system in 1949, a topic to which we will soon turn. Very often, the

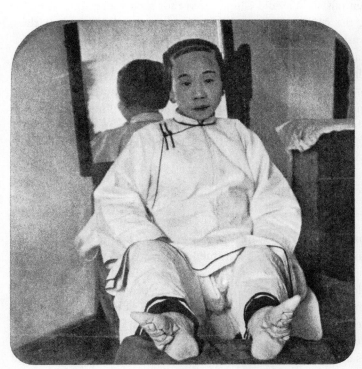

■One indication of female oppression was foot binding. Women's feet, bound from childhood, were reduced to three inches in length from toe to heel. Binding restricted the woman's movement. This was another means of establishing male dominance.

Confucian ethic was countered with Buddhist religious values that tend to be anti-aristocratic, have often entered the dynastic cycle at the beginning of conflict, and formed the core beliefs of the secret societies. (Buddhism is discussed more extensively in the section on India.)

During each cycle, the Han Chinese feudal system remained intact. While it might contract during a period of conflict, the same centralized bureaucracy would emerge with the success of a new dynasty, even though the dynasty might belong to another ethnic group, such as the Mongols of the northland. This system of overarching political and social control, based on Confucian values, incorporated many other distinct ethnic groupings with a fair degree of success.

During the 1950s, the communist government of Mao Zedong studied ethnic groupings in China and discovered that, including the Han, there are fifty-six national minorities in China. Through the millennia of Chinese culture, the dominant trend has been to leave the various ethnic groups alone, but with the underlying expectation that they would become sinified; that is, they would imitate the Han Chinese. In the 1960s, during the Cultural Revolution (to be discussed), the customs of minority peoples were censured or forbidden. People were not allowed to use their own language. Traditional healing practices, art, and literate traditions were outlawed (Maybury-Lewis 1992, 83).

Chinese social organization and culture remained relatively unchanged for three thousand years, despite repeated rebellions and periods of disintegration followed by new periods of consolidation and reintegration. Numerous dynasties rose and fell in this fashion as less and less effective and more corrupt descendants followed a successful emperor until there was another revolt and a new dynasty. However, the basic Confucian traditions and lifeway remained the same.

The question is often raised: Why did China survive for such a long time while the civilizations of Europe, the Middle East, and Africa rose and fell? There are three answers. First, while invasions did occur from outside China, the invaders viewed Chinese culture as superior and adopted it as their own once in power. Second, Chinese culture has always been relatively tolerant of ethnic differences within its borders. Third, Chinese culture is flexible and adaptive. Confucianism, the core of Chinese values, is not a supernaturalistic religion and does not lend itself to fanaticism. The Chinese, over their long history, have been more pragmatic than dogmatic. However, there have been exceptions, such as the Chinese communist period that lasted from 1949 to 1975.

COLLAPSE OF THE EMPIRE AND THE RISE OF COMMUNISM

In the nineteenth century, beyond the cyclical pressures which troubled all dynasties, there was added the heavy pressure of foreign influence which weakened the ability of the Ch'ing dynasty to resist disintegration and made it more difficult to achieve cohesion. Africa and the Middle East had been incorporated as parts of a European colonial empire. China, and its neighbors in Asia, did not collapse as easily to the Europeans, putting up great resistance. Under pressure from the Europeans, the Chinese government agreed to open **treaty ports**, or ports of trade where Europeans were restricted to walled-in compounds and only allowed to trade with officials. The Chinese hoped this technique would allow them to keep the rest of China intact. Yet, these ports of trade made China a satellite of the industrializing world, and they expanded despite the tactics of the Ch'ing to keep China pure against outsiders.

treaty port

A port of trade where Europeans were restricted to walled-in compounds and allowed to trade only with officials

In 1795, a peasant revolution in the northwest and Honan province spelled the beginning of the end. The Ch'ing, like the Ming, had come to suffer from corruption; public finance had been squandered without counting the cost. The court and state had lived beyond their means, and corruption "favored by the centralization of power in the hands of the emperor … had known no bounds from 1775 onwards" (Gernet 1996, 533). As the central court weakened, European traders were at the doors of the trade cities of the coast.

Once the European traders had their foot in the door, they monopolized trade and then used foreign investment to gain control over Chinese industries near the treaty ports. Slowly, the ports became bastions of foreign interest within China (an example here would be English controlled Hong Kong). Chinese dynastic power was further weakened by a series of wars carried on by outside powers: the Anglo-French War against China in 1860–1861; the annexation of Vietnam by the French; the Japanese war against China in 1894–1895; and the Russo Japanese war of 1904–1905, which was fought on Chinese soil. In each of these wars, China lost territory to outside imperialist interests. There were also internal rebellions—the Taiping Rebellion (1850–1865) and the rebellion of the Nien (1852–1868), which foreshadowed the peasant-based Communist revolution of the twentieth century (Wolf 1969, 119). These revolutions were led by secret societies, such as those mentioned above. However, the root of Chinese disintegration and the despair of the Ch'ing dynasty was the introduction of opium into Chinese society. The British East India Company had gained a monopoly over the production of opium in India, which they exported to China. By 1810, four to five thousand cases of opium were being imported into Canton, and imports were to continue to increase rapidly despite attempts by the Chinese government to end the trade (Gernet 1996, 536). A series of Opium Wars (especially 1839–42) were fought by the British to prevent China from closing its doors to this drug. Opium was smuggled into China despite draconian efforts to stop the trade. China used silver to pay for opium, causing a budget deficit that crippled the Chinese government.

By 1870, the Ch'ing empire had practically disappeared. The fighting between the government, revolutionary forces led by secret societies, and the colonial forces who took various sides led to an enormous loss of material wealth caused by the bitter fighting. The losses in human lives were unparalleled in human history. Whole rich and densely populated areas in Nanking and Hangchow were ravaged: between twenty and thirty million people died.

■Raw opium

The Warlords   The last Chinese dynasty collapsed in 1911 due to both internal and external pressures, and nationalist rebels took over the diminished government. The collapse of central authority led to the increased power of regional warlords. In the period from 1911 to World War II, China was divided into territories controlled by warlords, each attempting to capture the state with his army. Many warlords were the leaders of anti-Manchu, anti-monarchic political movements that supported democratic reform. Many of the leaders, such as Sun Yat-sen, were intellectuals with connections to Europe and the United States (Sun Yat-Sen founded the Society for the Rebirth of China, which later became the Kuo Min Tang). The military governors or warlords collected taxes, seized loot from opponents, and produced and distributed opium. They also borrowed money from foreign banks to keep their wars alive. They recruited their armies from the impoverished peasantry, some of whom were no better than bandits (Wolf 1969, 127).

At the same time, industrial capitalism grew in the urban regions of China, but it did not grow fast enough to incorporate peasants leaving the countryside. Foreign banks funded industries run by Chinese workers and protected by the warlords, who lived off the taxes they imposed on both urban and rural populations. The control of agriculture by banks with international connections led to the increased production of export commodities, such as tobacco and opium, but a decrease in food production. Much of the land came to be controlled by absentee landowners who were protected by warlords, and who used their resources to finance their struggles with each other. The introduction of commercial crops and the commercialization of land led to an increase in the value of land, and rents increased. Prices for land doubled and tripled in some regions in the late nineteenth century (Wolf 1969, 130).

The Communist Dictatorship and the Cult of Mao   The struggles between the warlords just prior to World War II were reduced to two powerful leaders in contention to gain control of China: Chiang Kaishek, the heir and brother-in-law of Sun Yatsen and creator of the Kuo Min Tang or Nationalist Party, and Mao Zedong, the Communist leader of the Share Production Party. Both parties were founded on Soviet models. These two warlords formed a brief alliance, but in 1927, Chaing Kaishek attempted to destroy Mao Zedong and his Communist followers. In World War II, Chaing Kaishek made himself an ally of the United States but was not successful in his battle with the Japanese invaders of China; instead he retreated to western China. Mao Zedong was to prove much more successful fighting the Japanese in northern China and Manchuria. At the end of the war, the two leaders faced each other. The success that Mao Zedong had against the Japanese drew enormous support from peasants recruited to his Red Army; and in 1949, Chiang Kaishek was forced to flee to Formosa (Taiwan), where he organized a new government and established Nationalist China (the new name of Taiwan).

The Communist Revolution of 1949 restructured mainland China according to a Millenarian dream (Wolf 1969, 154). The origins of Mao Zedong's communist ideas are not in Karl Marx but rather are tied to China's ancient past: an anti-Confucian core philosophy of revolutionary, egalitarian, and utopian aspirations. What *communism* came to mean after 1949, however, was Marxist: collective discipline, indoctrination to state ideology, public works of gigantic scope, and a highly centralized statist form of social structure dominated by the Communist Party. In China, as in the former Soviet Union, state institutions were completely controlled by the Communist Party. The party came to be everywhere and directed everything—government administration at all levels, commercial enterprises, rural communes, factories, hospitals, schools and universities— even when it had no competence to do so. As in the Soviet Union, the leaders were the most elderly members of the Communist Party, and the only criterion to promotion appears to have been devotion to political orthodoxy (Gernet 1996, 662). In contrast, the socialism of Africa and the Middle East appears mild, more a matter of state control of basic industries than the thorough control of every organization and social structure.

Beginning in the 1950s, China went through a series of attempts to push economic growth. In 1958, Mao announced the Great Leap Forward to accelerate production. Attempts were made to establish iron and steel foundries in the countryside, to force urban dwelling intellectuals to live like peasants, and to forcibly communalize and collectivize all agriculture. Intellectuals, especially those with Western educations, were viewed as threats to the state. The Communist state attempted to outlaw Confucianism, viewing this philosophy as the dead hand of tradition, which held back the new state. Ancestor worship was outlawed, and the temples of the ancestors desecrated or destroyed. There was considerable resistance to the attack on ancestral temples and the collectivization of agriculture, and thirty million people died or were killed between 1959 and 1962 (Ogden 1991, 9).

The most extreme period came between 1966 and the early to mid 1970s when Mao Zedong, his wife, and close followers (the Gang of Four) launched the Great Proletarian Cultural Revolution. This was really the cult of Mao Zedong. Mao and his followers tried to radically restructure society through the Red Guard (not to be confused with the Red Army), an elite force of young radicals. It was during this phase that state terrorism was used on the Chinese people. *The Red Book of Mao* was printed by the millions and distributed free to the masses. It consisted of epigrams supposedly written by Chairman Mao. The Red Guard went on rampages breaking into homes, stealing or destroying property, shearing long hair off young women, and attempting to eradicate all signs of European or American culture, including classical music. People with formal degrees, such as educators, doctors, and lawyers, were arrested and imprisoned with no charges made against them. It has been estimated that 10 percent of the population, about 100 million people, were the targets of the Red Guard, and that tens of thousands of those targeted were killed (Ogden 1991, 11).

Mao Zedong's theory of economic development consisted of cutting off trade connections to the outside world and attempting to achieve overnight urban development on the back of the rural peasantry. China became economically isolated, even making itself into an enemy of its one ally, the Soviet Union. Instead of urban economic development, the whole of China's economy suffered one economic disaster after the other until after Chairman Mao's death.

The Cultural Revolution was a colossal failure, both in human life and in a lack of economic growth. Industrial and agricultural production dropped dramatically. There was also a cultural loss. The Red Guard not only attacked western institutions, they also attempted to destroy Chinese traditions. Since Confucianism had been specially targeted, and there was no real alternative except for Mao's little Red Book, by 1976, there was an almost total breakdown in both traditional Chinese morality and in Marxist-Leninist values (Ogden 1991, 11).

Economic Reforms Without Political Reform Under Deng Xiaoping

The end of the Cultural Revolution came with the death of Mao Zedong in September of 1976. Deng Xiaoping, who became chairman of the Communist Party, replaced Mao Zedong in 1977. Upon Mao's death, the Gang of Four was arrested and removed from power. Deng began the deradicalization of Chinese society with the introduction of new free market policies. Deng restructured Chinese society without developing a new cult of personality and has come to strikingly resemble the successful monarchs of Chinese history whose personal qualities are often a complete mystery to following generations. Deng has become the most enigmatic leader China has had in over a century.

Mao was accused of making serious mistakes. Maoism was rigorously questioned. Since traditional Chinese culture had been practically destroyed by the Red Guard, the new attack on Maoist thought left China without any strong belief system. Western values began to filter back, but were viewed as "spiritual pollution." Deng Xiaoping attempted to open the door to western style free markets within a communist dictatorship.

Deng established five special economic zones (SEZs), predominantly in southern China, and allowed small businesses to open in the major cities. He also allowed farmers to lease state lands and to utilize market principles in growing and selling crops. The strongest of the economic zones are located in Guangdong province, which is located in south China just to the north of the island-city of Hong Kong. Deng's theory was that free market economies could be developed within a socialist framework and that economic reforms should precede political reforms. Free markets were in, but democracy was out for the time being.

The question is how successful can the new market system be without democracy? Economic reforms in China have led to enormous economic improvements, but open markets have led to corruption as bureaucrats sold special favors to successful "capitalist entrepreneurs." Many new capitalists took advantage of the corruption of government to make themselves wealthy. While democratic reform is not attractive to the old oligarchy of China, part of the problem is the fear of the political collapse next-door in the former Soviet Union. China is equally multi-cultural, and there are many ethnic republics in China that would like to have their independence.

There are many analysts who believe China is reluctant to implement western style democracy due to a fear of the collapse of the Chinese state. On the other hand, it has become apparent that there are new freedoms in China and that corruption is being attacked. Local committees, originally organized by the Communist Party to oversee the activities of people in the countryside, are becoming openly critical of Communist Party officials in the political centers. Far from being closed down, the government in Beijing is listening to complaints, much as did the old Confucian Mandarins.

This opens an interesting debate: Can Confucian ethics allow the efficient growth of a capitalist society without corruption? Is the democratic-capitalist connection a necessary and sufficient one, or can Oriental societies operate ethical governments without democracy? The position taken in this book is that democratic reform eventually is necessary to support successful capitalist development. South Korea's recent turn toward democracy, and also more limited shifts in Malaysia and the Philippines, support this view. On the other hand, Singapore's success with a one party, Confucian-based society is a challenge.

The lack of democratic reform culminated in a protest in Tiananmen Square in Beijing in April 1989. This protest began as a gathering intended to mourn the death of Hu Yaobang, a party leader that supported democratic and free market reforms. Youthful university students idolized him. Students gathered at Tiananmen Square in central Beijing to mourn Yaobang's death, and thousands of students streamed into Beijing from across the country. Sympathetic railroad workers let them ride the trains free. The mass memorial soon turned into a student protest, and a tent city was set up. Students demanded democracy but were not sure what that meant. When asked what they really wanted, they said that what they wanted was what the United States stood for (as reported at the time by Dan Rather of CBS News).

This protest was brutally crushed, with the army killing four hundred people and the government destroying pro-democracy movements and blocking the transition to democracy. Moreover, after an unsuccessful attempt by hardliners to stem the tide of capitalism, China is now one of the fastest growing economies in the world, expanding at a rate of 7 to 10 percent annually. However, continued rapid economic growth may come at a high price in environmental damage. China's construction of a huge hydroelectric dam on the Yangtze River is a case in point (see "Ecological Maladaptation: The Three Gorges Dam in China").

Ecological
Maladaptation

The Three Gorges Dam in China

The Three Gorges Dam project on the Yangtze River was a source of bitter controversy between the bureaucrats who control China and environmentalists in China and around the world. Mostly completed in 2008 after construction began in 1994, it is expected to be fully operational in 2011. At an estimated cost of over $22 billion, it will be the world's largest dam. Environmentalists claim that the Chinese government has all but ignored environmental considerations in creating this colossus.

The region of the Three Gorges has inspired Chinese poets and painters for centuries with its serenity and breathtaking beauty. All this has changed. The dam has dramatically increased water levels in the three gorges—Qutang, Wu, and Xiling—and inundated eight thousand archaeological sites from China's Warring States period (475–221 BC) and many sites of even more ancient cultures. Thirteen cities, 140 towns, and 1,352 villages are submerged or partially submerged by a reservoir that is six hundred kilometers long (equal in length to Lake Superior) and covers about one thousand square kilometers (386 square miles). The new lake rises over 175 meters (574 feet) above current river levels, inundating the narrow canyons and rapids for which the region is famous.

More than the natural beauty of the region was threatened. Once residents were relocated, logging in the region greatly expanded to supply the Three Gorges project. Much of the land surrounding the project site is susceptible to erosion and landslides, and deforestation on a large scale is exacerbating these problems, while contributing to a rapid buildup of sedimentation in the lake. Environmentalists warn that high levels of sedimentation will increase the danger of severe flooding upriver, even though flooding below the dam may be better controlled. Changes in water flow may damage the existing downriver dike system because of the serious channel scouring that will be cause by water released from the dam. The dam will endanger several species, including the Yangtze River sturgeon and alligator, the freshwater finless dolphin (whose numbers are already down to about three hundred), the cloud leopard, and the Siberian white crane.

Environmentalists argue that the mentality of old-line Communism that permeates the bureaucracy leads to reckless exploitation of nature for economic development and an almost total lack of regard for the country's most magnificent scenery.

Paradoxically, the Three Gorges Dam may have some ecological benefits. The dam will produce over 18,000 megawatts of power and thus will ease China's dependence on coal for three-quarters of its electrical power needs. This will reduce the country's greenhouse gas emissions. Currently, China is first in the production of greenhouse gases. The dam will protect the middle and lower reaches of the Yangtze from devastating floods. A flood in 1954 left thirty thousand people dead and one million homeless. Development experts point out that the dam will provide electricity for China's inland central-southern region, opening a relatively backward area to economic development.

Environmentalists, however, insist that the environmental costs will outweigh the economic benefits; but the government silences Chinese environmentalists. They have been systematically excluded from consultative groups, especially after the Tiananmen Square military crackdown on political dissidents. Their proposals for smaller dams and dike control were never seriously considered in policy deliberations that led to the 1992 approval of the dam. China's grassroots environmental movement has been severely repressed by current political leaders, who view such movements as threats to their authority. There was little chance that popular movements would emerge with enough force to stop the massive construction project. China is still gripped by the Great Leap Forward mentality of Mao Zedong, a mindset that inspires support for extravagant and ecologically destructive projects, not unlike those that characterized the Soviet Union before its collapse. Soviet projects have left a legacy of ecological devastation from which it will take decades to recover. (Source: Sullivan 1995)

bride price

Gifts paid from the groom's clan to the bride's clan

dowry

Wealth, including material possessions, the bride brings into her marriage, which is often appropriated by the groom's clan

Women and the Family Under Communism

While Communism may have failed economically and politically in China, sincere attempts were made to emancipate women from traditional Confucian codes. In 1950, new laws abolished the feudal marriage system, which was based on the supremacy of men over women. A new democratic marriage system was established based on the free choice of partners, monogamy, equal rights for both sexes, and protection of the lawful interests of women and children. The laws further prohibited bigamy, concubinage, child marriage, interference in the remarriage of widows, and the extraction of money or gifts in connection with marriage (Chao 1977). The 1980 law raised the minimum legal age from eighteen to twenty for women and from twenty to twenty-two for men, relaxed restrictions on divorce, and stipulated that both husband and wife are obligated to practice family planning. The new laws faced the reality of China's burgeoning population growth.

The laws have had significant impact. Monogamy has become a reality. Free choice is the rule in the cities, and young people tend to marry at a later age. Family size has been reduced; more women have obtained jobs, and the great inequality between men and women has been reduced. However, while many oppressive traditional norms have been abandoned, inequalities remain. Women's subordinate position is reflected in the preference for sons, in women's double-burden of full-time, paid employment and major responsibilities for child care and housework, the lack of representativeness in political affairs, and in violence against women in the form of infanticide and wife-battering (Eschleman 1994, 144).

Particularly noticeable are the differences between urban and rural cultures. The clan was never as important in the cities as in rural villages. Not only does the clan remain important in rural areas, but also many of the traditional values described above remain. In urban regions, major changes have taken place, moving dramatically from the arranged pattern to one of greater freedom and personal choice. **Bride price** (gifts from the clan of the groom to the clan of the bride) has almost disappeared in urban regions, as has the **dowry**. The dowry, which was common in early European history, included material possessions the bride brought into her marriage, such as clothes, jewelry, and land. The groom's clan often appropriated this wealth. However, there is little in the form of a dating culture, even in the cities; it is still considered inappropriate for males and females to have contact with each other in public, and the opportunities to get to know each other are limited (Eschleman 1994).

While communism may have emancipated women to some extent, the puritanical nature of Chinese culture survives. In one report, Liu Dalin, a scholarly pioneer in the study of human sexuality in China, reported that women had little knowledge of sexual matters. One in three women reported never having an orgasm and not even knowing what the question meant. Because of the absence of foreplay, many wives found sex bothersome and painful. Only 13 percent of married couples had ever made love naked; and when sex did occur, it was restricted to less than a minute (Eschleman 1994, 146).

■Some aspects of the American lifestyle are vastly different from Chinese culture. Certain behaviors accepted as 'normal' in the U.S. could be considered punishable in China. What we think of as traditional dating or public affection, is unheard of in China.

China, along with Cuba, is one of the few nations in the world that has managed to slow down the rate of population growth without the wealth increases that usually accompany the demographic transition to small families. As a result of intensive Chinese family planning, the birthrate was reduced from 34 per 1,000 in 1970 to an estimated 12.29 in 2011. The Chinese government not only tells couples that they must practice birth control, it also tells them what contraceptive they must use.

A one-child policy has had several unintended consequences. Because of the high value placed on male children, women routinely use ultrasound devices to test the sex of a fetus; if it is female, they abort it. Female infanticide is also reported as routine in the countryside. While the government has special incentives for one-daughter families, the desire for male children has had the consequence of a distorted population pyramid. In the younger generation, there are fewer women of marriageable age today than there are in the older generations. This is also true in India for similar reasons. The distortion in the population pyramid means that many grown men can anticipate living their lives out without wives. Some writers speculate that this change may finally alter the way that Chinese and Indians view boys and girls; in the short run, however, the low value given women is having a profound impact on the future of the family in China.

PEOPLE ON THE PERIPHERY: CHINA'S MINORITIES

While China is passing through the transition from socialism to capitalism, the lack of democratic reform and persistent human rights violations remain major concerns. As China grows economically, what is happening to its ethnic minority populations? The Han Chinese majority makes up about 94 percent of the population of China; the other 6 percent is divided among fifty-five officially recognized ethnic minority groups (called ethnic nationalities in China) with a total population of some 60 million. Some groups such as the Hani number more than one million while others number only about one thousand.

The 1950s was a period during which minority nationalities were recognized, autonomous regions were established, and democratic and agrarian reforms were instituted. This was followed in the 1960s and 1970s by harsher measures such as collectivization, the People's Commune reorganization, and finally persecutions and human rights violations

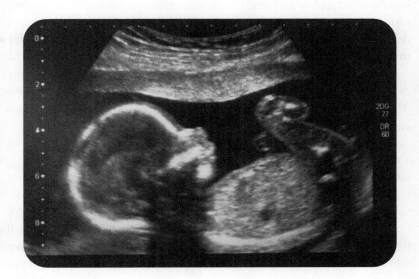

■Because of the high value placed on male children, women routinely use ultrasound devices to test the sex of a fetus; if it is found to be female, they abort it.

designed to eliminate cultural and ethnic differences. The 1980s witnessed a return to the autonomous structures for ethnic minorities and the opening of free markets in place of the severe collectivism of the previous decade (Lemoine 1989).

The Chinese government counts the Tibetans as a national minority, arguing that China liberated the Tibetans from harsh feudalism in the 1950s (Fei 1981). The Tibetans view their condition as forced subjugation by China, and the Dalai Lama administers the government-in-exile of Tibet from India (French 1994).

The Hani   The Hani are people of Tibeto-Burman ethnic heritage who live in southern Yunnan province and some of the adjacent northern parts of Vietnam, Myanmar (Burma), Thailand, and Laos. There are over 1.2 million Hani in China alone. Traditionally, the Hani lived in small settlements of thirty to forty households in forested areas and practiced slash-and-burn agriculture in some areas and rice paddy cultivation on narrow terraces in other areas. Rice and maize are their main staples; but they do raise several cash crops, including cotton, sugar cane, and ginger. The Hani were organized in patrilineal clans that claimed great genealogical depth. Only men inherited property. Hani religious beliefs consisted of polytheism, animism, and ancestor worship; and neither Buddhist nor later Christian missionaries had much success in converting them (Notar 1994). China's revolution not only profoundly affected China, it also affected people like the Hani, who were accused of local national chauvinism because of their religious and cultural practices. Subjected to religious and cultural oppression from the late 1950s through the 1970s, in the 1980s the Chinese government allowed the Hani to return to some of their ancient traditions. However, a more subtle threat to their cultural identity may be the incorporation of younger people to national life through education and government jobs. In other countries, such as neighboring Thailand, the Hani appear to be worse off than in China, suffering poverty, lack of citizenship and land rights, and the deceptive recruitment of their young women into prostitution (Tooker 1993, 119).

Tibetans   In 1950, the Chinese army invaded eastern Tibet and claimed sovereignty but left the Dali Lama, religious and political leader of the Tibetan people, as chief administrator. After several years of negotiations, punctuated by violent encounters, the Dali Lama fled to India in 1959 and has ruled in exile since then. The Chinese government has, since 1953, brutally attempted to eradicate Tibetan culture and is responsible for the death of about one-fifth of the population. Thousands have been tortured and imprisoned. Although China declared Tibet a Chinese Autonomous Region in 1965, its own Han peoples were moved in to displace Tibetans. The population of Lhasa, the capital, is already more than half Chinese.

The influx of Han Chinese (the dominant ethnic group of China) has led to a decline in the use of the Tibetan language and has produced increased pressure on Tibetan resources. Pro-independence activists continue to be imprisoned and tortured, and Buddhist monks and nuns are targets of Chinese abuse.

The environment has suffered as well. A major hydroelectric project on Yamdrok Tso, a sacred lake, has caused major environmental loss to the Tibetan people. Tibetan communities in exile have raised international awareness of human rights violations, including religious persecution, international funding for destructive development projects, and forced abortion and sterilization of Tibetan women (McGranahan 1993, 125–126). Although the United States government declared the Chinese occupation of Tibet to be illegal, its desire to continue to foster the Chinese free market economic reforms has prevented human rights activists from having any impact on policies favoring trade with China.

Modernizing India: The Response to Colonialism

India, in pre-colonial times, occupied a much larger territory than it does today although the exact size expanded and contracted as trade, hegemonic control, and agricultural production waxed or waned. British interests, which controlled the South Asian subcontinent until 1947, carved modern India out of pre-colonial India

ORIGINS OF INDIA

India was and is the core of South Asia, and has dominated the subcontinent for over three thousand years. The cultural area of South Asia is extensive, covering such modern countries as Pakistan, Bangladesh, India, Nepal, Bhutan, and the large island of Sri Lanka to the south of India. The dominant religions have been Hinduism and Islam, and it is the region where Buddhism emerged. Buddhism is an offshoot of Hinduism which has been integrated into most of these regions and became, with Confucianism, a dominant religion of China. Karla Sinopoli has shown how the ideologies and power structures of ancient and comparatively recent Indian Hindu states were determined by such factors as distance from the central core, long distance trade, control over the production and the distribution of trade goods (Sinopoli 1994a). When trade was successfully monopolized and tied to tank style irrigation agriculture, powerful city-states emerged. When either of these was threatened, the civilizations contracted, often becoming the vassals of other powerful Hindu states.

South and central India lie within the tropics, while northern India is influenced by the Himalaya-Kush Mountains, which separate India from China, and is more temperate. The major rivers of the Indian subcontinent, the Indus, the Ganges, and the Brahmaputra, have their origins in the Himalayas and have been used for long distance water borne trade for thousands of years. These rivers carry alluvial soils down to the plains where Indian society originated. Tropical rainforests in the south, interspersed with arid uplands, were the home of tribal societies that were not integrated into states until modern times.

The earliest city-states in South Asia were Harappa at the northern end of the Indus River valley and Mohenjo-Daro in the south, both manifestations of what archaeologists

■The Himalaya-Kush Mountains separate India from China.

call Harappan civilization (and both in what is today Pakistan). Both cities were built according to similar plans and their populations, supported by irrigation agriculture, hovered around thirty thousand. Each contained a large, walled citadel made of bricks and had special buildings, pools for ritual baths, and temples that were probably used as storehouses. The two cities were located on a flood plain, which lacked any mineral resources; however, they produced finely crafted objects made of copper, bronze, and jewels. These objects were used in maintaining extensive trade contacts with China and the region of the Persian Gulf. Like China and other ancient civilizations, trade was one of the factors that stimulated the growth of hierarchical social organization. Ceramic representations of humans and animals may have been forerunners of important Hindu deities, and the still undeciphered writing may be early versions of the **Vedas**, texts upon which the Hindu religion is based. Hinduism is one of the two major religions of South Asia; the other is Buddhism.

Harappa and Mohenjo Daro appear to have collapsed around 1500 BC. According to one theory, the manufacturing of bricks for the extensive fortifications and temples may have denuded local forests and led to extensive flooding and salinization, of which there is evidence (Fagan 1989). The problems of irrigation, deforestation, and salinization are also modern problems in South Asia.

THE RISE OF HINDUISM AND THE CASTE SYSTEM

The core of South Asian civilization shifted to the Ganges River Valley, but many elements of Harappan civilization, including beliefs, survived and formed an important part of ancient Hindu states. Hindu civilization developed after Indo-European speaking Aryan nomads from the Iranian plateau spread over much of western South Asia. They brought with them Sanskrit, which is the originating language of European civilizations. Hegemonic control by the invading Aryans, rather than irrigation, brought Hindu society into being. The **caste system** (a hierarchical social structure based on the Hindu religion, explained below) emerged; and a mythology, which rationalized it, became formalized as the Hindu religion, much as the Koran formulated the Islamic state in Southwest Asia and North Africa, and Confucianism conceptualized the state to the north in China.

The origins of the Hindu religion are extremely ancient and underlie much of civilization in South Asia, Southeast Asia, and in the western Pacific in Indonesia, Malaysia, and the Philippines. Hinduism underlies many other religions of these regions, including Buddhism and Islam. Hinduism is associated with three major beliefs and objectives. The first one is that of reincarnation, called *Samsara*, which holds that one's soul, or **atman**, is reborn each generation in a new organism, but not necessarily as a human being. Whether one is born again as a higher order spirit escaping the cycle of life, as a lower or higher human of the caste system, as an animal, or as an insect depends on the second major belief: *karma*. **Karma** is destiny, which is only partially influenced by one's behavior; it can also be influenced by the often capricious desires of dozens of cosmic gods. These must be worshiped, and their special support petitioned to achieve the third objective: *moksha*. **Moksha** is the ultimate release from the cycle of birth and rebirth, and it is the ultimate aim of the Hindu religion. The Hindu religion explains much of Indian society, including the caste system and the very high regard given to animals, as the rebirth of the soul into a new being. The creatures into whose bodies the souls are born could be one's unsuccessful relatives who are beginning the life cycle again due to a lifetime of corruption (the cow in the road or the bug under your shoe may be your aunt or uncle). Thus, life is sacred.

Vedas

Texts upon which the Hindu religion is based

caste system

A hierarchical social structure based on the Hindu religion

atman

The Hindu term for soul, which is reborn every generation

karma

The Hindu term for one's destiny

moksha

The Hindu term for the ultimate release from Samsara, the cycle of birth and rebirth

The Hindu model resembles the Chinese Confucian classics in laying out a powerful ethic of rule, showing when power should be used to control the lower castes and when it should not, and providing the moral authority to rationalize the caste system. The Indian state, in its various manifestations, depended on Hinduism for the rationalization of the activities of the rulers.

According to Hindu belief, cities and villages were divided according to the specialized activities of people; people were expected to marry within their occupational group (called **caste endogamy**). There were four **varnas** or castes, each assigned to specific locations and tasks. Traditionally, the lowest varna was that of the cultivators and serfs or **Sudra**. The **Brahmans** were the priests and teachers. The **Kshatriya** were also elites, assigned the role of warriors and rulers, while the **Vaisya** were the landholders and merchants (Basham 1959; Keesing 1976). Below the four varnas and outside the class system, according to some Indian authorities, were the so-called "untouchables." Each varna came to contain within it numerous subdivisions which designated more specific occupations. It is these subdivisions that came to be known as castes (and subcastes) and whose status within the caste hierarchy shifted from region to region. This basic model has remained stable in Hindu ideology for over two thousand years.

The caste system cannot be separated from the Hindu religion; both appear to have evolved together and reinforced one another. The Hindu religion is based on the twin ideas of hierarchy and purity. The Hindu term *jati* refers to a biologically based kinship group, which is culturally ascribed to a hierarchical position according to a theory of purity. Those at the bottom are least pure, and those at the top are the most pure; and purity is designated by the practice of rituals leading to **nirvana**, escape from this world by the upper castes at death. Only those at the top are allowed to practice the highest rank principles of purity, relegating all others to lower levels.

Virginity is an ideal expectation at marriage. A young woman that has lost her virginity may be stoned to death by her own relatives. Families arrange marriages to link individuals by caste level. Infant betrothal and the prohibition of divorce were common, and still are in rural areas, as is *sati*, the custom whereby a wife is supposed to throw herself on her husband's funeral pyre.

The entire Hindu caste system is held together by the *jajmani* system, which links local castes in a series of traditionally determined exchanges of goods and services. In these relationships, one party is viewed as the patron or *jajman* and the other as the worker or *kamin*, conforming to pervasive notions of hierarchy. In many parts of village India, jajmani relationships between families were hereditary. Technological change, new jobs in cities, and increased participation in the cash economy have caused the breakdown of the jajmani system in recent years.

BUDDHISM: THE SEARCH FOR EQUALITY

Another important religion, which began in India and spread across the entire mainland of Asia to Korea and to Japan, is Buddhism. Buddhism was born out of Hinduism but differs from Hinduism, fundamentally, in its disregard for hierarchy. The religion of Buddhism is largely ascribed to one person, Siddartha Gautama, who was born about 563 BC in southern Nepal. He was a member of an elite caste, who sought religious enlightenment at age twenty-nine, abandoning his wife and child to become a wandering monk. After wandering throughout northeastern India for six years, imposing self-denial and self-torture on himself, he is said to have sat under a shady bo or *bodhi* tree and experienced enlightenment; hence the name Buddha was applied to him.

---

caste endogamy

Marriage to a member of one's own caste

varna

The Hindu term for caste

Sudra

A member of the lowest Hindu caste, which was comprised of cultivators and serfs

Brahman

A member of the Hindu caste containing priests and teachers

Kshatriya

The elites in the Hindu caste system, including warriors and rulers

Vaisya

The landholders and merchants in the Hindu caste system

nirvana

Escape from this world by the upper castes at death, achieved by purification rituals

■After wandering throughout northeastern India for six years, imposing self-denial and self-torture on himself, he is said to have sat under a shady bo or *bodhi* tree and experienced enlightenment; henceforth he was given the name *Buddah*.

The Buddha's basic message is called **dharma**, which means saving truth. The Buddha, like Hindu preachers, taught that existence is a cycle of death and rebirth. However, the Buddha discounted hierarchy, and also self-torture or self-denial; he argued that only by abandoning the attachment to worldly goods could one escape into nirvana. During the 200s BC, Indian emperor Asoka made Buddhism a state religion; and it then spread to China, Nepal, and to the rest of Asia. In the meantime, Buddhism became a minor religion in India.

Four schools of Buddhism developed, all with much in common, beginning with **Theravada Buddhism** or *The Way of the Elders*, which is the only one of the early schools to survive. Found today in Burma, Cambodia, Sri Lanka, Laos, and Thailand, this school emphasizes the life of Buddha and the virtues of the monastic life, a practice common in these countries. The second way is **Mahayana Buddhism**, which stresses the existence of many Buddhas that can save people through grace and compassion. Mahayana Buddhism is found primarily in Japan and in other countries of East Asia. Finally, **Mantrayana Buddhism**, found in Mongolia and Japan, stresses a special relationship between a **guru** (spiritual leader) and his followers. Finally, **Zen Buddhism**, practiced in Japan, is much like Mantrayana Buddhism but emphasizes a special state of enlightenment called **satori**, a special flash of insight into oneself and the universe.

dharma

The Buddha's basic message

Theravada Buddhism

An early school of Buddhism found today in Burma, Cambodia, Sri Lanka, Laos, and Thailand

Mahayana Buddhism

A school of Buddhism that stresses the existence of many Buddhas that can save people through grace and compassion

ISLAM AND TRADE IN INDIA

The caste system was a form of labor exploitation; and from time to time, it was replaced by trade-oriented Islamic rule when Moslem invaders took over India, such as in the Mughal period just before British rule. The Mughal period began in the ninth century, with the gradual expansion of Islam into the trade-based cities of the west coast of India, and then expanded in the eleventh century when the city-states of Bengal and Gujarat were brought under Moslem control. Islam later spread into the Malay straits and east as far as the Philippines and Indonesia. By the fourteenth century, all of India except the Hindu kingdom of Vijanagar was under Islamic control. The Moslem religion considers its members equal, and it appealed to many Hindus, who converted to Islam. As Eric Wolf put it, "Islam and trade thus went hand in hand in the Asian seas" (Wolf 1982, 234).

While trade cities were brought under the control of separate Moslem leaders, the Mughal Empire brought the separate states under the control of a single hegemonic state, created by Timurid Turks from Turkestan. Chief Babur became the first Mughal emperor in 1527. The Mughal system was further organized by his grandson, Akbar, who placed the power over the new kingdom in the hands of a military elite, called the **Mansabdars.** Most of these were recruited from Turkestan and Persia, but many were local Muslims and Hindu chieftains. The Mansabdars formed a cosmopolitan elite that was rewarded with lifetime grants (not unlike the *ejido* system described in the next chapter for Latin America). Under them came the **Zamindars**, local elites drawn from the upper castes of each region. Many Hindu leaders, including Nanak the founder of Sikhism, opposed the Mansabdars. The Mansabdars were at first tolerant of ethnic and religious differences; however, later they became increasingly intolerant, giving an opening to British interests, which used the divisions between Hindus and Moslems to gain support for the expansion of the British Empire.

COLONIAL RULE

The English came to India in search of trade, not conquest, in the seventeenth century. They acquired **entrepots** (trade enclaves) from the Mansabdar elites. The British had the right to trade with Indian traders, but the rulers of the cities had control over that trade (determining price, profit, volume traded, etc.). When the British first established their fort cities along the coasts in the sixteenth century, the Moslem dynasty was declining in power (Stavrianos 1982, 274). Slowly, Hindu leaders from the southern provinces challenged the power of the northern Moslem elite. The British supported the Hindu elites in order to undermine the Moslem rulers, and the region came to be controlled by an alliance of local Hindu princes (the Zamindars) and British merchants (members of the East India Company who were the traders mentioned above). At the Battle of Plassey in 1757, the Moslem Mansabdars were overthrown by English troops, who were financially supported by Hindu Zamindar merchants (Wolf 1982, 244).

Conversion to a Capitalist Economy   By 1818, the British were in total control but preferred to rule through the Zamindar elites. This type of indirect rule is characteristic of trade and tribute empires. However, the British converted the tributary economy into a capitalist, private property economy, with the Zamindars becoming the owners of the land but required to pass along most of the tribute to the British. According to Eric Wolf:

> In the Permanent Settlement that the English introduced in Bengal in 1793, however, the *Zamindars* were turned into outright property owners, required to turn over to the British administration nine-tenths of the tribute received from their peasants, and retaining one-tenth for their own personal use. The English thus created, at one stroke, a class of three thousand Indian landlords who held the same property rights as English landlords, including the right to sell, mortgage, and inherit land (1982, 247).

Thus, English rule converted a diffuse tributary system into a centralized tax system based on rights to private property by an upper caste. These changes occurred after private property rights had been established in Great Britain, but their impact in India was quite different. The average peasant was stripped of all his or her traditional rights and was placed into a forced contractual relationship with the new owners of the land who were now only interested in cheap labor, not with tribute and rights (Wolf 1982, 247–248). The lands of previous tributary tribes and states were made the private property of the old elites of India. The British created a new political system in which the old regional elites were transformed into national elites who owned almost all of the resources of their region.

Many of the local populations were clearly disturbed by increased British control and by the transfer of resources to old elites. The Indian military rebelled against British garrisons in the Great Mutiny of 1857. The British put down the mutiny at a great cost of life and imposed a more direct form of British rule, which lasted until independence in 1947. For close to one hundred years, British rule favored policies supporting the landowning Zamindars and exports of agricultural products, particularly opium, which

■Mohandas Ghandi led India to its liberation from British rule. As a result, India was divided into Hindu India and Moslem Pakistan in 1947

was exported to China. The Zamindars forced the peasants to grow poppies (for opium), tea, and cotton for export instead of their traditional foods. The development of Indian industry was discouraged, and so India "underdeveloped" in contrast to the core (Stavrianos 1982, 277). The new land laws were to have the long-term effect of reinforcing the Indian caste system and the Hindu religion, instead of weakening them (capitalism is thought to have weakened traditional institutions in western Europe, which did not really happen in India).

Liberation and the Rise of State Socialism

Mohandas Ghandi led India to its liberation from British rule, and the subcontinent of India was divided into Hindu India and Moslem Pakistan in 1947. (In 1971, what had been East Pakistan became the independent nation of Bangladesh.) After 1948, India came to be controlled by the Congress Party. While there were other parties, a monopoly of power was held in the hands of elite members of the Congress Party, most of whom were members of the landowning classes.

Thus, the British created a hybrid political system. The new system, which dominated the Indian subcontinent after partition, can also be found in other regions under British control, such as Burma (Myanmar) and Egypt. The British colonial system wedded traditional tributary hierarchical bureaucracies to a private property capitalist model. After British abandonment of colonial control, former British colonies in Asia remained under the control of those elites who owed their dominant positions to British policies. In most cases, the bureaucracies created prior to British abandonment of the colonial system survived to the present time (an exception is Burma which went through a socialist revolution in 1961).

India chose to move in the direction of state socialism, modeling its economy on a blend of British democracy and an Indian form of state capitalism and socialism. The private sector was not outlawed, and the economic system of India constrained the growth of the private sector by allowing it to expand only with government permission. Heavy industry was reserved for the public sector and was stunted by quotas and high tariffs. Controls were placed on land use, on trade in farm products, and on the price of agricultural commodities. In the 1980s, India tried to expand the economy by borrowing and produced large-scale debt. On the political side, the Congress Party, while arguing it was democratic, controlled India much as the Institutional Revolutionary Party (PRI) controls Mexico. Corruption and economic development went hand in hand.

ETHNIC POLITICS: SIKH STRUGGLES FOR INDEPENDENCE

The Congress Party reserved the most important political and commercial positions for its party members: this meant the members of the upper economic classes. Other ethnic and religious groups, such as the Sikhs of Punjab and lower ranked Hindus and Moslems, felt discriminated against. The government and the Congress Party, striving to create a secular, socialist state, came into conflict with various Hindu and Moslem communities. Attacks on the government and counter attacks on ethnic and religious groups grew through the 1980s and 1990s.

Sikh ethnic identity dates to the fifteenth century. Guru Nanak, born to a Punjabi Hindu family in 1469, developed the Sikh religion and distinct way of life. Sikhism is not, strictly speaking, an ethnic identity but is a way of life based on a religion which is similar to Hinduism, out of which it grew; and it differs, primarily, in rejecting caste and rank (McLeod 1989). Many writers believe Sikhism is a variation on the Hindu religion as Protestantism is a variant of Christianity.

Sikhs distinguish themselves from Hindus by abjuring polytheism and the caste system. Sikhs believe in one god, Akal Purakh, who reveals himself through *sat*, both truth and reality. According to Guru Nanak, man's duty is to meditate on the revelation of *sat* (Kapur 1986). Nine gurus followed Guru Nanak, teaching an egalitarian, anti-caste ethic that put the new religion into conflict with Hindus and the ruling Mughal dynasties (which were Moslem). The Sikhs of Punjab constructed the Golden Temple of Amritsar, a large palatial structure, to serve as both a religious and political center (Kapur 1986).

Attacks by the Mughal elites on the Sikh religion, including the assassination of one guru, led to the development of specialized militancy by Sikh males. After the conquest of India by the British, Sikh political power in the state of Punjab was shattered. However, Sikh men were recruited to the army where they earned a special reputation as fighters. Sikhs were extremely successful economically in Punjab, primarily as farmers of wheat and barley. Throughout the nineteenth and early twentieth century, Sikhs demanded the return of control over what they believed to be their province, although they did not represent more than one-third of the population of Punjab. Their demands were based on financial and other contributions to India.

After India won its independence from Great Britain, the debate continued between Sikhs and the Congress Party, which gained control over India. Sikhs wanted to control that region of the Punjab where they were numerically dominant. The Congress Party responded by imposing controls on Sikh religious temples, particularly the Golden Temple of Amritsar. Sikh temples are very wealthy. The Sikhs demanded autonomy for their temples, but the Indian state continued to impose its control, taxing the temples.

In October 1984, Prime Minister Indira Gandhi's handpicked Sikh bodyguards assassinated her. This extraordinary and violent act was the Sikh's response to the Indian army's storming of a Sikh shrine, the Golden Temple at Amritsar in the state of Punjab. In 1984, debate over temple control exploded as militant Sikh radicals took over the Golden Temple and used it as a base for terrorist activities against Hindus. The Indian military invaded the sacred temple in an attempt to remove Sikh terrorists; several hundred Sikhs were killed, including a militant fundamentalist Sikh preacher, Jarnail Singh Bhindranwale (Kapur 1986, 226; Hardgrave 1992, 106).

For some time, Sikh terrorists have been killing Hindu victims in the state of Punjab, while Sikhs living outside Punjab have been the targets of reprisals by Hindu terrorists. Killings and reprisals have been a part of ethnic animosities for centuries. In 1991 alone, more than five thousand people were killed in the Punjab due to terrorist and counter terrorist activities (Hardgrave 1992, 112).

The demands by Sikhs for an independent state, to be called Kalistan, must be put into perspective by mention of similar demands and violence by Muslims in the State of Kashmir and by tribal groups in Assam and other regions. One tribal group, the Nagas, was promised an independent state at the time of partition, but instead was split between three new Indian states: Assam, Arunachal, and Manipur. The Nagas demand a new state of Nagaland and are becoming increasingly embittered by Indian repression and human rights abuse (Maybury-Lewis 1997, 42). In addition, there are other ethnic and religious movements toward separatism in Bilhar, Uttar Pradesh, and Tamil Nadu.

How can ethnic violence be explained in India and elsewhere? Let's think back to the models presented in Chapters 7 and Chapter 9: primordialism, instrumentalism, and relative deprivation. At first glance, ethnic violence in India appears to be the consequence of the first model. Many describe India as an ideal democratic society based on the philosophy of Mohandas Gandhi and his protests against British colonial policy. India appears to have adopted the British system of secular democracy with a prime minister and two houses of parliament. With such a democratic social system, only a primordialist model makes sense since political differences should be settled democratically. However, a deeper reading of Indian history reveals a very different picture. Selig S. Harrison shows India to be a highly centralized and socialistic society, one in which the elite Hindu castes have long controlled the economy to their advantage and discriminated against other castes and ethnic groups (Harrison 1992). This being the case, the point to be made here is that ethnic violence in India is the consequence of ethnic repression by the institutions of the state, not some kind of primordialist urge, and thus is better explained by the institutional model, with the deprivation resulting from domination by elites.

The problem of ethnic conflict is widespread in Asia, and as we have learned, in Africa, the Middle East, and in Eastern Europe. It has become particularly destructive in the island nation of Sri Lanka, just to the south of India, where the Tamil Tigers, terrorists from Hindu communities, are attacking Buddhist communities in a country which is dominated by the Buddhist religion, much as India is dominated by the Hindu religion. One general lesson to be learned from these conflicts is that in our globalizing world, there may be a great need for decentralized or federal states (such as is being experimented with in Ethiopia). Yet territorial states feel they must remain highly integrated to fight against economic competition from other states, presenting a real dilemma in the management of national institutions.

Indonesia: An Emerging Tiger

Indonesia, a country in Southeast Asia that consists of more than 13,600 islands, is also ethnically very complex; its political system is far from democratic. It includes the large islands of Borneo and Java, half of the island of New Guinea, and the newly incorporated island of East Timor. It is a region that, while experiencing considerable ethnic conflict, has also had successful and rapid economic growth. In the sixteenth century, the islands of Indonesia belonged to independent Islamic principalities; and before that, most of the urban centers were Hindu. When the Dutch imposed their rule on Indonesia in the seventeenth century, it was a complex mix of religions, peasants, and tribes of many ethnic backgrounds.

The Dutch imposed their political system on the varied peoples of Indonesia. The anthropologist, Clifford Geertz, described the Dutch colonial pattern of paddy rice agriculture in Indonesia as a form of agricultural involution (Geertz 1963). What he meant is that instead of evolving into a more complex and prosperous economy, Dutch export policies had the consequence of forcing the economy to grow in on itself, becoming ever more complex as the population grew, but producing poverty for the peasants since most of the rice they grew was exported, not eaten (Geertz 1963).

Geertz lived in the Indonesian town of Pare, which is on the island of Java, studying the relationship between Islam and social structure. He was there during a violent anti-Dutch revolution under President Sukarno, who attempted to bring about a socialist style government, and a counterrevolution in 1965 led by President Suharto. During Sukarno's revolution and Suharto's counterrevolution over five hundred thousand Communists were slaughtered. When President Suharto overthrew Sukarno, the people of Indonesia were among the poorest in the world with an average income of about $100.00 a year. Today the population has expanded to over 200 million, making it the world's fourth most populous country as well as the world's largest Islamic country. The economy is no longer involuting. Instead, Indonesia has become one of the Asian Tigers, growing at a rate of 6 percent per year with an average income of almost $1,000 a year, making it the largest South-East Asian economy.

Geertz, who lived through the bloodbath of the Sukarno/Suharto revolutions, recently reflected on his return to Pare after the killings in 1971:

> … the killing fields had come and gone, the national regime had changed from civilian to military, and what politics existed was dominated by a semi-official umbrella party promoting a semi-official civil religion. Pare was still physically about what it had been. With a net outflow of population nearly matching natural increase, it was not even much larger. The same people, the same groups (though there were no Communists and fewer Sukarnoists), the same bureaus, were still in charge, and most of them operated with the same, formal and status ridden ideas of right and propriety. Daily life, except for the fact that the ideologues were quiet or silenced, was not much different … what was different, or anyway seemed different to me, was mood, humor, the color of experience. It was a chastened place (Geertz 1996, 5).

Clifford Geertz also worked on the nearby island of Bali, which is not Islamic but Hindu, to describe the culture of its people. Margaret Mead and Gregory Bateson had studied Bali dances two decades before. Mead and Batesons' photographic study of the Hindu folk dances caught the importance of status and style, of balance and intricate customs such as the complex **legong**, a girls' dance about ancient longings of love and of battle, and the **bjauk**, which uses masked dancers. These theatrical, courtly, and formal dances are usually accompanied with bands called **gamelans** of cymbals, drums, and keyed instruments. The Dutch colonial government did not intervene in the economy of the Balinese, but it did impose its political organization, bringing about the deaths of many of the ritual kings who ruled Bali at the beginning of the twentieth century. The culture of Bali had been left alone by the first Islamic dynasties of Indonesia and was largely allowed to continue practicing its Hindu culture by the Dutch. Mead, Bateson, and Geertz—all studied the relationship between the Hindu religion and the theatrical expression of Balinese culture, which has largely survived today. Hindu culture in Bali is extremely intricate and ornate, and attracts the attention of many visitors.

Because of its protected position, Bali did not suffer the agricultural involution described by Geertz for the other islands. Today, eco-tour guides take European, Japanese, and American tourists to view the dances with the same intricate paddy fields in the background once photographed by Mead and Bateson back in the 1930s. Many travel guides are from mainland Java, and the Balinese do not particularly care for the attention they receive, continuing to grow and export rice and fine cloth.

Indonesia in the 1990s, however, was not the Indonesia of the 1940s. The tourist to Bali, if he or she read Indonesian, may have picked up the local newspaper and read

legong

A Balinese girls' Hindu folk dance about ancient longings of love and battle

bjauk

A Balinese Hindu folk dance using masked dancers

gamelan

A Balinese band consisting of cymbals, drums, and keyed instruments

accounts about the battles in East Timor or Iran Jaya (Western New Guinea) where an aging President Suharto tried to suppress revolutionaries and was critiqued by Amnesty International for human rights violations. The reports read strangely like Dutch newspaper accounts of the uprising in far off colonies of Indonesia in the 1940s, prompting the reader to wonder about colonialism in the modern age where the colonist is the one colonized.

Changing Vietnam

Vietnam has struggled for two thousand years to maintain its independence. For most of its history, it has been China that dominated Vietnam either directly or through puppet emperors. The Khmer Empire, a hydraulic civilization based on paddy rice agriculture and long distance trade, arose along the Mekong River in modern Cambodia, and gave rise to the distinct cultures of southeast Asia combining Hinduism, Buddhism, and Confucianism. Most northern Vietnamese were ethnically Chinese, but over the years have created a separate identity (Collingwood 1991, 93).

North Vietnam was conquered by China as early as 214 BC, and again in 111 BC, when Han Chinese established firm control. The Chinese dominated the region of North Vietnam (known as Tonkin) for a thousand years (*viet* means people, *nam* is Chinese for south); and Chinese culture, particularly Confucius values, dominated. A people, known as Champa, ruled the southern part of Vietnam as a separate kingdom. Both the north and south were brought under the control of a separate ethnic group known as Annamese in the sixteenth century. By 1700, two distinct Vietnamese dynasties founded by Annamese gained control and separately ruled North and South Vietnam.

In 1787, Nguyen-Anh, a general, signed a military aid treaty with France, which was interested in opening trade along the Red and Mekong Rivers (Collingwood 1991, 93). France soon dominated Vietnam and also the neighboring countries of Cambodia and Laos. France called these three countries Indochina. France was to have a difficult time ruling this rich region. Not only is it geographically very rugged with mountains, rivers, and marshlands, it also has a highly diversified mixture of ethnic Chinese, Indonesian, Malaysian, Thai, Vietnamese, Laotians, and Khmers who were traditional enemies long before the French arrived (Collingwood 1991, 93).

France became the authoritarian ruler of Vietnam. Its policies toward the Vietnamese people were to have important ramifications in the twentieth century. French policy, for over half a century, created extreme forms of deprivation throughout Vietnamese society: peasants, middle classes, and elites all suffered at French hands. The result was a classic peasant revolution whose origins were misinterpreted by American foreign policy makers. That misinterpretation resulted in what is perhaps the most disastrous foreign policy decision of all time for the United States.

The imposition of French rule on Vietnam did not produce an easy union. There were continuous uprisings, which led the French sociologist Paul Mus to warn the French against the "convenient notion" that Vietnamese peasants were "a passive mass, only interested in their daily bowl of rice, and terrorized into subversion by agents" (Karnow 1983, 99). Karnow writes concerning the military capabilities of the Vietnamese peasants:

> Their country's frequent wars also infused in the Vietnamese a readiness to defend themselves, so that they evolved into a breed of warriors (Karnow 1983, 98–99)

■The French were warned that the Vietnamese peasants were not "a passive mass, only interested in their daily bowl of rice." These people, though not soldiers, would indeed rise up and defend themselves.

The French turned rice into an export commodity. Exports in 1860 were 57,000 tons; by 1937, exports had risen to 1,548,000 tons. To make this increase possible, the French supported the development of a class of large landowners:

> The result was that in Tonkin five hundred large land owners—both French and Vietnamese—came to own 20 percent of the land; another seventeen thousand owned a further 20 percent. The remaining small holders, about one million in strength, divided the rest among themselves; the average holding amounted to less than half a hectare per family (Wolf 1969, 166).

Land was also drained and irrigated by the French in the Vietnamese South, and then sold at low prices in an attempt to recover costs. By 1938, half of the South's arable land was planted in rice, and about 50 percent of this was owned by only 2.5 percent of the landowners. More than half of the southern population of about seven hundred thousand families was landless (Wolf 1969, 166).

Deprivation ran high among peasants and middle class Vietnamese alike, and provided fuel for nationalist social movements. Vietnamese intellectuals found weapons for their battle in Western teaching. Children who went to school in France and returned to Vietnam soon found themselves taking increasingly more radical political positions, often based on theories and ideologies they had learned abroad. One these, Ho Chi Minh (Nguyen ai Quoc), trained in China by Maoist leaders, organized the League for the Independence of Vietnam (or Viet Minh) in 1941 to fight the Japanese invaders. Upon their defeat in 1945, he and his followers assumed they would take over the government. Instead, a civil war ensued, eventually involving the United States.

The war in Vietnam can now be looked back upon with the hindsight of history. It was an anti-core, nationalist revolution much like that fought in Russia and China. The Marxism of the new Vietnamese state did not bring it prosperity, but it did bring the people a sense of dignity. Now Vietnamese leaders are introducing some democratic policies and new open market systems. The Vietnamese refer to the new policy

doi moi

A Vietnamese term, similar to the Russian word peristroika, meaning the "restructuring" of markets and economy away from closed socialist practices

as **doi moi,** a term that has the same meaning as the Russian word peristroika, that is, restructuring. In many ways paralleling events in China, the Vietnamese economy has begun to improve dramatically; however, the Communist government insists on maintaining control, much to the anger of the younger Vietnamese who do not remember the war. The government of Vietnam is attempting to attract foreign investment, but foreigners are reluctant to invest in a country that is controlled by an authoritarian government. As in China, the pressure for democratic reform by outsiders and by the young is intense, but the old Communists are afraid to let go control of the country for fear it will dissolve into its constituent ethnic and religious regions.

Vietnam's economy is still among the poorest of Southeast Asia; however, the model for the future has shifted from China to neighboring Thailand, whose economy is booming. The United States maintained an economic boycott of Vietnam until December 1992, when President Bush decided to lift it as a gift to the Vietnamese leaders who had produced extensive new information on MIAs (Americans missing in action between 1960 and 1975) and POWs (former prisoners of war).

The Vietnamese revolution and the war with the United States had the effect of destabilizing all of Southeast Asia, particularly neighboring Kampuchea (Cambodia) and Laos, both of which went through violent revolutions and are still seeking to return to a normal existence. Had the United States, in its policy decisions, taken more account of the culture history of Vietnam and less of the chimera of Communism, it is likely that much senseless conflict could have been avoided. One of the lessons history provides is that the Vietnamese people feared China, the assumed ally of North Vietnam, as greatly as they feared France or the United States. China, in turn, was much too involved with its own internal disputes to overrun the whole of Asia and to transform it into a giant communist state.

Japan: The Leading Asian Tiger

Americans are increasingly concerned with competition from Japan and with Japanese investment in the economy of the United States, including the purchase of baseball franchises and urban real estate. While Americans focus on the success of Japan, the larger story is that the core-periphery set of relationships of the last century and a half is being tilted in a new direction as the countries of the Pacific Rim begin to co-participate in the development of a new core with two or three centers, Japan being the most powerful of the centers.

Japan is one of only three major Asian countries to escape domination and colonization by the west (China and Thailand are the other two), although none completely escaped western influence. Like China, Japan deliberately isolated itself economically and politically from the West in the early eighteenth century; but by the late nineteenth century, Japanese leaders realized that China's strategy was not working and that China was being partitioned by European powers. When Japan was forced to open its doors by Commodore Matthew Perry in 1853, the Samurai elite decided to abandon the feudal system and to introduce capitalism, which transformed Japan after the Meiji Restoration of 1868–1911.

TRADITIONAL JAPANESE CULTURE

Japan has the oldest constitutional monarchy in the world dating back to Foundation Day, February 11, 660, when Jimmu was enthroned as the first emperor. The Japanese language developed from an ancient Chinese dialect. Japanese culture combined rice cultivation,

Confucianism, and Buddhism on top of an earlier nature worshiping religion called Shintoism. These continue today as the core of Japanese culture.

During World War II, Japanese culture became of central interest to American anthropologists, particularly Ruth Benedict, whose book, *The Chrysanthemum and the Sword* (1946), attempted to explain the nature of Japanese institutions. Her book became highly controversial because of its psychoanalytic approach, but much of what she described showed how anthropologists could study the institutions of modernizing societies. Benedict and many more recent writers have shown how Japanese culture developed as a type of decentralized feudalism, which differed from the highly centralized state of China. The emperor was basically a figurehead, and the royal family was a symbol of Japanese unity rather than the real rulers. Symbols of power and ritual became very important in Japan, many based on traditional religion. Feudal lords, who developed a culture based on hierarchy, regard for family, and ancestor worship within a framework of Shinto, Buddhist, and Confucian values, held the power. The **samurai** (derived from the Japanese word for servant) sustained the feudal rule. In 1192, the leader of one of the feudal clans seized control of the country and declared that he was the supreme military leader, or **shogun**. Japan evolved a militaristic culture within which Zen, a special version of Buddhism, placed a unique emphasis on self-discipline, a Japanese value that has remained through to the present. Anthropologists and historians largely agree that the most important Japanese value became **bushido**, or the way of the warrior, a concept obligating the warrior to carry out his lord's wishes or commit **seppeku**, or ritual suicide.

THE WESTERNIZATION OF JAPAN

Commodore Perry's opening of Japan made the feudal elite realize that the decentralized power structure would not work in a modern world. Japan centralized its political system during the Meiji Restoration, beginning with the abandonment of the samurai feudal system and the restoration of the Emperor of Japan. Japan sent students and researchers to study in Western universities, and it hired foreign engineers and intellectuals to help design a new Japan. Japanese leaders tried to model the country's new institutions on the most successful institutions of the core. For example, it borrowed its financial institutions from Germany and its educational institutions from France (Reischauer 1988).

While Japan imported western capitalism, it only imported a few democratic ideas. Japanese leaders, in the 1880s, felt that it would be several decades before the people of Japan would be ready to understand democratic institutions. The British concept of a parliament was turned into a Japanese institution, the Diet, with 1 percent of the population having the right to vote and the prime minister being selected by special advisors to the emperor. Western ideas, such as the separation of government from business enterprises and the development of labor unions to protect workers, were foreign. The Japanese cultural ideal was the *ie*, or "house," (the direct opposite of the American emphasis on the individual and his or her success):

> Simply put, this is the Japanese socio-psychological tendency that emphasizes (in the sense of protecting, cherishing, finding needs for, or functioning best in) "us" against "them" (Yamamura 1987, 133).

In Japan, a close working relationship evolved between the most powerful commercial families, called the *zaibatsu* (combines which organized finance, business, and industry), and the government. Government made investments in the private sector by subsidizing

---

samurai

A class of warriors that sustained Japanese feudal rule

shogun

A supreme military leader in feudal Japan

bushido

A Japanese concept that obligated a warrior to carry out his lord's wishes or commit ritual suicide

seppeku

Japanese ritual suicide

such powerful families as the Mitsubishi clan in the development of industry. Employees hired to work for the powerful, family-owned corporations became like members of the family, and their jobs were secure for life. Labor unions were disdained, both by the industrialists and by the workers who considered themselves to have quasi-kinship connections to the business houses which employed them.

At the turn of the century, Japan had caught up to the West in the use of many industrial technologies. In 1905, Japan and Russia fought a naval battle that proved the superior technology of Japanese battleships (Reischauer 1988). However, Japan lacked natural resources to support its growing industry, and Japanese leaders decided they should develop colonies on mainland Asia. In the 1930s, Japan gained hegemony over many of its neighbors, particularly Korea, Taiwan, and China. Japan also forced economic dominance on much of eastern Asia. Japanese expansionist tendencies, particularly in Manchuria, made it a feared nation and brought threats to it from the core countries. In the late 1930s, the Japanese military gained control of the government. Threats, counter-threats, and cultural misunderstandings on both sides brought Japan into World War II on the side of the Axis powers, and against the United States and its allies.

From a technological point of view, the War in the Pacific was close. Japanese air and sea technology took the United States by surprise. Many have argued that Japan lost the war, not because of inferior technology, but because of poor strategies at several battles, such as the battle of Midway, which were based on Japanese assumptions about the poor fighting capacity of the American military.

The occupation of Japan led to new political and economic innovations imposed on Japan by the American military. One of these was the introduction of American style democracy (Cohen 1987). General Douglas MacArthur rewrote the Japanese constitution to reflect his own vision of an Americanized Japan. A new British style "Diet" (parliament) was developed with a separation of powers among the three branches of government: legislative, executive, and judicial. Attempts were made to break up the zaibatsu and destroy the power of the old entrepreneurial families.

However, the fear of communism in Asia led the United States to support the rapid reindustrialization of Japan. Reforms to government and industry were soft peddled so that while the political system was reformed to allow greater democratic participation, the bureaucracies were left alone. In addition, the old zaibatsu were allowed to reconstitute

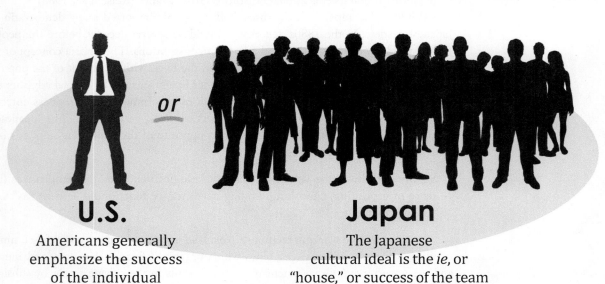

U.S.	Japan
Americans generally emphasize the success of the individual	The Japanese cultural ideal is the *ie,* or "house," or success of the team

themselves in the early 1950s into informal *keiretsu* (networks of affiliated companies) (Reischauer 1988, 306–307). Of particular importance was the continued evolution of a financial relationship between government and industry, which was and is radically different from that which exists in the United States. In Japan, newly developing business enterprises have been systematically supported by the government until they are able to stand on their own feet. Businesses in crisis are often met with financial help from the government. Furthermore, politicians, government bureaucrats, and businessmen help each other in ways which Americans would label "corrupt" but which Japanese perceive as "doing business."

The *keiretsu* are central to Japan's postwar growth and success. Western scholars tend to confuse the keiretsu with the more familiar conglomerates of the western core, which attempt to monopolize a single industry (such as AT&T's attempt to monopolize the communication industry of the United States prior to 1984). However, the keiretsu is peculiarly Japanese. Keiretsu consist of sets of firms that specialize in different economic tasks such as banking, manufacturing, energy production, export-import marketing, etc., in cooperation with each other. One can think of these different business enterprises as distinct rooms within a single house. Keiretsu attempt to set up firms in every important segment of the economy. Such organizations in the United States would be subject to antitrust laws, but antitrust laws have little importance in Japan. The existence of keiretsu allows Japanese firms to integrate the latest developments on matters related to financing, technological development, personnel, purchasing, marketing, and planning in the most efficient and cooperative style possible (Yamamura 1987). Competition between firms in the United States drives up the cost of innovations and their use. The Japanese keiretsu, as an inter-firm organization, makes Japanese production less expensive than in old core countries.

In addition to the keiretsu, the Japanese have developed new techniques of personnel management, which are also highly efficient. American social science research during the Depression years of the 1930s produced many studies suggesting ways to improve corporate decision-making (particularly the Western Electric studies in Chicago) which were never implemented in the United States. Japanese corporate managers utilized several of these studies to redesign manufacturing techniques in Japan after World War II. The most important innovation was the concept of "quality circles" which brought managers and workers into cooperative relationships with each other in manufacturing. Instead of vertical relationships between management and labor, the quality circle approach put managers and workers together on the same level to solve problems in manufacturing. This approach is currently being reintroduced to the United States.

Japan also created one of the most efficient educational systems in the world. Unlike the American educational system, which is highly decentralized and controlled by local school boards, the Japanese educational system is run by the Ministry of Education which sets all standards and policies. The cost of education in Japan is comparatively lower than in the United States, but more children receive a better education (Tasker 1987).

Japan has succeeded as a capitalist member of the world system since World War II because of the close financial relationships between business and government, the keiretsu, the quality circle management strategies, and its educational system. Part of Japan's success is due to a general agreement on the part of the Japanese people that they must cooperate if they are to successfully compete in the modern world, an "us" versus "them" point of view largely lacking in the western core countries.

Chapter
Summary

Asia: The Emerging Tigers

In many parts of Asia the development of agriculture in the Neolithic before 6000 BC gave rise first to settled tribal communities, and later, between 4000 and 2000 BC, to chiefdom level political organizations. Some time between 2000 and 1000 BC state level organizations, supported by intensive agriculture and extensive trade, began to appear. These early states quickly developed complex systems of class differentiation, highly developed craft specialization, trade networks reaching far to the west into Europe, and great religious traditions such as Hinduism, Buddhism, and Islam, which were intimately connected to the state bureaucracies.

The great civilizations of Asia were subjected to waves of Western capitalist expansion and colonization beginning in the sixteenth century, which transformed their societies and economies. Europeans colonized many of the Asian nations; and even the few that were spared direct colonization were greatly influenced by European contact. Market economies spread to the furthest reaches of the rural hinterlands. Numerous independence and nationalist movements arose which attempted to throw off the yoke of colonialism and domination. Under the able leadership of such well-known figures as Mohandas Ghandi in India, Ho Chi Minh in Vietnam, and Mao Zedong in China, many Asian nations had achieved political independence by the 1950s; but they remained economically peripheral to the Western core nations. Some, such as China and Vietnam, experimented with forms of socialism in an attempt to develop outside what had already become a global economic system. These experiments were unsuccessful; and as the twentieth century drew to a close, all of the nations of Asia were involved (but to varying degrees) in the world capitalist economy. Several nations, Japan and Thailand among them, have come to be known as the Asian Tigers because of their rapid rise as world-class economic powers. It appears that Indonesia is an emerging tiger, and Vietnam may very well be another.

Like much of the rest of the world, many of the nations of Asia are struggling with internal problems of ethnic and religious conflict that have resulted in numerous instances of violence. In India, major confrontations have occurred between Hindus and Sikhs. China, too, confronts problems with its ethnic minorities while struggling to enter the capitalist economy on its own terms. China continues to receive criticism from international human rights organizations and western governments for its invasion and occupation of Tibet more than forty years ago, while paradoxically continuing to receive "most favored nation" trade status from the United States.

Chapter
Terms

atman	373	Mandarin	361
bjauk	380	Mansabdar	376
Brahman	374	Mantrayana Buddhism	376
bride price	369	moksha	373
bushido	384	nirvana	374
caste endogamy	374	peasant	361
caste system	373	samurai	384
Chou dynasty	360	satori	376
dharma	375	scapulimancy	359
divination	359	seppeku	384
doi moi	383	shogun	384
dowry	369	sinification	361
entrepot	376	Sudra	374
filial piety *(hsiao)*	360	theocracy	360
foot binding	361	Theravada Buddhism	375
gamelan	380	Ti	359
gentry	361	treaty port	363
guru	376	tsu	361
jajmani	357	Vaisya	374
karma	373	varna	374
Kshatriya	374	Vedas	373
legong	380	Yang-shao	358
Lungshan	358	Zamindars	376
Mahayana Buddhism	375	Zen Buddhism	376

Check out our website
www.BVTLab.com
for flashcards,
chapter summaries,
and more.

Chapter 11

Latin America: Political Bosses, Dependency, and Democratic Reform

Latin America stretches from the Rio Grande in the north, forming the United States-Mexico border, to Tierra del Fuego, a large island that is the southernmost part of Chile. Mexico's topography may be compared to a large funnel with the western and eastern mountain ranges of the Sierra Madre Occidental and Sierra Madre Oriental converging just south of Mexico City, forcing all north-south trade into a narrow region where the great core centers of Mesoamerican history emerged: Teotihuacan, Tenochtitlan, and colonial and modern Mexico City. South of Mexico City, mountainous basins occur regularly to Guatemala, and each of these was occupied by a city-state in pre-Columbian times. Lowland civilizations were linked to the highland civilizations, following overland trade routes through lowland Mexico to the central Yucatan.

Central America links the Western Hemisphere's two continental ecosystems, acting as a land bridge between North and South America. It is a thin strip of extremely heterogeneous climates, soils, landforms, vegetation, animal species, and peoples. South of Panama, the Andes mountains contain a series of highland basins running south to north, where most populations are concentrated, while the great Amazon basin to the east forms a lightly inhabited tropical region of threatened indigenous peoples and resources.

We may divide the history of Latin America into five distinct time periods, each characterized by significantly different political and economic institutions: (1) The prehistoric period, characterized by indigenous economies and polities ranging from subsistence-based tribal agriculturalists to city-states and tributary empires such as those of the Maya, Aztec, and Inca; (2) the colonial period which began with the conquest of Tenochtitlan

Figure 11.1

☐ Physiographic Map of Latin America

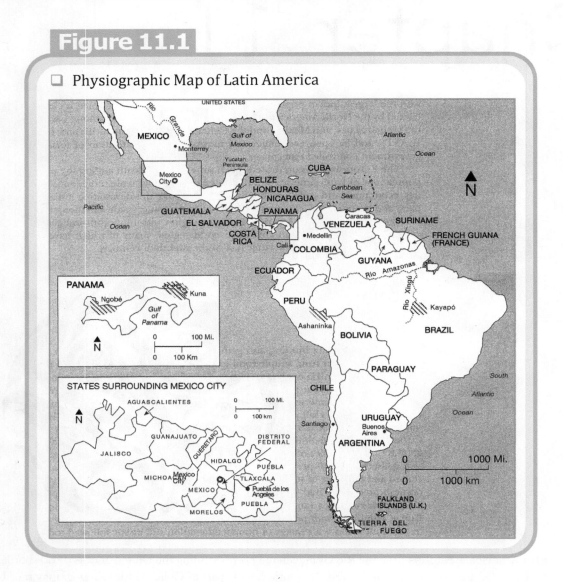

caudillo

Spanish term for a man of power or authority, supreme commander, a head of state, a political boss

in 1521 and ended with the beginning of the wars of independence against Spain in 1810, and during which the institutions of Latin America were determined by Iberian models from Spain and Portugal; (3) the period of the **caudillos** (political bosses), which lasted roughly from the end of the wars of independence (1810–1820) to the 1930s, during which time Latin America developed its own internal forms of political organization, primarily based on the colonial **haciendas**, but with economic and political control being exercised by regional caudillos rather than peninsular Spanish administrators; (4) the period of state capitalism or state corporatism from 1930 to 1986, during which the state further developed and protected its industrial base through closure of the Latin American economies; and (5) the period of neoliberal reform beginning in 1986. During the later phase of the caudillo period, from 1870 to 1930, there was considerable industrialization in the most progressive Latin American countries, which also became the wealthiest (Mexico, Colombia, Venezuela, Argentina, Brazil, and Chile). The rural sector was affected by the tendency toward privatization of Indian **ejidos** (communally held land), and the decimation and sometimes destruction of the Indian communities in Mexico, Guatemala, El Salvador,

hacienda

Traditionally, a large Latin American estate, generally found in the highlands, self-sufficient but producing for local markets, and supported by a slave-like caste of peon laborers

ejido

A term in Mexico for a collective estate, usually owned by Indian communities and found mostly in the highland regions of Latin America

Mesoamerica

Refers to the area of sophisticated pre-Hispanic civilizations in Mexico and upper Central America, which includes the southern two-thirds of Mexico, all of Guatemala and Belize, and the northern third of Honduras and El Salvador

Bolivia, Peru, and Ecuador—the countries with the largest Indian populations. The period of neoliberal reform is characterized by the North American Free Trade Agreement (NAFTA) among Canada, the United States, and Mexico, the General Agreement on Tariffs and Trade (GATT), and by open economies and moves toward privatization of formerly government controlled enterprises.

The European invasion caused much suffering and death among the native populations of Latin America and disrupted, on a massive scale the indigenous polities, economies, and social and family life. Yet, despite this devastating initial impact, and despite over five hundred years of domination by a succession of colonial and state governments, Latin America remains a region with numerous indigenous cultures, perhaps more than any other world region, many of which have displayed renewed vitality in the latter half of the twentieth century.

From Tribes to States in Mesoamerica

The transition from a hunting and gathering way of life to one based on agriculture, a transition from simple food extraction to food production and from band to tribal organization, began in the arid highlands of Mexico some time before 5000 BC. By about 3400 BC, the plants that would later form the agricultural base of Mesoamerican civilization had already been domesticated—maize, beans, squash, and chili peppers—all seed crops. Several other plants of lesser importance were also domesticated. The transition from heavy reliance on food extraction to overwhelming dependence on food production was gradual. By 2300 BC, the peoples of the Tehuacan Valley in Mexico still relied on hunting and gathering for 70 percent of their food. But by 1500 BC the balance had shifted, and evidence of sedentary village life permits us to infer that reliance on domesticated foods had become dominant. Sedentary villages begin to appear all over **Mesoamerica** (and lower Central America) at this time. The herding of llamas, combined with potatoes and maize agriculture, had a similar early date in the Andes, and is a strategy of human adaptation still widely followed today.

Between 1500 and 1100 BC, tribal societies in Mesoamerica (Mexico and the northern part of Central America) and the Andes were transformed into the more complex sociopolitical entities of chiefdoms, as described in Chapter 5. For example, archaeological

■The people of Mesoamerica transitioned from a hunting and gathering way of life to one based on agriculture. Crops included maize, beans, squash, and chili peppers.

Figure 11.2

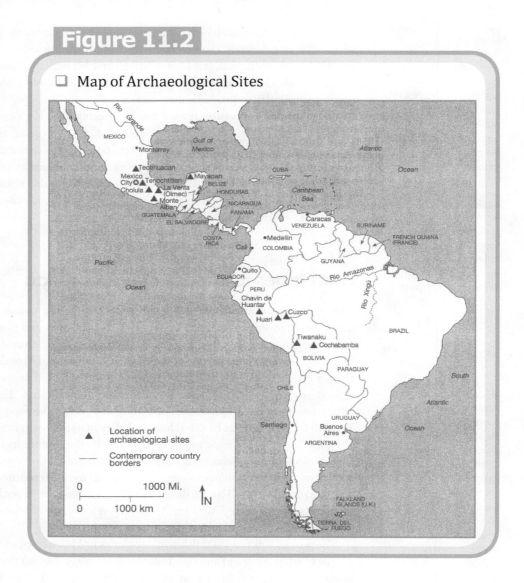

❑ Map of Archaeological Sites

excavations at the sites of La Venta and San Lorenzo, on the tropical east coast of Mexico revealed giant basalt heads, giant buried masks, and a pyramid in the form of a volcano all within a preplanned plaza. The art style and associated artifacts at these two sites are known as Olmec culture. While both of these sites were ceremonial centers with only small residential areas, enough is now known about the Olmec culture to be certain that social stratification and craft specialization were present (Culbert 1983). These are characteristics usually associated with a chiefdom level of sociopolitical organization.

Exotic objects of obsidian and jade found at Olmec sites, as well as Olmec style art found in the state of Morelos in central Mexico and also on the southern periphery of Mesoamerica in El Salvador, provide clear evidence that the Olmec were engaged in long distance trade (Culbert 1983). The site of San Jose Mogote in the valley of Oaxaca, for example, shows strong Olmec influence and evidence of trade between 1100 and 850 BC. During this time period, San Jose Mogote was the largest site in the Oaxaca valley, with more than 80 percent of the population living there, while 20 percent lived in the country-side in small villages. Similar chiefdom type societies emerged throughout Mesoamerica at about the same time. Some scholars, such as Michael Coe (1962), believe that the Olmec were the first to develop a state level of organization and were the "mother culture" from which all Mesoamerican civilizations sprung. Others, such as Flannery (1968) and Culbert (1983), favor the idea that class stratification emerged in many places in Mesoamerica at about the same time and that, rather than Olmec influence causing this class stratification, it was the stratification that enhanced widespread trade relations and made Olmec influence possible.

Not long after, as in Mesopotamia, chiefdoms were transformed into states with great drama and speed. This happened not in one place but throughout Mesoamerica at roughly the same time period, about 700 BC. By 500 BC, San Jose Mogote was abandoned; the population moved to the nearby mountain of Monte Alban and established another chiefdom on top of it, after excavating a flat surface on top and building a series of temples. The population of the valley increased seven to eight times *after* (not before) the chiefdom of Monte Alban was established, an extraordinary growth rate of about 1.3 percent per year for the valley. The population growth rate for Monte Alban is calculated at 6 percent per year, two or three times that of modern industrializing countries (Blanton et al. 1981, 71).

To the north in the Valley of Mexico, the giant city of Teotihuacan grew in an even more explosive fashion. Teotihuacan is the most spectacular site in Mesoamerica, occupying a large portion of the Valley of Teotihuacan (it became the largest city in the world at the time Rome was at its height). However, the city did not evolve slowly; rather it appears that most of the people of the city had once been rural dwellers.

The implications of the dramatic increase in the size of the city and the depopulation of the countryside are enormous because there is no other instance in history where a city grew by suddenly swallowing most of its rural population. In fact, this shift in populations flies in the face of most evolutionary and demographic theories about the growth of cities. Cities are supposed to appear when population densities in the countryside pass a certain critical maximum and the surplus populations develop cities. However, it is obvious this process did not occur at Teotihuacan. Some of the population came from outside the Valley, from cities in Tlaxcala and Puebla. Teotihuacan went through a phase of enormous expansion shortly after it destroyed its chief rival, Cuicuilco, during the first century. From a population of twenty thousand to thirty thousand, Teotihuacan grew to more than one hundred fifty thousand by about AD 500 (Carmack, Gasco, and Gossen 1996, 57). On the other hand, the rural population in the basin of Mexico dropped from one hundred thousand to fifteen thousand. Eighty-five thousand people moved into Teotihuacan! There is no evidence that the move was forced on the rural population, and many of these urban dwellers remained farmers. Abundant natural springs in the area were used to support an elaborate irrigation system that produced abundant agricultural yields.

There is evidence that the city of Teotihuacan was planned before any major building occurred. The Street of the Dead was constructed before construction began on the enormous pyramids. Anyone who has visited Teotihuacan has to be impressed by the planning that went into the design of the city. The city itself is laid out so that the Street of the Dead lies on an axis to a monument found on one of the nearby mountains. The giant city of Teotihuacan, as well as Monte Alban in the highlands of Oaxaca and the lowland Maya states in the region of the southern Yucatan and the Peten of Guatemala, all collapsed between AD 600 and 1100. Teotihuacan was burned in the seventh century. Evidence of selective burning of administrative and religious structures at Teotihuacan argues for internal revolt (Carmack et al. 1996, 60). This is the same time period in which there is a significant shift towards sea trade around the Yucatan Peninsula and ecological pressures on resources. After the collapse of the theocratic and large states, smaller towns and cities

■When the Spaniards arrived in central Mexico the Aztec, (Nahuatl-speaking peoples) had established control over most of the central Mexican highlands and adjacent coastal regions.

emerged forming alliances, such as that of Tenochtitlan and its sister cities along ancient Lake Texcoco or Mayapan and its allies in the northern Yucatan.

By the time the Spaniards arrived in central Mexico, Nahuatl-speaking people, known as the Aztec, had established control over most of the central Mexican highlands and adjacent coastal regions. The saga of the conquest of Tenochtitlan, capital of the Aztecs, is well-known. The Aztec emperor, Montezuma, had visions, portents of the coming of the Spanish. These were confused with the legend of Quetzalcoatl, a mythical ruler-god, reputedly bearded, who, upon his departure several hundred years before, declared his eventual return. However, it was really the horse, firearms, and the skillful use of the enemies of the Aztecs that allowed the Spanish their bloody successes, not magic.

The Emergence of Civilizations in the Andes

The transition from hunting and gathering to agriculture in the Andes and adjacent Pacific coast and *montaña* (eastern slopes of the Andes) areas was similar to that in Mesoamerica. By 4200 BC, there is some evidence of plant domestication along the Peruvian coast. At about the same time, somewhere in the river basins of northern South America, the pattern of root crop agriculture that emphasized reproduction by cuttings developed. By 1500 BC, the pattern of root crop agriculture was fully developed in the Amazon-Orinoco lowlands and had spread over the Andes to the Pacific coast; and the pattern of seed crop agriculture—maize, beans, squash, and chili peppers, but particularly maize—had spread south out of Mesoamerica and was well established in the Andean area. This felicitous conjunction of root crop and seed crop agriculture, combined with such native Andean cultigens as the potato and quinoa (a grain) and a varied climate, led to a rapid expansion of population and rapid development of social organizational complexity.

Stone houses, ceremonial centers, and temples were present by 900 BC at the site of Chavin de Huantar, located 16,000 feet above sea level in the northern Peruvian Andes. This spectacular religious center is not unlike La Venta, and authorities have speculated that there may have been contact between the two cultures as early as 800 BC. At Chavin de Huantar, a stone sheathed platform containing a maze of narrow passages and galleries surrounded a central plaza where stood an amazing stone pillar. The pillar, called the **Lanzon**, depicted a mythological jaguar with serpents for hair. The symbolism was strikingly like that of the Olmec culture of Veracruz, Mexico. The Chavin culture dominated the Central Andes for seven hundred years, and then disappeared about 200 BC; the pattern of later states and empires and exploitation had been set.

Chavin was followed by a florescence of small states such as that called Mochica in the Viru Valley of Peru. Thousands of people lived in this and other similar theocratic states located in the coastal river valleys. In southern Peru, another spectacular civilization evolved called the Nazca. The people of Nazca constructed gigantic stone sketches of a

Lanzon

A temple at the site of Chavin de Huantar in the Peruvian Andes depicting a feline deity, dated to about 800 BC

■Nazca stone sketches of animals and ancestors were discovered on the coast of Peru and northern Chile from aerial photographs.

variety of animals and ancestors on the coast of Peru and northern Chile. Most of these were not recognized for what they are until aerial photographs were made of them.

From AD 600 to 1000, a classic tributary conquest state emerged known as Tiwanaku (Tiahuanaco in earlier literature), located on the southern shores of Lake Titicaca. It had a ceremonial center of over twenty thousand people, massive stone sheathed courts and platforms, and immense carved stone statues. Tiwanaku controlled a large trade network, which spread as far away as Argentina. According to some scholars a second "twin" empire emerged in northern Peru with similar characteristics called Huari. Alan Kolata, however, argues that Huari was just a regional center of the one far-flung empire of Tiwanaku that, at its height between AD 750 and 1000, had regional centers in coastal Chile, coastal Peru, and the Cochabamba Valley of Bolivia. A significant climate change, a great drought lasting from AD 1000 to 1400, severely affected agricultural production and gradually brought an end to the Tiwanaku Empire by AD 1100. Smaller, less spectacular, states arose in the coastal river valleys and some of the highland basins (Kolata 1993).

In the fifteenth century, the final pre-Hispanic empire came into existence, that of the mighty Inca. The name Inca was given to the ruling family, which could supposedly trace its origin back several centuries, and for those several centuries apparently ruled little more than Cuzco and its immediate environs. Pachacuti Inca Yapanqui, the ninth Inca, who ruled from AD 1438–1471, unified the southern Peruvian highlands and was succeeded by his son, Topa Inca Yupanqui (1471–1493), who continued to expand the empire in all directions. When Topa Inca Yupanqui's son, Huayna Capac, succeeded him, he expanded the Inca realm to its greatest extent, imposing hegemony over an empire that stretched more than three thousand miles from northern Colombia to central Chile. It included the coastal lowlands, the most inaccessible upper reaches of the Andes up to 15,000 feet, and the upper reaches of the *montaña* (Fagg 1963).

At the peak of his glory, Huayna Capac died in an epidemic in 1527 or 1528. His most probable heir, Ninan Cuyuchi, died in the same epidemic. This left two sons, Huascar Inca, by Huayna Capac's Peruvian wife, and Atahualpa Inca by his Ecuadorian wife. Huascar was officially crowned Inca in the southern capital of Cuzco and apparently had the loyalty of the populace. Atahualpa had control of most of the professional army and took over the northern part of the empire, establishing his capital at Quito. After five years of bitter civil war, Atahualpa defeated Huascar, captured him, and before his own death at the hands of the Spaniards, had him killed. On November 15, 1532, Francisco Pizarro and his small band of Spaniards arrived on the plains of Cajamarca, through trickery captured Atahualpa, and held him for ransom for a time. Finally, Atahualpa was accused by the Spaniards of numerous crimes, among them polygyny (which was not a crime in Inca society), usurpation (because he had taken the throne from his brother), fratricide (because he had his brother killed), and idolatry (because he did not worship the Spanish god). As a pagan, he was to be burned at the stake. However, at the last minute Father Valverde, the priest who accompanied Pizarro, talked Atahualpa into being baptized, and so he was

■Pizzaro ordering Inca ruler Atahualpa to be executed.

entitled to be hanged instead—and he was, on July 26, 1533. This was the beginning of the end for the Inca state, but it was not superior force of arms that brought the mighty Inca Empire to its knees. It was disease. As Michael Moseley wrote in the following:

> In 1532, the quintessence of native civilization toppled with the impact of a single European state. The basic impact came neither from advanced technology nor sophisticated corporate organization. The most effective weapons arming the conquistadors were smallpox, measles, and other Old World diseases. These first under-mined and later virtually destroyed the demographic foundations of New World society.... (1983, 236).

The Invasion and Its Aftermath

The invasion of Latin America was a staggering event. (The indigenous peoples of Latin America argue that they were invaded but never conquered, so we refrain from using the term "conquest.") It occurred a full century before the English colonies were established in North America. Latin America was the first non-European con-tinental area to be confronted by the forces of Western-ization, and it was the most dramatically changed. From the very beginning, there was a violent and continuous clash of cultures. Christianization of Latin America's Indian populations resulted in the imposition of one set of institutions from Monterrey, Mexico, to Santiago, Chile. The gold and silver mined out of Mexico, Colombia, Bolivia, and Peru paid for several European wars and made the Industrial Revolution possible. New trade routes established to facili-tate the mining industry had the consequence of destroying all other trade routes, such as those that existed throughout Latin America in pre-European times. The wealth robbed from the New World and the imposition of imperialistic institutions condemned Latin America to a future of underdevelopment.

Perhaps the most notable consequence of the invasion, of contact between the New World and the Old, the consequence with the most far-reaching repercussions for the native cultures of Latin America was the demographic impact. First to feel the impact were the native populations of the Caribbean islands. Diseases and inhuman working conditions in the mines and plantations resulted in near total extinction within fifty years after initial con-tact (by 1550). Later, African slaves were brought in to provide a labor force, and cattle ranchers and large sugar plantation owners dominated the islands economically (Wolf 1982).

As Eric Wolf has pointed out, the invaders and colonists wanted native labor, the crown of Spain wanted native subjects, and the friars wanted native souls. The "conquest" that was to have produced utopia, instead resulted in the collapse of native cultures and biological catastrophe (Wolf 1959). In Middle America during the first one hundred years after the invasion, native populations declined by as much as 90 percent. While the decline was not this drastic elsewhere in Latin America, most areas did suffer at least a 50 percent

■A sugarcane plantation in Cuba.

decline before recovery began. While in some areas native populations began a slow demographic recovery after 1800, in others the recovery did not begin until a century later.

The litany of reasons for the decline of native populations is long and includes all of the following: excessive labor requirements, excessive tributes, mistreatment in general, drunkenness, starvation, flood, drought, disease, and divine providence. While mistreatment certainly accounts for some deaths, it is no longer seen as the principal cause of population decline. Various European diseases to which the native populations had no initial immunity or resistance were the paramount cause of native deaths. Even a short list of known major epidemics in New Spain presents a grim picture: smallpox epidemics in 1520, 1531, and 1545; typhoid in 1545, 1576, 1735, and twenty-nine more times before 1821; a great measles epidemic in 1595; and malaria and yellow fever, apparently from Africa, spread quickly through the New World tropics and became endemic (Wolf 1959, 196).

Population decline seriously disrupted all aspects of native society and culture in Latin America, but it was not the sole cause of such disruption. The Spanish practice of *reducción*, concentrating native populations into nucleated villages, was especially disruptive for those native populations that were semi-nomadic and those who lived in small, widely dispersed settlements. In addition, inhuman living conditions and brutal treatment did take its toll in areas close to mines and plantations. Mestizoization, a process of biological and cultural blending, while disruptive of native life, produced new cultures neither Indian nor European.

The Colonial Period

By the middle of the sixteenth century, Latin America had three power centers: one at Mexico City, one at Cuzco, Peru, and one in Brazil (which was ruled by Portugal). Later other centers would develop at Buenos Aires, Argentina, and Caracas, Venezuela. As a means to exercise control over the native populations from these centers, the Spanish Crown merged communitarian traditions from Spain with traditional Mesoamerican and Andean ideas of collective land ownership. Lands were allocated to Indian communities as collectives, their exploitation was carefully regulated, and they could not be sold. The native communities gradually developed internal mechanisms to control this process of

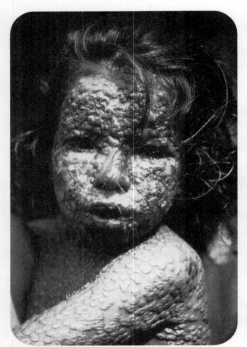

■Little girl infected with smallpox. The Spanish brought with them many diseases from Europe to which natives of Latin America had no immunity.

plantation

Similar to haciendas but organized for the production of export commodities such as sugar, cotton, or hemp (for cordage); tend not to be self-sufficient and depend on local farmers for food

rancheria

A small Latin American farm, usually containing cattle and/or maize and owned by people of Indian ancestry

domination. (See below.) During the colonial period, the domination of the landscape by Spanish colonial institutions so profoundly altered the human ecology as to allow us to collapse the two categories of human ecology and political economy into one: political ecology.

POLITICAL ECOLOGY: MINES, HACIENDAS, AND PLANTATIONS

In previous chapters we have seen how human institutions defined the political ecology of distinct regions of the world after the development of states, but that underlying state institutions were earlier traditional forms of human adaptation (that is, human ecology). Nowhere is the outstanding impact of human political institutions on human ecology more clear than in Latin America. By 1570, Spain had imposed an entirely new political economy on the whole of Latin America based on bureaucratic cities, haciendas, plantations, and mining. For this reason, in this chapter we combine the categories of human ecology and political ecology to just political ecology. By the end of the colonial period, the mine, the hacienda, and the plantation dominated the political ecology of Latin America. The *haciendas* (large agricultural or cattle estates found primarily in the highlands and sometimes the size of small countries) were formed out of former Indian lands and specialized in growing subsistence goods for local markets. Meanwhile, plantations and mines produced for export (cochineal, cotton, sugar, coffee, silver, and gold). The **plantations** (these are large lowland estates, often run by slave labor in earlier centuries or by indebted peons today) and haciendas were, and still are, interspersed by small independent farms called **rancherias** (small farms, usually in cattle or a combination of cattle and maize, or just maize) also called open communities, which were owned by Creoles of mixed Spanish-Indian ancestry. In the highlands of both Mesoamerica and the Andes, there were "closed" communities with communal lands, owned by vestiges of the original Indian population. It is in these communities that the religious cargo system flourished (see below).

The rancherias and ejidos, as well as haciendas, produced food for local markets—maize, beans, squash, rice, tomatoes, meat. Their members also produced household-made objects such as ceramic pots and dishes, candles, rope, woven rugs, and clothing. The difference between rancherias and ejidos is that individual mestizo families usually owned the former, while Indian villages and/or clans collectively owned the latter. Sometimes the open and closed communities were in competition for land, and even today tensions exist between the two. To sum up a variety of studies, the haciendas relied, basically, on labor from the regions of rancherias and ejidos, although they also depended on those who lived on the larger estates, who were often drawn both from open and closed communities (the resident laborers on plantations or haciendas are known as **colonos** in Guatemala). Colonos were paid less than subsistence wages, not enough to live on. In some cases, workers were allowed to farm small plots on hacienda lands. These plots are often known simply as *milpa*, the same term used for family owned fields. Ethnographically, it is often difficult to tell when a community was made up of independent ranchero farmers or of colonos, and often these are so intermarried as to make little difference. In all cases, workers were perpetually in debt to the hacendado or to the company store on the plantation. Coffee and cattle were the products of the highland haciendas.

colono

A term used in Guatemala on either haciendas or plantations for the resident laborers that usually farm a small plot of land given to them by the landowners to make up for low wages

latifundia

Term used for haciendas or plantations, large and elite-owned estates

minifundia

Small estates, usually owned by independent farmers, whose labor is used by large estates

ayuntamiento

The Latin American colonial form of local administration, usually controlling a *municipio* or municipality that consists of a large *cabecera* or head village, where the ayuntamiento is located, and smaller towns and villages

debt peonage

Debt slavery where workers are loaned food, clothing, and other goods at high interest rates and are then trapped by their debt, often as near-slaves

Lowland plantations were highly commercial; and through to the mid-twentieth century, they had workers who were either slaves or debt peons. Plantations exported cotton, sugar, cochineal, and bananas or other tropical fruits grown on the lowland plantations (Wolf and Mintz 1956).

The traditional literature on Latin American land ownership once stressed the difference between the **latifundia** and the **minifundia**. The latifundia were the gigantic estates, both plantations and haciendas, owned by the elites of Latin America, while the minifundia were the rancherias and ejidos. The two were viewed as separate societies, often contrasted to the manors and peasant estates of Europe in the Middle Ages. However, from studies beginning in the 1960s, there emerges quite a different picture. Rather than forming two separate societies, *latifundistas*, the owners of the large estates, depended on the labor of *minifundistas*, owners of small estates (both Indian ejido and mestizo rancheria communities). The latifundistas controlled all political power by appointing their representatives to the local **ayuntamientos**. The ayuntamientos are like American counties, and outside of the major cities were the only units of government that, for all intents and purposes, ruled all communities except the Indian towns. These were ruled by their own elders. Minifundistas of either community type were never allowed to serve on the ayuntamientos, and thus were relegated to second or third class social status, often at the level of virtual slaves.

The type of economic relationship between the two groups has been given the name **debt peonage**. Administrators on large estates would loan out food or money at exorbitant interest (30 percent per year or more was not unusual); the *minifundistas* would be expected to pay back the sum. Because wages were never enough to pay principal and interest, entire villages of ejiditarios and rancheros were stuck with perpetual debts. It was these debts that spawned the many revolts by the lower classes against their elites from Mexico to Chile.

In recent years, the distinction between plantations and haciendas, and between closed and open communities has faded, primarily due to legislation protecting workers, but also due to the fragmentation of the hacienda system through inheritance, or in the case of Mexico, the redistribution of lands. However, the regions that were originally in plantation or hacienda tenure remain very poor today. Historic and ethnographic data from Mexico and elsewhere show a clear and constant relationship between the existence of large haciendas or plantations and regional underdevelopment. It is becoming increasingly clear that not only did plantations and haciendas produce poverty instead of wealth but that they held back the modernization process which might have occurred had the regions in question been allowed to evolve a family farm estate system such as found in the United States during similar time periods.

The contrast between the Latin American pattern of land ownership and that in North America (including Canada) is very revealing. North American farmers were always able to control local town boards and councils. While they might get into debt to banks, they had the political power to fight corporate interests on the east coast to their own benefits. Most important, the American farmers owned their own land. If the unit of land became too small due to technological innovations, the small farmer could sell out to a large farmer and sell his labor in the small towns. In Latin America, the minifundista was tied to land, which he could not own, and to debts he could not pay. No wonder modern Latin America has a heritage of rural exploitation, which is difficult to overcome. Finally, as the industrial revolution proceeded, efficiencies of rural production drove down the cost of food in North America. The food was purchased by urban workers in greater amounts, and of higher quality as time went by, while farmers continued to produce ever-larger harvests. While the price of food went down, the income of farmers went up. With cheaper food, worker salaries stretched further. Finally, farmers could afford to buy what urban workers made, stimulating the urban/rural markets. Both rural and urban workers became progressively more prosperous, buying from each other.

In Latin America, this type of rural-urban market relationship never materialized. Instead, plantations were geared to sell their produce as cheaply as possible to European and American markets, while the hacienda owners were not interested in increasing efficiency because they had all the cheap labor they wanted. Small farmers used most of what they produced to meet their own subsistence needs and sold their scant surplus in local markets.

THE EMERGENCE OF HYBRID CULTURES AND CLASS STRATIFICATION

Clearly underlying Latin American social structure was the political ecology described above. Even though the native populations fell dramatically, especially in the first one hundred years after the invasion, they also began to grow again in the centuries that followed. Spanish immigration to the New World was fairly light, rarely accounting for more than 2 percent of the total population. Spanish men took Indian women as wives, and Indian maids and cooks were forced into concubinage. Sexual unions between Spanish men and Indian women led to the rapid rise of mixed blood or **mestizo** populations. By 1825, about a quarter of the population of Spanish-speaking America was **Ladino** (another term for mestizo). By 1950, the Ladinos were three-quarters of the population.

The hacienda and plantation social structures of colonial Latin America were highly stratified with a small number of Whites of European descent dominating a pyramid of Ladinos, Blacks, and Indians until early in the nineteenth century when the wars with Spain shifted power in favor of upper caste Ladinos (usually of light complexion). The Ladino population continued to expand and became numerically dominant at the turn of the twentieth century.

Where the Spaniards and Indians mixed cultures and genes, mestizo (Ladino) communities arose which have been called "open" communities. The Indian communities were largely "closed." It was and is the open communities that participate in the national political culture of Mexico, Central America, Bolivia, Peru, and Ecuador, while the closed communities by and large have historically not played a role in national political cultures of these same countries.

In those regions where both Indian and Ladino populations were substantial, mixed or **syncretic cultures** developed. A syncretic culture is one that combines elements of two or more cultures. An example would be the Tarascans of western Mexico in the state of Michoacan, who maintained their independence during Aztec times and have only incorporated those elements of modern Mexican culture that they wish to adopt. They are expert silversmiths and use their traditional skills to sell in the modern tourist markets. There are many examples of syncretic cultures throughout Mexico. The syncretic cultures, combining important elements of both Indian and Hispanic culture, are concentrated in the highlands of Mexico; however, some are found also in lowland regions in southern Mexico and northern Central America, and Andean Bolivia, Peru, and Ecuador. These cultures have usually retained Indian languages. The Spanish Crown allowed the Indians to organize themselves into special Indian towns with their own customs, which survived until the late nineteenth century. During the colonial period, Hispanic towns and Indian towns often coexisted in the same regions. For example, Puebla de los Angeles, just south of Mexico City, was built to be specifically Spanish with its own ayuntamiento or municipal council governed by the citizens of the city. However, it was not able to maintain its Span-

---

mestizo

Originally meant mixed blood, hybrid, usually of Indian and Spanish descent; often the term used instead of *Creole*, which refers to a hybrid language, and today meaning anyone of Indian and Spanish heritage

Ladino

Spanish term used in Guatemala meaning the same thing as mestizo or Creole

syncretic culture

A culture that combines elements from two or more cultures

ish purity and like all Mexican cultures is today a blend of the native and Spanish cultures. Only a few kilometers away were the mostly Indian cities of Cholula and Tlaxcala that were organized and run by Indian *"caciques"* (chiefs).

The independence of the Indian towns was never complete. Spanish institutions, particularly the courts, dominated Indian priests and caciques. Churches were forced on Indian towns, and the children of elite Indian families were taught the Spanish language and indoctrinated in the Catholic faith. The Catholic faith was universal to most regions of Latin America by the turn of the seventeenth century. The closer the Indian towns were to the Spanish towns, the greater was the acculturation to Spanish norms. Remote Indian towns and villages retained much more of their traditional cultures until relatively late in the nineteenth century, when nationalistic political movements precipitated a new wave of acculturation.

THE CARGO SYSTEM

cargo (fiesta) system

Refers to the civil-religious system of the highland Indian towns of Mexico, Guatemala, Bolivia, Peru, and Ecuador, where syncretic religions of mixed Catholic and traditional Indian practice redistribution of wealth and commit participants to membership in their closed communities

Today, in many of the Indian communities of both the highland Andes and Mesoamerica, men must serve their communities by passing through a series of offices, which usually involve considerable individual expenditure. This system is known as the **cargo** or **fiesta system,** or the civil-religious hierarchy. Both the structure and the functioning of the system have evolved since colonial times; and there are now, and probably have always been, differences in the system between communities as well. The most detailed description of a modern cargo system is that provided by Frank Cancian for the Maya community of Zinacantan in the highlands of Chiapas, Mexico (1965, 1992). The Spanish term *cargo* means burden; and basic to all variations of the cargo system is the expenditure of wealth in the sponsorship of religious fiestas in order to accumulate prestige within one's community. The cargo system has been compared to the potlatch of the Northwest Coast and the Big Man redistribution system of the Pacific Islands. Like these other redistribution festivals, the cargo system reduced the wealth of all in exchange for status in the community. In the nineteenth century and later, in many Indian communities, there existed a ladder-like arrangement of sets or levels of civil and religious offices, with many positions in the bottom sets and usually only two or a very few in the top sets.

alcalde

In the cargo system the highest rank, that of mayor

Adult married men were obliged to serve in alternating positions in the civil and the religious hierarchy of offices until they had served in the top sets. The period of service for each office was one year. The lower level cargos were usually low status community services such as acting as policemen at the fiestas, sweeping out the church, buying drinks for the elites to be used in celebrations, or for the women, preparing the clothing of the saints for holy days. The upper level cargos were those of managing the entire cargo system, and only a handful of men achieved this high status. The elite men usually alternated the religious cargos with civilian political positions, usually ending their careers as **alcaldes** or mayors at the top of a civilian cargo system. Considerable expense was involved in fulfilling the obligations of office, so most men did not serve in successive years but "rested" for several years in between cargos. Anthropologists, such as George Foster (1965), theorized that the cargo system acted as a leveling mechanism to make everyone equal (it did not), but also had the impact of producing an image of limited good, which acted against individuals trying to invest in their land because their profits would have to go into the cargo system. (In Chapter 7 we learned how, among the modern Maya, there are political differences between the Catholics who support the old cargo system and the evangelicals who do not.)

It has long been thought that the cargo system had its beginnings in the early colonial period when Spanish civil authorities imposed a set of civil offices on Indian communities and the Catholic Church established the *cofradía* (religious brotherhood) system to insure the proper care of church property and proper celebration of religious holidays. However, this is not a universally accepted view. Many have argued that the cargo system had pre-Hispanic antecedents that combined with the Spanish system imposed in colonial times. In colonial times, positions in the hierarchy of civil offices seem to have been separate from the religious brotherhoods, and the civil offices were usually occupied by the indigenous elites. The brotherhoods were entrusted with the sponsorship of religious fiestas, which were supported partly from the yield of corporate properties controlled by the brotherhoods and partly through the contributions of the members. Individual sponsorship of cargos does not appear to have been characteristic of the colonial period (Chance and Taylor 1985). Individual sponsorship emerged as the brotherhoods gradually lost control of corporate community lands in the late colonial period, when the protections provided by the Spanish Crown weakened.

Interestingly, as modern inflation has impacted indigenous communities, there has been a return in some communities to more collective forms of sponsorship of religious fiestas. Beverly Chiñas describes this shift for the Isthmus Zapotec of San Juan Evangelista (1973). Chiñas also notes that while, strictly speaking, it is a man who publicly serves a cargo, the Zapotec view is that the man and his wife, together, fulfill the responsibilities and that the man could not do it alone. For the Peruvian Andes, Catherine Allen notes that a man only accepts a cargo if his wife agrees because it is she who is responsible for providing the elaborate meals and the chicha (corn beer) that must be served on the ritual occasions throughout the year (1988). In Sonqo, the community Allen studied, a man and his wife are not considered to be fully adult members of their community until they have served one cargo.

The Breakdown of the Closed, Corporate Community

In addition to the different views on the origin and evolution of the cargo system noted above, there have been different interpretations of its function; and it is apparent that these closed communities may be disappearing. Originally, Eric Wolf (1959) argued that the cargo system functioned to redistribute wealth within the Indian community and to protect it from outside forces. However, Cancian (1965) conclusively showed for Zinacantan that the cargo system did not level wealth differences. Wealth differences continue to exist, and it is the well-to-do who can serve the higher-level cargos, with their enormous expenditure requirements for food and drink throughout the year, without going deeply into debt. Studies in many other communities have confirmed that while the cargo system may serve to redistribute some wealth in the community, it does not level wealth differences. Recent writers argue that these communities were never as closed as once thought; if they were, they have lost their closure in the last two decades. They argue that the cargo system was a means by which the Spanish Crown and the Church and, later, other outsiders exploited indigenous communities. Marvin Harris (1964) contends that the cargo system never protected Indian communities from exploitation by outsiders. In fact, much of what is needed to fulfill cargo obligations, especially alcoholic beverages, must be purchased from outsiders; thus, the system drained wealth from the community and enhanced the process of domination.

It is also obvious that the revolutionary violence in Guatemala, and economic pressures on the Maya of southern Mexico, have permanently changed whatever once might have been. Modern studies show that while the cargo system clearly developed as part of a process of domination and exploitation of Indian communities in the highlands of Mesoamerica and the Andes, it has been adapted by the plantation elites as a means to maintain political and economic domination. Research in recent years has shown that the debt developed by Indians as part of their cargo systems were purchased by agents working for lowland plantations, and that members of these communities were subsequently forced to work off their debts on the plantations. It has also come to light that the plantations often owned the lands of the Indian communities, and exchanged the use of these lands for working on the plantations (Smith 1982). Thus, the contrast between the closed corporate Indian communities and the open Creole rancherias is less clear than it once was. It is becoming clear that if these communities were once closed, modern elites, plantation owners, and tourists are rapidly opening them today. Their corporate social structure may be more a part of the past than the present.

The Period of Caudillos in Latin America: 1810–1930

Porfirismo

The liberal philosophy of Porfirio Dias, the dictator of Mexico from 1876–1911, of industrializing rapidly by opening countries to outside investment

The Wars of Independence in Latin America ushered in the *caudillos*, men of power, who opened the economies to outside market forces (particularly after 1870). This period lasted until the Great Depression of 1929. The economic philosophy of this time period is well illustrated by **Porfirismo**, named after the liberal Mexican dictator, Porfirio Diaz, who ran Mexico from 1876 to the Mexican Revolution of 1910. His point of view was that Latin American countries should open themselves to outside investment, migration, and scientific knowledge.

Indigenous peoples were viewed as economically backward and openly criticized. When possible, elite mestizo landowners who further expanded the hacienda and plantation systems of Latin America took their lands. The liberal dictators allowed land to become increasingly concentrated into the hands of the few. Concessions to foreign corporations became common; and in Chile, Peru, and Mexico, the control of mines passed from local families to British and American interests. In Mexico, twenty-nine companies obtained possession of over 27.5 million hectares, about 14 percent of the total land area of the Republic. One-fifth of Mexico was given away in this manner. In Mexico, northern Central America, and in the Andean countries, much of the land taken over by haciendas was the former ejido land of Indian corporate communities. Where such estates were not forcibly taken, they were broken up and individual families were given titles to the land. Once the Indians were

■Research in recent years has shown that the debt developed by Indians as part of their cargo systems were purchased by agents working for lowland plantations, and that members of these communities were subsequently forced to work off their debts on the plantations.

given individual plots of land, they could be made to sell those lands to pay off debts incurred by community cargo rituals (Wolf 1969, 16–17). Many of the landless peasants went to work on the growing railroads and in the mines and the new factories.

CLASS AND RITUAL KINSHIP

compadrazgo

Co-parenthood, the relationship between the parents of a child, the child's sponsors, and the child

compadre

A co-father or a co-parent generally; usually a wealthy relative, neighbor, or friend

comadre

A co-mother, the female sponsor of one's child, for example, at baptism

Crosscutting upper and lower classes is a ritual kinship relationship known as **compadrazgo** or godparenthood. This ritual relationship, with its origins in the sacraments of the Catholic Church, requires men and women to assume responsibility for the religious education of their baptized child. In the ritual, men and women are linked by common involvement in the baptism of a child, and call each other **compadre** or **comadre**. Sponsors are chosen by the parents of the child to oversee his or her spiritual growth. However, while the relationship of sponsorship for the child is crucial (the godfather-godchild relationship), the sociologically more important relationship in most of Latin America is that between the parents and the godparents. Between *compadres* (co-fathers) or *comadres* (co-mothers) of the same social class, the relationship may be one of drinking buddies or women helping each other in the harvest or in sewing projects. The tie of co-parenthood, then, links the two couples, not just the child and godparents. People who are very popular usually have many *compadres*.

Compadrazgo relationships may be between members of the same class, and as such are symmetrical; or they may be between upper and lower class families, in which case the relationship is asymmetrical. In the second type of relationship, called a patron-client relationship, the upper class compadre is always the sponsor of a lower class child. The wealthy compadre is expected to help the family of his *compadre* of the lower class, as well as his godchildren, never the other way around. Caudillos, rich landowners, powerful politicians, and wealthy industrialists often have dozens, or hundreds, of compadres whom they help out in exchange for political support, forming one of the many patron-client relationships found in Latin America. The help for the lower class compadre and his family (and godson) can be in the form of education, health maintenance, or financial help during crises. Typically, modern politicians have many *compadres* in the working classes whom they depend on for political support (Wolf and Hansen 1972, 134).

In one study done by Robert Murphy of the rubber-gathering town of Ita at the mouth of the Amazon River, rubber gatherers, whose lives were very unstable, had storekeepers as their compadres or patrones. The storekeepers depended on their lower class compadres to gather rubber for them, which they then sold upriver for a profit, and in exchange granted them credit in their stores (which is also a form of debt-peonage, cited in Wolf and Hansen 1972). Hacienda owners also typically develop compadre relationships with colonos living on their estates.

LATIN AMERICAN SEXUAL RELATIONS: MACHISMO, VIRGINITY, AND PROSTITUTION

In traditional Latin American society, it was common for members of the elite classes to acquire another wife or wives. Once married, a man would become attached to a young woman, usually of a lower social class, and would set her up in another house or apartment, taking care of her financial needs. The man was responsible for taking care of his mistress' children. Thus, polygyny, the marriage of a man to more than one woman was common, although not legally recognized. Because members of the lower classes could not afford this luxury, this de facto polygyny was primarily an upper class trait. While the Catholic Church attempted to impose its morality on Latin American men, male chastity was and is ignored and scorned, an attitude that is part of the **machismo** complex.

The machismo complex has a second side, however. For, in addition to a man being expected to act like a man by having many mistresses and prostitute lovers, he was also expected to stand up to others who might wish to exploit his own female relatives and friends. His mother and his sister were sacred, beyond reproach; pistol duel, knife thrust, or fists could meet any insult towards them. This complex code is expressed in many **charro** folk songs in Mexico, where the women of his own class are beyond his grasp, for they must be protected and treated with respect, while the women of the bars and of the night are fair targets. However, the women of the lower classes also have their fathers, sons, and male relatives, who must protect them, adding up to codes of behavior which produce, even today, considerable interclass conflict.

Reflecting the feminine side of the machismo complex is what Emilio Willems refers to as the **virginity complex** (Willems 1975). This is centered on the upper class idea that the virginity of unmarried (and upper class) females should be preserved at all cost through segregation of the sexes, chaperonage, and closely controlled courtship. Men felt that to marry a girl who had lost her virginity would make them appear foolish. After marriage, a woman's behavior was socially restricted by the husband's strict control over her social activities. The wife was expected to remain home, to raise her children, to reject any advances by other men, and to participate in elite social activities, while remaining in the background with other women supervising cooks, maids, and the household staff. She was also expected to look the other way when her own husband paraded his machismo through the brothels and had his little affairs with the cook, the maid, and the school girl on the other side of town. These escapades would inevitably produce gossip between networks of upper class women, and they are the subject of many novels and plays. Within the husband's male networks, the same activities brought approval, a clap on the back, and offers of drinks. Yet, within the man's household, the woman's commitment to family would bring the man's friends to compliment her virtues, emphasizing the theme of the woman as mother.

Lower class sexual ideas were more relaxed, and lower class men did not attach the same importance to virginity. Prostitution was and is an answer to the expectations of machismo and the virginity complex of the elite and the lower sexual mores of the lower class. The virginity complex and the prostitution of lower class women are a symbolic antithesis, but in curious ways are not really that opposite from each other. From Boys' Town in Matamoros' Mexico to the red light districts in Medellin, Colombia, and Buenos Aires in Argentina, the practice of prostitution is widespread throughout Latin America; however, prostitutes are not viewed as immoral degenerates, as happens in the United States. Americans find the acceptance of prostitution in Latin America to be at odds with their own values, but Latin Americans find the puritanical anti-prostitution laws in the United States to be a contradiction to the open sexuality of Americans.

Prostitution has a long and complex history in Spain, Portugal, and in Latin America; and it is not always what it appears to be, for it too is tied to the virginity complex. While the elite women of society held the prostitute in low regard, in men's songs, especially the Mexican **rancheras**, and **corridas** (folk ballads), the prostitute is often the emotional and brave antithesis of the coldly virginal daughters of the elite. She is the woman of passion, the fallen but meritorious woman, often standing by her beloved who may be a revolutionary, warrior, soldier, scoundrel, or general, while the man's calculating wife spends her time trying to trap her amorous husband or planning on ways of moving the status of her family up in the world of social elites. Novels, short stories, and today, telenovelas (the Latin

---

machismo

The Latin American expectation that a man will exploit those women he can and protect those he must which is based on the term macho, meaning strong male

charro

A Mexican cowboy dance or the name for the Mexican cowboy

virginity complex

The Latin American expectation that women will maintain their virginity at all cost and found primarily among the elite classes

rancheras

A popular form of Mexican folk music associated with the western frontier, particularly the state of Jalisco

corrida

A Latin American dance associated with the music played during bullfights, called the *paso doble* (two step)

■Once married, wives were expected to look the other way when her own husband visited brothels and had affairs.

American version of the soap opera), tell the stories of women who have fallen on hard times, who are virginal in mind but must prostitute themselves to make ends meet (thus the Bezit's opera about Spain, *Carmen*, with its prostitute cigarette-making heroine). In these stories, women often support their illegitimate children, who are raised by other kinswomen, such as the prostitute's sisters, in distant cities. The mother's shame and her profession is kept a secret, as is her identity, and she is often identified as the maiden aunt.

The ambivalence between men and their wives, and men and their prostitute lovers, is often symbolized by the image of Mary Magdalene, the fallen woman forgiven by Christ, who is also considered a saint and who washed the body of the dead Christ. The identities of the two Marys are often run together, and the symbolic qualities of prostitutes and virgins have been central themes for centuries. One very famous opera that captures much of the heroics and ambivalence of marriage and loose women, rigid codes, and the men and women who dare challenge them, is *Don Giovanni*, by Mozart. This tale of an Italian count could take place in Madrid, in Mexico City, or in Buenos Aires.

While the growing independence of women and their ability to find employment has produced a challenge to machismo, as well as the virgin complex, daily stories in Latin American newspapers of real life Don Juans, sainted prostitutes, cold wives, and vengeance make one realize that these codes of behavior are not going to disappear overnight. In early 1997, a chauffeur was arrested in Mexico City for killing his rich employer and wife in retribution for the seduction of his sister, a maid in the rich man's home.

RELIGION AND COMMUNITY

The values that formed the institutions of religiosity in Latin America from the sixteenth century until today range from the formal hierarchies of the Roman Catholic Church to the individualistic shamanism of the Amazonian tribalist or highland Andean llama herder or the Candoble of the Bahaian spiritualist. Between these two poles ranged other formal and informal institutions that framed the religious behavior of the peoples of Latin America. The writer, Carlos Fuentes, points to Iberian Catholicism, the religion of the Spaniards who migrated from Spain to the New World, as the font of religion for the Latin societies of the New World. It was composed of medieval cults such as the cult of the saints, the fiesta complex (which resembles the cargo complex, but dates back to medieval times), and religious **sodalities** (associations of men and women which cut across families' ties and bound both to the church). These were transplanted to the New World where they found fertile ground. One characteristic of medieval religiosity was the unconditional and spontaneous acceptance of doctrine and sacraments. Impiety, atheism, and agnosticism were inconceivable (Willems 1975).

In addition to the formal hierarchy of the Catholic Church and its doctrines, and perhaps more important, were Iberian folk beliefs such as witchcraft, fear of the evil eye, werewolves, and devil spirits of the cold night. In addition, numerous folk religious beliefs of the New World and of Africa became part of the syncretic religions of Latin America. In early December 1531, on Tepeyac Hill near Mexico City, Tonantzin, the Aztec goddess, was transformed into the Virgin of Guadalupe and appeared to the shepherd, Juan Diego, carrying miraculous roses in winter. Nothing has proved as consoling, unifying, and worthy of respect as the figure of the Virgin of Guadalupe in Mexico. She became the Virgin of La Caridad de Cobre in Cuba, and the Virgin of Coromoto in Venezuela. Paralleling the female goddess, Quetzalcoatl, the feathered serpent, the priest of knowledge and self-sacrifice evolved into Jesus Christ. According to Carlos Fuentes, it is impossible to tell who is being worshipped in the baroque altars of Puebla, Oaxaca, and Tlaxcala: Christ or Quetzalcoatl (Fuentes 1992, 146).

Christ, in turn, was transformed into many Christs, just as there were many Quetzalcoatls. There is a Cristo de Entierro, the buried Christ; there is Cristo de Saquipulas, or the sacrificed Christ; and there is Christ in heaven. While the Latin American Christs are dead or in agony, the Virgin is surrounded by perpetual glory and adoration. The attitude towards the Virgin Mary is one of celebration, while that toward Christ is more profoundly ambiguous, a combination of suffering, sacrifice, and forgiveness.

The churches were organized around male and female sodalities that handled distinct tasks of the yearly round of fiestas with their spectacular services and processions. Among the middle and upper classes, the belief in the cult of the saints was elaborately developed. The effigies of the patron saints, Christ, and the Virgin Mary were carried on the backs of men and women through the streets of Mexico City, Guatemala City, San Salvador, Bogota, Medellin, Caracas, and other cities of Latin America. To different saints were attributed different powers. For example, *Nuestro Señor de los Temblores* of Lima and Cuzco, who is Jesus Christ of Earthquakes, protected the faithful against the agitations of the mountains (Willems 1975).

The wealthy, fearing for their mortal souls, donated money and property to the Church and to the associated brotherhoods and sisterhoods (sodalities). They financed the construction of the beautiful temples of Latin America. In addition, hospitals, usually attached to churches, were also financed in this fashion. In this way, the church became very wealthy, often loaning money (with interest) and serving as the premier banking institution.

Church and state were closely linked. During the colonial period, appointments by the crown had to be confirmed by the Vatican. In post-colonial times, highly placed political authorities were closely connected by kinship to church authorities. There is an old saying in Mexico that in the most aristocratic families one brother was the landowner, one brother was the general, and one brother was the archbishop. The alliance of church and state was highly developed, and both estates reinforced each other except during periods of revolution when the relationships between church and state were severed. There were

sodality

An association based on common interest; in tribal society cross cuts clans and other unilineal lineages; in modern society, any type of fraternity or sorority based on common interest, such as male or female groups in Latin America supporting the Catholic Church and its religious celebrations

schisms in the church that often broke into open conflict. Native-born priests identified themselves with Creole interests, and the wars of revolution produced a conflict between native clergy and Iberian clergy. The Church also engaged in commercial enterprises, and anti-clerical factions wanted to confiscate its wealth, as occurred after the revolutions against Spain. The Church only regained its power and prestige in the post-revolutionary years through persuasion and compromise.

In more recent times, the schism in the Church is between the conservative views of the priests who represent the views of the upper classes and those who espouse **liberation theology**. Liberation theology is a largely socialist movement within the Catholic Church of priests who identify with the human rights needs of the working classes. Liberation theology argues that the Church should intervene to prevent human rights abuses, while the conservatives argue that the role of the Church is to save human souls, not to interfere in politics— a blatantly hypocritical position. In very recent years, many Latin Americans have broken with Church doctrine to create new religious movements tied to **evangelical protestantism**. A more conservative movement than liberation theology, evangelicals argue that one should not politicize religion, and that socialism is evil. Evangelical Protestantism has become a threat to Church interests, and government authorities, particularly in Central America, have persecuted leaders.

liberation theology

A political movement within the Catholic Church in Latin America supporting the interests of the poor and often associated with a socialist point of view

evangelical protestantism

A religious movement in Latin America which offers an alternative to the Catholic Church in the form of Protestantism and often has a conservative political perspective, the opposite of liberation theology

Dependency, Revolution, and the Rise of State Capitalism

The Depression of the 1930s brought about the disintegration of the power of the liberal caudillos, which was based on a coalition of landowning elites, who controlled exports, and commercial importers; both benefited from low tariffs. Before the 1930s, the liberal caudillos with their patron-client political systems ran Latin America as personal fiefdoms. Attempts to compare these systems to feudal European societies are common, but the two systems are not analogous. Latin American societies were not feudal, socialist, or capitalist. They were highly bureaucratic and centralized, like their colonial antecedents, but run by caudillos, who ruled by the powers of their armies and personalities. One writer, Claudio Veliz, has described these societies as centralist, and argues that the tradition of centralism dates back to the Spanish colonial period, with its large and expensive bureaucracies. However, the one-man, personalistic, caudillo-based centralism shifted in the 1930s to a new type of political economy, one based on the impersonal technocrat at the head of an enormous state apparatus: state capitalism.

State capitalism was Latin America's response to dependency, much in the same way that socialism in China and Russia were responses to the same threat. Yet state capitalism is not to be confused with socialism, for it has different roots, as will be described. As the importance of industry increased, trade unions developed power and the industrial working class became a dominant force, particularly in countries with large industrial bases, such as Mexico, Argentina, Chile, Venezuela, Colombia, and Brazil. A wave of political movements, mostly with leftist rhetoric, supporting state corporatist capitalism swept Latin America in the 1930s; but these were not uniform and were very weak in the countries of Central

America and in the Andean countries of Peru, Bolivia, and Ecuador (where the quasi-slave labor of large Indian populations undercut the development of trade unions).

After the 1930s the economies of Latin America, primarily in industrial countries, have been called corporatist or state capitalist, both terms having roughly the same meaning. The highly centralist caudillo governments of the pre-1930s, with their personalized one-man rule, gave way to centralized governments. Ostensibly these were organized by political parties, but really controlled by faceless bureaucrats who remained in power decade after decade while new elections changed the apparent leaders, the presidents and the governors of the states, but really changed little. The state capitalist systems were a response to dependency theory, which was primarily developed by Latin American economists to explain the poverty of the Latin American countries. The dependistas (dependency theorists) explained that as long as Latin America had to compete with European and American corporations, Latin American economies would continue to suffer the trade imbalances fostered by exports of raw materials from haciendas, mines, and plantations.

It is easy to confuse Latin American state capitalism with socialism or Asian systems of the same name, but they differ in certain key respects. One of these is the importance of trade unions, which are often part of the corporatist structures of Latin American societies. Trade unions are often illegal or barely tolerated in capitalist Asian countries, and Asian systems tend not to be corporatist. Latin American political economies are also not socialist because they do not have centralized state planning. The easiest way to conceptualize corporatism is to think of a giant political pyramid with every interest group having a niche, with its own defined rights, ranks, and privileges. The pyramid has cleavages running vertically: church, state bureaucracy, industrialists, the army, trade unions, peasant unions, political parties—all with their specialist interests and privileges informally defined, and each one in turn stratified by wealth into a class of elites and non-elites. The corporatist model clearly depends on the colonial model with its social classes and communities, each clearly defined according to royal prerogatives; however, this model has been updated to deal with the complexities of the twentieth century, primarily by the addition of the faceless technocrat or bureaucrat. This special class, which is not to be confused with the constantly changing politicians, is a permanent group which runs the economies by adjusting import/export tariffs, duties, borrowed money, taxes, and other aspects of the economies so that they will continue to function decade after decade.

In the corporatist states, trade unions, businessmen, the military and governments came together, often under one party states (PRI in Mexico, Peronismo in Argentina) or multi-party democracies (Colombia, Venezuela, Brazil, Chile, Venezuela) to protect nascent industries against outside competition. This was done by erecting high tariff walls, Latin America's answer to dependency theory, and giving the control of business organizations to the state. Often the old industrialists of the pre-1930s period became the managers of state run enterprises in the period that followed. They and their families benefited by the protection of the state and by the many perquisites extended to them, such as free university education in state-run universities for their children. The university students, their jobs secured by their parents and the state, often paraded as Marxists for their few years at the university and then silently replaced their fathers as leaders in state run businesses (or as faceless bureaucrats). Business elites married into the families of well-known politicians, and the two groups became indistinguishable through the fifty years during which state capitalism dominated. Outside business groups, such as transnational corporations, were only brought into the state capitalist enterprises to the degree that they agreed to protectionist state policies and to dominant ownership by the state. Thus, we have the curious example of the supposedly German run Volkswagen of Puebla, Mexico, whose trade unions could strike and close down the city of Puebla with impunity, while the governor of the state would declare that there was nothing he could do, and the managers of the plant would stand around with their hands in their pockets.

Unfortunately, the rural poor, as well as the urban poor, were locked out of the new political machines, or politicians in standard patron-client relationships manipulated them. In response, during the 1960s, the disenfranchised poor became involved in radical political movements to overthrow the corporate state and replace it with a socialist state representing all classes. These movements were countered by state terrorism until the early 1980s. By then, most of the radical leaders had disappeared, the victims of faceless and nameless death squads.

The development of state capitalism cannot be understood as a movement of the left or of the right. In certain countries, leftist trade unions were dominant; in others, rightist business interests. Generally, the more industrial the society, the greater was the influence of the left; and the more agricultural the society, the greater was the influence of the right. The 1930s was a time of seething discontent. New political groups made radical promises and many new political parties developed: social democrats, communists, syndicalists, business groups, student associations, fascists, and corporatists—all attempted to change the structure of society. The elites attempted to accommodate the old to the new. Yet, in the end, the corporatist state grew larger and more powerful.

Important economic changes occurred during the phase of state corporatism. States expanded to include new industries, which became part of state structure. Heavy industry was built up and was subsidized or owned by the state, particularly energy production. Prosperity increased during World War II because the countries of the core shifted to manufacturing war material, and Latin American countries began to make their own goods and brought about the growth of a new industrially oriented middle class. Political instability continued after the war, but so did economic growth. The **Gross Domestic Product (GDP)** rose. In addition, there were many changes with important political implications: Literacy went up, life expectancy increased, new transportation was constructed, the middle sectors grew, organized labor became stronger, peasants migrated to cities, the rural proletariat became more organized and more vocal, social problems multiplied, and workers demanded more goods and services. The state grew proportionately to meet the demands of all sectors of society that had been incorporated into the state.

However, state capitalism has not worked well. Latin American countries, borrowing to keep the business enterprises functioning, have approached bankruptcy; and control by elites has led to revolution. Overall, there is a fragmented social order in Latin America—the old corporatist pyramid no longer works well. During the 1960s and 1970s, Latin America became, increasingly, a conflict-ridden society with numerous groups challenging the power of elites. New elites, with models borrowed from the Asian tigers, are insisting on privatizing industry, introducing real free markets, and reducing the power of the state through democratic reform. Russia is also experimenting with these two transitions toward capitalism and democracy, but from the very different base of state socialism. Mexico is battling to keep the two transitions on course. Threats to the survival of both countries are daily newspaper fare.

Gross Domestic Product (GDP)

The value of all final goods and services produced within the borders of a country, usually calculated on the basis of a common currency such as the U.S. dollar

Case
Study

Invention of the Corporatist State in Mexico

The liberal caudillo, Porfirio Diaz, ruled Mexico from 1876 until 1911 when, with the Mexican Revolution a few months old, he resigned and fled to Paris where he died four years later at the age of 85. Before he fled, he stated that the revolutionaries had let a tiger loose. For six years, revolutionary armies fought each other and destroyed the Mexican economy in the process. The Mexican Revolution had two storm centers; one in the southern region around Morelos led by Emiliano Zapata, and one centered in the northern state of Chihuahua, led by Doroteo Arango, otherwise known as Pancho Villa. The southern storm center was a region of hacienda agriculture where expanding estates had driven small holders off their own lands and forced many to become wage workers on lands of the elite (Wolf 1969, 27). Villa and Zapata represented claims for revolutionary social change, but more moderate forces became dominant. A constitutional assembly was called at Queretaro at the end of 1916. The writing of the resulting constitution was dominated by radical General Obregon who called for secular education, separation of church and state, liquidation of the haciendas and plantations, land reform, wide ranging labor legislation, and an assertion of the eminent domain of the nation over resources (Wolf 1969, 43).

Obregon's constitution was an explicit statement of state capitalism, but it existed in name only until 1929, when President Plutarco Calles organized the National Revolutionary Party (now known as the Partido Revolucionario Institucional, or PRI, the Institutional Revolutionary Party), which has ruled Mexico since that time. The PRI was founded as a modern mass based party with a structure radically unlike nineteenth century parties. Yet, Mexico foundered until 1934 when General Lázaro Cárdenas, a new and radically leftist president, moved the country towards the left and initiated land reform and labor organization on a massive scale. He dismantled the power of the hacienda owners and distributed hacienda lands to the peasantry. Cárdenas nationalized the railroads, the oil fields, and many foreign firms without compensating the foreign owned corporations. Although he ignored the anti-clerical laws of the preceding Calles regime, he maintained a separation of church and state and encouraged the teaching of atheism in the schools. Mexico was the first Latin American society to organize itself explicitly around a corporatist model, and its major symbol became the great pyramid of the sun at Teotihuacan.

The ability of the PRI to survive was dependent on its ability to reward supporters with jobs in government-run industries, and in government itself (federal, state, and municipal). By 1970, government, in its many forms, accounted for close to 75 percent of all jobs. As long as Mexico was able to borrow money, it was able to expand economically. Until 1980, Mexico's economy grew at rates ranging between 6 to 8 percent per year; however, in the early 1980s, international banks refused to loan more money to Mexico, and its economy went into a tailspin. The rate of inflation soared. The rationale for public support of the PRI was weakened (Purcell 1992, 54). In addition, by 1980, it was apparent that state capitalism was exacerbating the wealth differential between the elites and masses. Despite all of the rhetoric, the rich got richer and the poor got poorer—and Mexico sank deeper and deeper into debt.

President Miguel de la Madrid Hurtado took office in 1982. De la Madrid opened the economy, determined to bring Mexico into the global economy by becoming a signer of the General Agreement on Tariffs and Trade (GATT). He also ended the government's anti-American rhetoric, which had dominated Mexico for decades. The immediate impact of his policies was to almost scuttle the 1988 election of his handpicked successor, Carlos Salinas de Gortari. Many former PRI supporters voted for the left-of-center candidate, Cuauhtémoc Cárdenas Solorozano (the son of General Lázaro Cárdenas, the President of Mexico from 1934 to 1940) because of de la Madrid's austerity measures. Cárdenas had created the PRD (The Revolutionary Democratic Party) as a leftist and populist split off from PRI. Strongly supporting Cárdenas were PRI-affiliated labor union workers whose jobs were threatened (Purcell 1992, 54–55).

As we read in Chapter 6, the well-intended reforms of both NAFTA and democratization are having unintended consequences in the lowlands of Chiapas with the rise of the Zapatista movement. Similar political movements are occurring elsewhere, many of them advocating a restoration of state capitalism or a move toward socialism. The rewards of capitalism and democracy may be long in coming, or they may not come at all; the social structure of Mexico has deep roots in exploitation and in class stratification. To change these structures is not going to be an overnight affair, but the changes that are happening in Mexico are widespread in Latin America. At least Mexico no longer has to be concerned about the power structure being in the hands of a landed elite, as is still true in Central America.

From Caudillismo to State Terrorism in Central America

The problems with caudillos in Central America were even more severe than in Mexico. Unlike Mexico, there was very little industrialization in Central America until quite late in the 1920s and 1930s; and even then, industries were limited to clothing, shoes, and concrete. The economies of the Central American countries, particularly Honduras, Guatemala, El Salvador, and Nicaragua, were based on agricultural exports from plantations, many of which were controlled by foreigners or wealthy elites. Communication and transportation systems (telegraph, railroads, etc.) were in foreign hands. Labor organizations were extremely weak and kept that way. The countries tended to be made up primarily of the extremely rich (landowners) and extremely poor (workers of the land and landless workers). There was a small middle class of service personnel, but it tended to identify with the conservative landowners (Woodward 1976). The indigenous peoples of the region were left to fend for themselves when they were not being actively oppressed as in El Salvador in the 1930s.

At a time when Mexico was redistributing agricultural land and expropriating the oil lands of Americans and foreign investors, the elites of the Central American republics were finding ways to concentrate even more agricultural land and other resources into their own hands. During the first half of this century, the transitions to modernization became increasingly more blocked by the oligarchies. Those arguing for an equitable distribution of resources were accused of being communists and persecuted (Blackman, et al. 1986).

During the 1930s, the Central American pattern of land-owning caudillos dramatically changed due to the world depression. New and powerful labor unions developed in the agricultural sector as the wages of agricultural workers plummeted. A war in Spain between Francisco Franco's fascists and leftist forces alerted the Central American oligarchy to the possibility that radical social movements might occur in the Central American republics. New right wing dictators, such as Jorge Ubico in Guatemala, Tiburcio Carías Andino in Honduras, General Maximiliano Hernández Martínez in El Salvador, and Luis Somoza in Nicaragua came to power. In short, in the 1930s, Mexico and the Central American republics went in opposite political directions: Mexico to the far left and the Central American republics to the far right (Blackman et al. 1986, Booth 1990, Baloyra 1990, Ebel 1990).

Following World War II, a radical change in Central America in the direction of liberal democracy appeared eminent. In country after country, with the exception of Nicaragua (where the Somoza clan clung to power), the right wing dictators of the Depression were overthrown. During the late 1940s, labor movements and left wing political movements grew, infiltrating the universities and the governments. The landed oligarchies found their positions of total control threatened.

The pressing demand of government critics in Central America (and Cuba in the Caribbean) was land reform. Most of the land had been alienated from Indian and mestizo farmers, creating a gigantic rural proletariat. Workers in agriculture were reduced to a serf-like existence on the haciendas and plantations. Critics compared their situation to nineteenth century slavery in the Deep South of the United States.

The owners of the land, like the plantation owners of the Deep South, tended to be absentee landowners. They lived in the central cities and visited their estates every two or three weeks to confer with largely illiterate administrators. Only profits interested these owners, and they invested little in the regions from which they took their livelihood. Many of these lands, particularly on the south coast of Central America, are among the richest agricultural lands in the world. Colonos and wandering landless laborers worked the estates of the rich for as little as a dollar a day. The wealthy lived in luxury in Guatemala City, Antigua, Tegucigalpa, Managua, and other large cities (Smith 1982, 1985).

Revolutionary movements broke out after World War II, not unlike those in Mexico two decades before. Rural and urban guerrillas battled right-wing governments for the next half-century. In two instances, Cuba in 1959 and Nicaragua in 1979, revolutionaries came to power. The Cuban revolution is the only one to have survived. The Sandinistas lost the election of 1990 to Violeta Barrios de Chamorro and her party, UNO, in Nicaragua.

Today, without American support for right-wing governments, and without Soviet support for left-wing movements, the violence in Central America abated. Left-wing political movements and right-wing governments came to uneasy truces, both sides realizing that their goals were not obtainable. Yet the conditions that produced the conflicts remain. The vast majority of the people of Central America live in grinding poverty. Unemployment remains high, the landless are still landless, crime has increased steadily, and corruption remains a major problem. In addition, there is notable ecological degradation with forests destroyed, land and water poisoned, and soil eroded.

Democratization and Privatization in South America

Until the early 1980s, military governments that used state terrorism dominated Brazil, Argentina, and Chile, as well as many other South American countries. They are now moving in a radically new direction, trying to follow Mexico's example and abandon state capitalism. In Brazil, the military returned to the sidelines and allowed elections, but state capitalism continued under civilian rule for almost another decade. Politicians were big spenders who dramatically boosted public sector pay. Inflation reached 227 percent in 1985, and was brought down by a price freeze; however, by 1990 it had reached almost 1500 percent. A spurt of economic growth was brought to a complete standstill, where it stayed for the next three years.

In 1990, Brazil's fortune appeared to improve. On March 15th, a new president, Mr. Fernando Collor, the governor of the tiny state of Alagoas, promised economic and political reforms. He sounded the same tune as Salinas de Gortari in Mexico. He had triumphed over Francisco da Lula Silva, a socialist, with an anti-socialist campaign, much to the shock of the left. However, halfway through his administration, he was impeached for corruption, and his place taken by his vice-president, Itamar Franco. President Franco appointed, as his finance minister, Henrique Cardoso. Mr. Cardoso was famed as one of Latin America's foremost leftist sociologists. Cardoso's early writings were the heart of dependency theory, and his theory was the basis for much of the state corporatist responses throughout Latin America. It came as something of a shock when, in 1992, Cardoso pushed through the legislature a set of policies which favored private industry and leveled inflation. He developed a new currency, the *real* (replacing the cruzeiro), and prices, which had been rising at 30–50 percent a month, slowed to single numbers.

Finance minister Cardoso ran for the presidency of Brazil in October 1994, on an anti-corporatist, anti-state capitalist platform. His chief opponent was Francisco de Lula Silva, who clearly expected to win by a landslide with his socialist platform. Much to Lula Silva's stunned surprise, Cardoso won easily with 54 percent of the vote, twice Lula's share.

Ecological
Maladaptation

Destruction of the Rainforest in the Amazon Basin

The Amazon rainforest is the largest in the world. Covering about 7 million square kilometers (about 2.7 million square miles—slightly smaller than the contiguous United States), it makes up about a third of South America. However, new development projects are destroying this rainforest at an alarming rate. During the mid 1990s more than twenty thousand square miles of rainforest were being cleared annually to make way for farmland and pasture land for ranches (DeBlij and Muller 1997, 255).

The slash and burn agriculture, traditionally practiced by the indigenous peoples of the area, was sustainable because of the small scale of such operations. Temporary stress on one part of the system by small groups of people was followed by long periods of abandonment in which the forest would regenerate itself. These soils cannot support the kind of massive development projects that are now common in the Amazon. Access to these remote areas has been made relatively easy by the rapid expansion of Brazilian highways, which have penetrated the Amazon with a vengeance. Almost two hundred thousand settlers move into this region annually.

The military rulers of Brazil, who are now out of favor and out of power, decided to open the great Amazon Basin in the 1960s. Brazil borrowed large sums of money in order to invest in the Amazon, particularly in the construction of the Trans Amazon highway. Farmers were given low interest loans to move into the Amazon to build farms. Many farmers experimented with expensive fertilizers, pesticides, herbicides, and other chemicals to increase productivity and maintain soil fertility (and continue to do so), putting many into debt. The chemi-

cals do considerable ecological damage, contaminating rivers, streams, and subsurface aquifers.

The process is ongoing and continues the cycle of exploitation. Settlers move into the Amazon basin, lured by the cheap land prices and promises of fertile land. However, within two to three years, the soil is depleted and sold to ranchers who can grow pasture grasses for their herds. This leads to a concentration of most of the land in the hands of the large agribusinesses (deBlij and Muller 1997, 255), as the small subsistence farmers keep clearing new areas in search of fertile soil. It has also led to the destruction of the forest habitat of indigenous peoples throughout the Amazon.

In addition to the land development schemes denuding the tropical rainforest, mining and logging concerns are also active in projects throughout the Amazon. The largest and most rapidly developing subregion is the seven States of the Amazon, where population has tripled since 1980 to about 1.5 million. In this region, a huge project, known as the Grande Carajas Project in eastern Pará State has transformed the environment from a tropical rainforest to an industrial complex. This project was designed to exploit one of the world's largest known deposits of iron ore in the Serra dos Carajás hills. It includes a mining complex, the Tucuruí Dam, and a 535-mile (860 km) railroad to the Atlantic port of Sao Luis. The infrastructure built for the mining operation, and the workers it has attracted, has led to a related development of the nearby city of Manaus, which is now a major industrial center, specializing in the production of electronic goods. (DeBlij and Muller 1997, 255)

A second leading development scheme is the Polonoreste Plan located five hundred miles to the southwest of Grande Carajas along the 1500-mile long highway BR 364 corridor that parallels the Bolivian border. Most of the settlement is within Rondônia State. This project is appealing to plantation workers who have lost their jobs due to mechanization, wealthy ranchers and agribusiness, and subsistence farmers. These groups have been fighting for land in this region, while the Brazilian government is trying to establish some land reform policies.

In the meantime, the rainforest continues to disappear. While this pattern of rainforest destruction is worldwide, the problem is most severe in the Amazon, accounting for over half of all tropical deforestation. Massive rainforest destruction causes the extinction of plant species that could be useful to cure human diseases, alters patterns of rainfall and has a climatic impact worldwide, and exposes fragile tropical soils to massive erosion. It is clear that the development underway in the Amazon is not sustainable and that continued destruction of the tropical forest will indeed have global consequences.

Cardoso rightly singled out formal indexation of wages as a major reason for inflation, and attempted to stop it. However, Cardoso ran into significant opposition by the state corporatist bureaucrats and politicians who manned the Brazilian political machine. Brazil remains far behind its neighbors, Chile and Argentina; that is stimulating the Brazilian electorate to examine the economic advances of these two Latin American tigers.

In Argentina, the military returned the government to the civilians in 1983 after torturing and executing over twenty-five thousand civilians. In the election of 1989, the government decided to allow the Peronist Party to compete; and Carlos Saul Menem, leader of the Peronist Justicialist Party, won but did a very un-Peronist thing. He opened markets, reduced tariffs, and privatized the economy. Basically, Menem jettisoned fifty years of Peronist corporatism. The story in Chile is almost identical to Argentina's. General Pinochet, who overthrew Marxist President Salvator Allende in 1973, had decided to rule in Chile until 1999; however, a plebescite in 1989 showed that the majority of the Chilean people were tired of his one man dictatorship. On December 14, 1989, in a multi-party election, Chile elected Patricio Alwyn as president and state terrorism came to an end. Alwyn, like Saul Menem, decided to follow Mexico's lead. The problems of inflation, international debt, and the crimes committed by the Pinochet regime against its own people, posed major hurdles for the Alwyn administration. However, having finally achieved democracy after a sixteen-year dictatorship, the Chilean people have been moving through the economic and political transitions successfully.

Similar changes have occurred in most of the countries of South America. Suddenly, democratic capitalism is bursting out all over. Are the new governments really democratic, however? The reason for the state terrorism in the first place was to destroy the left wing, and it was thoroughly destroyed. Are the countries of South America practicing true democracy, or is it a fiction as in the past? At the present time, it appears that elections are open and that mass, participatory democracy is a fact of life. Only time will tell what will happen after the left reorganizes.

Indigenous Strategies of Cultural Survival

As mentioned at the beginning of this chapter, Latin America has more surviving, distinct indigenous cultures than any of the other world regions. Within the past twenty-five years there has been a dramatic rise in the formation of indigenous organizations whose purposes are to negotiate with the nation-states of Latin America for various legal rights and protections—especially land rights—and to protect and preserve, and in some instances rejuvenate, native cultures and traditions. The strengthening of ethnic and cultural identity has become an important universal survival strategy for Latin American indigenous peoples from Mexico to Chile. Native peoples have renewed their efforts to control the processes of domination and exploitation that have beleaguered them for the past five hundred years. In many countries, such as Ecuador and Panama, the various indigenous groups have formed countrywide, pan-indigenous organizations to promote the welfare of their communities; and some native organizations have formed networks of links with their compatriots in other countries, including the United States, and with sympathetic human rights organizations.

Beyond this, the responses of particular indigenous cultures to renewed oppression from territorial states in the late twentieth century have varied considerably. These varied responses we term "strategies for cultural survival." They range from the peaceful, and effective so far, political negotiations of the Kuna with the government of Panama to religious

Case
Study

The Drug Trade in Latin America

As revolutions came to an end in Central America and political and economic changes occurred in Brazil, Argentina, and Chile, they brought an end to state terrorism and ushered in democracy in other regions of South America. Drugs, terrorism, and revolution came to be tied together in a complex web, corrupting governments and threatening the way of life of peasants and indigenous peoples.

The smuggling of drugs into the United States is a relatively young enterprise. In the 1960s, the primary drug imported into the United States from Latin America was marijuana. Few hard drugs were smuggled across the Mexican border until the 1970s, when Americans began to import cocaine and other hard drugs. Smuggling has always been a part of life in the Colombian Andes. Since 1979, however, it has evolved into narcoterrorism, corrupting many officials at a time when the Colombian government is attempting to follow the leadership of Mexico, Brazil, Argentina, and Chile.

The Medellin drug cartel was organized in 1979. Personal armies were organized by the Medellín cartel made up of *sicarios*, hit men, who used motorcycles and small but powerful machine guns to assassinate designated enemies of the cartel. Within a very short time, the city of Cali, in the southern Department of Cauca, developed its own cartel for largely similar reasons. A third cartel, known as the Atlantic or coastal cartel, also evolved in Cartagena. The three cartels spilled over in their interests, and territorial disputes began to occur. These led to violent confrontations between the sicarios of the drug "mafias." Law enforcement personnel began to intervene and became the targets of sicarios. Judges, lawyers, and policemen were assassinated. Journalists for Colombian newspapers were

also targeted and killed. The Medellín, Cali, and Atlantic drug cartels have acted as brokers in the drug trade, with both the drug trade and narcoterrorism having spilled over into neighboring countries, particularly Peru.

Cocaine is a derivative of the coca plant. Poor peasant farmers, many of Indian ancestry, grow the coca plants on the lower slopes of the eastern Andean foothills in Peru, Ecuador, and Bolivia. Many of the regions where the coca is now grown for the drug trade are traditional coca growing districts where the crops have been grown for millennia and traded into the highlands. As a result of the new demand, there has been some expansion of coca growing into higher valleys in northern Ecuador and Peru. Less addictive and much less powerful, the leaves of the coca plant have been mixed with lime and chewed by the Indian populations of the Andean highlands for centuries, at least since the time of the Inca. Coca leaves had been distributed by an internal Indian marketing system until the late twentieth century, when the international marketing of cocaine intruded into the local peasant agricultural and marketing system.

Processing plants were set up in the coca growing areas, and the coca leaf is now transformed on the spot into raw coca paste. This is done by adding several chemicals including kerosene, benzene, and acetone. The coca paste must then be transported to more sophisticated laboratories, many of which are located in the Colombian Llanos (eastern plains) and the Magdalena River valley. Here the raw paste is treated again and turned into cocaine and other coca products. It is then smuggled by plane from these lowland regions in eastern Colombia up to various other distribution points, such as the Cayman Islands, Central America, or Mexico where it is transhipped to the United States (Gugliotta and Leen 1989).

The coca growing districts of Ecuador, Peru, and Bolivia were almost entirely in regions that were relatively free of state government control because they were far away from the central capitals and had little to offer the caudillos and caciques. They developed their own cacique elites made up of indigenous leaders. In the mid to late twentieth century all of this changed dramatically, and the regions attracted the organizational talents of the cartels. The cartels stepped in and offered money and protection to isolated and largely poverty stricken Indian and mestizo populations. In exchange for the raw coca leaf, the cartels have offered local producers money, goods, and protection, and incorporated the traditional caciques as long as they accept control by more powerful caciques at the top.

In the Upper Huayanga Valley of Peru, the *Sendero Luminoso* (Shining Path) revolutionary movement has become a major dealer in drugs and violence, with the Medellín and Cali cartels on the receiving end of the drugs. In exchange for "protecting" the local coca growers, the cartel pays the Sendero revolutionaries with weapons.

Because the regions in question are isolated and the jurisdictions of the Peruvian, Bolivian, and Ecuadorian national administrations have not reached them, soldiers and administrators are considered outsiders. American Drug Enforcement Agency (DEA) operatives and others working for the United States, Colombian, Peruvian, Ecuadorian, and Bolivian administrations are alleged to be trying to destroy the peasant drug economies.

The Sendero Luminoso is a relatively unknown revolutionary movement that depends on its ability to terrorize the rural populations, especially in the old Indian regions. It uses extreme violence to intimidate the peasants, the military, and the police. President Alberto Fujimori, put into power through democratic elections, overthrew his own government in order to deal with the Sendero Luminoso. He has not had much success until recently, when the leader, Anibal Guzman, was captured and jailed.

The most recent American policy is to try to help peasant coca growers find alternative export crops to grow and market. It is hoped that this strategy will take power away from the Shining Path. However, American foreign policy, the demand of the drug cartels, and the brutal policies of the government of Peru have already had a devastating impact on such tribal groups as the Ashaninka (Campa), Peru's largest lowland Indian group.

revitalization movements like that of the Ngóbe of Panama in the 1960s, and to armed rebellion as in the case of the Maya Zapatistas of Chiapas, Mexico (discussed in Chapter 7).

Here we will examine two cases of cultural survival strategies: the Kayapó of Brazil in South America, and the Ngóbe of Panama in Central America.

Case Study

The Kayapó of Brazil, South America

Brazil's indigenous population, estimated to have been between 3 and 5 million in the early sixteenth century, is now only about 250,000—and even this number represents an increase over the estimated 150,000 to which the population had been reduced by the 1950s. Among the survivors are the Kayapó. Today, many of Brazil's indigenous communities have formed organizations to fight against further encroachment on their territories by outsiders and to protect their human rights. The Kayapó are unusual in that they have successfully appropriated modern technology in their struggle for self-preservation. Anthropologist Terence Turner has con-

ducted research among, and worked closely with, the Kayapó since the early 1960s; and while not the only source of information on them, his numerous publications are certainly among the most thorough and reliable accounts. Turner has carefully documented both traditional Kayapó social organization and their remarkable—and so far successful—struggle for cultural survival against miners, loggers, and the development plans of the Brazilian government.

The Gê-speaking Kayapó live in the southern part of the Brazilian state of Pará on the southern edge of the Amazon rainforest, along tributaries of the middle course of the Rio

Xingu. Their population of about four thousand is divided among fourteen villages, the largest of which is Gorotire with about one thousand inhabitants. Traditional Kayapó villages are circular with a men's house in the center of a large public plaza, which is surrounded by a circle of houses, two or three concentric circles in very large villages. Most villages have between two hundred to four hundred people and are usually separated from one another by distances of over one hundred kilometers. The villages remain politically autonomous, as they have always been. Kayapó lands have almost all been designated as legal reserves during the past ten years, with a total area of about one hundred thousand square kilometers. (Turner 1995)

Despite recent income from mining and logging concessions, almost all Kayapó continue to rely on their traditional economic activities of slash-and-burn agriculture, hunting, fishing, and gathering as their main sources of livelihood. For stretches of several weeks at a time, the Kayapó communities still go on hunting/gathering treks, traveling substantial distances from their base villages.

Monogamy and extended family households characterize family organization, with matrilocality being the preferred form of post-marital residence. Young boys around eight years of age are ceremoniously removed from their mothers' households, inducted into an age grade, and reside with their age mates in the men's house until they marry. At marriage, a man takes up residence in his wife's father's household. Kinship is reckoned bilaterally; there are no unilineal descent groups. After the birth of his first child, a man joins one of the men's associations, often that of his wife's father. Women have corresponding associations. It is the men's associations that are responsible for the organization and sponsorship of all, and it is these men who are the "chiefs" of the village.

Regular contact with outsiders began around the 1850s and was mostly conflictual. More or less peaceful contact with Brazilians began in the 1950s. In the early 1960s, when Terence Turner conducted his initial research among them, the Kayapó had not yet developed the forms of social consciousness that they would later use successfully in their campaigns of political resistance (Turner 1991). However, this was soon to come. In the 1970s, recognizing that their cultural survival in the future would depend upon their ability to deal successfully with Brazilians, many of the Kayapó village chiefs sent their sons and nephews out for schooling. At the same time, the extended visits of anthropologists and other professionals, who clearly valued Kayapó culture for its own sake, heightened their awareness of "the potential political value of their "culture" in their relations with the alien society" that surrounded them. (Turner 1991, 301)

In the 1980s, the nature of Kayapó contact with outsiders shifted as miners and loggers invaded the area. After an initial period of armed resistance, the literate young leaders of some of the Kayapó villages established contractual arrangements with the miners and loggers and began to receive a percentage of the profits. At this time, Kayapó lands had not yet been granted official reserve status by the government, although the villages were technically under the protection of Brazil's National Indian Foundation (FUNAI), formerly the Indian Protection Service (SPI).

With funds from the mining and logging concessions, the young leaders were able to make trips to Brasília to lobby in the halls of government for the Kayapó cause and also to travel abroad, attracting the interest and support of humanitarian and environmental organizations. The Brazilian government, under great pressure as a result of the international media coverage of the Kayapó cause, financial and political support from NGOs (both Brazilian and foreign), and the militancy of the Kayapó themselves, granted a series of reserves to the Kayapó villages in the late 1980s and early 1990s. (Turner 1995, 103)

After a few years, during which contracts for the extraction of gold and timber continued to be renewed, the Kayapó seemingly had enough of deforestation and severe environmental pollution (mainly from the mercury used in the gold extraction process). They cancelled all contracts and expelled miners and loggers from their reserves. Only a few small mining ventures continue, operated by the Kayapó themselves and a few miners who agreed to teach them. The Kayapó have also begun to explore the possibilities for income from environmentally sustainable activities such as the extraction of Brazil nut oil and ecotourism.

Perhaps the most remarkable aspect of the Kayapó battle for cultural survival has been their use of modern technology, particularly video cameras. They make use of short-wave radios these days to communicate among their distantly scattered villages. Since obtaining their first video camera in 1985, some of the Kayapó have received professional training as cameramen and videotape editors. They have progressed from a "home movie" to a professional level of skill, in large measure due to Terence Turner's Kayapó Video Project, begun in 1990. Turner stresses that the training focused on skills and that the Kayapó editors, in particular, "retain control of both form and content." (Turner 1992, 7)

The Kayapó have used video as a medium to document their own cultural practices, particularly the numerous ceremonies that are spectacular performances with elaborate body painting and colorful feather and fiber costumes and masks. They have become aware of the political power of these external displays of their culture, which attract much public interest, particularly at the international level. They have also used video as a means of documenting their political encounters with representatives of the Western world. As Turner points out (1992, 7), they are aware of the international leverage they achieve by having their own cameramen filming events that are being covered by the international press, thus assuring that their cameramen will themselves be a center of media attraction. Two examples, recounted by Turner, nicely illustrate Kayapó political astuteness in the use of video.

Throughout their continuing struggle for cultural survival, using the technology of the modern Western world to help them achieve their social and political ends, it should be noted that the Kayapó have operated within their own traditional cultural structure of chiefly leadership and authority in politically autonomous villages.

Case
Study

The Ngóbe of Panama, Central America

There are over forty-three distinct indigenous peoples of Central America with a combined population of between 4 to 5 million. These peoples have been marginalized politically, and with the exception of the Maya of Guatemala, are largely unknown. El Salvador has more than a half million Indians, largely silent due to a fear of government reprisals. Other indigenous groups live along the coastal plains along the Caribbean. Among the better known are the Miskito, who became prominent due to their conflict with the Sandinista government in Nicaragua, and the Kuna of Panama who are known for their colorful applique cloth panels known as *molas* (Miller 1993, 218–219).

The indigenous peoples of Central America largely choose to live in rural backlands in relative isolation, preferring a lower standard of living to the loss of their cultural heritage. Yet isolation is disappearing. Investment schemes, which may help the majority urban populations and are strongly supported by the governments of Central America, often target the natural resources located in the lands of the indigenous peoples. Often looked down upon by Spanish speaking peasants, whose populations are rapidly expanding, indigenous peoples are finding there are no places left to retreat to. The remaining forests are being cut down, and native peoples are being displaced and driven into cultural extinction. Two-thirds of Central America's forested lands have been cleared since 1950. Central American peasants look hungrily at the lands of the natives.

What is now the Republic of Panama had an estimated indigenous population circa AD 1500 of six hundred thousand to one million. The impact of the Spanish invasion was disastrous. Within one hundred years many native groups had disappeared altogether, and those remaining were greatly reduced in numbers—by as much as 80–90 percent—and suffered severe disruptions of their lifeways. Population recovery did not begin until the early nineteenth century. Like the Kayapó, the Ngóbe were among the survivors. Their population may have actually reached a low point in the late eighteenth century when the Ngóbe may have numbered as few as four thousand to five thousand (Young 1985).

In recent decades, their numbers have dramatically increased so that now the Ngóbe are the second most numerous indigenous groups in all of Central America, second only to the Maya. Today there are over one hundred thousand Ngóbe living within the approximately eleven thousand square kilometers of the mountainous region of western Panama that they claim as their remaining traditional territory, and at least another twenty thousand living

permanently elsewhere in Panama. In the heart of their territory is Cerro Colorado, a mountain containing what may be the world's fourth largest deposit of low-grade copper ore. This copper deposit has figured prominently in Ngóbe struggles for cultural survival since the 1970s, as will be discussed below.

As their numbers have outstripped their resource base, more Ngóbe have permanently moved out of their traditional territory; and many more who have remained have sought to supplement their livelihood with part-time wage labor in a highly inflationary economy with a surplus of unskilled labor and wages that remain well below the inflationary curve. It is not only the economy of Panama that threatens the survival of Ngóbe culture, however; the global economy is affecting them as well. What have been their strategies for cultural survival and how successful have these been to date? In some ways, their story parallels that of the Kayapó; in other ways, it differs.

Even today the majority of Ngóbe depend on slash-and-burn agriculture and the raising of a few cattle and other barnyard animals, supplemented by some hunting and gathering, as their major source of livelihood. They live in small hamlets—most too small even today to be called villages—scattered throughout the mountains at distances of a kilometer and more. Traditionally, each hamlet consisted of the members of a single kin group and in-married women, for the Ngóbe practiced postmarital **virilocality** (residence after marriage on the lands of the husband's kinsmen). Ideally polygynists, a man often housed his two or more wives and their respective children in separate dwellings in the same hamlet. Today two or more kin groups may occupy many hamlets, and this has led to an increase in disputes over land. The kin group as a whole owns land, with both men and women receiving use rights. In theory, this could involve a lot of people using the land because the Ngóbe reckon descent, and thus land use rights, bilaterally, that is, through both mother and father equally. In reality, land use rights are constrained by actual place of residence and generational continuity of use (see Young 1971, Chapter 5, for details).

In the early 1960s, patterns of sharing (reciprocity) of food and labor among kinsmen, near and distant, were still reasonably effective as a means of redistributing goods and services to relieve temporary shortfalls in times of local scarcity, as was the redistribution of food that took place on ritual occasions. However, social and economic strains that had been building up since the 1930s in the context of greater involvement with the agencies and institutions of the outside world were beginning to take their toll. Between the 1930s and the 1970s, the Ngóbe went from marginal involvement with the outside world and its economic system to dependency upon it. The first response to crisis occurred in the early 1960s in the form of a revitalistic religious movement. (Young 1971, 1975, 1978)

This social movement came to be known as the religion of Mama Chi (little mother), after the young Ngóbe woman who, in 1961, saw a heavenly vision and received a message from the Christian god. The Ngóbe have been subjected to Christian influence in one form or another since the time of the Spanish invasion, but it would not be accurate to say that very many of them are "Christianized" in the conventional sense of the term. Nonetheless, many Christian elements are incorporated into their belief system. According to Mama Chi, the Ngóbe were to withdraw from contact with the outside world, including the removal of those of their children who were attending outside schools, cease the performance of their traditional rituals and the consumption of alcohol—an integral part of the rituals— and treat each other, henceforth, as one big family of brothers and sisters. If these teachings were followed, then at the end of a five-year period of trial the Ngóbe would be the recipients of great good fortune; if the teachings were not followed, then misery and ill fortune was to be their lot. As is often the case with religious prophecy, the nature of both the good fortune and the bad was quite vague.

Although her teachings spread throughout the Ngóbe country, and at its height in the mid-1960s the Mama Chi religion affected all Ngóbe living both within and outside the traditional territory, in the end the movement failed to become an established religion. By the mid 1970s, only a very few followers remained. Today the Mama Chi religion retains a small number of followers and has the status of what we would call a cult. The Mama Chi religion progressed through a variety of changes and offshoot interpretations before it ceased to be a significant force for change. However, its accomplishments in terms of a restructuring of Ngóbe internal and external relationships were far-reaching. Later political resistance was born of this revitalistic religious movement.

During 1964–1965, young men with some formal education began to dominate the movement. Within a year the concerns of the movement shifted from predominately religious to political, from seeking salvation through supernatural means to seeking it through political means. This shift in orientation marks the beginning of a still continuing process of politicization and political restructuring among the Ngóbe. There is no longer any formal connection between the remaining adherents of the Mama Chi religion and the new political organization of the Ngóbe. It is this political structure that represents the current Ngóbe strategy for cultural survival.

Although Mama Chi's teachings did not succeed as a religion, the movement had an enormous impact on the Ngóbe during its active life. It stimulated a fundamental transformation in social consciousness in at least four impor-

tant ways. First, by seeking withdrawal from contact with the outside world, the Mama Chi religion forced the Ngóbe into full awareness of the relations of subordination and dependency that existed between them and the outside world. This fostered conscious consideration of alternative means of adaptation to the cash economy.

Second, by ordering the removal of all Ngóbe children from schools, an order that was initially complied with during the early stages of the movement, the Ngóbe quickly realized the importance of knowing Spanish and of literacy as a powerful tool in dealing with government officials, merchants, and other outsiders.

Third, by prohibiting traditional rituals and advocating pan-Ngóbe sister- and brotherhood, the movement forced an assessment of the very foundations of Ngóbe culture as they understood it. This fostered a newfound sense of self worth, solidarity, and ethnic identity. The Mama Chi religion, as is the case with all indigenous social movements, represented an attempt to restructure relations with the non-indigenous world. In the process, the Ngóbe came to realize that subordination is a state of mind rather than an unalterable condition of life.

Fourth, an emphasis on political autonomy that occurred during one phase of the movement, while even at the time viewed as impractical and unattainable by many, certainly produced in the process a greater appreciation of the potential for using political means to achieve socio-economic ends. However unintentionally, the Mama Chi religion initiated the process of politicization among the Ngóbe.

Prior to the political restructuring that came about within the context of the Mama Chi religion, the Ngóbe had no recognized chiefs. Decisions were made and disputes settled by kin groups. Temporary arbitrators were chosen by kin groups on the basis of their reputations as men who could render judgments that would be acceptable to both sides. Action oriented decisions were taken by consensus. Ngóbe appointed by the government as **corregidores** (civil judges) served mainly to record births and deaths in the civil registry, in actuality. Only if they were known to be good traditional arbitrators did they also serve in that capacity. This system worked well to settle disputes and arrive at decisions internally. It was essentially maladaptive in relations with government agencies and other outside organizations because no one could speak for the Ngóbe as a group.

By 1970, a chief (cacique) had been selected to represent each of the three Panamanian provinces in which the Ngóbe claim territory: Bocas del Toro, Chiriqui, and Veraguas. The selection of these men is reported to have occurred at a regional congreso (meeting) in Veraguas Province, sometime in 1968. Each chief appointed local representatives known as jefes inmediatos. By 1970, General Omar Torrijos, then leader of the Panamanian government, had officially acknowledged the three chiefs as the legitimate leaders/representatives of the Ngóbe. However, as late as 1978 many Ngóbe still questioned the authority of the provincial chiefs and were thus still unable to present a united front to outside agencies. However, the impending negotiation for an open-pit copper mine at Cerro Colorado was making their need for unity more critical.

Between 1970 and 1981, three mining companies in succession contracted with the Government of Panama for exploration rights in the Cerro Colorado area. These were Canadian Javelin, Texas Gulf, and finally Rio Tinto Zinc. Each company in turn conducted extensive explorations. An access road to Cerro Colorado was constructed through Ngóbe territory from the Pan American Highway, which skirts their territory in Chiriqui Province. During this same period, the Ngóbe were also the object of several national and international development projects. Ignored by the government for most of their history, the Ngóbe became the object of assimilationist policies disguised as "development" and concern for their welfare. In the late 1970s, as mining exploration intensified and the opening of a mine looked likely, some Ngóbe leaders, some of whom were attending the national university in Panama City, requested and received technical guidance from a Jesuit-affiliated organization known as the Panamanian Center for Study and Social Action, regarding the potential social and environmental impacts of a large open pit copper mine in their territory.

Within this rather ominous context of transnational mining companies and mega-projects, the Ngóbe were still struggling to achieve consensus about the representativeness and scope of authority of their restructured political system. It was not clear, for example, whether the chiefs and their subalterns should concern themselves with internal affairs or only with external affairs, and whether they should supplement or supplant existing forms of authority. Local and regional congresses were held to discuss these matters, as well as to discuss the one issue on which all were agreed—the need to obtain a legally established *comarca* (reservation) from the government. As mining exploration expanded, the issue of the mine also became a widespread concern and was linked by the Ngóbe to legal title to their land.

Gradually, there came to be widespread acceptance of the chiefs and their representatives; and, by unspoken process rather than deliberated decision, the new political structure focused on external affairs. The Ngóbe held their first General Congress with representatives from all three provinces in 1979. At this congress, the Ngóbe were still not of one mind on the issue of the mine. Some believed the government's promises of benefits; others were certain that the mine would bring only social and environmental disaster; and still others felt they did not have enough information to make an informed decision. However, one clear result of this first General Congress was that the leadership realized that the Ngóbe alone could not control the political dynamics involved in dealing with transnational corporations, and they actively began to seek outside support and use the public media to promote their cause and denounce government and corporate duplicity.

At the second General Congress in 1980, solidarity in opposition to the Cerro Colorado mine was achieved; and the Ngóbe leaders publicly declared that they would con-

tinue their opposition to the mine until the government granted them their *comarca,* as Torrijos had promised them a decade before. The Ngóbe (with some help from sympathetic Jesuits and other friends) had also drawn international attention to the human rights and environmental issues related to the proposed copper mine. While this strengthened their position, it is not likely that this international outcry alone would have stopped Rio Tinto Zinc had the potential profits been great enough. High inflation which dramatically raised initial investment costs, negotiation problems with the Panamanian government, and world market prices of copper that were both low and volatile combined to force Rio Tinto Zinc, in 1981, to suspend plans to open the mine. (Gjording 1991)

Throughout the 1980s and early 1990s, the Ngóbe continued to demand legal title to their lands and to openly oppose government development plans. In the 1990s, they added public demonstrations, roadblocks on the Pan American Highway, marches to Panama City (a distance of about five hundred kilometers), and hunger strikes to their forms of political resistance and as means of drawing public attention to their plight. They also publish a newsletter, use tape recorders at their meetings, especially those with representatives of government and transnationals, and actively seek support from international environmental and human rights organizations. Despite this, by 1995 the government had granted mining concessions for 80 percent of Ngóbe territory without any consultation with the Ngóbe. (Sarsanedas 1995) In February 1996, the government signed an agreement with yet a fourth mining company, Panacobre, a subsidiary of Tiomin Resources, which is a Canadian corporation for exploration and exploitation of the copper deposit at Cerro Colorado, again without including the Ngóbe in the process. This precipitated a march to Panama City of three hundred Ngóbe and a demand for an audience with President Pérez Balladares of Panama, which was reluctantly granted. At this meeting the President agreed to submit a proposal to the legislature to demarcate Ngóbe territory as a legal reserve. In late November 1996, Pérez Balladares did submit the proposal, but it specified only half the hectares the Ngóbe were claiming and did not suspend the mining contract with Panacobre. The Ngóbe rejected the proposal and continued to protest.

In late January 1997, the Panamanian Legislative Assembly approved the proposal to give the Ngóbe legal title to their land as a *comarca* (reserve); but the government did not rescind the mining contract with Panacobre to exploit the copper deposit at Cerro Colorado.

The long process of learning to use their cultural identity as a political tool in a multicultural world, a process that began with the Mama Chi movement, is now complete. At one of their general congresses about 1992, those present decided on "Ngóbe-Buglé" as their official cultural identification to the outside world; and this is how they are now referenced in the Panamanian daily, *La Prensa*. No longer are they referred to as "Guaymí." (The Buglé are a small indigenous population in Veraguas Province who are culturally related to the Ngóbe.) They have clearly learned the value of political alliances. In a letter enclosed with the June-July 1996 issue of their newsletter, *Drü*, the letterhead reads "Congreso General Ngóbe-Buglé y Campesino," a public declaration of the fact that they have joined forces with the non-indigenous *campesino* (peasant) population of the region on issues of joint concern. The letter itself is signed by a Ngóbe who identifies himself as "secretary of international affairs"! The Ngóbe have not yet achieved the success of the Kayapó, and they have had to build an entirely new political structure to deal with external affairs. However, like the Kayapó, they have developed new forms of social consciousness, and these have resulted in similar strategies for cultural survival.

virilocality

Residence after marriage on the lands of one's kin

corregidor

The political position of civil judge, a ceremonial post in the traditional cargo system with no real power, and within an *ayuntamiento*, the same term applied to positions analogous to councilman or alderman

■   ■   ■

Chapter
Summary

Latin America: Political Bosses, Dependency, and Democratic Reform

The earliest adaptations of humans in the New World were those of big-game hunting, dating to at least 10,000 BC. The transformation of these hunting/gathering societies into tribal agricultural societies occurred gradually, between 3000 and 2000 BC. With great speed, chiefdoms emerged about 1500 BC, followed by states by 700 BC. These developments were stimulated, as was true in other world regions, by trade. City-states emerged in both Mesoamerica and the Andes with some remarkable parallels, such as the worship of feline deities.

In the early sixteenth century, the indigenous civilizations of Latin America collapsed as Spanish and Portuguese invaders imposed a political ecology of bureaucratic cities, mines, plantations, and haciendas, while at the same time destroying the indigenous trade connections that had supported millions of people. A population collapse followed which may have destroyed up to 90 percent of the New World's people. The slow population recovery took centuries.

The Spanish Empire, along with that of Portugal, collapsed in the early nineteenth century and was followed by a century of strong–man rule (caudillos). State capitalism replaced caudillo rule after the 1930s, in response to the Great Depression and the theory of dependency. State capitalism began as a promise to improve the lot of the poor, but instead made the rich richer and the poor poorer.

In the last decade, state capitalism is being challenged by new forms of political economy, which are also appearing in Asia, Africa, and Eastern Europe. These new systems depend on open markets and democracy, but they are proving very difficult to implement. There is a great fear that these new systems will only mean more poverty and violent social movements. However, there is also hope that Latin America, in the next century, will begin to live up to its promise as a region of prosperous countries, within which indigenous groups and the poorer social classes will gain democratic rights not available to their ancestors.

Chapter
Terms

alcalde	402	Ladino	401
ayuntamiento	400	Lanzon	395
cargo (fiesta) system	402	latifundia	400
caudillo	391	liberation theology	409
charro	406	machismo	406
colono	400	Mesoamerica	392
comadre	405	mestizo	401
compadrazgo	405	minifundia	400
compadre	405	plantation	399
corregidor	423	Porfirismo	404
corrida	406	rancheras	406
debt peonage	400	rancheria	399
ejido	392	sodality	408
evangelical protestantism	409	syncretic culture	401
Gross Domestic Product (GDP)	411	virginity complex	406
hacienda	392	virilocality	423

Check out our website
www.BVTLab.com
for flashcards,
chapter summaries,
and more.

Chapter 12

Global Problems, International Development, and Anthropology in the Third Millennium

We are leaving so many problems to the next generation—poverty, conflict, damage to the environment, abuse of human rights—that long term solutions will be possible only when there is better understanding of peoples and communities, the subject-matter of *anthropology*. (From a Royal Anthropological Institute advertisement in *Anthropology Today*, vol. 12, no. 6, December, 1996)

While we entered the twenty-first century on January 1, 2001 (contrary to popular belief that this event occurred one year earlier), January 1, 2000, *was* the beginning of the *third millennium AD*. What are the prospects for humanity into this third millennium? Will there be widespread Malthusian pestilence, plague, and famine, or prosperity for all? Realistically, the year 2000 brought neither, but the half-century to century beyond might. It depends largely on the choices us humans make. If we are to achieve sustainable resource management and thus ensure a livable world for future generations, we must stop abusing nature, as we have most seriously done since the beginning of the industrial era. This does not mean that we have to return to a hunting and gathering lifestyle, but it may mean that many of us, especially those of us living and doing well in the developed world, will have to change our habits of consumption. Anthropology is one of several sciences that can provide the knowledge to support informed policy and personal choices, thus showing the way to prosperity and a sustainable future. The achievement of sustainability, in its broadest sense, would clearly be the crowning achievement of humankind. However, it is difficult to be an optimist in today's world.

In several of the preceding chapters, we have examined the historical rise and fall of cultures and civilizations in various regions of the world. We have looked at the factors that influenced cultural evolution in one direction or another in the various regions; we have shown how trade and tribute empires were transformed into territorial states under the influence of economies of scale; and we have examined some of the causes of unrest, conflict, and various other issues within each region. We have suggested that a growing process of globalization is now influencing all people everywhere and that at least some of the disharmony evident in the world today is a reaction to this process. We suggest that, as you read what follows, you think about the extent to which the ethnic conflicts in many regions may be politically motivated resource wars.

The desire for economic and political advantage produces policy inconsistencies and distortions that the cynical among us see as giving the lie to supposed humanitarian goals of development. For example, Cuba and China have both been accused of extensive human rights violations. As a result, U.S. policy toward Cuba has included an economic blockade for more than three decades. On the other hand, we have granted China "most favored nation" status for purposes of trade. A clear, if macabre, example of radically different interpretations of the same data is the case of human rights violations in El Salvador in the late 1970s. At one point the U.S. Congress was to vote on whether to continue to provide economic (and military) aid to this tiny Central American country. Human rights organizations pointed to the dismal record of human rights violations, including thousands of outright killings by the El Salvadorean government, and lobbied congress to deny further aid. Those in favor of continuing aid did not dispute the figures on the killings and other violations of human rights; instead they argued that aid should be continued because the total number of killings was less than reported the year before, and this showed that the government had improved the human rights situation! Congress voted to continue providing aid.

In this final chapter, our focus will be on two closely interrelated themes that are with us today and that will have a profound influence on the future of human cultures: (1) global environmental issues, particularly as these relate to development; and (2) international development—what it means, its problematic nature, and whether **sustainable development** is possible. Briefly, sustainable development means development that meets current needs without compromising the needs of future generations. More will be

sustainable development

Development or improvement in the quality of human life that is economically viable (benefits are greater than costs), socially and culturally acceptable, and ecologically viable (resources used at a rate equal to or less than the rate of renewal); strategy that is designed to meet current needs without compromising the needs of future generations

■Cuba and China have both been accused of extensive human rights violations. U.S. policy toward Cuba has included an economic blockade for more than three decades. On the other hand, we have granted China "most favored nation"

said about sustainability below. In the case of both environmental issues and the elusive goal of sustainability, but particularly the latter, we will be looking at how anthropology can contribute to solutions to the world's problems.

Global Problems

No one knows exactly how many different species of life there are on this earth. About 1.4 million species have been named and described. However, these are thought to be only a small fraction of the total, with estimates of the total varying from a few million to upwards of 100 million. Likewise, estimates of yearly species extinction vary from four thousand to forty thousand (Southwick 1996). Why is this important? For many reasons, but perhaps the two most important, practical reasons are that species diversity represents a great storehouse of untapped potential for both human food and medicine. All of our current domesticated foods, both plant and animal, and an overwhelming number of our medicines are refined versions of, or derived from, wild species. To the extent that we diminish the biodiversity of our planet through human action, we decrease the potential for our own well-being in the short term, and that of our descendants in the long term. As Charles Southwick puts it: "Ultimately, good economics will have to involve sound ecology." (1996, 4)

In our view and that of many others, particularly professional ecologists, humans are currently using Earth's renewable resources at unsustainable rates, and contaminating air, land, and water everywhere. That is, renewable resources such as forests and soils are being used more rapidly than nature can replenish them. However, we should point out that not everyone agrees on which resources are most at risk of **depletion** or **degradation**, or on the magnitude of the risk. Even when risks are generally acknowledged, as in the case of deforestation or species extinction, there is little agreement on what might be the best course of action. Many countries have recognized both of these problems and have signed international agreements to work together, but they are struggling to establish mutually acceptable goals and policies that will work. The difference between the optimists and the pessimists is reflected in widely varying estimates of such things as food production potential and population growth rates, in strikingly different interpretations of the same data, and in the amount of faith one places in technological innovation as the key to human survival and well-being.

"Most ecologists consider human population growth to be one of the greatest problems in global ecology and a major driving force of environmental degradation. They see excessive consumption as an equally important cause of pollution and environmental deterioration. Most agree that the two factors work hand in hand to threaten the world's ecological integrity" (Southwick 1996, 159–60). Pollution of air, land, and water, water scarcity, population growth, agricultural production, energy consumption, and deforestation are among the problems of global scope that humankind faces today. Other problems could be added to this list.

In the following sections we focus our gaze on population, food production, and deforestation. We begin with a case study that examines the complex interrelationships among these factors in the Mexican states of Puebla and Tlaxcala, both bordering the Federal District about thirty miles south of Mexico City. This study also considers the employment needs of the population and the difficulty of balancing these needs with the need to mitigate environmental degradation. This study provides a striking example of the clash between the short-term perceived needs of the people and institutions responsible for environmental degradation and the long-term vision of the institutions responsible for protecting the environment. It also illustrates well the complex links among the political, economic, ecological, and demographic transitions discussed in Chapter 2, and why these transitions are so difficult to achieve.

---

depletion

A human-induced reduction in the quantity of a natural resource or for renewable resources such as forests, a reduction at a rate greater than the natural rate of regeneration or replacement

degradation

A human-induced reduction in the quality of natural resources, such as soil, water, and air, that reduces the capacity of these resources to support life

Case Study

The Political Ecology of Puebla-Tlaxcala

The central highlands of Mexico consist of fertile basins and valleys separated from each other by forested mountain chains. The small adjacent states of Puebla and Tlaxcala are located in the fertile Puebla basin just south of Mexico City. Forested mountains surround the basin. To the north are the volcanic mountains of Popocatepetl, Ixtaccihuatl, and La Malinche. Ranching, agriculture, lumber, coffee production, mining, and industry, particularly textile and automobile manufacturing—all are the economic activities in these states. Unfortunately, all are currently creating environmental problems. The Mexican government realizes this and has passed hundreds of laws designed to address these problems. However, the laws are not enforced, and the problems just get worse. In 1987, Smith began the ongoing Puebla Tlaxcala Project in political ecology, which is an attempt to understand why non-compliance is so rampant. The project is one of the few of its kind that focuses on the interaction of human institutions and regional ecosystems over an extended time period.

There are 217 *municipios* (municipalities) and thus 217 *ayuntamientos* (town halls) throughout the state of Puebla. Each has its local construction of *caciques* and connections to local power structures and to the PRI at both state and national levels. The present cacique structure came into being during the presidency of Lázaro Cárdenas (1934–40) and solidified its power during the term of his

successor, Manual Avila Camacho (1940–46). The power structure of each municipio differs, depending on the local economy. In some districts, the agricultural ejidos (cooperative farming estates) dominate, in others the industrial unions *(sindicatos)*, and in yet others businessmen and industrialists dominate through local chambers of commerce. SARH, (the federal and state bureaucracy controlling irrigation and water use), SEDUE (Mexico's Environmental Protection Agency), the governor, the president, and other members of the "elite" government structure—all must play intricate political games with the various local caciques to achieve minimal public goals.

The state of Puebla, the city of Puebla, the 217 municipalities and their mayors, the governor, the ayuntamientos, and the hundreds of local caciques face two very real problems: the need for economic development to create jobs for a growing population and the need to mitigate existing environmental problems. At times these two sets of policy goals, job creation and environmental protection, contradict each other at the local level.

Attempts to reform the local power structure have largely failed because the reforms must come from Mexico City down to the local level. Recent reforms by the national PRI have yet to "trickle down" to the local level, and the lack of political and economic reform has blocked any possibility of mitigating ecological problems.

ENVIRONMENTAL ISSUES

Puebla's most serious environmental problems are contamination of the water supply, deforestation, and air pollution. In the northern mountains, particularly in and around the municipality of Huauchinango, there are over five thousand coffee cultivators, who use the local rivers to process coffee and thus contaminate the water supply. Contamination is so bad that one river, the Arroyo Amarillo or Yellow Arroyo, has been renamed Arroyo Negro or Black Arroyo. The women of the region complain that there is no potable water and that they cannot wash clothing in local rivers because of the bad smell. The San Marcos and Necaxa Rivers are dying, and the fishing economy has been killed off (Smith 1994).

Further south in the fertile Puebla valley, farmers have turned from growing maize and wheat for local consumption to growing exportable products, such as strawberries and tomatoes, for the U.S. market. These farmers have greatly increased their use of irrigation, fertilizers, herbicides, and pesticides in recent years, at a time when community populations are increasing. More food is being imported to feed people, while at the same time the water of the region is being contaminated by the agrochemicals used to produce crops for export (Smith 1994).

The textile and automobile industries contribute to regional water pollution. A study of thirty-five wells in the municipio of Puebla showed that ground water is contaminated with bacteria, fecal material, and industrial chemicals. The water supply in Lago Valsequillo, once a huge man-made lake formed by the construction of the Valsequillo Dam, has dropped dramatically; and the fish in it have died from pollution (Smith 1994).

Deforestation by the peasants living on *ejidos* (communal farms) and by lumber companies is seriously depleting the forests of northern Puebla, especially parks found on the volcanic slopes of Popocatepetl and Ixtaccihuatl. Smugglers steal whole logs and take them out of the state on logging trucks, and they are often armed with machine guns. A major cause of deforestation is the cutting of evergreen trees for Christmas. There is a major industry in cutting and smuggling these trees out of state parks where they are supposed to be protected.

The diminished forests no longer absorb rain so that water cascades directly into rivers, significantly increasing rates of soil erosion. This and irrigation agriculture has produced a severe drop in the level of the aquifer, causing shortages of drinking and irrigation water. Potable water is becoming so difficult to obtain for the growing population that it has to be brought in from outside of the region. Millions of pesos are paid for diesel fuel used to truck water. Furthermore, deforestation has led to a reduction in rainfall, which in turn has further reduced the aquifer. (Trees release water vapor into the atmosphere through **transpiration**. Large-scale deforestation can significantly affect rates of precipitation.)

Fueling the environmental problems has been a demographic explosion. People have been leaving rural regions for the last generation and moving into cities. In 1960 Puebla de los Angeles was a city of seven hundred thousand; by 1989 its population was over two million. A million people had migrated into the Puebla region in less than five years because of the earthquake in Mexico City in 1985. As is true for all over populated cities of the periphery, the air over Puebla is badly polluted as a consequence of industrial and automobile emissions. Over two hundred fifty thousand automobiles, buses, and trucks contaminate the air of Puebla de Los Angeles. Few of the vehicles have anti-pollution devices and unleaded gasoline is rare, and 250 tons of contaminates go into the air each day.

Adding to these already serious environmental problems, in the mid 1980s companies from the northern industrial city of Monterrey began to invade the valley of Puebla, mining

transpiration

A loss of water vapor into the air by plants that eventually returns to the earth as precipitation (rain or snow)

■Over 250,000 automobiles, buses, and trucks contaminate the air of Puebla de Los Angeles.

riverbanks for silica sand (used in making glass for beer bottles) and other minerals. The mining of silica and other minerals has led to further contamination of the rivers of the region.

East of the old Indian city of Cholula (which is next to the largest pyramid in the world), ejido owners have converted thousands of acres of prime agricultural land into a moonscape by mining soils for brick manufacturing. The bricks are then exported to Mexico City and used locally to house people in the growing fringes of the two cities.

SEDUE AS DON QUIXOTE

With this picture of environmental damage in mind, let us examine the relationship between the institutions that attempt to mitigate environmental degradation in the long term and those which are causes of the degradation in the short term.

Mexico has passed hundreds of laws to protect the environment, but is unable to enforce them. The one-party political structure means that the party and the government are the same thing. It is thus exquisitely difficult for the government to punish anyone for breaking its laws. The reason is simple. The law-breaker is a voter, often a member of the PRI—often a very important member. For the government to move against the PRI is the same as moving against itself.

In the early 1980s, Mexico passed a law to protect the environment called the "law of ecological equilibrium." President Miguel de la Madrid (1982–1988) created a new cabinet level agency called the Secretariat for Urban Development and Ecology (*Secretaria de Desarrollo Urbano e Ecologia*, or SEDUE). SEDUE was charged with enforcing compliance to the law of ecological equilibrium. In 1986, de la Madrid appointed an aggressive lawyer to head up the SEDUE branch in Puebla. One of his first acts was to lock up many of the machines (road graders and bulldozers) used to scavenge minerals along the riverbanks of Puebla. Although he received support from the PRI and local businessmen against the exploiting outsiders from Monterrey, many of these law-breaking outsiders simply pried the locks off of their machines and went back to work.

In 1988, SEDUE officials throughout Mexico decided to attack air pollution. In Puebla, new regulations were passed forcing taxicab and bus drivers to tune their engines and use good fuels. In addition, SEDUE began to irritate local businessmen (who are important contributors to PRI) as it shut down one contaminating local company after another, including several plants of the giant Volkswagen of Mexico, a Chevrolet dealership, and a few textile firms. By 1989, SEDUE had closed down sixty-five contaminating businesses including textile, ceramic, and wood manufacturers, grease and oil service stations, and sections of Volkswagen of Mexico. In September 1989, one textile union leader complained SEDUE had put forty families out of work by shutting down a textile firm.

Deforestation was tackled with the same energy. SEDUE officials joined with the governor of the state and the president of the city council of Puebla to stop deforestation. Thousands of new trees were planted in parks. One cement factory donated sixty thousand trees to the project, but deforestation continued apace as though nothing were being done. The governor appointed a military unit to protect the forests, but little came of this. Peasants belonging to remote mountain based *ejidos* publicly complained to the governor that PRI officials were looking the other way when the lumber thieves destroyed the forests.

The attempt to alleviate environmental problems was blocked in Puebla in 1990 due to pressure from a political movement made up of taxicab and truck driver unions, Marxist university students, peddlers called the October 26th Movement, and local businessmen. Taxicab and truck drivers hijacked trucks and buses, which they parked across the interstate running down from Mexico City, effectively paralyzing the city of Puebla. A less aggressive lawyer from PRI replaced the aggressive SEDUE lawyer from PRI. By July 1990, businesses were no longer being shut down for violating pollution laws. Slowly, the movement to protect the environment was stopped by local labor unions and business enterprises as well as Marxist university students. The response of the peasants, who had been complaining about the lack of potable water, was mixed. The peasant farmers of this region generally side with the leftist students, and many did in this case. However, those living in ejido communities in the forested areas of northern Puebla, which were being illegally logged, remained strongly environmentalist, especially on the issue of preserving local forests, and asked SEDUE to help.

This demonstrates the great difficulty of enforcing national laws at the local level when those who benefit from loose environmental regulation control local power structures. Local recognition of this problem has led to the emergence of a new political movement called *Patronato Puebla Verde*, a "green" political movement that is trying to force city leaders to comply with national environmental laws. Still, SEDUE and the *Patronato Puebla Verde* have been unable to challenge successfully the political machine that runs the city.

The North American Free Trade Agreement (NAFTA) added another dimension to the political ecology of Mexico, but it has so far failed to alter the workings of the political machine where environmental problems are concerned. American environmentalists initially tried to block the NAFTA because of its lack of environmental protection provisions. A side agreement, which was added during debates in the U.S. Senate, could be considered a part of the NAFTA. Thus, the Mexican government is, in theory, bound by the NAFTA to enforce environmental regulations similar to those in the United States. However, despite what both U.S. and Mexican environmentalists might want, the Mexican government is still hampered in its enforcement efforts by local politics, as the Puebla-Tlaxcala case illustrates. Yet with the new international pressure of the NAFTA, in particular, the sanctions the U.S. government may impose on businesses that violate environmental regulations, there is some hope. Susan Bilello, a journalist, suggested that the economic pressures produced by the NAFTA are forcing a shift in Mexican politics in the direction of the rule of law (1996).

The links among economics, politics, and environmental resources are complex, as the Puebla example shows. The enforcement of environmental laws by an authoritarian government is problematic, as is the enforcement of political or economic laws. The NAFTA, an imperfect agreement at best, may nonetheless provide Mexico with the international leverage necessary to move toward compliance with environmental laws that it already has on the books.

Population   The world of the third millennium faces several challenges, global in nature, and all related to the activities of humans in relation to their environment. At the core of these problems is that of population growth. The human population is rapidly reaching the point, if it has not already been reached, when we will overwhelm the resource base.

Current net worldwide population increase is somewhere between 85 and 90 million persons annually (Southwick 1996; World Resources 1996). Net increase means that deaths worldwide have already been subtracted from this total. Deaths worldwide were about 51 million in 1993 (WRI 1996). The human population has gone from about one billion in 1800 to almost 6 billion today. We may believe that we have considerable control over ecosystem dynamics, and we may believe that we can therefore disassociate ourselves from the rest of nature. Ultimately, however, we cannot do so. An ecological principle from which we cannot escape is that a species that grows in numbers beyond its available food supply will suffer a reduction in numbers, often a sharp reduction from starvation and disease. Humanity may be able to postpone such a fate by means of its undeniable genius for technological innovation, but in the end we live in a world of finite resources.

Looking at global population trends is an important way to estimate future demands for food, water, and energy. Projections of the size of the world population by the year 2025 vary from about 7.9 to 11.9 billion, according to the World Resources Institute. The differences in the projections are due largely to different assumptions being made about **fertility rate** trends, as well as mortality rates. The world fertility rate has shown a general decline since the 1960s and currently stands at an estimated three children per woman. Population stability requires a rate of two; and even if/when this rate is reached on a worldwide basis, demographic momentum will cause the population of the world to continue to increase for several decades thereafter. Table 12.1 provides a simple illustration of world fertility rate trends. Figure 12.1 shows projected population growth to the year 2150. Both show that populations are continuing to increase most rapidly in the poorest countries. This illustrates a relationship between population growth and poverty. What the experts dispute is the direction of the causal arrow. Does poverty cause population growth, or does population growth cause poverty? We hope that you realize, having gotten this far through this book, that such simple formulations mask the complexities and multiple connections of variables in the real world. Anthropology, through an examination of the relationships between values, world views, and the demographic profiles of different cultures, helps us understand that there is more to poverty than simply population growth, and vice versa.

Many scientists believe that if we do not take steps to curb human population growth, nature will do the job for us. Even if it is true that as the economies improve in those countries where the population is growing most rapidly that the population growth rate will decrease, the view of those who see poverty as the cause of population growth (see discussion of the postulated relationship between wealth and family size in Chapter 2)—and there are those who doubt this (some of whom view population growth as the cause of poverty)—it still might be wise for governments to consider population control policies. Such policies would certainly help to hasten the arrival of a sustainable future.

Can the world produce enough food to continue to meet the needs of the growing human population? Let's look at some things that affect agricultural production.

Agriculture and Food Production Between 1990–1995, only thirteen countries of 157, all in Europe, had reached annual population growth rates close to zero. Today, in may other areas of the world, including parts of the Middle East, Africa, Asia, and Latin America, the population growth rate remains above 2 percent. This

fertility rate

The average number of living children a woman will have during her lifetime

Table 12.1

☐ World Fertility Rate Trends (using data from WRI 1996, 174)

	1950s	1990s
Developed countries	2.8	1.7
All developing countries	6.2	3.4
Poorest developing countries	---	5.6
WORLD	4.5	3.6

Figure 12.1

❑ Trends and Projections in World Population Growth, 1750–2150

Sources: 1. United Nations (U.N.) Population Division. *Long-Range World Population Projections: Two Centuries of World Population Growth. 1950–2150* (U.N., New York, 1992), p22. 2. Carl Haub, Director of Information and Education. Population Reference Bureau. Washington, D.C., 1995 (personal communication).

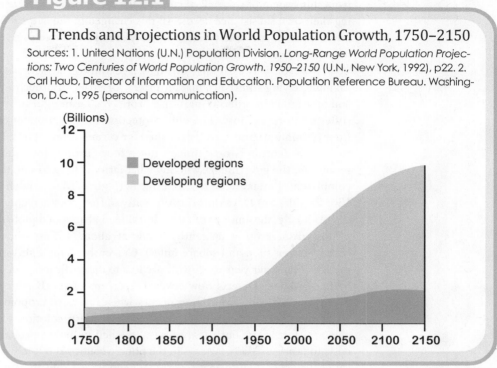

means, among other things, that the world would need a lot more food. However, food production is not just a simple matter of using appropriate, sometimes innovative, agricultural technology to plant and harvest and to increase yields. The agricultural policies of governments also can have a significant impact on production.

In Egypt, for example, until the late 1980s, the agricultural system was completely government controlled. Farmers received their inputs from the government at controlled prices and sold their production to the government at similarly controlled prices. The

■Until the late 1980s, the agricultural system in Egypt was solely run by the government. Now, farmers buy the inputs at market prices and they are free to sell their crops to anyone at whatever prices the market will bear.

result was that the government made a fortune and the farmers, who were not benefitting from this system of centralized control, tried to produce as little as possible beyond meeting their own subsistence needs. All this changed in the late 1980s; and now farmers must buy the inputs at market prices, and they are likewise free to sell their crops to anyone at whatever prices the market will bear.

However, it is clear that this new freedom for farmers also includes new risks, for example, trying to predict market prices for crops in order to determine what to plant and how much in order to maximize profit. If a farmer guesses incorrectly, he or she can suffer a substantial loss. The only protection the government currently provides is that floor (minimum) prices are established for certain crops. Thus, if world market prices on such crops (cotton is one, though not a food) drop below the government-established minimum, the government will buy what farmers have to sell; this reduces (but does not completely eliminate) the risk to farmers. (Source: Max Goldensohn, anthropologist and Vice President of Development Alternatives, Inc., personal communication).

Annually, the amount of agricultural land abandoned globally due to soil exhaustion or loss from erosion currently stands at about seventy thousand square kilometers (twenty-seven thousand square miles). Currently about eighty-six thousand square kilometers of land per year worldwide are lost to desertification, an area about the size of the State of Maine. Deserts now cover 17 percent of the Earth's land surface (Southwick 1996, xvii, 85). Soil exhaustion occurs when intensive cropping depletes soil nutrients faster than nature can replace them. The modern solution to this problem has been chemical fertilizers, but these cause watershed pollution problems as well as increasing costs to farmers. Many farmers in the poorer countries of the world cannot afford chemical fertilizers without heavy government subsidies. Thus they must abandon plots after a few years due to sharply declining yields. However, soil erosion is a far greater problem.

"The first global survey of soil erosion showed that since World War II, more than 3 billion acres of cropland—an area larger than China and India combined—have been damaged by human activity and will prove costly, if not impossible, to reclaim" *(Science News* 1992, 215).

■Deserts now cover 17 percent of the Earth's land surface.

Soil erosion on agricultural land was causing an estimated loss of more than 20 billion tons per year in the 1980s. By the 1990s, the loss was estimated to be about 75 billion tons of topsoil per year. Depending on local conditions (temperate, tropical, type of vegetation cover, etc.), it will take between two hundred to one thousand years for one inch of new soil to form. That inch can be lost in as little as ten years. It is estimated that soil in the United States is being lost at seventeen times the formation rate. In Iowa, it is being lost at thirty times the formation rate; and Iowa had, by 1981, already lost *half* of its original topsoil (Southwick 1996, 101). Forty percent of all U.S. cropland currently under production has already eroded to the point of declining productivity (Council on Environmental Quality 1991, cited in Southwick 1996). The relevance of these facts about soil loss and yield declines in the United States becomes evident when we consider that the United States is a major supplier of food grains to developing countries. For example, the U.S. exported

United States is a major supplier of food grains to developing countries.

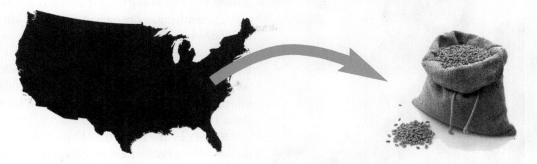

more than 84.6 million metric tons of cereal grains annually between 1991–1993, most of it to developing countries. This is down from 103.6 million metric tons annually exported between 1981–1983, and not all of the difference can be attributed to increased yields and thus declining need for grain imports in the developing countries (WRI 1996, 245).

In developing countries, a combination of overgrazing, overcropping, deforestation, and destruction of other vegetation cover is producing massive soil loss. Salination, from flooding and overuse of irrigation, is also a major problem in many watersheds (Southwick 1996, 104). The countries of the Middle East suffer from widespread problems of desertification due to overuse and misuse of irrigation and the farming of marginal lands formerly used only for grazing by pastoral nomads (see discussion in Chapter 9). Both Latin America (see Chapter 11) and many countries in Southeast Asia (see Chapter 10), for example, Thailand, the Philippines, and Vietnam, have suffered massive deforestation and consequent soil erosion due to a combination of legal and illegal logging, and the need to open up new agricultural land to keep up with population growth. All three of these Southeast Asian countries, as well as many in Latin America, have enacted strict laws to conserve their forests, but enforcement has been difficult. Africa (Chapter 8) has suffered from numerous large-scale development projects that have focused on export agriculture to the detriment of small farmers. However, development planners are now beginning to recognize the value of local knowledge of the environment in designing projects, so there is some hope that new projects will prove more environmentally sound than those of the 1960s and 1970s.

Land provides 99 percent of the food we consume; aquatic systems provide only 1 percent (Pimental et al. 1995, cited in Southwick 1996, 99). Yet only 11 percent of the earth's land surface can be used for agriculture. Worldwide, we are already using about 40 percent of the arable land for crops and pasture (World Resources 1996, 201). However, we have no guarantee that the soils and water resources of the other 60 percent will be sufficient to support sustainable agriculture. We must also realize that any additional land brought under cultivation or turned into pasture will be at the expense of existing forest, grasslands, and wetlands. Yet, clearly, massive food production increases will be necessary to feed the rapidly growing human population. Can most of the needed increased yields be got from improved agricultural technology? Despite shortcomings and even failure in some areas, the Green Revolution (a combination of improved varieties achieved by genetic engineering and scientifically controlled applications of fertilizers, pesticides, and herbicides) did manage to produce crop yields that kept ahead of population growth from the 1950s through the late 1970s. During the 1980s increased yields from all sources (improved varieties, more intense cultivation,

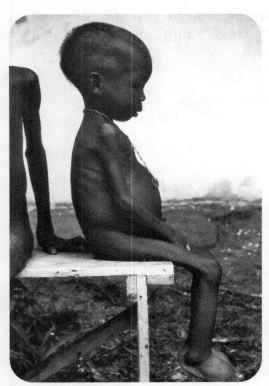

■Currently, millions of people in the world are malnourished or literally starving. Food production is the answer, but this also has a cost; therefore, the problem remains.

and bringing new land under production) only barely managed to keep apace of population growth. In the 1990s, population growth was beginning to outpace increases in yields.

Currently, many people in the world are undernourished or malnourished. Several million are even worse off; they are quite literally starving. In Mexico, for example, the Latin American Economic Commission estimates that, of Mexico's 45 million people living below the poverty line, 9 million have only one-fourth of what is needed to purchase food for a day (Latinamerica Press 1996).

Studies by the FAO, the World Bank, and the IFPRI (International Food Policy Research Institute), a part of CGIAR (Consultative Group on International Agricultural Research) are optimistic about the possibility of food production keeping up with population growth, at least until about 2020. Lester Brown and Hal Kane of the Worldwatch Institute, on the other hand, count themselves among the pessimists. They see as serious constraints no recent significant improvements in agricultural technology, declining fisheries productivity, degeneration of rangelands, and steadily increasing water scarcity. (WRI 1996) One can certainly add to this list soil loss, resulting in agricultural lands being taken out of production. While worldwide agricultural yields are currently still continuing to show a small increase, they are definitely showing signs of leveling off. Furthermore, some experts argue that fragile tropical and subtropical environments cannot sustain further production increases.

Most studies agree that agricultural production can continue to meet "effective demand," at least in the near term. What does this mean? "Effective demand" is the "demand that corresponds to purchasing power irrespective of food needs." (WRI 1996, 229) Translated from the unfeeling prose of economics, this means that the hungry poor will continue to go hungry because they do not have the "purchasing power" to buy the food they need. What might be done? Boosting food production at the *household level* would help, but it would not solve the problem of those many urban poor who cannot grow their own food. The World Resources Institute suggests that increasing food production in the developed countries will not meet the food needs of the poor in developing countries (229). Given the recognized constraints, where will the food production increases come from?

According to the FAO, which the World Resources Institutes considers to be optimistic, 66 percent of the increases in developing countries will come from increased yield, 21 percent from expansion of land under cultivation, and 13 percent from greater cropping intensity (meaning the shortening of fallow periods and growing more than one crop per year on lands that currently only produce one yearly crop). Leaving aside the question of whether these sources of increase in agricultural yields represent a realistic scenario, such increases will increase pressures on land and water resources, and contribute to deforestation (at least one-half of the potential agricultural land in developing countries is currently forested). Some of the yield increase will come from an expansion of irrigated lands, adding to the water scarcity and salination problems that already exist in some areas.

Many countries are already facing serious food security problems that are not likely to go away in the near future. "Famines and temporary food deficiencies can result from drought, flood, war, political strife, or poor harvests." Such events are increasing, especially in the developing countries of the world. Africa presents the bleakest picture, with a recent severe drought affecting more than 13 million people. South Asia is also a problem area. (WRI 1996, 235)

Production gains can be made by minimizing soil loss, improving the efficiency of water use, reducing post-harvest losses, and generally improving agronomic practices. But will this be enough? High input agriculture has already proven to have numerous environmental disadvantages. The alternative, integrated farming systems moving toward more organic farming, is certainly much more environmentally friendly. However, there is considerable doubt about whether organic farming can produce the required yield increases to meet the needs of the world's growing population. Once again we suggest that policies to control rates of population growth must be a part of the solution, along with a reduction in rates of consumption among the affluent.

The affluent of the world must learn not only to consume less food but less energy in general. While rates of energy consumption are difficult to calculate and will always be approximations, it is still instructive to compare such "relative" rates by country. Energy consumption is often calculated in gigajoules (gJl), approximately the equivalent of 6.9 gallons of oil, and based on both commercial and domestic use of electricity, petroleum products and other fossil fuels, and other energy sources of significance in particular countries. Without going on at length about the need for the most developed nations to reduce energy consumption if we are to move toward world-wide sustainability of resource use, we offer a simple comparison to demonstrate the point: Energy consumption in the United States is more than five times that of Mexico, almost fifteen times that of Brazil and China, thirty-five times that of Indonesia, forty times that of India, and an astounding 140 times that of Haiti and Bangladesh, the poorest nations in the world. (Southwick 1996, 271)

Deforestation   Charles Southwick, an ecologist, estimates that forests in 1990 covered about 4.3 billion hectares (28.7 percent) of the earth's land surface. As he also points out, forests covered an estimated 45.5 percent of the Earth's land surface about ten thousand years ago, when the transition from food extraction (hunting and gathering) to food production (agriculture and animal husbandry) began. (1996, 117) Rates of deforestation steadily increased from 1960 to 1990 in the developing countries of the world, and fully one-fifth of all natural tropical forest cover was lost during those three decades. Asia lost 33 percent while Africa and Latin America each lost about 18 percent. Between 1980 and 1990 alone eight percent (163 million hectares) of natural tropical forest cover was lost. (World Resources Institute, et al. 1996)

What drives this process of deforestation? Population growth and poverty are the usual suspects. The poor do contribute to deforestation by clearing land for agriculture and because wood is their chief—often

■Deforestation in Southern Mexico.

the only—source of fuel for cooking. However, compared to other sources of tropical deforestation, the damage done by the poor is minuscule. It is also true that, at least in an indirect sense, population growth contributes to deforestation. As many developing countries struggle to keep food production apace with population growth, governments establish policies that encourage the conversion of tropical forests to agricultural use. The tragedy of this solution to the food problem is that most tropical forest soils are thin and not well suited to prolonged or permanent use for agriculture or pasture. The indigenous peoples who inhabit these forests in places like the Amazon basin of South America have understood the limitations of these lands for centuries and have evolved sustainable forms of shifting cultivation (also called swidden or slash-and-burn cultivation), utilizing tiny plots scattered throughout the forest and interspersing root crops, seed crops, and tree crops to, in some sense, duplicate the natural biological diversity of the tropical forest itself. Attempts at permanent agriculture on these same lands became economically nonviable after just a few short years. Unfortunately, by the time such plots are abandoned, there is little chance that the forest will return.

Logging, cattle ranching, and commercial-scale export agriculture are the major causes of tropical deforestation (Southwick 1996). About 60 percent of tropical forest loss in Mexico is due to ranching (Renner 1997), and much of the beef does not feed Mexicans but is exported. The timber trade has argued for years that its role in deforestation is negligible and that land clearing and fuel wood collection are the chief causes. A new study by the World Wide Fund for Nature (WWF), which assesses illegal as well as legal logging, comes to the conclusion that the international timber trade is the primary cause of forest loss and degradation, not just in the tropics but worldwide (1996). It is the industrial nations of the world that are the major consumers of lumber and timber products.

While the spotlight has recently been on tropical deforestation, the situation is not much better in the temperate forests of the developed countries. The U.S., for example, lost 1.1 percent of its remaining forest between 1980 and 1990 (World Resources Institute 1996); and this forest is, like that of other developed countries, already less than half of what it was in the seventeenth century. In the United States and most of Europe, remaining forests are second growth and plantations. Very little old growth forest remains.

> In 1989 the U.S. Forest Service, charged with the management and conservation of forests representing 8.2 percent of the nation's land area, opened approximately 2.6 million acres to timber cutting. In the same year, the U.S. Forest Service reforested 148,600 acres through tree planting programs (*Report of the U.S. General Accounting Office*, 1990). Thus, over seventeen times more acreage of Forest Service land was used for deforestation than for reforestation (Southwick 1996, 121).

Ineffective management policies, coupled with the desire for short-term gains and a certain amount of corruption, raise the prospect of massive cutting of Siberia's extensive forests (WRI 1996). Illegal logging is already underway in some areas.

"Forests, not floods" was the chant being repeated at a street demonstration on the University of Oregon campus, January 13, 1997, following the disastrous floods of December 1996 throughout the Northwest and California. Decades of clear cutting have left many steep slopes in the Northwest unstable, causing massive mudslides, and exacerbating

■The international timber trade is the primary cause of forest loss and degradation. It is the industrial nations of the world that are the major consumers of lumber and timber products.

flooding throughout many watersheds, despite the numerous dams constructed for flood control by the U.S. Army Corps of Engineers. While some believe that damming of major watersheds has contributed to the problem, in the aftermath of the greatest floods of this century others are arguing for more dams.

Beyond the wood and non-wood products they provide for human use, forests serve many ecologically beneficial purposes. Natural forests are complex ecosystems containing many species. Great biodiversity is especially true of tropical forests. Forests capture and slowly release water, thus protecting watersheds and keeping rates of soil erosion low. Through transpiration, forests also release great quantities of water into the air that eventually returns as rain or snow. Forests release oxygen and lock up carbon dioxide gas (CO_2), considered to be a major contributor to the greenhouse effect. Some ecologists and climatologists believe that the massive deforestation in the tropics since the 1950s is causing global warming. Forests are essential to the health of our global ecosystem and thus to the well-being of all cultures and nations. Thus, deforestation, currently taking place on a massive scale in the tropics, as well as forest degradation, an all too common phenomenon in the developed countries of the temperate zone, are global problems that must be addressed. Forest degradation occurs as a result of air pollution that produces acid rain, and also through reduction in natural species diversity due to logging and then replanting forests with only one kind of tree so that they can be easily logged again in a few years.

Sustainable forest management is essential to the health of the planet. Anthropologists and ecologists are aware that indigenous peoples in Latin America, North America, and throughout Asia and Southeast Asia have practiced sustainable forest management for centuries. The Kayapó of Brazil (see Chapter 11) and the Guaraní of Paraguay are just two examples. Their model has always been that of agroforestry, a model that incorporates the use of the non-timber products of the forest interspersed with their subsistence plots. In recent years, some groups such as the Guaraní have been able to sell rubber, yerba mate, and other forest products commercially without damaging the forests upon which they depend (Reed 1997). Studies have shown that the sustained yields of forest products that do not require damaging the trees are economically much more beneficial in the long term than are the short term gains realized from selling the logs. The modern world has much to learn about forestry from the indigenous world.

International agreements went into place in 1994, specifying that by the year 2000 all forest products in both the tropical and temperate forests should come only from forests that are being sustainably managed (World Resources 1996, 212). Since then, the practice of sustainable forest management has increased greatly.

International Development and Development Anthropology

The post-World War II phenomenon of international development aid was supposed to eliminate poverty and result in general economic well-being for the countries of the underdeveloped Third World. Almost a half-century of development, economic and technological, has had the opposite effect and has produced many of the problems that we face today—and that will be with us for the foreseeable future. Development aid has produced the seeming paradox of increased poverty. To understand why this is so, is not an easy matter, and experts do not agree on the relationship between causes and consequences. Anthropology can contribute to an understanding of these problems, dealing as it does in interrelationships and cross-cultural comparisons. However, it will require the collective knowledge of many disciplines and many cultures, and the political will in policy making of many nations to solve these problems because they are truly global in scope. Policy failures have certainly contributed significantly to current problems.

International Development Aid

According to the tenets of capitalism, the only healthy economy is a growing, expanding economy. In other words, economic growth is the engine that drives us toward greater prosperity. Since the end of World War II, the First World has provided, through bilateral and multilateral agencies, an enormous amount of financial, material, and technical aid to the so-called underdeveloped or lesser-developed countries of the Third World. Economic development was (and for many economists and politicians still is) seen as the force that would produce social development (often phrased as an improvement in the quality of life, especially for the poor) and political development (which, for the countries of the First World, unequivocally meant a transition to democracy). However, for a period much longer than the seventy years since the end of World War II, economic growth, despite its benefits, has led to the destruction of thousands of life-sustaining ecosystems on all parts of the planet, and the growth of poverty rather than the alleviation of it. Many scientists—ecologists and anthropologists, in particular—are concerned that the current process of economic globalization is exacerbating existing environmental and social problems, and if not checked, may result in global ecological collapse and the end of life as we know it.

While the early goals of development aid were to stimulate the economies of the lesser developed countries (LDCs), to alleviate poverty, and to improve the standard of living in general for the peoples—especially the poor—of the LDCs, the overall effect of six decades of development projects, mostly in the Third World countries of Africa, Asia, and Latin America, has been the opposite. Poverty has increased. The rich have gotten richer and the poor poorer in relative terms; that is, while in some countries the standard of living of the poor may be somewhat better than it was a half-century ago, the gap between the rich and the poor has increased. In some countries, such as Rwanda and Somalia in Africa, the poor are poorer now than they were fifty years ago in *absolute* terms. Throughout much of the world, the percentage of the population living in poverty has increased rather than decreased. This is even true in the United States.

A later rephrasing of the goals of development stressed improvement in the "quality of life"; but given the value-laden nature of this concept, it would seem impossible to use

■Though the standard of living of the poor may be somewhat better than it was a half-century ago, the gap between the rich and the poor has increased.

it as a cross-culturally valid measure. How, exactly, would one go about measuring the "quality of life" when the concept itself means different things in different cultures, depending on what is valued? The United Nations Development Programme has developed what is called the *Human Development Index (HDI)*. This index is supposed to assess progress in a way that is more relevant to sustainable development than strictly economic indicators such as **Gross National Product (GNP)** and **Gross Domestic Product (GDP)**. Particular attention is given to issues of equity, poverty, and gender. The HDI is an aggregate indicator, based on national life expectancy, educational attainment, and GDP, and measured in terms of **purchasing power parity** (World Resources 1996, 160, 176). While it provides a basis for comparison of countries in terms of "progress," it is, like all other such indices, culturally insensitive and does not measure the quality of life from different cultural perspectives. "Progress" is defined strictly in terms of the goals of the Western (First) world.

Sustainable Development

Today the focus of development aid is on sustainable development. What, exactly, does this mean and how much is being done to achieve it, assuming that it is a worthwhile goal? There is also talk, mostly among politicians, economists, and some businessmen, of sustainable growth. This is clearly wrong-headed, however, for growth cannot continue indefinitely; that is, growth cannot be sustained in a world of finite resources. However, as anthropologists we must attempt to understand the social and cultural context of this kind of thinking and work to engender other more sensible modes of thought. Our life quite literally depends on it. Herman Daly, formerly an economist with the World Bank and currently a professor at the University of Maryland, has repeatedly said that the oft-used phrase "sustainable growth" is an oxymoron, a contradiction in terms. Yet among economists, Daly is a lonely voice crying in the wilderness. Most economists, as we have said, believe that the only healthy economy is a growing economy, and most equate growth with development. However, this need not be so. Development can be defined as

---

Gross National Product (GNP)

The value of all final goods and services produced within the borders of a country, plus net income from abroad

Gross Domestic Product (GDP)

The value of all final goods and services produced within the borders of a country, usually calculated on the basis of a common currency such as the U.S. dollar

the realization of potential (Brooks 1990), which does not necessarily imply continuous economic growth. In fact, given that the resources of the earth are finite, though many are renewable, successful development, that is, sustainable development, cannot possibly mean continuous economic growth. Sustainable development must mean something other than economic growth.

What do we mean by sustainable development? What would it take to achieve it? Many scholars in various disciplines—anthropologists, ecologists, economists, political scientists, sociologists—as well as development planners, policy makers, politicians, and bureaucrats—all have commented on the first question, or attempted to answer it. Yet no matter how they have defined it, few have proposed a plan to achieve sustainable development. Indeed, it was only in the late 1980s, in the Bruntland report, *Our Common Future* (1987), that a basic definition of sustainable development was proposed. In this report, sustainable development was defined as "development that meets the needs of the present without compromising the ability of future generations to meet their own needs." Today, sustainable development has become the buzzword and the most popular concept in the field of international development.

In our view, sustainable development should, at a minimum, be defined as development that is the following:

- *Environmentally sustainable* Ecosystems and resources are maintained in a healthy state over a long period of time, biodiversity is preserved, and the natural capacity of ecosystems is protected.

- *Economically sustainable* Net benefits over costs are realized in the long term.

- *Socially sustainable* This includes cooperation of resource users, institutional capacity, and political will, among other things. (Young 1991, 27–28)

David Brooks defines sustainable development in terms of five broad requirements: "integration of conservation and development; satisfaction of basic human needs; achievement of equity and social justice; provision for social self-determination and cultural diversity; [and] maintenance of ecological integrity." (1990, 24).

These two ways of defining what sustainable development is, or should be, are not all that different. To achieve sustainable development requires working closely with the intended beneficiaries of development at the local level, and taking local cultural context and local knowledge into account in project design. Anthropologists working in development have been advocating this approach for a long time.

Development Anthropology and the Anthropology of Development

An oversimplified but still useful way to characterize what cultural anthropologists do is to divide them into those who do basic research, most of whom are employed in academic institutions, and those who do applied work, most of whom are employed outside of academe (with the caveat that some anthropologists do both during the course of their careers). A substantial number of anthropologists of both kinds currently concern themselves with the processes and problems of international development. Again oversimplifying, we can say that those inclined toward basic research focus on the anthropological analysis of the processes, projects, and outcomes of international development. In other words, they do the anthropology of development. Some of those who call themselves applied anthropologists (remember that applied anthropology can be defined as the application of anthropological knowledge to the solution of contemporary human problems, and it encompasses much more than just international development) do development anthropology. They are actually employed on development projects, by public and private agencies that provide development assistance, in a variety of capacities, ranging from short-term consulting to project management to regional oversight responsibilities.

Those concerned with the anthropology of development tend to be hypercritical of development both as process and product. Some, for example, Arturo Escobar (1995), focus on development as a profoundly colonial discourse, as a contrived reality designed to perpetuate the economic domination and subordination of the Third World by the First. It follows that such critics are also very critical of development anthropology, that is, of the active involvement of anthropologists in the development process. As the number of anthropologists working in development has increased since the mid-1970s, the critique has become more strident. The agenda of development agencies are seen as ethnocentric, as having policies and programs that link progress to capitalism, industrialization, and modern technology (Warren and Bourque 1991). This is considered a very one-sided and very "Western" view, which fails to take account of differences in cultural perspectives about what is valued. Development anthropologists do not necessarily disagree. As Moreno-Black and Young have pointed out,

> There is no escaping the fact that ... in development agencies [there is] no shortage of officials and technicians who hold ethnocentric viewpoints, although there are also many who do not. Anthropologists who work within the development establishment know in more detail than their critics the sins of the establishment. But they believe they can be effective in countering ethnocentric biases and that they can have a positive impact on the process of development.... [Development] anthropologists have chosen to confront the dragon while their critics apparently prefer to hide from it in the hope that it will go away. (1992, 84)

Both development anthropologists and their critics agree on two points. One is that development project planners have generally not given sufficient (if any) attention to the importance of cultural differences and their potential (or actual) impact on project outcomes. Second, those planners have generally not sought the active involvement of the intended beneficiaries early on in the project design stage, much less in prior consultations to determine whether development is desired at all and, if so, what kinds of projects are wanted. Small nongovernmental organizations (NGOs) have a much better record in this regard than bi-lateral and multilateral aid agencies, such as USAID and the World Bank.

The case of the fish processing plant at Lake Turkana in Kenya provides an example of development gone wrong. More important, it shows how the failure to incorporate existing anthropological knowledge into project planning and implementation can have disastrous consequences.

THE EMPLOYMENT OF ANTHROPOLOGISTS IN DEVELOPMENT

Large funding agencies, such as the World Bank, the United Nations, and the Agency for International Development, have in the past been reluctant to have anthropologists participate in development projects other than as trouble-shooters when something goes

Case Study

The Frozen Fish Plant in the Desert

In the early 1970s, Norwegian developers became concerned about the lack of available high protein food among the Turkana pastoral nomads who live just south of the Sahara desert in the Sahel in northern Kenya. A project was formulated that was designed to catapult the Turkana out of susceptibility to drought and protein scarcity, and into a commercially viable venture which would utilize a renewable, environmentally safe, high protein, low cholesterol resource, namely fish. It would also settle the Turkana in permanent villages. According to the United Nations Food and Agriculture Organization (FAO), pastoral nomadism threatened the fragile ecosystems of the Sahel. Specifically, settling nomadic pastoralists into permanent communities would address this problem. The British government published a handbook on rangeland management, which argued "since the ecologically unsound dependence on milk is at the root of [the pastoralists'] problem, that is the most obvious point of attack. Reduce the dependence on the milk diet, and the battle is at least part won" (Harden 1990, 178).

There happened to be a gargantuan natural fish tank in Turkana territory in northwest Kenya called Lake Turkana, which teemed with Nile perch as well as *tilapia*, a delicious white fish. The perch can grow to four feet and longer. The Kenya Fisheries Department confidently predicted huge catches every year for decades. Norwegian developers took up the challenge to convert the Turkana pastoralists into fish farmers. A severe drought in the 1960s had killed eleven thousand head of Turkana cattle, and many herders had turned to fishing. Norway, through its development agency, Norad, tried to systemize the conversion (Harden 1990).

Salaried Norad fishing experts arrived in 1972 with twenty fiberglass boats, four motor boats, and the *Iji*, a thirty-six-foot research vessel which had been trucked overland more than seven hundred miles. It was determined that the most desirable product would be frozen fish fillets. Consultants recommended the construction of an "ice-making, freezing, and cold storage plant." The government of Kenya liked the idea, and Norad invested two million dollars in the construction of a fish plant, which looks like an upscale Lutheran church according to Blaine Harden, a journalist who studied the history of the project:

> Although it was surrounded by tin-roof shacks, desert scrub, and the odd camel, it would not have looked out of place in the upper middle-class suburbs of Oslo or Washington or Los Angeles. The Norwegians also built a road connecting the remote fish plant to Kenya's highway system

and to Nairobi. That cost $20 million. The idea was for the Turkana Fishermen's Cooperative Society to sell quick-frozen fish fillets in Kenya's cities and abroad (Harden 1990, 180).

When the plant was completed in 1981, the Norwegians discovered that chilling the fish from 100 degrees to below freezing, using diesel powered generators, cost more than the fillets were worth. Production also demanded more clean water than Turkana District had. The plant only operated for a few days before its freezers were turned off. "It became Africa's most handsome, most expensive dried fish warehouse" (Harden 1990, 180).

Then, as happens every thirty years, part of Lake Turkana disappeared when the Omo, the major river that feeds the lake, ran low because of drought. Twenty thousand Turkana, whom the Norwegians had lured to the lake to become fishermen, were stuck without fish; and their livestock were dying due to overcrowding on the barren, overgrazed banks of the lake. In addition, nearly every tree near the lake had been chopped down for firewood. To top things off, the research vessel became stranded in the middle of the lake.

According to Harden, the Norwegians could have driven thirty-five miles to the town of Lodwar where colonial records would have shown that the lake had dried up once before in 1954:

> No one checked. Nor did Norad take the trouble to learn—from mountains of available anthropological studies—that the Turkana people consider fishing to be the last resort of an incompetent who cannot handle his livestock. Unless they are very hungry, they do not eat fish. They consider as beneath contempt those who are forced to survive as fishermen without livestock (Harden 1990, 181).

Norad had attempted, in good faith, to help the Turkana. However, ignorance of local climatic conditions and fluctuations made the project ecologically unsustainable; ignorance of local cultural values made it culturally unsustainable; and overconfidence in modern technology made it economically unsustainable. High technology answers to problems of poverty are common, and they are very attractive to government officials. Such projects come with a lot of money that can be siphoned off for relatives and political cronies of the bureaucrats. There is little doubt, in these cases, that once the developers leave the projects will collapse. Anthropologists are quite wary of large ticket, high tech approaches to the transformation of poor societies.

wrong. The attitudes of these agencies have been changing, however; and more and more anthropologists are being hired both as permanent employees and as consultants who work as part of a project team from the early design phase of the project. There has been a realization that the anthropologist can supply a perspective and a type of technical expertise not normally found among economists, agronomists, engineers, or other technically trained individuals. The perspective includes the knowledge that an understanding of the local culture is essential to project success, and that the local culture must be understood in its own terms (cultural relativism), as well as in the context of the regional and the national, and often the international (cultural dynamics). It also includes a focus on thinking small, that is, taking a bottom-up approach. The technical expertise of anthropologists varies; but for those working in development, it includes methods for arriving at an understanding of local (or indigenous) knowledge systems and methods for building project activities upon such local knowledge. Local or indigenous knowledge has always been at the core of ethnography; only recently has it become a popular topic in the world of international development (see, for example, Warren, Slikkerveer, and Brokensha, eds. 1995 for a recent selection of essays on the topic).

The reason people are poor usually has little to do directly with a lack of knowledge about how to improve their economies. It has a lot to do with the institutions that govern their lives, particularly those at the national level. If the anthropologist cannot change the national rules, and he or she usually cannot, then it is smarter to work on small projects, particularly those that may initiate change from the ground up. In other words, the reason most people in the periphery are poor has a lot to do with the political economy of the world and the institutions within the peripheral nation state. Up until very recently, the political economy of the world allowed the core to monopolize wealth. Under such circumstances, massive aid projects were unlikely to achieve positive results. While this is changing, there is still not a great deal that massive aid projects can achieve, as illustrated by the Turkana fish project and many other massive development projects around the world. The environmental and social costs of many large projects often outweigh the economic benefits, despite favorable environmental impact assessments and social soundness analyses (both required for all USAID projects) at the project design stage.

A far better approach is to suggest small changes. For example, Peter Little, a development anthropologist with the Institute for Development Anthropology, did a study of Somalia cattle markets and recommended that cattle herders in Somalia would do better if they sold their cattle across the border in Kenya rather than on the overseas market. He argued that just a few traders in Mogadishu controlled the profits of trade to their own benefit (Little 1988). Unfortunately, Somalia descended into a civil war shortly after Little published his report on his study of cattle markets, and his idea could not be implemented.

Patricia Vondal's research on Indonesian duck farming, conducted between 1981 and 1983 (Vondal 1989), illustrates how local innovations can have desirable regional consequences and how the anthropologist's holistic approach can reveal not just what happened but how it happened and what the important interconnections are. Vondal's work is a good illustration of how basic anthropological research can inform the development process by providing a systematic account of local knowledge, practice, and innovation.

■　　■　　■

Case Study

The Duck Farmers of Borneo

Present day Indonesia is a kaleidoscope of three hundred languages and more than one hundred ethnic groups. While primarily Muslim, and with a small minority of Christians, many of its people believe in animism or nature worship. About 75 percent of the population live in rural areas, and more than one half engage in fishing and small plot rice and vegetable farming. After enduring centuries of control by Portuguese and then Dutch colonists, and ravaged by the Japanese army during World War II, Indonesia won its independence in the 1950s. Its revolutionary President Sukarno, tried to move the country towards socialism, but Army General Suharto overthrew him in 1966. Suharto institutionalized capitalistic reform measures that are beginning to transform Indonesia into a modern market oriented nation state.

Patricia Vondal, a development anthropologist with the Agency for International Development, studied changes that had taken place in Indonesian duck farming. Her study on the marketplace economy of South Kalimantan province in Indonesian Borneo showed how improved economic conditions, which were the consequence of a stable government, led to entrepreneurial innovations in duck farming (Vondal 1989). The traditional farm management strategy of the farmers of Southeastern Borneo's interior swamplands was to produce duck eggs in combination with the exploitation of forest, swamp, and riverine resources, as well as traditional rice and vegetable farming. Duck farming was a specialization in a seasonally flooded riverine and swampland ecosystem where rice and vegetable farming is limited to the dry season. Duck eggs are a major alternative to fresh food in the diets of the people of South Kalimantan during the rainy season. The eggs are held in high regard as a healthy food that promotes strength and are favored in baking many types of pastries, which are a product of the region.

Traditional flock management strategies were determined by the availability of resources used for duck feed. These included freshwater snails and fish, swamp vegetation, and sago palm. The ducks were herded to forage in the rivers and swamplands, and the farmers supplemented this feed with additional fish that they caught. However, the annual depletion of fish in the dry season severely disrupted duck farming. Fresh water fish breed at the beginning of the rainy season in November. During the rainy season, floods spread out from the rivers, and fish densities also increase, which benefits the ducks. Towards September and October, however, the dry season reduces the water supply and fishing sharply increases, depleting stocks. Available fish exceed local demand, and much is salted, dried, and sold in the provincial capital of Banjarmasin. As the dry season progressed, however, lack of fresh

fish forced most farmers to sell their duck flocks and turn to other occupations, such as trading or timber cutting, both of which take them away from their families for periods up to half the year. A sudden change in diet causes ducks to stop laying eggs for six to eight weeks.

With the improved economy of Southeastern Borneo in recent years, more people have been able to afford duck eggs, and the price for these has risen. Moreover, as the human population grew, there was also an increased demand for duck eggs. Duck eggs are not the food of the poor, but of a growing middle class, which places a high value on this form of food. Thus, duck farming has become increasingly more attractive, but the limitation placed on the farmers by the depletion of fish in the dry season appeared insurmountable.

One of the most important points of Vondal's work is that she showed how, with stable (or expanding) markets, these peasant farmers searched for alternatives to fresh fish as a food source for their ducks. A few duck farmers began experimenting with the use of slightly rotted, dried fish not fit for human consumption and with dried fish purchased from the local market. Local traders were quick to respond. Fish that were too old or too small for human consumption were increasingly sold at local markets to duck farmers.

The discovery of how dried fish could be used for duck feed had a dramatic impact on egg production. Villagers could now duck farm on a year round basis and hold production relatively constant by manipulating the type and amount of fish, either dried or fresh, which they gave to their mature flocks, thus breaking the environmental and biological constraints which had limited duck farming to a part-year activity. In addition, salt-water fishermen found a new market for their dried fish stocks, selling to duck farmers, and thus further increasing the regional economic impact of this innovation in duck farming.

Vondal's research demonstrates that under conditions of market predictability, due in large part to a stable government insuring a lack of corruption, transaction costs are low and offer the opportunity for people to experiment. Innovative experimentation, which always involves a certain amount of risk, becomes economically feasible under such low risk conditions. The anthropologist, with her holistic approach, can offer valuable insights for the design of small-scale development projects and a reasonable account of the conditions that will enhance their likelihood of success.

The unanswered question in this case: What environmental impact is year-around duck farming likely to have?

Chapter
Summary

Global Problems, International Development, and Anthropology in the Third Millennium

There exists much tension between the short-term needs of the growing human population and the need to achieve sustainable resource management on a worldwide basis, if the needs of future generations are to be adequately met. Among the requirements to achieve sustainable development will be policies that serve to eventually reduce the size of the human population and policies that serve to reduce rates of consumption among the overly affluent.

Throughout this book, we have explored the processes that have influenced the rise and fall of nations and civilizations. In this last chapter, we have examined some, but by no means all, of the global environmental problems facing humankind in the third millennium. International development, intended to alleviate poverty and create worldwide economic well-being, has instead led to greater poverty and environmental degradation in the process. Economic growth, despite its benefits for some, has served as the engine of resource depletion and environmental contamination. Human population growth has contributed to resource depletion as food production technologies struggle to keep apace of our growing numbers, often at the expense of existing natural forests and grasslands.

Anthropologists working in development have stressed the need to understand the processes involved within their varied cultural contexts and the need to integrate local knowledge in development planning. Anthropology does not have definitive answers to the global problems facing humanity, nor does any other scientific discipline. However, we are certain that any viable solutions will have to incorporate an understanding of cultural values and cultural context; and in this sense we are certain that an anthropological perspective can contribute, indeed *must* contribute, to a better future for humankind.

We have met the enemy and they are us.

—Pogo

Chapter
Terms

degradation	430	Gross National Product (GNP)	444
depletion	430	purchasing power parity	445
fertility rate	435	sustainable development	429
Gross Domestic Product (GDP)	444	transpiration	432

Check out our website
www.BVTLab.com
for flashcards,
chapter summaries,
and more.

Glossary

1967 Six Day War   Also known as the June War of 1967, this short battle was won by Israel against the combined armies of Egypt, Syria, and Jordan. It led to the second diaspora of Palestinian peoples and the occupation of the West Bank.

A-cosmic   The belief in principles or forces which are not cosmic, such as the basic principles (Ten Commandments) of the three monotheistic religions

Acculturation   The adaptation of one culture to the culture of another society

Acephalous   Headless tribes; social structures in which there are no apparent leaders and decision-making depends on egalitarian relationships

Achieved status   Status in a society that is determined by virtue of accomplishing those things that the society values

Alcalde   In the cargo system the highest rank, that of mayor

Allophone   A sound contained in a phoneme that has variations due to the context of other sounds in which it occurs

Alterative movement   A social movement with the limited goal of changing some aspect of the individual (partial change of the person, not the society)

Amratian   This is the second stage following the Badarian producing the first decorated pottery; burials show increased stratification but this is still a tribal society. This site is also from Upper Egypt, near Abydos, and is dated between 4000 to 3500 B C. There is evidence that these people may have used natural irrigation of the Nile and that villages were organized into totemic clans. Men wore little clothing; both sexes used cosmetics ground up on stone palettes.

Anthropoid   A term that can be used for the ancestors or characteristics of monkeys, apes, and humans

Anthropology   The study of humankind

Anthropology of art   The study of folk art

Anthropology of religion   The comparative study of how humans view the supernatural

Applied anthropology   The use of anthropological knowledge to solve the problems of human societies around the world

Arabs   Peoples speaking any of the language, derived from the Arab languages spoken at the time of Mohammed in southern Saudi Arabia, now found in North Africa, Egypt, Saudi Arabia, Palestine, Syria, Iraq, and elsewhere

Articulation   The connection (articulation) between increasing levels of efficiency in production and financial rewards to the workers found in Western Europe and the United States

Artifact   Items created by humans that have definite forms and functions created by culture

Ascribed status   Status in a society that is determined by birth

Assimilation   The surrender of ethnic markers or identity (or culture) to a dominant ethnic group, which may be forced or voluntary

Astrolabe   An instrument used to measure the altitude of the sun or stars used in navigation

Atman   The Hindu term for soul which is reborn every generation

Australopithecines   The earliest hominids

Authoritarian power   Structural power found in state capitalist societies with some degree of authority given to non-elite or non-government groups, as long as they do not challenge the means of authority of the elites

Ayuntamiento   The Latin American colonial form of local administration, usually controlling a municipio, or municipality, that consists of a large cabecera or head village, where the ayuntamiento is located, and smaller towns and villages (Traditionally controlled by hacienda owners, today it is a unit of local political organization in most of Latin America.)

Badarian   This is the first of three stages of the pre-dynastic period in Egypt dating to 5000 BC. These tribal farmers and gatherers lived in mud huts and practiced burials in wooden tombs, probably tied to an ancestor cult much like the cultures of Dynastic Egypt. They cultivated emmer wheat and barley which they harvested with reaping knives made of microblades. This site is found in Upper Egypt.

Bands   Peoples on the peripheries of ancient and modern states and chiefdoms who practiced hunting and food gathering, had egalitarian societies, and were largely nomadic (Band societies probably preceded the development of tribes, chiefdoms, and states. Property rights are public.)

Bedouin   A speaker of Arabic who lives in the desert

Bilateral kinship   Relationship to others (relatives) traced from an individual through his/her parents (see Bilateral Network) (The difference between bilateral kinship and unilineal descent is that in the first relationships are traced from a individual to others and in the second relationships are traced from a founding ancestor through either a line of females or a line of males to an individual.)

Bilateral networks   Networks of relationships to relatives that are traced from a man or woman through both parents; also called a personal kindred

Bjauk   Balinese dance dependent on masked women and men

Bound morpheme   Units of meaning that must occur attached to another morpheme

Brahmins   The caste of priests, usually considered the highest caste

Bride price   Common in societies practicing patrilineal descent; wealth that is paid to the family or clan of the bride in recognition of her status and the loss she represents to her family of orientation and clan

Broad spectrum hypothesis   A hypothesis by Kent Flannery that argued that domestication and village life were part of a complex of factors

Caliph   Also calif, kaliph, or khalif, a title for the head of a Moslem state

Cargo system   Refers to the civil-religious system of the highland Indian towns of Mexico, Guatemala, Bolivia, Peru, and Ecuador, where syncretic religions of mixed Catholic and traditional Indian practice redistribution of wealth and commit participants to membership in their closed communities; also referred to as the fiesta system (Indians carry symbolic cargos each year of ceremonies that are ranked and create status levels for successful participants.)

Caste   This rank and status distinction is made in hegemonic societies where members of the same caste are expected to marry one another (castes are, in theory, endogamous) and practice the same occupation. Rank and status are inherited, usually through the father, and are coupled to rituals and ceremonies established by religion, such as the Hindu religion in India.

Caste endogamy   Marriage to a member of one's own caste.

Caste system   Four basic Indian castes: Brahmin (priests), Ksaitryas (warriors), Vaisyas (merchants), and Sudras (laborers or peasants) that are subsequently subdivided and can be considered supercastes, or over-ranking categories. (Into the four castes are ranked thousands of castes, each of which is an endogamous group practicing a specific profession. In addition, there is a fifth class of untouchables, those generally not considered part of the four-caste system and outside of society.)

Caudillo   Spanish term for a man of power or authority, supreme commander, a head of state, a political boss

Charismatic phase   The first phase in a redemptive movement when followers believe in their messianic or charismatic leader when the leader is believed to have special knowledge of the word of God, the meaning of nature, or the future revealed by history (The term charismatic refers to the special powers a person appears to have.)

Charro   A Mexican cowboy dance or the name for the Mexican cowboy

Chou   The first state or empire in China that dated to between 1100 BC to AD 220 (Ironworking was common, as were mass burials and extensive warfare. Confucius taught his message, and Buddhism spread through China. The Great Wall was built to keep nomads out.)

Civil Rights Movement   A reformative social movement designed to ensure the rights of minorities (including women) and to create an egalitarian social order

Class   This is a social category used for modern industrial societies and refers to ranking of the population into distinct levels based on wealth or achievement. Most modern societies have a three-class system composed of upper, middle, and lower classes. In modern states, the majority of the people belong to the middle class.

Classic phase   In the history of anthropology, the period in which anthropologists became employed in colleges and universities; began just before World War I and lasted until a few decades after World War II

Cognatic descent   Descent traced through any combination of male and female links to a common ancestor (Membership in cognatic descent groups may overlap because of the different pathways through which descent can be traced to common ancestors. In societies with cognatic descent groups, an individual may choose to be a member of one or a small number of groups and such choice usually means that membership in other such groups is precluded, or cannot be activated.)

Cognitive anthropology   The study of folk taxonomies of human and natural phenomena

Cognitive science   The scientific study of cognition

Colonos   A term used in Guatemala on either haciendas or plantations for the resident laborers that usually farm a small plot of land given to them by the landowners to make up for low wages

Comadre   A co-mother, the female sponsor of one's child, for example, at baptism

Compadrazgo   Co-parenthood, the relationship between the parents of a child, the child's sponsors, and the child (The godparents theoretically share the responsibility with the parents for the religious training of the child. In actuality, the social significance of the relationship goes beyond religious training. It is sometimes the basis for patron-client relationships common in Latin America between elites and non-elites. Also in Latin America the relationship between co-parents is usually more significant socially than that between godparent and godchild.)

Compadre   A co-father or a co-parent generally; usually a wealthy relative, neighbor, or friend

Comparative linguistics   The study of the origins of different languages and the genetic relationships among languages

Complementary opposition   A process whereby groups with distinct interests at a low level are tied to each other by common membership in a higher level category which draws their cooperation

Compradors   The commercial elites in the Middle East who were enriched by links to European colonial governments, usually as importers of European goods (The children of this class often became the revolutionaries driving out colonial governments.)

Connectivity   The "adaptations" of cultures to each other

Conquistadores   "The Conquerors," a Spanish term, referring to the first wave of colonists to the New World (which included soldiers and non-soldiers alike) whose actions were based on mercantilist beliefs and the interest of Spanish colonists to the capture of wealth, not its creation

Corporate ownership   Rights to the use of a resource are limited to those who are members of a group and are much more specific, in contrast to public ownership. In tribal societies, lineages or clans or other groups based on a principle of descent may be corporate owners of property.

Corporations   In capitalist societies, corporations are fictions based on the extension of private property rights from individuals to groups or associations of individuals. This protects the rights of any one member by distributing liabilities to all.

Corporatism   This means the same thing as state capitalism, except the society is conceptualized as formed into a giant pyramid-like corporation.

Corregidor   The political position of civil judge, a ceremonial post in the traditional cargo system with no real power, and within an ayuntamiento the same term applied to positions analogous to councilman or alderman

Corrida   A Latin American dance associated with the music played during bullfights, called the paso doble (two step)

Cosmic   A form of polytheism very common to non-monotheistic peoples who believe that the forces of the cosmos are supernatural beings (winds, rains, stars, sun) (Roman and Greek Hellenism is a cosmic religion.)

Crusades   Any of the military expeditions undertaken by the Christians of Europe in the eleventh, twelfth, and thirteenth centuries to recover the Holy Land from various Islamic states

Culture   The shared knowledge, beliefs, and patterns for behavior, the resulting behavior, and the resulting material products

Cybernetic theory   The interdisciplinary study of the structure of regulatory systems

Debt peonage   Debt slavery where workers are loaned food, clothing, and other goods at high interest rates and are then trapped by their debt, often as near-slaves; supposedly outlawed after World War II, but still common in remote rural regions

Degradation   A human-induced reduction in the quality of natural resources, such as soil, water, and air, that reduces the capacity of these resources to support life. (Contamination of soil with toxic waste is an example of soil degradation.)

Deity   A supernatural being or god; a being with powers which are beyond those of nature

Democratic capitalism   Economies characterized by private property rights, free or open markets, competition for profits, and democratic government and not to be confused with monopoly capitalism which dominated Western Europe and the United States until the early twentieth century (Important: ideally, democracy balances the worst excesses of exploitation produced in capitalist societies, but this ideal has often been betrayed by sundry interest groups found on both the left and the right of the political spectrum where left is labor and right is capital.)

Depletion   A human-induced reduction in the quantity of a natural resource or for renewable resources such as forests, a reduction at a rate greater than the natural rate of regeneration or replacement. (Erosion is an example of soil depletion.)

Descriptive linguistics   The analysis of the structures of language into agreed-upon components in order to provide descriptions that are comparable

Dharma   A person's essential quality or character or destiny, according to Buddha

Diaspora   This term refers to several different occasions during which the Jewish peoples were dispersed from their homelands, the first of which occurred after the Babylonian destruction of Jerusalem in 597 BC (Another diaspora was the expulsion of the Jews from Spain in the late fifteenth century. The same term is often applied to Palestinians driven out of Palestine at various times, beginning with the 1948 creation of Israel.)

Diffusion theory   The idea that cultures have devolved or degenerated from earlier, advanced civilization(s), such as ancient Egypt

Disarticulation   The lack of a connection between efficiency in the workplace and wages (Disarticulation is usually produced when wages are set by global market forces or by state managers, not by national economies. Countries, which are increasingly drawn into the global economy, are challenged by disarticulation. Worker salaries in the United States and Western Europe are increasingly disarticulated. State capitalist and state socialist economies both tend to be disarticulated before they begin the transition to democratic capitalism. Disarticulation may be the greatest challenge of globalism.)

Dispersed clan   A clan whose members live in many villages

Divination—scapulamancy   The use of ox and other scapulae to foretell the future (Symbols, which later became Chinese writing, were painted on the scapula; then these were heated, and the future was read by studying cracks in the symbols.)

Doi moi   Vietnamese parallel to the Russian word *perestroika,* meaning to open markets or restructure the economy away from closed socialist practices

Dowry   The wealth that is given by the family of orientation of the bride as an endowment to the groom or to compensate the bride for her loss of rights when she marries out and often confused with bride price

Ecological circumscription   A theory developed by Robert Carneiro who argues that agricultural societies evolve because growing populations are prevented from migrating due to mountains, deserts, or jungles. The growing populations produce increased conflict due to land limitations, which is resolved by developing hierarchy and castes or classes based on the wealth of the landowning group.

Economic anthropology   The comparative study of economic systems

Economic liberalization   The transformation of state capitalist or state socialist societies into democratic capitalist societies, and in general, refers to the introduction of free or open markets to societies that have closed markets

Ejido   A term in Mexico for a collective estate, usually owned by Indian communities and found mostly in the highland regions of Latin America

Emic analysis   The analysis of what a native thinks about his culture as an insider

Encomiendas   Rights given to the Conquistadores and their immediate descendants to the labor of Indians, but not to their lands (The right to the exploitation of Indian labor led to a population collapse and to the opening of lands, which became the haciendas discussed above.)

Enculturation   The term used by anthropologists to describe the general process whereby children learn what their parents and others around them know

Endogamy   Marriage within a specified group like a clan or a lineage (Clan endogamy is more common than lineage endogamy.)

Entrepots   Trade centers (*See* Treaty Ports)

Ethnicity   Regional or national identity based on language, religion, or heritage, with ethnic identities usually identifiable by self-defined "ethnic markers," such as flags, speech patterns, costumes, beliefs, or other criteria which separate one ethnic group from another

Ethnocentrism   The common feature of all people to think their own culture is superior to others

Ethnocide   The destruction of the ethnic markers, ethnic identity, or culture of an ethnic group or groups

Ethnographer   The researcher who conducts field research among a particular group of people

Ethnographic present   The presentation of an ethnography as static and unchanging

Ethnographic relativism   Also called cultural relativism, the tendency to write about people as though they had always existed, and to do so with a sense of moral ambiguity

Ethnography   A study produced by an ethnographer

Ethnohistory   The study of the lifeways of past populations

Ethnolinguistics   The study of the ways in which people from different cultures organize, categorize, and classify the things that make up their worlds

Ethnology   The comparison of the features of two or more societies or cultures

Ethnonationalism   Separatist social movements that are transformative and redemptive at the same time, and are often ethno religious and call for a total change in the nature of society while doing the same for the state of the individual. (The movements tend to be separatist because the leaders often consider that contact with other groups will weaken or reduce the legitimacy of the movement. Such movements often fade as it becomes apparent that separatism is not a possible option.)

Etic analysis   The comparative analysis of a culture with other cultures by an outsider to the cultures

Evangelical Protestantism   A religious movement in Latin America which offers an alternative to the Catholic Church in the form of Protestantism and often has a conservative political perspective, the opposite of liberation theology

Exogamy   Marriage outside of some specified group like a lineage or clan (In societies with descent groups, marriage must usually be with someone who is not a member of one's own descent group. In societies with only bilateral kin groups, marriage must usually be with someone who is not a close relative, or who does not share the same surname.)

Family of orientation   The family into which one is born

Family of procreation   The family one creates

Female infanticide   Causing the death of a female infant either through ritual murder or through neglect (In societies where this occurs, it is usually permitted because sons are considered more valuable than daughters.)

Fertile Crescent   A 1500-mile region that stretches from the mouth of the Tigris and Euphrates rivers down through the Levant and through Mesopotamia (modern Iraq)

Fertility rate   The average number of living children that a woman will have in her lifetime

Feudalism   In general, this refers to the manorial system of Western Europe and differs significantly from the tributary systems found in Asia. Feudal societies are not highly centralized; and while a king/queen can demand tribute from the manorial lords, he/she cannot count on them for political support. The Asiatic model, on the other hand, tends to have a large bureaucracy and army that is directly dependent on the ruler and obedient to his/her demands. It is theorized that the reason for the difference between these two models is that the Asiatic model was based on irrigation agriculture, which could be controlled by the ruler.

Filial piety (*hsaio*)   The devotion of the child to the father and the father to the emperor in the Confucian religion of China

Five Pillars   The five major expectations of those who practice Islam

Food extraction   The hunting and gathering of food

Food production   The creation of food through horticulture, agriculture, and pastoralism

Footbinding   The mark of male control over the female in the Mandarin classes, when infant girls had their feet bound while young, crippling them as adults, and generally not practiced by the peasant class (The grown-in foot was considered a sign of beauty.)

Forensic anthropology   The identification of human skeletal remains that may be evidence of a crime

Formative phase   In the history of anthropology, the period in which anthropologists were primarily trained to collect, classify, and describe cultural and biological materials for museums; primarily occurred in the nineteenth century

Free morpheme   a word that stands alone and has meaning

Gamelans   Balinese percussion instruments

Gaucho   An Argentine cowboy, usually of Indian descent (Araucanian), who specialized in cattle herding on the great cattle haciendas (called estancias)

Genocide   The systematic extermination of a people group

Gentry   The wealthiest and most powerful upper segment of the Chinese clan and the group from which the Mandarins were recruited

Gerzean   Gerzean culture probably represents a chiefdom society and rose from the preceding Amratian. It was widespread found in both Upper and Lower Egypt between 3500 BC and 3100 BC when Egypt was unified. The Gerzean is known for the use of metallurgy, casting flat axes and ribbed daggers out of copper. There is evidence for long distance trade since copper came from the Sinai to the east along with lead and silver which probably came from Asia. There is evidence for contact with Mesopotamia in the form of a cylinder seal, and there is evidence for the use of boats with sails.

Global anthropology   The current phase of anthropological history, which seeks to answer questions about the nature of culture by reaching out to global processes

Grammar   The way the sentences of a language are constructed

Gross Domestic Product (GDP)   The value of all final goods and services produced within the borders of a country, usually calculated on the basis of a common currency such as the U.S. dollar (*See also* purchasing power parity)

Gross National Product (GNP)   GDP plus net income from abroad

Guru   A spiritual leader among Buddhists

Hacienda   Traditionally, a large Latin American estate, generally found in the highlands, self-sufficient but producing for local markets, and supported by a slave-like caste of peon laborers; also refers to modern cattle ranches not unlike those of the modern American West (The Spanish term *finca* is often used in reference to haciendas. An owner is a *finquero*.)

Haciendas   Large estates, somewhat similar to the manors of Western Europe, which grew out of the encomiendas granted to the Conquistadores in exchange for their loyalties to the Hispanic and Portuguese crowns. (The control of land became the most important single vehicle for wealth in Latin America, and those who controlled the haciendas controlled the political system.)

Hadith   Authenticated accounts of Muhammad's sayings and actions that have been compiled and are recognized as Muslim scripture along with the Quran

Hegemonic cores   This is the heartland of tributary empires, usually tribute-taking states (or cities) which control a periphery made up of tributary states.

Hilly flanks theory   The theory developed by Robert Braidwood that agriculture was developed in a region where the wild ancestors of food plants occurred naturally, as apparently supported by excavations in the hilly flanks of the Qalat Jarmo site in 1948

Historical anthropology   A subfield of archaeology that examines the sites occupied by human populations during the historic period, and the artifacts the sites contain, in order to supplement the written records of history

Historical particularism   The name given to early anthropological approaches in which ethnographers would omit fine details in their writings

Hominid   A term that can refer to ancestral or modern humans

Hominid   Primates, including humans and their ancestors, belonging to the family hominidae

Hominoid   A term that can mean ancestors or characteristics of apes and humans

Human or cultural anthropology   The study of the relationship between cultural systems and physical habitats

Ideal culture   What people think they ought to do

Il Rah   An invisible road followed by pastoral nomads, which is often compared to a giant carpet laid over the landscape of grasses and water

Incest taboo   A prohibition against sex with a close relative

Indigenismo   Initially, in the early twentieth century, a transformative movement in Latin America to liberate the communities of Indians, but later a means of co-opting Indian communities within conservative and state capitalist political parties

Indigenous   Refers to contemporary reformative social movements and not to be confused with indigenismo, which seeks to restore rights to the original inhabitants of various world regions ranging from Malaysia to Latin America

Infix   A bound morpheme that occurs within a word

Inkatha   A nationalist and conservative political movement in South Africa which is opposed to the Africa National Congress and composed of supporters of Zulu Chief Mongosutho Buthelezi and his cousin, King Goodwill Zwilithini, the titular head of the Zulu tribe (Kwa Zulu). (Inkatha supports the independence of the Natal Province in eastern South Africa, as a state for the Kwa Zulu.)

Interpretivism   An approach to ethnography that emphasizes the interpretation of the meaning and values of a culture's symbols

Islam   The religious system of Allah according to his Prophet Mohammed

Jajmani   A redistribution economy that focused on the role of the *jajman*, usually an member of the elite Brahmin landowning caste, who collected the surplus production of members of distinct castes as taxes and distributed them back (The non-agricultural castes were given grain in exchange for the products or services.)

Karma   One's destiny within the Hindu religion

Kerese   Shallow well that is dug vertically to tap into an aquifer, usually adding horizontal tunnels at the bottom of a well, and can be manned by a single clan

Khan   The hereditary chief or leader of a clan or chiefdom among pastoral nomads, but also applied to the chiefs of settled towns throughout the Middle East and Inner Asia

Kibbutz   Collective farms in Israel that were organized during the early or Zionistic phase of Israeli history with roots in socialist philosophy

Kshatriya   The second level caste of warriors and rulers

Ladang   The term used in Indonesia to refer to swidden plots (*See* swidden)

Ladino   Spanish term used in Guatemala meaning the same thing as mestizo or Creole

Lanzon   A temple at the site of Chavin de Huantar in the Peruvian Andes depicting a feline deity, dated to about 800 BC

Late or Upper Paleolithic   The last phase of the "Stone Age," also known as Upper Paleolithic, coinciding with the appearance of biologically modern humans (Homo sapiens sapiens) and lasting from 40,000 to 9000 BC

Later Iron Age   A term used by anthropologists and historians for the region of Central Africa between AD 1000 and 1500. (It was a period of great economic, social, and political development with a characteristic emphasis on cattle-keeping and the mining and smelting of iron ore. Inter-regional trade was particularly well-developed.)

Latifundia   Term used for haciendas or plantations, large and elite-owned estates

Legal anthropology   The comparative study of law among cultures

Legong   A Balinese court dance of young girls

Lexicon   The vocabulary of a particular language

Liberation theology   A political movement within the Catholic Church in Latin America supporting the interests of the poor and often associated with a socialist point of view

Linguistic anthropology   The study of the relationship between language and culture

Lungshan   A Chinese early chiefdom that appeared between 4000 to 2000 BC and distinguished by highly burnished, wheel-made, thin-walled pottery; pit houses surrounding a central long house; temples of pounded earth; and the use of permanent fields instead of slash and burn (Of particular importance is evidence for shamanism and ancestor worship in the form of scapulimancy. There is also important evidence of household manufacturing and long distance trade.)

Machismo   The Latin American expectation that a man will exploit those women he can and protect those he must which is based on the term macho, meaning strong male

Mahayana Buddhism   Buddhist tradition that is found in Tibet, China, Vietnam, Korea, and Japan

Mana   A Polynesian word that is used in anthropology to refer to a powerful magical force, which can be manipulated by humans who have the appropriate ritual knowledge

Mandarin   Those from the gentry who passed the state exam (usually based on Confucian philosophy) and became the bureaucracy (This class was ideally separate from the Chinese aristocracy or ruling class, an ideal which was often broken.)

Manorial system   Dating back to Roman rule in Western Europe, the manorial system consists of large landed estates (manors) ruled by lords, who were under the tributary control of a single king/queen and his/her clan or lineage. The lords of the manors did not own them but were granted the right to use them in exchange for tribute to the king (the manorial system is a tributary state).

Mansabdars   The Muslim upper caste in India, controlled both the army and bureaucracy

Mantrayna Buddhism   Stresses the relationship of a guru to his followers

Mastabas   Cut stone tombs with flat roofs housing mummies, these Pre-dynastic monuments presaged the development of Egyptian pyramids in the Dynastic period.

Matrilineal descent   Descent traced through a line of females (Both women and men acquire membership in a matrilineal descent group from their mothers, but only women can pass membership in the group on to their children.)

Mechanical solidarity   Durkheim's idea that "primitive" societies were less diversified than "modern" societies and had little division of labor

Menhirs, dolmens, and passage graves   These are a similar type of burial monuments, usually associated with chiefdom level social structures. They are found in Western Europe for the Mesolithic and Neolithic. They are also found in Asia. Usually consisting of three vertically placed rocks overlaid by a fourth roof layer, these monuments are thought to have been the burial sites of chiefs.

Mercantilism   This economic philosophy determined European international policies during the colonial period and was based on the idea that wealth was limited and could only be divided, and not created. A further characteristic was the idea that money (specie) was the store of wealth, particularly in the form of silver and gold. Those societies that controlled the distribution of specie would become rich and powerful. These two ideas drove European countries to control as many other countries and regions as possible.

Meroe   A chiefdom or state which arose directly south of Egypt between 1500 BC and AD 350 with very Egyptian characteristics

Mesoamerica   Refers to the area of sophisticated pre-Hispanic civilizations in Mexico and upper Central America, which includes the southern two-thirds of Mexico, all of Guatemala and Belize, and the northern third of Honduras and El Salvador

Mesolithic   The Middle Stone Age, the period during which the domestication of plants and animals took place, generally characterized by microlithic tools, dating from about 9000 to 7000 BC (The period following is called the Neolithic, or New Stone Age.)

Messianic   Term that is used to refer to transformative or charismatic movements led by a leader or leaders, who promise deliverance or redemption

Mestizo   Originally meant mixed blood, hybrid, usually of Indian and Spanish descent; often the term used instead of Creole, which refers to a hybrid language, and today meaning anyone of Indian and Spanish heritage

Microblade   A type of implement found in European Mesolithic cultures and formed by snapping a blade into smaller pieces and forming those pieces into composite tools; also called a microlith.

Millet   Under the Ottoman Empire, a term for a religious and political unit defined by its adherence to a religion and granted certain rights and privileges (The Islamic millet had the highest rank, while Christians, Jews, and members of other communities were granted lower ranks. Nonetheless, non-Islamic communities or ethnic groups were allowed to keep their practices as long as they did not contradict the Islamic state.)

Milpa   The term used in Mesoamerica to refer to swidden plots (*see* swidden)

Minifundia   Small estates, usually owned by independent farmers, whose labor is used by large estates

Modernization   This is a theory, popular in the 1950s and 1960s, that capitalism and industrial technology can transform traditional societies into democratic capitalist modern societies. The fallacy lies in the lack of attention by theoreticians to traditional social structures that are ruled by non-democratic elites whose vested interest is in controlling power (structural power).

Moiety   A division of society into two social groups, usually based on a rule of unilineal descent (In other words, all of the lineages or clans in a society will belong to one or the other of these two moieties. Usually, the lineages or clans belonging to a moiety share descent from a common (usually mythical) ancestor in the distant past.)

Moksha   The ultimate release from Samsra, according to Hindu belief

Monogenesis   A theory of human origin that argues the existence of a single "mound builder" race that degenerated into many races over time

Monotheism   The doctrine or belief that there is a single high God. (This is the belief of the people of the Book or Old Testament: Jews, Christians, and Arabs.)

Morpheme   A unit of sound that has meaning and is composed of phonemes

Multiculturalism   A reformative social movement with the objective of granting distinct ethnic groups the right to retain some, or all of their heritage (markers, identity, culture), and in general, can be considered a type of civil rights movement which goes beyond the demand for equality before the law and seeks a degree of recognition from the larger society of its distinct heritage

Municipio   Spanish term for a political division that is the equivalent of a township

Neolithic revolution   A term coined by Vere Gordon Childe to describe his assumption that people moved to the lowland oases along the Tigris and Euphrates rivers because of the desiccation of the climate and that they developed agriculture when they came into close proximity with plants, animals, and water

Nirvana   The Hindu idea of escape from the caste system and of birth and re-birth or samsara

Organic solidarity   Durkheim's idea that modern societies are more heterogeneous and cohered than earlier societies because people play many different roles that require them to cooperate

Paleoecology   The relations and interactions between ancient life forms and their environment

Paramount chief   The central office of a chiefdom is an ascribed role which is inherited by either the oldest or most talented of a set of offspring who can claim descent from the founding ancestor of the chiefdom. The office of the chief differs from that of a king or head of state in that power does not inhere to the office, which is primarily ritualistic; and he/she cannot initiate a political act, such as a declaration of war, without support from other less powerful chiefs and close kinsmen.

Patrilineal descent   Descent traced through a line of males (Both men and women acquire membership in a patrilineal descent group from their fathers, but only men can pass membership in the group on to their children.)

Patrilocality   The relocation of a woman to her husband's house upon marriage

Peasant   The lowest classes, ranks, or castes of the tsu or clan; those who worked the land as distinct from the Mandarin or merchant classes

Perennial irrigation   More complex irrigation/well/tunnel structures requiring state support

Phone   A discreet sound that is part of a language

Phoneme   The significant sounds in a language that convey meaning when speaking

Phonetic alphabet   An alphabet based on the sounds of a spoken language

Phonology   The study of the phonemes of a language

Phratry   A grouping of two or more lineages or clans into a larger group based on a belief in common descent, like a moiety except that the lineages or clans form more than two groups, called phratries

Plantations   Similar to haciendas but organized for the production of export commodities such as sugar, cotton, or hemp (for cordage); tend not to be self-sufficient and depend on local farmers for food

Political anthropology   The study of the emergence and development of public policy and political culture

Polygenesis   A theory of human origin that argues that God created many distinct races to fit into the distinct environments of the world

Polygyny   Marriage between one male and two or more females forming multi-family social structures

Polytheistic   The doctrine or belief in many gods or powers

Pongid   A term that can refer to ancestral or modern apes

Porfirismo   The Liberal philosophy of Porfirio Dias, the dictator of Mexico from 1876–1911, of industrializing rapidly by opening countries to outside investment

Potlatch   A redistribution feast, traditional among some Native peoples of Northwestern North America, in which an individual gives away wealth in order to achieve prestige or higher status

Prebendalism   A political system based on a ruler giving offices to his followers as gifts, rewards, or stipends for political support

Process   The focus by anthropologists on the problems of human adaptation to physical habitats

Proletariat   Those without property (The rural proletariat are those without land, and the urban proletariat are those without wealth or the opportunity to acquire wealth.)

Public ownership   Rights to the use of a resource are public to anyone (analogous to the use of highways or parks in Western culture).

Purchasing power parity   The amount of a common "market basket" of goods and services that can be purchased locally, using local currency, including goods and services not traded internationally (GDP adjusted on the basis of purchasing power parity is often significantly higher than GDP calculated solely on the basis of U.S. dollars.)

Qanats   Horizontal wells that are dug into hills or mountains to tap aquifers (subterranean pools of water) and can be manned by a single clan

Quran   The Koran, the sacred scripture of Islam, that was believed by orthodox Muhammedans to be the revealed word of God, spoken in Arabic

Rancheras   A popular form of Mexican folk music associated with the western frontier, particularly the state of Jalisco

Rancheria   A small Latin American farm, usually containing cattle and/or maize and owned by people of Indian ancestry

Real culture   What people actually do

Reciprocity   Economic transactions between individuals or groups where exchange is based on trust that the person to whom something is given will be equally willing to give in return (moral relationships) (Generalized reciprocity occurs among close kinsmen: there is no expectation that something of equal value will be returned, and there is no expectation that the return will take place within a specified period of time. The only expectation is that at some time something will be given back. Balanced reciprocity occurs among close and more distant kinsmen, and sometimes among good friends. There is the expectation that something of equivalent value will be given within an agreed upon period of time. Reciprocity is the opposite of market exchange, which is based on profit (a-moral relationships).

Redemptive movement   A social movement with the goal of completely changing the individual—changing the state of the person, not the society (Generally, redemptive movements are religious or psychological in nature.)

Reductionism   The tendency to explain human communities through theories that viewed them as though they existed in isolation

Reference group   The social environment of a movement made up of other people (reference) who are used as a contrast or a basis for comparison to establish relative deprivation

Reformative movement   A social movement which has goals limited to targeting certain aspects of society for change (again, change is to the social system, not the self)

Reification   Turning an abstract idea into a concrete idea with cause-and-effect aspects

Relative deprivation   A social science theory that explains the motivation of people involved in social movements and found in the feeling of alienation by a people who feel that they are illegitimately deprived of status, property, power, or worth

Religious statement   An attempt to explain non-observable phenomena

Renaissance   The period marking the transition from the medieval to the modern world, roughly from the fourteenth through the sixteenth centuries, when the arts and philosophies of the ancient world, particularly Greece and Rome, were rediscovered and made the basis for a new birth of European culture

Resource mobilization   The resources that a group must control in order to succeed in its goals (It is not enough that a group is deprived; it must also have the capacity to succeed. One block to success is structural power. (See Chapter 6.)

Salinization   Term for the process of irrigation water in deserts picking up salts from basic sources and depositing those salts again in concentrated form so that after several generations of use the soils lose their fertility

Samsra   The Hindu belief in reincarnation

Samurai   The Japanese military aristocracy during the feudal period

Satori   The flash of insight which distinguishes Zen from other Buddhist schools

Scala Naturae   Also called natural ladder of life, the taxonomy of animal and plant species developed by Greek and Roman thinkers, which gradually became an evolutionary paradigm

Scapulamancy   *See* divination

Scientific statement   A logically related set of propositions that attempt to explain the relationships between certain observable facts

Sectarian   The opposite of secular; movements which have a religious basis

Semantics   The study of the meaning of words, phrases, sentences, and even larger units of discourse

Seppeku   One of the ritual codes of bushido requiring the warrior to commit suicide if he could not complete a mission

Settled farming   In Africa, the farming that is village farming, where peasants use rainfall or irrigation resources to support themselves and their families, usually selling their surplus on regional markets connecting them to herding peoples

Shaman   A religious specialist, male or female, who is able to communicate with and control natural and supernatural forces and mediate between humans and these non-human forces

Shogun bushido   The Japanese commander in chief, supreme military ruler during the feudal period or a code of behavior of Japanese warriors during the feudal period in Japan

Sinified   Process of enculturation whereby non-Chinese learned Chinese culture; often used to refer to Mongol invaders who took over the Chinese state but became Chinese

Social anthropology   The study of kinship

Social movement   An attempt by people to organize themselves to effect change in the face of resistance

Social structure   The rules (institutions) governing social relationships and organization in human societies (In bands and tribes, these relationships are based on kinship. In modern societies, they are based on kinship and broader community relationships defined by expected roles and statuses.)

Socialization   The term used by sociologists to describe the general process whereby children learn what their parents and others around them know

Sociolinguistics   The study of language in relation to its social context

Socionatural systems   The relationship among ecosystems, cultural institutions, and political economy

Sodality   A form of social group which cuts across kin groups and unites people on the basis of mutual interests. An association based on common interest; in tribal society cross cuts clans and other unilineal lineages; in modern society, any type of fraternity or sorority based on common interest, such as male or female groups in Latin America supporting the Catholic Church and its religious celebrations

State capitalism   Often confused with corporatism in Latin America, state capitalism is non-democratic and tends to be characterized by state ownership of industrial capital (but not land, which is often in the hands of the elite). Also confused with state socialism, state capitalist economies do not have central economies managed and planned by bureaucratic elites. They do have markets; however, these tend not to be free but are controlled by the elites to their advantage. Private property rights are restricted to the wealthy classes (and thus are scarce).

State socialism   Often confused with communism, state socialist societies tend to be non-democratic (although they often claim lofty democratic goals) and are characterized by state ownership of industrial capital and land (all means of production). State socialist societies differ from state capitalist in having neither free markets nor private property rights, but having centrally controlled and managed economies. Communist and socialist societies differ in the myth that the working class owns the former while bureaucratic managers control the latter. In fact, most socialist or communist societies are state socialist.

Stratified   This primary characteristic of states is one where status relationships fall into a minimum of two stratified classes (but often many more), also known as political classes or as social classes. In tributary states, also known as primitive states, status relationships are ascribed and the upper class (aristocracy) is endowed with power, while the lower class (peasantry) is not. In modern industrial societies, status relations are achieved (in theory).

Structural power   Structural power is control over the political process by the elites who control state capitalist or state socialist economies; it is also the residual control over power by former elites once economic systems no longer exists.

Sumptuary laws   Laws found in chiefdoms and hegemonic states and specify privileges of the elite or nobility while simultaneously prohibit commoners from exercising the same privileges. For example, the elite may wear certain types clothing and jewelry that the commoners are not allowed to wear. Such items then symbolize class or rank differences.

Supernatural   A belief in principles or forces which are not part of the natural universe but are beyond, found among the Peoples of the Book

Sustainable development   Development or improvement in the quality of human life that is economically viable (benefits are greater than costs), socially and culturally acceptable, and ecologically viable (resources used at a rate equal to or less than the rate of renewal); strategy that is designed to meet current needs without compromising the needs of future generations

Swidden   Shifting between agriculture dependent on cutting down and burning a small patch of forest, planting crops on the plot for two or three years, and then allowing the plot to lie fallow (remain unused) for a number of years until the forest has grown back

Symbolic anthropology   A subdiscipline of anthropology that emphasizes the interpretation of the meaning and values of symbols in a culture; also called interpretivism

Syncretic   The blending of elements of two or more distinct traditions that may refer to religion, music, other aspects of culture, or culture as a whole

Syntactics   The study of the organization of words into phrases and sentences

Teleology   The ascription of values to "systems," whether human or physical

Territorial clan   A clan which claims ownership of a territory in which its members are concentrated

Theocracy   A form of government in which a sacred deity is viewed as the supreme ruler

Theravada Buddhism   Early school of Buddhism that is found in Burma, Sri Lanka, and elsewhere in Southeast Asia

Ti   Also, T'i or Shang-ti, a superior being in the Chinese pantheon of gods during the during the Lungshan period

Totalitarian power   Structural power found in socialist or communist societies where no political autonomy is allowed to non-government or non-elite groups

Trade/raid nexus   These are the two sides of the coin of pastoral nomadic adaptations: when the tribe succeeds in protecting its herd and has a surplus of animals, it trades with settled town dwellers. When it is not successful, it raids.

Transformative movement   A social movement which has as its goals the radical and total change of the social order (the system outside the self)

Transhumance herding   Transhumance herding is often viewed as the opposite of settled farming with herders driving cattle, camels, horses, or goats over a changing landscape dependent on their knowledge of local ecosystems for survival. But settled farming and transhumance herding are tied together symbiotically. The markets of the farmer are supplied by goods carried by the drover, and both exchange the appropriate goods with each other (grain for meat, and vice versa). Transhumance herders have a permanent base village, unlike true pastoral nomads who do not.

Transpiration   A loss of water vapor into the air by plants that eventually returns to the earth as precipitation (rain or snow)

Treaty ports   Also known as ports-of-trade, which were entrepots or trade centers where European traders were protected by the state as long as they did not interfere in politics

Tributary empires   This is another name for pre-modern world systems (Wallerstein). Tributary empires are based on hegemonic cores controlling trade and warfare and receiving tribute from those societies in the periphery, which they dominate.

Tributary states   These are states found in the peripheries of hegemonic empires that pay tribute to the cores of empire. Also known as theater states, often they are not distinguishable from chiefdoms.

Tsu   The traditional multi-generational Chinese clan or extended family based on patrilineal descent, which incorporated the elite Mandarin as well as peasant lower classes

Ulema   A council of men who are experts on Islamic religion and law

Unilineal descent   Descent that is traced from a founding ancestor through either a line of females (matrilineal descent) or a line of males (patrilineal descent) to determine one's membership in a unilineal descent group (Unlike cognatic descent groups where an individual may belong to more than one group, membership in a unilineal descent group is exclusive and based on either the group membership of the mother (matrilineal) or the father, patrilineal.)

Unilinear evolution   The idea that all of the most advanced cultures had passed through the same stages—savagery, barbarism, and civilization—or had stopped at one of the first two stages

Untouchable   This is a social category in the Indian caste system made up of those people whose occupations are considered ritually unclean such as leatherworkers, those who dispose of dead animals, those who handle the dead, those who clean latrines, and so on. Since only the four central castes were considered acceptable aspects of Indian society, the Untouchables were considered a fifth category outside of the social system.

Vaisya   The third level caste of landholders and merchants

Varnas   The term for the four Indian castes

Vedas   The sacred scriptures of Hinduism that are the four Books of Wisdom: Rig- Veda, Yajur-Veda, Sama-Veda, and Atharva-Veda.

Villeins   The peasants living on the manors who worked the land and were at the bottom of the manorial status pyramid.

Virginity complex   The Latin American expectation that women will maintain their virginity at all cost and found primarily among the elite classes

Virilocality   The relocation of a woman to the lands of her husband's kin upon marriage

Yang-shao   The first neolithic, probably tribal, culture of China, circa 6000 to 5000 BC, characterized by partially subterranean houses, domesticated rice, millet, pigs, dogs, chickens and water buffalo (They made stone sickles, mortars, pestles and ceramics, and probably practiced slash and burn agriculture.)

Zamindars   The Hindu elite under the control of the Mansabdars during the first phase of British colonialism

Zen Buddhism   A form of Buddhism that stresses personal enlightenment and is found in Korea and Japan

Zionism   The plan outlined in the Balfour Declaration of November 2, 1917, to colonize Palestine with Hebrews

References

Aberle, David F. (1991). *The Peyote Religion among the Navaho.* Norman: University of Oklahoma Press.

Acheson, James M. (1996). Household organization and budget structures in a Purepecha pueblo. *American Ethnologist* 23(2):331–351.

Acheson, James M. (1995). Coase among the Purepechas: Transaction costs and institutional change in a Mexican Indian pueblo. *Journal of the institutional change in a Mexican Indian pueblo.* Journal of Institutional and Theoretical Economics 151(2):3–43.

Aciieson, James M. (1986). Social organization of the Maine lobster market. In S. Plattner (Ed.), *Markets and Marketing (pp.* 105–132). Monographs in Economic Anthropology, No. 4. Lanham, MD: University Press of America.

Acheson, James M. (Ed.) (1994). *Anthropology and Institutional Economics.* Monographs in Economic Anthropology, No.12. New York: University Press of America.

Acheson, James M., and James A. Wilson (1996). Order out of chaos: The case for parametric fisheries management. *American Anthropologist* 98(3):579–594.

Adams, Robert Mc. (1975). The emerging place of trade in civilization studies. In J. A. Sabloff & C. C. Lamberg-Karlovsky (Eds.), *Ancient Civilization and Trade (pp.* 451–464). Albuquerque: University of New Mexico Press.

Adams, Robert Mc. (1974). Anthropological perspectives on ancient trade. *Current Anthropology* 15(3):239–258.

Al Khalil, Samir (1989). *Republic of Fear.* New York: Pantheon Books.

Algaze, Guillermo (1993). *The Uruk World System.* Chicago: University of Chicago Press.

Allen, Catherine J. (1988). *The Hold Life Has: Coca and Cultural Identity in an Andean Community.* Washington, DC: Smithsonian Institution Press.

Anthropology Today (1996). 12(6). [Advertisement].

Arensberg, Conrad (1961). The community as object and as sample. *American Anthropologist* 63:241–264.

Arensberg, Conrad, and Solon T. Kimball (1972). *Culture and Community.* Gloucester, MA: Peter Smith.

Armstrong, G. Patrick (1989). Gorbachev's nightmare. *Crossroads* 29:21–30.

Balovra, Enrique (1990). El Salvador. In Howard Wiarda and H. F. Kline (Eds.), *Latin American Politics* and Development, 3rd ed. (pp. 183–197). Boulder, CO: Westview Press.

Barfield, Thomas (1993). *The Nomadic Alternative.* Englewood Cliffs, NJ: Prentice-Hall.

Barnett, Homer (1953). *Innovation: The Basis of Cultural Change.* New York: McGraw-Hill.

Barth, Fredrik (1961). *Nomads of South Persia: The Baseri Tribe of the Khamseh Confederacy.* Boston: Little, Brown.

Barth, Frederic (Ed.) (1969). *Ethnic Groups and Boundaries.* Boston: Little, Brown.

Basham, A. L. (1959). *The Wonder That Was India.* New York: Grove Press.

Baxter, Craig (1992). Bangladesh: A parliamentary democracy if they can keep it. *Current History* 91(563):132–137.

Bellah, Robert, et al. (1985). *Habits of the Heart.* New York: Harper & Row.

Benedict, Ruth (1946). *The Chrysanthemum and the Sword .* Boston: Houghton Mifflin.

Benjamin, Medea (Trans. & Ed.) (1989). *Don't Be Afraid Gringo: A Honduran Woman Speaks from the Heart The Story of Elvia Alvarado*. New York: Harper Collins.

Bennett, John W. (1998). *Classic Anthropology: Critical Essays, 1944–1996*. New Brunswick, NJ: Transactions Publishers.

Bennett, John W. (1993). *Human Ecology as Human Behavior*. New York: Transaction Publishers.

Bennett, John W. (1985). The micro-macro nexus: typology, process and system. In Billie R. DeWalt and Pertti J. Pelto (Eds.), *Micro and Macro Levels of Analysis in Anthropology: Issues in Theory and Research* (pp. 23–54). Boulder; CO: Westview.

Bennett, John W. (1976). *The Ecological Transition*. Chicago: Aldine.

Bennett, John W. (1969). *The Northern Plainsmen*. Chicago: Aldine.

Bennett, John W. (1958). Economic aspects of a boss-henchman system in the Japanese forestry industry. *Economic Development and* Cultural Change 7:13–30.

Bernard, H. Russell (1995). *Research Methods in Anthropology: Qualitative and Quantitative Approaches*, 2nd ed. Walnut Creek, CA: Altamira Press.

Berthrong, Donald J. (1948). La Crosse, a Case Study in Social History, 1900–1910. Unpublished MA Thesis, Department of History, University of Wisconsin, Madison.

Bilello, Suzanne (1996). Mexico: The rise of civil society. *Current History* 95(598):82–87.

Blackman, Morris J., William M. Leo Grande, and Kenneth E. Sharpe (Eds.) (1986). *Confronting Revolution: Security through Diplomacy in Central America*. New York: Random House.

Blanton, Richard, and Gary Feinman (1984). The Mesoamerican World System. *American Anthropologist* 86:673–682.

Blanton, Richard E., Stephan A. Kowalewski, Gary Feinman, and Jill Appel (Eds.) (1981). *Ancient Mesoamerica*. Cambridge: Cambridge University Press.

Block, Maurice (1994). Language, anthropology, and cognitive science. In Robert Borofsky (Ed.), *Assessing Cultural Anthropology (pp.* 276–282). New York: McGraw-Hill.

Bodley, John H. (1982). *Victims of Progress*. Menlo Park, CA: Cummings Publishing.

Bohannen, Paul, and P. Curtin (1995). *AFRICA AND AFRICANS*. Prospect Heights., IL: Waveland.

Boorstin, Daniel J. (1983). The *Discoverers*. New York: Random House.

Booth, John A. (1990). Nicaragua: Revolution under siege. In Howard Wiarda and H. F. Kline (Eds.), *Latin American Politics and Development*, 3rd ed. (pp. 467–482). Boulder, CO: Westview.

Borofsky, Robert (Ed.) (1994). *Assessing Cultural Anthropology*. New York: McGraw-Hill.

Bourgois, Philippe (1996). Confronting anthropology, education, and inner-city apartheid. *American Anthropologist* 98(2):249–265.

Brooks, David (1990). Beyond catch phrases: What does sustainable development really mean? *International Development Research Centre Reports* 19(1)24–25.

Brown, Lester R., Nicholas Lenssen, and Hal Kane, et al. (1996). Vital Signs 1996: *The Trends That Are Shaping Our Future*. New York: W. W. Norton.

Brumfiel, Elizabeth (1994). *The Economic Anthropology of the State*. Monographs in Economic Anthropology, No. 11. Lanham, MD: University Press of America.

Burg, Steven (1993). Why Yugoslavia fell apart. *Current History* 92(577):357–363.

Burgos-Debray, Elizabeth (see Menchu, Rigoberta).

Busby, Annette (1995). Kurds. In J. Middleton and A. Rassam (Eds.), *Africa and the Middle* East (pp. 174–177). Encyclopedia of World Cultures, Vol. 9. Boston: G. K. Hall & Co.

Buxbaum, Edward (1967). The Greek-American group of Tarpon Springs, Florida: A study of ethnic identification and acculturation. Unpublished Ph D. Dissertation, Department of Anthropology, University of Pennsylvania.

Calhoun, Craig, Donald Light, and Suzzane Keller (1994). *Sociology*, 6th ed. New York: McGraw-Hill.

Campbell, John (1964). *Honour Family, and Patronage*. Oxford: Clarendon Press.

Cancian, Frank (1965). *Economics and Prestige in a Maya Community*. Stanford: Stanford University Press.

Cancian, Frank (1992). The *Decline of Community in Zinacantan*. Stanford: Stanford University Press.

Carmack, Robert M., Janine Gasco, and Gary H. Gossen (1996). *The Legacy of Mesoamerica: History and Culture of a Native Civilization*. Upper Saddle River, NJ: Prentice-Hall.

Carneiro, Robert (1961). *Slash-and-Burn Cultivation among the Kuikuru and its Implications for Cultural Development in the Amazon Basin*. Caracas: Editorial Sucre.

Carneiro, Robert L. (1973). Slash-and-burn cultivation among the Kuikuru and its implications for cultural development in the Amazon Basin. In Daniel Gross (Ed.), *Peoples and Cultures of Native South America* (pp. 98–123). New York: Doubleday.

Carneiro, Robert L. (1970). A theory of the origin of the state. *Science* 169:733–738.

Carroll, John B. (Ed.) (1956). *Language, Thought, and Reality: Selected Writing of Benjamin Lee* Wharf. Cambridge, MA: MIT Press

Carter, Gwendolen M., and P. O'Meara (1986). *African Independence: The First Twenty-Five Years.* Bloomington; Indiana University Press.

Chagnon, Napoleon (1968). *Yanomamo: The Fierce People* New York: Holt, Rinehart and Winston.

Chagnon, Napoleon (1974). *Studying the Yanomamo.* New York; Holt, Rinehart and Winston.

Chance, John K., and William B. Taylor (1985). Cofradias and cargos: An historical perspective on the Mesoamerican civil-religious hierarchy. *American Ethnologist* 12(1):1–26.

Chang, K. C. (1975). Ancient trade as economics or as ecology. In J. A. Sabloff and C. C. I.amberg-Karlovsky (Eds.), *Ancient Civilization and Trade* (pp. 211–224). Albuquerque: University of New Mexico Press.

Chao, Paul (1977). *Women under Communism: Family in Russia and China.* Bayside, NY; General Hall.

Childe, V. Gordon (1936). *Man Makes Himself.* London: Watts and Company.

Chinas, Beverly L. (1973). *The Isthmus Zapotecs: Women's Roles in Cultural Context.* New York; Holt, Rinehart and Winston.

Claessen, Henri J. M., and Pieter Van De Velde (Eds.) (1991). *Early State Economics.* New Brunswick, NJ; Transaction Books.

Clark, Grahame, Stuart Piggott, et al (1961). *The Dawn of Civilization: The First World Survey of Human Cultures in Early Times.* New York: McGraw-Hill.

Clifford, James, and George E. Marcus (Eds.) (1986). *Writing Culture: The Poetics and Politics of Ethnography.* Berkeley: University of California Press.

Coatsworth, John (1979). Obstacles to economic growth in nineteenth-century Mexico. *American Historical Review* 39;939–960.

Coatsworth, John (1974). Railroads, landholding, and agrarian protest in the early Porfiorato. *Hispanic American Review* 54:48–71.

Coe, michael D. (1962). *Mexico.* New York: Praeger.

Coe, Michael D., Dean Snow, and Elizabeth Benson (1986). *Atlas of Ancient America.* New York; Facts on File.

Cohen, Theodore (1987). *Remaking Japan: The American Occupation as New Deal,* New York: Free Press.

Cohen, Yehudi (Ed.) (1968). *Man in Adaptation: The Cultural Present.* Chicago; Aldine.

Collier, George A. (1994). Roots of the rebellion in Chiapas. *Cultural Survival Quarterly* 18(l):14–18.

Collingwood, Dean (1991). *Japan and the Pacific Rim.* Sluice Dock, Guilford, CT; Dushkin Publishing Group.

Comaroff, John (1994). Democracy, fried chicken and the anomic bomb. *Cultural Survival Quarterly* 18(2/3):34–39.

Commins, Stephen K., Michael F. Lofchie, and Rhys Payne (Eds.) (1986). *Africa's Agrarian Crisis: The Roots of Famine.* Boulder, CO; Lynne Rienner.

Conklin, Harold C. (1961). The study of shifting cultivation. *Current Anthropology* 2(1)27–61.

Coon, Carleton (1962). *The Origin of Races.* New York: Knopf.

Cossali, Paul, and Clive Robson (1986). *Stateless in Gaza.* London: Zed Books.

Cramer, Christopher (1994). Rebuilding South Africa. *Current History* 93(583);208–212.

Cressey, George B. (1963). *Asia's Lands and Peoples.* New York: McGraw-Hill.

Culbert, T. Patrick (1983). Mesoamerica. In Jesse D. Jennings (Ed.), *Ancient North Americans* (pp. 495–555). San Francisco; W. H. Freeman.

Cunliffe, Barry (1979). *The Celtic World.* New York: McGraw Hill.

Cunliffe, Barry (1974). *Iron Age Communities in Britain.* London; Routledge & Kegan Paul.

Daly, Herman (1996). *Beyond Growth: The Economics of Sustainable Development.* Boston: Beacon Press.

Daniel, Glyn (1962). *The Idea of Prehistory.* London: C.A. Watts.

Dart, Raymond (1925). Australopithicus Africanus: The Man-Ape of South Africa. *Nature 115,* 2884: 195–199.

De Blij, H. J., and Peter O. Muller (1997). *Geography: Realms, Regions, and Concepts,* 8th ed. New York; John Wiley and Sons.

De Janvry Alain (1981). *The Agricultural Question in Latin America.* Baltimore, MD: John Hopkins University Press.

De Tocqueville, Alexis (1957). *Democracy in America.* New York: New American Library.

De Waal, Alex (1996). In the disaster zone. In William Haviland and Robert J. Gordon (Eds.), *Talking About People,* 2nd ed. (pp. 241–251). Mountain View, CA: Mayfield.

De Waal, Alex (1994). Genocide in Rwanda. *Anthropology Today* l0(3);1–2.

De Waal, Frans (1995). Bonobo Sex and Society. *Scientific American* 272,3: 82–88.

Dean, Warren (1969). *The Industrialization of Sao Paulo, 1880–1945.* Austin: University of Texas Press.

Des Forges, Alison (1994). Burundi: Failed coup or creeping coup. *Current History* 93(583)203–207.

Divale, William, and Marvin Harris (1976). Population, warfare, and the male supremacist complex. *American Anthropologist* 78(3)521–538.

Douglas, Mary (1966). *Purity and Danger.* London: Routledge & Kegan Paul.

Downs, James F. (1971). Spirits, power, and man. In Y. Cohen (Ed.), *Man in Adaptation: The Institutional Framework* (pp. 187–194). New York; Aldine.

Drennan, Robert D. (1976). Religion and social evolution in formative Mesoamerica. In Kent Flannery (Ed.), *The Early Mesoamerican Village* (pp. 345–368). New York: Academic Press.

Drewal, Margaret Thompson (1992). *Yoruba Ritual.* Bloomington; Indiana University Press.

Duncan, Kenneth, and I. Rutledge (1977). *Land and Labor in Latin America.* Cambridge: Cambridge University Press.

Earle, Timothy (1987). Chiefdoms in archaeological and ethnohistorical perspective. *Annual Reviews of Anthropology* 16:299–308.

Ebel, Roland (1990). Guatemala: The politics of unstable stability. In Howard Wiarda and H. F. Kline (Eds.), *Latin American Politics and Development,* 3rd ed. (pp. 498–518). Boulder, CO: Westview.

Economist, The (1996). August 31.

Economist, The (1995). April 8.

Economist, The (1992). October 19.

Eickelman, Dale (1981). *The Middle East: An Anthropological Approach.* Englewood Cliffs, NJ: Prentice-Hall.

Eiseley, Loren (1958). *Darwin's Century.* Garden City, NY: Doubleday.

Elashmawi, Fared, and Philip R. Harris (1993). *Multicultural Management.* Houston, TX: Gulf Publishing.

Ensminger, Jean (1992). *Making a Market: The Institutional Transformation of an African Society.* Cambridge: Cambridge University Press.

Erickson, Paul A. and Liam D. Murphy (2003). *A History of Anthropological Theory.* Orchard Park, NY: Broadview Press.

Eschleman, J. Ross (1994). *The Family.* Boston: Allyn & Bacon.

Escobar, Arturo (1995). Encountering *Development: The Making and Unmaking of the Third World.* Princeton, NJ: Princeton University Press.

Esman, Milton J., and Itamar Rabinovich (Eds.) (1988). *Ethnicity, Pluralism, and the State in the Middle East.* Ithaca, NY: Cornell University Press.

Etzioni, Amital (1993). *The Spirit of Community.* New York: Crown.

Evans-Pritchard, E. E. (1940). *The Nuer.* Oxford: Clarendon Press.

Fagan, Brian (1985). *In the Beginning: An Introduction to Archaeology.* Boston: Little, Brown.

Fagan, Brian (1995). *People of the Earth: An Introduction to World Prehistory,* 8th ed. New York: Harper Collins.

Fagan, Brian (1989). *People of the Earth: An Introduction to World Prehistory.* Glenview, Il.: Scott Foresman.

Fage, J. D. (1995). *A History of Africa,* 3rd ed. London: Routledge.

Fagg, John E. (1963). *Latin America: A General History.* New York: Macmillan.

Fei Hsiao-Tung. (1981). Toward a People's Anthropology. Beijing: New World Press.

Fishlow, A. (1965). *American Railroads and the transformation of the antebellum economy.* Cambridge: Harvard University Press.

Flannery, Kent (1968). The Olmec and the Valley of Oaxaca: A model for interregional interactions in formative times. In Elizabeth P. Benson (Ed.), Dumbarton Oaks Conference on the Olmec (pp. 79–110). Washington, DC: Dumbarton Oaks Research Library.

Flannery Kent V., and Joyce Marcus (1983). The growth of site hierarchies in the valley of Oaxaca, Part 1. In Kent Flannery and J. Marcus (Eds.), *The Cloud People* (pp. 53–64). New York: Academic Press.

Fogel, Robert W. (1964). *Railroads and American Economic Growth.* Baltimore: Johns Hopkins University Press.

Fortune, Reo (1932). *Sorcerers of Dobu: The Social Anthropology of the Dobu Islanders of the Western Pacific.* London: G. Routledge and Sons, Ltd.

Foster, George M. (1965). Peasant society and the image of limited good. *American Anthropologist* 67: 293–315.

Frank, Andre Gunder (1978). *Dependent Accumulation and Underdevelopment.* New York: Monthly Review Press.

Frank, Andre Gunder (1969). *Latin America: Underdevelopment or Revolution.* New York: Monthly Review Press.

Frank, Andre Gender (1967). *Capitalism and Underdevelopment in Latin America.* New York: Monthly Review Press.

Frankfort, Henri (1956). *The Birth of Civilization in the Near East.* New York: Doubleday.

Freeman, Charles (1993). *The World of the Romans.* New York: Oxford University Press.

French, Rebecca R. (1994). Tibetans. In Paul Friedrich and Norma Diamond (Vol. Eds.), *Encyclopedia of World Cultures, Volume VI. Russia and Eurasia/China* (pp. 493–496). Boston: G. K. Hall.

Fuentes, Carlos (1992). *The Buried Mirror: Reflections on Spain and the New World.* Boston: Houghton Mifflin.

Gasco, Janine, and Barbara Voorhies (1989). The ultimate tribute: The role of the Soconusco as an Aztec tributary. In Barbara Voorhies (Ed.), *Ancient Trade and Tribute: Economies of the Soconusco Region of Mesoamerica* (pp. 287–303). Salt Lake City: University of Utah Press.

Gearing, Frederick O. (1970). *The Face of the Fox.* Chicago; Aldine.

Gearing, Frederick O. (1971). The structural poses of 18th-century Cherokee villages. In Y. Cohen (Ed.), *Man in Adaptation: The Cultural Present* (pp. 181–187). New York: Aldine.

Geertz, Clifford (1996). *After the Fact: Two Counties, Four Decades, One Anthropologist.* Cambridge: Harvard University Press.

Geertz, Clifford (1968). *Islam Observed.* New Haven, CT: Yale University Press.

Geertz, Clifford (1963). *Agricultural Involution.* Berkeley: University of California Press.

Gernet, Jacques (1996). *A History of Chinese Civilization.* Cambridge: Cambridge University Press.

Gilbert, Martin (1993). *The Dent Atlas of Jewish History.* London: J. M. Dent.

Gilbert, Martin, (Ed.) (1990). *The Illustrated Atlas of Jewish Civilization: 4000 Years of Jewish History.* New York: Macmillan.

Givens, David B. and Timothy Jablonski (1995). 1995 survey of anthropology PhDs. In *The AAA Guide: A Guide to Departments, A Directory of Members* (pp. 306–317). Arlington, VA: American Anthropological Association.

Givon, Talmy (1979). *On Understanding Grammar.* New York: Academic Press.

Gjording, Chris N. (1991). *Conditions Not of Their Choosing: The Guaymi Indians and Mining Multinationals in Panama.* Washington, DC: Smithsonian Institution Press.

Glazer, Nathan, and Daniel P. Moynihan (1975). *Ethnicity: Theory and Experience.* Cambridge: Harvard University Press.

Glazer, Nathan, and Daniel P. Moynihan (1970). *Beyond the Melting Pot.* Cambridge: MIT Press.

Goldman, Minton F. (1992). *Commonwealth of Independent States and Central/Eastern Europe.* Sluice Dock, Guilford, CT: Dushkin Publishing Group.

Goldschmidt, Arthur (1983). *A Concise History of the Middle East.* Boulder, CO: Westview.

Goldschmidt, Walter (1978). *As You Sow: Three Studies in the Social Consequences of Agribusiness* [orig. 1947]. Montclair, NJ: Allenheld, Osmun.

Gossen, Gary (1994). Comments on the Zapatista movement. *Cultural Survival Quarterly* 18(1):19–21.

Grove, David (1981). The formative period and the evolution of complex culture. In J. Sabloff (Vol. Ed.), *Archaeology, Supplement to the Handbook of Middle American Indians,* Vol. 1 (pp. 373–391). Austin: University of Texas Press.

Gugliotta, Guy and Jeff Leen (1989). *Kings of Cocaine.* New York: Harper & Row.

Hall, Edward, and Mildred Hall (1990). *Understanding Cultural Differences.* Yarmouth, ME: Intercultural Press.

Halliday Frank E. (1989). *England: A Concise History.* New York: Thames & Hudson.

Harden, Blaine (1990). *Africa: Dispatches from a Fragile Continent.* Boston: Houghton Mifflin.

Hardgrave, Robert L. (1992). After the dynasty: Politics in India. *Current History* 91(563):106–112.

Harris, Marvin (1994). Cultural materialism is alive and well and won't go away until something better comes along. In Robert Borofsky (Ed.), *Assessing Cultural Anthropology* (pp. 62–76). New York: McGraw-Hill.

Harris, Marvin (1992). Distinguished lecture: Anthropology and the theoretical and paradigmatic significance of the collapse of Soviet and East European Communism. *American Anthropologist* 94(2):295–303.

Harris, Marvin (1979). Cultural Materialism: *The Struggle for a Science of Culture.* New York: Random House.

Harris, Marvin (1968). *The Rise of Anthropological Theory.* New York: Thomas Crowell.

Harris, Marvin (1964). *Patterns of Race in the Americas.* New York: Walker.

Harris, Philip R., and Robert T. Moran (1987). *Managing Cultural Differences,* 2nd ed. Houston: Gulf Publishing.

Harrison, Selig S. (1992). South Asia and the United States: A chance for a fresh start. *Current History* 91(563):97–106.

Hatch, Elvin (1985). Culture. In Adam Kuper and J. Kuper (Eds.), *The Social Science Encyclopedia* (pp. 178–180). London: Routledge & Kegan Paul.

Headland, Thomas, Kenneth Pike, and Marvin Harris (Eds.) (1990). *Emics and Etics: The Insider/Outsider Debate.* Newbury Park, CA: Sage.

Hegel, Georg W. F. (1956). *The Philosophy of History.* New York: Dover.

Herrnstein, Richard J., and Charles Murray (1994). *The Bell Curve: Intelligence and Class Structure in American Life.* New York: Free Press.

Himmelstein, Hal (1984). *Television, Myth, and the American Mind.* New York: Free Press.

Hobsbawm, E. J. (1962). *The Age of Revolution 1789–1948.* New York: Mentor.

Hockett, Charles F. (1960). Logical considerations in the study of animal communication. In W. E. Lanyon and W. N. Tavolga (Eds.), *Animal Sounds and Communication* (pp. 392–430). Washington, DC: American Institute of Biological Sciences, Publication No. 7.

Holloway, Thomas (1977). The coffee colonos of Sao Paulo Brazil: Migration and mobility. In K. Duncan and I. Rutledge (Eds.), *Land and Labor in Latin America* (pp. 301–321). Cambridge: Cambridge University Press.

Homans, George Caspar (1941). *English Villagers of the Thirteenth Century*. New York: Russell and Russell.

Homans, George [1941] (1968). English villagers of the thirteenth century. In Y. Cohen (Ed.), *Man in Adaptation: The Cultural Present* (pp. 466–477). Chicago: Aldine.

Hourani, Albert (1991) A History *of the Arab Peoples*. Cambridge: Cambridge University Press.

Howell, Nancy (1990) *Surviving Fieldwork*. Washington, DC: American Anthropological Association.

Hughes, Johnathan (1987). *American Economic History*. Glenview, IL: Scott Foresman.

Hunt, Shane (1973). Growth and guano in nineteenth century Peru. Discussion Paper No. 34, Princeton, University.

Huntington, Samuel P. (1996). *The Clash of Civilizations and the Remaking of World Order*: New York: Simon & Schuster.

Huntington, Samuel P. (1993). Democracy's third wave. In L. Diamond and M. F. Plattner (Eds.), *The Global Resurgence of Democracy* (pp. 3–25). Baltimore: Johns Hopkins University Press.

Hutchinson, Sharon (1996). Nuer Dilemmas: *Coping with Money, War and the State*. Berkeley: University of California Press.

Jannedy, Stefanie, Robert, Poletto, and Tracey L. Weldon, (Eds.) (1994). *Language Files: Materials for an Introduction to Language & Linguistics,* 6th ed. Columbus: Ohio State University Press.

Jennings, Jesse D. (Ed.) (1983a). *Ancient North Americans,* San Francisco: W. H. Freeman.

Jennings, Jesse D. (Ed.) (1983b). *Ancient South Americans*. San Francisco: W. H. Freeman.

Johnson, Allen W. and Timothy Earle (1987). *The Evolution of Human Societies: From Foraging Group to Agrarian State*. Sanford, CA: Sanford University Press.

Johnson, Gregory (1973). Locational exchange and early state development in Southwestern Iran. University of Michigan Museum of Anthropology, Anthropology Papers #51.

Joseph, Richard (1996). Nigeria: Inside the dismal tunnel. *Current History* 95(601):193–200.

Kapur, Rajiv (1986). *Sikh Separatism: The Politics of Faith*. London: Allen & Unwin.

Kanow, Stanley (1983). *Vietnam: A History*. New York: Viking.

Keddie, Nikki (1981). *Roots of Revolution: An Interpretive History of Modern Iran*. New Haven, CT: Yale University Press.

Keesing, Roger (1981). *Cultural Anthropology*. New York: Holt, Rinehart, Winston.

Keesing, Roger M. (1976). *Cultural Anthropology: A Contemporary Perspective*. New York: Holt, Rinehart and Winston.

Kehoe, Alice (1981). *North American Indians*. Engelwood Cliffs, NJ: Prentice-Hall.

Kimball, Solon, and W. Partridge (1979). *The Craft of Community Study: Fieldwork Dialogues*. Gainesville: University of Florida.

Kimmerling, Baruch and J. S. Migdal (1994). *Palestinians: The Making of a People*. Cambridge: Harvard University Press.

Knight, Virginia C. (1992). Zimbabwe: The politics of economic reform. *Current History* 91(565): 219–223.

Kolata, Alan (1993). The *Tiwanaku: Portrait of an Andean Civilization*. Cambridge, MA: Blackwell.

Krader, Lawrence (1968). *Formation of the State*. Englewood Cliffs, NJ: Prentice-Hall.

Kroeber, Alfred (1948). Anthropology. New York: Harcourt Brace.

Kroeber, Alfred (1917). The superorganic. American Anthropologist 19:163–213.

Kroeber, Alfred (1909). Classificatory systems of relationship. *Journal of the Royal Anthropological Institute* 39:77–84.

Kroeber, Alfred and Clyde Kluckhohn. (1952). *Culture: A Critical Review of Concepts and Definitions*. New York: Vintage Books.

Kuhn, Thomas (1962). *The Structure of Scientific Revolutions*. Chicago: University of Chicago Press.

La Lone, Darrell E. (1994) An Andean world System: Production transformations under the Inka empire. In Elizabeth Brumfiel (Ed.), The Economic Anthropology of the State (pp. 17–41). Monographs in Economic Anthropology, No. 11. New York: University Press of America.

Lacey, Robert (1981). *The Kingdom: Arabia and the House of Sa'ud*. New York: Avon.

Lanternari, Vittorio (1963). *The Religions of the Oppressed: A Study of Modem Messianic Cults* (Trans. from the Italian by Lisa Sergio.) New York: Mentor.

Lapidus, Ira M. (1988). *A History of Islamic Societies*. Cambridge: Cambridge University Press.

Larson, Gerald J. (1995). *India's Agony over Religion*. Albany: State University of New York Press.

Lasky, Harold (1948). *The American Democracy, a Commentary and Interpretation. New* York: Viking.

Latinamerican Press (1996). Mexico: Restless poor are hungry. Vol. 28, no. 34 (Sept. 19), pp. 1, 8.

Laughlin, Charles and Eugene D'Aquili (1974). *Biogenetic Structuralism*. New York: Columbia University Press.

Laughlin, Robert (1994). Mayan Resistance: Sna Jtz'ibajom, The House of the Writer. *Cultural Survival:* 13–15.

Laughlin, Robert (1995). Sna Jtzs'ibajom, the house of the writer. *Cultural Survival Quarterly* 19(2):9.

Leach, Edmund (1954). *Political Systems of Highland Burma*. Boston: Beacon Press.

Leach, Edmund (1961). *Pul Eliya: A village in Ceylon*. Cambridge: Cambridge University Press.

Lee Richard (1984). *The Dobe !Kung*. New York: Holt, Rinehart and Winston.

Lee, Richard (1972). The *Dobe !Kung*. New York: Holt, Rinehart and Winston.

Lee, Marion (1969). Long-term Brazilian development. *Journal of Economic History* 29:473–93.

Leibenstetn, Harvey (1957). *Economic Backwardness and Economic* Growth. New York: Wiley.

Lemarchand, Rene (1994). *Burundi: Ethnocide as Discourse and Practice*. New York: Cambridge University Press.

Lemoine, Jacques (1989). Ethnicity, culture and development among some minorities of the People's Republic of China. In Chien Chiao and Nicholas Tapp (Eds.), *Ethnicity and Ethnic Groups in China* (pp. 1–9). Hong Kong: Don Bosco Printing Co., Ltd.

Levy Jr., Marion J. (1966). *Modernization and the Structure of Societies*. Princeton, NJ: Princeton University Press.

Lewin, Roger (1992). *Life at the Edge of Chaos*. New York: Macmillan.

Lewis, Bernard (1995). The *Middle East*. New York: Scribner's Sons.

Lieberman, Devorah, and Mel Gurtov (Eds.) (1992). *Revealing the World: An Interdisciplinary Reader for International Studies*. Dubuque, IA: Kendall/Hunt Publishing Co.

Little, Peter (1988). Preliminary observations of rural-urban linkages in southern Somalia. Development Anthropology Network. *Bulletin of the Institute for Development Anthropology* 6(1):4–10.

Lodge, George C. (1990). *Perestroika for America*. Boston: Harvard Business School.

Lofchie, Michael F. (1986). Africa's agricultural crisis: An overview. In Stephen K. Commins, Michael F. Lofchie, and Rhys Payne (Eds.), *Africa's Agrarian Crisis: The Roots of Famine (pp. 3–18)*. Boulder, CO: Lynne Rienner.

MacDonald, Charles (1989). The Kurdish challenge in revolutionary Iran. *Journal of South Asian and Middle Eastern Studies* 13(1/2):52–68.

Magnarella, Paul J. (1993). *Human Materialism*. Gainesville: University of Florida Press.

Mair, Lucy (1974). *African Societies*. Cambridge: Cambridge University Press.

Malinowski, Bronislaw (1917). *Baloma: The Spirits of the Dead in the Trobriand Islands*. London: Royal Anthropological Institute of Great Britain and Ireland.

Malinowski, Bronislaw [1944] (1960). *A Scientific Theory of Culture and Other Essays*. New York: Oxford University Press.

Malotki, Ekkehart (1983). *Hopi Time: A Linguistic Analysis of the Temporal Concepts in the Hopi Language*. Berlin: Mouton.

Mango, Andrew (1979). The multiple crisis in Turkey. *Asian Affairs* 10:125–31.

Marcus, George E., and Michael M. J. Fischer (1986). *Anthropology as Cultural Critique: An Experimental Moment in the Human Sciences*. Chicago: University of Chicago Press.

Marx, Karl (1936). *Capital, a critique of political economy*. New York: The Modern Library.

Masters, William H., and Virginia E. Johnson (1966). *Human Sexual Response*. Boston: Little, Brown.

Masuda, Shozo, Isumi Shimada, and Craig Morris (Eds.) (1985). *Andean Ecology and Civilization: An Interdisciplinary Perspective on Andean Ecological Complementarity*. Papers from the Wenner-Gren Foundation for Anthropological Research Symposium No. 91. Tokyo: University of Tokyo Press.

Maybury-Lewis, David (1997). *Indigenous Peoples, Ethnic Groups, and the State*. Boston: Allyn & Bacon.

Maybury-Lewis, David (1992). Millenium. New York: Viking.

McCorkle, Constance M. (1989). The context of the cotton/cereal equation in Burkina Faso. In S. Smith and E. Reeves (Eds.), *Human Systems Ecology* (pp. 81–106). Boulder, CO: Westview.

McGranahan, Carole (1993). Tibetans. In Marc S. Miller (Ed.), *State of the Peoples: A Global Human Rights Report on Societies in Danger* (pp. 125–126). Boston: Beacon Press.

McGreavy, William (1971). *An Economic History of Colombia, 1845–1930*. Cambridge: Cambridge University Press.

McLeod, W. H. (1989). *The Sikhs*. New York: Columbia University Press.

McNeil, Robert and William McNeil (2003). *The Human Web: A Bird's-eye View of World History*. New York: Norton and Co.

McNeill, William (1974). *The Shape of European History*. New York: Oxford University Press.

McNeill, William (1963). *The Rise of the West*. Chicago: University of Chicago Press.

Mead, Margaret and Ruth Leah Bunzel (1960). *The Golden Age of American Anthropology*. New York: G. Braziller.

Meggers, Betty J. (1971). *Amazonia: Man and Culture in a Counterfeit Paradise*. Chicago: Aldine.

Menchu, Rigoberta (1984). *I, Rigoberta Menchu*. (Elizabeth Burgos-Debray, ed.; Ann Wright, trans.) London: Verso.

Michael, Robert T., John H. Gagnon, Edward O. Laumann, and Gina Kolata (1994). *Sex in America: A Definitive Survey*. Boston: Little, Brown.

Middleton, John (1995). Introduction to Africa. In John Middleton and Amal Rassam (Eds.), *Encyclopedia of World Cultures, Volume IX, Africa and the Middle East* (pp. xxiii–xxxiv). Boston: G. K. Hall.

Migdal, Joel S. (1996). Society-formation and the case of Israel. In Michael Barnett (Ed.), *Israel in Comparative Perspective: Challenging the Conventional Wisdom* (pp. 173–198). Albany, NY: SUNYPress.

Miller, Marc S. (and Cultural Survival staff) (1993). *State of the Peoples: A Global Human Rights Report on Societies in Danger.* Boston: Beacon Press.

Miller, Robert *(1959).* A History of La Crosse, Wisconsin, 1900–1959. Unpublished Ph.D. Dissertation, Peabody College.

Mintz, Sidney *(1985). Sweetness and Power.* New York: Viking Penguin.

Mintz, Sidney *[1960] (1974). Worker in the Cane.* Westport, CT: Greenwood Press.

Mintz, Sydney and Eric Wolf (1957). *Haciendas and Plantations in Middle America and the Antilles.* Jamaica: Mona.

Moore, Sally Falk *(1994). Anthropology and Africa: Changing Perspectives on a Changing Scene.* Charlottesville & London: University Press of Virginia.

Moran, Emilio *(1982). Human Adaptability: An Introduction to Ecological Anthropology.* Boulder, CO: Westview.

Moran, Emilio *(Ed.) (1990). The Ecosystem Approach in Anthropology.* Ann Arbor: University of Michigan Press.

Moreno-Black, G., and Philip Young *(1992). Anthropology and* international development in *the late* twentieth century. In Devorah Lieberman and Mel Gurtov *(Eds.), Revealing the World: An Interdisciplinary Reader for International Studies* (pp. 53–91). Dubuque, IA: Kendall/Hunt.

Morgan, L. H. (1876). *Ancient Society.* New York: World Publishing Society.

Morgan, L. H. (1870). *Systems of Consanguinity and Affinity of the Human Family.* Washington, DC: Smithsonian Institute.

Moseley, Michael E. (1992). *The Incas and Their Ancestors.* London: Thames & Hudson.

Moseley, Michael E. (1983). *Central* Andean civilization. In Jesse D. Jennings (Ed.), *Ancient South Americans* (pp. 179–239). San Francisco: W. H. Freeman & Co.

Murdock, George P. (1967). *Ethnographic Atlas.* Pittsburgh, PA: University of Pittsburgh Press.

Muslih, Mohammed (1994). Jericho and its meaning: A new strategy for the Palestinians. *Current History 93(580):72–77.*

Nash, June (1994). Global integration and subsistence insecurity. *American Anthropologist 96(1): 7–30.*

Nash, Manning (1989). *The Cauldron of Ethnicity in the Modern World.* Chicago: University of Chicago Press.

Nickels, Martin K., David E. Hunter and Phillip Whitten (1979). *The Study of Physical Anthropology and Archaeology.* New York: Harper and Row.

Niehoff, Arthur, and Conrad Arensberg *(1963). Technical Cooperation and Cultural Reality.* Washington DC: Department of State and Agency for International Development.

North, Douglas (1990). *Institutions, Institutional Change and Economic Performance.* Cambridge: Cambridge University Press.

North, Douglas (1981). *Structure and Change in Economic History.* New York: W. W. Norton.

Notar, Beth E. (1994). Hani. In Paul Friedrich and Norma Diamond (Vol. Eds.), *Encyclopedia of World Cultures, Volume VI: Russia and Eurasia/China* (pp. 449–452). Boston: G.K. Hall.

Nuccetelli, Susana (2002). *Latin American Thought: Philosophical Problems and Arguments.* Boulder. CO: Westview Press.

Ogburn, William F. (1938). *Machines and Tomorrow's World.* New York: Public Affairs Committee.

Ogden, Suzanne (1991). *China.* Guilford, CT: The Dushkin Publishing Group.

Oliver, Symmes (1962). Ecology and cultural continuity as contributing factors in the social organization of the Plains Indians. *University of California Publications in American Archaeology and Ethnology* 48:13–49. Reprinted in Yehudi Cohen (Ed.), *Man in Adaptation: The Cultural Present.* Chicago: Aldine.

Overbeek, Johannes (1974). *History of Population Theories.* Rotterdam: Rotterdam *University Press.*

Park, Kyeyoung (1996). Use and abuse of race and culture: Black-Korean tensions in America. *American Anthropologist 98(3):492–499.*

Park, Robert E. (1936). Human ecology. *American Journal of Sociology* 42:3–49.

Park, Robert E., E. W. Burgess, and R. D. McKenzie (1925). *The City.* Chicago: University of Chicago Press.

Peacock, James and A. Thomas Kirsch (1980). *The Human Direction: An Evolutionary Approach to Social and Cultural Anthropology.* Englewood Cliffs, NJ: Prentice-Hall.

Pehrson, Robert (1966). *The Social Organization of the Marri Baluch. Chicago:* Aldine.

Peletz, Michael G. (1995). Kinship studies in late twentieth-century anthropology. *Annual Review of Anthropology* 24:343–72.

Peretz, Don (1977). *The Palestinian State.* Port Washington, NY: Kinniket Press.

Pike, Kenneth (1954). *Language in Relation to a Unified Theory of the Structure of Human Behavior, Vol. 1.* Glendale, CA: Summer Institute of Linguistics.

Pilbeam, David (1984). The Descent of Hominoids and Hominids. *Scientific American* 250, 3: 84–88, 93–96.

Pilcher, William (1972). *The Portland Longshoremen: A Dispersed Urban Community.* New York: Holt, Rinehart and Winston.

Pimental, D., et al. (1995). Environmental and economic costs of soil erosion and conservation benefits. *Science* 267:1117–1123.

Pinault, David (1992). *The Shiites: Ritual and Popular Piety in a Muslim Community.* New York: St. Martin's Press.

Polanyi, Karl [1944] (1962). *The Great Transformation: The Political and Economic Origins of Our Time*. New York: Beacon Press.

Portes, Alejandro, and J. Walton (1976). *Urban Latin America*. Austin: University of Texas Press.

Prunier, Gerard (1995). *The Rwanda Crisis: History of a Genocide*. New York: Columbia University Press.

Purcell, Susan Kaufman (1992). Mexico's new economic vitality. *Current History* 91(563):54–58.

Rappaport, Roy A. (1994). Humanity's evolution and anthropology's future. In R. Borofsky (Ed.), *Assessing Cultural Anthropology* (pp. 153–165). New York, McGraw-Hill.

Rappaport, Roy A. (1979). *Ecology, Meaning and Religion*. Berkeley, CA: North Atlantic Books.

Rassam, Amal (1995). Introduction to the Middle East. In John Middleton and Amal Rassam (Eds.), *Encyclopedia of World Cultures, Volume IX, Africa and the Middle East* (pp. xxxv–xxxix). Boston: C. K. Hall.

Redfield, Robert (1941). *The Folk Culture of Yucatan*. Chicago: University of Chicago Press.

Redfield, Robert, Ralph Linton, and Melville J. Herskovits (1936). A memorandum on acculturation. *American Anthropologist* 38:149–152.

Redman, Charles (1978). *The Rise of Civilization*. San Francisco: W. H. Freeman.

Reed, Richard (1997). *Forest Dwellers, Forest Protectors: Indigenous Models for International Development*. Boston: Allyn & Bacon.

Reeves, Ed (1989). Market places, market channels, market strategies: Levels for analysis of a regional system. In Sheldon Smith and Ed Reeves (Eds.), *Human Systems Ecology* (pp. 58–80). Boulder, CO: Westview.

Reich, Robert B. (1991). *The Work of Nations*. New York: Alfred Knopf.

Reischauer, Edwin O. (1988). *The Japanese Today*. Cambridge: Cambridge University Press.

Renfrew, Colin (1979). *Problems in European Prehistory*. New York: Cambridge University Press.

Renfrew, Colin, and J. M. Wagstaff (Eds.) (1982). *An Island Polity: The Archaeology of Exploitation in Melos*. Cambridge: Cambridge University Press.

Renner, Michael (1997). Chiapas: An uprising born of despair. *World Watch* 10(1):12–24.

Riesman, David (1950). *The Lonely Crowd: A Study of the Changing American Character*. New Haven, CT: Yale University Press.

Rosenberg, Nathan, and L. E. Birdzell, JR. (1986). *How the West Grew Rich*. New York: Basic Books.

Rousseau, Jean Jacques (1994 [1755]). *Discourse on Politcal Economy*. New York and Oxford; Oxford University Press.

Roy, Sara (1994). The Gaza Strip: Past, present, and future. *Current History* 93(580):67–71.

Royal Anthropological Institute (1951). *Notes and Queries on Anthropology*. London: Routledge & Kegan Paul.

Rust, William, and R. J. Sharer (1988). Olmec settlement data from La Venta, Tabasco, Mexico. *Science* 242:102–104.

Sabloff, Jeremy A., and David F. Friedel (1975). A model of a pre-Columbian trading center. In Sabloff and Lamberg-Karlovsky, *op cit.*

Sabloff, J. A., and C. C. Lamberg-Karlovsky (Eds.) (1975). *Ancient Civilization and Trade*. Albuquerque: University of New Mexico Press.

Sahlins, Marshall (1994). Goodbye to tristes tropes: Ethnography in the context of the modern world. In Robert Borofsky (Ed.), *Assessing Cultural Anthropology* (pp. 377–393). New York: McGraw-Hill.

Sahlins, Marshall (1977). Culture and environment: The study of cultural ecology. In Sol Tax and Leslie G. Freeman (Eds.), *Horizons in Anthropology*, 2nd (revised) edition (pp. 215–23]). Chicago: Aldine.

Sahlins, Marshall (1965). On the Sociology of Primitive Exchange. In Association of Social Anthropologists of the Commonwealth (Eds), *The Relevance of Models for Social Anthropology* (pp. 139–236). New York: F.A. Praeger.

Sahlins, Marshall (1972). *Stone Age Economics*. Chicago: Aldine.

Sahlins, Marshall (1968). *Tribesmen*. Englewood Cliffs, NJ: Prentice-Hall.

Sahlins, Marshall (1961). The segmentary lineage: An organization of predatory expansion. *American Anthropologist* 63:322–345.

Sahlins, Marshall, and E. R. Service (Eds.) (1960). *Evolution and Culture*. Ann Arbor: University of Michigan Press.

Sanford, Albert, and H. J. Hersheimer (1951). *A History of La Crosse, Wisconsin*. La Crosse, WI: La Crosse Historical Society.

Sarsanedas, Jorge (1995). Basta Va! Drü 8(44):2.

Schneider, David M. (1980). *American Kinship: A Cultural Account*, 2nd ed. Chicago: University of Chicago Press.

Science News (1992), No. 141, p. 215.

Scott, Shaunna L. (1995). *Two Sides to Everything*. Albany, NY: State University of New York Press.

Service, Elman (1966). *The Hunters*. Englewood Cliffs, NJ: Prentice-Hall.

Service, Elman (1962). *Primitive Social Organization*. New York: Random House.

Shillington, Kevin (1989). *History of Africa*. New York: St. Martin's Press.

Shubane, Khehla (1992). South Africa: A new government in the making? *Current History* 91(565):202–207.

Simpson, George Gaylord (1949). *The Meaning of Evolution: A Study of the History of Life and of its Significance for Man*. New Haven, CT: Yale University Press.

Sinopoli, Carla (1994a). Political choices and economic strategies in the Vijayanagara Empire. In Elizabeth Brumfiel (Ed.), *The Economic Anthropology of the State* (pp. 223–242). Monographs in Economic Anthropology, No. 11. Lanham, MD: University Press of America.

Sinopoli, Carla (1994b). The archaeology of empires. In W. H. Durham, E. V. Daniel, and B. Schieffelin (Eds.), *Annual Review of Anthropology*, vol. 23 (pp. 159–180). Palo Alto, CA: Annual Reviews, Inc.

Sinopoli, Carla (1995). The Archaeology of Empires: A View from South Asia. *Bulletin of the American Schools of Oriental Research* 299/300: 3–11.

Sklar, Richard L. (1986). The colonial imprint on African political thought. In Gwendolen M. Carter and Patrick O'Meara (Eds.), *African Independence: The First Twenty-Five Years* (pp. 1–30). Bloomington: Indiana University Press.

Smith, Richard, (1974). Los Cafeteros. Unpublished Ph.D. Dissertation. Department of Anthropology, University of Oregon.

Smith, Robert (1988). *Kingdoms of the Yoruba*. Madison: University of Wisconsin Press.

Smith, Sheldon *Los Cafeteros* (1974). Doctoral dissertation, University of Oregon

Smith, Sheldon (1995). *World in Disorder: An Anthropological and Interdisciplinary Approach to Global Issues*. Lanham, MD: University Press of America.

Smith, Sheldon (1994). Politics and ecology in Puebla. In Elizabeth Brumfiel (Ed.), *The Economic Anthropology of the State* (pp. 325–348). Monographs of the Society for Economic Anthropology, No. 11. Lanham, MD: University Press of America.

Smith, Sheldon (1993). *World in Disorder: An Interdisciplinary Approach to Global Issues*. Lanham, MD: University Press of America.

Smith, Sheldon (1985). The re-establishment of community: The emerging festival system of the American Midwest. *Journal of American Culture* 8(3):91–100.

Smith, Sheldon (1982). Human ecology, socionatural systems, and the central-satellite plantation system of Guatemala and Colombia. *Studies in Comparative International Development* 17(l):3–21.

Smith, Shelon and Richard L. Smith (1989). Horizontal and vertical linkages in highland Antioquia, Colombia: The architecture of the landscape. In S. Smith and E. Reeves (Eds.), *Human Systems Ecology: Studies in the Integration of Political Economy, Adaptation, and Socionatural Regions* (pp. 170–201). Boulder, CD: Westview.

Smith, Sheldon, and Ed Reeves, (Eds.) (1989). *Human Systems Ecology: Studies in the Integration of Political Economy, Adaptation, and Socionatural Regions*. Boulder, CO: Westview.

Smith-Ayala, Emilie (1991). *The Granddaughters of Ixmucané: Guatemalan Women Speak* Toronto, Canada: Women's Press.

Sneider, Daniel (1992). The Soviet 'ecocidal' legacy. *Christian Science Monitor*. June 11.

So, Alvin (1990). *Social Change and Development*. London: Sage.

Southwick, Charles H. (1996). *Global Ecology in Human Perspective*. New York & Oxford: Oxford University Press.

Sowell, Thomas (1981). *Ethnic America: A History*. New York: Basic Books.

Spencer, Robert F. (1959). The North Alaskan Eskimo: A study in ecology and society. *Ethnology Bulletin* 171. Washington: Smithsonian Institution Bureau of America.

Spooner, Brian (1982). *Desertification and Development*. London: Academic Press.

Spooner, Brian (1979). *Environmental Problems and the Organization of Development in the Arid Lands of South-West Africa*. Bangkok: United Nations.

Staples, Robert (1985). Changes in Black family structure: The conflict between family ideology and structure conditions. *Journal of Marriage and the Family* 47:1005–1013.

Stavrianos, L. S. (1982). *The World since 1500*. Englewood Cliffs, NJ: Prentice-Hall.

Steward, Julian H. (1968). The Great Basin Shoshonean Indians: An example of a family level of sociocultural integration. In Y. Cohen (Ed.), *Man in Adaptation. The Cultural Present* (pp. 101–115). Chicago: Aldine.

Steward, Julian H. (1955). *Theory of Culture Change*. Urbana: University of Illinois Press.

Steward, Julian H. (1951). Levels of sociocultural integration: An operational concept. *Southwestern Journal of Anthropology* 7:374–390.

Steward, Julian H. (1949a). South American cultures: An interpretive summary. In J. H. Steward (Ed.), *Handbook of South American Indians*, vol. 5 (pp. 669–772). Smithsonian Institution, Bureau of American Ethnology, Bulletin 143. Washington, DC: U. S. Government Printing Office.

Steward, Julian H. (1949b). Cultural causality and law: A trial formulation of the development of early civilizations. *American Anthropologist* 51:1–27.

Steward, Julian H. (Ed.) (1967). *Contemporary Change in Traditional Societies* (3 vols.). Urbana: University of Illinois Press.

Steward, Julian (Ed.) (1956). *The People of Puerto Rico*. Urbana: University of Illinois Press.

Stone, Irving (1977). British direct and portfolio investments in Latin America before 1914. *Journal of Economic History* 37:690–722.

Stonich, Susan (1993). *1 Am Destroying the Land: The Political Ecology of Poverty and Environmental Destruction in Honduras.* Boulder, CO: Westview.

Sullivan, Jo (1989). *Africa.* Guilford, CT: Dushkin Publishing Group.

Sullivan, Lawrence R. (1995). The Three Gorges project: Dammed if they do? *Current History* 94(593):266–269.

Tambiah, Stanley J. (1994). The politics of ethnicity. In Robert Borofsky (Ed.), *Assessing Cultural Anthropology* (pp. 430–442). New York: McGraw-Hill.

Tasker, Peter (1987). *The Japanese* New York: E. P. Dutton.

Temu, Arnold and Bonaventure Swai (1981). *Historians and Africanist History: A Critique.* London: Zed Press.

Thornton, Arland (1989). Changing attitudes towards family issues in the United States. *Journal of Marriage and the Family* 51:873–893.

Thurow, Lester (1992). *Head to Head: The Coming Economic Battle among Japan, Europe, and America.* New York: William Morrow.

Tishkov, Valery A. (1994). Inventions and manifestations of Ethno-Nationalism in Soviet academic and public discourse. In Robert Borofsky (Ed.), *Assessing Cultural Anthropology* (pp. 443–453). New York: McGraw-Hill.

Tooker, Deborah (1993). The Hani of China. In Marc S. Miller (Ed.) *State of the Peoples: A Global Human Rights Report on Societies in Danger (pp.* 118–119). Boston: Beacon Press.

Turner, Terence (1995). An indigenous people's struggle for socially equitable and ecologically sustainable production: The Kayapó revolt against extractivism. Journal *of Latin American* Anthropology 1(1):98–121.

Turner, Terence (1992). Defiant images: The Kayapo appropriation of video. *Anthropology Today 8(6):5–16.*

Turner, Terence (1991). Representing, resisting, rethinking: Historical transformations of Kayapó culture and anthropological consciousness. In George W. Stocking, Jr. (Ed.), *Colonial Situations: Essays on the Contextualization of Ethnographic Knowledge, History of Anthropology,* vol. 7 (pp. 285–313). Madison: University of Wisconsin Press.

Tylor, Edward B. [1871] (1958). *The Origins of Culture.* Part I of *Primitive Culture.* New York: Harper & Brothers.

United States General Accounting Office (1990). *Report.* Washington, D.C.: U.S. General Accounting Office.

Van Buren, Mary (1996). Rethinking the vertical archipelago: Ethnicity, exchange, and history in the South Central Andes. *American Anthropologist* 98(2): 338–351.

Van Willigen, John (1993). *Applied Anthropology:* An Introduction. Westport, CT: Bergin & Garvey.

Vanstone, James W (1974). *Athapaskan Adaptations: Hunters and Fishermen of the Subarctic Forests.* Chicago: Aldine.

Veliz, Claudio (1980). *The Centrist Tradition of Latin America.* Princeton, NJ: Princeton University Press.

Vondal, Patricia (1989). The ecology of farm management in a swampland region of Indonesia. In Sheldon Smith and Ed Reeves (Eds.), *Human Systems Ecology* (pp. 107–123). Boulder, CO: Westview.

Waldrop, M. Mitchell (1992). *Complexity: The Emerging Science at the Edge of Order and Chaos.* New York: Simon & Schuster.

Wallerstein, Immanuel (1979). *The Capitalist World Economy.* New York: Cambridge University Press.

Wallerstein, Immanuel (1976). *The Modern World System: Capitalist Agriculture and the Origins of the European World Economy in the Sixteenth Century.* New York: Academic Press.

Warner, W. Lloyd (1949). *Democracy in Jonesville: A Study of Quality and Inequality.* New York: Harper.

Warner, W. Lloyd, and Paul S. Lunt (1942). *The Status System of a Modern Community.* New Haven, CT: Yale University Press.

Warren, D. Michael, L. Jan Slikkerveer, and David Brokensha (Eds.) (1995). *The Cultural Dimension of Development: Indigenous Knowledge Systems.* London: Intermediate Technology Publications.

Warren, K. and D. Bourque (1991). Women, technology, and international development ideologies: Analyzing feminist voices. In M. di Leonardo (Ed.), *Gender at the Crossroads of Knowledge. Feminist Anthropology in the Postmodern Era* (pp. 278–311). Berkeley: University of California Press.

Weber, Max [1930] (1958a). *The Protestant Ethic and the Spirit of Capitalism.* New York: Scribner.

Weber, Max (1958b). *The Religion of India.* Glencoe, IL: Free Press.

Weber, Max (1951). *The Religion of China.* Glencoe, IL: Free Press.

Weber, Max (1949). *The Methodology oil the Social Sciences.* (Trans. & Ed. by Edward H. Shills and Henry A. Finch). Glencoe, IL: Free Press.

Weeks, Dennis (1992). The AIDS pandemic in Africa. *Current History* 91(565):208–213.

Weiner, Annette B. (1988). *The Trobrianders of Papua New Guinea.* New York: Holt, Rinehart and Winston.

Wexler, Bruce (2006). *Brain and Culture: Neurobiology, Ideology, and Social Change.* Cambridge, MA: MIT Press.

White, Leslie (1959). *The Evolution of Culture.* New York: McGraw-Hill.

White, Leslie (1949). *The Science of Culture.* New York: Grove Press.

Whorf, Benjamin L. [1936] (1956). An American Indian Model of the Universe. In John B. Carroll (Ed.), *Language, Thought, and Reality* (pp. 57–64). Cambridge, MA: MIT Press.

Willems, Emilio (1975). *Latin American Culture: An Anthropological Synthesis*. New York: Harper & Row.

Wilson, William J. (1996). *When Work Disappears*. New York: Alfred A. Knopf.

Wilson, William J. (1991). Studying inner-city social dislocations: The challenge of public agenda research. *American Sociological Review* 56(1): 1–14.

Wilson, William J. (1987). *The Truly Disadvantaged: The Inner City, The Underclass, and Public Policy*. Chicago: University of Chicago Press.

Wittfogel, Karl (1957). *Oriental Despotism*. New Haven, CT: Yale University Press.

Wolcott, Harry F. (1994). *Transforming Qualitative Data: Description, Analysis, and Interpretation*. Thousand Oaks, CA: Sage.

Wolf, Eric (1994). Facing power, old insights, new questions. In Robert Borofsky (Ed.), Assessing Cultural *Anthropology (pp* 218–228). New York: McGraw-Hill.

Wolf, Eric (1982). *Europe and the People without History*. Berkeley: University of California Press.

Wolf, Eric (1969). *Peasant Wars of the 20th Century*. New York: Harper & Row.

Wolf, Eric (1966) *Peasants*. Englewood Cliffs, NJ: Prentice-Hall.

Wolf, Eric (1959). *Sons of the Shaking Earth*. Chicago: University of Chicago Press.

Wolf, Eric, and E. C. Hansen (1972). *The Human Condition in Latin America*. London: Oxford University Press.

Wolf, Eric, and S. Mintz (1957). Haciendas and plantations in Middle America and the Antilles. *Social and Economic Studies* 6:380–412.

Wolfe, Alvin (1977). The supranational organization of production: An evolutionary perspective. *Current Anthropology* 18:615–635.

Woodward, Ralph (1976). *Central America*. New York: Oxford University Press.

World Commission on Environment and Development (1987). *Our Common Future*. New York & Oxford: Oxford University Press.

World Resources Institute, United Nations Environmental Programme, United Nations Development Programme, and World Bank (1996). *World Resources 1996–97*. New York & Oxford: Oxford University Press.

World Wide Fund for Nature (1996). The timber trade and global forest loss. WWF article at URL http://www.panda.org/tda/forest/forest2.htm.

Worsely, Peter (1957). *The Trumpet Shall Sound*. London: Marc Gibbon and Kee.

Wright, Ann (see Menchu).

Yamamura, Kozo (1987). Behind the 'made in Japan' label. In M. Hyoe and J. Hirschmeir (Eds.) *Politics and Economics in Contemporary Japan* (pp. 127–142). Tokyo: Japan Cultural Institute.

Yergin, David (1991). Oil: The strategic prize. In Micah Sifry and C. Cerf (Eds.), *The Gulf War Reader* (pp. 21–26). New York: Random House.

Young, Philip D. (1991a). Conceptual frameworks, sustainable development, and the management of fragile lands. In Philip D. Young (Ed.), *Fragile Lands Management in Latin America and the Caribbean: A Synthesis* (pp. 21–58). Bethesda, MD: Development Alternatives.

Young, Philip D. (1985). Guaymi socionatural adaptations. In William G. D'Arcy and Mireya D. Correz (Eds.), *The Botany and Natural History of Panama La Botánica e Historia Natural de Panama* (pp. 357–365). St. Louis: Missouri Botanical Garden.

Young, Philip D. (1978). La trayectoria de una religion: El movimiento de Mama Chi entre los Guaymies y sus consecuencias sociales. *La Antigua* 11:45–75. Panama: Universidad Santa Maria La Antigua.

Young, Philip D. (1975). Guaymi nativism: Its rise and demise. *Proceedings of* the XLI International Congress of Americanists, vol. 3 (pp. 93–101). Mexico, DF: Instituto Nacional de Antropologia Historia.

Young, Philip D. (1971). *Ngawbe: Tradition and Change Among the Western Guaymi of Panama*. Illinois Studies in Anthropology, No. 7. Urbana: University of Illinois Press.

Young, Philip D. (Ed.) (1991b). *Fragile Lands Management in Latin America and the Caribbean: A Synthesis*. Bethesda, MD: Development Alternatives.

Photo
Credits

Front Matter   iStockphoto (both), i; iStockphoto (both), iii; Shutterstock, xvii

Introduction   AP Photo, 1; iStockphoto, 2; iStockphoto, 3; Wikipedia photo, 4; iStockphoto (all), 5; iStockphoto (both), 6; Wikipedia photo, 10; Shutterstock, 11; Wikipedia photo, 12; iStockphoto, 13; Wikipedia photo, 16; iStockphoto, 17; Shutterstock, 21; iStockphoto, 23; iStockphoto, 26; iStockphoto, 27; iStockphoto (both) 29; iStockphoto, 31; iStockphoto, 33; AP Photo, 36; iStockphoto, 37

Chapter 1   iStockphoto, 39; iStockphoto, 40; Wikipedia photo, 42; AP Photo, 43; iStockphoto, 44; iStockphoto, 46; iStockphoto, 48; iStockphoto (top), iStockphoto (frame), Wikipedia photo, 49; Shutterstock, 50; Wikipedia photo, 52; iStockphoto, 53; iStockphoto, 59; iStockphoto, 65; Wikipedia photo, 67; Wikipedia photo, 68; iStockphoto, 70; iStockphoto, 72

Chapter 2   AP Photo, 75; iStockphoto, 76; Wikipedia photo, 77; Wikipedia photo, 78; Wikipedia photo, 80; Wikipedia photo, 81; Wikipedia photo, 83; iStockphoto (both), 84; iStockphoto (all), 85; iStockphoto, 89; Wikipedia photo, 90; iStockphoto, 91; Wikipedia photo, 92; Wikipedia photo, 95; iStockphoto, 97; iStockphoto, 98; Shutterstock, 100; Wikipedia photo, 103; iStockphoto, 105; iStockphoto (all), 107; iStockphoto, 110

Chapter 3   iStockphoto, 111; iStockphoto, 112; iStockphoto, 113; Wikipedia photo, 114; Wikipedia, 115; iStockphoto, 117; iStockphoto, 120; iStockphoto, 126; Shutterstock, 132; Wikipedia photo, 135; Wikipedia photo, 139; iStockphoto, 142; Wikipedia photo, 144; iStockphoto, 147; iStockphoto, 149

Chapter 4   AP Photo, 151; iStockphoto, 152; Shutterstock, 153; AP Photo, 155; iStockphoto (both) 159; iStockphoto, 167; iStockphoto, 173; iStockphoto, 178

Index